THE MAGUS:
KUNDALINI AND THE GOLDEN DAWN

A COMPLETE SYSTEM OF MAGICK THAT BRIDGES EASTERN
SPIRITUALITY AND THE WESTERN MYSTERIES

NEVEN PAAR

The Magus: Kundalini and the Golden Dawn
Copyright © 2022 By Neven Paar. All Rights Reserved.

No part of this book may be reproduced in any form or by any electronic or mechanical means including information storage and retrieval systems, without permission in writing from the author. The only exception is by a reviewer, who may quote short excerpts in a review.

Cover Art by Emily Paar
Illustrations by Neven Paar

Printed in Canada
First Printing: October 2022
By Winged Shoes Publishing

ISBN—978-1-7770608-4-8

Disclaimer: All material found in this work is provided for your information only and may not be construed as professional medical advice or instruction. No action or inaction should be taken based solely on the contents of this information; instead, readers should consult appropriate health professionals on any matter relating to their health and well-being. Although the author and publisher have made every effort to ensure that the information in this book was correct at press time, the author and publisher do not assume and hereby disclaim any liability to any party for any loss, damage, or disruption caused by errors or omissions, whether such errors or omissions result from negligence, accident, or any other cause.

I dedicate this work to the seeker of Hidden Knowledge, with the hope that it will shine Light on the many subjects of the Western Mysteries, and give you the necessary tools to undertake the process of Spiritual Alchemy yourself—the Great Work.

—Neven Paar

Other books by Neven Paar

Serpent Rising: The Kundalini Compendium

www.nevenpaar.com

Winged Shoes Publishing
Toronto, Ontario

List of Figures:

Figure 1: Kundalini Energy Raised to the Crown..17
Figure 2: The Seven Chakras...26
Figure 3: The Qabalistic Tree of Life...34
Figure 4: The Fylfot Cross..37
Figure 5: The Path of the Flaming Sword 60
Figure 6: The Serpent of Wisdom..61
Figure 7: The Human Being as a Mini Solar System..65
Figure 8: The Tetragrammaton—YHVH..72
Figure 9: The Pentagrammaton—YHShinVH (Yahshuah)..74
Figure 10: The Four Worlds: Atziluth, Briah, Yetzirah, and Assiah 77
Figure 11: Hermes and the Caduceus 83
Figure 12: Qabalistic Correspondences of the Caduceus of Hermes......................84
Figure 13: The Garden of Eden Before the Fall 88
Figure 14: The Garden of Eden After the Fall 90
Figure 15: The Tree of Life and the Kundalini 95
Figure 16: The Chakras and the Elements 101
Figure 17: The Tree of Life and the Major Arcana of the Tarot.............................106
Figure 18: Keys of the Tarot (Zero to Three)..110
Figure 19: Keys of the Tarot (Four to Seven)...118
Figure 20: Keys of the Tarot (Eight to Eleven) 124
Figure 21: Keys of the Tarot (Twelve to Fifteen)...130
Figure 22: Keys of the Tarot (Sixteen to Nineteen) 139
Figure 23: Keys of the Tarot (Twenty and Twenty-One).....................................147
Figure 24: The Tetragrammaton in the Circle Spread Divination 157
Figure 25: The Microcosmic Operation in the Circle Spread Divination 158
Figure 26: The Macrocosmic Operation in the Circle Spread Divination 160
Figure 27: The Present and Future Cards in the Circle Spread Divination..........161
Figure 28: The Pentagram and its Correspondences..169
Figure 29: Traditional Golden Dawn Regalia (Outer Order)...............................197
Figure 30: The Author's Personal Golden Dawn Temple 198
Figure 31: Banishing Pentagram of Earth..209
Figure 32: LBRP Magickal Gestures..213
Figure 33: Four Forms of the Hexagram in the BRH 215
Figure 34: Middle Pillar Exercise 220
Figure 35: Invoking and Banishing Pentagrams of the Elements........................223
Figure 36: Invoking Pentagrams of the SIRP 226
Figure 37: Banishing Pentagrams of Spirit..230
Figure 38: The System of Advancement in "The Magus" 236
Figure 39: Grade Signs of the Four Elements...240
Figure 40: Three Steps of the Portal Grade Signs 242

Figure 41: "The Magus" Emblem..244
Figure 42: The Twelve Zodiac..253
Figure 43: The Twelve Houses and their Correspondences............................266
Figure 44: The Seven Ancient Planets 271
Figure 45: Lesser Invoking Hexagrams for Saturn, Jupiter, and Mars.............288
Figure 46: Lesser Invoking Hexagrams for Venus, Mercury, and the Moon......289
Figure 47: Lesser Banishing Hexagrams for Saturn, Jupiter, and Mars............290
Figure 48: Lesser Banishing Hexagrams for Venus, Mercury, and Moon..........291
Figure 49: Greater Hexagram Planetary Attributions 292
Figure 50: Symbols of the Zodiac Signs 294
Figure 51: Greater Hexagrams for Saturn, Jupiter, and Mars..........................295
Figure 52: Greater Hexagrams for Venus, Mercury, and the Moon 296
Figure 53: Greater Invoking Hexagrams for the Sun.....................................297
Figure 54: Greater Banishing Hexagrams for the Sun 298
Figure 55: I.N.R.I. in Hebrew: Yod, Nun, Resh, Yod (right to left)..................302
Figure 56: The L.V.X. Signs 304
Figure 57: The Forms of Hermes 312
Figure 58: The Ouroboros—Orphic Egg 362
Figure 59: The Three Alchemical Principles: Sulfur, Mercury, and Salt 368
Figure 60: Ceremonial Magick of the Golden Dawn 382
Figure 61: The Four Watchtowers and the Tablet of Union 387
Figure 62: The Eighteen Enochian Keys 417
Figure 63: The Ego as a Reflection of the Soul in BAG................................424
Figure 64: The King's Chamber Initiation of ZEN 432
Figure 65: The Thirty Enochian Aethyrs 451
Figure 66: The Olympic Planetary Spirits 468
Figure 67: A Permanent Kundalini Awakening...472
Figure 68: The Bindu and the Kundalini Circuit...474
Figure 69: The Merkaba—Optimised Torus...480

List of Tables:

TABLE 1: The Seven Chakras and their Correspondences..29
TABLE 2: The Ten Sephiroth and their Correspondences..35
TABLE 3: The Twenty-two Tarot Paths and their Correspondences................................36
TABLE 4: The Seven Ancient Planets and their Correspondences 286
TABLE 5: The Planetary Hours of the Day 307
TABLE 6: The Planetary Hours of the Night..307
TABLE 7: Divine Names Attributed to the Seven Ancient Planets 462
TABLE 8: Divine Names Attributed to the Sephiroth 463
TABLE 9: Invocation of the Forces of the Zodiac Signs 463

THE MAGUS: KUNDALINI AND THE GOLDEN DAWN
By Neven Paar

Contents

AUTHOR'S INTRODUCTION 1
    Awakening the Tree of Life 1
    Overcoming Desire 3
    The Kybalion 4
    My Kundalini Awakening 5
    The Golden Dawn System 7
    Sharing Knowledge and Wisdom 10
    A Man On a Mission 11

PART I: THE QABALAH 15
EASTERN AND WESTERN SPIRITUAL SYSTEMS 16
    Kundalini and Magick 16
    The Chakras 18
    Karmic Energy 19
    Chakra Cleansing and Tuning Practices 20
    The Kundalini Crisis 21
    The Five Elements 23
    The Seven Chakras 25

THE QABALAH AND THE TREE OF LIFE 30
    Qabalah and Magick 32
    The Qabalah and the Elements 37
    The Three Pillars of the Tree of Life 39
    Ain Soph Aur (Limitless Light) 40
    Kether (The Crown) 41
    Chokmah (Wisdom) 42
    Binah (Understanding) 43
    Daath (Knowledge) 45
    Chesed (Mercy) 47
    Geburah (Severity) 48
    Tiphareth (Harmony/Beauty) 50
    Netzach (Victory) 52
    Hod (Splendour) 53
    Yesod (The Foundation) 55
    Malkuth (The Kingdom) 57
    The Path of the Flaming Sword 59
    The Serpent of Wisdom 60
    The Thirty-Two Paths of Wisdom 62
    The Hebrew Alphabet 63

THE TREE OF LIFE AND THE SOLAR SYSTEM 64
THREE PARTS OF THE SELF 67
TETRAGRAMMATON AND PENTAGRAMMATON 71
FOUR WORLDS OF THE QABALAH 76
THE CADUCEUS OF HERMES 82

THE GARDEN OF EDEN 86
- The Garden of Eden Before the Fall 87
- The Garden of Eden After the Fall 89
- The Tree of Life and the Kundalini 92

THE SEPHIROTH AND THE CHAKRAS 96

PART II: THE TAROT 103

THE MAJOR ARCANA OF THE TAROT 104
- The Tree of Life and the Major Arcana 105
- Tarot Cards and Divination 107
- Rider-Waite and the Golden Dawn 108
- The Fool 111
- The Magician 112
- The High Priestess 114
- The Empress 116
- The Emperor 117
- The Hierophant 119
- The Lovers 120
- The Chariot 121
- Strength 123
- The Hermit 126
- Wheel of Fortune 127
- Justice 128
- The Hanged Man 131
- Death 132
- Temperance 135
- The Devil 136
- The Tower 138
- The Star 141
- The Moon 142
- The Sun 144
- Judgement 147
- The Universe 149
- Scrying the Tarot 151

THE CIRCLE SPREAD DIVINATION 153
- Pre-Divination Preparations 154
- The Divination Method 156
- Spiritual Influences and Magick 162
- Cleansing and Storing Your Tarot Cards 163

PART III: CEREMONIAL MAGICK 165

THE FIVE ELEMENTS 166
- The Soul and the Ego 166
- The Pentagram 168
- The Earth Element 170
- The Air Element 173
- The Water Element 176
- The Fire Element 181
- The Spirit Element 184

CEREMONIAL MAGICK RITUAL EXERCISES 189

- The Hermetic Order of the Golden Dawn 189
- High and Low Magick 190
- The Origins of Magick 191
- The Power of Magick 193
- Spiritual Initiation 195
- Ritual Wear and Setting 196
- The Ritual Process 199
- The Magickal Journal 202
- The Four-Fold Breath 204
- The Mind's Eye Meditation 205
- Lesser Banishing Ritual of the Pentagram 206
- Banishing Ritual of the Hexagram 214
- Middle Pillar Exercise 217
- Lesser Invoking Ritual of the Pentagram 222
- Supreme Invoking Ritual of the Pentagram 225

THE GREAT WORK 231

- Spiritual Alchemy Program I—The Five Elements 232
- Accelerating the Spiritual Alchemy Program 238
- Grade Signs of the Five Elements 240
- *The Magus* Emblem 243
- The Next Step in the Great Work 246
- A Warning On Enochian Magick 247

PART IV: ASTROLOGY 249

ASTROLOGY AND THE ZODIAC 250

- The Horoscope 251
- The Four Elements Within the Zodiac 252
- Aries—The Ram 254
- Taurus—The Bull 255
- Gemini—The Twins 255
- Cancer—The Crab 256
- Leo—The Lion 257
- Virgo—The Virgin 258
- Libra—The Scales 259
- Scorpio—The Scorpion 260
- Sagittarius—The Archer 261
- Capricorn—The Goat 262
- Aquarius—The Water Bearer 263
- Pisces—The Fish 264
- The Twelve Houses 265

THE PLANETS WITHIN OUR SOLAR SYSTEM 270

- Saturn 272
- Jupiter 273
- Mars 274
- The Sun (Sol) 275
- Venus 277
- Mercury 278
- The Moon (Luna) 279

    The Earth 281
    The New Planets—Uranus, Neptune, Pluto 282
ADVANCED PLANETARY MAGICK 284
    Lesser Ritual of the Hexagram...287
    Greater Ritual of the Hexagram 292
    Analysis of the Keyword 300
    Spiritual Alchemy Program II—The Seven Ancient Planets 305

PART V: THE KYBALION-HERMETIC PHILOSOPHY 309
INTRODUCTION TO THE KYBALION 310
    The Wisdom of Hermes Trismegistus 311
THE SEVEN PRINCIPLES OF CREATION 315
    I. Principle of Mentalism 315
    II. Principle of Correspondence 319
    III. Principle of Vibration 321
    IV. Principle of Polarity 323
    V. Principle of Rhythm 325
    VI. Principle of Cause and Effect 328
    VII. Principle of Gender 330
THE ALL-SPIRIT 333
THE MENTAL UNIVERSE 336
THE DIVINE PARADOX 339
THE ALL IN ALL 342
PART VI: HERMETIC ALCHEMY 347
THE EMERALD TABLET 348
    Analysis of The Emerald Tablet 349
THE ART OF ALCHEMY 360
    The Ouroboros..362
    The Philosopher's Stone 363
    Duality and the Trinity in Alchemy..364
    Alchemical Stages and Processes 366
    The Three Principles in Nature 367
    The Four Elements and the Quintessence 370
    As Above, So Below 370
    The Alchemical Metals 371
THE STAGES OF ALCHEMY 373
    Calcination 374
    Dissolution 375
    Separation 375
    Conjunction 376
    Fermentation 377
    Distillation 378
    Coagulation 379
    The Magus Spiritual Alchemy Formula 380

PART VII: ENOCHIAN MAGICK 383
THE ENOCHIAN MAGICK SYSTEM 384

    John Dee and Edward Kelley 385
    Enochian (Angelic) Language 385
    The Four Watchtowers and the Tablet of Union 386
    The Golden Dawn and Enochian Magick 388
    The Aim of Enochian Magick 389
    The Cosmic Planes 390
    The Body of Light and the Subtle Bodies 391
    The Cosmic Elements 393
    Enochian Magick and Dreams 394
    Astral Travel 395
    Enoch and Hermes 396
    Enochian Armies of Angels 397
    Angels and Demons in Enochian Magick 398
    Defeating Demons in your Dreams 399
    The Enochian Elemental and Sub-Elemental Keys 400

THE EIGHTEEN ENOCHIAN KEYS 402
THE THIRTY AETHYRS (19th ENOCHIAN KEY) 418
    Sexual Energy Currents in the Aethyrs 419
    Babalon in Enochian Magick 420
    Descriptions of the Enochian Aethyrs 421
    The Call of the Aethyrs (19th Key) 449

WORKING WITH THE ENOCHIAN KEYS 452
    Scrying the Keys and the Aethyrs 453
    Spiritual Alchemy Program III—The Enochian Keys 454

EPILOGUE 458
APPENDIX 461
ADDITIONAL ADEPT MATERIAL 462
    Supplementary Tables 462
    Olympic Planetary Spirits 464

KUNDALINI AWAKENING ARTICLES BY THE AUTHOR 469
    The Nature of the Kundalini 469
    Kundalini Transformation—Part I 473
    Kundalini Transformation—Part II 477

CEREMONIAL MAGICK TESTIMONIALS 482
GLOSSARY OF SELECTED TERMS 486
BIBLIOGRAPHY 498

AUTHOR'S INTRODUCTION

AWAKENING THE TREE OF LIFE

The Caduceus of Hermes is a Western Mysteries symbol used in medicine in modern-day society. You had seen it many times when you went to see a doctor, but most of you are probably unaware that the Caduceus has various hidden meanings. It symbolises healing but also indicates a Spiritual awakening mechanism, or process, that the Easterners call the Kundalini.

After I experienced a Kundalini awakening and searched for answers, it took me some time to determine how it corresponded with the Caduceus of Hermes. However, once I figured it out, I was able to get more answers about the Kundalini, but through a Western lens—this was helpful to me since I live in North America and not somewhere in the Eastern part of the world.

From the Western Mystery school that I was a part of for many years, the Golden Dawn, I learned that the Caduceus of Hermes is the Tree of Life of the Qabalah. With this information, I realized that I did not need to study the Kundalini through Hindu books and practices (as is the norm in today's day and age), but I had all the answers I needed in the Qabalah and the Western traditions. Furthermore, once I made other parallels between the Kundalini and the Tree of Life, I concluded that an awakening of the Kundalini is a complete awakening of the Tree of Life within the individual.

The ten Sephiroth, or Spheres, on the Tree of Life are states of consciousness, with the lowest being called Malkuth (the Earth) and the highest being called Kether—the *White Light*. (Note that terms in the italic text are further defined in the Glossary at the back of the book.) The Inner World of a human being consists of the states of consciousness between Malkuth and Kether, with Kether as the highest manifestation of the Divine energy.

Full awakening of the Kundalini brings about an activation of the entire Tree of Life within the individual. Through this experience, the consciousness gains access to all the Spheres instantly. Still, since the inner Laws are mental, one must mentally travel upwards into the higher Spheres of the Tree of Life to align their consciousness with their *Higher Self* and completely transform. Thus, it is a process, not an overnight endeavour. But awakening the Kundalini starts this process.

The Kybalion: Hermetic Philosophy is an occult book written in the early twentieth-century that elucidates the Principles of Creation. It states the truth of our existence: the "All is Mind, the Universe is Mental." In recent years, science has learned that the nature of the physical Universe is virtually empty space and that what we see and classify as *Matter* may be a Hologram. Many scientists and philosophers even say we may live in a digital simulation.

If the nature of the world around us is a Hologram inside a simulation, then my theory that we live inside the "Dream of God" may be correct. We are reminded of this reality nightly as we dream, just as God dreams us—through the mind. Only our mind is a finite one, while the mind of God is infinite. As we dream, our Creator dreams us. The difference is a matter of frequency of vibration, but the substance is the same. The Ancients called this substance Spirit. Spirit is the substantial reality underlying all things in existence.

Interestingly, a full Kundalini awakening (when the energy becomes localized in the brain permanently) brings forth a state of existence whereby the awakened person can perceive the world around them as a digitally enhanced one. Visually, a silvery glow and heightened sharpness in objects are seen in the same way as one would perceive an immaculate virtual reality simulation—this occurs because of the awakening of the inner Light that permeates all things that the physical eyes see.

After the very intense Kundalini awakening that I had earlier on in my life, I see the world in this way. I can personally attest that the world around us has a Holographic nature, which may very well be a digitally enhanced simulation. Whatever its true nature is, one thing is sure; it is *Maya*—an illusion.

Even though our world may be illusory, it is through the Spirit (which connects all aspects of the world at a deep level) that we experience unconditional love. Unconditional love unites all living things and has no bounds, just like the Spirit energy. It is a Spiritual kind of love energy without conditions, limitations, or expectations. This unconditional love is what we all seek deep inside, whether we are consciously aware of it or not.

The Kundalini awakening is an awakening to the Fourth Dimension, the *Dimension of Vibration*. Here, the mind becomes the connecting link between the Spiritual reality and the material one, while the physical body is the vehicle of consciousness. The mind is the receiver that can tune in to different levels of vibration that comprise the Cosmic Planes. These Cosmic Planes consist of but are not limited to the Lower Astral Plane (Etheric), Higher Astral Plane (Emotional), Lower Mental Plane, Higher Mental Plane, and the Spiritual Plane. These five Planes are commonly grouped into the three Cosmic Planes of the Astral, Mental, and Spiritual. And the Sephiroth of the Tree of Life are embodiments of those Planes and the Planes in between. After all, each Plane has Sub-Planes related to its nature.

"Everything in the Universe, throughout all its Kingdoms, is conscious: i.e., endowed with a consciousness of its own and on its own Plane of perception." — H. P. Blavatsky; excerpt from *"The Secret Doctrine: The Synthesis of Science, Religion, and Philosophy"*

Going back to my life's journey after the Kundalini awakening and learning about the Tree of Life—I have made certain conclusions about my own life and how I accessed the different Spheres on the Tree of Life in the past, often unconsciously. The experience of polarizing my consciousness in the Sphere of Hod (the domain of Mercury or Hermes) led to my Kundalini awakening in the first place. I will briefly share some other life experiences that coincided with the Spheres of the Tree of Life, which all led to this most grand of events.

OVERCOMING DESIRE

I experienced the Sphere of Netzach and the Planet Venus when I was with my first love in high school—this was when my Spiritual journey started. Having her in my life allowed me to travel upwards in consciousness. I was in love, and the feeling of love connected me with my *Holy Guardian Angel* (Higher Genius), who guided me at the time. At this time, I intuitively realized that thoughts regulated how I felt about life, so I wanted to gain control over them on a deeper level.

I saw the process of destiny, which allowed me to go with the flow of life without emotionally attaching myself to anything. I understood that attachment would result in fear of losing the object(s) of my desire—this was a very Buddhist approach to eliminate desire and quiet the Ego. I had to remove fear from my life if I was to reach *Nirvana*. That became my ultimate goal after connecting to the Spirit for the first time.

I took every living moment as a test of my faith in God-the Creator and the higher reality, which I seemed to understand at a deep level. As I passed more tests, I was taken higher in levels of consciousness until my entire world was utterly transformed. Passing these tests had a cumulative effect, increasing the positive energy and momentum needed to reach my goal. I remember saying to myself, "If only the rest of the people in the world could see what I saw and believe what I believed, the world would be a better place, and the power of the Divine would not be doubted."

I lived in a state of perpetual bliss. Nothing could disturb my new worldview. Because of this act of letting go of all expectations, I felt unconditional love for everyone and everything. I began reframing daily mundane events to view them through a positive lens—this was the key to building and maintaining my momentum—reframing any negative thing into a positive one.

Many things occur throughout the day that the Ego does not like, and in turn, it wants to convince us to get upset somehow. Learning to regulate the Ego and to use the intellectual, rational Self when processing life events is the key to overcoming negative emotions. According to *The Kybalion*, in this way, we can neutralize emotions, which naturally swing from positive to negative and back again in a rhythmic fashion consistently throughout the day. This rhythmic swing of the emotions is because of the Ego's perception. Like a child that does not get what it wants, it becomes upset. Realistically, we react like children our whole lives; the only difference is that we learn to curb our emotions and act logically and rationally as adults. Still, we experience a low in the emotions when we do not get our way.

The Sphere of the logical, rational mind is called Hod on the Tree of Life. Its opposite is Netzach, which is the Sphere of emotion. Hod contains both positive and negative viewpoints on life; it is our duty as Spiritual human beings to reconcile the two by applying the energy of unconditional love. We can choose an optimistic viewpoint at any given moment if we only focus our minds in the right direction and apply our willpower correctly. In this way, we overcome the pull in the negative direction, which the Ego tries to sway us towards so that it can tap into our fears. The Ego feeds on fear in the same way as the Higher Self feeds on unconditional love. The two are opposites of each other.

THE KYBALION

After accessing the Sphere of Netzach through being in love, I became curious about other possibilities. As my relationship with my first love ended, I met new people and got in touch again with some friends who all had common characteristics that enabled them to exert power over others and their own reality. I sought to learn what they knew and beyond. Whether it was my Ego seeking power or curiosity about what is possible and attainable in the world, I decided to explore this idea of personal power, learn from it, and grow. In this way, I polarized myself entirely in the Hod Sphere, distancing myself from my emotions.

In 2004, *The Kybalion* came into my possession. As mentioned, this book outlines the Principles governing *Creation* and how they operate on all Planes of existence. After reading it countless times and practising its Principles in the real world, I started to understand its ideas and concepts at a deep level. And that was the key right there—understanding. I saw the wisdom of the Principles at the deepest levels of my intuitive capacity. I particularly became attracted to *The Kybalion's* Principle of Vibration and how it fits in with Polarity, Rhythm, and Gender—the other Principles in the book.

As I kept reading this book, I became wholly absorbed into the Sphere of Hod and my mentality. My existence vanished from my heart and emotion, and I started living exclusively from my head and intellect. I could only intellectualize my emotions at this point, as I lost the ability to feel them. It may seem like a downgrade at first, but it felt like an upgrade as it was happening since I attained a degree of control over my reality that was otherwise impossible before. After all, perception determines your reality. Hence, by controlling how you perceive the outside world and events within it, you can control your own experience of what reality is for you.

And so, I became a sorcerer of the mind. By applying my willpower, my imaginative capabilities were increased, and I could control my perception of reality to a degree unfathomable to most people. Thus, I exerted dominance over the Mental Plane, reframing every adverse event into a positive one. As the old Hermetic axiom states, "As Above, So Below"—by controlling my mind, I was directing my emotions and manifesting any reality I desired.

With this newfound ability to control my reality, I handled every life situation and interaction with other people in a way where my reality came out on top. I learned that within any group of people on the same wavelength, there is only one reality, and that reality belongs to the person who vibrates their willpower higher than others. In other words, they believe in themselves more than others do. As I was learning these Principles, my confidence rose to an extraordinary level. I always used my quick rational mind to say the right thing at the right time. I felt on top of the world and saw that anything was possible with this new mindset.

I realized that I could only feel defeated if I believed that I was since my perception of life events was just a matter of polarity, nothing more. If I believed that I could do something, I was right. And if I thought that I couldn't, I was also correct. My mind could give me all the reasons why I was right or why I was wrong; it all depended on what I asked it for. So, I never lost my cool in any situation, always focusing on the positive outcome. This way of controlling your mind can achieve wonders, and it did for me.

"Thought is a force—a manifestation of energy—having a magnet-like power of attraction." — *William Walker Atkinson; excerpt from "Mind-Power: The Secret of Mental Magic"*

I developed a strong affinity for Hermes Trismegistus since *The Kybalion* Principles are his teachings. He is called Trismegistus for being "Thrice Great," meaning he has control over the three Inner Planes of existence. To govern your reality, you must control your thoughts since thought predates all things. And since emotions are a by-product of thoughts, by managing your thoughts, you also have authority over how you want to feel as well. Also, by being in charge of your thoughts, you create a link to the Spirit energy and the field of infinite potential. Thus, life becomes very exciting and enjoyable since you invariably are learning to live in the present moment, the *Now*. And what greater gift is there from the Divine than this knowledge?

The summer of 2004 was unravelling like a movie, with me as the main character. The things happening in my life got so unreal that I started to believe that I was truly special. I mean, it was hard not to. I had just developed superhero-like abilities by mastering *The Kybalion* Principles and putting them into practice. I learned that knowledge is the most excellent source of power. Anything is possible in life, and you can manifest your deepest dreams when you maximize your personal power through the application of knowledge.

If you are interested in reading more about the details of the extraordinary events that took place and unravelled my fate, I encourage you to read my autobiography, *Man of Light,* which I worked on at the same time as this book. It is the only way you will understand the level of momentum that I generated by learning and applying the Principles of *The Kybalion* since this momentum was to reach its pinnacle that same year with a life-changing event.

MY KUNDALINI AWAKENING

After the grandiose summer of 2004, I regularly re-read *The Kybalion*, getting something new from it every time. One night, in October of 2004, I had a few profound realizations about the Principles that led to a very intense Kundalini awakening that evening. This event was a spontaneous activation as I knew nothing of this subject at the time. But in retrospect, everything in my life's journey led up to that event, so it was not a coincidence.

The Kundalini energy rose to the Crown (Sahasrara), activating the Seven Chakras along the way. The awakening process was completed once the Kundalini invigorated the *Seventy-Two Thousand Nadis*, or energetic channels, discussed in the Hindu tradition—thereby fully activating my *Body of Light* (or Light Body) and awakening all of its latent potential. I was raised to the level of *Cosmic Consciousness* in a matter of a few minutes. In terms of the Tree of Life, I had awakened all of its ten Spheres at once. Afterwards, I could experience the Sephiroth by using my Body of Light as a vehicle (to travel in those Inner Planes). Also, by awakening the entire Tree of Life, I had awakened the higher, Spiritual energy Spheres. Thus, the transformative process of integrating all the parts of the Self with the Spirit began.

However, my past conditioning up to that point had to be cleared. The time had come to learn a new way of living. A complete transformation of mind, body, and Soul was in order so that I could integrate with the newfound Cosmic Consciousness that became a part of my everyday life. And although this was not an easy task, it was a necessary one.

The Kundalini awakening activated all the latent potential inside of me. Because it awakened the Seven Chakras simultaneously, negative Karma stored in each Chakra came to the forefront of my consciousness. Note that other than the Seven Chakras, otherwise called Major or Common Chakras, there are also various Minor Chakras along the energetic points of the body, which also got activated upon awakening the Kundalini. Minor Chakras are auxiliary energy centres that work with the Major Chakras as energy flow conductors and regulators. They assist the Major Chakras in carrying out their duties; thus, they are interconnected with them. For simplicity, though, since this book deals only with the seven Major Chakras, I will be referring to them as Chakras only, unless I distinguish that they are Minor Chakras.

Because the entire Tree of Life was now awakened inside me, it brought out a lot of fear and anxiety. Everything in life started to worry me. Having the Kundalini awakening before you are ready to receive such an influx of energy can, and will, be very challenging because, to attune to the higher Spheres of the Tree of Life, you will have to overcome the negative Karma from the lower Spheres. There is no other way. The process of Spiritual Evolution is Universal.

"Worry is the child of fear—if you kill out fear, worry will die for want of nourishment." — William Walker Atkinson; excerpt from "Thought Vibration or the Law of Attraction in the Thought World"

Although I felt blessed to have had such a profound experience, with many transformations of mind, body, and Soul right from the start, I still had fear and anxiety present within me. I could feel it in every action I was performing, and it became crucial that I find a way to help myself. Nobody could understand what had happened to me when I told them of my experience. Some even suggested I seek therapy and get on prescription medication because my thoughts and emotions were in disarray. I chose not to follow their advice and sought to find another way to help myself.

My brain felt broken, and the constant fear and anxiety made it difficult to live. The old model of functioning ceased to exist, and I seemed lost. I had no control over my thoughts or emotions anymore. Depression soon set in because I was at the mercy of energy that I did not understand—the Kundalini. I cried myself to sleep many nights and felt alone.

Nevertheless, because of the profound changes in how I started perceiving the world, I became determined to help myself at all costs. So I started seeking and looking for Spiritual practices to help my mental and emotional Self get into balance again. I was going to overcome my fear and anxiety and learn to enjoy my new Self, and nothing would stop me.

THE GOLDEN DAWN SYSTEM

After dedicating myself to learning more about the Kundalini and *Hermeticism* through books, I was drawn to a Western Mystery school called the *Esoteric Order of the Golden Dawn*. The Golden Dawn is a school of occult sciences that teaches its students Qabalah, Hermeticism, Tarot, Astrology, *Geomancy*, the Egyptian and Christian Mysteries, and most importantly, Ceremonial Magick. I say most importantly because the Chief *Adept* (of the Toronto Temple) told me that the purpose of Ceremonial Magick within the school is to undergo a process of Spiritual Alchemy to cleanse and purify the Chakras, thereby removing the negative Karma stored in each. Since I needed exactly what the Golden Dawn had to offer, I decided to join the Order.

As every new Order member is given a Magickal name, I was named Frater Prudentia de Animus Lux, or Frater P.A.L. for short. The name is Latin, and its English translation is "Wisdom of Spiritual Light." The Chief Adept told me that he channelled the name from Divine Realms, which inspired me. From that moment on, I decided it was my solemn duty to live up to my Magickal name at all costs.

It was time that I changed who I was and who I had become up to this point. Using others for personal gain and seeking power over them became something I had to neutralize within myself to attune my Chakras. I learned that every action which does not come from a place of unconditional love is an Egoic action that carries Karmic consequences. At this time, I had been experiencing my Karma in real time, moment to moment, because the Kundalini awakening made all my negative thoughts and emotions appear more real than ever.

The Kundalini energy bridges the conscious and subconscious minds so that you can't hide from your thoughts anymore. Everything has to be dealt with and overcome. I could not mess around with any more energy that was not pure and of the Light since it stimulated fear within me. The Kundalini awakening process forced me to change, clear my thoughts, and quiet my mind like never before.

Since I was still polarized in Hod and living a somewhat mental existence up to this point, I started a shift back to Netzach to get in touch with my emotions and with the power of love again. As the Sphere of Hod filters the energies of the above Spheres before they manifest, this aspect of my personality had to be amended. The daily ritual exercises presented to me by the Golden Dawn started positively impacting me right away. After searching for a year, I finally found my self-healing tool.

In the first grade of the Golden Dawn, Neophyte, I was introduced to the Lesser Banishing Ritual of the Pentagram (LBRP). Its purpose was to clear my Aura (egg-shaped personal energy field) of positive and negative energy influences and get me in touch with my Soul through silence and peace of mind. I also was given the Middle Pillar (MP) exercise that brought Light into the Aura by invoking the Middle Spheres of the Tree of Life. I worked directly with the Tree of Life through the Middle Pillar while having this Kundalini energy active within me. The Middle Pillar exercise is a gradual process of bringing Light in, but a powerful one. I did these two ritual exercises for about a month, and for the first time since awakening Kundalini, I felt better and better daily. There were no negative consequences to using these two exercises, I found. I had energy alignments in my Light Body almost nightly as the Kundalini energy worked through me.

The following month, I started working on my Karma and the Chakras themselves after being initiated into the Grade of Zelator, the grade of the Earth Element. This Element corresponds with the Base Chakra-Muladhara. I was given the Lesser Invoking Ritual of the Pentagram (LIRP), whereby I invoked the Earth Element directly into my Aura. The LIRP is used to invoke the four Elemental energies. The purpose of the LIRP is to activate Karmic energy and tune the Chakra pertaining to the Elemental energy being invoked.

In Zelator, I was also given the Banishing Ritual of the Hexagram (BRH) that removed Karmic Planetary influences from my Aura and got me in touch with my Soul more. The Lesser Banishing Ritual of the Pentagram works to clear the Microcosm, while the Banishing Ritual of the Hexagram clears the negative influences from the Macrocosm. The Microcosm is the world inside of man, while the Macrocosm is the world outside. One reflects and affects the other—As Above, So Below.

"Everything that can be found in the Universe on a large scale is reflected in a human being on a small scale." — Franz Bardon; excerpt from "Initiation into Hermetics"

In the Zelator grade, I had many energy alignments in my Light Body, primarily through grounding my thoughts and the energy lines connecting to the Minor Chakras in the soles of my feet. The energy lines in the Foot Soles need to link back to the Earth on which we walk, meaning there needs to be an alignment in Muladhara Chakra. The Kundalini continued to transform me, and the ritual exercises I was working with were helping considerably with the transformation.

In the next Grade of Theoricus, I started working with the Air Element. Air allowed me to connect with my thoughts more. It proved to be a hugely transformative experience and removed much of the fear and anxiety I had before. The Air Element directly connects to the Ego and the lower thoughts and desires. Invoking Air allowed me to connect with my Heart Chakra-Anahata, and tune and purify it.

I became highly attuned to my dreams and was Lucid Dreaming almost nightly. *Lucid Dreams* were my first taste of Out of Body Experiences (OBE's) since my consciousness embodied my Body of Light to travel in these enigmatic, inner Cosmic Realms. My thoughts became much calmer and more peaceful after spending three months working with the Air Element and overcoming the Karmic challenges present within it.

In Theoricus, I connected more with the Spirit energy. I experienced energy alignments in my newly formed Light Body as a cooling, Spirit energy permeated the Minor Chakras at the soles of my feet and the palms of my hands. This experience enabled me to awaken new psychic powers and become One with everything I looked at in the Physical World. Purifying the Air Element within the Self is crucial when undergoing the Kundalini awakening process. In fact, the Caduceus of Hermes is the representative emblem of the Air Element. Air is connected to healing as well as Light—the ultimate healer.

The next grade, Practicus, was when I started to get in tune with unconditional love through the Water Element, which corresponds to Swadhisthana-the Sacral Chakra. I felt the soothing, loving energy of Water permeate my Light Body that put my mind in a state of profound calmness. Fear and anxiety washed away in the presence of this beautiful, loving Water energy. I spent many nights crying in the warm embrace of this process of Spiritual transformation that I was undergoing. Everything I was experiencing with these ritual exercises worked wonders to elevate my Kundalini experience and further my Spiritual Evolution.

After being in Practicus for two months, I was ready to embrace the Fire Element and tune my Solar Plexus Chakra-Manipura; thus, I entered the following grade of Philosophus. Manipura was the last of the lower four Chakras. Mastery over the Fire Element and my willpower meant that I was ready for invocations of Spirit. This Fire energy seemed (in a sense) similar to the energy of the Kundalini when I first awakened it but more balanced. Up to this point, because I had done so much work in attuning the lower Chakras and removing fear and anxiety from my energy system, working with Fire was fun and relatively easy. My biggest challenge in the Fire grade was overcoming any anger issues.

Since I was working on attuning my willpower, I had to align it with my Higher Self and not my Ego. The challenge of distinguishing between the impulses of the two was part of the work that I was undertaking. The dichotomy of Ego and Spirit is present at all times. We have to use the Element of Water and unconditional love as an anchor and foundation for our actions.

At this point in my Magickal journey, I left the Golden Dawn Order since politics within the organization were beginning to overshadow the crucial personal work that I was doing. From that moment onwards, I decided to be a solitary Magus. Once I had spent seven months working with the Fire Element, I was ready to undertake invocations of the Spirit. I used the Supreme Invoking Ritual of the Pentagram (SIRP) to invoke the Four Elements under the presidency and direction of the Spirit energy. Spirit is not an Element in and of itself, as it works through the other Four Elements. The Chakras of the Spirit Element are the three highest ones—Vishuddhi, Ajna, and Sahasrara.

In reality, you learn to function through the three highest Chakras by awakening the Kundalini. As you become in tune with your Higher Self (through Sahasrara), you learn to operate through intuition and the direct experience of energy—otherwise known as Gnosis. You must let go and become a channel for the Light to speak through you. Learning to attune the lowest four Chakras and remove the negative Karma from each is paramount in furthering your Spiritual Evolution after awakening Kundalini.

I worked with the Supreme Ritual of the Pentagram for nine months before taking my Magickal journey to the next level by beginning to work with Enochian Magick. The Enochian Magick system enabled me to further my Spiritual Evolution and Spiritual Alchemy process. I found the experience with this system to be invaluable, especially working with the Thirty Aethyrs. These concentric circles inside the Aura stimulated and directly worked with the Ida and Pingala *Nadis*—the masculine and feminine currents that regulate the Kundalini energy.

I had many profound mystical and transcendental experiences while working with Enochian Magick. I found the Thirty Aethyrs to be the key to taking my consciousness across the Abyss, which is a process I will discuss in great detail in this book because of its importance. However, I am presenting Enochian Magick practices for the advanced aspirant only in this book. I will explain why that is later on.

I have also included Planetary Magick as part of the curriculum presented in *The Magus*. In my experience, Planetary Magick has been very useful in isolating the different parts of my psyche pertaining to Archetypal forces that make up my character and personality. These can be seen as the higher powers of the Chakras, although they are more related to the powers of the Sephiroth on the Tree of Life. Through the use of Planetary Magick, I built up my ethics and morals, which helped shape my new beliefs about myself and the world I live in. This work was essential to my Spiritual Alchemy process with Ceremonial Magick.

SHARING KNOWLEDGE AND WISDOM

I worked with Magickal rituals for over five years and then spent two years leading my own Golden Dawn group in Toronto, Canada. Afterwards, I broke away from the organized system but continued to teach Ceremonial Magick to many people who had come along my path seeking Spiritual Evolution. I had fallen in love with the subjects in this book as I journeyed through the Western Mysteries. Due to my passion, I dedicated all of my energy to mastering all of them. Now I am presenting this much-anticipated work here for you, the reader. I want other seekers (such as myself) to get the full benefit from using Ceremonial Magick. Therefore, I am presenting the mentioned ritual exercises, along with their complementary theoretical knowledge.

As a herald of good news, a messenger of the Gods, I am excited to share my discoveries with others, especially Kundalini awakened individuals. I hope to bless their lives the same way I was blessed when I walked into that Golden Dawn Temple in Toronto sixteen years ago, seeking inner healing after awakening the Kundalini energy. Over the years, I accepted that the Magickal name I was given within the Golden Dawn Order (Frater P.A.L.) is also symbolic of my role as being a "pal" or "friend" to all people who seek Spiritual guidance and teachings. As the embodiment of the "Wisdom of Spiritual Light," it has been my duty to share this Light with others in their quest for sacred knowledge and Spiritual transcendence.

My seventeen-year journey of living with awakened Kundalini is a testament to the power of Hermetic teachings, from *The Kybalion* to the Qabalah and Ceremonial Magick. These three powerful tools are invaluable to any aspirant who desires to evolve Spiritually and realize their true potential. I am thrilled to share this with you, the reader, knowing that if you devote the recommended time to learning about these subjects and practising the ritual exercises yourself, you will evolve Spiritually.

Whether you are a Kundalini awakened individual looking for a practice to help deal with the fear and anxiety that arise upon the awakening (as I was), or you want to help yourself grow Spiritually and expand your consciousness, these ritual exercises and teachings are for you. Thus, I am honoured to be presenting this information to you and excited at the same time to take part in helping with your Spiritual Evolution.

When it comes to practising Ceremonial Magick, the best advice I have ever received is to be determined, persistent and consistent in working on the ritual exercises daily because the cumulative effect of daily practise yields the most positive results. If you merely glance over the exercises but don't try them, or try them a few times and deem them too tedious to be consistent with them daily, you will not get anything from them. However, if you stick to it and follow the prescribed program, you will benefit greatly in many ways.

I have presented everything clearly and concisely so that you can follow the steps easily and can achieve the desired results. Be persistent in your study and in working with the ritual exercises daily, and allow yourself a few weeks to a month to start seeing some results. I guarantee you that you will not be disappointed in the long run. You will most likely develop a deep love and admiration for these exercises because of the positive effect they will have on your life and your ability to reach your true potential.

A MAN ON A MISSION

I have tried here to condense my Spiritual journey in as few words as possible so that you have some idea of who I am and how I got here. I wanted you to know the background behind my Kundalini awakening and my journey in Magick, and how it had helped me when I needed it most. After the Kundalini awakening, I was forced by the Divine to transform on all levels of Self so that I could become a conduit and vessel for this newfound Kundalini energy. Silence of mind became my prime objective. I was no longer concerned with controlling my reality, as was the case before the awakening. I learned to overcome my Ego so that I could align with my Higher Self, as that became my destiny after the awakening.

I wrote this book during a three-year writing period that commenced in October of 2016, precisely twelve years after the awakening of the Kundalini. During those three years, I also worked on three other bodies of work. This writing period continues to this day and may prove to be a lifelong endeavour. Nonetheless, during those three years, my ideas solidified, and the bulk of the text for each of the four bodies of work was written.

Man of Light is my autobiography—my life's journey. It is an in-depth look at my life leading up to the awakening and everything that followed. It is a chronological sequence of events in my life that all shaped me into who I am now. In these pages, I have given you only a small, diluted version of my full life story. There is much more to my journey than what you have read thus far, but at least now you understand how I came to write *The Magus*. *Man of Light* is presented in a series of novels where I recount all of my life stories, some entertaining and informative, and others hard to believe. Although the content of the *Man of Light* books can be perceived as fiction, it is not. Every story and every event in the series happened to me at some point. My transformation is ongoing even after seventeen years of living with an awakened Kundalini, and *Man of Light* deals with how I have integrated these monumental changes into my personal life.

My second body of work, *Serpent Rising: The Kundalini Compendium*, features everything you need to know on the topic of Kundalini, including the science of bioenergy crossed with human anatomy, the philosophy and practice of Yoga (with Ayurveda), Crystals, Tuning Forks, Aromatherapy, Tattvas, Merkaba Mysteries, and so much more. I also discuss the Kundalini awakening and transformation process in detail, including permanent and partial Kundalini awakenings, Lucid Dreaming, the role of food, water, nutrients, and sexual energy during integration, and peak events in the overall transfiguration process.

This book contains all of my knowledge and experience acquired over the past seventeen years, including the all-important meditations on different energy points inside and around the head area that I discovered while encountering energy stagnations and blockages. Knowing how Ida, Pingala, and Sushumna operate within the

Kundalini system will enable you to be your own mechanic and "fix the engine" when it malfunctions. You can use these special Kundalini meditations to troubleshoot the system if you have a short-circuit, which can happen after a traumatic event or with drugs, alcohol, or other substances.

Lastly, having helped many Kundalini awakened people over the years who were "groping in the dark" looking for answers, I have included their most common questions and concerns as part of the book as well. *Serpent Rising: The Kundalini Compendium* is a thorough and advanced exposition on the Kundalini that is a must-read for anyone interested in the subject and their Spiritual growth. As a preview of this book and to give you an idea of the kind of psychic gifts you can receive by awakening the Kundalini, I have included a few articles I wrote for a blog in the back of *The Magus*.

Serpent Rising II: Kundalini in the Ancient World continues my Kundalini exploration journey; it includes historical research that proves that our Ancestors had full knowledge of the Kundalini as depicted symbolically in their art, sculpture, and scriptures. Furthermore, by examining Ancient traditions and religions, I have found that the Kundalini is a common thread that unites their Spiritual systems, practices and beliefs. I am excited to share this work alongside the first part, which will stand the test of time as the world's most comprehensive body of work on human energy potential.

My third body of work, *Cosmic Star-Child*, tackles perhaps the most critical question about the Kundalini—why do we have it in the first place? Why are we not born with an awakened Kundalini but instead have to activate it ourselves in this lifetime? To answer these difficult questions, I have travelled the world to Ancient sites to gain insight into the Kundalini from our Ancestors. By finding out where we came from, we can figure out where we are going. My findings over the years have made me question our history and humanity's origins. Much of what I have seen and experienced firsthand does not add up with what we are led to believe is the truth about who we are.

In *Cosmic Star-Child*, I challenge the old beliefs imposed by the Darwinian theory of evolution and offer insights into a more esoteric version of humanity's roots with Ancestors who are not of this world. This work contains rigorous exploration and research, supported by the latest scientific and archaeological findings. All conclusions in this work are fact-checked—they correspond with what many scholars in modern times accept as the truth regarding human history and origins. I believe that only by getting to the truth of the matter concerning who we are and how we got here can we honestly answer the most critical questions relating to the existence and purpose of the Kundalini energy.

I have expounded upon my own life experiences and the topics I am most passionate about in all four bodies of work to share my insights with you, the reader. Together, all of my books go hand in hand, although each tackles different subjects in detail.Thank you for deciding to make me a part of your Spiritual journey. I am confident that you will benefit greatly from my knowledge and experience and that if you devote yourself to the work presented in this book, you will further your Spiritual Evolution.

Fiat Lux,
Neven Paar

"O people of the Earth, men born and made of the Elements, but with the Spirit of the Divine Man within you, rise from your sleep of ignorance! Be sober and thoughtful. Realize that your home is not in the Earth but in the Light. Why have you delivered yourselves over unto death, having power to partake of Immortality? Repent, and change your minds. Depart from the Dark Light and forsake corruption forever. Prepare yourselves to climb through the Seven Rings (Chakras) and to blend your Souls with the Eternal Light."

—Hermes Trismegistus

from "Poimandres," the "Vision of Hermes"

PART I:
THE QABALAH

EASTERN AND WESTERN SPIRITUAL SYSTEMS

KUNDALINI AND MAGICK

Kundalini is a Sanskrit word which means "coiled one"—it refers to a form of primal energy called *Shakti*, said by Hindus to be located at the base of the spine, and coiled three-and-a-half times in a state of potential. This energy centre corresponds with Muladhara, the Earth Chakra. When the Kundalini is raised, Shakti meets *Shiva* at the top of the head, and their Divine Marriage represents the union of the individual consciousness with the Cosmic Consciousness. Kundalini energy is Life energy, and its overall purpose is to expand human consciousness. It is dormant in most people and can be awakened through meditation techniques, or even spontaneously, without any conscious effort of the individual.

> *"When you succeed in awakening the Kundalini, so that it starts to move out of its mere potentiality, you necessarily start a World which is totally different from our World. It is the World of Eternity."* — Carl Gustav Jung; excerpt from *"The Psychology of Kundalini Yoga: Notes of the Seminar Given in 1932 by C. G. Jung"*

Kundalini is interchangeable with the Western term "Serpent Power" and has been likened to a serpent for various reasons. Firstly, when the energy rises, to the person experiencing the awakening, the inner sound it makes is similar to the hissing of a snake. Secondly, its movement and expansion happen in the spinal column, which is shaped like an upright serpent or snake. Thirdly, the snake sheds its skin monthly, thereby renewing itself continually. The Kundalini, once activated, enables one to continuously transform and "shed their skin" until they are perfected Spiritually.

Once the Kundalini energy reaches the top of the head (Figure 1), it breaks the *Cosmic Egg*. It activates the Light Body and the Seventy-Two Thousand Nadis that flow like spider webs from each Chakra to our Body of Light—this is what is referred to as a "full" or "permanent" Kundalini awakening. A "partial" Kundalini awakening is when the Kundalini rises into a particular Chakra and then drops back down to the base of the spine, only to rise again sometime in the future. Though there are practices capable of inducing a Kundalini awakening, ultimately, it is something that is chosen for you in this lifetime by the Divine.

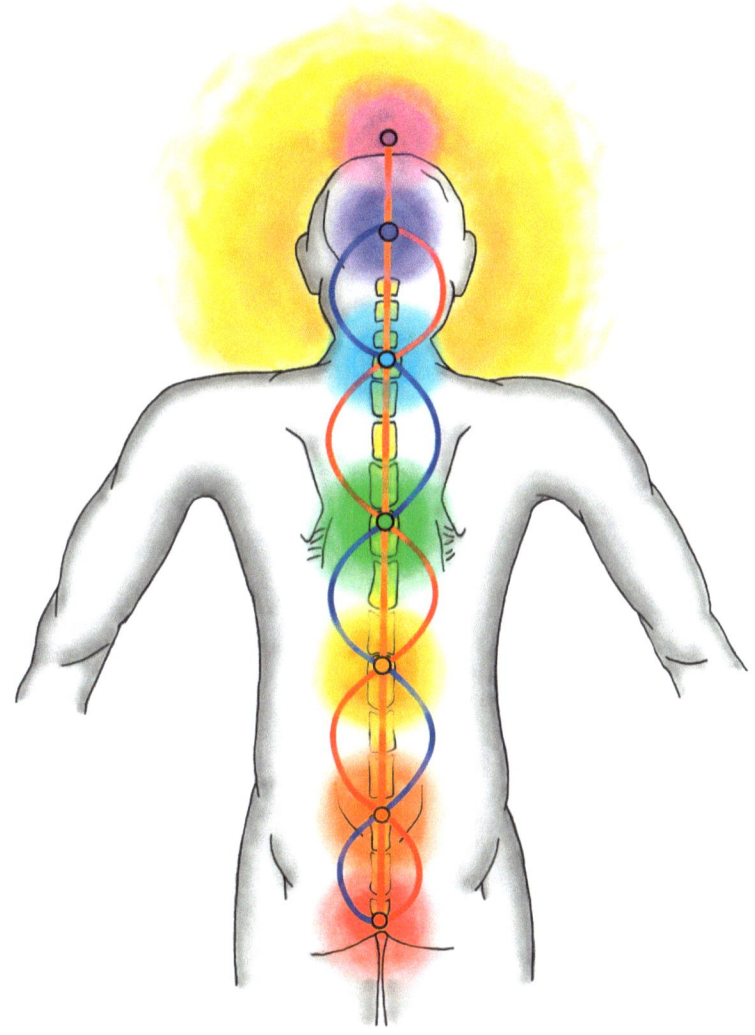

Figure 1: Kundalini Energy Raised to the Crown

As I mentioned in the "Author's Introduction," a powerful method of cleansing and purifying the Chakras is the use of Ceremonial Magick ritual exercises. Along with the Qabalah and the Tree of Life framework, these exercises are of Western origin. In this book, I will walk you through what Qabalah and Ceremonial Magick are and how they can help you. I will also give you these ritual exercises so that you can become familiar with them and use them on your awakening journey. Ceremonial Magick is the key to evolving beyond the negative Karma of the first four Elemental Chakras and learning how to attune, and operate, from the three higher Spiritual, or Aetheric, Chakras.

Ceremonial Magick is a sacred art of energy invocation and evocation. The ritualistic invocations it employs invoke (call-in) different energies from the Macrocosm (Solar System) into the Microcosm (human Aura) with the purpose of Spiritual Evolution. The ritual evocations allow the practitioner of Magick to access inner states of consciousness that they are otherwise unable to access. These ritual techniques, or exercises, consist of magical formulas (incantations) that involve the use of symbols, numbers, and the vibration (chanting) of Divine Names. Ceremonial Magick exercises focus on the Karmic evolution of the Chakras, which are synonymous with the energies of the Elements and Sub-Elements. In this way, the Eastern and Western systems describe the same ideas, just in different terms.

Eastern and Western philosophies may seem utterly unrelated on the surface, but there is much correlation between them in reality. They both serve to bring about a common goal—the expansion and evolution of human consciousness and union with the Divine. Discussing the energies of the Seven Chakras of the Eastern system is the same as talking about the energies of the Five Elements of the Western system. In *The Magus*, we will be examining the Western Mysteries (including Qabalah, Ceremonial Magick, and Hermetic philosophy) while corresponding everything to the Eastern system of the Seven Chakras and the Kundalini.

THE CHAKRAS

Chakra is a Sanskrit word for "spinning wheel" or "vortex" and is an Eastern term. This word is used to describe the invisible energy centres along the spinal column, comprised of multi-coloured flowing energy. These are the centres that balance, store and distribute the energies of life throughout our various Subtle Bodies. The Subtle Bodies are expressions of the different inner Cosmic Planes as each Subtle Body has a corresponding Cosmic Plane. Chakras are conductors of energy coming from the Cosmic Planes, and each is responsible for overseeing particular aspects of a human being's life. When cleansed and balanced, the Chakras offer exceptional extrasensory abilities.

"The Chakras or Force-Centres are points of connection at which energy flows from one body of a man to another...all these wheels are perpetually rotating, and into the hub or open mouth of each a force from a higher World is always flowing." — Charles W. Leadbeater, excerpt from "The Chakras"

Chakras are not physical. They are located in the Body of Light. They manifest in a circulating pattern in seven major areas of the Body of Light. They can be imagined as being shaped like flowers in full bloom. Each Chakra has a certain number of petals, wheel-like energy vortices radiating outwards that form horizontal, right angles. The Chakras spin clockwise, and the rate of their spinning determines how tuned or out of tune they are. The faster the spin, the more Light they channel, and the better they function.

Chakras regulate consciousness. Whether you have awakened the Kundalini or not, your Chakras are active to some extent, but if you are not using particular Chakras daily, they may be so stagnant that they seem practically at rest. Once you have awakened the Kundalini and raised it into the brain, your Chakras become invigorated by the Light from the Kundalini energy. They become like light bulbs functioning at maximum capacity. If a Chakra is filled with negative energy, it emits a dim Light rather than a bright one. Personal Karma stands in the way of the inner Light shining brightly, which is why the Chakras need to be cleansed and purified. Once this process is complete, the Light can shine brightly again.

KARMIC ENERGY

In the context of this book, Karmic energy refers to negative energy stored somewhere in the Aura that manifests through one of the Seven Chakras. This Karmic energy dims the Light of whichever Chakra it pertains to. Therefore, to cleanse the Chakra and tune it, we have to remove the negative Karma stored within it. Once this happens, the energy flow in the Aura will be robust and vibrant, and the Chakras will be functioning at their most optimal level.

Karma is an Eastern term defined in Hinduism and Buddhism as "the sum of a person's actions in this life and previous lives, viewed as deciding their fate in future existences." The word itself has become internationally recognized over time, and today we all understand what it means to some extent. If you have heard the saying, "You reap what you sow," or "What goes around comes around," then you understand how the Law of Karma operates on a human level—we get back what we put in essentially.

Karma is also defined as destiny or fate, following as an effect of a cause. According to the Law of Karma, every action is the effect of one or more previous actions and will be the cause of one or more future actions. Thus, if you have negative energy in a Chakra, it means that you acted negatively towards someone at some point in your past and accumulated bad Karma. Therefore, our behaviour and actions determine our fate. Through the work presented in this book, you are learning to develop and heighten your moral compass and ethics. By overcoming your Karmic burden, you become a better person, which cleanses your Chakras and improves their efficiency.

"Life will give you whatever experience is most helpful for the evolution of your consciousness. How do you know this is the experience you need? Because this is the experience you are having at the moment." — Eckhart Tolle; excerpt from "A New Earth: Awakening to Your Life's Purpose"

The notion of Karma is usually accompanied by the idea of reincarnation—that each life is the effect of previous lives and will be the cause of future lives. Maybe you are a good person in this lifetime, but you were not in one of your past lifetimes. You still would have Karmic energy to overcome, stored somewhere in your Chakras.

Our present incarnation on Earth is to gain experiences and learn the lessons of nature that allow us to continue our Spiritual Evolution. And we express those lessons (or lack thereof) from our past lives. In this sense, Karma is cyclical—it involves life events of similar quality, from which you are meant to learn something and evolve. Interestingly, these events will keep repeatedly occurring until you learn the intended Karmic lesson.

As each Chakra is a part of how you express your personality and character to the world, then the Karma of each Chakra is negative energy attached to how you express yourself in the world. Therefore, the Chakra needs to be cleansed and tuned so that your actions are coming from a place of unconditional love. If they are coming from a place of love, you are enlightening the Chakra of that expression of Self.

So if you are acting selfish, angry, lustful, fearful, greedy, arrogant, and so on, you need to work on those parts of Self and turn these actions into their positive, loving counterparts. In other words, you need to evolve the Karma particular to those Chakras that express these specific behaviours. This book aims to teach you how to turn negative (or bad) Karmic energy into positive energy and evolve Spiritually.

CHAKRA CLEANSING AND TUNING PRACTICES

Ceremonial Magick ritual exercises from the Western system are one of the practices for cleansing and tuning the Chakras, but there are other Spiritual healing practices worth mentioning. All of these practices address the stagnation of energy in the Aura. They also help in optimizing the energy flow of the Chakras. I will cover only a few here that I have found most helpful on my Spiritual journey, although there are many more. The Spiritual practices I have found most valuable work on invoking or evoking energy into the Aura, similarly to Ceremonial Magick exercises.

A powerful tool for cleansing and tuning the Chakras is the use of Gemstones, otherwise called Natural Stones or Crystals. A Gemstone is a precious or semi-precious stone produced by nature, found in rock formations. Most Gemstones are mineral crystals, though not all of them. Gemstones have been used for thousands of years by Ancient people from the East and the West for Spiritual healing. Each Gemstone emits a different type of energy which has various healing properties when applied to the human Aura. However, since the science of Gemstones is not exact in terms of the type and quantity of energy that each stone emits, it is much harder to isolate individual Chakras to work on them. In addition, many Gemstones can be used for more than one Chakra, making it a haphazard process compared to Ceremonial Magick ritual exercises.

Another Spiritual practice, or tool, for working with the Chakras is Tuning Forks used in Sound Healing, which is both an Eastern and Western practice. Since each Chakra vibrates at a particular frequency, a Tuning Fork that resonates at that same frequency can be used to tune the Chakra and heal the energies in the Aura.

The Tuning Fork matches the frequency of a Chakra and "entrains" it, thereby returning it to its optimum, healthy vibration. The limitation of this practice is that it is relatively new (under forty years), and the frequencies of the Tuning Forks may or may not be accurate in terms of their application to Spiritual healing. So far, though, what has been proven is that it works quite efficiently.

The use of Tattvas is an Eastern practice that has been around for over two-thousand years. The very word "tattva" is a Sanskrit word meaning "essence," "principle," or "element." Tattvas represent the Four Elements of Earth, Water, Air, and Fire, along with the fifth Element of Spirit. They are easy to use while also being very effective. There are five primary Tattvas, each of which has five Sub-Tattvas, making a total of thirty. Tattvas are best looked upon as "windows" into the Cosmic Planes, which correspond to the energies of the Chakras.

Tattvas are beneficial in working with the Chakras and the Karmic energy contained therein. They do not generate any energy in and of themselves, like Gemstones and Tuning Forks do, but they are useful to zero in on the inner Cosmic Planes and work on the corresponding Chakras. In my experience, working with the Tattvas goes hand in hand with using Ceremonial Magick rituals pertaining to the Elements.

These are a few of the practices worth mentioning that apply to Spiritual healing. Other healing practices include but are not limited to Yoga, *Reiki*, Acupuncture, Qigong, Tai Chi, Aromatherapy, Reflexology, Biofeedback, Ruach Healing, Past Life Regression, Hypnosis, Transcendental Meditation, and Neuro-Linguistic Programming. What you choose is up to you. As I said, though, in my personal experience, after having tried just about every method out there, I have found Ceremonial Magick to be the most precise and effective way of working with the Chakras and Spiritually healing and evolving.

THE KUNDALINI CRISIS

Whether you have awakened the Kundalini energy or not, you will have Karmic energy to deal with in your life. Everyone needs to cleanse their Chakras of negative energy to advance Spiritually. For non-awakened people, their consciousness operates from one Chakra at a time in most cases. Depending on which inner faculty you use, you will jump from Chakra to Chakra to express those faculties. Your emotions belong to a different Chakra than your imagination, for example, or your willpower. But in all cases, you can fine-tune those inner faculties so that your personal power increases.

Those individuals, who have had a full, permanent, Kundalini awakening, are dealing with a much more challenging situation. All of their Chakras are streaming into consciousness at the same time. Having gone through this myself years ago, I can safely say that this state of Being is a form of crisis. For these people, it is crucial to start working on clearing the Karmic energy from each Chakra immediately to overcome this uncomfortable state.

After a full, permanent, Kundalini awakening, all fears are magnified since every thought in these individuals' minds appears as real as you and I. This happens because, as the Light is projected from the inside, it magnifies all thoughts, animating them and giving them life. When the Kundalini rises into the brain, a bridge is created between the conscious and the subconscious minds, linking them and giving them unity.

However, in unawakened people, their consciousness oscillates between the conscious and subconscious minds, with a clear division. So to clear the Karmic energy, we need to work primarily on clearing the harmful content in the subconscious mind since this is where most of the negative energy is stored.

We all have our Demons (adverse thought senders) that we hide from. We lodged them somewhere in the back of our subconscious mind and tried to forget about them sometime in the past. They surface occasionally, but these Demons are left alone for the most part. "Out of sight, out of mind," as the saying goes. They are still a part of us, though and need to be confronted. Until we overcome them, we will not be tapping into our highest potential as Spiritual human beings.

The work presented in this book aims to help you face your Demons and fears and overcome them. We are trying to give our Demons wings, metaphorically speaking, and turn them into their loving opposites, the Angels (positive thought senders). We can make our Demons allies in life and use them to increase our personal power drastically.

Also, by overcoming your Demons, you remove fear from your system since Demons feed on fear energy while the Angels feed on love energy. Unmastered Demons and Karmic energy go hand in hand; thus, you have to learn to confront your Demons and subdue them if you want to overcome your Karmic energy and evolve Spiritually.

"F.E.A.R. is False Evidence Appearing Real." — Anonymous

For the Kundalini awakened individuals, though, those who have had a full and permanent awakening, no choice is given in this matter. As this bridge between the subconscious and conscious minds is created, all of their Demons have full access to their consciousness daily. They cannot run nor hide from them anymore. And as all of this negative subconscious content is released to be dealt with, it can make for a very uncomfortable living experience. I remember because I was there seventeen years ago. It became crucial for me to find a way, practice or tool to deal with my Demons if I would enjoy my life again. And, as destiny would have it, I stumbled upon Ceremonial Magick, and my prayers were answered.

In full and permanent Kundalini awakened individuals, there is also a constant vibratory sound heard inside the head that sounds like a jet engine or a swarm of bees. This continuous vibration, which is present 24/7 following a Kundalini awakening, is very alarming at first and requires adjusting. Furthermore, fear of the Unknown adds to the overall fear and anxiety once these other inner transformations have taken place.

Unfortunately, no medical doctors can help in the matter since the Kundalini phenomenon is still relatively new, meaning that not much is known about it in our society. We are not dealing with something physical but with energy—an intangible substance. Most psychologists or psychiatrists cannot help either because unless they have had a Kundalini awakening, they cannot possibly understand what these individuals are going through. The work of overcoming the Karmic energy in each Chakra is paramount to helping these individuals advance and move forward with their Spiritual Evolution.

THE FIVE ELEMENTS

The Five Elements correspond with the Seven Chakras (Figure 2). The first four correspond with Earth, Water, Fire, and Air, respectively. The three higher Chakras correspond with Spirit or *Aethyr* (the two terms are interchangeable). By invoking the energy of the Five Elements, Ceremonial Magick ritual exercises work to tune and purify their associated Chakras. The tuning process occurs once the Elemental energies are brought into the Aura via these exercises and worked through in consciousness. This process influences your psyche, activating Karmic level events meant to be overcome so that you can purify and exalt the Chakra(s) corresponding with its Elemental energy. Thus, the Ceremonial Magick exercises presented in this book speed up your Karma in its process of unfoldment, accelerating your Spiritual Evolution process.

You will have a lot of Karmic energy coming your way from working with the Elements, but this is a good thing when trying to grow Spiritually. It may be uncomfortable at first, but you will soon welcome the process as you start overcoming your Karmic energy. Also, as you open doors to your inner psyche, you will find that more doors will open that you did not even know existed. In this way, you will be developing yourself into a Spiritual Warrior.

The path of Enlightenment is only for the strong. The work with Ceremonial Magick exercises will make you resilient and resistant to negative energy. You will learn to live with negative energy and use it productively instead of being used by it. By learning not to fear the negative energy, the anxiety that arises when faced with confrontations in life will lessen, resulting in your personal power rising.

As you evolve Spiritually due to this work, you will discover a whole new way of living. You learn to live in synch with the Cosmos and the Universal Laws by mastering the Elements of your Being. And when you are living in this way, the Universe will bless you by making all of your dreams come true. Sounds too good to be true? It is not. But you have a lot of work ahead of you to get there.

"Man is a Microcosm, or a little World, because he is an extract from all the Stars and Planets of the whole firmament, from the Earth and the Elements, and so he is their Quintessence." — Paracelsus; excerpt from "Hermetic Astronomy"

The Universe outside of us, including the energy composition of every human being, consists of the Four Elements (five including Spirit). Hermetic Qabalah states that the Microcosm directly reflects the Macrocosm, and vice versa—As Above, So Below. The Microcosm is the Aura and the energetic composition of a human, which finds its reflection in the Universe and, more particularly, in the Solar System we are a part of (located in an outer spiral arm of the Milky Way Galaxy).

Through this Hermetic axiom of, "As Above, So Below," we work our Magick, knowing that if we affect something outside of us, we affect something inside of us, and vice versa. The Elements are found in the physical Universe that we partake in and inside of us. Inside of us, they are expressed through the Chakras. Outside of us, they are expressed through the land, the sea, the air, and the Sun.

Spirit is not technically an Element in and of itself but is the composition of the sum of the Four Elements—it is the building block, the medium, the glue which holds them all together. It is the Prima Materia, the First Substance, and the Source of everything in existence. Everything manifested came from the Spirit, and everything is meant to go back and be re-absorbed into the Spirit. Spirit vibrates at the highest vibration frequency; hence, it is invisible to the senses. As the vibration slows down, the Spirit manifests as the four primary Elements of Fire, Water, Air, and Earth, sequentially. As Spirit is manifesting as the lower Elements, it retains its original energy in a state of potential. It is up to us to Spiritualize our Elements and raise our consciousness back to the Source—God-the Creator.

The four primary Elements can be seen as Realms, Kingdoms, or divisions of nature. They are the basic modes of existence and action—the building blocks of everything in the Universe. However, even the Four Elements are not technically four but three; since the fourth Element of Earth is the composition of the three foundational Elements in their densest form. Earth and Spirit, therefore, are like opposites of each other—they are at opposite ends of the vibratory scale. The three foundational Elements are Fire, Water, and Air.

Fire is purifying. It destroys the old, making way for the new. All new things come out of Fire, and all old things are transformed by it. The Fire Element is the masculine Principle, and the Father energy—the driving Force of the Universe. Fire represents Force and Will, and it is the closest of the three foundational Elements to Spirit. The active part of the Self relies on the Fire Element. It is the conscious mind, the willpower, and the vitality of a human being. Fire is combustion within the Physical World, manifesting both heat and Light. Through burning, Fire brings about transmutation, regeneration and growth. Fire's direction in Space is the South.

Water is the feminine Principle, the Mother energy, in partnership with the Father energy, the Fire. It contains the Astral blueprint of all solid bodies in the Universe. The Water Element is Form; the Force of Fire cannot exist without it. The two are opposites of each other and exist as a duality. The Water Element is the passive, receptive part of the Self—the subconscious. It is what comprises feelings and emotions. Water is love, consciousness, and the infinite possibilities that exist before Form and Creation. Within the Physical World, Water is made up of hydrogen and oxygen molecules. Its direction in Space is the West.

Air is all around us and is always in motion. All of life depends on Air, the offspring of the Fire and Water Elements. As the offspring, it is the Son energy. Within the physical reality, Fire and Water come together to create Air in the form of steam. Therefore, the Air Element is the balancing point between the other primary Elements, Fire and Water. Air is action, and it is closely related to Fire. Like Fire, the Air Element is also masculine, representing activity and energy. Differing from Fire, Air is associated with the intellect and the logical mind. Thinking and thoughts, just like the Air Element, are rapid, quick to change, and without Form. Air is also associated with the sense of smell. As the Fire Element acts, Air communicates. With the use of vocalized language, Air is the breath of life. Air makes up the Earth's atmosphere within the Physical World as a mixture of gases. Its direction in Space is the East.

Earth is the Three-Dimensional World in which we all exist. It is the ground on which we walk, the material expression of the Universal energy. The Earth Element was manifested once the energy of Spirit had reached the lowest point of density and frequency of vibration. It represents growth, fertility, and regeneration concerning *Gaia*—the Planet Earth. Earth is the synthesis of the Fire, Water, and Air Elements in their most dense Form, and the container of those Elements on the Physical Plane. In a general sense, the Earth Element represents grounding and stability. It is passive and feminine, just like the Water Element. Within the Physical World, Earth is our Planet's organic and inorganic compounds. Earth's direction in Space is the North.

THE SEVEN CHAKRAS

Muladhara, the first Chakra, is attributed to the Element of Earth. Its location is between the perineum and the coccyx (tailbone). Muladhara is directly linked to the base of the spine, where the Kundalini resides, coiled three-and-a-half times in a state of potential in the unawakened individuals. Muladhara is also called the Root or Base Chakra. It is related to the physical body and its expression in the material world. This Chakra's energy is the densest as it vibrates at the lowest frequency of all the Chakras. Muladhara has four petals, or vortices, and is the colour red. The Subtle Body of Muladhara is the Lower Astral Body as it functions through the Lower Astral Plane just above, but touching upon, the Physical Plane. Note that the Lower Astral Body is invariably connected to the physical body and not something completely separate from it. Many people say that Muladhara is the Chakra that expresses only the physical body, although it also has an Astral or invisible component. The Lower Astral Body is frequently called the Etheric Body.

Swadhisthana, the second Chakra, is attributed to the Element of Water. Its function is to process our lower emotions projected from our subconscious mind. The location of Swadhisthana is in the lower abdomen. It is often called the Sacral, Spleen, or even Navel Chakra, and it deals with social interaction, sexuality, and empathy toward others. This Chakra contains the lower parts of the Self, as it is the seat of the Ego. Its primary mode of functioning is to feel since it is the source of emotionality. Swadhisthana is the place where our stability and our foundation are. It is a place of no thought, only action—action in the direction of our expression in the outside world. An emotional response triggers this action, though. Swadhisthana has six petals and is the colour orange. The Subtle Body of Swadhisthana is the Higher Astral Body, and it functions in the Higher Astral Plane, which is above the Physical and Lower Astral Planes. There is no clear division between the Lower Astral and Higher Astral Planes, but one leads into and corresponds with the other in the same way as the emotions affect bodily actions and vice versa. The Higher Astral Body is often referred to as the Emotional Body.

Manipura, the third Chakra, is attributed to the Element of Fire. Its function is to drive and motivate us while powering our creativity since Manipura is the birthplace of our imagination. Manipura is the source of our willpower, and it is located at the solar plexus; hence, it is called the Solar Plexus Chakra. It deals with intelligence, mental clarity, and harmonizing the will and emotions. Manipura works with the Chakra above it, Anahata (which is related to thought), to activate the imagination, which requires both willpower and thought. Manipura is the "Seat of the Soul"—it uses the Element of Air (above it), as well as the Elements of Water and Earth (below it). Manipura acts on the emotions of Water and the stability and actions of Earth. Fire acting on Earth is how we animate the physical body in the material world. Manipura has ten petals and is the colour yellow. The Subtle Body of Manipura is the Higher Mental Body, and it functions on the Higher Mental Plane. The mind is above the involuntary emotions of the Astral Plane.

Figure 2: The Seven Chakras

Anahata, the fourth Chakra, is attributed to the Element of Air. Also known as the Heart Chakra, Anahata's location is in between the two breasts. Its function is to process the emotions of our imagination and fantasies while powering our thoughts. Through it, we feel love, but we also experience the Karma of the three lowest Chakras. In Anahata, we also understand our life's work and purpose. As the Air Element is thought, Anahata is related to willpower and emotion (below it), as it exalts the Fire and Water Elements. Air moves and sustains both Water and Fire, as related to the Elements and their physical manifestations. Air maintains equilibrium between the Fire and Water Elements also. As this Chakra is the place where we feel love, it is the place where we feel compassion toward others once activated correctly. If this Chakra is inactive, we turn to selfishness and "feeding" the Ego. Anahata has twelve petals, and its colour is green. The Subtle Body of Anahata is the Lower Mental Body, functioning on the Lower Mental Plane. Note that the Lower and Higher Mental Planes are, in reality, one Plane of existence, although a division can be made in their expression. The Ego expresses itself more through the Air Element, while the Soul expresses itself through the Fire Element.

Vishuddhi, the fifth Chakra, is attributed to the Element is Spirit (Aethyr). Otherwise known as the Throat Chakra, Vishuddhi's location is in the throat. Vishuddhi works in conjunction with the following two Chakras above it, Ajna and Sahasrara. All three of the highest Chakras are of the Spirit Element. Vishuddhi is related to the expression of the Self and written and oral skills. It generates the vibration of the spoken word, as it is the centre of communication. Vishuddhi controls discernment and the intellect as well. It has sixteen petals, and its colour is blue. The Subtle Body of Vishuddhi is the Spiritual Body within the Spiritual Plane. The three highest Chakras work in unison with one another as they channel the Light downwards from Sahasrara (Kether on the Tree of Life). I will discuss this process in greater detail in the next chapter on the Qabalah.

Ajna, the sixth Chakra, is also attributed to the Element of Spirit, or Aethyr. Also known as the Brow, or Mind's Eye Chakra, Ajna is located at a point within the head between and just above the eyebrows. Ajna is the primary Chakra concerning the Inner Worlds or Planes. Through this Chakra, we reach the Crown/Sahasrara and exit out of our physical body to travel in different dimensions of Time and Space. These travels occur in the higher Cosmic Planes where we use our Light Body as the vehicle. Lucid Dreaming and Astral projection are two types of Spiritual travel dependent on Ajna. Ajna is also the centre of intuition because it receives information from the higher realms above it that come through Sahasrara, the Crown Chakra. Ajna has two petals and is the colour indigo. The Subtle Body of Ajna is the Spiritual Body within the Spirit Element.

Sahasrara, the seventh Chakra, is also attributed to the Element of Spirit, or Aethyr. Otherwise known as the Crown Chakra, Sahasrara is located at the top of the head, in the centre. It is the last of the personal Chakras relating to the consciousness concerning the physical body. Sahasrara is the highest Chakra of the Spirit Element. As the highest in human consciousness, it is the source of ultimate understanding and knowledge. Just as the Root Chakra connects us to the Earth, the Crown Chakra is our connection to the Universe above us. Sahasrara is White Light and the source of it. Light comes in through Sahasrara, and it gets dimmer depending on how much Karma there is in the lower Chakras. The dimmer the Chakras below it, the more Ego is present, and the less the Higher Self is present. The source of the Higher Self is Sahasrara. Traditionally, this centre is like a wheel with one thousand (countless) petals or vortices. As the source of everything, it is also the source and totality of all the powers and the Chakras. In some schools of thought, the colour of Sahasrara Chakra is white, whereas, in others, it is violet. Sahasrara is the gateway to the Divine Worlds that are beyond comprehension. The Subtle Body of Sahasrara is the Spiritual Body.

***

Now that you have been given the colours of each Chakra, you will find something peculiar about their specific pattern. All the colours follow the pattern found in the rainbow, starting with red, and ending with violet. The rainbow is caused when water droplets in the air refract the White Light from the Sun. The result is the spectrum of Light with seven distinct colours. The totality of the Chakras then is the White Light from the Sun, which comes in from above (through Sahasrara Chakra) and filters downwards into each Chakra, thereby powering them. The Buddhists refer to the Body of Light as the *Rainbow Body*.

According to many Spiritual schools of thought, other than the Major and Minor Chakras, there are also Transpersonal Chakras. These are Chakras outside of the Light Body that the human being is connected to energetically. If we extend the energetic column of the Seven Chakras upwards and downwards, this would mean there are various Transpersonal Chakras above Sahasrara and one below Muladhara, in varying degrees of consciousness. Transpersonal means that they transcend the realms of the incarnated personality. However, I will not get into these Chakras in this book since it is outside the scope of work to be undertaken here. For information related to the Transpersonal Chakras, refer to my second book, *Serpent Rising: The Kundalini Compendium*.

Above the Spiritual Plane, there also exists the Divine Planes, to which Chakras above Sahasrara belong. Once you have come far enough with your Spiritual Evolution, you may be granted entry into these Divine Planes. Regardless, although there are some shared characteristics from one experience to the next, no two experiences of the Divine Planes are the same. Thus, what you see, feel, and hear will be personal to you only.

TABLE 1: The Seven Chakras and their Correspondences

Chakra #	Chakra Name (Sanskrit & English)	Location on body	Colour and # of Petals	Element & Tattva, Cosmic Plane	Body/ Being	Tuning Fork Hz- Cosmic & Musical	Gemstones
1	Muladhara, Root or Base	Between perineum and coccyx	Red, 4	Earth (Prithivi), Lower Astral/ Etheric	Survival, Grounding, Security, Kundalini (Origin)	194.18, 256.0 & 512.0	Hematite, Black Tourmaline, Red Jasper, Snowflake Obsidian
2	Swadhisthana, Sacral or Spleen	Lower abdomen	Orange, 6	Water (Apas), Higher Astral/ Emotional	Emotions, Subconscious Mind, Sexuality	210.42, 288.0	Carnelian, Orange Calcite, Tiger's Eye, Septarian
3	Manipura, Solar Plexus	Solar Plexus	Yellow, 10	Fire (Tejas), Higher Mental	Willpower, Creativity, Vitality, Conscious Mind	126.22, 320.0	Citrine, Golden Topaz, Yellow Jasper, Yellow Opal
4	Anahata, Heart	Between breasts	Green, 12	Air (Vayu), Lower Mental	Thoughts, Imagination, Love, Compassion, Healing	136.10, 341.3	Green Aventurine, Green Jade, Malachite, Rose Quartz,
5	Vishuddhi, Throat	Throat	Blue, 16	Spirit (Akasha), Spiritual	Communication, Intelligence	141.27, 384.0	Amazonite, Aquamarine, Blue Lace Agate, Blue Topaz, Turquoise
6	Ajna, Brow/ Mind's Eye/ Third Eye	Between eyebrows (slightly above)	Indigo, 2	Spirit (Akasha), Spiritual	Clairvoyance, Intuition, Psychic Senses	221.23, 426.7	Lapis Lazuli, Sapphire, Sodalite
7	Sahasrara, Crown	Top of head (centre)	White/ Violet, 1000	Spirit (Akasha), Spiritual	Oneness, God-Self, Understanding, Cosmic Consciousness	172.06, 480.0	Amethyst, Diamond, Clear Quartz, Rutilated Quartz, Selenite

THE QABALAH AND THE TREE OF LIFE

"In brief, the Tree of Life is a compendium of science, psychology, philosophy, and theology." — Dion Fortune; excerpt from "The Mystical Qabalah"

The word, Qabalah, originates from the Hebrew "QBL," meaning "an oral tradition." The Qabalah is the esoteric component of Judaism, referred to by Dion Fortune as the "Yoga of the West." The Qabalah encompasses an entire body of Hebrew mystical principles that are the cornerstone and foundation of the Western Esoteric tradition. Most Western Mystery schools use the Qabalah as their primary framework in the same way that Eastern schools practice Yoga and meditation. The purpose of both schools of thought is Enlightenment.

There are a total of twenty-four different spellings of the term "Qabalah," the following three being the most common. Kabbalah (with a K) is the Jewish Kabbalah, in reference to how this Ancient practice is studied within the Jewish tradition. Cabala (with a C) is a term used to signify the use of the Qabalistic teachings within Christianity. Qabalah (with a Q) is the Hermetic Qabalah, as part of the Western Esoteric tradition involving mysticism and the occult. The many subjects covered in this work all fall under the heading of the Hermetic Qabalah. Thus, this form of spelling will be used.

As it is with most occult knowledge, the exact origins of the Qabalah are unknown. However, it is quite clear from its study that it contains the influence of the Egyptian, Greek, and Chaldean traditions. The Qabalah brings forth a symbolic representation of the origins of the Universe and humanity's connection with God-the Creator. It is based upon the notion that all things in Creation are derived from this Source (God).

The Tree of Life (Figure 3), which is the basis upon which virtually all Western Spiritual systems are laid, is the key component of the Qabalah. Qabalists consider it as the blueprint of all existence. Ain Soph Aur, the "Infinite White Light" (according to the Qabalah), is the highest imaginable Source of all that is. It manifests in sequential order through ten distinct Sephiroth on the Tree of Life. The Sephiroth are also known as Spheres or emanations. The word "Sephiroth" refers to multiple Spheres, while the word "Sephira" refers to a single Sphere. In essence, the Sephiroth are states of consciousness.

Israel Regardie, the author of *The Golden Dawn*, called the Tree of Life a "Spiritual filing cabinet," containing within itself the perfect method for classifying all the phenomena of the Universe and recording their relationships. Qabalists say that everything in nature can be categorized on the Tree of Life since everything in nature exhibits a particular state or frequency of vibration. As such, everything has a level of consciousness which can be mapped somewhere on the Tree of Life.

Qabalah has been passed on by word of mouth for thousands of years. Its origins are veiled in mystery. Legend has it that the *Godhead* taught the Qabalah to a select group of Angels. These Angels then established a theosophical school in the Garden of Eden—to preserve and pass on this knowledge. Following humanity's Fall from Eden, the Angels took on the responsibility of teaching us the Qabalah so that we could Spiritually transform and return to Eden (Paradise) once again. This story reveals the intention and potential of the Qabalah.

Adam is said to have been the first Qabalist, followed by Abraham, who is credited with bringing the doctrine to Egypt. Qabalah's influences are present within Egyptian mysticism. The Egyptians were an evolving, esoteric society continually expanding and growing on all fronts. It was there that Moses was initiated into the Qabalah by the Angels themselves. David and Solomon are also among some of the earliest Qabalists. Through direct communication with the Divine (Gnosis), the Qabalistic tradition was first given to the people of the Earth. Then, it was passed down to each subsequent generation through word of mouth (and, in some cases, directly from the Divine).

The doctrine of the Qabalah consists of four unique parts:

I. Practical Qabalah—Talismanic and Ceremonial Magick
II. Literal Qabalah—The study of Gematria, Notarikon, and Temurah
III. Unwritten Qabalah—The Qabalah that is only imparted orally
IV. Dogmatic Qabalah—The doctrinal portion of the Qabalah; the three essential books on Jewish Mysticism: *The Sepher Yetzirah*, *The Zohar*, and *The Aesch Mezareph*

The Qabalistic system relies on the energy of numbers and letters. *The Sepher Yetzirah*, known as "The Book of Formation," is attributed to the patriarch Abraham. It presents the ten numbers and twenty-two letters of the Hebrew alphabet. These thirty-two symbols are known as the Thirty-Two Paths of Wisdom.

Containing a wealth of insight, *The Zohar*, or "Splendour," is the most quoted of the Qabalistic books. Essentially, it is a group of publications, including discourses on the mystical aspects of *The Torah* and scriptural interpretations, mysticism, Cosmology, and mystical psychology.

The Aesch Mezareph, or "Purifying Fire," is the Hermetic and Alchemical Fire. It also contains mystical knowledge concerning the different aspects of the Tree of Life as applied to Spiritual Alchemy.

The Qabalah's ultimate purpose is to answer the primary, fundamental, existential questions that we have as human beings concerning Creation. These questions relate to God-the Source, its nature and attributes, our

Solar System, the creation and destiny of Angels and humans, the nature of the human Soul, the Five Elements, the Universal Laws, transcendental symbolism of numerology, as well as the hidden truths contained with the twenty-two Hebrew letters.

According to the Qabalah, all aspects of Creation have their origins in Ain Soph Aur. The ten emanations of God-the Source (ten Sephiroth) reveal the many aspects of the nature of the Divine. However, the system is monotheistic, with the androgynous One God, from whom all of Creation emanates. The ten Spheres are presented in three columns (or Pillars), connected by twenty-two paths attributed to the twenty-two Major Arcana of the Tarot. As you can see, twenty-two is the number of the Hebrew letters and the Major Arcana of the Tarot, meaning there is a correspondence between them.

It will become evident to you right away that the Tree of Life is a beautiful system of mathematics, symmetry, and balance. The Sephiroth express the Divine attributes, which are presented in an Archetypal pattern, serving as the model for everything within Creation. There are ten Sephiroth because ten is a perfect number, containing every digit without repetition while also including the total essence of each digit.

QABALAH AND MAGICK

The purpose of Ceremonial Magick is Spiritual Evolution. The Qabalistic Tree of Life offers the "roadmap" towards this goal, while Magick provides the means. As such, Ceremonial Magick and the Qabalah are inextricably intertwined. As individuals evolve Spiritually, their willpower becomes heightened over time since the ability to affect change in the real world is an integral part of Spiritual Evolution. Both Ceremonial Magick and the Qabalah teach the individual how to conform reality to will and manifest their desires.

"Magick is the art and science of causing change to occur in conformity with will." — Aleister Crowley; excerpt from "Magick in Theory and Practice"

The Qabalah has a Spiritual link with Gnosticism since Gnosis is the direct communication with the Divine through the invocation or evocation of energy and communion with it. It is understood that nearly three-quarters of the Qabalah must be learned within oneself, through experience, instead of through the study of literature. This fact emphasizes the value of Ceremonial Magick and the invocation (and evocation) of Universal energies as the best way to receive Gnosis. Using Ceremonial Magick and memorizing the correspondences of the Tree of Life will provide the best method of studying the Qabalah. It will also enable the practitioner to understand the relation between the Chakras and the Elements, as is one of the intended purposes of *The Magus*.

Every man and woman also has their own Tree of Life since the Divine made us in its image. Therefore, your level of Spiritual Evolution can be mapped somewhere on your Tree. The different energies of the

Sephiroth resonate with active forces within your psyche. You can work with your Tree of Life by using Ceremonial Magick ritual exercises to help you evolve Spiritually.

By working with the different energies of the Tree of Life, you can restructure your mind in an organized fashion so that you can easily access the forces of each Sephira. Thus, you can attain an incredibly high degree of self-control by studying and practising the Qabalah.

Qabalah is a form of active psychology, especially when exploring it with the aid of Ceremonial Magick. As you invoke the energies of the Tree of Life, you will be able to map out all aspects of your inner Self and gain new degrees of control over the different components which comprise it. Included are your willpower, imagination, reason, emotions, desires, memories, thoughts, intuition, and overall inner power.

By committing the Tree of Life and its correspondences to memory, you will have easy access to the fundamental Archetypes, which are the primordial structural elements of the human psyche. Archetypes are universal, meaning that all humans partake of them. They give us the mental foundation on which to build our realities. And as you work with the energies invoked through Ceremonial Magick exercises, you will be able to connect with these Archetypes, learn from them, and use them proactively in your own life.

Through the practical study of the Tree of Life, Spiritual progress and the Spiritual path itself becomes much smoother and more understandable. Without this knowledge and experience, the road can be unclear. The Qabalistic system offers the mental foundation while Ceremonial Magick provides the energy to work with it actively. Together, you have the necessary tools that can unlock the hidden potential within you so that you can be a Co-Creator in this reality and manifest your innermost desires. The aim is to become a cause instead of an effect by consciously applying the Universal Laws.

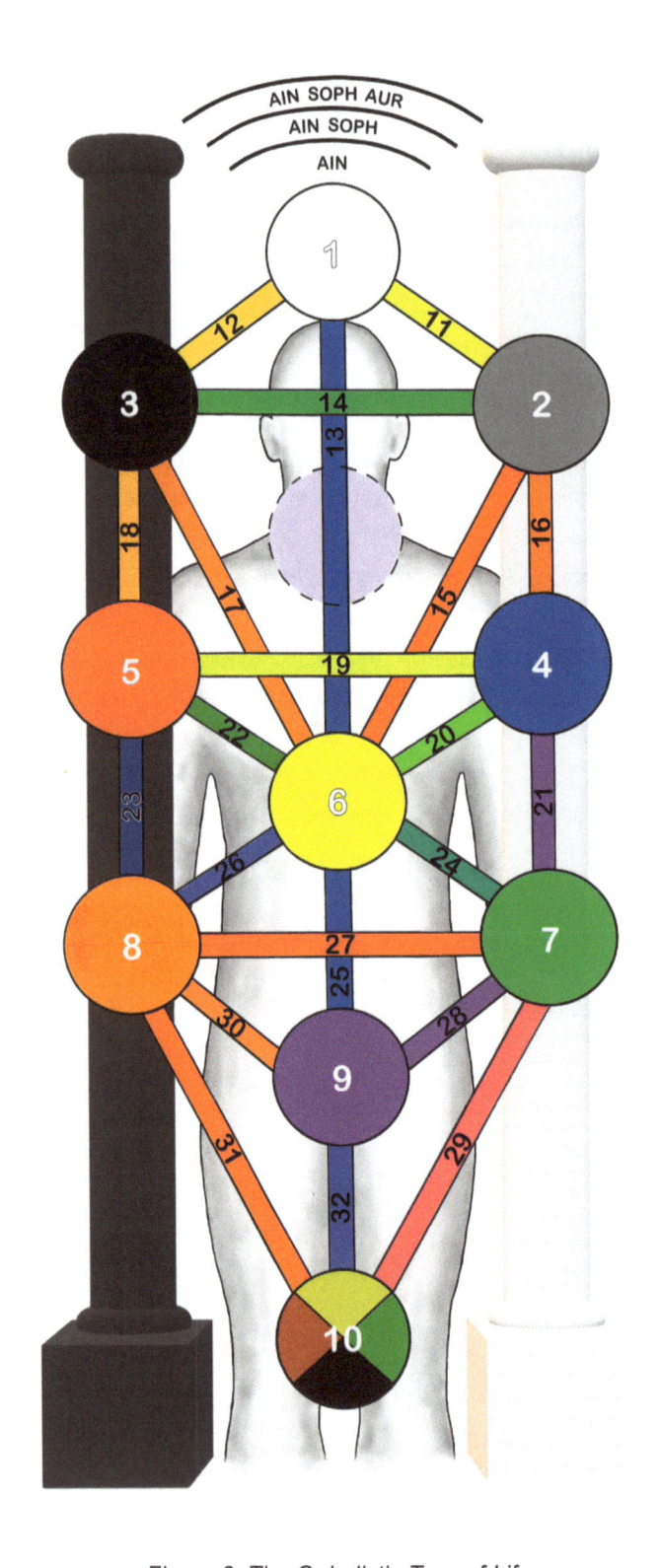

Figure 3: The Qabalistic Tree of Life

TABLE 2: The Ten Sephiroth and their Correspondences

Sephira #	Hebrew & English Names	Intelligence (Sepher Yetzirah)	Spiritual Experience	Symbols	Colour (Briah)	Body/Being	Planet & Element Quality
1	Kether, Crown	Admirable/ Hidden	Union with God	Crown, Point, Fylfot Cross	White	Real Self, Oneness, Spirituality, Truth	No Planet, Spirit
2	Chokmah, Wisdom	Illuminating	Vision of God Face to Face	Straight Line, Yod, Phallus	Grey	Spiritual Will, Purpose, Intelligence	No Planet, Spirit
3	Binah, Understanding	Sanctifying	Vision of Sorrow	Cup-Chalice, Womb, Triangle, Heh	Black	Intuition, Awareness, Clairvoyance, Faith	Saturn, Spirit
4	Chesed, Mercy	Cohesive/ Receptacular	Vision of Love	Crook, Scepter, Pyramid, Square, Orb, Eq.-Arm Cross	Blue	Unconditional love, Consciousness, Memory	Jupiter, Water
5	Geburah, Severity	Radical	Vision of Power	Sword, Spear, Scourge, Pentagon	Scarlet (Red)	Willpower, Fortitude, Drive	Mars, Fire
6	Tiphareth, Beauty	Mediating	Vision of Beauty/ Harmony	Rose and Calvary Cross, Truncated Pyramid, Cube, Vav	Golden Yellow	Personal Self, I-Centre, Vitality, Healing	Sun, Air
7	Netzach, Victory	Occult	Vision of the Triumph of Beauty	Rose, Girdle, Lamp	Emerald Green	Emotions, Desire, Romantic love	Venus, Fire
8	Hod, Splendour	Absolute/ Perfect	Vision of Splendour	Names of Power, Masonic Apron	Orange	Logic and Reason, Intellect	Mercury, Water
9	Yesod, Foundation	Pure/Clear	Vision of the Machinery of the Universe	Perfume, Sandals	Violet	Thoughts, Subconscious, Illusions, Sexuality, Kundalini	Moon, Air
10	Malkuth, Kingdom	Resplendent	Vision of the Holy Guardian Angel	Altar, Mys. Circle, Triangle of Art, Heh-Final	Citrine, Olive, Russet, Black	Physical Body, Survival instinct, Grounding	Earth-Planet and Element
Hidden	Daath, Knowledge	-	Dominion Over Darkness	Prism, Empty Room	Lavender	Communication, Transformation	No Planet, Spirit

TABLE 3: The Twenty-two Tarot Paths and their Correspondences

Path #	Tarot Card	Tarot Title	Hebrew Letter & English Name	Ruler & Colour (Atziluth)	Intelligence (Sepher Yetzirah)	Body/Organs
11	The Fool	Spirit of the Aethyr	Aleph, Ox	Air, Bright Pale Yellow	Scintillating	Respiratory System
12	The Magician	Magus of Power	Beth, House	Mercury, Yellow	Transparent	Cerebral Nervous System
13	The High Priestess	Priestess of the Silver Star	Gimel, Camel	Moon, Blue	Uniting	Lymphatic System, All Fluids in Body
14	The Empress	Daughter of the Mighty Ones	Daleth, Door	Venus, Emerald Green	Illuminating	Tactile Organs, Inner Sex Organs
15	The Emperor	Son of the Morning	Heh, Window	Aries, Scarlet (Red)	Constituting	Head-Face, Brain, Eyes
16	The Hierophant	Magus of the Eternal Gods	Vau, Hook/Nail	Taurus, Red-Orange	Triumphal	Throat, Neck, Thyroid, Vocals
17	The Lovers	Children of the Voice Divine	Zayin, Sword	Gemini, Orange	Disposing	Arms, Lungs, Shoulders, Hands
18	The Chariot	Child of the Powers of the Waters	Cheth, Fence	Cancer, Amber	Influencing	Chest, Breasts, Stomach
19	Strength	Daughter of the Flaming Sword	Teth, Serpent	Leo, Greenish Yellow	Spiritual Activities	Heart, Chest, Spinal Column, Upper Back
20	The Hermit	Magus of the Voice of Light	Yod, Hand	Virgo, Yellowish Green	Willful	Digestive System, Spleen, Intestines
21	Wheel of Fortune	Lord of the Forces of Life	Kaph, Palm/Fist	Jupiter, Violet	Conciliating	Liver, Adrenals, Sciatic Nerves, Feet
22	Justice	Daughter of the Lords of Truth	Lamed, Ox Goad	Libra, Emerald	Faithful	Kidneys, Skin, Buttocks, Lumbar
23	Hanged Man	Spirit of the Mighty Waters	Mem, Water	Water, Deep Blue	Stable	Organs of Nutrition
24	Death	Child of the Great Transformer	Nun, Fish	Scorpio, Green Blue	Imaginative	Outer Sex Organs, Reproductive Sys.
25	Temperance	Daughter of the Reconcilers	Samekh, Prop	Sagittarius, Blue	Tentative	Hips, Thighs, Liver
26	The Devil	Lord of the Gates of Matter	Ayin, Eye	Capricorn, Indigo	Renewing	Knees, Joints, Skeletal System
27	The Tower	Lord of the Hosts of the Mighty	Peh, Mouth	Mars, Scarlet (Red)	Active or Exciting	Muscular Sys., Nose, Testicles, Sinews
28	The Star	Daughter of the Firmament	Tzaddi, Fish	Aquarius, Violet	Natural	Ankles, Circulatory System
29	The Moon	Child of the Sons of the Mighty	Qoph, Back of Head	Pisces, Crimson	Corporeal	Feet, Toes, Adipose, Lymphatic System
30	The Sun	Lord of the Fire of the World	Resh, Head	Sun, Orange	Collective	Heart, Eyes, Vitality, Circulatory System
31	Judgement	Spirit of the Primal Fire	Shin, Tooth	Fire, Orange-Scarlet	Perpetual	Organs of Intelligence
32	The Universe	Great One of the Night of Time	Tav, Tav-Cross	Saturn, Indigo	Administrative	Skin, Hair, Teeth, Bones, Joints, Spleen

THE QABALAH AND THE ELEMENTS

The Four Elements are an intricate part of the Qabalah, and their energies are contained in the Tree of Life. I will break down the different levels of manifestation of the Elements as pertains to their functions within the Tree of Life. This will aid in understanding the overall system of the Qabalah and the process of manifestation of Divine energy. Although you will be hearing most of these Qabalistic concepts for the first time, I will not go into their descriptions now but later on, as I am discussing them individually. Use this information as a reference and an introduction to the Elements within the Qabalah.

Figure 4: The Fylfot Cross

Primordial Elements are found in Kether. Considering that Kether is the potential of all things in existence, the Elements at this level are undifferentiated and in a state of pure potential. Since the Fylfot Cross (Figure 4) represents the Kether energy, it explains how the Elements function at this level. It has four arms equal in length, each attributed to one of the Elements of Earth, Air, Water, and Fire. Within the Four Elements are to be found the Twelve Zodiac in triplicities, as each Zodiac sign belongs to one of the Four Elements.

Each arm of the Fylfot Cross is continued at a right angle, symbolic of motion around a centre. In the centre is the Star of our Solar System, the Sun. The four arms are spinning on the Sun centre so fast that they seem practically at rest. In this way, the Spirit energy is invisible to the senses since its vibration is so high in frequency.

The Fylfot Cross is otherwise called the "Hammer of Thor" or the Swastika. The Swastika was used as a symbol of Divinity and Spirituality in Indian religions long before the Nazi Germans adopted it as part of their movement.

Primal Elements are the Tetragrammaton—the Hebrew letters YHVH (Hebrew God Jehovah) applied to the Four Worlds of the Qabalah. Primal, in essence, means Primary. Within the Primary Elements, the letter Yod is attributed to Fire, Heh to Water, Vav to Air, and Heh-final to Earth. Each of the Four Worlds has a Tree of Life, and these are called Atziluth, Briah, Yetzirah, and Assiah.

Atziluth is attributed to the Fire Element, Briah to Water, Yetzirah to Air, and Assiah to Earth. I will discuss the Four Worlds of the Qabalah in greater detail in a later chapter of this book. All you have to understand at this point is that when I am talking about the Primal Elements, I am referring to the Four Worlds.

Specific Elements are the Tetragrammaton or YHVH as applied to Chokmah, Binah, Tiphareth, and Malkuth in any of the Four Worlds. For example, Chokmah is attributed to the Fire Element, Binah to Water, Tiphareth to Air, and Malkuth to Earth. Therefore, in the World of Atziluth, we have Fire (Specific) of Fire Primal, Water (Specific) of Fire Primal, Air (Specific) of Fire Primal, and Earth (Specific) of Fire Primal. And the same goes for the other three Primal Elements.

Transitional Elements are the Yod, Heh, and Vav, or the Fire, Water, and Air, as applied to the paths of the Tree of Life. The Transitional Elements are always in transit between the Sephiroth. They help in understanding the Tarot cards differently since the twenty-two Major Arcana of the Tarot are attributed to the twenty-two paths of the Tree of Life.

Astral Elements are the Tetragrammaton of YHVH applied to the four lowest Sephiroth of Netzach, Hod, Yesod, and Malkuth, which comprise the Astral Plane.

Base Elements are found in Malkuth—this is the final manifestation of the Elements in their densest Form, which comprise the World of Matter.

Sephirothic Elements relate to the general Elemental quality of each of the ten Sephiroth on the Tree of Life. When discussing each of the Sephiroth, I will refer to their general Elemental quality and any other Elemental attributions they have.

Note that the fifth Element of Spirit is not a part of the Qabalah in a way where it can be broken down and separated from the whole. Spirit is (in a sense) the glue which holds the whole system together. It is also the primordial essence, the First Substance, and the Source of all manifestation. Within Spirit are to be found the Four Elements in their state of potential. Conversely, within the Primordial Elements is found the Spirit as the substance from which they emanate. When something emanates from something else, it carries the potential of the very thing it originated from—this means that Spirit is a part of everything in existence. The goal of the Alchemist is to bring out the Spirit from all aspects of its manifestation through Transmutation. Transmutation is the action of changing or the state of being changed from one form to another.

THE THREE PILLARS OF THE TREE OF LIFE

The Ten Sephiroth of the Tree of Life are divided into three pillars. On the right is the Pillar of Mercy while on the left is the Pillar of Severity. In the centre is the Pillar of Balance (or Mildness). Together, these three pillars symbolize the play of duality in all of Creation and the balancing force that unites them.

The Pillar of Mercy on the right is described as masculine, active, and positive. It is the Pillar of Force, and the colour white, representing the Light. It contains the Sephiroth of Chokmah, Chesed, and Netzach. The Pillar of Severity on the left is described as feminine, passive, and negative. It is the Pillar of Form, and the colour black, representing darkness. It contains the Sephiroth of Binah, Geburah, and Hod. Together, The Pillar of Mercy and the Pillar of Severity represent duality in all its aspects—*Yin* and *Yang*.

The Pillar of Balance, otherwise called the Middle Pillar, represents balance while bringing equilibrium to the other two columns. It brings unity to the many dualistic, contending forces in life. It is grey in colour and relates to the Middle Pillar exercise, whose purpose is to bring in the Light from Kether to balance the mind, body, and Soul. The Pillar of Balance (Middle Pillar) contains the Sephiroth of Kether, Tiphareth, Yesod, and Malkuth.

The Sephiroth also carry the qualities of the three Elements of Fire, Water, and Air. The Pillar of Force is of the Fire Element quality, the essence of Wisdom and Knowledge. Conversely, the Pillar of Form is of the Water Element as the essence of Love. Finally, the Middle Pillar is of the Air Element quality, as it serves to balance the Fire and Water Elements. The energetic nature of the Air Element is Truth.

In the Golden Dawn tradition, the Pillar of Form is called Boaz, while the Pillar of Force is called Jachin. The Pillar of Form represents Matter and darkness, while the Pillar of Force represents Spirit and the Light. The Middle Pillar represents the mystic consciousness that equilibrates the two.

In the Kundalini system, the Pillar of Mercy represents the masculine Pingala Nadi of the Fire Element. In contrast, the Pillar of Severity represents the feminine Ida Nadi of the Water Element. The central column, Sushumna, is the Middle Pillar which reconciles them, corresponding with the Air Element. As the Kundalini rises through the human spine, its hollow tube-like nature carries the energy upwards, terminating inside the brain. Sushumna is the channel which expands and regulates consciousness.

The Sephiroth are all perfectly balanced on the three pillars. The opposing Sephiroth on the Pillar of Severity and the Pillar of Mercy are meant to balance each other out, while the Middle Pillar is self-balancing. While the three pillars represent the qualities of the Elements of Fire, Water, and Air, the Elements interchange as you scale down the Tree of Life. Each Sephira contains within itself all the Sephiroth above it when looking upwards at the Tree of Life. Once reflected through the Middle Pillar, an Element found in one Sephira will be included in the Sephira after it, although in a lower form of that same Element. In this way, the Pillar of Severity and Mercy will have the Fire and Water Elements interchanged within them.

The Middle Pillar works a little bit different, though, as it stays true to the Air Element for the most part. The two manifested Sephiroth of Tiphareth and Yesod are both of the Air Element quality, with each receiving an influence of either the Fire or Water Elements. Tiphareth receives the energy of the Fire Element and is related to the Soul, while Yesod receives the energy of the Water Element and is related to the Ego.

The Middle Pillar is a perfect representation of *Heaven* and Earth. At its lowest point is Malkuth, the Earth, while at its highest point is Kether—the pure, undifferentiated Spirit energy. Within it is found the Air Element, with the influence of the Fire and Water Elements. In the same way, we have our own Earth and the atmosphere enveloping it, containing the air necessary for us to breathe and live, followed by the Heavens (sky) above. I will explore some of these ideas in further detail as I describe each Sephira. Proceeding down from the Godhead (Ain Soph Aur) to the manifested world are the ten Sephiroth.

AIN SOPH AUR (LIMITLESS LIGHT)

The Universe is the sum total of all things in existence and the living creatures it contains. It is conceived of as having its primaeval origin in infinite Space. This unlimited Space is the Ain, which translates as "Nothing."

"Before having created any shape in the world, before having produced any Form, He was alone, without Form, resembling nothing. Who could comprehend Him as He then was, before Creation, since He had no Form?" — *"The Zohar"*

The Ain is not a Being; it is simply a "No-thing." We cannot comprehend it, and we cannot know it. As far as our limited human consciousness is concerned, it does not exist. The idea here is that the human mind is limited in scope to understand the Ain. Therefore, we should not even attempt such an endeavour. It is unspeakable, unknowable, and unthinkable. The number zero is allocated to the Ain. It is the highest *Veil* in the process of Creation.

To become conscious of itself and make itself comprehensible to itself, the Ain becomes Ain Soph, which means "no limit" or "Infinity." As there is nothing, then there are no boundaries or limitations. It is the limitless foundation, the Eternal in its purest essence. The Ain Soph is the second Veil after the Ain.

Further still, the Ain Soph manifests as Ain Soph Aur, which means "Limitless or Eternal Light." Ain Soph Aur proceeds from Ain Soph as a necessity. It is the lowest of the Three Veils situated closest to the Tree of Life. Light plays a vital role in the Qabalah, and Ain Soph Aur is its Source.

According to Albert Einstein's Theory of Relativity, if you were to travel at the speed of Light, some fascinating things would occur in Space/Time—you would be in all places and times at once. In other words, you would become Eternal and experience what Light experiences from its perspective. You would be able to travel vast distances in a split second and even move backwards and forwards in time.

To manifest Creation, the Ain Soph Aur contracts itself into a central point without dimension through a process that *The Zohar* calls Tzim Tzum. In this way, the first Sephira on the Tree of Life is formed—Kether, the Crown. Following Kether, the other nine Sephiroth are formed in sequence, as the Light filters downwards, until the physical Universe is created.

Ain Soph Aur is also known in the Qabalah as the Three Veils of Negative Existence. This is because everything upwards of Kether (the highest Sephira on the Tree of Life) is in the outer limits of existence, as the initial impulse of Creation, and has not been created yet.

KETHER (THE CROWN)

Kether corresponds with Sahasrara, the "Crown" Chakra. Situated at the apex of the Pillar of Balance, Kether is the head of the Sephiroth on the Tree of Life. Its Element is Spirit/Aethyr, and it is the first point of *Non-Duality*. As such, Kether is also the gateway to the Beyond and the Transpersonal Chakras above the Crown. Note that the Chakras above the Crown, within the Divine Planes, would still be part of Kether and not within the Three Veils of Negative Existence since nothing can exist within Ain Soph Aur. The Primordial Elements are found in Kether as the Four Elements in their state of unmanifested potential. The Hebrew Divine name of Kether is Eheieh, while the *Archangel* is Metatron. In the Golden Dawn system of Magick, Kether pertains to the Ipsissimus (10=1) Grade of the Third Order.

> *"The First Path is called the Admirable or the Hidden Intelligence (the Highest Crown), for it is the Light giving the power of comprehension of that first Principle which has no beginning; and it is the Primal Glory, for no created Being can attain to its essence."* — *"The Sepher Yetzirah"* (on Kether)

The term "Hidden Intelligence" implies that Kether is unmanifest, having no beginning point and that no one can attain its essence while living in the physical body. Kether can only be experienced through the next two Sephira of Chokmah and Binah (Wisdom and Understanding), through intuition. One's consciousness must be pure to experience a glimpse of the "Primal Glory" of Kether since the duality of thoughts must be transcended. Kether is the first cause behind all causes, referred to in *The Zohar* as the *Macroprosopus*, the "Vast Countenance," or Arik Anpin. It is God in Heaven, above duality, as the Grand Architect of the Universe.

Kether is the undivided Source and the Absolute Truth of all that is. It is the essence of all of Creation. Everything emanates out of Kether, and into it, everything returns. Essentially, Kether is the channel for the Great White Light, and as such, the colour of Kether is a white brilliance. The number for Kether is one, as it contains within itself the nine digits of the decimal scale that remain.

The initial emanation of the Tree of Life is Kether, which is the state of consciousness in which Creation unites with the Three Veils of Negative Existence. Kether is the *Monad,* the singularity, and the highest conception of the Godhead. As the Divine life essence descends the Tree of Life, it is merely undergoing a process of transformation from one form of energy, or state of consciousness, to another.

Within mystical lore, the androgyny (male and female united in one form) symbolises Kether, representing a state of transcendence and union with the Divine. Kether is comparable to the Eastern notions of *Satori* and

Nirvana. Wisdom (Chokmah) is masculine, while Understanding (Binah) is feminine. Together, they lie immediately below Kether on the Tree of Life. However, Kether transcends the duality of both as the initial spark of the Divine.

A full Kundalini awakening which raises the energy and pierces the Crown Chakra, Sahasrara, is essentially an awakening to the Kether Sephira. This means that all the Sephiroth below Kether open up as reachable states of consciousness. A full, permanent Kundalini awakening is essentially an activation and invigoration of the entire Tree of Life within the individual—a concept I will refer to often.

Kether has no Planetary correspondence, as do most other Sephiroth. Its symbols are a crown, a point, and the Fylfot Cross. Kether's Deity correspondences from Spiritual and religious pantheons include Nudjer, Ptah, Aither, Aether, Dagda, Ymir, Brahman, Damballah, Ayida Wedo, and Olodumare.

CHOKMAH (WISDOM)

Chokmah is the second Sephira of the Tree of Life, situated at the top of the Pillar of Mercy. It functions through the Mind's Eye Chakra, and its Element is Spirit/Aethyr. "Wisdom" is necessary to reach Sahasrara, the Crown Chakra, along with its opposite, Understanding. The Hebrew Divine name of Chokmah is Yah, while the Archangel is Raziel. In the Golden Dawn system of Magick, Chokmah corresponds with the Magus (9=2) Grade of the Third Order.

> *"The Second Path is that of Illuminating Intelligence; it is the Crown of Creation, the Splendour of the Unity, equalling it, and it is exalted above every head, and named by the Qabalists the Second Glory." — "The Sepher Yetzirah" (on Chokmah)*

As Chokmah (Wisdom) cannot be known in the absence of its opposite, Binah (Understanding), it belongs to the dualistic realm. Chokmah is the masculine component of the Self. It is the Father energy, the Force, True Will, Holy Guardian Angel, and the first understandable aspect of the Self beyond Kether.

Chokmah is not the same as the White Light of Kether. Instead, it is the "Wisdom" which can perceive it—the "Illuminating Intelligence." Chokmah is the source of intelligence in human beings as it is the Fountain of Knowledge. It is the component of the Self that brings us to the passageway of the Light of Sahasrara, the portal into other, higher realms.

The colour of Chokmah is grey. The white brilliance of Kether is intermixed with its opposite, black, to create the grey Sphere of Chokmah. Chokmah is the highest Sphere that can comprehend the beauty of Sahasrara since it is closest to it. It is a tool that you use (as well as its opposite, Binah) to propel you into the world of Non-Duality of Kether (Sahasrara). Within Chokmah, the Holy Guardian Angel is located—the expression of your God-Self. Your Holy Guardian Angel can only be accessed through complete silence of mind and the shutting down of the senses.

The initial masculine aspect of Creation is the Fire (Specific) Element, which is expressed in Chokmah, as opposed to the androgyny of Kether. It is the Supernal Father and the Archetypal positive pole of existence. The energy of Chokmah is dynamic and giving, as it is the great cause of stimulation within the Universe. It is action and motion—the vital energizing element of all Creation.

The number of Chokmah is two, and this number was formed through Kether, the number one, reflecting itself. Out of the one, came the two and the three—Chokmah, and Binah, the Fire (Specific) and Water (Specific) Elements manifested through the Spirit.

The Zodiac is the physical representation of Chokmah since the Stars are a manifestation of the unmanifested White Light of Kether, which underlies all things in the Universe. The Stars channel the Fire (Specific) of Primal Fire Element that, in essence, are the Souls of all living things in the Universe. Chokmah's symbols are the phallus, the line, and the Hebrew letter Yod (as part of YHVH). The Deities that correspond with Chokmah include Thoth, Uranus, Caelus, Lugh, Odin, Vishnu, Nan Nan Bouclou, and Olofi.

BINAH (UNDERSTANDING)

Binah is the third Sephira of the Tree of Life, situated at the top of the Pillar of Severity. Like its counterpart, Chokmah, Binah functions through the Mind's Eye Chakra, and its Element is Spirit/Aethyr. One needs "Understanding" to traverse the path to Sahasrara to enter the realm of Non-Duality. The Hebrew Divine name of Binah is YHVH Elohim, while the Archangel is Tzaphqiel. In the Golden Dawn system of Magick, Binah pertains to the Magister Templi (8=3) Grade of the Third Order.

> *"The Third Path is the Sanctifying Intelligence: it is the foundation of Primordial Wisdom, which is called the Creator of Faith, and its roots are AMN (Amen); and it is the parent of Faith, from which doth Faith emanate." — "The Sepher Yetzirah" (on Binah)*

The above statement speaks of the connection of Binah to the concept of Faith, which is built on Understanding—we understand that a Spiritual reality exists even though we have no tangible proof of it. As it is the "Sanctifying Intelligence," it implies that it is Holy and free from wickedness. It is pure since its foundation is the Light of Wisdom (Chokmah).

Binah is the Great Mother and the feminine aspect of the Self—the Water (Specific) Element of consciousness. While Chokmah is active, Binah is passive. It is the negative pole of existence and the womb of all of Creation that brings forth life. Following Wisdom, Understanding is the second comprehensible aspect of the Self. In partnership with Chokmah, Binah serves to cultivate Understanding of our true essence and propel us into Kether (Sahasrara).

In terms of the personality on the Tree of Life, Binah gives rise to our intuitive faculties. It receives its impulse from Chokmah, the Holy Guardian Angel, who communicates to us when our minds are silent. Binah's Element is Spirit/Aethyr, and its colour is black. Since it is black, as is Malkuth (the Earth), there is a correlation between the two. Binah is the originator of the Holographic, Astral blueprint of all forms in existence. It is the "Sea of Consciousness" that contains all Matter in the Universe.

Force and Form are two respective male and female qualities repeatedly occurring on the Tree of Life, beginning with Chokmah and Binah. Together, they are the two initial building blocks of Creation—the proton and the electron. They also represent the highest Sephiroth on the two opposing pillars, the Pillar of Force and Pillar of Form, masculine and feminine components of Creation. Binah, being Understanding, brings forth the notion of the grasping of the ideas that are intrinsic to Chokmah (Wisdom) which is complete and infinite knowledge. It is only in Sahasrara, with Wisdom and Understanding, that we can experience Non-Duality and be immersed in the inner Divine Planes or Realms. However, we need a means of comprehending such experiences, and Chokmah and Binah serve as that means.

The initial three Sephiroth of the Tree of Life belong to what is known as the Supernal Triangle—otherwise called the "Supernals." The Supernals are the aspect of us that is beyond birth and death—the part of us that is Eternal—the Spiritual part of the Self.

The number of Binah is three, as the *Holy Spirit* of the Christian Trinity. The Father is Kether, the Unknowable, while the Son is Chokmah, His reflection. The Holy Spirit is the Sea of Consciousness of Binah and the substance upon which the Son reflects his Fire (Specific) energy. Binah becomes the "Sea of Love" once it receives and integrates the Light of Wisdom from Chokmah.

Chokmah animates all things in existence, creating the concept of Time, while Binah is the Space in which all things exist. Binah is therefore negative and dark, as is the outer Space of the Universe itself. The Trinity produced all living things and is their Source. In Alchemy, the Trinity are the Mercury, Sulfur, and Salt Principles.

Since Binah is the Great Mother, she must raise us and teach us how to live with other human beings. As such, Binah's Planetary correspondence is Saturn, the Planet of restriction, discipline, limitation, and Time. The symbols of Binah are the womb, the triangle, the cup, and the Hebrew letter Heh (as part of YHVH). Binah's Deity correspondences from other pantheons include Isis, Hera, Rhea, Juno, Danu, Frigga, Mahashakti, Guede, and Oya.

Although Saturn has an affinity to the Earth Element, Binah's corresponding Element is Spirit/Aethyr but with the influence of Saturn, as related to the Earth. There is also a correlation between Binah and the Sphere of Yesod. Binah is the beginning of all Form, while Yesod is the final Astral blueprint that comprises all the Sephiroth above it.

DAATH (KNOWLEDGE)

As the beginning of the Spirit/Aethyr Element, Daath serves as a separation point between Spirit/Aethyr and the lower Four Elements. Daath is the concealed eleventh Sephira of the Tree of Life. It is known as the "Great Chasm," or the Abyss. It divides the Supernals from all of manifested Creation. The Supernals are the component of the Self that is Eternal and beyond Time and Space, as they are its very Source. As such, Daath is the Sphere of "Knowledge" since we can transcend our bodily enclosures and raise our consciousness to Divine heights through knowledge. The source of all knowledge and wisdom is Chokmah.

The Supernals exist within the Spirit Element, and they function through the Four Elements, which are lower in the scale of manifestation of the Divine. The Ego also operates through these lower Four Elements, without the fifth Element of Spirit. Therefore, Daath separates the Ego from the Higher Self—the physical body from the Soul and the Spirit. Daath is, therefore, Vishuddhi the Throat Chakra, since this Chakra separates the Element of Spirit above from the lower Four Elements below.

Anything below the Sphere of Daath belongs to the realm of physical existence, being subject to the cycle of birth and death. The Supernals above Daath are above the birth/death cycle since they do not belong to the realm of duality. But as they are dual themselves, Chokmah and Binah are the aspect of the human being that is capable of understanding Non-Duality.

Daath is responsible for protecting the purity of the Supernal Triangle from the lower parts of the Tree of Life. It is an invisible Sephira, which means that it is not an official component of the Tree of Life. However, it is included within the Qabalistic philosophy and does play a significant role.

Daath is also the Sphere through which you access the negative side of the Tree of Life, called the Tree of Death. In *The Nightside of Eden* by Kenneth Grant, he describes the Abyss as a door that leads into the *Underworld*, the evil and distorted realm that is the abode of the Qlippoth. The Qlippoth is a Qabalistic term that equates with Demons. The Qlippoth exist inside of us but also outside of us. We had to have contracted them from the outside Universe for them to affect us. When you enter Daath and are crossing the Abyss, you must first traverse the Tree of Death, starting in Malkuth and climbing upwards before reaching the Supernal Triangle.

This means that when you metaphorically die, you must spend some time in *Hell* (the Underworld) and become a King or Queen of this infernal domain before being Resurrected and becoming a King or Queen of Heaven. You have to conquer your Demons and the fear inside yourself to be Resurrected in the Spirit. By overcoming your inner fears, you learn to command and control your Demons so that you can approach them without fear. Doing so will increase your personal power significantly since you will be able to use their negative energy constructively in life instead of being used and abused by it. To overcome your Demons means overcoming your vices and turning them into virtues.

In the Christian tradition, Jesus Christ descended into Hell right after the crucifixion (while his physical body was in the darkness of the tomb for three days) before he was Spiritually Resurrected. He had to establish dominance over the Demonic Kingdom (Hell) first before being crowned a King in Heaven. In the Egyptian tradition, *Osiris Onnofris* died inside a coffin as part of a ploy by his evil brother Set. Osiris Resurrected from the dead with the help of his wife, Isis. He became known among the Egyptians as the Lord of the Underworld and the Afterlife. In both stories, we have a connection between death, the Underworld (Hell), and a Resurrection that follows.

Interestingly, one of the symbols of Osiris is the Djed Pillar, which represents his spine. It was the Djed Pillar that Isis used to Resurrect Osiris from the dead. The Djed Pillar represents stability and strength within the Egyptian tradition, although its true meaning is veiled to the uninitiated. There is another symbolic meaning behind the Djed Pillar known to initiates of the Egyptian Mysteries—as an Ancient symbol for the Kundalini energy. The Kundalini energy acts as a force that activates the Spiritual Resurrection process. In Egyptian Mysticism, the Raising of the Djed Pillar is a ceremony whereby the initiate raises their Kundalini energy and obtains Spiritual transformation.

"The Abyss is passed by virtue of the mass of the Adept and his Karma." — Aleister Crowley; excerpt from "Magick in Theory and Practice"

Kundalini initiates know that the path of Spiritual Rebirth is emotionally and mentally painful and that they must first overcome their fears and anxieties before the Kundalini energy will make them at peace with themselves. These individuals must evolve past their Karma to enlighten the consciousness and raise it beyond the density of Matter. Only then can they pass through the Abyss successfully.

The first few years for anyone going through a full Kundalini awakening process are painful. The Spiritual process of rebirth requires you to work through your fear before becoming strong and being able to attain the beauty and transcendence that a Kundalini awakening brings. This process occurs in the Sphere of Daath, as it is the gateway to the Underworld or Hell. It is here that the Kundalini pierces the Throat Chakra on its way upwards through Sushumna, immediately "vaulting" you across the Abyss and onto your negative Tree of Life, metaphorically speaking. Always remember, though, that Hell is only real insofar as the mind is concerned since it is the mind which experiences the duality of Heaven and Hell. Outside of the mind and brain, Hell does not exist.

As Daath corresponds with the Throat Chakra, the notion of language and speech is significant here as it is through the spoken word that we can communicate with the Divine. Daath's colour is lavender. Daath is also connected with death, more specifically, the death of the Ego, making way for the subsequent rebirth of the Higher Self. The very words "Daath" and "death" are similar in pronunciation, which indicates a correspondence between the two. The symbols of Daath are the prism and the empty room. The Deity correspondences of Daath include Nephthys, Hypnos, Janus, Arianrhod, Heimdall, Aditi, Pushan, and the Barons.

CHESED (MERCY)

Chesed is the fourth Sephira of the Tree of Life, situated below Chokmah on the Pillar of Mercy. It is the first Sphere of our physical Universe because everything above the Abyss is unmanifest. Chesed's Elemental quality is Water. It functions through Swadhisthana, the Sacral Chakra, and represents the higher aspect of the Water Element. Chesed is the Spiritualized Sacral Chakra because of its connection to the Supernals through the Tarot path of The Hierophant. The colour of Chesed is blue—the colour of the Element of Water.

Chesed is the manifestation of the Water (Specific) Element from Binah, projected through Daath, manifesting as the tangible emotion of unconditional love. As such, the Sacral Chakra, Swadhisthana, is exalted through the Heart Chakra, Anahata. One of Anahata's functions is to experience the exalted states of the Fire and Water Chakras (Manipura and Swadhisthana), considering that Air moves both Fire and Water. For this reason, the emotion of unconditional love is felt in the heart. The Hebrew Divine name of Chesed is El, while the Archangel is Tzadqiel. In the Golden Dawn system of Magick, Chesed corresponds with the Adeptus Exemptus (7=4) Grade of the Second Order.

"The Fourth Path is named the Cohesive or Receptacular Intelligence; and it is so called because it contains all the Holy powers, and from it emanate all the Spiritual virtues with the most exalted essences: they emanate one from the other by the power of the Primordial Emanation, the Highest Crown, Kether." — *"The Sepher Yetzirah"* (on Chesed)

Chesed is of the same type of energy as Chokmah but on a more manifest level. While Chokmah is the all-powerful and knowing Father, Chesed is the Father's protective, forgiving, loving energy as he has been bathed in the Sea of Love of Binah. For this reason, Chesed is the Sephira of "Mercy." The supporting structure of everything within Creation is found within Chesed, as are all the Spheres preceding it. Thus, it is called the "Cohesive or Receptacular Intelligence," serving as a receptacle of the preceding energies.

Chesed is the first Sephira that can be grasped by the human mind, as it is where one experiences the clarification of the abstract ideas presented by the Supernals. Moreover, this clarification is expressed through the highest conceivable human emotion, which is unconditional love—one of the main building blocks of all things in existence.

Chesed is likened to the child of Chokmah and Binah, as it is their more densely manifested by-product. Having an affinity to the Water Element, Chesed is unconditional love, compassion, and the cultivation of wisdom. It is the highest conception of love for us as human beings (since there are many forms of love) and carries with it its counterpart Sephira, Geburah (Severity). To understand how these two Spheres operate, one must realize that when you love something or someone, you fight for them and in their name. It is an instinct to do so when love is concerned. The Watery emotion of love cannot exist without the Fire that fuels you to fight for that which you love.

Chesed and Geburah represent the triangle of the Fire Element (upright) and the triangle of the Water Element (inverted) superimposed one on top of the other. This symbol is the Hexagram, otherwise called the Star of David by the Hebrews—representing the perfected man and the highest Spiritual aspiration.

It is important to note that their opposing Spheres must balance all the Sephiroth on the Tree of Life. Only the Sephiroth within the Middle Pillar are self-balancing. Chokmah and Binah work together to produce Wisdom and Understanding, received through intuition. Chesed and Geburah produce the energy of Mercy and Severity. Intuition is an involuntary experience that is received through the Mind's Eye. There has to be a conscious application of the Water and Fire Elements in the case of Mercy and Severity to achieve a healthy balance between the two.

In terms of the human psyche, Chesed is the memory. It is right below the Abyss, as everything above the Abyss has no memory per se but is instead experienced entirely through intuition. Memory is what binds us to the Ego and the duality of the past and the present. The Ego is not present above the Abyss since the Supernals are timeless and Eternal. The Ego is tied to the manifested physical body; thus, it will eventually be annihilated when the physical body perishes.

The development of the Ego and memory produces the energy of unconditional love, the highest aspiration of human beings. Unconditional love gives us something to strive towards and fight for since, by doing so, we become absorbed in the unity of all of life in the Universe. By experiencing unconditional love, we transcend memory and the Ego and can taste the fruits of the Supernals.

The Planet attributed to Chesed is Jupiter, the Planet of expansion, morality, and ethics. Its symbols are the crook, the sceptre, the pyramid, the square, the orb, and the Equal-Armed Cross. Chesed's Deity correspondences include Amoun, Zeus, Jupiter, Llyr, Frey, Indra, Agwe, and Obatala.

GEBURAH (SEVERITY)

Geburah is the fifth Sephira of the Tree of Life, situated below Binah on the Pillar of Severity. It is the second Sphere of the known Universe. It functions through Manipura, the Solar Plexus Chakra, as the willpower of the individual Self. Geburah's Elemental quality is Fire. This Fire is not the same as the Fire (Specific) Element found in Chokmah but a manifestation of it on a lower level. Because it is right below the Abyss and the Supernals, it contains the Spirit energy (as does Chesed), in this case, received through the path of the Chariot Tarot card. The colour of Geburah is scarlet (red), the colour of the Fire Element.

The Fire (Specific) Element from Chokmah projects through Daath and manifests as the willpower in Geburah. At its most basic level, it is the motivation and drive to survive as a living organism in the Universe. Survival is dependent on personal power, which is an attribute of the Sephira of Geburah. Since willpower is an expression of the Fire Element, it is powered by the Fire Chakra, Manipura. When it is used in the name of the Higher Self, this Fire is exalted in Anahata, the Heart Chakra. The Hebrew Divine name of Geburah is Elohim Gibor, while the Archangel is Kamael. In the Golden Dawn system of Magick, Geburah pertains to the Adeptus Major (6=5) Grade of the Second Order.

> *"The Fifth Path is called the Radical Intelligence, because it resembles the Unity, uniting itself to Binah or Intelligence which emanates from the Primordial depths of Wisdom, or Chokmah."* — *"The Sepher Yetzirah"* (on Geburah)

Geburah's name is the "Radical Intelligence" because its action is extreme, as it seeks to create change. Geburah's role is to support evolution, and for this reason, it exacts justice at all times while tempering Chesed's merciful energy of love. Out of all of the Sephiroth on the Tree of Life, Geburah is the most feared and misinterpreted. Its role is to balance Chesed's benevolence, mercy, and Form-creating attributes through its application of brash and destructive actions.

Geburah is the restrictive feminine energy of Binah but on a more manifest level. Just as a mother protects her child, Geburah is the aspect of us that protects and fights for respect and honour in the world. Geburah imposes "Severity" and "Justice" (its other title). Often, it can bring destruction unless it is balanced by its counterpart, Chesed (Mercy). Geburah brings forth discipline through a purging Fire by challenging everything presented by its opposite, Chesed. It commands respect since its purpose is to cleanse the energy system (Aura) of impurities—as it plays the role of the "Right Hand of God," meaning it seeks to do God's Will.

An important lesson from the Golden Dawn Neophyte Initiation states that unbalanced Mercy is the barrenness of will, while unbalanced Severity is tyranny and oppression. So, in reality, you need to have a balance between the Mercy and Severity within yourself because if you do not, you will be unable to exercise your inner power. You will be a "doormat" for people to step all over as they please, or you will be of an ill temperament, jumping at every opportunity to fight with others, verbally and even physically.

Geburah powers the individual will. What you decide to use your willpower for in life is up to you. Since Geburah is the willpower, it is the domain that the *Fallen Angels* (Demons) have access to because Severity implies the use of that which is often considered negative energy. Geburah has a connection with Daath and the Demonic Realm of the Qlippoth since the Fire Element is closest to Spirit. Mastering Geburah implies the mastering of your inner Demons. Doing so will yield the most personal power.

Another important lesson from the Golden Dawn Neophyte Initiation says that if you do not punish evil when you are exposed to it, you become evil's accomplice. Hence, it is everyone's role in life to live justly, with respect to other people. When we are wronged or see the wrongdoings done to others, we must do our best to correct this behaviour; otherwise, we become an accomplice. Voltaire said it best, "With great power, comes great responsibility." We must take responsibility for our own lives and exact Severity when needed, to keep moving forward in life and strive. We must aid human evolution by being active Co-Creators with the Creator.

Anger comes from the Sphere of Geburah. It is a misuse of the energy of Geburah as it lacks the right dose of love and Mercy from Chesed. Whether you choose to be a tyrant, only seeking power to glorify the Ego, or a well-balanced individual who uses this Sphere to exact justice and punish and correct evil is totally up to you. However, a proper dose of Mercy always needs to be applied with Severity because using the Fallen Angels in Geburah without knowing how to temper them with love makes the difference between God-righteousness and Self-righteousness.

Geburah is the Sphere of honour and glory when properly applied. We must learn the true nature of the Fallen Angels and obtain authority over them instead of allowing them to control us. The Fallen Angels must always be used in God's name if you want to avoid negative Karma. Learning to control your Fire Element is one of the most significant challenges in life. Facing and overcoming this challenge will directly affect your level of success and accomplishment in life.

The Planet attributed to Geburah is Mars, the Planet of drive and action. Concerning the "survival of the fittest" concept, Mars is the Planet of war and competition. Symbols of Geburah are the sword, the spear, the scourge, and the pentagon. Geburah's Deity correspondences include Horus, Ares, Mars, Morrigan, Thor, Tyr, Shiva, Ogoun, and Oggun.

TIPHARETH (HARMONY/BEAUTY)

Tiphareth is the sixth Sephira of the Tree of Life, situated on the middle column, the Pillar of Balance. Tiphareth is found at the exact centre of the entire Tree. Being located in the centre, it is the recipient of the powers from all of the other Sephiroth. It represents the Air (Specific) Element, and it primarily functions through Anahata, the Heart Chakra.

It would be wrong not to assign Fire qualities to Tiphareth since its Planet is the Sun, the giver of Solar Fire and Light to our Solar System. Therefore, Tiphareth is best described as the Air (Specific) Element, acted on by the Fire Element. Anahata, the Heart Chakra as the primary expression, affected by the Chakra below it, Manipura—the Solar Plexus Chakra. The actual placement of the Tiphareth Sephira would be somewhere between these two Chakras.

Because Tiphareth is connected to Kether through the path of the High Priestess Tarot card, the Spirit Element is the motivating factor in Tiphareth, as you will see upon its examination. The colour of Tiphareth is a golden-yellow, the colour corresponding with the Air Element (yellow).

The Middle Pillar is attributed to the Air Element but is also the source of Spirit at the Crown (Kether). Hence there is a connection between Spirit and the Air Element, which I will explore in detail further on. When the Mercy of Chesed and the Severity and Justice of Geburah are balanced, "Harmony" and "Beauty" are attained. The Hebrew Divine name of Tiphareth is YHVH Eloah ve-Daath, while the Archangel is Raphael. In the Golden Dawn system of Magick, Tiphareth pertains to the Adeptus Minor (5=6) Grade of the Second Order.

"The Sixth Path is called the Mediating Intelligence, because in it are multiplied the influxes of the emanations, for it causes the influence to flow into all the reservoirs of the Blessings, with which these themselves are united." — "The Sepher Yetzirah" (on Tiphareth)

Tiphareth is the mediator between the Sephiroth due to its placement on the Tree of Life. Hence its name, the "Mediating Intelligence." The Air (Specific) Element is attributed to it since Air is thought, and thought is at the basis of all of the inner processes of man. As Chokmah and Binah are the Father and Mother, the Fire (Specific) and Water (Specific) Elements, Tiphareth is the manifested Son beyond the Abyss. The manifested Son is the Sun, the giver of Light and life in our Solar System. It is no coincidence that the word "Son" has a similar pronunciation as the word "Sun."

Tiphareth is the Sphere of Spiritual Rebirth. It is the abode of the Life-Death-Resurrection Deities, such as Osiris and Jesus Christ. The Reconciler (Redeemer) brings unity between that which is Above and that which is Below. As Tiphareth is located in the centre of the Tree of Life, it serves as the mediator of energies—as it receives energies directly from all the Spheres (except Malkuth-the Earth). As such, Tiphareth is the connection between the Lower and Higher Self. The name given to Tiphareth in *The Zohar* is the *Microprosopus* or the "Lesser Countenance."

Tiphareth is a Sphere of both illumination and healing. Since the Air Element moves both Fire and Water, Tiphareth serves as the place where the individual has contact with their Holy Guardian Angel from the Supernal Triad, above the Abyss. It is the Sphere of *Christ Consciousness*, where both Matter and Spirit are in perfect equilibrium. In terms of human personality, Tiphareth is the imagination.

The three Sephiroth of Chesed, Geburah, and Tiphareth form what is called the Ethical Triangle. The Ethical Triangle is the part of the Self that shapes the person's character. It is responsible for our morals and ethics, the building blocks of our character.

Building up the virtues within the Self is the highest manifestation of the Divine in humanity—this is why Chesed, Geburah and Tiphareth are called the "Ethical" Triangle. Because of their placement on the Tree of Life, these three Spheres are directly connected to the Supernals. Spirit energy is that which inspires us to act ethically and morally. The personality and the Ego are in the Astral Triangle below the Ethical Triangle.

As there exists a Veil separating the Supernals from the rest of the Tree of Life (Veil of the Abyss), there is also a Veil separating the Ethical Triangle from the lower Spheres (Veil of Paroketh). The Astral Triangle consists of Netzach, Hod, and Yesod. It is imperative to understand the difference between the Ethical Triangle and the Astral Triangle. A person with ethics and morals generally believes in what is good in this world. Therefore, they temper their Geburah with Chesed—their willpower and Severity with unconditional love and Mercy. If you do not use unconditional love as a motivating factor in your life, then by proxy, you are using Self-love, since opposites exist in everything, including expressions of love.

The Planet attributed to Tiphareth is the Sun, the Planet of vitality and creativity. As the Sun is the centre of our Solar System, Tiphareth is the centre of the Tree of Life. The Ancients called our Sun "Sol," which sounds like the word "Soul." The word "Solar" is derived from "Sol" as well. Our Sun gave birth to all the Souls in our Solar System, and it continues to nurture us through its Light by giving us heat and maintaining our Life energy. If the Sun were to cease its function one day, all the Souls in our Solar System would be annihilated.

Tiphareth also has a closer relation to Chokmah since it is the Holy Guardian Angel (your God-Self from Chokmah), projected into Tiphareth through the Emperor Tarot card path. Since Tiphareth is connected to all the Spheres other than Malkuth, it will contain the ideas found in all of them. The symbols of Tiphareth are the Rose Cross, the Calvary Cross, the truncated pyramid, the cube, and the Hebrew letter Vav (as part of YHVH).

Tiphareth's Deity correspondences include Osiris, Ra, the Buddha, Dionysus, Apollo, Sol, Angus Og, Balder, Krishna, Surya, Legba, and Eleggua.

NETZACH (VICTORY)

Netzach is the seventh Sephira of the Tree of life, situated at the bottom of the Pillar of Mercy. Netzach functions through Manipura Chakra, and it corresponds with the Fire (Astral) Element, which channels human instincts and desires. Netzach also relates to the feelings, which is a quality of the Water Element. As such, it uses the energy of the Chakra below, Swadhisthana, and the Chakra above, Anahata. Hence, it does not function through just one Chakra in particular, as is the case with most of the Sephiroth below the Abyss.

Netzach is the Fire found in Geburah projected through the Sphere of Tiphareth and the personality of the Astral Triangle, creating desire. "Victory" is attained when the Severity of Geburah is tempered with the Beauty of Tiphareth. Because of its placement on the Tree of Life, Netzach does not receive any Spirit energy directly from the Supernals. It only receives from the manifested Sephiroth below the Abyss. The Hebrew Divine name of Netzach is YHVH Tzabaoth, while the Archangel is Haniel. In the Golden Dawn system of Magick, Netzach pertains to the Philosophus (4=7) Grade of the First Order.

"The Seventh Path is the Occult Intelligence, because it is the Refulgent Splendour of all the Intellectual virtues which are perceived by the eyes of the intellect, and by the contemplation of Faith." — "The Sepher Yetzirah" (on Netzach)

The above reference to the "Occult Intelligence" points towards the "Hidden Intelligence" (Kether), something concealed within us that we must rediscover—our Divine nature, masked by our mundane emotions and thought processes. Thus, Netzach also represents the inner desire to attain Spiritual Illumination and to unite with our Higher Self. Desire becomes the manifested component of our Souls at this level of consciousness since we have lost our inherent birthright, the Spiritual Realm—the Garden of Eden. Through desire, we seek to be more than what we are.

Netzach has a connection with the Nephesh, the animal Self, and the Ego. It is the dynamic force that inspires and drives us. It is the part of the Self that is subjective and does not relate to unconditional love like Chesed, but personal or romantic love. Romantic love often involves the Ego, and thus, our insecurities are brought out to the surface to be dealt with. Since Netzach is the desire and the emotions, it can work to gratify the Ego or to exalt the Higher Self by inspiring ethical and moral behaviour. One needs logic and reason to make this decision, signified by Netzach's counterpart, the Sphere of Hod.

It is hard to attribute the Fire Element to Netzach without thinking of it in relation to the Water Element because Netzach is emotions, and its colour is emerald green, which is a combination of Chesed's blue and

Tiphareth's yellow. Hence, Netzach is connected to Chesed, unconditional love and Mercy. Netzach relates to desire, and it uses the Air Element and thoughts from Anahata, the Heart Chakra, to project. It is also connected to Yesod below, which is the source of our sexual energy. Thus, desire can be sexual love and lust, related to how the Ego loves, with attachment. Fortunately, it can be exalted to unconditional love, as is the nature of Chesed above.

Netzach is the abode of the Group Mind, which is the collection of symbols and images within each of us. It is the source of inspiration for the artist, the dancer, the musician, and the poet. The Planet attributed to Netzach is Venus, the Planet of desire, romantic love, and beauty. The symbols of Netzach are the rose, the girdle, and the lamp. Netzach's Deity correspondences include Hathor, Aphrodite, Venus, Brigit, Freyr, Lakshmi, Parvati, Erzulie, and Oshun.

HOD (SPLENDOUR)

Hod is the eighth Sephira of the Tree of Life, situated at the bottom of the Pillar of Severity. It functions through Swadhisthana Chakra and corresponds with the Water (Astral) Element, as pertains to logic and reason, which are primary attributes of Hod. But, as Netzach has an affinity with both the Fire and Water Elements, so does Hod, since logic and reason are a form of voluntary mental activity which uses the Fire Element as its driving force. Therefore, Hod functions through Swadhisthana but also through Manipura, tempered by the Air Element and thought in Anahata.

Hod is the Water Element from Chesed, projected through the Sphere of Tiphareth and the personality of the Astral Triangle. In other words, the Mercy of Chesed reflected through the Beauty of Tiphareth yields "Splendour." Because of where it is situated on the Tree of Life, Hod does not receive any Spirit energy directly from the Supernals. In the same way as Netzach, Hod only receives energy from the manifested Sephiroth below the Abyss. The Hebrew Divine name of Hod is Elohim Tzabaoth, while the Archangel is Michael. In the Golden Dawn system of Magick, Hod pertains to the Practicus (3=8) Grade of the First Order.

"The Eighth Path is called the Absolute or Perfect Intelligence, because it is the mean of the primordial, which has no root by which it can cleave, nor rest, except in the hidden places of Gedulah, Magnificence, from which emanates its own proper essence." — "The Sepher Yetzirah" (on Hod)

In the above excerpt, a position between Force and Form is implied, which creates the intellect. Hence it is called the "Absolute or Perfect Intelligence" since the source of the intellect's power is the White Light, perfect in every way. Chesed is frequently called "Gedulah" by Qabalists regarding the Water Element found therein. The intellect uses the Water Element to make an impression at the level of Hod. The formation of intelligence through logic and reason is an attribute at this level of manifestation since we no longer have the Spiritual component and have to rationalize to seek its attainment. Reuniting with the Spirit again is a choice that we have to make consciously and willingly while operating from Hod.

Through Hod, any writing, language, or communication comes forth, as it is the rational, organizing and categorizing aspect of the mind. It represents the left hemisphere of the brain, the intellectual component. Its counterpart, the right region, is the emotional part—Netzach. Logic and reason form the basis of intellect, which is different from intuition in receiving knowledge. Intuition is a direct knowing of truth, as the Archetypal Fire from the outside world makes an impression on the Soul.

On the other hand, intellect is based on learned knowledge over time. The Ego can use the intellect to deduce reality and make future life decisions. It is based on memory, which is the Element of Water from Chesed, while the intuition is an impulse, a Force that is from the Primal Fire Element from Chokmah. The intellect can be used to decide whether the person wants to work or fight for themselves or others. It looks for a reward in its actions. As such, it does not come from a place of unconditional love. Hence the very Egoic nature of the Sphere of Hod, because unless given the proper information from the higher Spheres, it may choose the Ego and rationalize to perform an action that is not in the name of good but instead may be seeking to gratify oneself and one's desires.

As Netzach is the abode of the Group Mind, Hod is the abode of the individual mind. It is the lesser form of the energy of Chesed, mediated through Tiphareth. Hod's energy is fluidic and Watery, just like the intellect. It needs Netzach to bring the intellect to life. Intelligence is dependent on its counterpart—emotion. The relationship between Netzach and Hod is a symbiotic one. Together, their balance supports a healthy personality. Unlike other Spheres above them, Netzach and Hod are the most commonly used and easily accessible for the average person daily.

Hod uses the Air, thought, and imagination from Tiphareth and the personal desires and emotions from Netzach to help it make its choices in life. Hod is orange, a combination of Geburah's red and Tiphareth's yellow. Hence the connection to Geburah and the Fire Element—with a link to Yesod, the primal impulses and sexual energy.

For many people, Hod and Netzach are the most widely used Spheres throughout their lifetime. The prevalent belief in society is that one must use logic and reason to guide them in life while tempering that with their emotions and their innate desire for sex and finding a mate. Society's collective level of Spiritual Evolution is somewhere between these two Spheres.

The Planet attributed to Hod is Mercury, the Planet of communication, logic, and reason. Mercury is otherwise called Hermes by the Greeks. The association of Hod to the Planet Mercury (Hermes) is fitting since it is Hermes who is regarded as the inventor of the many intellectual expressions such as mathematics, astronomy, language, etc. He is also the God of Wisdom and Knowledge who is connected to the Sephira Chokmah. As Chokmah is wisdom, the expression of the knowledge contained therein impacts Hod through the intellect.

The symbols of Hod are the *Divine Names of Power* (used in Magick) and the Masonic apron. Hod's Deity correspondences are Anubis, Khnum, Hermes, Mercury, Ogma, Loki, Bragi, Hanuman, Simbi, and Shango.

YESOD (THE FOUNDATION)

Yesod is the ninth Sephira of the Tree of Life, situated below Tiphareth on the Pillar of Balance. Yesod is the result of the unity between Netzach and Hod, as the Sephira of the Astral Plane, containing Astral Light. It is the receiver of the energies from each preceding Sephira, which, when combined, create a subtle, Astral blueprint comprised of Astral Light. Hence it is called the "Foundation" since it is the foundation of all things. The Hebrew Divine Name of Yesod is Shaddai El Chai, while the Archangel is Gabriel. In the Golden Dawn system of Magick, Yesod pertains to the Theoricus (2=9) Grade of the First Order.

"The Ninth Path is the Pure Intelligence, so called because it purifies the Numerations, it proves and corrects the designing of their representation, and disposes their unity with which they are combined without diminution or division." — "The Sepher Yetzirah" (on Yesod)

Yesod's role is to bring correction and purification to the preceding emanations before they manifest within the Material Realm, hence its name, the "Pure Intelligence." It is reflective in nature and omnipresent, as is the Astral Light, its substance. It is a medium of extremely subtle Matter, which is highly magnetic and electric, as it receives the impulses of the Spheres above it to create the Physical World. It is the changeless and endless ebb and flow of all the invisible forces in the world as it provides their very foundation of existence.

The intuitive faculties filter into Yesod—since Yesod has a connection to Binah (Understanding). The Earthly Plane is built upon Yesod, which is the Etheric Body double of everything in existence—the Foundation. Each worldly event unfolds within the Astral Plane before it manifests within the Physical Plane. For this reason, the Magus makes use of Yesod and the Astral Light to influence the world's activity before its physical manifestation. As the Hermetic axiom states, "As Above, So Below"—what we change in one Plane manifests in another. This process is the essence of Magick, which unfolds within Yesod—as does all Magickal work.

In terms of the human Aura, Yesod is the Air (Astral) Element. It functions through Anahata, the Heart Chakra, but on a much lower level than Tiphareth as it uses the sexuality and emotions found in Swadhisthana and Muladhara Chakras. Since Yesod's position is in the groin area, its placement would be somewhere between the Earth Chakra, Muladhara, and Water Chakra, Swadhisthana.

Some Spiritual schools of thought will assign sexuality to the Earth Chakra, Muladhara, since the source of the Kundalini is in the Earth Chakra, at the coccyx, at the base of the spine. The coccyx is the lowest point of the human energy system, which connects to the Minor Chakras in the foot soles, which, in turn, connect to the Earth. The Sphere of Malkuth would be precisely at the feet where they touch the earth on which we walk. As such, the Foot Sole Chakras activate the Earth Chakra centre at the base of the spine. Because Yesod is the abode of the Ego and the subconscious mind, it is related to the Water Chakra, Swadhisthana, as well. Again, it is challenging to assign Chakras to the Tree of Life Sephiroth since the Sephiroth are more complex in their function.

Because of its placement on the Tree of Life, Yesod receives no Spirit energy directly; hence, it is used most often by the Ego. The Ego is present in the Astral Triangle, separated from the Ethical Triangle by the Veil of Paroketh. It is otherwise known as the "Veil of the Temple" or the "Veil of Illusion." The Temple that is being referred to is one's Inner Temple that houses one's Inner God-Self. Our God-Self is of the Supernals. The Spirit energy is brought into the Ethical Triangle through the path of the High Priestess. The Veil of Paroketh, therefore, separates Spirit from Matter. Beneath the Veil, we live under the illusion that the World of Matter is substantial and real.

The Temperance Tarot card represents the path connecting Yesod to Tiphareth, the Moon and the Sun, that rends the Veil of Paroketh with the use of the Bow of Quesheth, which stands symbolically for a rainbow. The rainbow serves as a bridge between Heaven and Earth, Divinity and humanity. This bridge refers to the Chakras in the human Aura, which, when invigorated by the Kundalini energy on its upwards rise, activate the Rainbow Body, the Body of Light.

The word "Paroketh" is composed of four Hebrew letters, each of which represents one of the Four Elements: Peh (Water), Resh (Air), Kaph (Fire), and Tav (Earth). The Veil of Paroketh is lifted when we activate all the latent potential in the Body of Light by awakening the Kundalini and raising it to the Crown Chakra. Only then can we perceive the world around us as what it is—Maya, an illusion.

Sexuality is a function of the physical body, which is Malkuth—the lowest Sphere and one below Yesod. Yesod takes part in channelling logic, reason, and emotion from the two higher Spheres above it, Netzach and Hod. The Astral Triangle of Netzach, Hod, and Yesod is the most readily available energy for humanity and one that we use daily. The use of these energies forms our Ego and our personality.

Yesod serves as the beginning of the Astral Plane; the world of thoughts, emotions, imagination, willpower, memory, intuition and the Higher Will. It is everything that we contain inside us that is not the mere physical body we see in the mirror. The Universe Tarot card is the perfect representation of Yesod—it is the blueprint of the Outer Universe and the Inner Universe—including all the various aspects contained within the Sephiroth above Yesod. As such, Yesod is our gateway to the inner Self through the Astral World.

Sexuality is the driving force of the Ego but also our source of creativity. It is the mechanism that, when sublimated (transformed), can give us Spiritual Illumination. Sexual energy is fueled by Prana (Hindu), chi or qi (Chinese), mana (Hawaiian). It is at the very foundation of our existence. All three terms mentioned above essentially mean Life energy or Life Force. Consequently, we receive this vital energy through food and water as the nutrients in each transform into Light energy, which is the essence of Prana. This energy is then distributed through the Nadis—the energetic pathways or channels in the body. Light energy sustains our Inner and Outer Worlds. Its source is the Spirit energy.

In its state of potential, the Kundalini resides at the base of the spine, and it is triggered by sublimated sexual and Pranic energy from Yesod. The Kundalini is connected with Malkuth, the Earth, but stimulated by the thoughts and emotions of Hod and Netzach.

All parts of the Tree of Life need to be involved in the process if one is to experience a full awakening. The use of imagination (Tiphareth) must be present through the application of willpower (Geburah) and memory (Chesed). Most importantly, though, Wisdom (Chokmah) and Understanding (Binah) have to be involved in the process since the Kundalini energy needs to reach the brain on its upwards rise—this means that Ajna Chakra has to be engaged in some way during the Kundalini awakening process.

If the Supernals are not engaged in the process, the Kundalini energy will never reach the brain but will drop back down to the base of the spine instead—and the process will repeat itself in the future. All of these inner functions are accessed through Yesod, the Astral World—hence why it is the Foundation of all things concerning the inner Self.

The Planet attributed to Yesod is the Moon, while its colour is violet. The Moon is the Planet of feelings, moods, and instincts. The Moon makes perfect sense in describing Yesod because the Moon only reflects the Light of the Sun, as Yesod only reflects the Light contained in Tiphareth. Yesod has no direct contact with the Ethical Triangle other than its reflection through Tiphareth. It has no direct contact with Geburah and Chesed, but the fact that their colours are contained within it (red and blue make violet) shows that it does reflect those Spheres, although indirectly.

The Moon creates an illusion in one's mind since it cannot perceive the truth directly. The Moon is called "Luna" by the Ancients, and the word "lunatic" (describing chaotic and erratic behaviour) is connected to the function of the Moon. Now you see why—the illusions in one's mind trigger this kind of response.

The Spheres of Yesod, Hod, and Netzach form the Astral Triangle. The Astral Triangle is a reflection of the Ethical Triangle in the same way that the personality reflects the character of a person. The character is built upon virtues, and it exalts the Higher Self. Virtues belong to the Eternal part of us that was never born and will never die. Conversely, the personality belongs to the Ego and the realm of duality, including the cycle of death and rebirth. Each time a person dies, so does their Ego, only to be reborn again in another physical body and rebuilt from the ground up.

The symbols associated with Yesod are perfume and sandals. The Deity correspondences of Yesod are Shu, Khonsu, Artemis, Diana, Cerridwen, Nanna, Chandra, Soma, Masa, and Yemaya.

MALKUTH (THE KINGDOM)

Malkuth is the tenth Sephira of the Tree of Life, situated right under Yesod on the Middle Pillar of Balance. Malkuth's position is at the feet, which walk upon the Earth. Therefore, Malkuth is our connection to Mother Earth. The Minor Chakras at the soles of the feet connect with the base of the spine through the energy channels in the legs. Thus, Malkuth is directly connected to the Root Chakra, Muladhara, and the Kundalini energy. In terms of the human Aura, Malkuth is the Earth (Specific) Element.

In all of its designations, Malkuth is always of the Earth Element. It is the physical reality, the Universe, which we can touch, hear, see, smell, and taste. Everything past the point of Malkuth uses our internal sexual energy through the Tree of Life and its Sephiroth, which are the powers that work together to manifest our reality. Malkuth is the "Kingdom" in which we live, move, and have our Being. The Hebrew Divine name of Malkuth is Adonai ha-Aretz, while the Archangel is Sandalphon. In the Golden Dawn system of Magick, Malkuth pertains to the Zelator (10=1) Grade of the First Order.

> *"The Tenth Path is the Resplendent Intelligence, so called because it is exalted above every head, and sits on the throne of Binah. It illuminates the splendour of all the Lights, and causes an influence to emanate from the Prince of Countenances, the Angel of Kether." — "The Sepher Yetzirah" (on Malkuth)*

The term "Resplendent Intelligence" implies a close connection to Kether, as the number one is found in the number ten. Kether, the Spirit, exists in everything around us, from the smallest insect to the ground on which we walk. In terms of the Four Worlds concept (to be discussed later on), Malkuth becomes Kether in another Tree of Life on another level of reality.

There is also a connection between Binah, the Great Mother, and Malkuth, the Inferior Mother. Once Spiritualized, Malkuth, the Kingdom, becomes Binah, Understanding. This association can be found in the colours of Malkuth, which are citrine, olive, russet and black. Often, Malkuth is described as purely black, which gives it the association with Binah since it is also black. Binah is the Great Feminine Principle and the Holy Spirit in Christian terms, while Malkuth is the manifestation of that Holy Spirit in Matter.

Malkuth is synonymous with Gaia, as Mother Earth, although Malkuth represents all of Matter in the Universe. Also, notice the similarity in sound between the word "Matter" and "Mother." It tells you that there is a correlation between these two ideas.

As Binah is the Spiritual blueprint of Malkuth, our overall purpose as initiates of Light is to Spiritualize our own Earth (metaphorically speaking) and restore the Garden of Eden. We have to uplift our own Malkuth back into Binah. (The symbology of the Garden of Eden will be addressed later on.) But to do so, we have to Spiritualize all the Sephiroth between Malkuth and Binah. The overall purpose of our life here on Earth is Spiritual Evolution.

Malkuth, the Kingdom, is the World of Matter but also the gateway to the *Kingdom of God*. As Jesus Christ proclaimed, "Behold, the Kingdom of God is within you." (Luke 17: 21) The concept of the Kingdom of God not being something "out there" but something inside each of us is one of Jesus' most important messages to humanity. The Kingdom of God is already present within Malkuth because of its association with Binah and the Holy Spirit. It is up to each individual to raise their consciousness to its level, though. And it happens through Wisdom and Understanding, the understanding that we are Spirit and Matter in one.

Malkuth is the starting point of the Inner Worlds (Cosmic Planes) and inner workings of man. While Malkuth remains stable, the other Sephiroth above it are kinetic and mobilized. Malkuth's stability is a result of its low rate of vibration. All the Spheres above Malkuth vibrate at higher frequencies, with the vibration increasing from Sphere to Sphere as you are working upwards. Malkuth is the recipient of the Etheric framework of manifestation from Yesod. It is the container of the remaining nine Sephiroth as it grounds those energies within the Material Realm. As such, it is the ultimate Sephira of Form. Malkuth is the final receptacle for all of the different currents of energy that comprise the Tree of Life.

Malkuth is also more than just the Physical World and the Earth. It is also the Sephira where each of the other three Elements are based, only at a lower form of manifestation. In the Qabalah, they are called the Base Elements. They are portrayed in the colours of Malkuth as they reflect the powers of the three Sephiroth of

Yesod, Hod, and Netzach. Malkuth is only connected to these three Sephiroth on the Tree of Life. Malkuth is also assigned the Earth Element (Astral), meaning that although it relates to the Physical World, it also has a connection with the Astral World. Malkuth manifests through Muladhara Chakra, which also has a Subtle Body called the Lower Astral Body (Etheric Body).

For the Four Elements, there are three different states of Matter: solid (Earth), liquid (Water), and gas (Air). The Fire Element is given the principle of electricity. All physical phenomena fall under the Four Elements, giving us the means to understand their character and qualities. Each of the Four Elements is used to describe the physical, material essence of Malkuth.

The symbols of Malkuth are the Double Cubical Altar, the Mystic Circle, the Triangle of Art (Evocation), and the Hebrew letter Heh-final (as part of YHVH). The Deity correspondences of Malkuth include Geb, Demeter, Ceres, Cernunnos, Nerthus, Ganesha, Azaka, and Ochosi.

THE PATH OF THE FLAMING SWORD

The Path of the Flaming Sword (Figure 5) represents the sequence of manifestation of the Sephiroth. The Flaming Sword is often called the "Lightning Flash" by Qabalists. Essentially, the Path of the Flaming Sword signifies the process of Creation. Its sequence begins with Kether, followed by Chokmah, then Binah, Daath, Chesed, Geburah, Tiphareth, Netzach, Hod, Yesod, and ending with Malkuth.

According to Qabalist lore, when Michael banished Lucifer from Heaven, the Flaming Sword was put in place to block him from returning. Lucifer is known as the "Light of the Morning Star"—the spark of higher consciousness inside human beings that inspires us to strive for more than just a simple physical existence. The Fall of Lucifer is synonymous with our Fall from the Garden of Eden. We are Lucifer in this story.

If we are to reenter the Garden of Eden, we must ascend the Tree of Life by embarking upon the Path of the Flaming Sword in reverse. We begin in Malkuth and progress through the lower four Chakras before crossing the Abyss at Daath into the Spirit Realm. With a full Kundalini awakening, the whole Tree of Life is activated, including the Supernals. However, consciousness can only operate at the total capacity of the Light once the lower Spheres (corresponding with the lower Chakras) have all been energetically cleansed. One must traverse up the Tree of Life via the reversed sequence of the Path of the Flaming Sword.

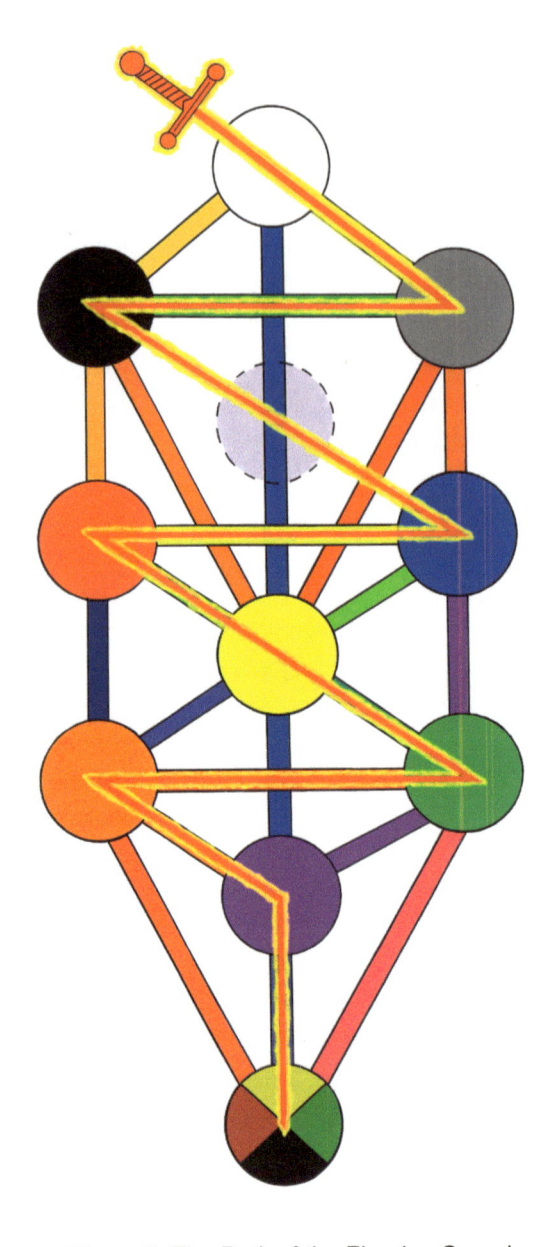

Figure 5: The Path of the Flaming Sword

THE SERPENT OF WISDOM

In the Qabalah, the Serpent of Wisdom (Figure 6) refers to the direction or course of the Hebrew letters as placed on the twenty-two Tarot paths of the Thirty-Two Paths of Wisdom. Together, these paths form a symbol—the Serpent of Wisdom. Therefore, the Tarot paths equal the Serpent of Wisdom while the Sephiroth equal the Path of the Flaming Sword. As the Path of the Flaming Sword represents Creation descending from the highest to the lowest (Kether to Malkuth), the Serpent of Wisdom climbs the Tree of Life from the lowest path (Tav) to the highest path (Aleph).

Figure 6: The Serpent of Wisdom

You can see now how the symbology of the Serpent is present within the Qabalah and the Tree of Life. It is the Kundalini energy that lights up the entire Tree of Life when awakened. It is the Serpent that tempted Eve to eat of the Tree of Knowledge of Good and Evil in the Garden of Eden, even though God strictly forbade this. Through their disobedience to God, Adam and Eve were banished out of the Garden.

Now, it is this Serpent again through whom we are to return to the Garden of Eden. We do so by awakening the Kundalini, the process of which is synonymous with activating and invigorating the entire Tree of Life and travelling upwards in consciousness. We ascend the Tree of Life in succession upwards, starting with the lowest Sephira, Malkuth, and ending with the highest Sephira, Kether.

"The Great Work, is before all things, the creation of man by himself, that is to say, the full and entire conquest of his faculties and his future; it is especially the perfect emancipation of his will."
— *Eliphas Levi; excerpt from "Transcendental Magic"*

This entire process is called the Great Work, or Spiritual Alchemy, and is the basis of this book. The purpose of the Great Work is Enlightenment or Spiritual Evolution and ascension. Performing the Great Work will unleash your personal power and maximize your potential in this life. And for those experiencing Kundalini awakenings, it will give them the tools whereby they will have a daily practice with which to combat the anxiety and fear that is unleashed when undergoing an awakening, especially a full, sustained one.

THE THIRTY-TWO PATHS OF WISDOM

To truly appreciate the Qabalah, you have to understand just how in-depth the system is. Thus far, I have elaborated on the Tree of Life and the ten Spheres. However, there are twenty-two connecting paths between them—the twenty-two paths along with the ten Sephiroth equal the Thirty-Two Paths of Wisdom. The twenty-two paths correlate with the twenty-two Major Arcana of the Tarot, which, in turn, correspond with the three main Elements of Air, Fire, and Water, the Twelve Zodiac, and the Seven Ancient Planets. The Elements, in this case, are called "Transitional" Elements since they represent energies in transit between the Sephiroth.

The twenty-two paths also correlate with the twenty-two letters of the Hebrew alphabet, which are considered very Magickal in their use, whether through writing or pronunciation of the Hebrew Divine Names. Everything I have just mentioned is regarded as Hermetic knowledge since Hermeticism is essentially the study of our Solar System and its energies.

As mentioned, the Qabalah is the blueprint of the Universe (our Solar System in particular), including the Cosmic Planes of existence. The ten Sephiroth are states of consciousness. The connecting paths are the energies that flow in and out of those states. Understanding these paths will offer you immense insight into your psyche and personality and give you a roadmap for going from one state of consciousness to the next safely and efficiently.

As each man and woman has their Tree of Life, this means that we can map our consciousness somewhere on our Tree. For example, if you are using logic and reason, your consciousness is in Hod, while if you are experiencing the emotion of desire, you are in Netzach. If you are experiencing the emotion of fear, you are in your subconscious mind, located in Yesod—this consequently is the place where your sexual energy is activated. If you are using your imagination, you are in Tiphareth, while if you are using your willpower, you are operating from Geburah. The process of remembering the past occurs in Chesed, as does the conscious application of the energy of unconditional love. Within the Supernals, intuition occurs as a direct knowing of truth. These are some of the correspondences of the Qabalah to our psychological makeup, but there are many more.

The Qabalah is all about correspondences between things we find in nature, and therefore memorizing these correspondences is the first step to attaining Gnosis. Through the process of Gnosis, your own Higher Self will become your teacher. Your own Higher Genius (Holy Guardian Angel) teaches you the true Qabalah—this is the part of you that is of God, the part of you that is Eternal—the Higher Self. The conscious work on your part is to memorize the correspondences. These memories will become like filing cabinets that the Higher Genius will use to teach you.

THE HEBREW ALPHABET

The Sepher Yetzirah separates the twenty-two letters of the Hebrew alphabet into three different classes: the Mothers, the Doubles, and the Simples. The three Mother letters are Aleph, Mem, and Shin. They form a trinity out of which everything within Creation arises. The three Mother letters correspond with the Elements of Air, Water, and Fire. Mem (Water) and Shin (Fire) are opposites, while Aleph (Air) is the balancing Element between them.

Spirit, although considered an Element for the sake of understanding, is essentially the glue of everything in existence but is not found in the Tree of Life in one of the twenty-two paths. The best way to understand Spirit is to understand it as the Supernal part of the Tree. Malkuth also is not a separate component since it is the World of Matter. Both Spirit and Matter represent the Alpha and the Omega—the beginning and the end of the Universe.

The seven Double letters include Beth, Gimel, Daleth, Kaph, Peh, Resh, and Tav. They are referred to as the Doubles since each letter contains a hard and soft sound within its pronunciation. Also, they each have a dual set of qualities. The Doubles represent the Seven Ancient Planets, the seven days of Creation, the seven orifices of the human being (used in perception), and the seven directions of Space (North, East, South, West, Up, Down, Centre).

The twelve Simple (or Single) letters are Heh, Vav, Zayin, Cheth, Teth, Yod, Lamed, Nun, Samekh, Ayin, Tzaddi, and Qoph. The twelve Simples represent the twelve different signs of the Zodiac, the twelve months of the year, and the twelve different organs within the human body.

As mentioned, the twenty-two Paths of the Tree of Life correlate with the twenty-two letters of the Hebrew alphabet. Their literal translations also have a very esoteric significance, allowing you to develop an even more in-depth understanding of the Qabalah. I will discuss these translations further in the section on the Major Arcana of the Tarot.

THE TREE OF LIFE AND THE SOLAR SYSTEM

"For the Sun is situated in the center of the Cosmos, wearing it like a Crown." — Hermes Trismegistus; excerpt from "Hermetica: The Greek Corpus Hermeticum and the Latin Asclepius"

People who inquire about the Tree of Life ask for the most practical description of what it is. The answer to their enquiry is simple; the Tree of Life is the blueprint of our Solar System. If we take the Tree of Life, lay it flat horizontally, and perceive each Sphere as the Planet it corresponds to, we will have a three-dimensional layout that is almost identical to the positioning of the Planets within our Solar System.

Keep in mind that the Ancients were unaware of the new Planets of Uranus, Neptune, and Pluto; hence, they were not included as part of the Qabalistic framework. Some modern-day Qabalists add them by corresponding Chokmah to Uranus and Kether to Neptune. Because of its size and irregular orbit, Pluto had been demoted as a Planet. In recent years though, it was again reinstated as one.

Although the Earth is in between Venus and Mars in our Solar System, if we put the Earth in place of the Sun as the centre from which all other Planetary energies emerge, we would get the exact numerical sequence as the positioning of the Planets on the Tree of Life. If Earth is the centre of our Solar System, we would have the Moon next (closest to the Earth), followed by Mercury, Venus, the Sun (in place of Earth), Mars, Jupiter, and Saturn.

This application makes a lot of sense when we apply the correspondence between the words "Soul" and "Sol," which is the Latin name used by the Ancients for the Sun. The Light of the Soul correlates with the Light from the Sun. Not the physical Light we see with our eyes but Light at a higher vibrational frequency. It is no wonder that the Ancients referred to the Soul as the "Eternal Spark from the Sun." Thus, since we have our physical existence on Earth, and our Soul originated from the Sun in our Solar System, the Light inside our Souls is our connecting link to our Creator. It is the highest Source inside us and who we are, in essence. This falls in line with the teachings of Jesus Christ and the first monotheist in history—the Egyptian Pharaoh Akhenaten.

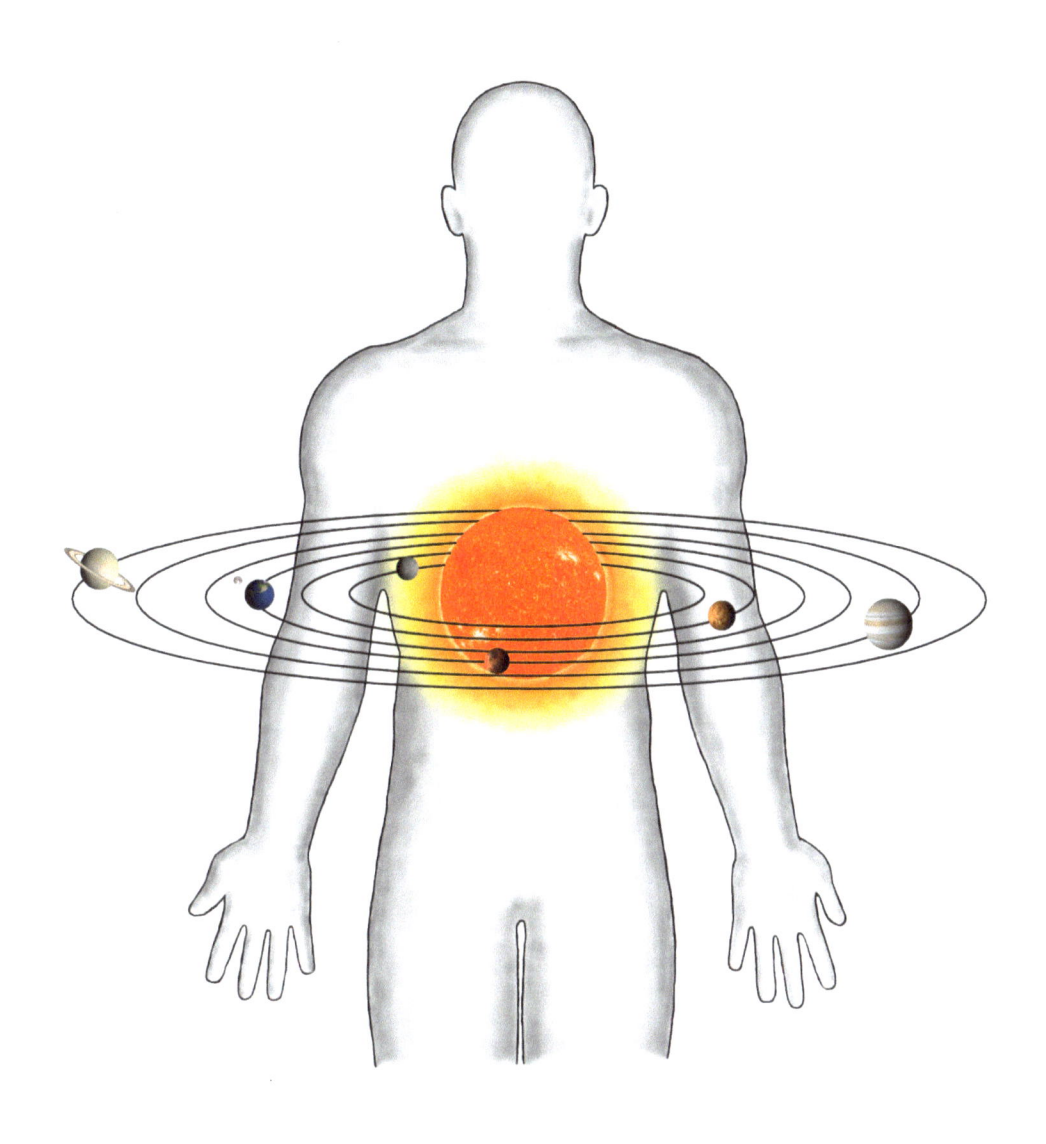

Figure 7: The Human Being as a Mini Solar System

Planets are held in orbit around the Sun by a spherical force that manifests as an invisible concentric sphere. Visually, this looks similar to how the layers of an onion overlay one on top of the other. If we imagine that the Earth is the centre of the onion, the Planetary energies are its layers, which follow the numerical sequence given by the Tree of Life. These energies form the Aura of the Earth, which corresponds with the human Aura. The Planetary energies are contained in both—As Above, So Below—the Microcosm reflects the Macrocosm.

As the Tree of Life is a reflection of our Solar System, our individual Tree of Life is a reflection of our Solar System as a whole—considering we were made in the image of our Creator. If you can imagine yourself as a Being of immense size (Figure 7), then the Sun (our central Star) is in your Solar Plexus area, the Seat of the

Soul and the Source of Light and the Fire Element. The correspondence Qabalistically would be the Sephira Tiphareth, the Air (Specific) Element acted on by the Solar Fire Element.

Tiphareth is the central Sephira which receives the influences of all the other Sephiroth, excluding Malkuth. As such, it is the Anahata Chakra acted on by Manipura Chakra. The exact Solar centre (Tiphareth) would be somewhere in-between those two Chakras—it is the Source of our Being through which we are connected to the Sun itself. This connection is attained through unconditional love—the binding energy of all things in our Solar System.

Around our own central Sun (in our Solar Plexus) are the Planetary energies, which manifest as our higher powers. These are the various components of our inner Self, the source of our morals and ethics. The Planetary energies are contained within the human Aura. Their impact on our Souls is directly affected by the motion of the Planetary bodies as they orbit around our Sun. We are connected to the powers of the Planets and, in this way, are a perfect Microcosm of the Macrocosm—a Mini Solar System which reflects the grand Solar System in which we have our physical existence.

Understanding the Planets and their powers is of paramount importance to this work. Knowledge of the Five Elements (which express themselves through the Seven Chakras) and the Seven Ancient Planets, and the Twelve Zodiac is the core, the basis of Hermetic Teachings and the Qabalistic Tree of Life.

THREE PARTS OF THE SELF

The Qabalists consider the ten Sephiroth and the connecting paths as a unity without division, forming what they call Adam Kadmon—the "Heavenly Man." In *The Zohar*, Adam Kadmon is also called the "Grand Old Man." He is a large, organic, Spiritual body in which each human being is considered a single cell, perhaps even less. Within Adam Kadmon is the potential of everything in our Solar System, and he is a manifestation of the whole and the unity of all things.

Adam Kadmon is also the prototype of a human being. The Sephiroth are the Cosmic Principles operating in the Macrocosm (our Solar System). They find their reflection in humanity as well—As Above, So Below.

The Self is the "I" that inhabits the physical body and uses it as its vehicle of manifestation. Without the Self, the human body is like a light bulb without electricity or a computer without any software that makes it run.

The human Self has three distinct components or parts, which function almost independently of one another but occupy the same Time and Space. Each of these parts of the Self functions simultaneously as all other parts, but we can only experience one of them at a time, and it is the one that gets our attention. Our awareness of one of the three parts of Self determines our state of consciousness. We experience these different parts of the Self through our thoughts, as thought is the basis of all reality. And we experience our thoughts through the mind—the connecting link between Spirit and Matter.

Since the three parts of the Self relate to the different Sephiroth on the Tree of Life, we have to superimpose the Tree of Life onto the physical body to understand the correspondences. According to the Qabalah, the first and highest division, or part of the Self, is known as the Greater Neschamah—which can further be broken down into the Yechidah, Chiah, and Lesser Neschamah. The Greater Neschamah resides in the brain. It is our True Self—the part of us that is Divine.

Yechidah is found in Kether, at Sahasrara Chakra, at the top of the head. It is Eternal—beyond Time and Space, and refers to the Freudian Super-Ego—the Higher Self. Yechidah is our connection to Cosmic Consciousness. It fuels our drive to evolve beyond our physical humanity and unite our consciousness with the Cosmic one. It is unknowable, as it is the White Light we are all a part of, but it can become known through the Chiah and Lesser Neschamah, which immediately lie below it.

Yechidah is also our connection to the Akashic Records, a type of memory bank contained within Cosmic Consciousness. It contains all human events, thoughts, emotions, and intentions that have happened in the past, are happening now, or will happen in the future. The future has already occurred from the perspective of God-the Creator, but since we are physical beings bound to Space and Time, we have yet to experience it.

The word "Akasha" in Sanskrit is a term for either "Space" or "Aethyr." It alludes to the Spirit Element—the animating Principle behind all of Creation. The Yechidah can access the Akashic Records through the Now, the present moment.

"A man who is doing his True Will has the inertia of the Universe to assist him."—Aleister Crowley; excerpt from "Magick in Theory and Practice"

The Chiah (found in the Sphere of Chokmah) is our True Will. It is the masculine, projective part of the Self, belonging to the Fire Element. It is our Holy Guardian Angel and the part of us that is continually fueling us to come closer to Divinity. The Chiah influences the functions of the left-brain hemisphere, such as analytic thought, logic, reason, science and math, reasoning, and writing skills. Since these functions happen through the mind, though, the part of the Self called the Ruach is involved. The Yechidah and Chiah are fundamentally Archetypal, meaning they are to some degree outside of our ability to understand them fully. We can use the left side of our brain, but we cannot understand why we know what we know nor the source of that knowledge.

The Lesser Neschamah is found within the Sphere of Binah. It is feminine and receptive, belonging to the Water Element. The Lesser Neschamah serves as our psychic intuition. It is the Self's highest aspiration and our deepest longing or most elevated state of consciousness. After all, our intuitive power links us directly to the Divine. In the average person, this aspect of the Self is relatively dormant and uncovered. Only after we begin to awaken Spiritually do we start to discover the powers of mystical understanding and transcendence. For this discovery to occur, though, a dialogue between the Higher Self and the *Lower Self* must take place first. The Lesser Neschamah influences the functions of the right-brain hemisphere, such as creativity, imagination, insight, holistic thought, and awareness of music and art forms in general.

Intuition is the highest part of the tangible Self. This part of us can channel information from the inner Cosmic Planes. The more Spiritually evolved you are, the more you function through intuition. Intuition is received through Ajna, the Mind's Eye Chakra. Those that are highly attuned to intuition become telepaths and empaths. Telepathy is the direct knowing of others' thoughts, while empathy is the direct knowing of others' emotions. Both take place through intuition since its function is to see and process energy. A Kundalini awakening is the awakening to a process of transforming the Self so that the individual functions mainly through intuition. Duality found in the lower parts of the Self is unified by the Holy Spirit energy released through the Kundalini.

The next component of the Self (after the Neschamah) is the Ruach, which is the conscious aspect of our Being. It is through the Ruach that reasoning powers are given. The Ruach is the mind, while the Neschamah is the Spirit. Between them lies the Abyss (Daath), separating Spirit and Matter. This separation occurs in Vishuddhi, the Throat Chakra, which separates the higher three Chakras of Spirit from the lower four Chakras of the Four Elements of Air, Fire, Water, and Earth.

The Ruach contains both the Soul and the Ego, which acts on behalf of the Lower Self. Through the Ruach, these two parts of Self battle each other for supremacy. The Soul's purpose is to raise the individual consciousness to the Higher Self (the Spirit) level, while the Ego's goal is to lower the consciousness to the level of Matter.

Nechamah lives in unity, as it is the undifferentiated Spirit, while duality is present at the level of Ruach and the mind. This duality gives rise to logic and reason, the tool that the Ruach uses to deduce reality. In this way, the intellect is formed, which is a lower manifestation of knowledge than the truth that only intuition can receive.

Ruach is the seat of what is known as "Outer-Consciousness." It is here that we can become aware of thought images before being able to transform them into actions. Ruach is related to most of our daily thinking. It is made up of five Sephiroth—Chesed, Geburah, Tiphareth, Netzach, and Hod.

Chesed is concerned with memory, and it lies on the left shoulder. It is the part of the Ruach that can memorize and retain information. Memory is related to Karma. Thus, its ultimate purpose is to teach us how to behave under the Universal Laws.

Geburah is concerned with willpower and fortitude, and it lies along the right shoulder. Strength of mind is necessary for us to learn to use our willpower in the name of our Soul, not the Ego. Tiphareth is imagination, and it is the balancing factor between willpower and memory since both are needed for it to function correctly. Its placement is within the Solar Plexus area.

Netzach is along the left hip, and it is concerned with our desires. Our ultimate desire is unity with the Divine, although desire can take many forms. And finally, Hod is along the right hip, and it is concerned with logic and reason. The ultimate purpose of the Ruach is to raise individual consciousness to the level of Cosmic Consciousness.

The Ruach signifies the intermediate level between the highest and lowest components of the Self. It is here that the ethical ability to make the distinction between good and evil is engaged. Within the Ruach, the person can concentrate on either temporary personal desires of the Ego or higher Spiritual aims and ideals of the Soul. The focused attention of the Ruach connects us to either our Lower or Higher Selves since it is the intermediary between the two.

The Ruach is connected to the Greater Nechamah as the Element of Air is connected to the Spirit. Primal Air is, in fact, a lower manifestation of the Spirit energy, as the Spirit manifested in a lower Element to serve as the reconciler of the other two Primal Elements—Water and Fire. Fire and Water need Air to survive as it fuels them both. Air then is the thought, active and passive, voluntary and involuntary, which is the source of both willpower and emotion—the Fire and Water Elements.

The next component of the Self is the Nephesh—the dark side and the subconscious mind, known as the Lower Self. The Nephesh, also understood to be the "Shadow Self," responds to the primal, animalistic instincts within us. The Nephesh is an essential component of the Self. It connects humanity to the Physical Realm of the Elements, as well as to our animal Ancestors. This part of us propels us to share in the same activities as all other animals—including sleeping, eating, and engaging in sexual activity. The Nephesh gave birth to the Ego, who is the adversary of the Soul since one of its primary functions is to continue carrying out the duties of the Nephesh while neglecting the Spirit.

The Nephesh is the first aspect of the Self, activated at birth. It can be found in the Sphere of Yesod, in the groin area, symbolized by the Moon. For this reason, it is somewhat misleading as it merely reflects the Light of the Sun in Tiphareth. Hence, the information it projects is deceptive since only the Light of the Sun is the real truth. Here, the Lunar energy is very significant as it is this sexual energy and force that serves to activate the Kundalini. Within the Nephesh area is where Prana, chi, mana (Life energy) is produced. In the Qabalah, this Life energy is also called Ruach, not to be mistaken with the Ruach as one of the three parts of the Self.

The Nephesh is symbolic of our fundamental impulses to oppose the societal whole—including society's conceptions of ideal behaviour. The Nephesh is the dark side of the consciousness within the Ruach, the mind. It can be likened to the Freudian ID.

The Ruach must always maintain control of the Nephesh—the subconscious must always be under the conscious mind's control. The Nephesh feeds on fear and is its source. The Lower Self (the Nephesh) can evoke the Middle Self (the Ruach), which in turn can then activate the Greater Neschamah (the Divine, or God Self). This process causes the Greater Neschamah to come down into the lower portions of the Self to bring the individual up to a conscious recognition of the Divine Self. This operation is called "Spiritualizing the Ego."

Finally, the last component of the Self is known as the G'uph. Located in the Sphere of Malkuth, at the feet, the G'uph is connected to the physical body and the full spectrum of psychophysical functioning. Whenever there is a physical threat to the body, the G'uph communicates to the brain about what might be wrong. The G'uph is a lower level of the subconscious whose role is to inform the brain about the state of the body. It is essentially our "fight or flight" impulse. The G'uph and the Ego are allies, as are the Soul and Spirit. The origin of the word "goof" may relate to the G'uph since to behave like a "goof" means to operate at a lower level of human consciousness.

Understanding the three parts of the Self enables you to understand your psychological makeup, character, and personality. If you are to master the Self, it is of primary importance to know how the different components and energies within you function. Thus, understanding how psychology works is paramount to Spiritual Evolution and the accomplishment of the Great Work.

TETRAGRAMMATON AND PENTAGRAMMATON

The Tetragrammaton and Pentagrammaton concepts contain much symbolism related to the Kundalini awakening process and its overall purpose. To the Qabalists, the name of God is YHVH, which is called the Tetragrammaton in the Qabalah (Figure 8). Jehovah, the Hebrew God of *The Torah* (Old Testament), was named after the Tetragrammaton. Tetragrammaton is Hebrew for "four letters," which stand for Yod (Fire), Heh (Water), Vav (Air), and Heh-final (Earth). It is understood that no one knows the proper pronunciation of the name of God (YHVH) and that as human beings, we must unite with our Holy Guardian Angel or Higher Genius, Higher Self, to learn it.

There is a whole list of meanings and correspondences that fall in line with the four letters of the Tetragrammaton. Yod (Fire) represents Archetypal masculinity. Yod is the head, the illuminated mind, and our connection to the Heavens (the Stars). Heh (Water) represents Archetypal femininity. Heh is the shoulders and arms as our vehicle for manifesting the ideas from our minds. Vav (Air) represents physical masculinity. Vav is the torso carrying the spine, which serves as the channel for the Kundalini Fire. The Holy Spirit, when awakened, activates the Chakras and connects the Heavens above and the Earth below. And finally, Heh-final (Earth) represents physical femininity. Heh-final is the legs that walk on the Planet Earth itself.

Notice a correspondence between Heh (Water) and Heh-final (Earth). Both the legs and arms of the physical body are needed to manifest in this World of Matter. Also, each expression of the Heh letter implies a duality since both the arms and legs have two limbs each. Their mode of expression is towards the Physical World since this World of Matter is one of duality. The arms express the Air Element (the mind) since they are literally suspended in the air around us, mediating between the head (Heaven) and the legs (Earth). The legs serve all the Elements since they rest upon the Planet Earth and carry the torso, the arms, and the head.

Always keep in mind that the Qabalah is meant to be interpreted through symbols, allegory, numbers, and metaphors. If you see a similarity between any two ideas within the Qabalah, a correspondence also exists in the Spiritual Reality—As Above, So Below.

As mentioned in previous lessons, the Four Elements are found in the lowest four Chakras. The highest three Chakras are of the Aethyr. What is the Aethyr? Very simply, the Aethyr is the Spirit Element. A Kundalini awakening is an awakening to the Spirit Element and its full integration within all of the Chakras.

Figure 8: The Tetragrammaton—YHVH

    The ultimate goal of the Kundalini awakening process is for the Kundalini energy to reach the Crown Chakra—for Shakti to reach Shiva. The Crown is Non-Dual; therefore, it does not contain Karma. When the Kundalini reaches the Crown, the Spiritual activation is complete. Once pierced by the Kundalini energy, the Crown opens up like a lotus flower, allowing the Divine Spirit from above to descend into the Chakras below, thereby infusing them permanently. The individual thus obtains a connection with their Higher, God-Self from the Supernals.

    The Chasm between the Ego and the Higher Self is called the Abyss. The Ego vanishes once you have crossed the Abyss and reached the Supernals. The Ego can never be annihilated while living in the physical body but its impact on the individual consciousness lessens drastically once the Abyss has been crossed. All the Sephiroth below the Abyss contain the Ego.

    The guardian of the Abyss is the infamous Devil, who represents duality and the material world in general. The Devil is the great tempter of the individual Ego since the Ego was born through the earthly body and is the intelligence that tends to it. Therefore, it is an accurate statement to say that the Ego is the by-product of the Devil.

Since duality is present in all things in our Universe, we can also find it in our understanding of good and evil. If there is God, who is pure Spirit and is All-Good, then it must also mean that God's Arch-Nemesis exists as a personification of "D(the)-evil" in the World of Matter. Hence the rise of the Devil as God's opposite. The Devil tempts us through the alluring qualities of the material world. I will explain the Devil energy in more detail in the Devil Tarot card.

Since good and evil are concepts experienced through the mind, the Devil also only exists in the mind. After all, the mind is humanity's link between Spirit (good) and Matter (evil) and our medium of experience of the World of Matter. And since the body cannot live without the mind, this means that we will have a mind for as long as we are alive on this Planet.

"Fundamentally, however, there is neither good nor evil; this is all based on human concepts. In the Universe there is neither good nor evil, because everything has been created in accordance with immutable Laws. The Divine principles are reflected in these Laws, and only through knowing these Laws will we be able to get close to the Divine." — Franz Bardon; excerpt from "Initiation into Hermetics"

Once you have crossed the duality of the mind and have reached the Supernals, the Devil and his Demonic minions (Fallen Angels) disappear. They were never even real in the first place but were only in your head, inside the mind. The Ego developed because of the illusion of the mind in perceiving this World of Matter as real. The Ego, in turn, gave rise to the dichotomy of good and evil, God and the Devil.

As the Ego feeds on fear, the Higher Self feeds on love. Fear, therefore, is subjective and is only experienced within the physical body, through the mind. The future of human evolution is for us to transform Spiritually so that we can extinguish all fear and function only through love. However, to accomplish this, we must learn to exercise our Free Will in life and consciously choose good over evil.

How you exercise your Free Will Principle determines how much negative Karmic energy you have in your Chakras. Those who don't know how to apply their Free Will are subject to their Karma being mainly a by-product of their past conditioning. Without using Free Will, you are like an automaton, repeating the same actions over and over, blindly, and without regard for personal evolution.

People who allow past conditioning to determine their fate rely on their memory to guide them in life. They are stuck in the old and have no room to allow new things to enter their lives. How they processed past events determines how they deal with current and future events. All events are the by-product of Time and Space in this Three-Dimensional World that our physical bodies partake of. Within all events, we have nothingness (Ain) and its opposite—pure unlimited potential, the Limitless White Light (Ain Soph Aur).

The vibratory state of our consciousness determines our level of experience of the limitless existence since we are connected to the White Light inextricably. The perceptions of our Egos are influenced by our past conditioning, which creates our limitations in life. Our Free Will, though can break through any limitations in a given instant and connect us with the limitless existence of the White Light. Free Will supersedes our conditioning and environmental factors and breaks down the Ego completely by putting us in the moment—the Now. When you are in the Now, your Higher Self can enter your consciousness and communicate to you.

One of the goals of the Great Work is to tune you into your Free Will and teach you how to use it. Your Free Will is your greatest Magical weapon in this world since it is the very part of you that is of the Godhead. In essence, your Free Will is the Word, whether spoken aloud or silently to yourself.

"In the beginning was the Word, and the Word was with God, and the Word was God." — "The Holy Bible" (John 1:1)

Many Christians believe that John the Baptist referred to Jesus Christ as the Word, which then gives this line a double meaning. Who was Jesus Christ, though? How are we connected to him? The answers to these questions are right before our eyes if we know where to look.

Figure 9: The Pentagrammaton—YHShinVH (Yahshuah)

The name of Jesus is very peculiar and symbolic. His Hebrew name is Yahshuah (usually translated as Joshua), spelt YHShinVH, otherwise called the Pentagrammaton in the Qabalah (Figure 9). In symbolic terms, YHShinVH stands for Fire (Yod), Water (Heh), Hebrew letter Shin, Air (Vav) and Earth (Heh-final). The Pentagrammaton is similar to the Tetragrammaton, the only difference being that the Hebrew letter Shin is added as the reconciler between the Four Elements.

The Hebrew letter Shin symbolizes the Element of the Holy Fire in the Qabalah. It consists of three strokes, representing three flames. The Qabalah refers to the three flames of Shin as the "Threefold Flame of the Soul." Shin, therefore, corresponds with the Holy Spirit and the Kundalini energy—Ida on one side, Pingala on the other, and Sushumna in the middle. Shin also means "tooth" in Hebrew. The tooth's function is to grind up food so that it can be ingested and digested into the system. Afterwards, the food transforms into Life energy—Prana, chi, mana, Ruach.

Shin represents a particular path on the Tree of Life, corresponding to the Judgement Tarot card, whose Magickal name is the "Spirits of God" or the "Spirit of Primal Fire". The Fire (Transitional) Element represents the path of Shin. When the letter Shin is placed in the centre of the Tetragrammaton (YHVH), it becomes a five-letter word that signifies the uniting of all opposites, masculine and feminine dualities—by way of the Holy Spirit/the Kundalini. As the Spirit integrates within the Self, the Cosmic Planes become activated within as reachable states of consciousness.

This Qabalistic mystery contains the secret of Jesus's true nature and why his myth is so important to us in this day and age. We must all assume the role of Jesus, as he prophesized when he said he would come back upon the Earth in the future after his death on the cross. Jesus was essentially saying that he would manifest through the initiate undergoing a Kundalini awakening transformation. We must be our own Saviour, our own Messiah, if you will. And to raise the Kundalini, we must learn to use our own Free Will and choose good over evil.

"Verily, verily, I say unto you, He that believeth on me, the works that I shall do shall he do also; and greater works than these shall he do; because I go unto my Father." — "The Holy Bible" (John 14:12)

The above saying by Jesus was preceded by him stating that he is in the Father and the Father is in him. Jesus wanted to convey that the people in the distant future would be able to perform the same works as him and even more remarkable since they will be connected to their Creator (Father), as he was. Jesus was aware that his power came from the awakening of the Kundalini energy and that the Kundalini was humanity's destiny. It is just a matter of time before all humans become transformed Spiritually, the same as Jesus was.

FOUR WORLDS OF THE QABALAH

The Four Worlds of the Qabalah model (Figure 10) exists to provide us with a key that allows a better understanding of the process of Creation and manifestation of the Divine energy. Furthermore, the philosophy that it expounds upon is instrumental in describing the states of consciousness that are reached once an individual has undergone a complete and permanent Kundalini awakening.

According to the Qabalah, the Universe is divided into four different Worlds. The Path of the Flaming Sword gave rise to the creation of the Sephiroth, which subsequently brought the Four Worlds into existence. Each of the Four Worlds evolved from the one that came before it, becoming more solidified as they attained manifestation within the physical reality.

The Four Worlds are synonymous with the Cosmic Planes. As mentioned already, there are three principal Cosmic Planes: the Spiritual Plane, the Mental Plane, and the Astral Plane. To them is added the Physical Plane to make up the Four Worlds. These Four Worlds are overlaid one on top of the other, the same as layers of an onion. Also, each World is signified by one of the Hebrew letters of the Tetragrammaton (YHVH)—which further reinforces the concept of the fourfold Qabalistic model of the Universe.

"All things manifesting in the Lower Worlds exist first in the intangible rings of the upper Spheres, so that Creation is, in truth, the process of making tangible the intangible by extending the intangible into various vibratory rates." — Manly P. Hall; excerpt from "The Qabbalah, the Secret Doctrine of Israel"

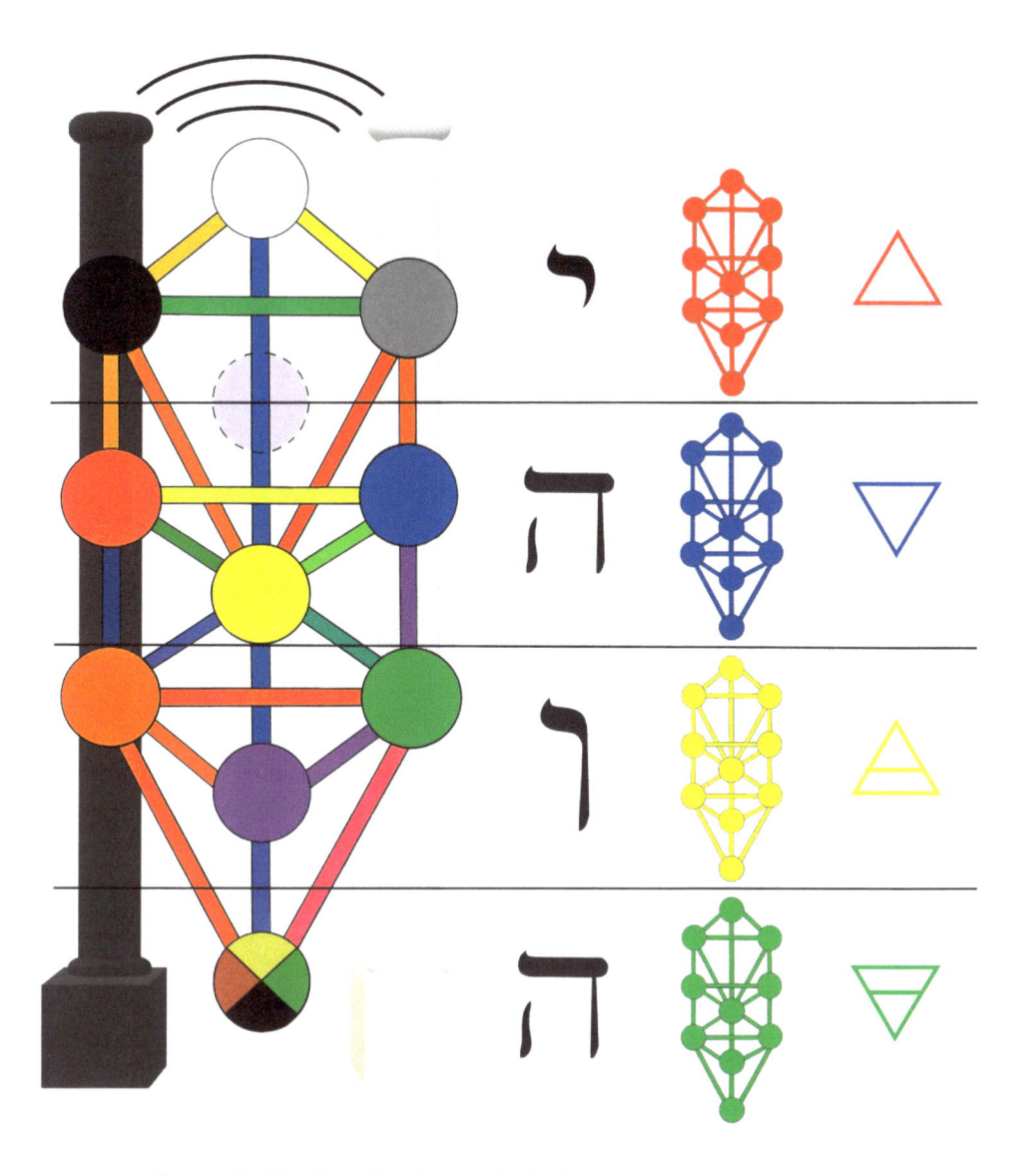

Figure 10: The Four Worlds: Atziluth, Briah, Yetzirah, and Assiah

    The first World is known as Atziluth. According to Qabalists, Atziluth is the World of Pure Spirit. It is the Archetypal World which initiates the other three Worlds. In other words, the other three Worlds evolved out of Atziluth. The letter Yod in the Tetragrammaton (YHVH) is given to Atziluth as the World of Primal Fire. Atziluth is ultimately beyond description, given its Spiritual essence, which is beyond Space, Time, and manifestation. Some Qabalists refer to the Divine Plane or the World where the thoughts of God are as Atziluth. Atziluth is the World of pure Divine energy. Whatever its designation, Atziluth gave birth to the other three succeeding Worlds below it in a descending scale of Light.

In terms of the Cosmic Planes, Atziluth would be the Spiritual Plane. Note that this World belongs to the Spiritual Plane but is considered the World of Primal Fire by Qabalists. The Spirit Element is omitted from the Four Worlds model in the Qabalistic framework since we lost our connection with it after the Fall from the Garden of Eden.

The Four Worlds model describes humanity's position right now, and the Spirit Element is something still to be obtained from our perspective. The two upcoming lessons on the Garden of Eden will further aid in describing humanity's current Spiritual state. For the sake of clarity, though, I am going to include the Spirit Element as part of the framework so that you can understand how the Four Worlds model relates to the Cosmic Planes. After all, one of the aims of *The Magus* is to bridge the Qabalah with the Chakric System.

Some Qabalistic schools of thought assign Atziluth to the three Sephiroth of Kether, Chokmah, and Binah, while some ascribe it only to Kether. The vital thing to take from this World is the notion and Archetype of it being a "Thought of God," which gives humanity a template that we can work from. Atziluth is beyond Time and Space as the first thing that filters through us when we relate to the world around us and look outwards. An apple is an apple, not an orange, the same way that a cup is a cup, not a spoon.

Having Archetypes we can all agree on enables us to build our realities. How we see the apple and orange depends on the lower Worlds that the Archetypes filter through since those Worlds are concerned with perception. In terms of the Tree of Life, the World of Atziluth has its Tree of Life, and the Malkuth of Atziluth is the Kether of the next World below it, called Briah.

The second World is Briah, also known as the Creative World. Qabalists refer to Briah as the World of pure intellect, the fluidic mind, and the World of Primal Water. The letter Heh from the Tetragrammaton (YHVH) is ascribed to it. Regarding the Cosmic Planes, Briah corresponds to the Mental Plane.

In the Qabalistic framework, Primal Water, in terms of Briah, is used to describe only the next phase of the manifestation of the Divine energy. As Fire represent Force, Water represents Form. This designation does not relate to the expression of the Water Element concerning the Cosmic Planes, though. If we imagine that the Spirit Element has been integrated as part of the whole, then the World of Briah belongs to the Elements of Fire and Air (the Higher and Lower Mental Planes).

Some Qabalistic schools of thought assign the Ethical Triangle of Chesed, Geburah, and Tiphareth to the World of Briah, and some even ascribe only Chokmah and Binah. Always keep in mind that the Qabalistic science deals with invisible forces that cannot be measured nor studied with physical instruments but only through abstract thinking. Thus, it is more of a philosophy used to best describe the different energies of the Solar System and our Aura, including the process of manifestation of the Divine.

Briah is the abode of the Archangels since it is those energies that move us to act morally and ethically. Water is best understood when relating to its opposite, Fire. So the Divine Force sends a thought impulse into Divine Form, thereby manifesting an Archetypal idea. This Archetypal idea is not a visual image (that relates to the next World), but we can experience it through intuition. It is still a thought, but more of an impulse, a hunch, something we can feel and experience at a deep level of our Souls. We feel this thought through the unconditional love energy in our Heart Chakra. Thus, Briah is best explained as the states of consciousness experienced through the Heart Chakra, Anahata.

The more unconditional love you carry in your Heart Chakra, the higher you are elevated and the more intuitive and empathic you are. You become a feeler instead of a thinker, which means that your consciousness resides in the World of Briah. Briah is the highest conception of God we can experience since the World above it, Atziluth, has no Form.

The human faculties can see the first glimpses of Form in the World of Briah through the Mind's Eye Chakra. This Chakra is the receptive part of the Self that receives from the World above it. The Mind's Eye Chakra, Ajna, is connected to Sahasrara, the Crown Chakra. That which is seen and experienced through the Mind's Eye Chakra filters downwards and is felt in the Heart Chakra. The World of Briah also has its Tree of Life. The Malkuth of its World is the Kether of the World below it.

In terms of how we perceive reality around us, there is still no illusion at the level of Briah. We intuitively agree on what the Mind's Eye sees, but when we start to break it down intellectually with our Egos, we filter down into the lower Worlds below Briah. The Light which shines from above begins to be tempered by illusion—the reflection of the truth. Our past conditioning comes into play now, and the thing we are seeing or intuitively feeling starts to get its visual form, resulting in our ability to see it inside our minds as images.

Visual images are manifested in the third World, called Yetzirah, the World of Formation. Yetzirah is where the subtle and flashing patterns behind physical Matter are found. The Qabalists call this the World of Primal Air and attribute the letter Vav to it in the Tetragrammaton (YHVH). Yetzirah is the abode of the various Orders of Angels. This World is attributed to the Astral Plane since the Etheric framework behind the physical Universe is found here. Many Qabalistic schools of thought assign this World to the Astral Triangle of Netzach, Hod, and Yesod.

In this World, the Ego starts to get involved in interpreting the reality around us. Although the Qabalists attribute this World to Primal Air, the Astral Plane belongs to the Water and Earth Elements in the Cosmic Planes model. In terms of how the Ego functions and expresses itself, though, this designation makes perfect sense since the Ego belongs to the Lower Mental Plane of the Air Element and the Higher Astral Plane of the Water Element in the Cosmic Planes model.

As the Spirit and Fire Elements are expressions of the Soul, the Ego expresses itself primarily through the Air Element since Air is considered a lower manifestation of Spirit. Air is essential because it gives life to the Water and Fire Elements, and they cannot exist without it as their medium of expression. To express themselves, Fire (Soul) and Water (consciousness) need Air (thought). Air is the firmament that holds the other two Elements in balance. Without Air, there is no life. This last statement is true symbolically and physically since every living thing needs air to survive—breath sustains all of life.

Through the Air Element, we see and feel the Astral World. The invisible Planes are experienced through the Mind's Eye Chakra because of our thoughts, which serve as conduits of information. They transmit that which is Above to that which is Below, and vice versa.

When acted on by the Fire of the Soul, thought becomes imagination. A human being without imagination is not a fully functioning human being. They reside wholly in the body, without motivation, drive, or inspiration. They live as a vegetable, tending to the physical body's needs and desires through the Ego but not fully partaking in the beautiful thing we call human life. To live a happy, balanced life, you need imagination. Imagination is at the core of all Creation.

> *"Imagination is the first step in creation, whether in words or trifles. The mental pattern must always precede the material form."* — William Walker Atkinson; excerpt from "The Secret of Success"

Sadly, many people lack imagination and reside entirely in their Egos, functioning through past conditioning. They do not live in the Now nor plan for a bright future. To do so, you need imagination. You need to use your thoughts with vitality and vigour actively.

At the point of the Astral World, what we see starts being tempered by illusion and our past conditioning. The illusion of the Moon acts on Creation, and thus, the Astral World contains many lies. The truth is only found in the Light of the Sun, while the Moon only reflects that Light; hence it cannot be trusted. The World of Briah can perceive the truth because of its positioning on the Tree of Life, while Yetzirah cannot. Therefore, truth is veiled by the illusion of the Moon in the World of Yetzirah. For this reason, the Ego is called the "False Self." The World of Yetzirah also has its Tree of Life. Its Malkuth is the Kether of the World below it, called Assiah.

The fourth and final World is Assiah, the active and Physical World of the senses and both seen and unseen energies of the Material Realm. The Twelve Zodiac and the Seven Ancient Planets are assigned to Assiah since it is the physically manifested World which we all engage in with our physical bodies and five senses.

The final letter Heh of the Tetragrammaton (YHVH) is ascribed to Assiah, the World of Primal Earth. The Earth Chakra corresponds to this World, but it also belongs to the Lower Astral Plane (Etheric). In Assiah, the Four Elements that make up the physical Universe exist both in sensation and in the hidden properties of Matter.

I will not talk much about Assiah because we have lived in it since birth. Because of our five senses, we can all agree on this World's existence and expression. The Ego evolved and attached itself to the consciousness because of the experience of our five senses. The Ego's function is to tend to the physical body and its needs and desires. It seeks to give to itself and defend itself from any threats from the outside world. Its primary mode of living is survival. In this way, the Ego and the G'uph are related.

Each of the Four Worlds having its own Tree of Life is an Ancient concept that helps us better understand the process of manifestation. In terms of the Kundalini awakening, once it is sustained and permanent, the Four Worlds (Cosmic Planes) open up as accessible states of consciousness for the individual. Remember always that a Kundalini awakening is a full awakening of the totality of the Spiritual Self. Therefore, all these Qabalistic concepts and Sephiroth become active within the awakened individual. The individual starts to function at the level of intuitively feeling the energy around them, which means they are operating from the Supernals (beyond the Abyss), and receiving information from the three highest Sephiroth.

The Supernals can best be described as existing in Atziluth or the World of Primal Fire. However, Fire is a mere Force without an opposite that enables it to register the idea that it is projecting into the mind—it is best to think of it as being able to receive directly from Atziluth and project into Briah at the same time. After all, Wisdom needs Understanding to comprehend itself—Force needs Form. A Kundalini awakened person lives in the Dimension of Vibration, and their consciousness reaches as far as the highest World of Atziluth.

By living in the Fourth Dimension, the Dimension of Vibration, the consciousness is untainted by duality and operates in the constant act of creating. The Kundalini system is in continuous motion, perpetually expanding the consciousness and being in the continual act of *Becoming*. The act of Becoming is the expression of the Water Element of consciousness—as it is continually changing, transforming and evolving once the Fire Element is perpetually acting on it.

Kether is entirely unlocked and open, and through Kether of the one World, you can reach into the Other Worlds. Thus, the whole system of the Qabalah and various states of consciousness are reachable. But this expansion of the Self and experiencing otherworldly dimensions entirely depends on how much influence the Ego has on the individual consciousness.

THE CADUCEUS OF HERMES

The Caduceus of Hermes is the medical symbol used in modern-day society to represent healing. This designation of the Caduceus is veiled in allegory, though. To the initiate of Light, the Caduceus of Hermes has many significant Spiritual meanings. The origin of the word "Caduceus" is Greek, meaning "Herald's Wand" or "Herald's Staff".

Hermes is the God of Wisdom and the Divine herald—the Messenger of the Gods to the Greeks. He is the second youngest of the twelve Olympian Gods, portrayed as carrying a staff intertwined with two snakes whose heads terminate in a winged disc. Hermes was known as the Divine Trickster, the God of boundaries and the breach of boundaries. He outwits other Gods, often for his satisfaction or the satisfaction of humanity.

Hermes' origin was from the Egyptian tradition. In the Egyptian pantheon of Gods, Hermes was called Thoth. He was portrayed as a man with the head of an Ibis bird. Thoth's duty was to act as a Scribe of the Gods. In Egypt, he was credited as the author of all works of science, religion, philosophy, and Magick. In the Roman adaptation of the Greek pantheon of Gods, Hermes became identified with Mercury. However, the designation of his attributes and powers stayed the same as the Greeks.

Hermes is most often portrayed as a younger man with a winged helmet on his head and winged sandals on his feet (Figure 11). Legend has it that Hermes used to carry a plain wand until he came across two fighting snakes one day. He separated them with his wand, after which they coiled themselves harmoniously around it. In this way, the Caduceus of Hermes was formed. The idea of reconciling opposites and balancing them is found in the Caduceus.

Hermes is the intermediary between the Gods and humans. He can move swiftly between the world of man and the world of the Gods. The wings on his helmet and sandals give him great speed and the ability to fly. As he moves freely between the worlds, he also guides the Souls of the dead to the Underworld and the afterlife in the Greek and Roman traditions.

Hermes is likened to the Archangel Raphael from *The Holy Bible*, the Archetype of the Air Element. Raphael is also pictured as carrying the Caduceus staff since it represents healing and the Astral Light. It is no coincidence that Hermes corresponds with the Air Element since the speed of thought represents his power.

Thought is the only thing that can travel between the Inner Worlds, and it is as fast as Hermes. One can even argue that Hermes can travel at the speed of Light, which is why thoughts can often see into the past and future through a process we refer to as clairvoyance. In the Qabalah, Hermes/Mercury is attributed to Hod—the Sephira related to the mind, and logic and reason.

Figure 11: Hermes and the Caduceus

As the two snakes intertwine a staff, they cross each other at five points, terminating with their heads facing each other and looking at the crowned disc at the top of the staff. The Caduceus of Hermes represents the Kundalini energy in man and the process of awakening, as this energy rises up the spine and coalesces in the centre of the brain. The two snakes of the Caduceus are Ida, the feminine current, and Pingala, the masculine current. Ida and Pingala represent duality and opposites found in nature.

Ida and Pingala also regulate the temperature in the body. Ida is the cold current, while Pingala is the hot current. They rise along the central column or staff, Sushumna, and cross at five points (the lower five Chakras) before terminating in the brain (where the highest two Chakras are found). They rise from the lowest Chakra, Muladhara, the seat of the Kundalini energy. When the Kundalini energy is activated at the base of the spine, it awakens from its state of potential. It rises upwards through the hollow tube of the spinal column, piercing each of the lower five Chakras along the way.

Ida and Pingala rise upwards simultaneously with Sushumna, crossing at the Chakric points until all three reach the brain and the Mind's Eye Chakra. Here, Ida and Pingala unite and rise together to the top of the head, the Crown Chakra, Sahasrara. The winged disc represents this action since, upon their termination at the Crown, the person undergoing a Kundalini awakening experiences an expansion of consciousness. Thus, the disc with wings represents the now elated, transcendental, higher consciousness.

The winged disc is a perfect symbol for Sahasrara, as this Chakra is Non-Dual and beyond opposites. In Ancient traditions, wings have always represented something of a Heavenly, Airy quality, belonging to the Angels and Gods. The wings on Hermes' helmet and sandals also represent the Spiritualized Elements. Thus, we can say that Hermes has his head in Heaven while having his feet planted firmly on the Earth.

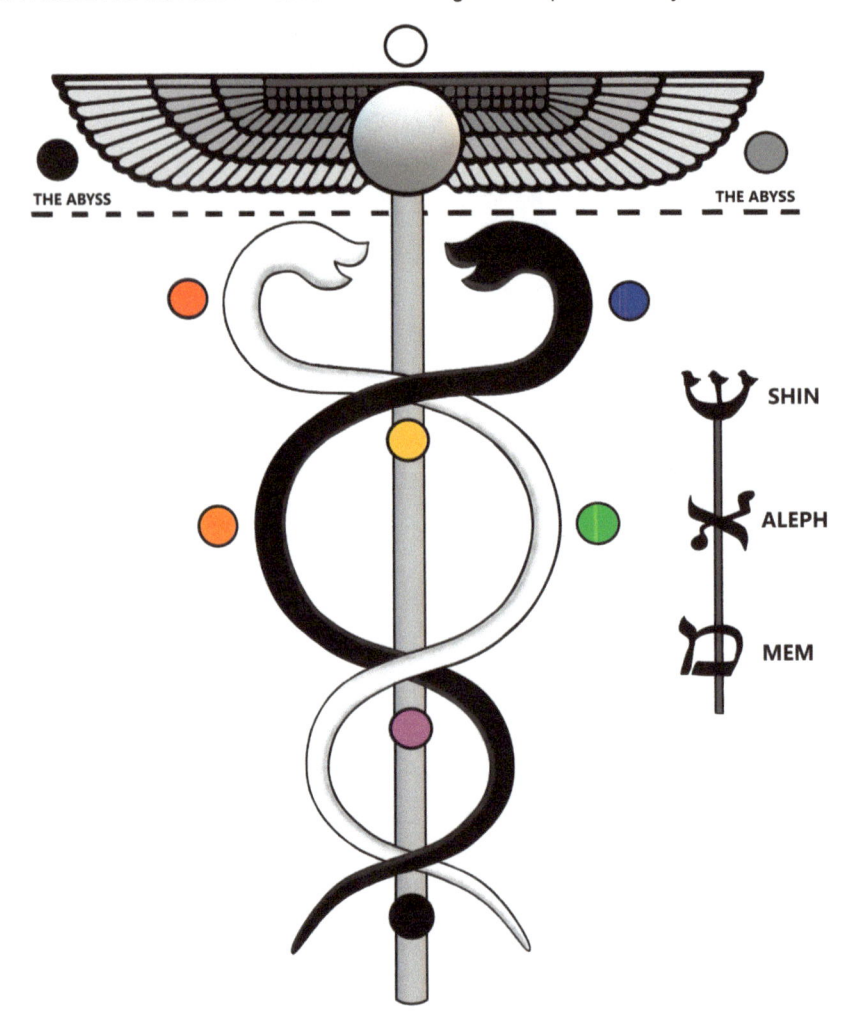

Figure 12: Qabalistic Correspondences of the Caduceus of Hermes

The Caduceus of Hermes is also a symbol of the complete Tree of Life in the Qabalah (Figure 12). The Hebrew letter Aleph is seen in the Caduceus as the heads and upper halves of the serpents. It is the symbol of the Air Element. Together, the two snakes' tails form the letter Mem, which symbolises the Water Element. The Hebrew letter Shin is formed with the wings and the top of the wand, representing the Fire Element and the Threefold Flame of the Soul and the three main Nadis of the Kundalini—Ida, Pingala, and Sushumna.

As you can see, the three Elements of Fire, Air, and Water are contained within the Caduceus. These are the three primary Elements of life, while Spirit is the combination of them in Heavenly form—the place where the Higher Self, or God-Self, resides. In their more dense form, the three Elements form the Earth Element, the aspect of the Self that relates to the Ego and the physical body.

The three Elements on the staff produce the Fire of Life Above and the Water of Creation Below. Air is in vibration between them—serving as their reconciler. There are two contending forces in all things within Creation, with a third force serving to balance them. So you see, in the Caduceus is hidden the mystery of Creation.

The highest point of the staff lies on the Crown (Kether), while the wings of the disc span outwards to both Wisdom (Chokmah) and Understanding (Binah). Together, they represent the Supernal Triangle and the Eternal, Divine aspect of the human being—our most high state of consciousness. Below the Supernals, the two snakes embrace the remaining seven Sephiroth of the Tree of Life. Considered as currents of Astral Light, they are also known as the "Twin Serpents of Egypt."

In terms of the Kundalini awakening, superimposing the Caduceus of Hermes onto the Tree of Life makes perfect sense. After the full and sustained awakening, the individual is propelled into a new state of consciousness, having awakened the entire Tree of Life within them. To clear the Karma of each Sephira, though, they must undergo some kind of purification process to help them rise from the lowest to the highest Sephira—since parts of their psyche are pulled in all directions. Their consciousness is operating at hyper-speed and is conflicting on many occasions. They are not localized in any one Sephira in particular. Instead, it feels like an experience of all Sephiroth at once.

Light is infused into each Sephira upon the rising of the three energy currents of Ida, Pingala, and Sushumna. It becomes imperative that the newly awakened initiate of Light finds some way to clear the negative Karma of each Element, which will, in turn, purify the Sephiroth and raise the consciousness beyond the Abyss—to operate solely from the Supernal Triangle.

This process will make the initiate be at One with their Holy Guardian Angel—their God-Self. However, to get there, the negative Karma of each Sephira has to be cleared first. Thus, the initiate must find a way to focus on, isolate, and work on their individual Chakras. They must rise from the lower to the higher Chakras by balancing their psyche and purifying their various Subtle bodies—the Astral, Mental, and Spiritual.

The ritual exercises contained within *The Magus* serve to aid in this purpose. The Spiritual Alchemy programs herein cleanse and tune the Chakras, enabling the Kundalini awakened individuals to attune to the higher, transcendental consciousness available to them.

THE GARDEN OF EDEN

The Garden of Eden story is from the *Book of Genesis* in *The Torah* and *The Holy Bible*. It is known throughout the world and is familiar to most people in North America, no matter what religion or Spiritual tradition they associate with. It is widely mentioned, as is the story of the Nativity of Jesus Christ, and over time it has become a part of modern-day society. As the story goes, as everyone understands it, we are currently living in a "Fallen" state Spiritually. Before the world as we know it, the Garden of Eden existed, where the first man, Adam, and the first woman, Eve, resided.

According to the Creation story from the *Book of Genesis*, God created the first man and woman and placed them in the Garden of Eden for them to guard the Tree of Knowledge of Good and Evil. Adam and Eve were both unclothed to represent their primordial innocence. God told them they could eat from any tree in the Garden except for the Tree of Knowledge of Good and Evil.

There is much that the Garden of Eden story can teach us if we look beyond the traditional framework as taught within Christianity and Judaism. By interpreting the story esoterically, it will become evident that the Garden of Eden is part of a much larger picture that connects with general mythological themes and aspects of other Spiritual traditions, human psychology, and more.

Although there are various perspectives of this story from an esoteric lens, some of which will be examined in my future works, what follows is the Qabalistic model, as taught within the Golden Dawn tradition. The two diagrams presented in the following pages will offer many new insights into the Garden of Eden story and give you the keys to your Spiritual Evolution. Additionally, it will provide you with many answers as to the nature of humanity and why we are currently living in this Fallen state.

THE GARDEN OF EDEN BEFORE THE FALL

The first diagram we need to examine is the Garden of Eden Before the Fall (Figure 13), when humanity was living in a state of perfection Spiritually. At the apex of the diagram was the Supernal Eden that contained the three Supernal Sephiroth of Kether, Chokmah, and Binah. Furthermore, Aima Elohim, the Supernal Mother, resided in Eden.

In the "Book of Revelation" from the New Testament of *The Holy Bible*, Aima Elohim is the woman of the Apocalypse. She carries a crown of Twelve Stars on her head, alluding to the Twelve Zodiac. She has the Sun in her chest and the Moon at her feet, representing the perfect balance between the masculine and feminine energies. The power of the Father, the Tetragrammaton (YHVH), is also contained in this diagram. These are the Four Elements of Fire, Water, Air, and Earth.

The Tree of Knowledge of Good and Evil springs out of Malkuth-the Earth, represented by the branches with leaves coming out of it, symbolic of the Seven Ancient Planets in their binary form. Seven branches rise upwards to the Tree of Life and the lower seven Sephiroth, while another seven rise downwards.

Below Malkuth lay the Kingdom of Shells, otherwise known as the Demonic Kingdom. It is represented by the Great Red Dragon, who has seven heads (seven infernal palaces), and ten horns (ten averse Sephiroth). He was coiled beneath Malkuth, the Earth, and had no place in the Tree of Life but was beneath it.

Within the diagram is a sense of balance as the Father is joined to the Mother. The Mother is present in the Supernals—Kether, Chokmah, and Binah. The crown of Twelve Stars is the Zodiac, and the Sun in her chest and the Moon at her feet represent balance and perfect function. Before the Fall from the Garden of Eden, we lived a Spiritual Reality and received energy directly from the Supernals. The whole Tree of Life was open to us, and our consciousness was aligned with the Higher Self of the Spirit energy.

The seven heads of the Red Dragon represent the Seven Ancient Planets and their powers in adverse form—since the Planets have dual powers. The ten horns are the ten Sephiroth of the Tree of Life also in their adverse form. As they lay below Malkuth, they did not participate in Creation. Thus, at some point in the past, we were not influenced by the Demonic Kingdom—this is the key.

The Tree of Life itself was above Malkuth, and it is represented by Eve holding the two pillars of polarity, the positive and the negative. Adam was in the middle with the Sphere of Yesod at his feet and Tiphareth at his head. His arms stretched out to Chesed and Geburah while Netzach and Hod were at his sides. Eve was supporting the whole Tree of Life and was holding Adam. Above Adam's head was the place of the invisible eleventh Sephira, Daath, which served as the reconciler of the forces of Chesed and Geburah.

The river Naher went out of the Supernals and Aima Elohim, which split into four heads at the point of Daath. The first head was Pison, flowing into Geburah, and it was the river of Fire. The second head was Gihon, which flowed into Chesed, and it was the river of Water. The third was Hiddekel, the river of Air, which poured into Tiphareth. The fourth river was Phrath, the Euphrates, which received the virtues of the other three rivers and flowed into Malkuth, the Earth.

Figure 13: The Garden of Eden Before the Fall

The Euphrates was the river of the Apocalypse. Its Waters of Life were clear as crystal, proceeding out of the Throne of God, with the Lamb on the other side, which was the Tree of Life. The Throne of God was the reigning centre of God that gave forth Eternal life. It was a place of sovereignty and Holiness.

The Tree of Life, in its perfection, gave forth twelve fruits, which are the Twelve Zodiac. Within the diagram, this idea is represented by the leaves coming out of the middle Sephiroth. The rivers of Eden formed a cross. On the cross was the great Adam, the Son. He was to rule the nations with a "rod of iron." In Malkuth is Eve, the Mother of All, the completion of all. Above the Universe, she supported the Eternal pillars of the Sephiroth with her hands. Thus was the Great Work complete, and everything was in perfect balance and harmony.

It is important to note that the eleventh Sephira of Daath was where the river Naher split into four heads, and it was a part of the Tree of Life. In the Tree of Life following the Fall, the Sphere of Daath is the Abyss. Within the Abyss, duality is separated from Non-Duality and the perfection of the Supernals, which are Eternal and infinite. The Abyss, therefore, protects the Spirit Element, and every single human being must re-integrate it within the Four Elements. Before the Fall, though, the Spirit Element was a part of Creation, and we were all perfect in every way.

Therefore, the Abyss, or Daath, is the separation point between the Spirit and the other Four Elements. We must understand this next point, as it is of utmost significance: Malkuth was in Daath before the Fall. Daath was a part of the Tree of Life, and there was no division between Spirit and Matter—they were One. Pure physical life was pure Spiritual life, and vice versa.

THE GARDEN OF EDEN AFTER THE FALL

Now that we have seen what our original state in the Garden of Eden was like, we can proceed with the second part of the story. As we examine The Garden of Eden After the Fall (Figure 14) from a Qabalistic perspective, we will be given the key to how we can apply this story to our own lives to further our Spiritual Evolution.

The Serpent tempted the Great Goddess Eve to taste the fruits of the Tree of Knowledge of Good and Evil. The branches of the Tree of Knowledge of Good and Evil rose upwards to the seven lower Sephiroth, but also downwards to the Demonic Realm. As Eve reached down to them, the two pillars she was holding in her hands were left unsupported. Without Eve's support, the pillars shattered, and the entire Tree of Life fell apart. This action marked the Fall of Adam and Eve.

The Great Red Dragon rose upwards, now with crowns atop his heads, symbolic of his dominion. Eden was desolated. The Dragon enclosed Malkuth and linked it to the Demonic Kingdom, the Kingdom of the Shells. Through this act, Malkuth, the Earth, became dual, containing the nature of both good and evil. The Qlippoth, whose literal translation means "Shells" or "Husks," are the impure and evil Spiritual forces operating from the Demonic Kingdom. They are the Fallen Angels, or Demons, who now infiltrated Malkuth, the Earth, to take part in Creation.

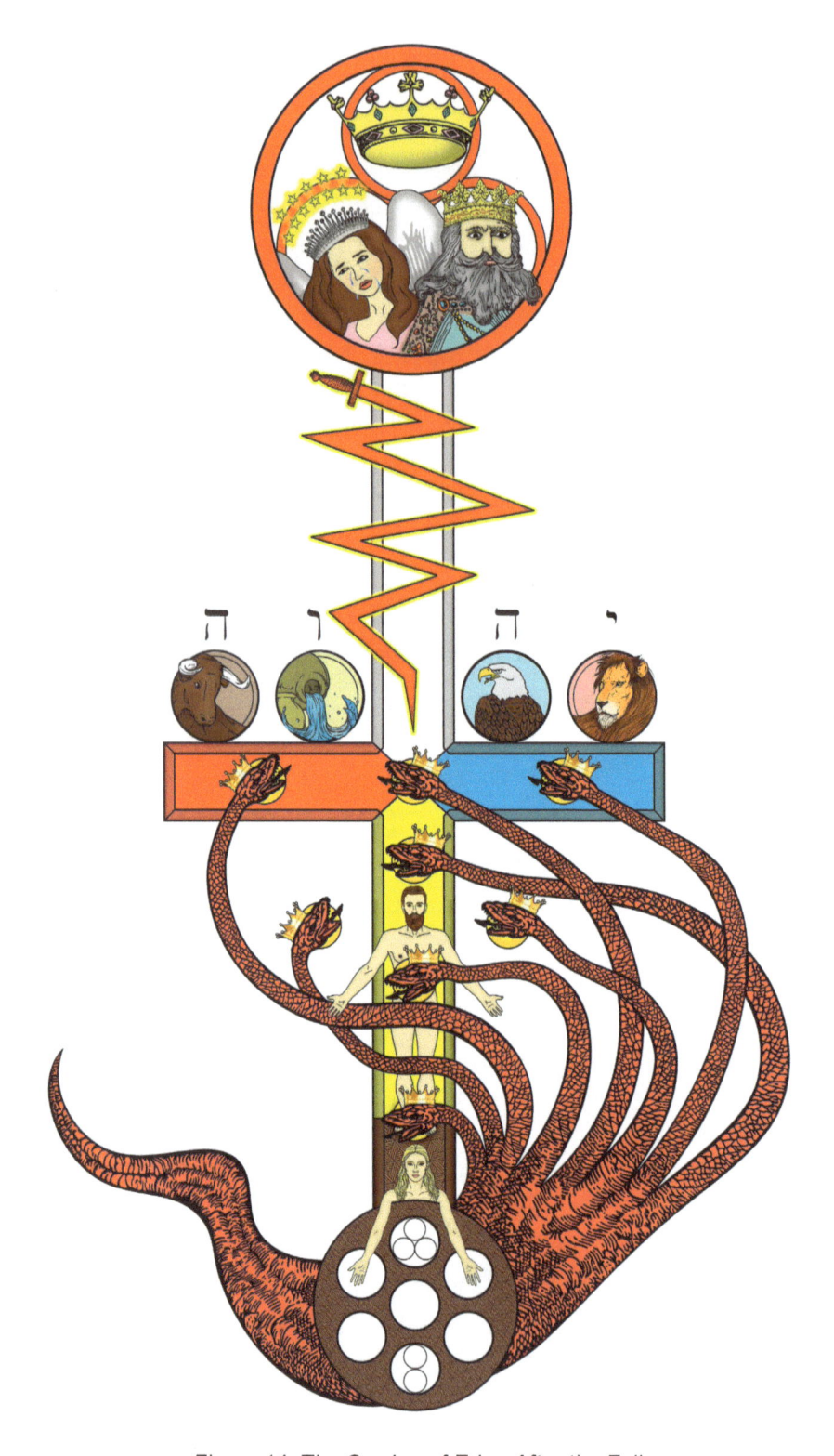

Figure 14: The Garden of Eden After the Fall

The heads of the Great Red Dragon rose into the seven lower Sephiroth, thereby giving the Qlippoth the power to operate from them as well. The Dragon went as far as Daath and the feet of Aima Elohim herself. The four rivers of Eden were defiled. The Dragon spilt out the Infernal Waters in Daath out of his mouth. These Infernal Waters are called "Leviathan," the piercing and crooked Serpent who now gained a foothold in the Tree of Life. In this way, the purity of the original Tree of Life was destroyed.

All was not lost, though. Tetragrammaton Elohim placed the Four Holy Letters YHVH and the Flaming Sword of the Ten Sephiroth between the devastated Garden and the Supernal Eden. Through this act, humanity was given a way back into the Garden of Eden. It became our destiny to taste its purity and beauty again.

To restore the system, a Second Adam needed to arise. As the First Adam was spread on the Cross of the Four Celestial Rivers, a Second Adam needs to be crucified on the Infernal Rivers of the four-armed Cross of Death. He must descend into the lowest Sephira, Malkuth, and then rise upwards following the reversed Path of the Flaming Sword. Then, as the Second Adam is purified and consecrated by the Four Elements (YHVH), he will be born again. The Second Adam may find his way back into the Garden of Eden through this process.

***

To best understand what is happening in this story from a Spiritual perspective, we must analyze its symbolism. The Serpent tempted Eve to eat of the Tree of Knowledge of Good and Evil. Symbolically, the Tree of Life she was supporting crashed down as she reached to pick the apple from the Tree of Knowledge. Notice here that the Serpent is found as the one who tempts Eve and is the initial cause of the Fall. Due to some innate curiosity or desire, Eve listens to the Serpent and does the one thing God told Adam and Eve not to do.

Firstly, the idea of the Serpent can be linked to the Kundalini energy in the human—the trigger that causes the evolution of consciousness and the full activation of the Body of Light. It is no coincidence that the Serpent is present in this cryptic story as one of the key players, along with Adam, Eve, and of course, God-the Creator. As the Serpent is the cause of the Fall, he must be found again in the effect—in restoring the Garden of Eden. Hence, we can say that a Kundalini awakening, awakening the Serpent Power, is our way back into the Garden of Eden.

Before the Fall, everything was in perfect balance. There was no division between Spirit and Matter, and all was One and Heavenly. The infernal Dragon was not involved in the Tree of Life but was kept below Malkuth, the Earth. It did not partake of Creation but stood outside of it. Once Eve reached down to eat the apple, the pillars were left unsupported, and the whole Tree of Life shattered.

At this point in the Creation story, God banned Adam and Eve from the Garden of Eden for disobeying him. We see that the Great Red Dragon rises above Malkuth and reaches up to Daath, where the one river splits into four. This one river, representative of the Spirit Element, is not involved in the Fall and remains untouched. The other four rivers, the Four Elements of Fire, Water, Air, and Earth, are included in the Fall and become desecrated.

Tetragrammaton Elohim places the Four Letters, YHVH, and the Flaming Sword of the Ten Sephiroth between the devastated Garden and the Supernal Eden. Daath now becomes the Chasm, or the Abyss, which separates the purity of the Supernal Eden (Pure Spirit) from the Tree of Life, which now becomes dual, containing good and evil within itself.

At one time, Daath was Malkuth, symbolically, and Spirit was Matter. But after the Fall, Daath becomes the separation point between the Spirit (Heaven) and the world of the duality of good and evil (Earth). This Chasm is in the mind as the mind is the connecting link to Spirit and Matter.

It is no wonder that Jesus Christ, who came after the *Book of Genesis* to take up the role of the Messiah, was crucified on the Cross of the Four Elements, the Infernal Cross. His act symbolizes the triumph of Spirit over Matter and the rebirth and return to the Garden of Eden. He became the Second Adam and the prototype for us to follow to return to the Garden of Eden—our true home. Now, each person has to be their own Messiah and take full responsibility for their Spiritual Evolution.

We must all start in Malkuth, the Earth, and traverse up our Tree of Life, following the Path of the Flaming Sword in reverse. As we do this, we are renewing ourselves through the Four Elements. The Garden of Eden story, from the Qabalistic perspective, gives us the key to the Spiritual Evolution process, whereby we must bathe ourselves in the Elements first before we are to be reabsorbed into Spirit, restoring the Garden of Eden within ourselves.

In the Golden Dawn and other Western Esoteric Mystery schools, this is accomplished systematically through Ceremonial Magick and invocation of the Elements through ritual exercises. The individual rises from Malkuth (Earth), into Yesod (Air), then into Hod (Water), and finally to Netzach (Fire). At this point in the Golden Dawn system, they are at the doorstep of Spirit. They then have to learn how to integrate the lessons of each Element into Spirit and become reabsorbed in it.

Once the entire Tree of Life has been fully activated and invigorated with Light during the Kundalini awakening, the transformation process has officially begun. The next step is to cleanse the lower four Chakras of Earth, Air, Water, and Fire, for the consciousness to operate from the top three Spirit Chakras—Vishuddhi, Ajna, and Sahasrara (the Crown).

The Garden of Eden story further affirms the importance of working with the Four Elements, which are synonymous with the Chakras, namely the four lowest Chakras, to ascend and elevate in consciousness. It is up to each one of us to restore the Garden of Eden within ourselves. Nobody can do it for us.

THE TREE OF LIFE AND THE KUNDALINI

There are two key verses in the Creation story from the *Book of Genesis* that offer further clues about the big picture concerning our Spiritual Evolution. I will be referencing the widely read King James Version of *The Holy Bible* to gain additional insights into the Garden of Eden story.

First, let us analyze the Serpent questioning Eve if she and Adam will eat from the Tree of Knowledge of Good and Evil. Eve tells the Serpent that the Lord God said that they would die if they were to eat from the Tree of Knowledge. The Serpent's response to this is intriguing.

> *"Ye shall not surely die. For God doth know that in the day ye eat thereof, then your eyes shall be opened, and ye shall be as Gods, knowing good and evil." — "The Holy Bible" (Genesis 3:4-5)*

It is interesting to note that the first step in the evolution of humanity took place right after our Creation as a species. We were perfect, living in a pristine state of existence in the Garden of Eden, where Spirit was Matter and Matter was Spirit. However, due to our innate desire for knowledge and curiosity about the Unknown, we were destined to Fall from the Garden of Eden. Our Fall was the effect, while the Serpent's temptation was the cause. He piqued Eve's curiosity and inspired her to do the one thing that God told her not to do—eat from the Tree of Knowledge of Good and Evil. Consequently, according to the words of the Serpent, it was the very thing that would make her and Adam "like" Gods and give them knowledge of good and evil.

The Lord God told Eve and Adam that they would die if they ate of the Tree of Knowledge. The death God was speaking of is a Spiritual death, a transformation of consciousness. Knowing the inner nature of his creation, God knew that Adam and Eve would disobey him and eat of the Tree of Knowledge. Nonetheless, since he gave them Free Will, he wanted it to be their decision. He knew that their disobedience would result in their ban from the Garden of Eden, putting them on a perilous Spiritual journey that would eventually result in their symbolic death, followed by a rebirth and re-entrance back to the Garden.

At a distant point in time, the Chasm, or the Abyss (the place where duality exists, the mind), was not present as a mode of functioning. All of life was intuitional and instinctual. There was no need to think, but only to do. By entering into the realm of the mind (where duality takes place as a form of perception), Adam and Eve fell from the Garden. To make their way back again, they had to be reborn through the Elements, including the Spirit Element.

To know good and evil means to grow in knowledge. It means to activate your innate logic and reason—the part that is the intellect, which develops wisdom over time. To know good and evil means to be active participants (Co-Creators) and to make choices in life. By being Co-Creators in life, humans are "like" Gods, meaning they become the image of their Creator.

The Fall from the Garden of Eden was a way to test humanity's ability to do the right thing. To be exact, it was the beginning of this test—to see what humanity would do with Free Will. After all, we were designed to be Co-Creators in this reality. Thus, our ability to make conscious decisions about our future had to be tested.

Once Adam and Eve both ate the fruit of the Tree of Knowledge of Good and Evil, the Lord God found out what they had done. So he cursed both of them and told them that they are banned from the Garden of Eden. However, after banning them, the Lord God makes a peculiar statement involving the Tree of Life.

> *"Behold, the man is become as one of us, to know good and evil; and now, lest he put forth his hand, and take also of the Tree of Life, and eat, and live for ever." — "The Holy Bible" (Genesis 3:22)*

The Lord God says that humanity will be "like" God by knowing good and evil, but to live forever and be Eternal, we must eat from the Tree of Life. What he meant is that human beings must activate all the Spheres of the Tree of Life, which is something that can only be accomplished through a full and permanent Kundalini awakening.

A Kundalini awakening, which results in the full activation of the Body of Light by raising the energy to the Crown Chakra, Sahasrara, is an awakening of the entire Tree of Life within the individual. After the awakening, the different states of consciousness represented by the ten Sephiroth will become available as modes of functioning.

In this way, human evolution is a three-step process. The first step was before the Fall when everything was perfect; Spirit was Matter, and Matter was Spirit. Humans functioned on intuition and instinct alone. In this step, though, there was no knowledge of duality. Logic and reason did not exist because they are by-products of thinking about the past and future—a duality. Because the development of our intellect is inherent, since it is a crucial part of us, the next step had to be taken.

The Fall was the next step we had to undertake if we were to learn about duality and good and evil. This step involves the evolution of the mind and the application of our Free Will. It is the power of choice and what we will do with it. To evolve to the utmost of our potential, we were left alone to learn to take care of ourselves.

Humanity has been in this state for thousands of years and is still there. As a whole, we have not evolved yet to the third step. We are still learning about ourselves, our inner nature, and how to conquer evil on a mass scale. We have learned the power of good and unconditional love. In a way, our test has become to overcome Self-Love with unconditional love, as it is a necessary step in the evolution of consciousness.

The third step of our evolution is the awakening of the Kundalini. It is the activation of the complete Tree of Life and raising of individual consciousness to the Supernals (Figure 15). Once we accomplish this, we will reenter the Garden of Eden. We will live forever, as God said. Not our physical bodies of course, but by Spiritualizing our Egos, we will liberate our Souls from the pain and fear of living in the material world. Our consciousness will expand and become united with the Cosmic Consciousness of the Godhead.

Very few people in the world have undertaken this third step. Nevertheless, this trigger switch of the Kundalini energy is present in everyone. It is a matter of choice to evolve Spiritually and rise above the mind and duality. As the Kundalini rises to the Crown, the mind becomes bypassed yet again. Consciousness begins to function in the same way as before the Fall—through intuition and instinct. The main difference is that logic, reason, and the intellect are still available to us as modes of functioning. In other words, the lesson has been learned, and man has consciously chosen good over evil, love over fear.

In a way, Spiritual Evolution tests our ability as human beings to love one another before all things. It is a way to test our choices in life and safeguard the Spirit. If we choose to love each other and do good for the purpose of doing good, we will overcome evil, allowing us to reconnect with the Primal Spirit energy.

We are each to become our own Messiah and be reborn Spiritually. We must activate and enlighten our Tree of Life with the Kundalini energy and raise our consciousness to the Supernals. Each person's duty is to find their way back to the Garden of Eden from the Fallen state they are in—this is the most profound yet veiled meaning we are to derive from this cryptic story.

Figure 15: The Tree of Life and the Kundalini

THE SEPHIROTH AND THE CHAKRAS

Over the years, many Spiritual teachers have attempted to reconcile the ten Sephiroth of the Tree of Life with the Seven Chakras to find common ground between the two systems. Their method was to superimpose the ten Sephiroth of the Tree of Life onto the Chakric system—and reconcile the opposing Sephiroth. Unifying the Pillar of Mercy and Pillar of Severity into the Middle Pillar does yield seven Sephiroth, which corresponds with the number seven of the Chakras. This method works in theory, yes. Upon examination of the results, though, the correspondences of the unified Sephiroth to the Chakras simply don't match.

From my personal experience working with the energies of the Tree of Life and the Chakras, I believe there is a way to reconcile the two systems. It is a lot more complicated than the method mentioned above, though. I think that the people who teach this first method are limited in their understanding of both systems since they have no direct experience but instead make their conclusions based purely on their intellect and other people's works. The only way to truly understand the energies of the Tree of Life is to practice a viable method of energy invocation that deals with these particular energies—such as Ceremonial Magick. In my case, I have had the privilege of living with an awakened Kundalini while practising Ceremonial Magick, which enabled me to experience the energies of both the Tree of Life and the Chakras to an incredibly high degree through Gnosis.

After many years of directly working with the energies mentioned above, I believe I have found common ground between the Eastern and Western systems and a way to unify and reconcile them. After all, there is only one Creation, and there is only one Creator, no matter what name we give him/her. Every human being is built the same, irrespective of our cultural or religious upbringings. We are all composed of the very building blocks of Creation, which are found in both the Eastern and Western systems—the energies of the Five Elements of Spirit, Fire, Water, Air, and Earth. These five energy types are found in both the Tree of Life and the Chakric system (Figure 16) and are the unifying factor between the two schools of thought.

The Magus contains a one of a kind, comprehensive, and all-encompassing invisible science of energy that we all partake of as human beings and the methods (ritual exercises) that you can use to invoke/evoke these Elemental energies to further your Spiritual Evolution. To best explain how the Eastern and Western systems are related, I will examine each of the ten Sephiroth of the Tree of Life by scaling the Tree upwards following the reversed Path of the Flaming Sword while comparing them to the energies of the Chakras.

> *"...some of the Sephiroth and the Chakras are similar, but not exact. Take all of the ten Sephiroth into consideration and this similarity is diminished. The Sephiroth and the Chakras have different functions, different correspondences, and a host of other attributes that are specific to the cultural roots of each system." — Israel Regardie; excerpt from "The Middle Pillar: The Balance Between Mind and Magic"*

We begin our exercise in the lowest Sephira, Malkuth—the Earth. As mentioned, Malkuth is the Physical World in which we live, the World of Matter. As such, it corresponds with the Earth Chakra, Muladhara. The Earth Chakra partakes of the Physical World of Matter and the state of consciousness of the Astral Plane, namely the Lower Astral Plane. The Earth Chakra then is the connecting link between the Physical Plane and the Astral Plane, and not just the Physical World, as many Spiritual teachers have concluded.

Going upwards, we have the Sephira Yesod, the Astral Plane, accessed through the sexual energy of a man or woman. Its location on the Tree of Life is in the groin region. In the Chakric system, though, this region is the position of Muladhara, the Earth Chakra. The sexual energy certainly comes from the abdomen since when we feel any sexual arousal, we can feel it there as an emotion first. Thus, we have the connection to the second Chakra, Swadhisthana, since that is where the lower emotions are experienced. Lower, in this case, means they are in some way connected to the expression of sexual energy. The genitals power this sexual energy, and their placement is below the coccyx. The coccyx is the place of the Kundalini energy at the base of the spine, where it is said to be coiled three-and-a-half times in its dormant state and originating from Muladhara Chakra of the Earth Element.

There is confusion about whether Yesod is simply the Swadhisthana Chakra and the Water Element, or perhaps Muladhara, the Earth Element—since that is what we get if we directly superimpose the Chakric system onto the Tree of Life. Additionally, according to the Qabalah, Yesod is attributed to the Air Element. This attribution further adds to the confusion since Anahata, the Heart Chakra, is also assigned to the Air Element—and Yesod is way below Anahata. We have only scaled up to Yesod, and already there is a great deal of confusion concerning which Chakra is which Sphere—the correspondences are all over the place. This confusion persists as we continue going upwards on the Tree of Life and examining the energies and attributes.

As we go upwards past Swadhisthana Chakra, we reach the Fire Chakra-Manipura, in the Solar Plexus. It is here that many teachers have said that the Spheres of Hod and Netzach, in their opposition, represent the Fire of Manipura. I would argue the validity of their statement since Fire, according to the Four Worlds concept, is the highest of the four Elemental Worlds (excluding Spirit) and is Archetypal, meaning that it is without Form. However, we have Form with Hod and Netzach since they are the most accessible parts of Self throughout the day—logic and emotions. Both are thought-based, expressing themselves through the Astral and Mental Planes. The Fire Element manifests itself through the Higher Mental Plane only, and that Plane is particular to the Soul, not the Ego. In contrast, the Ego is linked to emotion, which belongs to the Astral Plane and the Water Element, not the Fire Element.

Going upwards, we have Tiphareth, which many Spiritual teachers have said is the Heart Chakra, Anahata. This statement may be the only accurate one since Tiphareth is attributed to the Air Element, and so is Anahata.

But even here, in the Qabalistic framework, Tiphareth is placed in the Solar Plexus, the Soul centre, which corresponds with Manipura Chakra. Moreover, as I have mentioned before, Tiphareth has Fiery qualities since it is Qabalistically attributed to the Sun, the source of Light and heat in our Solar System. Thus, its placement should be somewhere between the two Chakras of Manipura and Anahata, where it primarily expresses the Air Element and has a close association with the Fire of the Soul.

And what of the following two Spheres above it, Geburah and Chesed? The attributes of Chesed and Geburah being reconciled as the Throat Chakra, Vishuddhi, do not make sense since Vishuddhi is attributed to the Spirit Element. At the same time, Chesed and Geburah belong to the Water and Fire Elements. According to the Qabalah, the attributes of Geburah are the colour scarlet (red), Planet Mars, severity, strength, and willpower. Are these not the qualities of the Fire Element? And is Chesed not the Water Element? According to the Qabalah, it is blue, Planet Jupiter, mercy, and unconditional love, all of the qualities of the Water Element. Also, the attributes of Hod and Netzach being unified to represent the Fire Chakra of Manipura makes no sense since these are also clearly Water and Fire Elements, but on a lower level than Chesed and Geburah.

Instead of Chesed and Geburah being integrated as one Chakra and Netzach and Hod joining to represent another Chakra, it is more accurate to say that Chesed and Hod come together to power the Water Element, operating from Swadhisthana (the Water Element Chakra). In contrast, Geburah and Netzach, in combination, express the Fire Element, working through Manipura (the Fire Element Chakra). And both of these pairs of reconciled/unified Sephiroth are filtered through the Sphere of Tiphareth (the Air Element Chakra).

And Tiphareth is not just the Anahata Chakra since Anahata pertains to unconditional love, which is an emotion and is of the nature of the Water Element, hence the connection to Swadhisthana Chakra. But Manipura, the Fire Element Chakra, powers that emotion once there is an influx of White Light from the Chakras above.

Remember, Manipura is the Seat of the Soul. White Light must supply the lower four Chakras with energy if the Soul is to dominate the consciousness instead of the Ego. Once the Crown is open and the Light descends, the Chakras will be Spiritualized, and the individual can experience higher emotions and thoughts, such as unconditional love. Without the influx of Light, the individual will be prone to Self-love, which means the Ego will be in charge.

The three Chakras of Manipura, Swadhisthana, and Anahata seem to work in unison, powering each other and providing the distinct energies of the five Sephiroth of Chesed, Geburah, Tiphareth, Netzach and Hod, which comprise the Ruach—the animating principle of the person. Breathing and taking in Pranic energy via food and water activates these principles and Sephiroth, or Spheres.

Muladhara and Swadhisthana Chakras are most often used by the Nephesh, the Lower Self, which is powered by the sexual energy from Yesod. The Nephesh becomes neutralized once the White Light is brought into the lower four Chakras. They become exalted and start operating at their optimal capacity, allowing the Soul to govern over consciousness.

The statement that the Spheres of Chokmah and Binah reconcile in Ajna Chakra is relatively accurate. Chokmah and Binah are Wisdom and Understanding working in unison and received through intuition. Ajna Chakra is the entry point into the Higher Worlds past the five senses (using the sixth sense and the Mind's Eye, which operates through intuition). Ajna is also the gateway to the Cosmic Planes in general and contains forms and pictures found in Yesod (the Astral World). So even here, the attribution is not entirely accurate. Again, the Sephiroth seem to work together to produce the results that are found in the Chakras. Still, the only way to truly reconcile the two systems is with the Five Elements of Earth, Air, Water, Fire, and Spirit, since the Elements take part in both the systems.

Sahasrara Chakra being the Sphere of Kether is an accurate statement since in both the Eastern and Western systems, this Chakra, or Sephira, is attributed to Spirit in its purest sense, which is unknowable, Eternal, and ineffable. Therefore, in reality, not much is known about it nor is meant to be understood without personal experience of the White Light. Hence, its experience is not applied to our everyday life and our function in the world around us. We can only experience Kether when we enter mystical states of consciousness—either through meditation or through inspired and elevated thinking. Obtaining a close connection with Kether is the aim of every human being on this Planet since it can result in the descent of the Spirit energy and a permanent transformation of consciousness.

We know with certainty that the first four Chakras carry the Four Elements of Earth, Water, Fire, and Air. We also know that the next three Chakras are of the Aethyr/Spirit Element—they start in the Throat Chakra and end at the top of the head, the Crown. The throat and neck separate the head from the rest of the body. Therefore, it makes the most sense to conclude that it is the area where Spirit begins and the lower Elements end.

The Throat Chakra is Vishuddhi, whose primary purpose is to aid in communication. In Vishuddhi, we generate vibration in our voice to communicate with the outside world. The spoken word is our link with the Divine. And since it is Divine, it belongs to the Spirit Element. Thus, everything in Vishuddhi and above it must also be of the Divine, while everything below it is not. Below Vishuddhi, according to the Chakric system, we have the Four Elements. So you see, the ten Sephiroth or Spheres of the Tree of Life cannot be broken down by just uniting the opposing Spheres into the middle column.

I propose to impart an entirely different concept of how to look at the Tree of Life to the reader. Instead of viewing it from Malkuth, imagine yourself standing in Tiphareth, your Sun centre and Soul core, and looking at the Tree of Life from a three-dimensional point of view by laying it flat horizontally. This will allow you to overcome the limitations of reconciling the opposing Spheres by systematically scaling the Tree of Life upwards.

From this viewpoint, Chesed can be integrated with Hod, while Geburah can be united with Netzach. One has a higher function than the other, but both pairs of opposites operate from either the Water or Fire Elements. The Element of Air connects the Spirit above and the lower Elements below. And this connection, as well as separation, occurs in Vishuddhi, the Throat Chakra.

The Eternal part of the Self exists beyond the Abyss (Vishuddhi Chakra), separating the Supernal Self with the reincarnated, manifested Self. As mentioned, the Supernal Self is the Element of Spirit. It is separated by the invisible eleventh Sphere of Daath, which is the Abyss itself, signifying the death of the Ego that is required to reach the Spirit. To die to the Ego is necessary to align with the Spiritual Self. Water and Fire Elements exist as dual opposites, masculine and feminine energies, the building blocks and tools that the Spiritual Self uses to extinguish the Ego.

Once we go below the Supernals and Daath, we find the Ethical Triangle, Astral Triangle, and the physical body. Air is the connecting medium, the link between Spirit and Matter, which makes sense because Air gives life to all living creatures. Without breath, we cannot live longer than a few minutes. The Air Element is in Anahata Chakra, and it is also connected to the groin and the place where we receive Prana, our Life energy.

The Middle Pillar of the Tree of Life is the connecting link between Heaven and Earth. Air is the connecting link between the Divine and man. Our Prana is fueled by breath, food, and water, which is activated and directed in the groin region by our sexual energy, the source of all creativity. Thus, a physical manifestation of Pranic energy is sexual expression, while a Spiritual one is the activation of the Kundalini. Both are fueled by sexual and Pranic energies, which are distinct from one another yet intimately related.

The Kundalini becomes the vehicle whereby we connect the Sephiroth of our Middle Pillar and rise through Daath into the Supernals to connect to our Sahasrara Chakra and open ourselves to the influx of Spirit above. Daath represents the symbolic death necessary to be reborn into the Spirit. The Fire Element Chakra that operates through the Spheres of Geburah and Netzach is now tempered by the Water Element Chakra and the Spheres of Chesed and Hod. These create the inner functions that comprise the Self, which we use to raise our consciousness to reach the Higher Self that is of the Godhead.

Remember that Life is a play, a Divine game, and we need a reason to perform actions in the Physical World—the Fire and Water Elements give us those reasons. One is unconditional love, and the other is willpower—love under will. Willpower needs a reason to act, and that reason is unconditional love. Unconditional love needs an action whereby it can know itself and that action is willpower. These two statements imply the dichotomies of the God and Goddess, masculine and feminine, Fire and Water, Manipura and Swadhisthana—one working for and with the other. For this reason, Manipura and Swadhisthana are one on top of the other in the Chakric system. The firmament, the connecting link, is found in the heart, representing the Air Element Chakra, Anahata.

Yesod is also Air, so we see that the Air channel does not stop—it is immediately produced right after Earth. Our Life energy, our Prana, is permanently active. One does not have to be sexually aroused to feel it, as it is always present. Ingested food transforms into Prana, serving as the primary fuel of the physical body and the Subtle Bodies of the Cosmic Planes.

Pranic energy, coupled with sexual energy, activates our imagination. Imagination gives us the ability to create the same way as we were created—through thought. As a man thinketh, so he is. And according to the *Book of Genesis*, we were made in the image of our Creator.

Life is the constant impregnation of the subconscious mind through imagination, continuously fueled by Pranic and sexual energy and tempered by the Fire and Water Elements. By sublimating our Pranic and sexual energy, we can awaken the Kundalini and break through Daath by encountering an Ego death, opening us up to the Supernals and the Godhead, our Source.

The Kundalini is man's "activation switch" and our goal and mission in this lifetime. Its awakening is an attainment that occurs when the Ethical Triangle has been perfected; when imagination has filled the subconscious with thoughts that resonate with Wisdom and Understanding, and when one has risen past the bodily desires and Egocentric points of view.

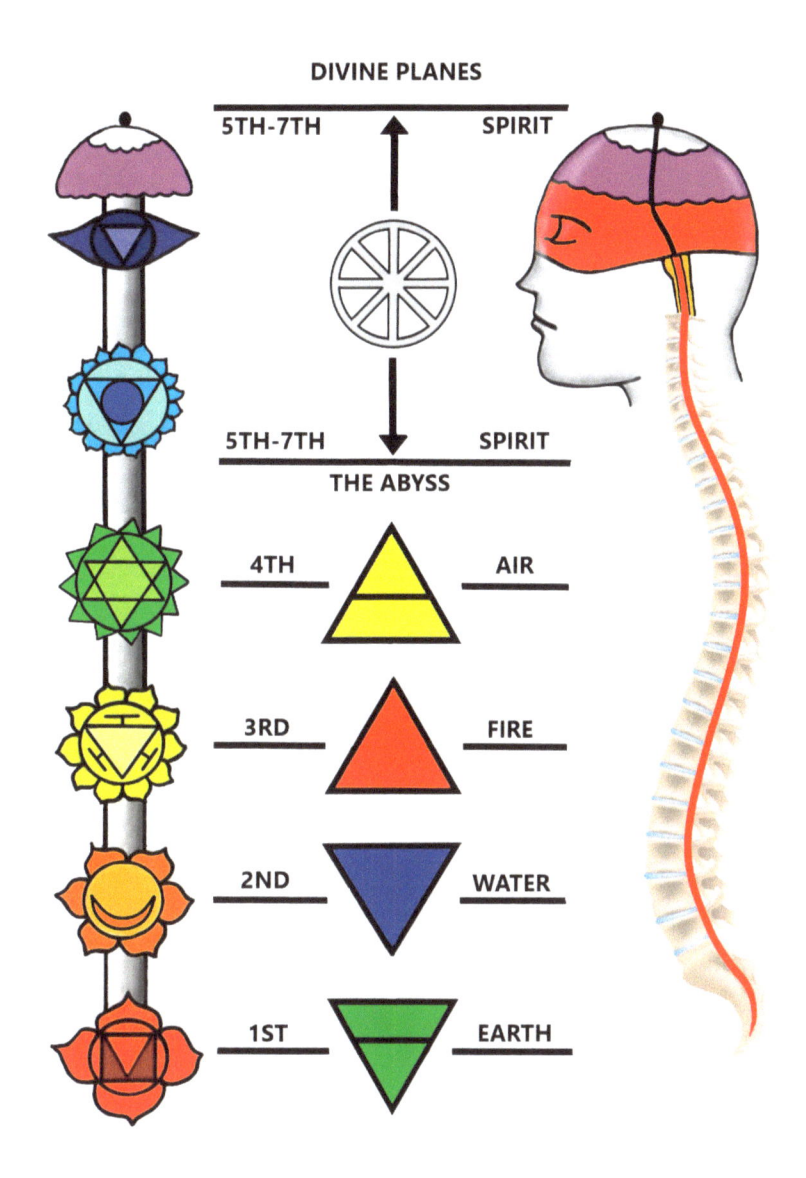

Figure 16: The Chakras and the Elements

Although the Chakric system does not superimpose perfectly on the Tree of Life, we can see how the Five Elements of Life are present in both, just displayed differently. Both the Chakric system and the Tree of Life represent the same Creation process.

Let us begin by breaking everything down into the three primary Elements. Firstly, Fire and Water, which are in perfect conjunction, symbolically form a Hexagram. Then, the Air Element serves as the firmament that supports them by breathing life into them. Next, as the base of it all, the foundation, is the physical body of the Earth Element whose essence is the denser combination of those three Elements. What follows is the Chasm-the Abyss, represented by the Throat Chakra. The Abyss separates the head and brain from the rest of the body in the human being.

The Throat Chakra, Vishuddhi, uses the Air Element (thought) to connect to the Element above it—the Spirit Element. Spirit uses the Throat Chakra as the starting point of manifestation and sublimation of energy. Next, through the second last Chakra, the Mind's Eye (Ajna), it uses Wisdom and Understanding to rise to the Non-Duality and beauty of Sahasrara—the Sphere of Kether. Kether is the summit of our Spiritual Evolution. It signifies Nirvana—the Crown of Achievement and goal of the Yogi, the Sage, and the Seeker of Light.

The goal of the Kundalini mechanism is to sublimate Pranic and sexual energy and raise it into the head—to enlighten the Supernals and expand the individual consciousness. The Kundalini energy awakens the whole Tree of Life and all the Chakras so that the consciousness can access all of the Cosmic Planes particular to each Chakra. Once the energy has blown through Daath, an Ego death occurs, and the awakened individual starts to attune more and more to the Supernals. Wisdom and Understanding become the main guiding force in the lives of these awakened individuals.

I will not discuss the Transpersonal Chakras above the Crown since they are incomprehensible to the human mind. Still, impose on your mind the existence of Divine Worlds far above ours, which are attainable in this lifetime. Trying to describe their experience is similar to a human trying to explain its existence to an ant. Human consciousness is so vast and able to stretch to such great heights that it is impossible to put into words the beauty of what lies beyond our mere, physical existence.

In *The Magus*, we will adhere only to the discussion of the ten Sephiroth, the Seven Chakras, the Four Elements, and the Spirit. The purpose of this book is to help you reach the greatness of Sahasrara. What you experience through Sahasrara is left for you, and you only, to explore.

PART II:
THE TAROT

THE MAJOR ARCANA OF THE TAROT

"The Tarot embodies symbolical presentations of Universal ideas, behind which lie all the implicits of the human mind, and it is in this sense that they contain a secret doctrine, which is the realization by the few of truths embedded in the consciousness of all." — A. E. Waite; excerpt from "The Pictorial Key to the Tarot"

Tarot cards are an integral part of the Western Mystery tradition that feature incredible imagery, containing timeless, esoteric wisdom concerning all of Creation. It is a complete and intricate system used to describe the unseen, invisible forces that influence the Universe.

Tarot cards serve as a key to a better understanding of the occult sciences. For centuries, mystics, Magi, and others involved with the occult have used Tarot cards to aid their Divinations and meditations. Since they encompass the Macrocosm and the Microcosm, Tarot cards also offer us a map of the different components of the human psyche. In Divination, Tarot cards allow us to have direct communication with our Higher Self as we glean into the Unknown.

The Tarot has an inextricable connection with the Qabalah and the Tree of Life. In 1850, Eliphas Levi recognized the relationship between the twenty-two Trumps, or Major Arcana of the Tarot, and the twenty-two letters of the Hebrew alphabet. This recognition inspired a revival of the occult sciences. Occultists from across the globe engaged in an in-depth study of the Tarot and its connection to the Qabalah.

Though the connection between the Tarot and the Qabalah is visible, the origins of the Tarot are still unknown. Some claim that the Tarot has its roots in Egypt, from "The Book of Thoth." Others insist that it was created by a group of Adepts who, intending to ensure the preservation of their esoteric philosophy, hid it within a deck of playing cards. Ultimately, the complete history of the Tarot remains a mystery.

Traditionally, the Tarot contains seventy-eight cards, divided into four suits of fourteen cards each, plus twenty-two Trumps (Major Arcana). The Major Arcana serve to map the journey of the human Soul. In *The Magus*, we will only be focusing on the Major Arcana since their knowledge goes hand-in-hand with knowledge of the Qabalah and the Tree of Life.

The Minor Arcana contains forty Small, numbered cards and sixteen Court cards. The Small cards are numbered from ace to ten and are divided into four different suits—Wands, Cups, Swords, and Pentacles. These four suits signify the Four Elements, the Tetragrammaton, and the Four Worlds of the Qabalah. Also, each of the ten Small cards is associated with one of the ten Sephiroth. Although I will not get into the Minor Arcana in the following lesson, it is up to the reader to further learn about them. Their knowledge will allow for a more comprehensive overview of the Tarot and its relation to the Qabalah and the Tree of Life.

THE TREE OF LIFE AND THE MAJOR ARCANA

The twenty-two Major Arcana of the Tarot are the main cards used in Divination, and their energy represents the twenty-two paths that unite the ten Sephiroth of the Tree of Life (Figure 17). These twenty-two paths, including the ten Sephiroth, represent the Thirty-Two Paths of Wisdom. The twenty-two paths represent the energy connecting and pouring out from one Sphere to the next, and as mentioned, the Spheres represent states of consciousness.

The Major Arcana are forces in transition—Karmic forces that have influenced the incidents of the past and will affect the events in the present and future. They represent Spiritual lessons or experiences as you go through life. As such, it is essential to learn about the Major Arcana as this knowledge will help you on your Spiritual journey. Merely knowing about them can trigger and unlock latent, subconscious forces that will help you progress further in your Spiritual Evolution.

The highest purpose of the Tarot is as a system of Self-initiation and Enlightenment. The twenty-two Trumps are considered the keys of Universal Wisdom. To those practising this sacred art, the Tarot is a sacred mirror into which they could see themselves and the deeper aspects of the Self. It is a map into the realms of Spiritual bliss and a record of man's relationship with the Cosmos.

Due to the knowledge contained therein, the Tarot can be considered a textbook of occult teachings. The Major Arcana are a symbolic map of inner Space, describing various states of consciousness, from the lofty Spiritual heights of Divinity down to the material world of human beings and Matter. In this way, the Tarot encompasses all of existence.

The twenty-two paths can be broken down into the three Transitional Elements of Fire, Water, and Air, the Twelve Zodiac, and the Seven Ancient Planets. The twenty-two Major Arcana cards are said to contain the totality of the energies of our Solar System. The knowledge of the Tree of Life and the Major Arcana, coupled with the knowledge of *The Kybalion's* Principles of Creation, is the basis of Hermeticism.

Another critical point to mention is that one of the twenty-two letters of the Hebrew alphabet is assigned to each of the Major Arcana cards. The twenty-two Hebrew letters are a complete Qabalistic philosophy and a system of its own. Each letter is a symbol with many ideas associated with it. These ideas bring forth certain Archetypes that are resonant with the energy of the Tarot cards. Archetypes unlock the doors of our subconscious mind to communicate with our inner Self. Therefore, constant communication occurs between the conscious and subconscious minds with the use of the Tarot, which helps us evolve Spiritually.

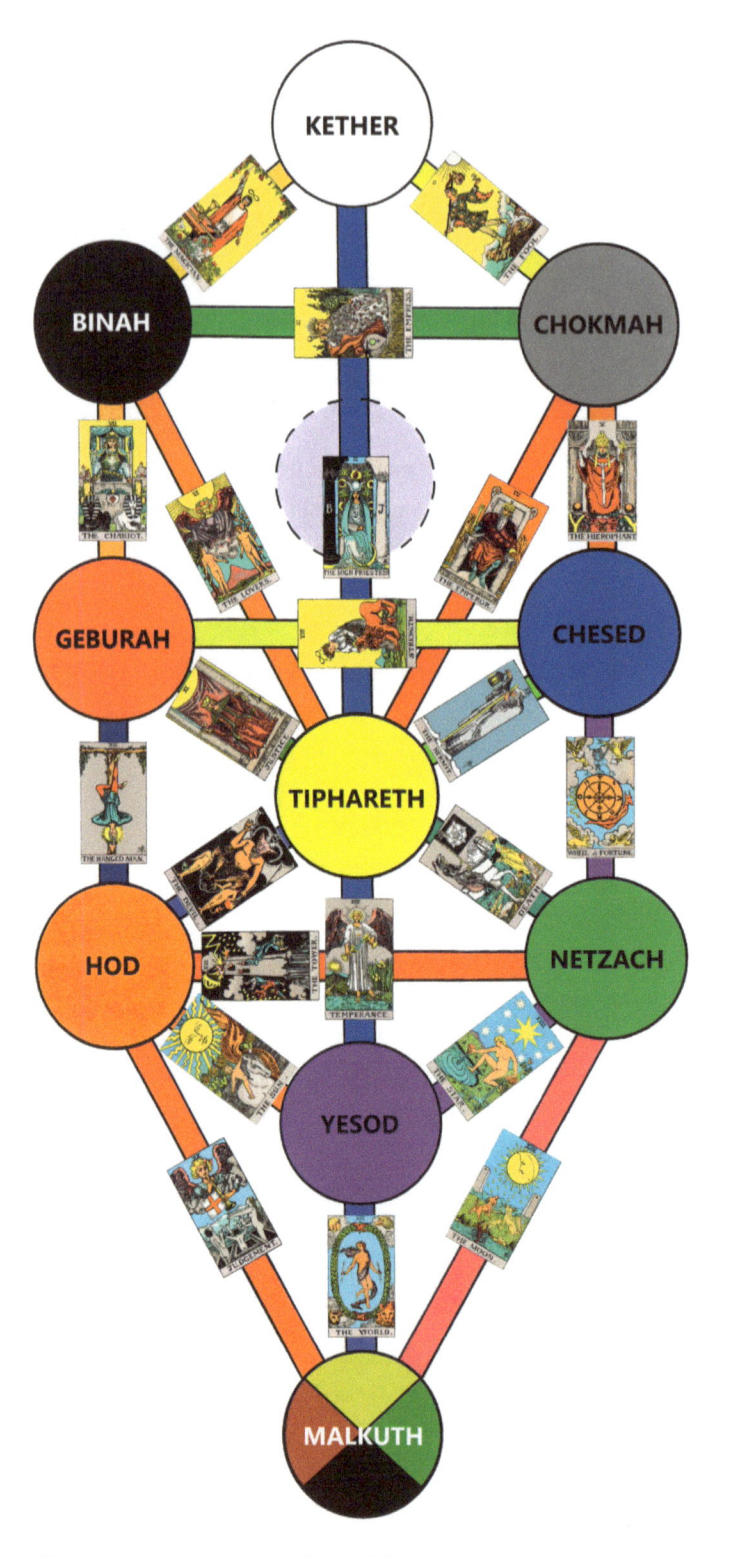

Figure 17: The Tree of Life and the Major Arcana of the Tarot

What is also of importance is the breakdown of the twenty-two Hebrew letters into the three Mother letters, the seven Double letters, and the twelve Simple letters. This breakdown is synonymous with the Tarot's association with the three Elements, the Seven Ancient Planets and the Twelve Zodiac, totalling twenty-two.

In this section, I will give you the breakdown of each Tarot card, with a brief description of the energy that it represents. Keep in mind that this is merely a general introduction to the world of the Tarot. It is recommended that you learn about the Tarot further on your own, and there are many books and resources available that can enable you to continue your studies.

"Symbolism is the language of the Mysteries. By symbols men have always sought to communicate to each other those thoughts which transcend the limitations of language." — Manly P. Hall; excerpt from "The Secret Teachings of All Ages"

The twenty-two Trumps of the Tarot communicate through visual images—which contain symbols, numbers, and metaphors. Since the Tarot cards have Archetypal imagery, they speak to us from the highest of the Four Worlds, the World of Atziluth or Primal Fire. Hence, by using the Tarot, we are communicating directly with the Divine. Furthermore, the pictures of the Tarot represent the Spiritual truths of our existence. For this reason, the Tarot is considered the most used Divination tool by the initiates of the Western Mysteries.

The colours used in the Tarot cards are essential as well, which for the most part, relate to the colours of the Tree of Life paths that each Tarot card corresponds with. Also, they feature the colours of the Elements present in each card and Planetary and Zodiacal attributions. Although this is not the case for all Major Arcana cards in the myriad of decks available, most of them do hold to this rule.

TAROT CARDS AND DIVINATION

The word "Divination" is derived from the Latin "divinare," which means "to foresee, to be inspired by God." Divination is the practice of extracting information from the Unknown regarding the past, present, and future. It allows you to transcend Time and Space and gain insight about an event, a situation, or even yourself or another person, through supernatural means.

Divination is found in all civilizations and cultures, old and new, and has been practised from time immemorial. It can be a clairvoyant process that employs a Crystal Ball or Scrying Mirror, or it can utilise different tools that require intuitive interpretations by the Diviner. Divination tools include I Ching, Runes, Spirit Boards, teacups, pendulums, and most notably—Tarot cards.

Tarot card reading is the most popular Divination method in the Western world. It works by formulating a question and then drawing and interpreting the cards. Spiritual forces affect the material world, and therefore, once you have a clear idea of the Spiritual forces at hand, you can ascertain certain truths in your life regarding your Inner as well as Outer Reality—the axiom of "As Above, So Below" is at play here as well. Through Tarot cards, we are trying to understand the "Above"—the Spiritual reality underlying all things. Once we understand that, we can know how it affects the "Below"—the material existence on Planet Earth. As such, Tarot cards read energy before it manifests.

The Circle Spread Divination is included as part of the lesson on the Tarot. Its purpose is to ascertain the Spiritual influences of any situation in your life. Also, since a large part of *The Magus* is working with different energies and invoking/evoking them into your Aura, it helps to have a method of determining how a Magickal operation will influence you (or a situation in your life) once it is completed.

The Circle Spread Divination only covers the twenty-two Major Arcana because it is a Spiritual Divination that only reveals the Spiritual nature of a particular action. Other Tarot Divinations can be more specific if their purpose is to gain insight into some future event or to get an exact answer to more mundane questions or inquiries. These wider-scope Divinations often include the Minor Arcana, which gives the Diviner more to work with to obtain the desired answer to a specific question.

After this brief introduction to the Tarot, I will describe each of the twenty-two Major Arcana cards. If you are working with the Circle Spread Divination, you are to use the card's meanings in Divination that are given at the end of each Tarot card's description. Keep in mind that the meanings associated with a Tarot card pulled upright are different than the meanings related to the same card drawn as reversed.

As there is a wealth of information on each Major Arcana card, the best way to study this subject is to contemplate and meditate on the names of each card, including its Qabalistic correspondences, symbols, numbers, and colours. By doing so, you will impregnate the Spiritual truth of each card upon your subconscious mind. To further this aim, I have included a method of "scrying" the Major Arcana. Scrying the cards is a powerful Divination method of obtaining Gnosis and furthering your understanding of the Major Arcana concerning the sacred Mysteries of the Universe and your psyche.

RIDER-WAITE AND THE GOLDEN DAWN

The two Golden Dawn Tarot decks that I will be referencing in the following descriptions of the Major Arcana cards are the *Golden Dawn Tarot* by Robert Wang and the *Golden Dawn Magical Tarot* by Chic Cicero and Sandra Tabatha Cicero. Students of the Western Mystery tradition widely use these two Tarot decks. Their Qabalistic correspondences and images hold to the timeless, esoteric wisdom contained within the world of the Tarot.

Apart from using almost the same symbols in each deck, the main difference between these two Golden Dawn decks is the use of colour. Ciceros' Tarot deck is richer and more vibrant, often displaying opposing Elemental colours not found in Wang's deck. Ciceros' Tarot deck is also more complex in imagery, containing extra symbols that Wang's deck does not have. The power of Wang's Tarot deck lies in its simplicity, as the symbols, images, and colours adhere to the basics of what each card means.

The symbols present in both decks are reminiscent of the Golden Dawn teachings and the Hermetic teachings passed on through the ages. As such, the two Tarot decks complement each other for the most part. Therefore, I will not focus too much on the differences in the Golden Dawn decks but use them as a frame of reference in comparison to the most popular and world-famous (in all of the twentieth-century) Hermetic Tarot deck—the *Rider-Waite* Tarot deck.

Initially published in 1909, Illustrator Pamela Colman Smith drew the cards in the *Rider-Waite* Tarot as per the instructions of occultist and mystic A.E. Waite. Interestingly, both Smith and Waite were part of the Hermetic Order of the Golden Dawn, which was the original Golden Dawn Order that all subsequent Golden Dawn Orders were based upon. (More on this subject in a later chapter.)

I have included the images of the *Rider-Waite* Major Arcana from the *Pictorial Key to the Tarot* (published in 1911) for reference. As for the two Golden Dawn Tarot decks, their images can be found online or by purchasing each deck.

One thing to note which differentiates the *Rider-Waite* deck and the two Golden Dawn decks is the use of colour in the cards. The *Rider-Waite* deck is not very focused on colour attributes pertaining to the Tree of Life as it is on imagery and symbols. Also, it is rather basic in terms of style of presentation and colour use, as it only uses primary and secondary colours.

The Golden Dawn decks use more elaborate depictions of images with intricate colours. What makes the Rider-Waite deck beautiful and powerful, though, is its simplicity. I will not go too deeply into the analysis of the colours but merely point out the differences for the sake of understanding each Tarot card. I invite the reader to do further research on their own into whatever else interests them about each Tarot deck.

As part of each description of a Tarot card, I have included an excerpt from one of the earliest and oldest Golden Dawn documents, titled "Notes on the Tarot." This document was written by one of the Hermetic Order of the Golden Dawn's founders, S.L. MacGregor Mathers, under the name G.H. Frater S.R.M.D. Because of its significance, this document was also made part of Israel Regardie's seminal work, *The Golden Dawn*.

Also, each of the twenty-two Tarot cards has a Magickal name derived from S. L. MacGregor Mathers' *Book T- The Tarot*, which is a manuscript given out to Adepts within the Hermetic Order of the Golden Dawn as part of the Adeptus Minor curriculum. The Magickal names of the paths retained their use as part of other Golden Dawn Orders that followed. Therefore, I include them here to help you further understand the energy of each path.

Figure 18: Keys of the Tarot (Zero to Three)

THE FOOL

The Fool is the Zero Key of the Tarot and the Eleventh path of the Tree of Life, which links Kether and Chokmah. This card represents the initial stream of energy from the unmanifested Creator. The Fool's Magickal name is "The Spirit of the Aethyrs" since it is the fiery intelligence and the first current of vibration in its potential state. This path is formed out of the Limitless Light of Ain Soph Aur and is the spark of thought. The Air (Transitional) Element rules this path. As such, the Fool represents the Baptism of Air. The Fool card represents Spirituality in its highest essence because of its close connection with the Source (God-the Creator).

"The Fool is the Crown of Wisdom, the Primum Mobile, acting through the Air on the Zodiac." — S. L. MacGregor Mathers; "Notes on the Tarot"

The above quote describes the energy of the path of the Fool on the Tree of Life. The Primum Mobile refers to the "First Whirlings" of manifestation that emanate from God-the Source. This process is best described as the commencement phase of the creation of the Universe; it is the action of the Cosmic energy at the beginning point of Creation.

The Primum Mobile is behind all motion in the manifested Universe. The Fool card represents the Primum Mobile as it acts through the Air (Transitional) Element on Chokmah, to which the Zodiac is associated. As the Light is channelled into the Stars from the Source-Kether, it becomes accessible through the Air Element and thoughts.

The Egyptian child-God, Harpocrates, is an excellent example of the energy of this path, as he has his index finger on his lips, signifying the concept of "silence" with this gesture. This gesture will be used as part of the ritual exercises within *The Magus* and is called the Sign of Silence. The Fool card signifies the silence of the mind, body and Soul, displaying the pure potential of the unmanifested Creator. Only through the silence of mind, body, and Soul can we contemplate the most important secrets and Mysteries of the Universe.

In the Golden Dawn Tarot decks, a child is shown naked, symbolizing its innocence. A wolf is shown in the card also to express the potential danger of innocence. He is on a leash, being guided by the child. The child seems unaware that the wolf can hurt him; hence, it is the growth and experience in life which will teach the child to avoid all dangers. The colour that predominates the card is yellow, symbolising the connection to the Air Element. Green is present as well to represent the natural element, as is white, symbolic of the Spirit.

In the *Rider-Waite* Tarot, a jester is shown in place of the child. The imagery alludes to another name given to the Fool card in some old versions of the Tarot—"the Jester." The jester has a small dog beside him instead of a wolf and is on the verge of walking off a cliff. Both the *Rider-Waite* Tarot cards and the Golden Dawn cards emphasize foolishness and the bliss of ignorance. Whether the jester is innocent or simply unaware of his surroundings remains a mystery. Whatever the case, his lack of self-awareness has put him in a dangerous situation. The same colour scheme is found in the *Rider-Waite* Tarot cards as the Golden Dawn cards.

This card offers a sense of mental, emotional, and Spiritual renewal. The Fool signifies the innocence of an infant or the ignorance of the jester and the vulnerability when embodying those mental states. Furthermore, The Fool represents the energy of a child before the formation of the Ego or a joker before he becomes Self-conscious. Hence there is a connection between attaining Self-consciousness and the birth of the Ego. To live in this world, we must become Self-conscious. But as we do this, we lose our Divine innocence.

The Hebrew letter attributed to the Fool card is Aleph, which means "ox," which is a worthy symbol for the procreative power of nature. Aleph is also the first letter of the Hebrew alphabet, thereby symbolizing new beginnings. The number of the Fool is zero, expressed by the tail devourer, the Ouroboros—a snake eating its tail. The Fool represents the unity of the manifested world and the Source of all Creation.

In the context of the Kundalini, this card represents the renewal of thought. It is the inspiration, as well as imagination. It represents Life energy, Prana, and the expansion of consciousness through the Air Element. In this card, all communication is through Gnosis—the direct imparting of information from the Divine to the human. Hence the silence, and the truth, which can only be communicated through it.

In a Divination, the Fool generally refers to Spirituality which is trying to rise above the Material Plane, unless it is a Divination of a material nature, where the Fool card takes on the reversed meanings. The Fool represents inspired thinking, new beginnings, spontaneity, wonder, awe, curiosity, and Spiritual freedom. If reversed, the Fool represents recklessness, negligence, the need for caution, and folly. The way to read the Fool in Divination depends on the nature of the question. If it is a Spiritual question, then the Fool (upright) has a very Airy, Spiritual nature and is considered a positive card.

THE MAGICIAN

The Magician is the First Key of the Tarot and the Twelfth Path of the Tree of life, which runs between Kether and Binah. The card's Magickal name is the "Magus of Power," which is ruled by Mercury—the Planet of the intellect. Once the Spiritual lessons have been learned through life experience, the Fool becomes the Magician; hence, he is directly opposite him on the Tree of Life. The Fool has learned to discern between good and evil through the development and evolution of the Soul. As a result, he has grown in wisdom and knowledge, becoming the Magician. The Spiritual journey begins with the Fool and ends with the Magician.

"The Magician is the Crown of Understanding, the beginning of material production, the Primum Mobile acting through the Philosophic Mercury on Saturn." — S. L. MacGregor Mathers; "Notes on the Tarot"

The above quote describes the essence of the path of the Magician. As the White Light of Kether acts on the mind, it is received through intuition, thus producing the Understanding in Binah. Since Mercury represents the mind, and Saturn represents the Three-Dimensional World, the mind becomes the connecting link between Spirit and Matter. The path of the Magician represents the power of having conscious control over events in Time and Space by using the intellect. Intelligence is built up by obtaining wisdom and knowledge through the mind.

The Magician is the thought becoming manifest since he invokes the Light energy and directs it. We are all seeking to become the Magician since he is the Master of the Elements. In some older versions of the Tarot, he is referred to as "the Magus." His other name is "the Juggler"—since he can control and balance the Elements. The Hebrew letter attributed to the Magician card is Beth, which means "house." The Magician is the house in which the Divine Spirit dwells.

The Caduceus of Hermes is shown in many examples of the Magician card as the primary Force. After all, Hermes is another name for Mercury. The Caduceus of Hermes is synonymous with Kundalini energy. The Magician is the Master of the Four Elements, including the fifth Element of Spirit, brought in through the Kundalini. The Magician's symbol is also the upright Pentagram, representing the Four Elements (the four lower points of the Pentagram) under the presidency of Spirit (the highest point of the Pentagram).

Hence, the Magician is the Kundalini awakened individual whose consciousness is elevated as they have progressed through the Chakras. The individual now operates through the Spirit Element in the highest three Chakras. For this reason, they are called the Magician—they can accomplish wonders and work Magick.

In the Golden Dawn Tarot decks, the Magician is presented as a man standing in front of a square altar. The square altar represents the four corners of Space in the World of Matter and the Four Elements of Being. On the altar are to be found the four Elemental tools (often referred to as the Elemental Weapons)—the cup (West), the wand (South), the dagger (East), and the pentacle (North). These symbolize the Water, Fire, Air, and Earth Elements. A symbol of Infinity is integrated within the image to represent the Eternal, Divine Energy. The colour that predominates the card is yellow to represent the connection to and dominance of the Air Element.

The *Rider-Waite* Tarot deck also features the same symbols in the image of this card. The main difference is that one hand points upwards while the other points downwards. This gesture symbolizes the Above and the Below, the Heaven and the Earth. "As Above, So Below" relates to the process of manifestation of the Divine energy. It also refers to manipulating this energy through the practice of Magick.

The Magician is reflected in the intellect, which gathers up and stores knowledge. Therefore, logic and reason are vital components present in this card. Within the *Rider-Waite* Tarot, red is present in the Magician's cape to symbolize the energized willpower.

While the Fool abides in silence and contemplation of the truth, the Magician engages in the act of manifestation—the Magician is representative of the creative force. He represents Thoth, the Egyptian God, also known as Hermes, the Greek God of communication, language, Magick, and wisdom. As mentioned, Hermes is called Mercury by the Romans to represent the same God energy.

This card has a most direct connection to the Kundalini in the totality of its overall experience. We are all aligning to the Thought of God—Thoth, the Egyptian God of wisdom. The pronunciation of both "Thoth" and "thought" are very similar, indicating a correspondence between the two ideas.

In a later section on *The Kybalion*, I will get into the power of thought and the concept of the Universe being a living Thought of God since thought is at the core of all existence. But, for now, impregnate upon your subconscious mind the relation between the Magician card, Hermes (or Thoth), and the Kundalini force—they are all One.

In a Divination, the Magician represents the power of manifestation, adaptation, wisdom, resourcefulness, skill, and the realization of potential. It is a very Mercurial card; thus, it relates to mental acuity. If reversed, it represents Egotism, unrealized talents and abilities, poor planning, conceit, manipulation, and even mania.

THE HIGH PRIESTESS

The High Priestess is the Second Key of the Tarot and the Thirteenth Path of the Tree of Life. It is the lengthiest path, beyond the Veil of the Abyss, from God the Crown (Kether) to the manifestation of God as the Resurrected Son (Tiphareth). The High Priestess is a very Watery path, ruled by the Moon. It is the root essence of consciousness and the substance and ultimate expression of the Element of Water. The High Priestess' Magickal name is the "Priestess of the Silver Star."

"The High Priestess is the Crown of Beauty, the beginning of Sovereignty and Beauty, the Primum Mobile, acting through the Moon on the Sun." — S. L. MacGregor Mathers; "Notes on the Tarot"

The above quote describes the essence of the path of the High Priestess on the Tree of Life. The Creator projects its White Light into the Sun through the Moon. As such, the Light of the Sun is only a reflection of the Light of Kether. This statement implies that the World of Matter is simply an illusion, a phantasmagoria—considering that all things in the physical world consist of Light particles projected by the Sun.

Gimel, the Hebrew letter meaning "camel," is associated with the High Priestess due to the camel's ability to travel across the desert (the Abyss) at length because of its gift of being able to hold water. Water represents consciousness, while the camel represents consciousness moving through the Abyss into the Spiritual Plane.

Traversing the High Priestess path is synonymous with raising the Kundalini energy from the Heart Chakra (Anahata) to the Crown Chakra (Sahasrara), which marks the completion of the full Kundalini awakening. Through a Kundalini awakening, we can perceive the world around us for what it truly is—Spirit energy.

To raise the Kundalini from the Heart into the brain centre, you must pierce the Throat Chakra, Vishuddhi. The Throat Chakra is where the lower Elements end and the Aethyr/Spirit Element begins. Upon activating the Spirit Element within yourself, you are crossing through the Abyss of the Mind. The mind contains duality while the Spirit exists in unity, in singularity. To attain the Spirit energy, you have to silence the mind and use the camel to cross the Abyss, metaphorically speaking. Once you do this, you will have raised the Kundalini into the brain centre. Once it rises into the brain, it never drops back down, which signifies a full, permanent Kundalini awakening.

The High Priestess is the symbolic form of the Great Feminine—Isis, Shekinah, and Mother Mary. Through self-sacrifice of the Slain and Resurrected God in Tiphareth, union with the High Priestess is the reward. You must first sacrifice the Ego and its lower impulses to be reborn. Without self-sacrifice, you cannot raise your consciousness to the level of the Spirit.

In the Golden Dawn Tarot decks, a woman is shown in a blue dress, holding a chalice of water, representative of the Water Element. She has a crescent Moon on her head and is covered with a veil. The veil is representative of the Veil of the Abyss, which is the boundary of the individual consciousness that separates the Supernals of Kether, Chokmah, and Binah, from the lower seven Sephiroth. The entire card has a predominantly blue colour to assert further the connection to and dominance of the Water Element.

The *Rider-Waite* Tarot deck features a similar image with the same symbols, including the two black and white pillars at Solomon's Temple—Boaz and Jachin (Severity and Mercy). The High Priestess is in between the pillars to symbolize balance and the card's placement on the Tree of Life, as it is on the Middle Pillar. She wears the crown of Isis on her head, meaning she is a believer in Magick. The Solar cross on her chest denotes that she is connected to the seasons of the Earth. The crescent Moon at her feet means that she has complete control over her emotions. The pomegranates on the drape behind her symbolize life, death, rebirth, and Eternal life.

The High Priestess is a card of mystery, passivity, and stillness. These are the Waters of Creation, which are boundless as is Cosmic Consciousness itself. The ideas of reflection and inner instincts are present in this card. In some older versions of the Tarot, the High Priestess is referred to as "the Popess."

The celestial body of the Moon is attributed to this card because of the power of visual thought that the Moon energy helps us form. This same power is used to raise the Kundalini energy from Muladhara. The creative force is channelled through the vehicle of the High Priestess, who then initiates its manifestation into Form.

Form is visual thought. For this reason, the High Priestess is the balancing force and the counterpart of the Magician. The Magician uses imagination, willpower, and thought to work his Magick. By imagining something and projecting energy into that thought, it will inevitably manifest—As Above, So Below.

In a Divination, the High Priestess represents the Divine Feminine, intuition, sacred knowledge, the subconscious mind, instincts, fluctuation, and change. This card is Lunar, and therefore you should be aware of the Moon cycles and whether the Moon is waxing (in increase) or waning (in decrease) at the time of the reading. If the High Priestess is reversed, it represents a disconnect from intuition, repressed feelings, ignorance, superficial knowledge of events in question, and secrets.

THE EMPRESS

The Empress is the Third Key of the Tarot and the Fourteenth Path of the Tree of Life. The Empress connects Chokmah and Binah, acting as the mediator between these two Spheres. The Magickal Title of this card is the "Daughter of the Mighty Ones." The Hebrew letter attributed to the Empress card is Daleth, which means "door." The Empress is the door to love. She represents the path of unity of Force and Form, the opposing Pillars of Mercy and Severity. This card represents the love between the Father and the Mother, Chokmah and Binah. The Empress is the force that brings together all opposing concepts, as love is the foundational energy of all of Creation.

"The Empress is the Wisdom of Understanding, the Union of the powers of Origination and Production; the Sphere of the Zodiac acting through Venus upon Saturn." — S. L. MacGregor Mathers; *"Notes on the Tarot"*

The above quote describes the energy of the path of the Empress on the Tree of Life. The projective power of the Father (Chokmah) is united with the receptive capacity of the Mother (Binah), thereby manifesting Light and consciousness, the Fire and Water Elements. Since Planet Venus represents the Universal energy of love, it becomes a binding force between Force and Form. The Empress then is the builder of Form and the womb in which manifestation is conceived.

The Empress is under the rule of Venus, the Planet of love. The Empress represents the essence of emotion in its most refined, pure form. Love is energy which generates emotions, which the Soul uses to steer its course through life. Love is also the energy found within all of Creation since all things were manifested through love.

In the Golden Dawn Tarot decks, a woman with a crown on her head is shown sitting on a throne. Her dress is red with green elements, while the background is predominantly green. She holds a sceptre in one hand and an *Ankh*, representing Eternal life, in the other. Furthermore, a dove is seen in the background, representing the Holy Spirit. The woman alludes to the Egyptian Goddess Isis, the positive side of nature. Qabalistically, she is Shekinah, the Divine presence of God-the Creator, representing our inner desire and yearning for unification with the Source of Creation.

In the *Rider-Waite* Tarot deck, a similar image is shown in this card. The main difference is that the *Rider-Waite* card has a predominantly yellow backdrop. In it are found grains and crops, as the Empress has dominion over nature. She wears a starry crown of twelve stars (the Zodiac), emphasizing her dominance over the Solar year. Her robe is pomegranate patterned, representing fertility. She represents growth in the natural world and the power of the heart and emotions.

In the context of the Kundalini awakening, the Empress card represents love in various forms. Love is the driving and motivating force behind our virtues, ethics and morals. Without love, our hearts turn to wickedness. The Empress' energy is the energy of rebirth. Love is the force that brings about our rebirth into the Spirit.

Hence, its connection with the dove and the Ankh. The Empress' Planet, Venus, encompasses each of the Sephiroth. Venus is the primary energy in the formation and unification of the many aspects of the Universe.

In a Divination, the Empress represents femininity, nature, nurture, sensuality, beauty, pleasure, fertility, abundance, and creative expression. If reversed, it implies the lack of individual willpower, neglect of one's needs, dependence on others, and creative blockages.

THE EMPEROR

The Emperor is the Fourth Key of the Tarot, and the Fifteenth Path of the Tree of Life, connecting Tiphareth and Chokmah. The Emperor is called the "Son of the Morning; Chief among the Mighty." The Emperor receives the energy of the Empress and channels it down into the Higher Self. As such, the masculine and feminine energies are balanced in this card. The Emperor was a warrior king who exchanged his sword for the wand in the past. He has matured and grown in wisdom over time. With this card comes a sense of control and guidance over the Self. The Emperor initiates energy and its creative force, as he is the stimulator of the dynamic current.

"The Emperor is the Wisdom of Sovereignty and Beauty, and the originator of them; the Sphere of the Zodiac acting through Aries upon the Sun, and initiating spring." — S. L. MacGregor Mathers; "Notes on the Tarot"

The above quote describes the energy of the path of the Emperor. It relates to the life/death/rebirth cycle contained within nature. This cycle is initiated by the Fire of Fire Sub-Element of Aries, the first Zodiac sign and the first sign of the first season in the Solar year. Since the Sun gives forth Soul and life to all living things in our Solar System, its Light regulates the cycles of time that we are all subject to.

The Hebrew letter attributed to the Emperor is Heh, which means "window." The Emperor is the window into personal power. This path is very fiery as the Zodiac sign of Aries rules it. Though this card may appear slightly masculine, its association with Aries and the beginning of spring reveals its feminine component, as the cycle of rebirth is a feminine process. However, since Aries is under the rule of Mars, this card is symbolic of powerful creative energy and rulership.

In the Golden Dawn Tarot decks, a man is shown sitting on a throne. He wears a crown on his head, similar to the Empress card. In Ciceros' version of the card, he is shown with a beard, while in Wang's, he is without one. He is clothed in red, holding a sceptre with a ram's head, representing sovereignty. His feet also are placed atop a ram. He holds a globe with an Ankh on top in his other hand. The predominant colours of the background are green and red. The different shades of red represent the energizing forces in this card. As the Empress is the positive feminine force, the Emperor is the positive masculine force.

Figure 19: Keys of the Tarot (Four to Seven)

In the *Rider-Waite Tarot Deck*, no ram is present, although the ram symbol is shown on the throne he is sitting on. He has a long beard, symbolic of his wisdom. He holds an Ankh sceptre in one hand and a globe, a symbol of domination, in his other hand. He sits atop a barren mountain, symbolic of dominion and unyielding power. In this card, there is no green present but grey instead to symbolize the wisdom and sovereignty of the Emperor.

In the context of the Kundalini awakening, the Emperor represents the Ego being under the guidance of the Higher Self. We are all striving to be the Emperor in our own lives and have control over our inner Selves, which will give us control over our outer reality. This card represents being in tune with the Higher Self and having dominion over the Ego and the material world. It represents being in control of the lower forces instead of being controlled by them.

In a Divination, the Emperor represents masculinity, Divine Knowledge, raw power, creative energy, control, structure, dominance, authority, discipline, stability, ambition, and conquest in a matter. If reversed, it represents the abuse of power, tyranny, anger, cruelty, rigidity, lack of discipline, excessive control, blind ambition, and self-righteousness.

THE HIEROPHANT

The Hierophant is the Fifth Key of the Tarot, and the Sixteenth Path of the Tree of Life, connecting Chesed and Chokmah. The card's Magickal title is the "Magus of the Eternal Gods." The Hierophant symbolizes the Higher Self, the connection between the Above and the Below. The Hebrew letter associated with this card is Vav, meaning "hook" or "nail." The Hierophant represents the binding force between the Above and the Below. To take this idea further, the binding energy of Spirit and Matter is "thought."

"The Hierophant is the Wisdom and Fountain of Mercy; the Sphere of the Zodiac acting through Taurus upon Jupiter." — S. L. MacGregor Mathers; "Notes on the Tarot"

The above quote describes the energy of the path of the Hierophant. Through the attainment of knowledge and wisdom, we can experience the mercy and compassion of the Creator. The Hierophant figure is none other than our Higher Self, a reflection of the Creator, who teaches us the Mysteries of Creation. The Higher Self uses the stable, grounded sign of Taurus (Air of Earth) to channel information to us, thereby impacting our emotions.

The Hierophant symbolises mercy, and he is depicted in the Golden Dawn Tarot decks as sitting upon a bull, signifying control over the Ego. He holds a scroll containing the *Logos* (the Word) while being illuminated by the Supernal Light from Above. The Hierophant is dressed in red—the same as the Empress and the Emperor. Red symbolizes his power and dominance. He holds a crook in his other hand, representing kingship.

The Hierophant is portrayed with a beard, symbolic of wisdom. His garb resembles that of a High Priest, and as such, he is the complement to the High Priestess. The colours in the background of the card vary considerably, with different browns present and maroon. These colours offer a more reflective feel, such as deep thought and contemplation.

In the *Rider-Waite Tarot Deck*, grey colour is predominant. The Hierophant figure in the card looks like a Pope, as is his name in some older versions of Hermetic Tarot decks. He is seated on a throne between two pillars, symbolizing law and liberty, or obedience and disobedience. He holds a triple cross with three horizontal bars, representing the Father, the Son, and the Holy Ghost (or Spirit). Seated before him are two acolytes illustrating the transfer of sacred knowledge within religious institutions. The Hierophant stands for all things which are righteous and Holy in the world. He is the leader of the human race and the head of any recognized hierarchy.

The grounded Zodiac sign of Taurus rules the Hierophant. It is the highest path on the Pillar of Mercy and a very masculine one. The Hierophant uses the stability of the energy of Taurus to communicate as the Great Teacher since Taurus is Air of Earth. He reveals the Mysteries, and his revelations are meant to be perceived through feeling and intuition, rather than the intellect, as he is the inner Light—the Higher Self. The Hierophant is the reflective or mystical aspect of the masculine energy—he is the thinker, while the Emperor is a man of action.

The notion of inner teaching is closely connected with this card. In the Kundalini awakening context, The Hierophant is the inner Light which is now unveiled to the initiate. Therefore, any communication of inner wisdom and knowledge is the work of the Higher Self—The Hierophant.

In a Divination, The Hierophant represents Spiritual Wisdom, morality and ethics, mercy, teaching, and conformity to traditional religious beliefs. If reversed, it represents rebellion, challenging the status quo, personal freedom, and new approaches to old beliefs and ideals.

THE LOVERS

The Lovers is the Sixth Key of the Tarot, and the Seventeenth Path of the Tree of Life, connecting Tiphareth and Binah. The Magickal Title of this card is the "Children of the Voice Divine; Oracles of the Mighty Gods." The Lovers represent the personality in unity with the Higher Self. This unity is reached when the two opposing forces within the Light Body are sublimated and become One. Once this occurs, the Spirit energy can descend into the lower parts of Being.

"The Lovers are the Understanding of Beauty as well as the Production of Beauty and Sovereignty; Saturn acting through Gemini upon Sol." — S. L. MacGregor Mathers; "Notes on the Tarot "

The above quote describes the energy of the path of the Lovers. The unification of opposites occurs on the mind level, where duality occurs. The Lovers card represents the sublimation of thoughts and emotions since Gemini is of the Water of Air Sub-Element, representing the union of conscious and subconscious minds, the masculine and feminine aspects of Being. By unifying all opposites within the Self, the Soul achieves ultimate Understanding of its true nature, thus gaining a connection with the Higher Self.

The Golden Dawn Tarot decks are radically different from the *Rider-Waite Tarot Deck*. The Golden Dawn decks depict the Greek hero, Perseus, shown in combat with a sea monster, who represents the concept of fear. He aims to free the beautiful Andromeda from being chained to a rock. Here, Perseus is symbolic of the Higher Self, while Andromeda is the Lower Self. The stone signifies the Material Realm and mortality. Through the Planet Venus and love, the sublimation of energies occurs, giving reason to the theme in this card, which is the Divine Union. The predominant colours are blue and yellow, representing the Water and Air Elements present in the Gemini Zodiac sign.

In the *Rider-Waite Tarot Deck,* two figures are shown naked, showing they have nothing to hide from each other. The Divine Union is represented by the Archangel Raphael behind them in the clouds, protecting and blessing them. Raphael represents the Air Element, which is associated with mental activity and communication, as that is the foundation of any healthy relationship. There is a Tree of Knowledge of Good and Evil behind the woman, and a Tree with twelve trefoil flames, representing the Zodiac, behind the man. They appear to be in the Garden of Eden, which is a reference to Adam and Eve as the first Divine couple.

The Hebrew letter associated with this card is Zayin, which means "sword" or "armour." Sword and armour are the symbolic tools used to conquer fear. The dual Zodiac sign of Gemini rules this path. The Divine Love between the Gemini twins is not sexual in any way. The Lovers represent the uniting of the masculine (Sun) and feminine (Moon) energies within the initiate, acting through Gemini upon Sol (the Soul). The impact of inspiration and intuition results in liberation and illumination, removing the bonds of materialism and creating the Divine Union.

This card represents the reflection of the conscious and subconscious minds as they unite and return into the mirror as one. The Sea of Consciousness of Binah signifies this mirror. On one end of the spectrum of vibration is material form, while on the other is pure unmanifest consciousness. The Kundalini awakening is an awakening to both of these forces. The unification of opposites occurs over time as the conscious and subconscious minds learn to work in unison as one.

In a Divination, the Lovers card represents love, harmony, attraction, union, duality, and partnerships. If reversed, it means Self-love, loss of love, one-sidedness, disharmony, and imbalance.

THE CHARIOT

The Chariot is the Seventh Key of the Tarot, and the Eighteenth Path of the Tree of Life, connecting Geburah and Binah. The Magickal Title of this card is the "Child of the Powers of the Waters; The Lord of the Triumph of Light." The tenacious Zodiac sign of Cancer rules the Chariot. It is the first path that traverses the

Abyss from the lower Sephiroth. As the Chariot can move between all of the Cosmic Planes of existence with total ease, it represents the conquering of them. However, there must be a complete descent and integration of the Spirit energy before this can be achieved. This integration is what this path represents.

"The Chariot is Understanding acting upon Severity; Saturn acting through Cancer upon Mars."
— S. L. MacGregor Mathers; "Notes on the Tarot"

The above quote describes the energy of the path of the Chariot on the Tree of Life. As Binah acts on Geburah through the reflective Zodiac sign of Cancer (Fire of Water Sub-Element), the Higher Self is in control. This path exemplifies the conscious use of willpower by discerning the duality of the mind. Only by seeing "both sides of the coin" simultaneously can the Higher Self act with Understanding. And to achieve this, a proper dose of unconditional love must be applied.

In the Golden Dawn Tarot decks, a chariot moves through Space, guided by two horses. One horse is black, and the other is white, signifying the positive and negative forces within existence. The Chariot is powered by the union of these two opposing forces. The rider within the image symbolizes the Higher Self. He has sublimated both the negative and the positive energies and is now under the guidance of Spirit alone. He has penetrated the higher Sephiroth by rising above the clouds of illusion. The predominant colours are blue and yellow, along with a deep blue-violet, representing the sublimation of the psyche.

In the *Rider-Waite Tarot Deck*, the emphasis is on the horses, which appear as two Sphinxes, again with the same black and white motif symbolic of the opposites in nature. The figure in the Chariot is in armour to represent the warrior element of the Spirit. The crown on his head means that he is Enlightened and pure of will. On his chest is a square, representative of the Earth Element Tattva and the material world, which serves to ground all of his actions. The canopy of stars above the charioteer's head represents the influences of the celestial spheres and the Divine forces in the Heavens, which guide him. The colour scheme is the same as the Golden Dawn decks.

The Chariot symbolizes the Higher Self that moves through the Cosmic Planes of existence. It is a Watery path on the Pillar of Severity. The Chariot's counterpart is the Hierophant, found on the Pillar of Mercy. Its celestial body is the Moon, the Planet ruling Cancer, guiding the Chariot through the Cosmic Planes. The Hebrew letter associated with this card is Cheth, which means "fence" or "enclosure." The fence separates Binah and Geburah, the Supernals from the bodily enclosure.

The Chariot represents control over duality in all of existence, especially the mental reality. To accomplish this, though, you must be able to neutralize all opposing viewpoints by applying the energy of unconditional love. Furthermore, you must control how you perceive reality by seeing everything objectively and not subjectively since subjective perspectives only see "one side of the coin." As the Chariot is the path connecting the Willpower (Geburah) to Understanding (Binah), it represents using your willpower with understanding and not being tainted mentally and emotionally by the pain of duality.

In a Divination, the Chariot is a very positive card that represents willpower and strength of mind, mental control, victory, triumph, a sense of direction, and a need for determination. Its meaning, though, will be determined by where it falls in the Circle Spread. If it falls in Earth, it is usually long-lasting, while if it falls in Air, it can be transient. If the Chariot is reversed, it represents a lack of direction, lack of control, and opposition. It indicates that whatever obstacles you face will most likely not be overcome.

STRENGTH

Strength is the Eighth Key of the Tarot, and the Nineteenth Path of the Tree of Life, connecting Geburah and Chesed. The Magickal Title of the card is the "Daughter of the Flaming Sword; Leader of the Lion." Strength is a significant path below the Abyss that connects the two contending forces of the Higher Self—Mercy and Severity. This path represents passions under the control of the will and mastery of the Lower Self by the Higher Self. Leo is attributed to this card, the only Zodiac sign ruled by the Sun. As such, it represents vitality and authority.

"Strength is Mercy tempering Severity; the Glory of Strength; Jupiter acting through Leo upon Mars." — S. L. MacGregor Mathers; "Notes on the Tarot"

The above quote describes the energy of the path of the Strength card on the Tree of Life. When Mercy tempers Severity, Strength is achieved, which generates the feeling of Glory within the individual. Jesus Christ has referred to it as the *Glory of God*. It is the honour experienced and felt when an individual achieves a proper balance between Mercy and Severity. As Jupiter acts on Mars, through Leo's active, masculine sign (Air of Fire Sub-Element), a unity between the Water and Fire Elements occurs. Willpower falls under the governance of unconditional love, which is necessary to attain the correct balance within the mind, body, and Soul.

In the Golden Dawn Tarot decks, a lion is portrayed with a woman guiding him with her hand. In Ciceros' deck, the lion's tail is in the form of a serpent. It alludes to the Hebrew letter Teth, which is associated with this path, meaning "snake." More notably, it alludes to the shape-shifting energy of the path itself since the serpent and the lion are one. While the lion is a symbol of brute strength, available to be used for either good or evil, the snake represents the energy of the Kundalini. And the Kundalini is, of course, used to fully activate the Body of Light and its corresponding energy centres.

Figure 20: Keys of the Tarot (Eight to Eleven)

The Kundalini activation is meant to be guided by the will of the Higher Self, symbolized by the woman in the card. This woman is Aima Elohim—the Great Mother. She is the feminine Principle of Creation seen throughout the Major Arcana in her many forms. In this card, she holds flowers, symbolizing the innocence required to tame the lion. As this path is right below the Abyss, it is set in the desert. In Ciceros' deck, she is shown naked, with a green lion present, alluding to wild, raw energy, which is meant to be mastered by the Higher Self.

The Strength card represents the mastery of the Lower Self by the Higher Self. The Soul keeps the Ego in check, represented by the predominant brown colour of the desert Earth, on which the woman and lion stand. Endurance is necessary to master the Self, represented by the pale colours present in the card. We must overcome all of life's challenges to succeed in Spiritual growth.

In the *Thoth Tarot* deck, this card is referred to as "Lust." Lust is the psychological force producing an intense desire for something that can take many forms. We must focus our energy of desire on something that can yield a positive outcome in our lives.

The *Rider-Waite Tarot Deck* features the same symbolic elements as the Golden Dawn decks. The main difference is the symbol of Infinity on the woman's head, indicative of her being guided by the Eternal, Divine energy. She is holding the jaws of the lion open with her hands in a display of grace, love, courage and compassion. She is calm and collected while also showing dominance. Her gesture shows the need for discipline and control in the face of great adversity. There is an abundance of yellow colour in this card, representing the Air Element and thoughts, which need to be fine-tuned to gain control over the Lower Self.

When the Tree of Life is superimposed on the human body, the path of Strength connects the left and right arms. This connection is symbolic of the strength tapped into when both arms work together in harmony. Real strength is achieved when opposites unite. Such is the Law.

We need the strength of mind, body, and Soul to maintain our course on the Spiritual journey. This card represents the courage that is built over time after being tested by life's challenges and prevailing. Consequently, "Fortitude" is another name for this card in some older versions of the Tarot. Real strength is not determined by how fast you fall or fail in an attempt at an endeavour but by how quickly you get back up and try again. It is how fortitude, the strength of mind, is built. The Great Work is not for the faint of heart but for those willing to be determined, persistent, and consistent in their daily efforts to evolve in mind, body, and Soul.

In a Divination, the Strength card represents inner strength, power, bravery, determination, fortitude, endurance, courage, and compassion. Examining the other cards in the Circle Spread is crucial since power under the will of lousy judgment can be a negative thing. When reversed, the Strength card represents self-doubt, insecurity, weakness, and low energy.

THE HERMIT

The Hermit is the Ninth Key of the Tarot, and the Twentieth Path of the Tree of Life, connecting Tiphareth and Chesed. The Hermit's Magickal name is the "Magus of the Voice of Light, the Prophet of the Gods." The Hermit represents Divine Wisdom. He is the Sage and the Mystic—the messenger of the Divine Light. This very significant card represents the communication between the Higher Self of the Ethical Triangle and the Spiritual Self of the Supernal Triangle. For this reason, The Hermit is the *Light-Bearer* and the one who brings the message from the Higher Self.

"The Hermit is the Mercy of Beauty, the Magnificence of Sovereignty, Jupiter acting through Virgo upon Sol." — S. L. MacGregor Mathers; "Notes on the Tarot"

The above quote describes the essence of the path of the Hermit. The Word of God is found in the vibratory frequency of the Light and is the source of Universal wisdom. As the Light of the Sun spreads its energy across our Solar System, so does the Word of God. In the Hermit card, knowledge is imparted through the emotions through the passive, feminine energy of Virgo (Water of Earth Sub-Element).

In the Golden Dawn Tarot decks, an older man with a long, grey beard is portrayed, holding a lantern in one hand and a staff in the other. The Light from the lamp illuminates his path as he walks during the night. He wears a hood and mantle and stands on the desert Earth. The brown colour of the Earth predominates the lower portion of the card. His wardrobe is yellow-green with brown in Wang's Tarot deck and red and blue in Ciceros' deck. His staff depicts authority and power. The same snake found on the tail of the lion in the Strength card is found in this card at the Hermit's feet, representing the Kundalini energy and the Word received through it.

In the *Rider-Waite Tarot Deck*, similar imagery is portrayed, with the main difference being the colours that predominate, which are dark blue and grey. Also, the Hermit stands atop a mountain instead of the desert, denoting accomplishment and success. He is ready to share the high level of Spiritual knowledge that he has attained with the world. The lantern he holds contains a star with six points, known as the "Seal of Solomon," representing wisdom. Solomon was the wise king of Israel and also a powerful Magus.

The Hermit is associated with the Hebrew letter Yod, representing the Father Principle and Primal Fire in the Tetragrammaton. In Hebrew, Yod means "hand." There is also a phallic reference to Yod, which, when put together with the Virgo Zodiac as per the card's attribution, provides the symbol of sexual love in its virginal, unmanifested form. Its source is the unconditional love of the Universe. Furthermore, Yod represents the Logos, or the Word of Power, which connects the Lower Self and the Higher Self through the vibratory frequency of the Light. The vibration of the spoken word has the power to resonate to the ends of the Universe.

The Hermit is symbolized by Anubis, the Egyptian God, a lower form of Hermes/Thoth—the messenger to the Gods. In the Golden Dawn Neophyte Initiation, he is the Kerux, the Light-Bearer—one who holds the Lamp of Hidden Knowledge and one who guides the candidate.

The Hermit possesses the qualities of Fire (Yod) and Earth (Virgo). Therefore, it represents the beginning and the end of the Elements and the Tetragrammaton. The Hermit's lamp represents the Light that radiates out into all the Cosmic Planes and dimensions of Space/Time. In the context of the Kundalini awakening, the Word (now attained intuitively), which speaks through wisdom, is said to be a manifestation of the Hermit card.

In a Divination, the Hermit represents the search for truth, inner guidance, and introspection. When reversed, it implies loneliness, isolation, and losing touch with the inner Light that guides the way in life.

WHEEL OF FORTUNE

The Wheel of Fortune is the Tenth Key of the Tarot, and the Twenty-first Path of the Tree of Life, connecting the Spheres of Netzach and Chesed. The Wheel of Fortune's Magickal title is the "Lord of the Forces of Life." The Wheel of Fortune symbolises the Four Elements, crowned and unified by Spirit. This path represents the energy flow between the personality (the Lower Self) and the Higher Self on the Pillar of Mildness. The Wheel of Fortune is also a symbol of Karma and time, as it is in constant fluctuation, bringing past actions back into the present and further into the future. It is the cycling of human incarnation and destiny.

"The Wheel of Fortune is the Mercy and Magnificence of Sovereignty; Jupiter acting through Jupiter directly on Venus." — S. L. MacGregor Mathers; "Notes on the Tarot"

The above quote describes the energy of the Wheel of Fortune path on the Tree of Life. Since Jupiter is representative of mercy and compassion, it is the application of this energy or lack thereof that yields Karma. Since Venus represents the desires, it is the expression of those desires that yield good or bad Karma for the individual. Because of the cyclic nature of the Universe, which is continuously in motion, negative Karmic energy binds itself to our Aura so that we can work through it before being taken higher Spiritually.

In the Golden Dawn Tarot decks, the Cynocephalus, the Ape with the dog face, is depicted below the Wheel of Fortune, representing the lower, animalistic Self. He is a companion of Hermes, symbolizing time and Eternity. The Sphinx is shown above the Wheel of Fortune, serving as the Higher Self—the guardian of the occult mysteries. The Wheel is continually revolving, cycling energy between the Sphinx and the Ape, the Higher Self and the Lower Self. The twelve spokes on the Wheel of Fortune represent the Twelve Zodiac. The colour which predominates the card is blue, corresponding to the Element of Water. Deep purple and violet are also found in the card, symbolizing its mystic elements.

The same Wheel is found in the *Rider-Waite Tarot Deck* but with eight spokes instead of twelve. In it are ascribed the four letters of the Tetragrammaton (YHVH). Four winged creatures are found in each corner of the card. The Sphinx sits atop the Wheel, while on its bottom is a figure that could either be Anubis or the Devil. The Sphinx represents the wisdom of the Gods and Kings, while Anubis (or the Devil) represents the

Underworld or Hell. Light blue is the predominant colour in the card, representing the sky, accompanied by white clouds symbolising the Heavens. Each winged creature holds a book, which serves as a Holy scripture—the source of wisdom and understanding for humanity. To the left of the Wheel is a snake moving downwards, which indicates descending into the World of Matter.

Duality found in nature and the interaction between the extreme poles (positive and negative) is what makes the Wheel move. The Wheel of Fortune serves as the mediator between two opposites. It is referred to as the "Intelligence of Conciliation." In the action of the Wheel of Fortune is to be found the Hermetic Principle of Cause and Effect, which will be discussed in a later chapter on *The Kybalion*. Cause and effect and Karma are inextricably related.

The Hebrew letter assigned to this path is Caph, which means "palm" or "fist." It refers to riches and poverty, both influenced by the Planet Jupiter since it is the Planet of abundance. As Jupiter is the Planet of the Element of Water, this card shows the correspondences between the Water Element, Karma and consciousness.

The Wheel of Fortune is also the Wheel of life, death, and rebirth, as all things within Creation must go through this cycle. The notion of rebirth here alludes to the Spiritualization of all things in the Universe. Our inherent birthright is the Spiritual Realm, as it is our final goal. It is only a matter of time before all manifested things are reunited with their Source-Spirit.

In a Divination, the Wheel of Fortune is a positive Karmic card that indicates good fortune and happiness. But, depending on the question, it also represents change, life cycles, fate, destiny, and Karma in general. When reversed, the Wheel of Fortune represents bad luck, bad Karma, lack of control, resistance to change, and the breaking of cycles.

JUSTICE

Justice is the Eleventh Key of the Tarot, and the Twenty-second Path of the Tree of Life, connecting Tiphareth and Geburah. The Magickal Title of this card is the "Daughter of the Lords of Truth, the Holder of the Balances." This path is in charge of balancing the whole Tree of Life by equilibrating between the functions of each of its Spheres and the Sphere of its harshest, most severe action—Geburah.

"Justice is the Severity of Beauty and Sovereignty; Mars acting through Libra upon Sol." — S. L. MacGregor Mathers; *"Notes on the Tarot"*

The above quote describes the energy of the Justice card on the Tree of Life. Mars is the harsh, exacting, often destructive energy of the Fire Element. As it acts on the Sun, it checks and realigns all imbalances received from the other Sephiroth. The Libra energy (Fire of Air Sub-Element) represents the conscious weighing of opposites that tempers the Fire energy of Mars as it is brought forth into the Sun, the dispenser of

Light. Within the Light are to be found these qualities as part of its vibrational frequency. Thus, the concept of seeking justice in the name of something Higher is part of our human existence.

In the Golden Dawn Tarot decks, there is a feminine figure, robed in green. In one hand, she holds the "Sword of Justice." In the other, she holds the scales that weigh all actions. She stands between the two pillars of Hermes and Solomon, representing Form and Force, black and white, Yin and Yang. In essence, the pillars represent duality. At her feet is a jackal, representing Anubis, God of the Underworld. In the Egyptian *Book of the Dead*, he is tasked with taking away the Souls of the impure individuals in the Hall of Truth. Their Souls are weighed against the feather of the Egyptian Goddess Maat, who tests for impurity. In this card, Anubis symbolizes the removal of any impure actions that are not of the Light and cause imbalance on the Tree of Life. In Wang's deck, the floor is checkered, referring to the black and white floor of the Golden Dawn Temple.

In the *Rider-Waite Tarot Deck*, similar imagery in the Justice card conveys the same ideas. However, the feminine figure is robed in red instead of green, and there is no jackal present. She wears a crown also, to represent her authority. All three decks feature different colours in the background, ranging from greens to greys, blues, and even violet-purple. The violet-purple in the *Rider-Waite Tarot Deck* is representative of the intuition necessary to perceive the truth in reality. There needs to be a balance between intuition and logic for the individual to be able to exact true justice.

The Hebrew letter attributed to this path is Lamed, meaning "ox goad"; the stick used to encourage the Beast to continue moving forward. In this case, The Beast is our Ego and the physical body. Justice is connected to the Fool card since the ox, the Ego, is prompted with the ox goad. The Ego is found in the Air Element of the Fool card. The ox goad nudges us to continue advancing along the path in a balanced way, moving ahead in a positive direction. It checks us when we stray from the desired path.

Libra's Zodiac sign is associated with this path, continually weighing and judging, just like its symbol, the scales. It is highly active, forming part of the Universal Laws. The virtue of Justice accompanies two of the other cardinal virtues found in the Major Arcana cards, those of the Temperance and Strength Tarot cards.

This path's significance is that it brings the power of Mars and its harsh, direct, and fierce judgement upon Tiphareth, the Seat of the Soul. Thus, it ensures that the whole Tree of Life is in balance and equilibrium. This path is constantly correcting an imbalance. For example, if you are imbalanced in your actions and are overly merciful, the Sword of Geburah will swing to the side of Severity. If you are excessively severe and tyrannical even, the Sword of Geburah will turn to the side of Mercy.

The metaphorical Sword cuts away any signs of imbalance in a martial, necessary fashion. Its action is similar to the pendulum—swinging back and forth in compensation for the opposing sides. It continues to do so until a balance is reached. At all times, the Sword of Geburah perpetuates harmony, equilibrium, and forward movement. It is often called the Sword of Justice since its purpose is to maintain what is just in the eyes of God-the Creator.

In a Divination, Justice is a Karmic card representing fairness, truth, law, balance, equilibrium, clarity, and cause and effect. When reversed, it implies imbalance, lack of equilibrium, unfairness, unaccountability, and dishonesty.

Figure 21: Keys of the Tarot (Twelve to Fifteen)

THE HANGED MAN

The Hanged Man is the Twelfth Key of the Tarot, and the Twenty-third Path of the Tree of Life, connecting Hod and Geburah. Its Magickal title is the "Spirit of the Mighty Waters," thus, the Water (Transitional) Element is attributed to it. The path of the Hanged Man is a path of self-sacrifice and the notion of the Divine death. It relates to the Dying-God narratives, including the myth of Osiris and the crucifixion of Jesus Christ. In both stories, the God figure goes through a death and rebirth process, becoming something greater than their past Self. In this sense, the metaphoric death is a mandatory step to allow for something new and better to be reborn.

"The Hanged Man is the Severity of Splendour, and the execution of judgement; Mars acting through Water upon Mercury." — S. L. MacGregor Mathers; "Notes on the Tarot"

The above quote describes the essence of the path of the Hanged Man. The exacting power of the Fire Element in Mars uses the unconditional love energy of the Water Element to affect the Sphere of Hod, the intellect. Self-sacrifice becomes an act of compassion, applied either to oneself or other human beings. This action in the name of the Higher Self brings about the emotional aspect of suffering, which the intellect interprets as an honourable gesture. In this way, the mind learns the value of such an act and performing it becomes a Divine obligation, knowing that through suffering, you renew yourself.

In the Golden Dawn Tarot decks, the central theme is a figure of a man hanging upside down from a tree, in the shape of the Hebrew letter Tav, the final letter of the Hebrew alphabet. In this case, the tree symbolises both the beginning and the end of the Universe. The man's legs are crossed, suggesting the Fylfot Cross, an allusion to Kether and the First Whirlings. His arms are crossed, portraying the inverted symbol of Sulfur and the fiery energy of Geburah that filters downwards on this path. The predominant colour is blue, representing the Water Element. His bodysuit is orange, alluding to Hod, the Sephira of the intellect.

The *Rider-Waite Tarot Deck* features the same elements in the card, the only difference being that the man's hands are tied behind his back instead of above his head. Also, a halo is depicted around his head, symbolizing the descent of Spirit into Matter through self-sacrifice. This connection to Spirit is also shown in the predominant colour of the card, which is light violet, representing Sahasrara, the Crown Chakra. This card is one of transformation and incarnation of God into a man—the Higher Self descending into the Lower Self. The man wears red pants, representing the physical body and human passions, while his shirt is blue, representative of the calmness in his emotions. The yellow around his halo and his shoes represent a keen intellect.

> *"Esoterically, the Hanged Man is the human Spirit which is suspended from Heaven by a single thread. Wisdom, not death, is the reward for this voluntary sacrifice during which the human Soul, suspended above the world of illusion, and meditating upon its unreality, is rewarded by the achievement of self-realization." — Manly P. Hall; excerpt from "The Secret Teachings of All Ages"*

Despite being hung upside down, the Hanged Man's face is calm and peaceful, suggesting transcendence without suffering. In this gesture, the joy one experiences from self-sacrifice is suggested, which is not meant to be a burden as it might be initially perceived. This sacrifice takes place above the "Waters of Mem," exalting the Hanged Man through unconditional love. Mem, one of the three Mother letters, is the Hebrew letter associated with this card, which means "water."

The Hanged Man represents the Baptism of Water, the Element of unconditional love. This path is one of Self-crucifixion, an intellectual undertaking that is necessary to reach from the mind in Hod into the Fire of Geburah. You cannot attain the higher realms of the Self and align with your True Will without taking this step of crucifying and sacrificing yourself—the Ego and its impetus for action. Through self-sacrifice, you attain self-realization.

The Hanged Man is a relevant card that is constantly in operation in the lives of individuals undergoing a Kundalini transformation process. As a Kundalini awakening is a transformation of the Self on many levels, self-sacrifice becomes a key component in building up the unconditional love energy within the Self. It is also a primary ingredient in building ethics and morals by continually perpetuating the transformation sought after by the Kundalini energy.

As you keep humbling yourself in the name of unconditional love, your Spirit becomes exalted, allowing you to grow out of your Ego and transform. On the other hand, if you do not practice Self-sacrifice in this regard, you will dwell and cling to the Ego, which will cause much Spiritual, mental, and emotional suffering.

In a Divination, the Hanged Man represents sacrifice, martyrdom, surrender, and release. It is a card of suffering that results in the person emerging wiser. When reversed, the Hanged Man represents selfishness, the fear of sacrifice, needless sacrifice, stalling, resistance, and indecision.

DEATH

Death is the Thirteenth Key of the Tarot, and the Twenty-fourth Path of the Tree of Life, connecting Netzach and Tiphareth. The Magickal Title of this card is the "Child of the Great Transformer." Death is a significant path when climbing the Tree of Life upwards through the reversed Path of the Flaming Sword. It is an initiation during which the personality (the Ego) willingly dies to transform into the Higher Self and attain knowledge. The key idea here is the notion of transformation, as Egocentric points of view are changed into purified thoughts. The Ego is subdued over time as the Higher Self takes over the mind, body, and Soul.

> *Death is the Sovereignty and result of Victory; Sol acting through Scorpio upon Venus, or Osiris under the destroying power of Typhon afflicting Isis."* — S. L. MacGregor Mathers; "Notes on the Tarot"

The above quote describes the energy of the Death card on the Tree of Life. Scorpio is often associated with death because of the power of the scorpion to kill with its sting. This death is a type of regeneration as the thoughts and emotions are transformed, considering that Scorpio is the Air of Water Sub-Element. Victory is attained when the desires of the Self are focused on Self-transformation. The Ego bars the way to the Higher Self; thus, a transformation must occur before the Spirit can descend into the Self.

Typhon and Apophis (in Greek) are other names associated with Set, Osiris' evil brother who killed him to take his throne as Pharaoh of Egypt. Isis was the one who "re-membered" Osiris after Set cut him up into pieces and spread them all across Egypt. Once Osiris' body was restored, their son Horus was conceived posthumously. Horus then went on to fight and defeat Set, thereby taking back the throne.

Set represents the Ego, the adversary, in the above story, also alluding to Satan (the Devil). The word "sunset" corresponds with Set as it symbolizes the disappearance of the Light and the arrival of darkness. Osiris represents the Soul and the Higher Self. Since the Ego is the Soul's adversary in life, Set (the Ego) tears up Osiris (the Soul) into pieces and takes his throne in the Kingdom. The Kingdom is the physical body, while the throne is the seat of consciousness. Set ruling the Kingdom is symbolic of the Ego overtaking the consciousness, thereby gaining control of the physical body.

As Isis represents the female polarity of the Higher Self, it is her love, faith and wisdom that restores Osiris, reincarnating him as his son Horus. One of life's lessons is that we must go through darkness to see the Light. As our Egos develop and eventually usurp the Self, we acquire knowledge and wisdom along our life's journey that makes us seek a Spiritual transformation.

Horus is symbolic of the Sun and has the same birthday as Jesus Christ—December 25. This date is right after the Winter Solstice, representing the time of the year when days begin to get longer as the Light of the Sun is in increase. Horus symbolizes the Light present within, the Soul—originating from the Sun. The Soul leads the way in life as the source of ultimate wisdom and understanding. Horus also symbolizes Cosmic Consciousness, which we are connected to inextricably. By taking responsibility for our Spiritual Evolution, we realize we must become our own Messiah. We must transform the Ego and our old thoughts and emotions so that we can reconnect with our Soul and Higher Self and evolve in consciousness.

Since the Death card path leads from Tiphareth to Netzach, the Planet Venus also plays a role in its mystery. Venus, the Light of the Morning Star, has been associated with Jesus Christ but also with Lucifer, the Light-Bearer. There is a misunderstanding in society concerning the nature of Lucifer as he has received a negative reputation over the ages. In essence, Lucifer is the initiate of the Mysteries of the Cosmos—at the beginning of their path towards Enlightenment. He is the "Light in the Darkness" and the desire to be something more significant—a Spiritually exalted Being.

In the Golden Dawn Tarot decks, the Ego is portrayed as dismembered, with a skeleton figure wielding the *Scythe of Saturn*, cutting away its limbs, and leaving them on the ground. The skeleton is that which alone survives the destructive power of time. It is the foundation upon which our biological structure is built. The physical body can then house our Soul and consciousness. The skeleton survives the changeability of Time and Space as nature works from below upwards. On the other hand, the Hanged Man represents the transmuting power of the Spirit working from above to below.

Death represents the dismemberment of the former Self and the transformation into the new Self—the central theme of this card. It is a vital step that must be undertaken of your own volition before reaching the higher Sephiroth on the Tree of Life. Before you can experience Resurrection and rebirth within Tiphareth, you must attain victory over Netzach and the lower desires. For everything in the Universe, the death of the old is the rebirth of the new. Energy cannot be destroyed; it can only be transformed into different forms. The predominant colour in the Golden Dawn Tarot decks is blue-green, the two dominant shades of the visible World of Matter.

In the *Rider-Waite Tarot Deck*, a different depiction is shown to convey the same idea. A skeleton in armour is riding a white horse. The skeleton figure, in this case, represents the *Grim Reaper*—a symbol of death. His armour indicates invincibility—signalling that no one can avoid or destroy death. The white horse is symbolic of purity since the purpose of death is to purify the old. Surrounding him are dead and dying people of all classes, including kings, bishops, and commoners. He is carrying a black flag with a white flower in the middle. The flower and the setting sun in the background are symbolic of the act of death being a transformation into something higher and of the Light.

In Ciceros' depiction of the Death card, the skeleton's spinal cord terminates as a snake on the ground, thus being symbolic of the Kundalini energy in its state of potential at the base of the spine in the coccyx region. The entire Kundalini awakening process is one directly related to the Death card. Its purpose is to transform the Ego to reach the vibration of the Higher Self. The dross and negativity slowly burn away through the intense fire that is built up with the Kundalini energy. It is the same concept as when you bring water to a boiling point through the application of fire (heat); you change its state and purify it through the evaporation of impurities. Purification of the Self is a process of perpetual transformation. Death is a necessary step to be undertaken for something new to be created—something pure.

The Hebrew letter Nun, meaning "fish," is associated with this card. It alludes to the fluidic, Watery nature of the path, as it is the emotions of the Ego that you must overcome before you can rise higher in consciousness. The water present in this card is the water of putrefaction. In Ciceros' version of the Tarot card, an image of the scorpion is displayed (alluding to the Scorpio Zodiac sign), while in Wang's version, an eagle is found instead. The eagle is representative of the Water Element in its purified state.

In a Divination, Death represents the ending of a cycle, a new beginning, change, metamorphosis, transformation, and transition. Death usually brings forth some fluctuation and pain, whether of a mental, emotional, or even physical nature. When reversed, the Death card represents resistance to change, holding on, and stagnation.

TEMPERANCE

Temperance is the Fourteenth Key of the Tarot, and the Twenty-fifth Path of the Tree of Life, connecting Yesod and Tiphareth. The Magickal Title of this card is the "Daughter of the Reconcilers, the Bringer forth of Life." Temperance depicts a balancing of the Four Elements and a play on duality. The Hebrew letter Samekh, which means "prop," is assigned to the card. The prop is the female figure in the image, Aima Elohim herself, in one of her many forms. She represents the Supernal Triad, the Eternal part of the Self, who acts like a prop—support.

"Temperance is the Beauty of its firm Basis; the Sovereignty of Fundamental Power; Sol acting through Sagittarius upon Luna." — S. L. MacGregor Mathers; "Notes on the Tarot"

The above quote describes the energy of the Temperance card. Sagittarius is the energy of the Water of Fire Sub-Element and therefore represents balance—the willpower balanced by unconditional love. Also, it is logic and reason balanced by emotions. By using the opposing parts of the Self constructively, we can cut through the illusion of the Moon to attain the truth of the Sun. Temperance is essentially the process of achieving this aim, which can only be accomplished by the conscious application of the Fire and Water Elements.

In the Golden Dawn Tarot decks, there is a giant figure of a woman clothed in a blue garment, balancing two vases of Fire and Water, with a Tattvic symbol of Earth on her chest. She stands with one foot in water and one on the Earth. In this card, we find a balance between the Water and Fire Elements while operating from the foundation of the Earth Element. The Elements, in this case, represent the creative mind and physical Matter. A volcano in the background and the Sun above her head symbolize different aspects of the Fire Element present—terrestrial and Solar. In addition, she has Archangel wings to represent the Air Element and transcendence in thought.

The Bow of Quesheth is shown in Ciceros' version of the card—formed out of the three lowest parts on the Tree of Life. It represents the ascending of Ego, or Lower Self found in Yesod, which seeks to achieve Spiritual Union with the Higher Self in Tiphareth. As such, this card is attributed to Sagittarius, the Archer. The pulling motion of the Bow of Quesheth requires the counterchanged forces of the Fire and Water Elements found in the opposing Shin and Qoph paths—Judgement and The Moon. They are held together by the restraining power of Saturn, located in the path of Tav (The Universe card) below Temperance. The path which crosses Temperance is the Tower. It contains the energies of Mars, which focus the conscious and subconscious forces found in Judgement and The Moon paths. The Temperance card features colours representing the Four Elements, such as blue, red, yellow and green.

In the *Rider-Waite Tarot Deck*, a similar image is displayed within the card, the main difference being that a square replaces the Tattwic symbol of Earth on her chest with a yellow triangle within it. The vases also aren't red and blue as in the Golden Dawn decks, but gold instead. Here is represented the dilution of wine with water, symbolic of temperance—one of the cardinal virtues. The colour scheme is also a little different, with the addition of a violet sky, representing the connection to the highest Chakra—Sahasrara, the Crown. It represents the Supernal Triad as well as the Higher Self.

There is a similarity found between the path of Temperance and the path of the Lovers. They both involve the conscious tempering of the positive and negative energies within the Self, allowing you to transcend higher in consciousness. This unity of the contending energies creates a balance in the Self, which yields a "Vision of Beauty" experienced in Tiphareth. In the instance of the Temperance card, it may result in a conversation with the Holy Guardian Angel—the Higher Self. Before this can occur, though, you must attain a high degree of control over your sexual, animalistic nature, found in Yesod. Since this path leads from the Lower to the Higher Self directly, it is known as the *Dark Night of the Soul*.

In a Divination, the Temperance card represents patience, balance, and moderation. It means a combination of energies and things coming together. When reversed, the Temperance card represents imbalance, impatience, excess, extreme behaviour, and a general clashing of energies or interests.

THE DEVIL

The Devil is the Fifteenth Key of the Tarot, and the Twenty-sixth Path of the Tree of Life, connecting Hod and Tiphareth. The Magickal Title of the card is the "Lord of the Gates of Matter, the Child of the Forces of Time." There is a strong sexual feeling in this path. It alludes to the lust and perversion represented in the story of Sodom and Gomorrah from the Old Testament. Sex for the mere sake of bodily pleasure is a binding force to the Gates of Matter through the vice of lust. The Devil card's purpose is to bind our Souls to the World of Matter by appealing to our bodily senses. The Devil then is Matter itself and its enticing qualities. The more we align to the World of Matter and see it as the only thing which is real, the more we will distance ourselves from the Spirit.

"The Devil is the Sovereignty and Beauty of Material (and therefore False) Splendour, Sol acting through Capricorn upon Mercury." — S. L. MacGregor Mathers; "Notes on the Tarot"

The above quote describes the essence of the path of the Devil on the Tree of Life. Splendour is achieved through conscious comprehension of the Spiritual reality by implementing logic and reason. Using logic and reason to accept the World of Matter as real would yield false Splendour. The Beauty which is attained is transient and not Soul fulfilling. In the Devil card, we must always question what is real and unreal, without accepting the material Universe as the ultimate truth, but merely a manifestation of something much Higher.

Capricorn, the Fire of Earth Sub-Element sign, is attributed to this path. As Capricorn is ruled by the Planet Saturn, it is connected to Binah. Hence, duality is present in this card, the higher and lower manifestation—the Above and the Below.

In the Golden Dawn Tarot decks, an immense figure representing the Devil stands on the black cubical altar of the Universe, with two naked humans, male and female, chained to it. They each have horns on their head, representing the influence of the Demonic or negative energy. Yet, they seem happy and content being where they are. The Devil's body signifies the Elements of the Physical Realm. The wings allude to the Air Element, the hairy legs to Earth, the eagle talons to Water, and the torch in his hand to Fire. The torch points toward the Earth, symbolizing the terrestrial Fire and manifestation.

There is a Fire burning in the Devil's groin area, alluding to the raw sexual power of this path. The Devil's head is in the shape of the inverted Pentagram, suggesting the dominance of Matter over Spirit—the Ego exalted over the Higher Self. The Devil holds a ram horn of Aries, symbolizing the martial, fierce energy he possesses. The predominant colours of the card are golden brown, brown, black, grey and indigo. All the colours relate to the darker aspects of the Earth in its static state. In Ciceros' Tarot deck, gold and riches are displayed in the background, representative of the illusory goals of our mundane, physical existence.

Almost identical imagery and similar colours are used in the *Rider-Waite Tarot Deck*. In this case, though, the Devil figure has ram horns on his head instead of holding the ram horn. He holds one hand up, displaying to the humans that he comes from Above, which is a lie and trickery on his part. The male human in the card has a flame on his tail, while the female has grapes on hers. These are symbols of raw passions and being intoxicated by the alluring quality of the material world. The colour is pure black in the background, representing Malkuth-the Earth.

The inspiration behind the Devil card is derived in part from Eliphas Levi's famous illustration of Baphomet from *Transcendental Magic: Its Doctrine and Ritual*. Baphomet is an idol of a Deity that the Knights Templar were said to have worshipped, which subsequently found its way into various occult and mystical traditions. It is a symbol of the equilibrium of opposites found in nature.

The Devil works with the Death card; as Death represents the transformation and transmutation of the Lower into the Higher, the Devil card represents the binding force of the Lower Self to the World of Matter. One is centrifugal, seeking change, while the other is centripetal, as it wants things to stay as they are. The Lower Self fears and hates the process of change, and thus, it continually intends to keep us bound to the World of Matter. But our Spiritual Evolution is dependent on the disintegration and renewal of the Life Force. Thus, as the Devil card pulls us in, the Death card renews and regenerates our overall Being.

At first glance, this is a very confusing card, usually mistaken for something evil or negative, considering that within Christianity, the Devil is recognized as the antithesis of God. However, what the card truly represents is simply materialism. The Devil is the representative and ruler of manifested Form. He is an illusion of the mind, though, and nothing more since our brains are also made up of Matter, allowing us to accept the reality around us (in the World of Matter) as being real.

As humans, we have a misconstrued perception of the world and our concept of reality. On the path of the Devil card, we must move beyond our illusion of what we perceive as reality. We must overcome the lens of the Ego if we are to rise to Tiphareth, the Sphere of Resurrection. In *The Sepher Yetzirah*, this is described as the Path of "Renewing Intelligence." We attain new insights and a fresh understanding of the Beauty contained in Tiphareth by understanding the Devil card.

The Hebrew letter Ayin is associated with this path, meaning "eye." It alludes to the inner Mind's Eye having a clearer vision than that of the two physical eyes. In Ciceros' Tarot deck, the Devil figure has a large third eye on his forehead to refer to this mystery.

In the context of the Kundalini awakening, we aim to overcome the energy of the Devil, the binding of the Lower Self to the World of Matter through sex and bodily pleasures. The eyes are that which perceive the material world, which is the antithesis of the Spiritual World. Therefore, we must use the Mind's Eye, the singularity, to overcome the duality of the physical eyes.

As the Devil card signifies materialism, it represents the illusion of the manifested World of Matter. This world contains within itself the duality of good and evil. If we turn to the manifest world, it becomes evil since it is a false reality—a matrix. If we turn to the Spiritual aspect embodying all things, it becomes good since it feeds the Soul.

Throughout the Kundalini awakening, we learn to overcome Matter and attune to the Spirit. The Devil then becomes the great tempter because he appeals to the Ego and its needs and wants. Thus, we must always seek to overcome the Devil and the Ego, and this lesson is a test that we deal with daily. In overcoming it, we further our Spiritual Evolution.

In a Divination, the Devil card represents materialism, excessive sexual behaviour, addiction, obsession, and the Lower Self-the Ego. When reversed, the Devil card represents freedom, restoring control, detachment, and releasing limiting beliefs. Interestingly, the Devil is one of the few positive cards when reversed since it means overcoming the Material Realm in some way.

THE TOWER

The Tower is the Sixteenth Key of the Tarot, and the Twenty-seventh Path of the Tree of Life, connecting Hod and Netzach. The Magickal Title of this card is the "Lord of the Host of the Mighty." The card's main image is a Tower, symbolizing the programmed beliefs that we have about ourselves and the world around us. These beliefs have shaped our perception through childhood and into adulthood, under the influence of our parents, teachers, friends, and social institutions. In the same way, the Tower was built brick by brick. Our ego defends the Tower at all costs in adulthood, protecting its identity and belief structure. Thus, the destruction of the Tower represents the destruction of our old beliefs and concepts of reality. Only by destroying the old do we create room for something new to grow in its place.

Figure 22: Keys of the Tarot (Sixteen to Nineteen)

> *"The Tower is the Victory over Splendour; Venus acting through Mars upon Mercury; Avenging force."* — S. L. MacGregor Mathers; "Notes on the Tarot"

The above quote describes the essence of the path of the Tower on the Tree of Life. Victory represents the desire to attain a higher reality. It overtakes the intellect (represented by Mercury) since the mind uses logic and reason to rationalize why things should stay the same. The Ego uses intelligence to glorify itself. It seeks continuity in things staying as they are, thereby fearing change. Venus (the emotions) uses the power of Mars (the destructive Fire energy) to avenge itself and become renewed. If the intellect is predominant, the feelings suffer as they stay the same. The application of the Fire Element is necessary for there to be purging and purification of thoughts and emotions, which will result in the renewal and change in belief systems. Thought predates emotion, which over time forms habits, which eventually create a belief system.

In the Golden Dawn Tarot decks, a red flash of lightning is depicted, striking the Tower, indicating sudden realization or illumination. In an instant, the old realities and belief structures are changed forever. The lightning bolt signifies the powers of Mars and Geburah in action, as it destroys outdated beliefs and realities. Red is the predominant colour in the card, which represents Mars, Geburah, and the Fire Element. Brown is present to depict the terrestrial component since our beliefs are a part of our life in Malkuth, the Physical World. Yellow is shown to represent the Spiritual component as well as the Air Element, which are the thoughts that need to be renewed. And finally, the grey in the card connects us to the power of Chokmah—the Higher Self and our True Will.

The Crown at the top of the Tower is Kether, which is cut off by the lightning bolt. It symbolizes our mind opening up to new influences from Above that will replace the old influences Below. The card depicts people falling out of the Tower to express the old beliefs falling away. Many Tarot scholars say that these people represent the Kings of Edom who ruled in the land of Edom before a king ruled the people of Israel. Desolation and terror marked their reign, hence their other name, the "Lords of Chaos." Our role is to extricate them from the Tower, symbolically, thereby removing all unwanted, negative influences from our belief systems. On the right-hand side is the Tree of Life with ten Sephiroth, representing Light, while on the left-hand side is a Tree of Life with eleven Sephiroth, alluding to Daath, and the realm of the Qlippoth—the Demonic, dark Realm.

The *Rider-Waite Tarot Deck* features the same imagery, but instead of the different versions of the Tree of Life, the Hebrew letter Yod is used, with eleven Yods on the left and ten on the right. Yod is representative of the Primal Fire as the first letter of the Tetragrammaton, YHVH—Jehovah of the Hebrews. The colours here are different also, with black and grey predominating, representing the influence of Chokmah and Binah—Wisdom and Understanding. But also, the black is representative of Malkuth-the Earth.

The path of the Tower is the path of the destruction of limiting beliefs and old realities. Following this destruction, new creation, new ideas, new beliefs, and an overall new reality comes about. More and more aspects of the Higher Self are revealed in this new reality. This path balances the conflict between Hod and Netzach, the mind and the emotions. You have to have both in harmony to aspire to and attain the Higher Self.

The process of inner growth can be rather painful at times, as it requires us to shed our skin of what we once believed about the world around us and ourselves.

In the context of the Kundalini awakening, the Tower card is essential—it represents the constant purging of old realities and beliefs once the inner Fire of the Kundalini is released. Daily, this Fire burns away at impurities, both mental and emotional, and puts us in a constant state of renewal—a state of Becoming. Through this renewal, we rise in consciousness and align with the Higher Self.

The Hebrew letter Peh is associated with the path of the Tower, meaning "mouth." The mouth is the vessel of language and vibration. It represents the spoken Word, the most powerful tool and asset of the Magus, allowing communication with the Divine. Through the Word, realities are created and destroyed. Peh references the *Tower of Babel* story, which has a central theme around the limitations of language and the confusion that it can bring to the people.

In a Divination, the Tower card represents sudden change, revelation, and awakening to new ideas or thoughts. It implies the destruction of the old, for something new to take its place. When reversed, the Tower card represents the fear of change and clinging to old realities and ways of life.

THE STAR

The Star is the Seventeenth Key of the Tarot and the Twenty-eighth Path of the Tree of Life, which traverses from Yesod to Netzach. The Star's Magickal Title is the "Daughter of the Firmament, the Dweller between the Waters." The critical notion on this path is that of meditation, which is the conscious act of looking for the Divine Light. It requires the use of imagination and knowledge to undertake. The Astral personality of the Self uses the three lower Sephiroth of Yesod, Hod and Netzach to engage in meditation. Meditation reveals intuition, as the "fish hook" of the Hebrew letter Tzaddi is thrown into the Waters of Creation and pure consciousness to catch a glimmer of Divine Knowledge. The activity of meditation involves making the mind still. It seeks to draw the Divine Light into the Self from Cosmic Consciousness.

"The Star is the Victory of Fundamental Strength; Venus acting through Aquarius upon Luna; Hope." — S. L. MacGregor Mathers; "Notes on the Tarot"

The above quote describes the energy of the path of the Star on the Tree of Life. The regenerative power of Venus, through Aquarius (the Air of Air Sub-Element), acts on the illusory nature of the Moon. Venus applies the intuitive, Spiritual energy of Aquarius on the Moon to cut through illusion and get to the truth. A transformation occurs, and the Divine Light pours in since truth is of the vibratory frequency of the Higher Self. Connecting to the Holy Guardian Angel results in Divine information download, otherwise called Gnosis.

In the Golden Dawn Tarot decks, a feminine figure is depicted in this card, representative of the Great Feminine—Isis, Shekinah, and Mother Mary. She is the same figure as in the Empress and the High Priestess cards. However, in the Star card, she is wholly unveiled, as she is in a lower state of manifestation. The Star card implies that the Great Feminine is more easily accessible through the conscious act of meditation. She is seen holding two opposing vases, pouring the Waters of Life (pure, fluid consciousness), forming a river at her feet. These vases are attributed to the Primal Water and Primal Fire Elements—Binah and Chokmah. These Waters pour endlessly as they receive a constant energy supply from the Star of Venus above her head.

In Wang's version of the Tarot card, one foot is in water and another on land. Seven other stars surround the central Star, further alluding to Venus, since the number seven is the Sephira Netzach, corresponding with Venus. As Venus is a transformative, regenerative Planet, here it represents the transformation of the mind of the initiate through the act of meditation.

The Tree of Life and the Tree of the Knowledge of Good and Evil are portrayed behind the feminine figure. Here is implied that the setting of the Star card is the Garden of Eden—the source of the Waters of Life and Creation. In both Golden Dawn versions of the card, an Ibis bird sits atop one of the trees. The Ibis bird alludes to Thoth of the Egyptians, who is also Hermes/Mercury, the representative of the Divine Wisdom and thought. As mentioned, Aquarius is attributed to the path of the Star. Aquarius is the Zodiac of the "man," and its attribution to the Star alludes to the new Adam Kadmon, Resurrected after the Fall from the Garden of Eden.

The predominant colours in the card are violet-purple, green, and blue. The violet-purple refers to the transcendent, mystical energy present when one meditates since this colour relates to the Mind's Eye Chakra, Ajna. The green refers to the regenerative power of nature and of Venus. The blue refers to the Sea of Consciousness, while yellow is found in the Star of Venus. Since Venus represents love, this implies that the act of meditation is essentially an act of love.

In the *Rider-Waite Tarot Deck*, similar imagery is used, with the absence of the dominant violet-purple colour, replaced by a sky blue. One vase pours water on the land, while another in the water. Here is implied that the Waters of Creation can be found in both the Water and Earth Elements. Also, only one Tree is present, with a mountain in the background, representing the lofty heights of consciousness that can be attained.

As the Star is part of the Astral personality triad, it holds illusory Forms received from Yesod, the Moon. To align the Lower Self of the Astral triangle to the vibrations of the Higher Self, you must use both intuition and meditation, allowing the Divine Light to pour into your mind and raise your consciousness.

In a Divination, the Star card represents rejuvenation, hope, faith, renewal, and Spirituality. When reversed, it means the lack of faith, despair, and a disconnect with the Spirit.

THE MOON

The Moon is the Eighteenth Key of the Tarot, and the Twenty-ninth Path of the Tree of Life, connecting Malkuth and Netzach. The Moon's Magickal Title is the "Ruler of Flux and Reflux, the Child of the Sons of the Mighty." This path is known as the "Corporeal Intelligence," responsible for the formation of all bodies since it links the physical body with emotions. It is a highly sexual path, with lust, fantasy, and illusions, as it uses the Light of the Moon to reflect your desires onto you. The Moon card is best described as the subconscious, the area of the Self which projects fear and fear-based activities. The Hebrew letter Qoph is attributed to this path, literally meaning the "back of the head."

"The Moon is the Victory of the material; Venus acting through Pisces upon the Cosmic Elements; the deceptive effect of the apparent power of the Material Forces." — S. L. MacGregor Mathers; "Notes on the Tarot"

The above quote describes the essence of the path of the Moon on the Tree of Life. As the desires of Venus act through the Pisces Zodiac sign (Water of Water Sub-Element) on the physical body, they form instinctual emotions. The apparent power of the World of Matter has an alluring quality, whereby the consciousness is deceived by its forms, perceiving them as real. This lie, this illusion of reality, affects the lower emotions of the Astral World, creating fear deep within the subconscious mind. Fear then becomes that which binds the consciousness to the World of Matter. Overcoming fear is the first step in the journey towards Enlightenment.

In the Golden Dawn Tarot decks, two dogs are depicted standing on the land on opposite sides of a path. They serve to intimidate and scare the crayfish coming out of the water and onto the path. This path traverses through the two towers of Chesed and Geburah (Mercy and Severity), located on opposite sides. The crayfish begins its path of evolution, coming out of the Primal Waters of Creation, symbolizing the progression of all physical forms of life. As its consciousness is at a low level, it aims to evolve. It desires to rise out of the darkness and into the Light.

The Moon is above, waxing on the side of Chesed. There are four symbols of the Hebrew letter Yod falling from the Moon to the Earth. Here is implied a reference to the Four Worlds of the Qabalah and Primal Fire as the guiding force of the crayfish. The True Will seeks to evolve in consciousness so that it can perceive the boundlessness of the Light and Cosmic Consciousness. The Moon has sixteen primary and sixteen secondary rays, representing the permutations of the Four Elements and the duality of each. The Elements have to be purified within the Self to remove fear from the energy system.

It is important to note that the whole scene of the Moon card takes place at night since nighttime is when the Moon acts on the Earth and creates many illusions. The night also is the absence of the Light of the Sun and truth. The Moon card is a path of "blood and tears" in which fear and illusion and weakness of mind, body, and Soul must be overcome. It represents the life of the imagination, which is apart from the Spirit, hence creating the illusion. The predominant colours of the card are crimson, plum, and dark shades of blue, representing the water and the sky. The pale green of the Earth is present as well in the card.

In the *Rider-Waite Tarot Deck*, similar imagery is shown. The only difference is that the waxing Moon has fifteen letter Yods instead of four, further asserting the guiding power of the Primal Fire Element. The colours also are less pale in comparison to the Golden Dawn decks. The sky is light blue, although the scene is meant to be at night. There is a wolf and a dog, representing our animal nature. One is civilized, while the other is wild and ferocious.

The illusion of reality occurs once the Soul and individual consciousness are embedded into Matter. Once a Soul is born into this world, its consciousness accepts reality as what the physical senses can perceive. Over time, the Ego develops to shelter and protect the illusion of the Self as being the body. The Ego asserts that we are a separate component from the outside world. It then becomes necessary to evolve the consciousness back to the Source from whence it came, to liberate the Soul. The Moon Tarot card represents the beginning point of this journey.

The Moon card is the counterpart of the Sun card, whose Hebrew letter is Resh, meaning "head." Therefore, we have the subconscious mind of the Moon and the conscious mind of the Sun. The subconscious is the area of illusion—since the Moon only reflects the Light of the Sun. The Sun, on the other hand, projects the true Light. Therefore, there are no illusions present in the Sun, only the truth.

As Pisces rules the Moon card, it represents the deepest of the deep in the Water Element and the involuntary, instinctual emotions. On this card's path, you are faced with the subconscious content of your mind, the phantoms, illusory forms, and "skeletons in the closet", whose location is literally in the back of your head. This content consists of repressed memories and negative experiences that have been pushed away deep into your subconscious mind. The darkness is the ruler by night on this path, while the Sun rules by day. While travelling the path of the Moon, you must learn to overcome your fear of the night and the darkness and face and examine it directly, awaiting the sunrise.

In the context of the Kundalini awakening, the Moon card is the first path you encounter once you have had a full and permanent awakening. Darkness overtakes you as a bridge is formed between the conscious and subconscious minds through the influx of Kundalini energy. All fear and anxieties come out in "real-time" to be subdued as this happens. Astral Light, which is Lunar in quality, enflames your inner Being, exposing your fears and Demons and bringing them to the surface. It then becomes imperative to overcome your negativity to evolve Spiritually. This Astral Light, the Moon current, is brought into you through the Ida Nadi.

In a Divination, the Moon card represents illusions, the subconscious mind, fear, anxiety, and deception. When reversed, it means the release of fear, confusion, intuition, and overcoming deceit and illusion.

THE SUN

The Sun is the Nineteenth Key of the Tarot, and the Thirtieth Path of the Tree of Life, connecting Hod and Yesod. The Magickal Title of the card is the "Lord of the Fire of the World." It is the path of the Sun that reconciles the Divine aspect of the Self with the animal aspect. The Sun Planet is attributed to this path. Although considered as one of the Seven Ancient Planets in the Qabalistic framework, the Sun is, in fact, the central Star of our Solar System that all the other Planets within our Solar System revolve around.

> *"The Sun is The Splendour of a Firm Basis; Mercury acting through the Sun upon the Moon."* — S. L. MacGregor Mathers; "Notes on the Tarot"

The above quote describes the essence of the path of the Sun on the Tree of Life. Mercury imparts intelligence through the Light of the Sun, upon the foundation of the world—the Astral component of reality, represented by the Moon. Splendour is achieved as all living Astral forms are animated by the Light, which becomes accessible through the mind.

In the Golden Dawn Tarot decks, the card shows a boy and a girl, naked, holding hands, with one of them on the land and one in the water. The Sun shines above them, with twelve rays emanating from it. One-half of the rays are projected as wavy lines to represent vibration, while the other half are straight lines, which represent radiation. Together, the rays symbolize the masculine and feminine energies, as do the boy and the girl. Behind the boy and girl is a wall built out of many individual stones, representing the circle of the Zodiac that contains the children, keeping them bound under its influence. Once the children have increased in knowledge and intellectual capabilities, they will be able to climb over the wall. In other words, they will be able to overcome the Zodiacal energy influences on them.

There are seven Hebrew Yods on each side of the Sun, representing the influence of Primal Fire of the Father, Chokmah, descending onto the Earth through the Sun—his offspring (Son). The number seven represents the seven Planets and their powers. There are ten flowers on the ground, representing the ten Sephiroth of the Tree of Life. In Wang's deck, they are all on the Earth, while in Ciceros' deck, five are on the Earth while the other five are in the water.

The children represent the passive Elements of Water and Earth, while the Sun and the descending Yods represent the active Elements of Air and Fire. Thus, all Four Elements are present in this path. The predominant colours are sky blue, representing the Air Element; the yellow/orange Sun, representing the Fire Element; the green Earth, representing the Earth Element; and the blue water, representing the Water Element. The wall is grey, symbolising Chokmah and the circle of the Zodiac.

In the *Rider-Waite Tarot Deck*, slightly different imagery is portrayed. Only one male child is present, naked, riding a white horse. Sunflowers are in the background, and the child holds a red flag, representing the blood of renewal. The Sun is anthropomorphized as it is smiling, hinting at achievement. The card's imagery asserts that the conscious mind and intellect have overtaken the fears and illusions of the subconscious mind. As the child discovers a new mode of functioning, its innocence is renewed, bringing hope for the future. The predominant colour is yellow, red, white, and grey.

The Zodiac is highly influential on a person in terms of their character and personality throughout their life. While creating a person's Birth Chart, the Astrologers use the Zodiacal energies from the Sun to produce it. Thus, this path is known as the "Collecting Intelligence." It is best described as the intellectual energy or the thought process, and it is the first path of the Astral Triangle of the initiate's personality. This path creates a connection from Yesod—the Astral foundation of all Matter, to Hod—the mind and the intellect.

The Hebrew letter, Resh, meaning "head," is attributed to the path of the Sun card, which is the conscious mind that assimilates information and knowledge from the environment. The personality then uses this information to seek a reality higher than that of the Material Realm. Since Resh is a double letter, it has a double meaning, relating to what happens when you get too much Sun—it burns and scorches the Earth. As such, a necessary balance between the intellect (mind) and the emotions is implied in this path.

The myth of Icarus flying too close to the Sun and burning his wings exemplifies what happens if we are not careful with the Sun's energy. It must be approached with reverence and humility if we are to benefit from its power.

In terms of the Kundalini awakening, this path is the intelligence which is enhanced and evolving as the awakened individual receives the influx of the Kundalini Light, the very Light of the Sun itself, through the Pingala Nadi. It is not only the intelligence that evolves through the Kundalini awakening but also the character concerning speaking the truth, as it becomes a way of life naturally over time.

"There is no religion higher than truth." — H. P. Blavatsky; excerpt from "The Key to Theosophy"

Jesus Christ referred to himself as the Light of the World, and he was called the Son(Sun) of God. His twelve disciples were a symbolic representation of a higher truth contained in Jesus' overall teachings. Jesus was the central Sun, the Star of our Solar System, and the twelve disciples corresponded to the Twelve Zodiac—the other Stars in our Milky Way Galaxy. He was a Solar Deity, and his message was that the Sun is the highest representation of the Creator-God, and as such, we don't need any other Gods but him. Thus, his teaching was monotheistic. We are all Sons of the Sun (or daughters), as he was since we are all of the Light.

Jesus' teachings are a way of life, and their basis is unconditional love and compassion, which are qualities of the Light. To attain the Kingdom of God, which is Christ (Cosmic) Consciousness, we must become Resurrected (transformed) through the Holy Spirit. Only then can we walk in truth and embrace our true nature.

"I am the Light of the World; he that followeth me shall not walk in darkness, but shall have the Light of life." — "The Holy Bible" (John 8:12)

The Sun is the source of our Souls since our Souls are sparks of Light from the Sun. As mentioned before, the Ancients called the Sun "Sol," which may be the origin of the word "Soul." It cannot be a coincidence that the pronunciation is the same since coincidences don't exist if you are a student of the mysteries of the Cosmos. Every cause has an effect, and every effect has a cause, which runs like a chain, with every link being a past event that influenced some future event.

There is a correspondence between "Soul," "Sol," and another word with the same pronunciation—"sole," referring to the soles of the feet. The soles connect the human being to the Earth through the force of gravity.

We are all inextricably linked to the consciousness of the Earth, and the Earth itself has an Aeon, a vital force, an Auric body (field), to which we are connected.

Our Souls are attached to the Sun through our central core, our Solar Plexus—the Tiphareth Sephira. The Minor Chakras at the soles of our feet also connect our Souls to the Earth Aeon. Therefore, human beings are the connecting link between the Sun and the Earth, the Father and the Mother—via our consciousness. The whole operation is, in essence, an expression of the One thing, and that thing is God-the Creator, who is responsible for all of Creation. In Hermeticism, this operation is expressed through the axiom of "As Above, So Below."

In a Divination, the Sun card represents joy, happiness, success, vitality, warmth, optimism, and fun. When reversed, it represents sadness, negativity, being overly optimistic, and depression in general.

Figure 23: Keys of the Tarot (Twenty and Twenty-One)

JUDGEMENT

Judgement is the Twentieth Key of the Tarot, and the Thirty-first Path of the Tree of Life, connecting Hod and Malkuth. The Magickal name of this card is the "Spirit of the Primal Fire," thus, the Fire (Transitional) Element is attributed to it. Judgement is best described as a Baptism of the Fire Element. This card relates to the highest Cosmic expression of the Fire Element and the Spirit energy. Shin is the Hebrew letter associated with this path, meaning "tooth," alluding to the breaking down of food and its transformation into useable energy. The letter Shin also is called the "Three-Fold Flame of the Soul." The three flames that it alludes to are the three types of Fire—Solar, Astral, and Volcanic (Terrestrial).

"Judgement is the Splendour of the Material World; Mercury acting through Fire upon the Cosmic Elements." — S. L. MacGregor Mathers; "Notes on the Tarot"

The above quote describes the energy of the path of Judgement on the Tree of Life. The Divine Spirit descends from Binah and the Black Pillar of Form, through Hod, into Malkuth-the Earth. Thus, all things within the World of Matter contain a Spiritual counterpart, and the mind becomes the connecting link between Spirit and Matter.

In the Golden Dawn Tarot decks, the Judgement card features four naked figures in the water, receiving the Holy Fire from above, where Archangel Michael is seen blowing a trumpet with a white flag and a red cross on it. The trumpet radiates an influx of Spirit energy into the physical forms of the four figures. This image signifies the Judgement Tarot card as an act of initiation into the Holy Fire, with Archangel Michael serving as the initiator. The Fire triangle is also present in the card to further emphasize this idea. Each of the figures in the card is being charged by the Spirit energy coming from Michael's trumpet.

The land, the sea, the air, and the Sun are present within the Judgement card, representing the Four Elements. Two of the figures are beside one another, symbolizing the dual nature of the Astral Light. One figure represents Volcanic Fire, while the other two represent Astral Fire. Archangel Michael represents the Solar Fire. The central character has his back turned and is giving the Sign of the Theoricus, the grade of the Sephira Yesod within the Golden Dawn Order. He stands in an open coffin, representing Lazarus, rising from the dead. He is the initiate once he has climbed up to the level of Hod on the Tree of Life, as he receives the energy of the other three figures in the card. The colours of the Four Elements are found in the card, which include red, blue, yellow, and brown.

In the *Rider-Waite Tarot Deck*, similar imagery is depicted, with the main difference being that there are not only four naked figures but six of them. They are of a greyish complexion as they stand with arms spread, looking up at the Angel above them in awe. The Angel could be Michael, but he may also be Metatron since Metatron is related to the Spirit Element. Some of the figures emerge from graves with huge mountains or tidal waves in the background. Here may be a reference to the sea giving up its dead on the Last Day of Judgement, as described in the *Book of Revelation* in the New Testament of *The Holy Bible*. The entire scene is said to be modelled after the Christian Resurrection before the Last Judgement.

The Judgement card's path brings the experience of the Spiritual energy as it descends into Matter. It is an awakening to the Spirit and the presence of the Divine. Shin's Fire is a consecrating Fire that endlessly burns away the impurities of the body, mind, and Soul, leaving only the balanced and purified energy to remain.

When ascending the Tree of Life from Malkuth (through Ceremonial Magick), this card represents the first path off the Pillar of Balance since the Middle Pillar is self-balancing. All paths not on the Pillar of Balance (Middle Pillar) are supposed to be balanced by their opposites.

In terms of the Kundalini, the letter Shin is the direct representation of its energy. The three strokes on the letter stand for the three main Nadis or channels in the Kundalini awakening. Pingala, the masculine Nadi, relates to Solar Fire as the Light and the Father energy. In contrast, Ida, the feminine Nadi, relates to Astral Fire as the Sea of Consciousness and the Mother energy. Finally, Sushumna, the central Nadi (or channel) going along the human spine, is the Volcanic or Terrestrial Fire. It is the Earth as the offspring of the Father and Mother. Sushumna is Matter and the Physical Universe which regulates Light energy and consciousness.

The three strokes of the letter Shin also represent the Elements of Fire and Water, with Air as their reconciler. Therefore, it relates to the Hexagram, or Star of David, and the influx of the Holy Spirit in Christianity. Hence, Shin is considered initiatory energy since the Holy Spirit/the Kundalini Fire initiates the aspirant into something greater than themselves. The Kundalini Fire expands the consciousness and aligns the individual with their Higher Self—the part of them that is of the Godhead.

In a Divination, Judgement represents a Spiritual awakening, initiation, rebirth, inner calling, or a conclusion or decision that has to be made. When reversed, it means ignoring "the call," inner doubt, avoiding making decisions, and being too hard on yourself in general.

THE UNIVERSE

The Universe is the Twenty-First Key of the Tarot, and the Thirty-second Path of the Tree of Life, connecting Yesod and Malkuth. The Magickal Title of the card is the "Great One of the Night of Time." This path is the starting point of the Inner World, the Astral Plane, and it is named the Universe because it is a direct reflection of the outer Universe and all the components which comprise it—As Above, So Below.

"The Universe is the Foundation of the Cosmic Elements and of the Material World; Luna acting through Saturn upon the Elements." — S. L. MacGregor Mathers; "Notes on the Tarot"

The above quote describes the essence of the path of the Universe on the Tree of Life. The reflective power of Luna (the Moon) acts through Saturn (the Planet of Karma and Time) on the Earth Element and the World of Matter. As such, a reflection of the material Universe in Astral Form is created. The Astral Plane is the beginning point of going inwards and scaling the Tree of Life and its various, progressive states of consciousness. As the reflection of the Sun's Light, your thoughts are the medium of experiencing the Astral Plane and all the subsequent Planes above it. Negative Karmic energy you have accumulated over time is to be encountered in the Astral Plane, personified by personal Demons.

In the Golden Dawn Tarot decks, the woman depicted in the card is the Great Mother of Binah, with a crescent Moon on her head. She is a symbolic form of the Great Feminine—Isis, Aima Elohim, and Mother Mary. She holds the two double-headed wands of power in her hands, representing the positive and negative currents. She is primarily nude, with a scarf covering one side of her body. Her legs form a cross, symbolic of the Hebrew Letter Tav, to which this path is attributed. She serves as the doorway to life and death, Eternity and mortality, Spirit and Matter. She also represents the womb of all Creation, the Great Sea of Binah—pure, undifferentiated consciousness.

The Twelve Zodiac are portrayed in the card and the four *Cherubim* that represent the Four Elements—the man, the eagle, the bull, and the lion. Seventy-two stars adorn the Zodiac, representing the seventy-two fold name of God, the *Shemhamphorash*. A Seven-Pointed Heptagram or Star is present in the image, alluding to the Seven Palaces of Assiah—the Seven Ancient Planets. The Planet attributed to the Universe card is Saturn. To the Ancients, Saturn represented the confines of our Solar System since they had no means of measuring what lays beyond it. As such, the Universe card represents everything between the Planet Saturn and us. The background colour in the card is indigo, the colour of Saturn.

In the *Rider-Waite Tarot Deck*, the Universe card is called "The World." It is a fitting name since the Universe card represents the Astral duplicate of the World of Matter that we all partake in. Also, this card relates to the Physical World that we live in, where we commence our journey inward and upwards on the Tree of Life.

Similar imagery is portrayed in the *Rider-Waite Tarot Deck*, where a naked woman holds two wands and is covered by a scarf. The four Cherubim are in each of the four corners of the card. Instead of the Twelve Zodiac, a green wreath is depicted, symbolising Eternity and the unending circle of life. The background is sky blue instead of indigo, as in the Golden Dawn versions of this card.

The Hebrew Letter Tav is attributed to this path, and as it is the twenty-second letter of the Hebrew alphabet, it is the last letter. It means "cross," relating to the crossroads of leaving the Outer World of Matter to enter the inner Cosmic Planes.

The Astral Plane is the first of the Cosmic Planes to be encountered when going inwards. As it is the first path on the Tree of Life working upwards, it is like entering the Underworld, where we experience all the lowest forms of the Self. And since Tav, the last Hebrew letter, relates to the first Hebrew letter Aleph, it implies an association with the Fool card and the lack of experience and knowledge to discern between what is real and what isn't upon entering the Astral Plane.

In the beginning, you are given all of the keys of the Universe—the Twelve Zodiac, the Seven Ancient Planets, and the Four Elements. However, like an innocent child from the Fool card, you don't know what to do with these keys just yet. Therefore, you must ascend the Tree of Life and learn its lessons to use the keys with both wisdom and understanding.

In the context of the Kundalini awakening process, you are vaulted through the Universe card into the Astral World with the influx of the Astral Light, which bridges the conscious and subconscious minds. The Astral Light is brought in by the Kundalini energy. Therefore, every Kundalini initiate must begin with this path; it is the entryway to the Astral World and the beginning of the inward journey in exploring the Tree of Life.

Since this path represents the Astral Plane, it contains many shadows, ghosts, and repressed memories that we must confront before ascending the Tree of Life further. It offers a valuable lesson in balance and discrimination since we require both of these qualities to move ahead on our Spiritual journeys.

In a Divination, the Universe card represents completion, integration, fulfilment, harmony, and travel. It can also mean success and the end of a matter. When reversed, the Universe represents seeking closure, incompletion, disharmony, delays, and short-cuts.

***

Knowledge of the Tarot offers Universal Spiritual lessons that are beneficial for any individual concerned with their Spiritual progression. Furthermore, these lessons relate to all humanity since every human has their Tree of Life that regulates the expression of their various energies and consciousness. Thus, Tarot cards are the keys to Universal wisdom and the workings of your inner psyche.

Use the descriptions of each Tarot card as a meditative tool that you can refer back to often to gain the best understanding of this subject. These lessons will require a lot of revisiting to assimilate knowledge correctly and gain wisdom.

On the surface, these Tarot cards and their cryptic meanings may seem overwhelming and challenging to comprehend. Remember, the mind works like a filing cabinet; therefore, try to commit as much of this knowledge to memory. Once you have filed away the Qabalistic correspondences, numbers, and symbols of each Tarot card, you will start to understand at a deep level the meanings associated with each of them. Your memory belongs to the highest manifested Sphere of Chesed which borders on the Abyss of the Mind. Your Higher Self from the Supernals can reach into your consciousness and teach you through Gnosis once you have memorized enough information on the Major Arcana.

The purpose of the Tarot is to bring you one step closer to Enlightenment. If you dedicate yourself to learning the Tarot's mysteries, you will make profound changes to your mind, body, and Soul, furthering your Great Work. In essence, unity with the Higher Self, otherwise called the Holy Guardian Angel in the Qabalistic tradition, is the overall aim of the Great Work. This unity will bring forth Enlightenment—to be In-Light.

SCRYING THE TAROT

A powerful method of obtaining Gnosis from the Major Arcana Tarot cards is through "scrying." Scrying comes from the English word "descry," which means "to make out faintly" or to "reveal." Scrying is a form of Divination. It is a process of gaining Spiritual insight into a particular subject through supernatural means. This practice has been around for thousands of years, and all Ancient traditions practised it in one form or another.

Scrying requires using a scrying tool or medium, which includes Crystals, mirrors, stones, water, fire, and even smoke. The purpose of these items is to draw in your consciousness and activate and focus on your Mind's Eye Chakra so that you can channel information from Higher Realms through it, usually in the form of visions.

In the case of the Tarot, we will be using the Major Arcana cards as scrying tools. To perform the Tarot scrying method correctly, you should purchase a Tarot deck if you don't already have one. I highly recommend any of the three Hermetic Tarot decks mentioned so far, but any Tarot deck will suffice for this particular task.

Isolate the Major Arcana cards from the Tarot deck and pick one of the twenty-two cards you wish to scry. Hold the card approximately 12" to 14" inches away from you and start gazing at the card's image. Unfocus your eyes slightly while staring intently at the card. It will allow you to use your Mind's Eye during this process and for your consciousness to become completely absorbed and immersed within the Tarot card's image. Examine each detail of the card, including number patterns, symbols, and unique colours. Try not to rationalize what you are looking at but instead allow the images to speak to you while keeping an empty mind. Do this exercise for 3-5 minutes and focus on not letting any thoughts enter and break your concentration.

Very often, you will receive visions during your scrying session. It is not uncommon for the images you are gazing at to animate themselves right before your eyes. Even though they might appear random, these visions will correspond somehow with the theme and meaning behind the Tarot card you are scrying. In most cases, though, it takes a little bit of time for the symbols within each card to become embedded within your subconscious mind, which means that they will most likely communicate to you through your dreams. This communication is usually in the form of revelatory dreams with themes and images that tell some story that is influenced by the energy of the Tarot card you scryed that day.

The purpose of these visions through your dreams is to impart Gnosis to you and further your Spiritual Evolution. They are meant to teach you something about yourself and the Universe which you are a part of. They are also intended to inform you about the Spiritual meanings associated with the Major Arcana Tarot cards. Ultimately, the Gnosis that is imparted on you through Tarot scrying is dependent on your level of Soul progression and that which you need to know to keep evolving further Spiritually.

THE CIRCLE SPREAD DIVINATION

The Circle Spread Divination is an efficient Tarot reading that determines the Spiritual influences on you or on whomever you are doing the reading for. You can use it to gain insight into deeper aspects of your psyche or any situation, event, or action. The Circle Spread will help you understand who you are, what your intentions and motives are, and what energy influences surround you.

This powerful Divination cuts through surface knowledge about a subject, particular situation, or potential action, revealing the truth of the matter. As such, it can enlighten many areas of your life. It can also teach you more about yourself than any other Spiritual tool you may have at your disposal. This Divination is one that I made a part of my Spiritual journey many years ago and one that I do to this day because of its effectiveness.

The Emerald Tablet states, "As Above, So Below," meaning that everything that manifests in the Higher Planes will eventually filter itself down into the Physical World and either bring reward or havoc. The Circle Spread Divination isolates the source of an influence on you and lets you know whether Angelic or Demonic Beings are guiding this energy in a Higher Plane.

Suppose negative cards (Demonic energy) affect a situation in the Higher Planes. In that event, you can use specific Ceremonial Magick ritual exercises to tweak those negative energies and influence things before they happen. So, while the Circle Spread Divination can ascertain what type of energy affects you (or a situation) and in which Plane it exists, Ceremonial Magick exercises can be used to target that particular Plane and change the energy before it manifests. Using both methods to affect reality is the true path to becoming a Magus and gaining complete mastery over your life.

The Circle Spread Divination adheres to the Qabalistic Four Worlds model concerning the process of manifestation of the Divine energy. Since Divine energy needs to filter through the three principal Planes (Spiritual, Mental, and Astral) before manifesting in the Physical Plane, the Four Elements of Fire, Water, Air, and Earth are involved in this Divination. In this case, as in the case of the Four Worlds model, the Spirit Element is not included as part of the framework, and the principal four Planes are attributed to one of the Four Elements for simplicity.

The Fire Element is attributed to the Spiritual Plane (willpower), while the Air Element is assigned to the Mental Plane (thoughts). To the Astral Plane (emotions) is attributed the Water Element. Finally, the Earth

Element is assigned to the mundane, Physical Plane as the final stage of manifestation in the World of Matter. The designation of the Elements in the Circle Spread Divination is adjusted from the Cosmic Planes model to give the most optimal reading using the twenty-two Major Arcana.

To start, you must obtain a Hermetic Tarot card deck. I am specifying it being a Hermetic deck because the twenty-two Major Arcana must have the same attributes and titles as presented in the previous "Major Arcana of the Tarot" lesson. There is a myriad of decks available on the market today, and some of the more New Age decks are a system of their own, which do not hold to the arcane teachings of the Tarot. Thus, if you want to experiment with one of these decks on your own, that is fine, but to perform the Circle Spread Divination accurately, you must obtain a Hermetic Tarot card deck. Again, I recommend one of the three decks I described in the previous lesson on the Tarot. Any one of them is optimal for scrying or performing the Circle Spread Divination.

Once you have obtained a Hermetic Tarot deck, isolate the twenty-two Major Arcana from the rest of the cards. The Circle Spread Divination only uses the twenty-two Major Arcana, and you can use the Tarot descriptions in the previous lesson to aid your Divination.

Even though I gave you the meaning of each card in Divination, to truly become a successful Diviner, you must understand and memorize the entire esoteric, Alchemical, and literal meanings of each of the twenty-two Major Arcana. You will find that as you do this Divination more often, you will become better and better at it, and the process of obtaining insight will become easier. As with all things, practice makes perfect.

PRE-DIVINATION PREPARATIONS

Before engaging in a Tarot reading, it is essential to be in the right mindset and not be influenced by unbalanced energies. The mind should be neutral, where you are ready to receive information from Higher Realms. If you are angry before touching the Tarot deck or even overly joyous or excited, you will transmit this energy onto the deck, which will influence the reading.

Remember, the Tarot cards are meant to read energies from the Cosmos, and they can reach into the Unknown to give you insight about a future event or a force influencing you from Higher Realms. However, if you are coming into a Divination with excess energy affecting your psyche, the Tarot cards will read this energy instead. This is because the energy that the cards read is always the dominant energy in your Aura. If you are doing the reading for someone else, then the cards will read the dominant energy in their Aura instead, considering they are the ones who must shuffle the cards.

Before starting your Circle Spread Divination, you must address the space you are in and clear it of any stagnant or negative energies. Burning incense is helpful for this task, and its use will allow you to maintain a state of solemnity while performing the Divination.

Next, you must put yourself into a balanced state of mind, which means you must clear your Aura from any unbalanced energies. Therefore, before starting any Divination work, it is advised that you perform the Lesser Banishing Ritual of the Pentagram as well as the Banishing Ritual of the Hexagram. These two ritual exercises will enable you to become a "blank slate" so that you can interpret the energies correctly through the Tarot cards. You can find both practices in the following section on "Ceremonial Magick." In addition, both ritual exercises form part of the Circle Spread Divination in terms of the pattern of laying out the card spread.

To interpret the Tarot cards correctly, you must become a channel of information from Higher Realms; thus, your consciousness must be elevated to do this correctly. Your lower consciousness cannot interpret the Tarot cards, even though you may have memorized the meanings of each card. Remember, the intellect is only the Hod Sphere on the Tree of Life.

Therefore, to interpret the Tarot cards, you must elevate your mind to the Supernals and receive directly from Binah (Understanding) and Chokmah (Wisdom). For this reason, performing the Middle Pillar exercise before a Tarot reading is helpful. This exercise aims to infuse your Aura with Light energy, which will balance you out and raise the vibration of your consciousness. This ritual exercise can also be found in the "Ceremonial Magick" section and is best performed in sequence after the LBRP and BRH.

Your subconscious mind is the connecting link to the Higher Planes of existence, so it is imperative to be in a state where you are ready to receive from these Higher Realms. Since the Mind's Eye Chakra is a doorway into Higher Realms, it would be helpful to take a moment and connect with it. Aligning your consciousness with your Mind's Eye will enable you to use your intuition to interpret the Tarot cards, which is the optimal state of mind you should be in before a Divination.

Therefore, once you have centred and grounded yourself with the LBRP and BRH and infused Light into your Aura with the MP, the next step would be to spend a few minutes and do the Mind's Eye Meditation while performing the Four-Fold Breath. Again, you can find these practices in the following section on "Ceremonial Magick."

The Mind's Eye Meditation aims to connect you with the Mind's Eye Chakra; thus, a few minutes of this exercise should be enough. However, if you want to go into an extended meditation with this method, that is your choice. The stronger your connection is to your Mind's Eye Chakra, the more accurate your Divination will be since your intuition will be heightened.

Completing all necessary preparations is the key to a successful Tarot reading. As a final piece of the puzzle before starting a Tarot reading, it is helpful to do a small invocation to invoke the correct Spiritual energies that will aid you in accurately interpreting your Tarot reading. Since the Great Angel Hru is set over the operations of the Golden Dawn Order's secret wisdom, he is often called upon by many Tarot practitioners (in and out of the Order) for his guidance in Divination. His name is identical to that of the Egyptian Deity Horus (Ancient Egyptian "Hru"), and many Magi believe they are the same Being. It has even been suggested that Hru is the Angelic guardian of the Golden Dawn tradition; thus, his energy can be very impactful in the performance of a Tarot reading.

The following is an invocation of the Great Angel Hru, slightly modified from the original Golden Dawn version to best fit the intended purpose. As you perform this invocation, you should be standing upright and facing East while holding the Tarot deck in your hands.

> *"Under the Divine authority of **Yooohd-Heyyy-Vaaav-Heyyy** (YHVH), the Sole Wise and Sole Eternal One—I invoke **Heh-ru** (HRU), the Great Angel of the Secret and concealed Wisdom. Thou who ruleth the Mysteries of the Tarot, as the Sphynx is set over the land of Egypt. Thou whose mighty hand is imaged in the clouds of Book T, the sacred and mystical book of Hidden Wisdom. I invoke thee, be here now! Transform these Tarot cards from mere art images into true and accurate doorways unto Higher Worlds. Make each card a portal unto the true power that it portrays. Consecrate and purify this deck Hru. Make me a channel of your Divine Wisdom and give me insight into the Unknown so that I may obtain the necessary Knowledge that will aid in the exaltation of my Spiritual nature or that of another. Amen"*

Once you have completed the invocation of Hru, visualize a beam of Divine White Light descending from the sky onto your Tarot deck. The Light should be completely infusing itself into the deck. Imagine that the cards are being bathed in this Light as a final form of purification and consecration. Hold this vision for about ten to fifteen seconds while bowing your head and feeling thankful for this blessing from the Divine. After the Light beam has dispersed, draw a cross in the air over the cards with your dominant hand as you hold the cards with your other hand.

THE DIVINATION METHOD

The necessary preparations are now complete, and you have made yourself into a suitable channel to receive information from Higher Realms. All that is left is the actual Divination. To start the Circle Spread Divination, you will have to think of the question you want to be answered regarding yourself, a situation, an event, or an action you wish to perform. If you are only trying to gain insight into yourself and the energies surrounding you, then make that intention clear.

Once you are clear on the purpose of your Divination, keep this thought in your mind and start shuffling the cards. Keep repeating this purpose to yourself in your mind over and over while shuffling. This part is essential. Do not let outside thoughts enter your mind during the shuffling process since what you think about will determine what answer the cards will give you.

If you are doing the reading for someone else, then that person has to shuffle the cards themselves while thinking of whatever they need an answer on. The rule is that the person whom the Divination is for is the one who must shuffle the cards. Make sure to spend a few minutes doing this part of the process. Any method of shuffling works, so long as it is end for end. A popular way of shuffling is laying all the cards on whatever surface you are performing the Divination on, mixing them up thoroughly, and then picking them up.

Keep in mind that the Golden Dawn traditionally did not use reverse cards. The cards would always be placed in an upright fashion. The choice is yours, though, on whether you want to use reversed cards or not. I recommend that as you are learning, only lay them out upright, and as you get good at the Circle Spread Divination, do some experimenting with reversed cards as well.

Once the cards have been shuffled, you must cut them into four piles (Figure 24). These four piles signify the Tetragrammaton and the Four Elements—Yod (Fire), Heh (Water), Vav (Air), and Heh-final (Earth). You are to cut the cards from right to left, which is how Hebrew is read.

After you have cut the cards into four piles, take the right pile and place it on top of the next pile, followed by taking that pile and putting it on top of the next pile over. Finally, take the biggest pile and place it on top of the last pile on its left. By placing the piles one on top of the other, you are spelling out the name Tetragrammaton (YHVH), with Yod as the card on top. You are now ready to lay out the cards.

Figure 24: The Tetragrammaton in the Circle Spread Divination

The following descriptions of the placements and meanings of the Tarot cards in the Circle Spread Divination apply to the question or inquiry about something related to you. However, if the reading is for someone else, it would apply to them.

Turn over the first card on top, which is the Yod card. Here is the most important card of your Divination, the Significator Card. This card represents you at this particular moment in time regarding the specific situation you are inquiring about. It represents your energies at the time of the reading.

The next card that you turn over is the beginning of the formation of the Microcosmic portion of the Circle Spread Divination (Figure 25). In the Hermetic axiom, "As Above, So Below," the Microcosm is the Below (the Inner World), while the Macrocosm is the Above (the Outer World). The Lesser Banishing Ritual of the Pentagram represents the Microcosm, while the Banishing Ritual of the Hexagram represents the Macrocosm. The four Microcosmic cards are the Spiritual influences surrounding you within your sphere of influence, your Aura. These are the Spiritual influences that affect you internally at the present moment.

Turn over the next card and place it directly above the Significator Card. This card represents the Spiritual influences affecting you through the Air Element. Since the Air Element is expressive of your intellect and other mental operations related to your thinking processes, this card suggests the Spiritual influences on your thoughts in the Microcosm.

Turn over the following card and place it to the right of the Significator Card. This card represents the Spiritual influences affecting you through the Fire Element. As the Fire Element governs your drive, vitality, and raw energy, this card is expressive of the Spiritual influences on your willpower at the present moment.

The next card you turn over should be placed directly below the Significator Card. This card represents the Spiritual influences on you, filtered through the Water Element. The Water Element governs the emotions, which are expressive of how you feel. Emotions can be of a lower quality, motivated by the Ego and Self-love, or a higher quality, driven by the Higher Self and unconditional love. This particular card then is expressive of the Spiritual influences on your emotions and how you express love in your life.

The final card is to be placed to the left of the Significator Card. This card represents the Spiritual influences affecting you, filtered through the Earth Element. Since the Earth Element relates to your mundane, day-to-day life, this particular card is expressive of the Spiritual influences on your physical existence, including your physical body. And since the Earth Element is the combination of the Fire, Water, and Air Elements in a denser form, this card is representative of the Spiritual influences of those energies on your mundane life.

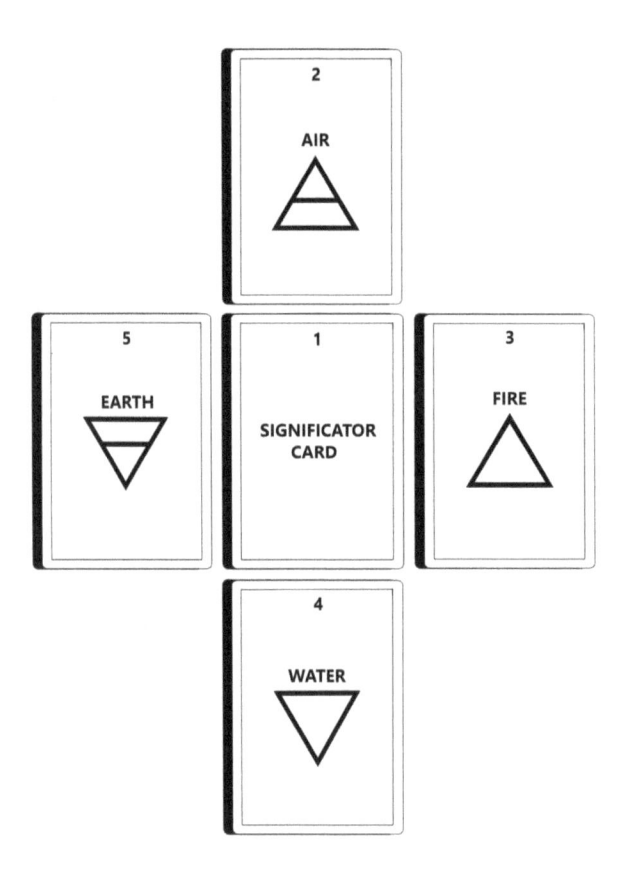

Figure 25: The Microcosmic Operation in the Circle Spread Divination

Now that you have laid out the five cards in front of you, you will see that their layout forms an Equal-Armed Cross. The Equal-Armed Cross is a symbol of Chesed, the first Sephira below the Abyss as the builder of Form, representative of our manifested, physical Universe. It depicts the Sun amid our Solar System, with each arm of the Cross corresponding with one of the Four Elements. The Yod letter of the Tetragrammaton is placed in the centre of the Cross as the Significator Card as it represents the Light of the Sun—your true inner nature.

The Equal-Armed Cross is also a symbol of the path of Tav, which is the Universe card of the Tarot. Through the Universe card, we enter the Astral Realm, where we can access the inner Cosmic Planes. Thus, the Equal-Armed Cross is a doorway into the Unknown and the Higher Planes of Spirituality.

The second part of the operation will show you the Spiritual influences around you from a Macrocosmic level (Figure 26). These energies are projected from the outside Universe, and they influence you or a situation you are inquiring about. Macrocosmic energies originate from the Mind of God and the Spiritual Plane, using the Planetary Spheres as their medium of expression. Thus, these are the Spiritual influences from the Higher Planes of existence.

As the Banishing Ritual of the Hexagram is Macrocosmic, it is based on the Zodiacal positions in the Heavens. The Elements, in this case, are arranged differently than in the Lesser Banishing Ritual of the Hexagram. I will explain how this works in later chapters when discussing the Hexagram Rituals.

The next card is to be placed in the upper left-hand corner, between the Microcosmic Earth and Air Elements. This card is attributed to the Fire Element in the Macrocosm, representing the Spiritual influences from the Higher Planes on your willpower. Since energies from the Higher Planes take some time to manifest in the mundane world, this card shows how your willpower is being affected and the direction in which it will change over time.

The following card goes in the upper right-hand corner, between the Microcosmic Air and Fire Elements. It is the angle of the Earth Element in the Macrocosm, representing the Spiritual influences from the Higher Planes on your mundane life within the Physical Plane of existence. In a way, this card sums up the other three Macrocosmic cards in terms of how these Elemental energies will manifest in your life in the future.

You are to place the next card in the lower right-hand corner, between the Microcosmic Fire and Water Elements. This card is attributed to the Air Element in the Macrocosm and the Spiritual influences from the Higher Planes on your thoughts. The pairs of Elemental cards (Microcosm and Macrocosm) represent the dichotomy between the present and the future. They are related to an expression of a particular Element within yourself or the situation you are enquiring about.

The final card is placed in the lower left-hand corner between the Microcosmic Water and Earth Elements. It is the angle of the Water Element in the Macrocosm, representing the Spiritual influences from the Higher Planes on your emotions. As the Microcosmic Water card represents where you are at with your feelings at the present moment, the Macrocosmic Water card represents the direction in which your emotions will change over time.

After placing the last card, we have now what appears to be a square or a cube. The Cube of Space is an essential concept in *The Sepher Yetzirah* since, according to Qabalists, it describes the physical Universe. The three axes of the cube, the centre point, the six sides, and the twelve edges are associated with the twenty-two letters of the Hebrew alphabet. These letters comprise the Macrocosm and the Microcosm, the Above and the Below.

Figure 26: The Macrocosmic Operation in the Circle Spread Divination

Thus, for Spiritual advice on a particular situation or to better understand the influences within and outside us, we have all the cards we need to make a proper enquiry. Therefore, at this point in the Divination, you should spend some time meditating and contemplating the cards that have been given.

If the question was solely to glean insight into yourself or a particular matter, then no further cards have to be laid out, and the Circle Spread Divination is complete at this point. If, however, you inquired about a particular action, decision, or a magickal operation and whether you should proceed with it, then you will need two more cards—one to the left side of the card spread and one to the right (Figure 27).

Proceed now to lay out the first card on the left of the card spread. This card indicates the probable outcome if no action is taken and if you let things stay on their current course without intervening. For this reason, this card is called the Present Card. Take a moment now to contemplate the Present Card concerning the matter of enquiry.

After doing so, lay out the final card to the right of the spread. This card indicates the probable outcome if you take the action that your initial question or enquiry was directed towards. It will tell you the Karmic effects of taking that particular action and the impact it will have on your mundane life. As such, this card is called the Future Card. Take a moment to contemplate the Future Card as it may be the most important card for you in the spread.

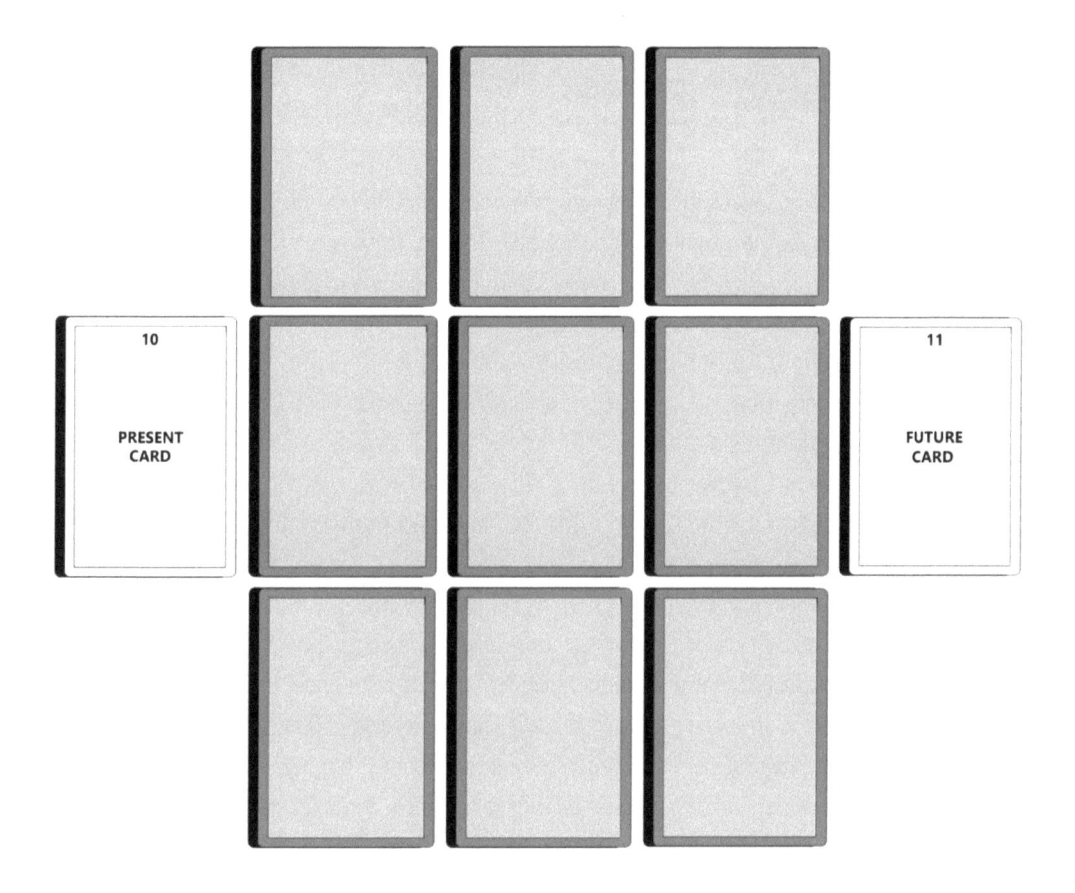

Figure 27: The Present and Future Cards in the Circle Spread Divination

    Contemplate the Present and Future Cards concerning one another and let your intuition and Higher Self guide you. Be honest with yourself, and don't let your Ego interpret the cards. For example, if the Future Card is negative, it may be time to leave the situation as it is. But if the Future Card is positive, the action is a go. And if both cards are positive, you have a choice whether to leave things as they are or to intervene since both options will yield positive results.

    If both cards are negative, you need to spend even more time examining the Spiritual influences surrounding you or the situation you inquired about. Perhaps there is something that you missed in your interpretation that can enlighten the whole Divination for you. Or maybe you need to change your own internal beliefs and attitudes if the Divination is in some way related to you.

Since we are the Masters of our destinies, we can use many available methods to change our energy and the Spiritual influences surrounding us. These methods include meditation, prayer, deep contemplation, and, most notably—Ritual Magick.

SPIRITUAL INFLUENCES AND MAGICK

An excellent method of affecting the Spiritual influences surrounding your cards is using Ceremonial Magick ritual exercises. Since the Pentagram ritual is related to your Microcosm and the Hexagram ritual pertains to your Macrocosm, you can use their invoking or banishing ritual exercises to alter and change the Spiritual influences surrounding the Elements of your Being.

Sometimes invoking a specific type of energy is all that is needed to ensure that the Microcosmic or Macrocosmic energy influences are positive and will yield the desired result. Now, if the Spiritual influences are a part of a long chain of causes and events, then the energy of the cards won't be able to be changed so easily. It all depends on the initial question or enquiry of the Divination. However, if it is to glean into yourself and the general Spiritual influences surrounding you, then this method of changing your energy is very efficient.

After performing a ritual exercise, it might take a few hours to an entire day for the invoked energy to penetrate the corresponding Chakra in your Aura and change your energy. For some people, this change would occur right away. If you were to do a follow-up reading with the same question or enquiry after performing a ritual exercise, you would find that your cards would be adjusted to the new energy in your Aura.

Keep in mind that you are permitted only to use the ritual exercises with which you have already completed the Spiritual Alchemy program (or if you are in the midst of one). You should not be working with any ritual exercises that you have not had any experience with so far since, by doing so, you will be negatively affecting your Spiritual Alchemy process and setting yourself back.

For example, if you are working with the LIRP of Water in your Spiritual Alchemy program but you wish to change the Spiritual influences on your Fire Element in the Microcosm, you should not perform the LIRP of Fire to do so since you have not reached its level yet. Thus, you should only work with the invoking or banishing Rituals of the Pentagram of the Earth, Air, and Water Elements. Although this will limit you to some extent, it will also motivate you to finish the entire prescribed program to have all the Microcosmic Elements available for use whenever you want.

To affect your Macrocosm, you can work with the invoking or banishing rituals of the Hexagram, as presented in the "Advanced Planetary Magick" chapter in *The Magus*. These are the energies of the Seven Ancient Planets that affect your Macrocosm through the Spirit energy.

Each of the Seven Ancient Planets is related to one of the Four Elements. You can use its invoking or banishing Hexagram ritual to tweak the desired Elemental energy in your Macrocosm. Note that two of the Seven Ancient Planets have an affinity with one Element (excluding the Earth Element, which has a correspondence to Saturn).

Feel free to experiment with the complementary pairs of Planets (working with one per day) to change your Macrocosmic energy influences. However, as with the Pentagram ritual, you are only to work with the Planets whose Spiritual Alchemy program you have completed and nothing above your level. Since to even embark on Planetary ritual invocations, you need to finish the prescribed Spiritual Alchemy program with the Five Elements (including Spirit), altering the energies of your Macrocosm is reserved only for the more advanced Magi in training.

Interestingly, depending on what energy you are working with (if you are following one of the Spiritual Alchemy programs from *The Magus*), that quality and type of energy will be present in your entire card spread. For example, if you are working with the Air Element, you may find that your card spread will be significantly influenced by this Element and may be unbalanced in the other Elements. The same applies if you are working with the Earth, Water, or Fire Elements. The Circle Spread Divination will read the dominant energy in your Aura; that energy will be highly influenced by whatever ritual exercises you work with daily.

CLEANSING AND STORING YOUR TAROT CARDS

Cleansing your Tarot cards is vital for maintaining positive energy in your Tarot readings and staying well-connected with your Tarot deck. When it comes to cleansing your cards, the most important two factors are how you store them and the method you use to cleanse (clear) them when necessary. Cleansing the cards should be done often since their energy must always be neutral for the Divination to be successful.

The initial cleansing of the cards should be performed once you have bought your Tarot deck, especially if you got it second-hand. Still, even if you purchased a brand new deck, I suggest cleansing the cards since you never know who handled your deck before you got it and what kind of energy that person (or people) infused into it. Remember, every time we look at something, we are affecting it with our energy, and if we make physical contact with an object, we directly infuse that object with our energy.

As a rule of thumb, only you should handle your Tarot deck unless you are doing a reading for someone else since that person will need to shuffle the deck themselves. In this case, or where someone accidentally touched your deck, you should cleanse it afterwards. Even if nobody touched your deck, but you feel disconnected from the cards for whatever reason, it is helpful to cleanse them and put their energy back into neutral.

There are many methods to cleanse your cards, and I will discuss a few that work best. The method that I like to use often is called a "Salt Burial Cleanse." Salt works great to draw out negative energy from Tarot cards. Wrap up your Tarot cards in a plastic bag and place them in the middle of an airtight container, covering them entirely with salt. Make sure that the bag has no holes since the salt should not be touching the cards directly. Close the container and leave the cards there for a few days before taking them out and disposing of the salt. Make sure the container is airtight because salt not only gathers the energies from a Tarot deck but also collects any moisture in the air, potentially damaging your cards.

Another method I find works well is the "Full Moon Cleanse." Since this cleanse is to be performed on a full Moon, it can only be completed successfully for one to two days during the month. I usually use the full Moon to cleanse my cards no matter what state they are in energetically. To perform the Full Moon Cleanse, place the cards beside a window or outside since the full Moon's rays need to penetrate the cards. Leave the cards there overnight and collect them in the morning, or leave them there an extra night and let them bathe in the Moon's rays. Note that the Salt Burial Cleanse, as well as the Full Moon Cleanse, are both very effective in clearing the energy of Gemstones as well.

There are other methods of clearing Tarot cards, such as prayer, meditation, incense cleansing, and even leaving them outside in the fresh air after a rainfall. However, I find that these methods are not as efficient as those I mentioned, but you are welcome to experiment with them and see what works best for you.

Once a Tarot reading is complete, you need to store your cards safely, whereby they are protected from outside energies and are ready to be used again when needed. There are many ways to store your Tarot cards safely, and I will mention a few that I believe are most optimal.

The method that I like to use is storing the cards in a white linen sheet. Since white is the colour of purity and Light, it will serve as a shield to protect against any outside energies. Foreign energies will bounce off your wrapped-up cards and return to whence they came. Another use of the white linen sheet is as a surface on which to perform the Divination. You unwrap the Tarot cards and use the same white sheet on a table surface (or whatever surface you wish to complete the Divination on) and lay the cards on it. Thus, the white linen sheet should be big enough to accomplish this double task (2'x2' minimum).

Some people like to store their Tarot cards in a special box. If you choose this method of storing instead, I recommend getting a box that is big enough for you to place a Quartz Crystal inside with the Tarot deck. A Quartz Crystal is an excellent absorber of energies, and you can use it to clear the energies of the cards and keep them always neutral. If you use a big enough Quartz Crystal for this task, you may never need to cleanse the cards since the Crystal will do all the work for you. Always remember, treat the cards with reverence and respect at all times and your Divinations will be successful.

***

The discourse on the Circle Spread Divination is now complete. I implore you to do further research on the Tarot on your own and make this a lifelong subject of study. Having the ability to read your energy or that of another person is one of the great gifts from the Divine and one that requires your utmost attention. There is a lot of great available material on the market that can enhance your skills and abilities as a Diviner.

Remember to practice this Divination method often, especially if you are working on one of the Spiritual Alchemy programs from *The Magus*. Having this tool at your disposal enables you to be aware of your energy at all times and be in charge of what you put out into the Universe. It allows you to know things before they happen and be a cause instead of an effect. Most importantly, it enables you to reach a deeper understanding of your True Will and your Higher Self and be one step closer to completing the Great Work.

PART III: CEREMONIAL MAGICK

THE FIVE ELEMENTS

THE SOUL AND THE EGO

Whether you have had a Kundalini awakening or wish to take the next step in your Spiritual Evolution, this section will give you the keys to working actively with the Five Elements of your Being for Self-transformation and exaltation of consciousness. The Ceremonial Magick ritual exercises presented here are techniques you can use daily to clear the negative Karmic influences on your Chakras, which keep you from progressing further in mind, body, and Soul. Before presenting the techniques, though, it is essential to give you an overview of each Element so that you can have a better idea of its nature and how it manifests in your life.

Throughout life, all humans have built up their Egos through past conditioning, which occurs naturally through our experience of life's events. Therefore, our Egos are a by-product of our environments and reactions to life events. With Ego development came the Karmic burden of allowing fear to enter our lives. This negative energy of fear manifests as Karmic blockages in our Chakras. Since fear is the antithesis to love, it means that any life event reacted to with fear instead of love carried with it Karmic consequences. The overall effect is that the Chakras became clogged with dark, negative energy (which impedes their functioning), and the Light of the Soul became dim over time.

The purpose of Ceremonial Magick exercises is to focus on the individual Chakras to purify them and remove any negative, stagnant energy so that they can function at their maximum capacity. As such, the purpose of this work is to reconnect with the Soul. The Light within must grow and expand inside the Aura. Removing the clutches of fear will leave us with unconditional love as our foundation. Herein is the meaning of Spiritual Evolution.

As we grew up and matured, we did so with the Divine inclination to develop our character, through which we express ourselves to the outside world. Keep in mind the difference between character and personality. A personality is used by the Ego to show itself to the outside world. Astrologically, it is linked to the Rising Sign at birth. A person's character is something different, though. It encompasses our deepest aspirations and beliefs and is more of a foundation of who we are, not who we think we are, which would be the personality. Astrologically, the character is our personal Sun Sign. The character expresses the Soul, while the personality expresses the Ego.

A person's character is built upon virtues, which form their ethical and moral beliefs. I will give you the basic breakdown of these virtues so that the picture can be clearer of how the Elements and Chakras relate.

Traditionally, there are seven virtues. They are chastity, temperance, charity, diligence, patience, kindness, and humility. The virtues are expressed through the Angelic part of us. Each of these seven virtues has a negative counterpart, called the seven vices. They are lust, gluttony, greed, sloth, wrath, envy, and pride. The vices express through the Demonic part of us. Angels channel Light and love energy, while Demons channel the energy of fear.

Now that you know the Qabalistic version of the Garden of Eden story, you know why we have both Angelic and Demonic counterparts. These Angels and Demons, known as positive and negative forces (or thought senders), express themselves through the mind. The mind is the connecting link between Spirit and Matter (the Above and Below). It is also a receiver that can tune in to all the Cosmic Planes between the two.

How a person chooses to express their humanity, whether through virtues or vices, is something personal to them and is usually a result of their past conditioning and Karma. Free Will also plays a role, but most people are not even aware they have Free Will, let alone know how to use it productively.

At our core, we are all Beings of Light. Whether we are in tune with our Souls or our Egos depends on where we are in our Spiritual Evolution process. Those people who are in tune with their Souls more are expressing their Free Will Principle, while those who are in tune with their Egos are like blind automatons, making decisions in their lives based on fear-based thinking. The biggest con the Ego ever pulled is to make you believe that you are it. Always remember this.

"Fear is nothing but idleness of the will." — Eliphas Levi, excerpt from "The Key of the Mysteries"

Because the doctrine of Karma is vital to the work presented in this book, it is worth mentioning a few more words on the topic. Karma refers to the Spiritual Principle of Cause and Effect, where the intentions and actions of an individual (cause) influence the future of that individual (effect). The Universal Laws imply that all activities not expressed through unconditional love and one of the seven virtues will yield negative consequences for the individual. The energy of the adverse action attaches itself to the individual's Wheel of Karma. It also gets lodged in the individual Chakra that deals with the expression of that particular action. It will then repeat itself in the future for the individual to do the right thing, which is to react accordingly by applying the energy of unconditional love.

I already discussed how negative, fear-based actions reduce the shine of the Chakra (or Chakras) particular to the expression of that action. As more and more negativity builds up inside the Chakras, their spin's intensity lessens, and the Light of the Soul gets dimmer. Remember, each Chakra is essentially a spinning wheel, radiating a type of energy pertaining to the colour of that Chakra. The Light of the Soul powers all the Chakras since Light contains all the colours within itself. Light disperses into one of the seven colours of the colour spectrum, which are synonymous with the colours of the Chakras. If the Light is strong and clear, then conversely, the spinning of the Chakric wheels is more powerful.

The Universal Law of the energy of unconditional love states that if you give Light and love to others and the Universe, you will receive that Light and love threefold. Light is love and wisdom— love and wisdom are Light. Therefore, someone with a lot of negative Karma in their Chakras will not radiate as much Light as someone with less negative Karma.

There are very few Beings with no negative Karma, but if you have a good foundation built on virtues and not on vices, you will be someone who generally has good Karma, which means that good things will happen to you. Good Karma means that we are in resonance with the Universal Laws, as the Universe wants to give us all that we desire in this world. Therefore, it is the natural inclination for Universal Energy to operate in the direction of making our wishes come true. However, when we accrue bad Karma by not performing actions in the name of Universal Love, the Universe punishes us by not giving us what we want and then makes us repeat the action until we get it right.

Remember, Karma is cyclic throughout various lifetimes and incarnations. Therefore, if you are a good person with positive Karma in this lifetime but you were a bad person in previous lifetimes, the Universe may still be giving you hurdles to overcome before showering you with its blessings once you have resolved your negative Karma.

Karma is the "safety switch" that the Universe uses to teach us who we are and how to behave. The Universe wants us all to love each other unconditionally—to be guided by wisdom in our lives. Because if we are punished for being selfish, angry, lazy, devious, manipulative, or ignorant, then we will think twice if next time we act selfishly and in the name of the Ego instead of in the name of the Light (Soul).

The Universe is our parent, and it wants us all to behave accordingly—and when we do not, we receive bad or negative Karma. Because the human psyche is a synthesis of the workings of the Four Elements and the infusion of the fifth Element of Spirit, we operate through those individual Chakras that, as shown earlier, are the expression of the individual Elements. Therefore, a well-functioning Chakra means the person is at a higher level of consciousness than someone with a Chakra filled with negative Karma.

In this section, I will give you the breakdown of the Five Elements, their correspondences, and how they express themselves in the human psyche. Then, in the following section, I will provide you with the exact techniques to invoke the energy synonymous with each Element so that you can attune that Chakra properly, remove the negative Karma from it, and raise the vibration of your consciousness.

THE PENTAGRAM

The Pentagram is a five-pointed star, with all the lines being the same length and the angles also being the same. It is one of the oldest and most potent symbols in human history. The Pentagram has played a part in almost all Ancient cultures and traditions, including the Babylonians, Egyptians, Hebrews, Greeks, Hindus, Chinese, and even Mayans in Mesoamerica. Moreover, it held various meanings for Ancient peoples, usually Astronomical and religious.

In Babylon, the Pentagram was used as a symbol that protects against evil forces. Early Christianity used it to represent the five wounds of Jesus Christ. Today, many Neopagan faiths, including Wicca, use the Pentagram as a symbol of faith. We can also find it within Freemasonry as one of its prominent symbols.

According to the Greek philosopher and mathematician Pythagoras, five was the number of the human being. Therefore, if we are to superimpose the Pentagram onto the human body, the two lowest points represent the legs, the two middle points represent the arms, and the top point represents the head.

The above concept is best expressed by Leonardo da Vinci's famous drawing, the "Vitruvian Man." His picture is based upon the proportions of the human body, featuring the human form perfectly inscribed within a circle and square. Conversely, the Pentagram is derived from a circle being divided into five perfect and equal points or parts. The symbol of the Pentagram within a circle is commonly known as a Pentacle.

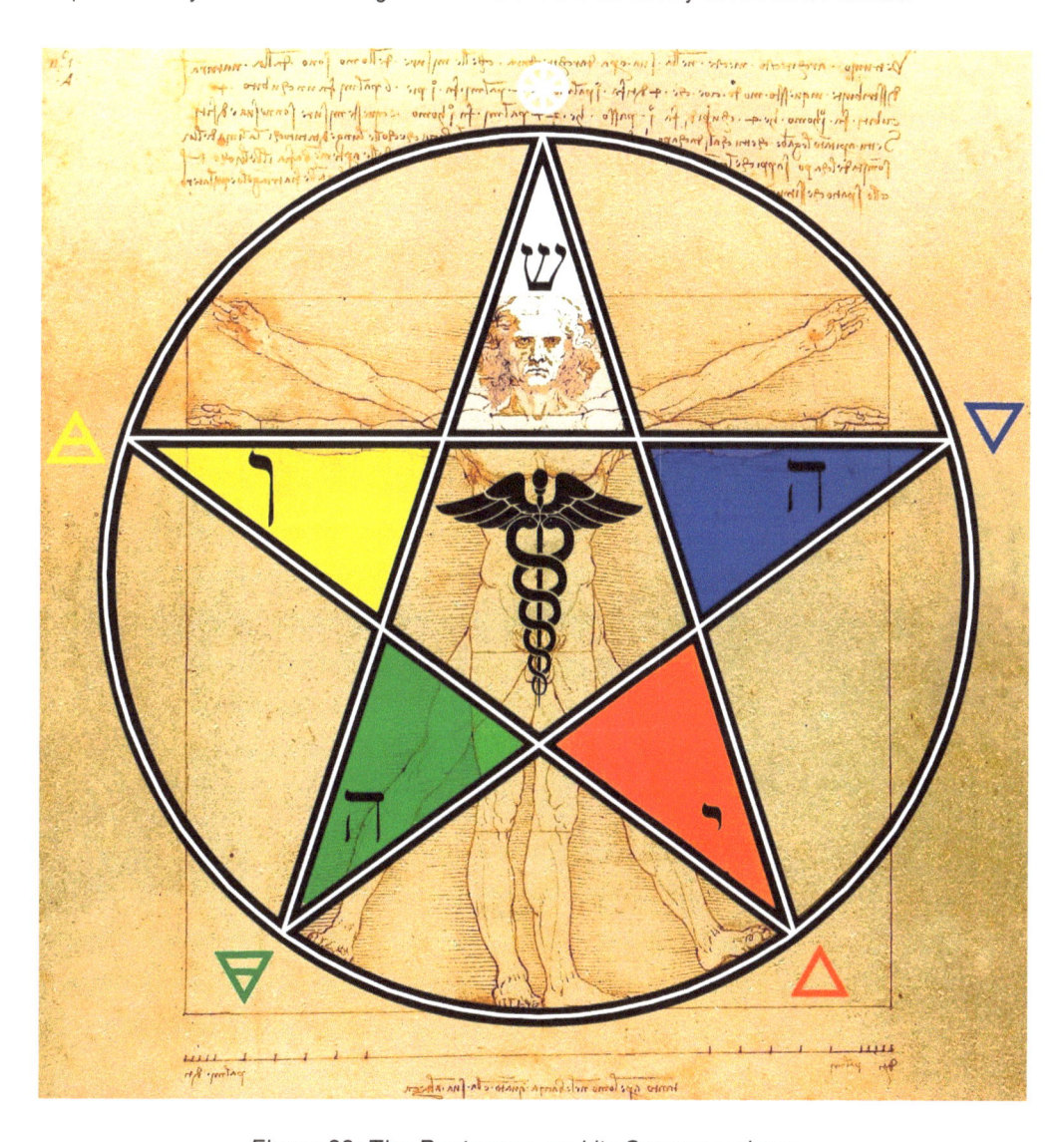

Figure 28: The Pentagram and its Correspondences

As the Greeks used the Pentagram to represent the Microcosm, the same meanings and associations found their way into Ceremonial Magick. The upright Pentagram (Figure 28) is called the Signet Star of the Microcosm. Each of its five points represents one of the Five Elements of Earth, Air, Water, Fire, and Spirit. The Five Elements, in turn, relate to the Pentagrammaton. And the totality of the power of the Pentagrammaton is contained within the symbolism of the Caduceus of Hermes. The Caduceus is expressive of the full awakening of the Kundalini energy within the human being.

The orientation of the Pentagram in Ceremonial Magick is of utmost importance. When upright, it represents Spirit over Matter as a symbol of the Light that invokes Angelic Beings and protects against evil forces. Conversely, when the Pentagram is inverted, it stands for Matter over Spirit and is considered an evil symbol since it invokes Demonic Beings. For this reason, you will see an inverted Pentagram used by Satanic groups or anyone involved in Black Magick.

When upright, the Pentagram symbol invokes benevolent powers that further our Spiritual Evolution. Therefore, as part of Ceremonial Magick ritual exercises, we will be using the upright Pentagram symbol in the invocations and banishings of the Five Elements.

THE EARTH ELEMENT

The Earth Element is Muladhara, the Root Chakra, corresponding Qabalistically to the Sphere of Malkuth. In the upright Pentagram symbol, the Earth Element is of the colour green, forming the lower left part of the Pentagram. Once we superimpose the human being onto the Pentagram symbol, the Earth Element represents the right leg.

Muladhara is the first Chakra, closest to the physical Earth. The Element of Earth is the physical body, the material world. Its expression in the psyche is always related to our connection to the material world. Some of the more mundane aspects of the Earth Element include having a job and owning a home and a car. Anything related to money and ownership of material goods is an expression of the Earth Element.

Earth is the opposite of Spirit—as the Spirit uses the energy of Fire, Water, and Air on a higher level, Earth uses those three Elements on a lower, denser level. Earth energy seeks to provide us with the things we need to make our material, physical existence a happy one.

As the Hermetic axiom states, "As Above, So Below"—Kether is in Malkuth, and Malkuth is in Kether. God is in everything we see before us, including the mosquito and the dirt on which we walk. Therefore, Earth is directly linked to Spirit since Spirit embodies the Earth. On the lower Plane of Earth, Spirit works by channelling the energy to work in the direction of survival and materialism.

The Earth Element is directly linked to the Ego since the Ego has its domain within the physical body. The Ego's primary purpose, its "modus operandi," is to protect the physical body and the personality. As such, the Ego uses the Earth Element to ensure the physical body's survival at all costs.

Unless you plan to leave your mundane life behind and go to Tibet or India to meditate in a temple, you must integrate into society and respect its workings. Being an outcast will jeopardize your survival; thus, the first lesson of the Earth Element is learning to function effectively, efficiently, and in cooperation with other people within society. You must learn to integrate into society and "blend in" before breaking apart and "standing out."

"To labour is the lot of man," as Homer said. Therefore, work is fundamental in our lives considering that most people in the world work five times a week, for eight hours a day on average. All people living in a civilized society need to earn money to survive and afford the luxuries of life that can make their lives on Planet Earth otherwise more enjoyable.

The Earth Element then includes satisfying our basic physiological needs vital to our survival, such as the need for air, water, food, and sleep. Physical exercise is also essential, as is the quality of the food and water we bring into our bodies. Bringing toxins into the body or being overweight, for example, can bring about health issues and jeopardise the body's life expectancy.

Once you have satisfied your basic survival needs, the next step is "standing out" and living the life you always dreamed of. We are all born with dreams and hopes for the future and of being extraordinary in some way. Nobody dreams of being average. We all want to be successful and have abundance in our lives. And success is not defined by how much money we make or have in the bank but by spending the twenty-four hours of the day doing what we love.

Being stuck in a job or career that makes you miserable may pay the bills, but it will not give you lasting happiness. You deserve to enjoy every moment of every day, meaning you must strive for a job or career that fills your Soul with joy. Your Ego may be content with where you are at in life since the Ego is only concerned with survival, whereas the Soul is concerned with inner happiness. Your Soul wants you to manifest an extraordinary life where you are in charge of your destiny, doing that which you love.

Since the Earth Element is related to the Three-Dimensional World of Space and Time, how you spend your time then is of utmost importance in your journey towards manifesting an extraordinary life. Therefore, once you have satisfied the bare essentials for living, your next step is setting some goals for yourself and organizing your time to achieve those goals.

Your goals should be geared towards giving you a more fruitful future, such as a job or career you would love. Being consistent daily with applying yourself to your goals will ensure you achieve them over time. In most cases, it is a gradual process that requires diligence and patience. You might have to sacrifice your comfort for the time being and apply all your free time to learning something new that can help you further your goals since knowledge is power.

You must learn to be resilient to life's challenges and remain motivated and inspired. After all, you cannot allow other people or the environment to determine your destiny if you want to succeed. However, maintaining momentum and working towards your goals will eventually yield your desired success. And once you have that dream job or career and spend your time doing what you love, you will be one step closer to mastery over the Earth Element in your life.

Since the Earth Element deals with the power of manifestation, this also includes manifesting the right relationships in your life. After all, if you are to lead an extraordinary life, you must spend your time with exceptional people. Your time is your most precious commodity; therefore, be careful who you give your time to.

Manifesting the right friendships in your life with like-minded people who share similar goals will provide the proper support to keep moving ahead on your journey. As the saying goes, "You are who your friends are." So surround yourself with positive people from whom you can learn something and avoid people who bring you down.

In terms of romantic relationships, manifesting a quality partner in your Earth life can further your Spiritual journey tenfold and bring you the joy and abundance you deserve. Falling in love is a process of unifying the masculine and feminine energies within yourself and gaining direct access to the Spirit energy. The right partner with whom you can share unconditional love can be the most significant source of inspiration in your life. They can bring healing on all levels, whether physical, emotional, mental, or Spiritual.

On the other hand, getting involved romantically with the wrong person can do the exact opposite. It can bring about unimaginable chaos in your life and drain you of your Life energy like nothing you have experienced before. Therefore, be wary of who you let into your life and who you get involved with romantically.

Keep in mind that when discussing the power of manifestation, I am not speaking strictly about the Earth Element since manifestation depends on the correct application of the Fire, Water, and Air Elements in relation to Earth. For example, to strive in life, you need drive, which comes from the Fire Element. Since manifesting your dreams requires imagination and mental acuity, a correct dose of the Air Element must also be applied. And since personal relationships are mainly matters of the heart, the Water Element and emotions are involved.

The Earth Element quiets our minds and offers us the energy to tackle our daily physical activities, whose purpose is to keep us moving forward in our Earthly existence. The invocation of the Earth Element brings about a grounding effect that focuses the mind. It removes the Ego's chatter that otherwise slows us down from performing our daily tasks with ease. When you invoke the Earth Element, your thoughts become grounded, and you can feel the density of your physical body. Being grounded enables the other Elements to manifest through you more efficiently.

As you are under the Earth Element's influence, you will have an easy time completing any daily tasks that involve physical labour. You may feel the need to join a gym or start doing some physical workouts at home. The idea of walking in nature will appeal to you as well as walking around the city or town you live within. As you do so, you will feel a heightened connection to the world around you.

The silence in your mind and the density of your physical body will enable you to hear the sounds of nature and feel plant and animal life like never before. Feel free to take off your shoes and socks and walk barefoot on the Earth or even hug a tree to try to further connect with our Planet. You may feel the Earth itself give off a slight aroma and a steady heat while you embody the energy of the Earth Element. As your ability to take in the world around you is greatly intensified, the buildings and structures of the city you live in will also appear more magnificent than ever.

You will notice that upon your first series of Earth invocations, you will manifest many different things in your life at an accelerated rate. You may be chatty at first, and the people in your life will react well to you, but you may appear stubborn sometimes. After a few weeks of Earth invocations, your thoughts will become denser as your Air Element slowly diminishes. Your ability to connect to your thoughts and emotions and those of other people will decrease as you continue invoking Earth.

Since Earth is the first Element you will be working with in your process of Spiritual Alchemy, the idea is to ground your thoughts and solidify the energy of your Aura. You will officially be in work mode, not thinking or contemplation mode. Since Earth energy is action-oriented (not thought or emotion-oriented), you will be unable to think too deeply about anything after a while. As a result, the Ego will become more prominent than ever. Not to worry, though; this part of the process is necessary since you will work on your Ego in the following Element of Air.

The virtue of the Root Chakra, Muladhara, is diligence, while its vice is sloth. Laziness in fulfilling the necessary tasks in your everyday life is an aspect of the bad Karma of the Earth Chakra. Every time you don't perform a physical action that you are supposed to do, you are making it more challenging to do that same action the next time around. Since laziness stores negative Karma in the Earth Chakra, use the Earth Element invocations to ground your thoughts so that you can perform your daily tasks with diligence. Doing so will gradually clear the negative Karma of Muladhara Chakra.

THE AIR ELEMENT

The Air Element is the fourth Chakra, Anahata, located in the heart centre—not the physical heart centre, but the centre of your chest between the two breasts. In the upright Pentagram symbol, the Air Element is of the colour yellow, forming the upper left part of the Pentagram. If we superimpose the human being onto the Pentagram symbol, the Air Element represents the right arm.

The Air Element corresponds with the Sphere of Tiphareth (whose Planetary attribution is the Sun) and the Sphere of Yesod (attributed to the Moon). Tiphareth is the centre of the Tree of Life, as it receives the energies of the other Sephiroth, except for Malkuth-the Earth. Malkuth is reached through Yesod-the Moon. The Air Element has a dual nature. It can be deceptive like the Moon, or expressive of the truth, like the Sun. The truth is received and perceived through intuition.

As the Earth Element Chakra (Muladhara) was about stability, the Air Element Chakra (Anahata) is about its opposite—thoughts. As thoughts are comprised of an ethereal substance, they belong to the mind. They are invisible, yet all of us share in them. Thoughts are most important to human beings since they give life to the Elements of Fire and Water within the psyche. Fire represents willpower, while Water represents emotion and love. One can have neither without Air since thought powers them both. Therefore, before you can accomplish anything in this world, you must first have had the thought of doing that thing. Thus, thought is at the root of all of Creation.

Air also directly correlates with the Element of Spirit/Aethyr and the Supernals. The Air Element is the Pillar of Balance on the Tree of Life since Air is the balancer of all things mental, emotional, and Spiritual. As such, it is directly linked to Kether, the source of the Spirit energy.

As Air is thought, it is also intelligence. The Sphere of Hod is linked to the intellect directly. However, in Hod, Air is tempered by the Water Element. Air is also connected to the Element of Fire and emotional thought or impulse. Thus, Air directly correlates to Netzach—emotions and desires. A well-functioning mind means that the individual is well balanced in the Element of Air.

The Air Element's workings are fundamental and encompass many things. Air is also Astral Light, an aspect of Spirit, so when you are invoking this Element, you will have Lucid Dreams very often. Lucid Dreams occur as the Aura gets infused with the Air Element through ritual invocations. While invoking the Air Element, you will also notice your physical body will be cooled down. You will be particularly sensitive to the air around you, which will feel like a constant cool breeze on your skin.

Since the Ego is present within the mind and is conditioned by things it interprets, once you invoke Air, you will feel very much in touch with your Ego, its needs, desires, and the nature of its thoughts. But on the other end of the spectrum, once a certain amount of Air invocations are completed, you will start to feel in touch with your emotions and the unconditional love energy projected through your Soul. To rise as high as the unconditional love energy, though, you first have to overcome the Ego since thought comes before emotion, and the Ego is found in thought, within the mind.

The Ego is fueled by sexual energy, which means that the Air Element invocations will tune you in to your sexual desires. Considering that an unpurified Ego naturally thinks about sex often, you may encounter sexual arousal as you amplify your thoughts with Air Element invocations. In addition, Air directly affects the subconscious mind, so whatever your deepest thoughts are will be heightened as you work with the Air Element.

You can spend many months invoking Air, and you will not be stagnating Spiritually but will instead be purifying your mind with every invocation. This is because the Air Element heals us mentally. Thought predates all emotion and action and is the foundation of our existence. Hence, there is a connection between the Air Element and the Spirit Element—our animating principle and the source of healing energy.

Air and Spirit Elements are connected because Anahata Chakra is right below Vishuddhi Chakra, the first Chakra of the Spirit Element. Air separates the lower three Chakras of the Earth, Water, and Fire Elements, with the higher three Chakras of the Spirit Element. Because it is the mediator and precursor of all things manifest, learning about the nature of your thoughts and getting in touch with them is a precursor to working with the other Elements.

Since Air is in the Heart Chakra, Anahata, and the higher emotions of the Heart are expressive of unconditional love; the Air Element acts as a medium of expression for the Spirit Element above, which channels these higher love energies. Remember always that Air fuels everything within the psyche as it animates the Fire and Water Elements. Therefore, as you clear the Ego's impulse through invoking the Air Element, the Higher Self will have an easier time communicating with you—which will manifest these higher vibrational feelings of love in your Heart Chakra.

Feelings of being elated, inspired, in thought, and intellectualizing the world around you are all attributes of the Air Element. Also, since Air is directly linked to Spirit, you will feel very Spiritual with invocations of Air. As the Air Element is of an Aetheric, invisible quality, you may find yourself doing inspirational writing, art, philosophizing, and other activities dealing with the inspiration of the mind. The Air Element fuels creativity and imagination; thus, activities that require creativity are most affected by Air. Creativity may be more of a Fire Element quality or expression, but remember that Fire needs Air to operate successfully.

People will generally react very well to you while invoking the Air Element. Your sense of humour will be heightened, and you may appear quirky and fun to others. Air is a fun Element to invoke; it brings inspiration and creativity to others when you are around them. However, since you will be very cerebral and thought-oriented, you may end up talking too much, thus neglecting the emotions of people around you. One of the downsides of working with the Air Element is that you may tune out of your feelings, which will make you appear cold and aloof to others.

In the Golden Dawn tradition, when one embarks on invocations of Air, they are said to be directly walking the path of Tav, the Universe Tarot card, which links Malkuth to Yesod. Tav is representative of the subconscious mind. This means that the first step when undergoing Spiritual Alchemy is connecting to the subconscious, involuntary mind and seeing what lies within it. It enables you to take a magnifying glass to your subconscious mind and "zero in" on the thoughts and emotions present in that area. And as the subconscious is the storehouse of buried and repressed psychological traumas, you will be working with your inner fears and Demons. As this path is very deceptive and illusory, overcoming your fears is mandatory in moving forward in your Spiritual Evolution.

Various vices and virtues are of the Air Element quality since Air relates to thoughts. Among them are patience and its counterpart vice of wrath. As one is quick to act and feel an emotion, which can sometimes lead to impulsiveness (especially in the case of anger or frustration), working with the Air Element enables you to build up your Heart Chakra quality and remove the impulses of the Ego. It allows you to learn to love stronger by realizing it is the ethical, right thing to do.

Temperance, as well as gluttony, are also expressions of this Element. Air enables you to take hold of your thoughts before engaging in frivolous actions through the Ego. Temperance requires mindfulness, as does patience. Performing Air invocations will infuse your Aura with the energy of Anahata, the Heart Chakra. It will enable you to tune this Chakra and the behaviours which are associated with it. Air also stimulates the sexual energy, which is felt in Swadhisthana, the Sacral Chakra.

The Air Element enables you to practice self-control. It can also be linked to the virtue of chastity since one requires self-control if they are not to fall prey to lust. Remember, Air is the great tempter since it is directly linked to sexual energy, so you may first go through lust before you can practice Self-control and chastity. All actions of the Ego to satisfy itself, from lust to gluttony to anger and wrath, require you to work with the Element of Air to balance your psyche and remove the negative Karma in this Chakra. Doing so will enable you to use your Air Element more constructively and live a healthier life.

Regarding the Spiritual Alchemy program, the Element you are working with gives rise to the following Element within you. First, Earth gave rise to Air, as the energy solidified within your Aura, enabling the Ego to come out. Then, Air purges the Ego until the Soul's emotions reveal themselves, signalling the emergence of the Water Element within your psyche. The feelings will then give rise to willpower, namely the True Will of the Fire Element. And the Fire will bring out the Eternal Spirit and the Higher Self.

As the Element you are working with gives rise to the following Element, it is not uncommon to feel you have completed its Spiritual Alchemy program earlier than expected. However, it is crucial to stick to the program presented in *The Magus* concerning the length of time you are to invoke each Element. A common mistake is getting excited to advance quicker through the Elements. Excitement is great, and you will encounter it while doing this work, but use it constructively to keep you moving forward instead of allowing it to deviate you from the prescribed program.

Advancing through the Elements faster than is recommended may Spiritually harm you in the long run by taking away from the Spiritual Alchemy process. Remember, this is an invisible science, proven over the ages; therefore, treat it with reverence and respect.

THE WATER ELEMENT

The Water Element is the second Chakra, Swadhisthana, located between the navel and the lower abdomen. In the upright Pentagram symbol, the Water Element is of the colour blue, forming the upper right part of the Pentagram. If we superimpose the human being onto the Pentagram symbol, the Water Element represents the left arm.

The Water Element's primary function is to generate emotions; its Qabalistic correspondence is with Chesed, whose Planetary attribution is Jupiter. Chesed is the expression of unconditional love, mercy, and altruism, which are the highest expressions of the Water Element.

Since it is related to emotions, the Water Element also encompasses other Sephiroth, the same as the Air Element (thoughts). Since the Sphere of Netzach is the form of lower, more instinctual emotions, such as lust and romantic love, the Water Element also expresses through this Sphere. Netzach corresponds to the Planet Venus and desire, which in this case is felt as an emotion tempered by the Fire Element.

The Water Element also powers the logical, reasoning mind of Hod, as Hod and Netzach work to complement one another. Hod corresponds to Mercury; therefore, in this aspect of the Water Element, it works in combination with the Air Element and thoughts.

The Water Element is also related to sexual energy and instincts found in the Moon, corresponding with the Sphere of Yesod. As you can see, the Water Element encompasses multiple middle and lower Sephiroth of the Tree of Life, as do the Air and Fire Elements.

It is crucial to understand that one form of love, Self-Love, seeks to gratify oneself and find romance while developing an Egoic attachment to its objects of desire. On the other hand, unconditional love is ethical and of the Higher Self. Therefore, it is more propitious to be able to share unconditional love with everyone, and quite a few of the virtues are built on it.

Interestingly, at the level of Netzach, romantic love becomes the kind of love that can create mental obsession—the need to own or control your object of desire. Netzach is naturally tempered by Hod (logic and reason), giving rise to a kind of love that needs a reason to express itself, which means it uses the Ego. In the case of romantic love, then, the sublimation of opposites happens only on the mental level.

At the level of Chesed, unconditional love is experienced since Chesed is moderated by Geburah, which is the individual willpower. Unconditional love is a type of love that is void of personal attachment; thus, it bypasses the Ego. It is of a higher vibration and quality and is more sought after than romantic love since it exalts the Spirit over the Ego. Unconditional love is experienced through the Soul.

The form of love in Netzach belongs to the Ego, as it is connected to Yesod, the Moon, and the animal Self. On the other hand, Chesed's higher form of love is connected to the Supernals through the path of the Wheel of Fortune, ruled by the bountiful Planet Jupiter.

The nature of the form of emotion from Netzach is exemplified by the beautiful woman, half-naked in a seashell, as is the portrayal of the Greek Goddess Aphrodite in classical art. Venus is her Roman equivalent, also portrayed half-naked in classical art. It is her physical form and its beauty that becomes the object of desire, but as we have seen so far, everything that has a connection to the World of Matter belongs to the realm of the Ego. Hence, the Ego's need to own, possess, and otherwise control its object of desire. It does not love for the sake of loving but to obtain and possess its object of desire.

Romantic love works both ways for men and women. It is only at the level of Chesed that we can love unconditionally, where the Water Chakra, Swadhisthana is exalted. On the other hand, expressing love at the level of Netzach and Hod keeps the Light of the Water Chakra vibrating at a lower frequency than that of Chesed. Both are emotions, and the nature of emotions is to love, but one can either love themselves internally or turn their love externally to love others.

In the second form of love, unconditional love, the person finds their True Self because when love is absent of a reason or cause, it is much stronger and more Spiritual. Therefore, the overall lesson in this Chakra of Water is learning how to love without attachment through the Soul. You must transform your lower love emotions into higher ones. You must choose your Soul over your Ego.

Since we are exploring the emotions, it is necessary to note that on the Tree of Life, emotions are primarily on the Pillar of Mercy. However, the Pillar of Mercy is masculine. Therefore, when you are on either the left or right Pillar, you must take into account the balancing energy of the Sphere on the opposite Pillar. Thus, in the case of emotions, it is willpower, logic, and reason that balance it.

Elemental invocations in *The Magus* connect with a particular type of energy from outside you and "call it" into your Aura. Water invocations zero in on Swadhisthana Chakra in particular. The purpose of invoking the Water Element is to tune and purify Swadhisthana Chakra. As your Aura becomes infused with Water energy, Karmic energy stored in this Chakra is activated, affecting future life experiences. Your mind and heart will then have to work through these experiences and learn life lessons from them. Once you learn the lessons associated with Swadhisthana Chakra, you will evolve past all blockages preventing it from functioning at its optimal rate of vibration. As such, the Water Element will heal your emotional Self over time.

In most cases, it is the Ego pulling you towards itself and preventing you from resonating and attuning with the Higher Self. Magickal operations with the Elements include learning about the Ego and evolving past it—since the Ego resides in the lower four Chakras (lower Four Elements) and does not partake of the Spirit energy. To have the full power of manifestation in your life, you must be living through your Soul and not your Ego. Your Soul can connect with your Higher Self, while your Ego cannot.

As you invoke the Water Element, you may notice a soothing feeling immediately in your emotions and a sense of love that overtakes you. Your Heart Chakra will be overcome with loving energy that sweeps over you like a wave. All intuitive emotions are felt in Anahata Chakra, even when an invoked energy is infusing a different Chakra. The Heart Chakra experiences energy directly, which you may feel immediately once new energy enters your Aura. Your ability to feel energies is determined by your level of sensitivity and intuitive capacity.

After invoking the Water Element for a few days, you will feel very comfortable with your Ego and showing it to the outside world. The Ego is usually the first part of the Self to come out when working with the Elements. Then, after you have spent some time embodying your Ego and showing its face to others, you will infuse the deeper aspects of the Water Chakra and start to tune into your Soul and the unconditional love energy.

As the previous step is the Egoic part of the invocations, this second step is the Chesed portion of the operation. Once this happens, you might feel powerful emotions of love towards people in your life. As a result, you will notice people lovingly reacting to you, and you will have an easy time creating bonds with others. The opposite sex will find you more attractive, naturally. You will be very accepting and non-confrontational with people. You may feel like an embodiment of a Saint or another Spiritual figure who exemplifies mercy, love, and truth. The concept of "turning the other cheek" will become very familiar to you as you will be in a passive, receptive mode, fully attuned to expressions of unconditional love.

You may often find yourself crying and feeling very emotional for no logical reason. Do not fear this state because crying is a method of purging emotions and is part of the Spiritual Evolution process. It is a form of rejuvenation. When you cry, you feel the totality of the emotion you are crying about, and in this act, you purify and release that emotional pain through love—since it is the love in our hearts that makes us cry in the first place. Crying involves using the Fire Element of the Soul, which acts on the Water Element and purges it. Every tear represents the act of purifying an old emotion. Crying is a good sign that you are moving forward in your Spiritual Evolution.

With Water invocations, you will notice your dreams taking on a different quality than with Air invocations. In your dreams, you will find yourself in different life situations in which you have to choose between the love of Self and the love of others. Thus, while invoking the Water Element, there are lessons to be learned from your dreams about developing ethics and morals. Your mind is playing tricks on you to allow the negative Karma to shed even while in the dream state. It is a good sign, as it means you are progressing further.

You will find yourself so filled with the unconditional love feeling that if you have experienced a Kundalini awakening, a complete surrender process will occur with invocations of the Water Element. The Sacral and Heart Chakras will be overtaken with love energy, allowing the Ego to let go finally.

Water energy also brings about the stimulation of sexual energy since it is felt in the abdomen. Now, this experience is not the same as with the Element of Air. In Water, the sexual energy is sublimated into love energy and is exalted. Therefore, you will find yourself sexually aroused at times but more from the notion of love than lust. Lust belongs to the Air Element, while love belongs to the Water Element.

It is imperative to note the association of the Water Chakra with the memory. Memory is to be found in the Sphere of Chesed, but its operation is through the Element of Water. Even the word "memory" corresponds to the Hebrew letter Mem—relating to the Water Element. Memory is something the Self uses to "re-member" itself. As such, it belongs to the realm of the past. You cannot have any memory of things happening in the Now since you are in the act of experience. And the future did not occur yet from our human point of view; thus, we cannot have any memory of it either. Memory provides the consciousness with a method of identifying itself.

Without memory, consciousness would lose itself. Consequently, losing oneself allows one to find their True Self—the Spirit.

You can say that the Ego uses memory to identify itself, which is not far from the truth. The Spiritual process is one of forgetting, and as you get more absorbed into unconditional love, you will lose the memory of the past more and more, which will enable you to be in the Now. Most elevated Spiritual people have little memory of the past and do not use it to relate to the world. Instead, they are continually living in the Now. However, as Chesed is the first Sephira past the Abyss and the Supernals, it brings forth memory and Form, a building block of the Self whereby it can know itself, learn from the past, and evolve.

If you have undergone a Kundalini awakening, you will find the Water Element very useful in furthering your transformation since it will enable you to "go with the flow." Going with the flow is challenging in the Kundalini awakening process because it is such a tremendous blow to the Ego, which then holds on for dear life to small fragments of the Self to maintain its identity.

In the Kundalini awakening, the fears are amplified at first and in the newly developing consciousness, the Ego will make many attempts to control the process. Because this is a new reality that you are now vaulted into, the Ego has difficulty finding itself. Building up the Water Element and infusing it within the Aura is crucial to getting past this stage and releasing yourself to the Kundalini energy.

In the Golden Dawn tradition, invoking the Water Element after working with Air means you are advancing from the Sephira Yesod to the Sephira Hod. The two Tarot paths which connect Yesod and Hod are the Judgement Tarot card path and the Sun Tarot card path. Judgement is the initiation into the Element of Fire, as you will experience once you keep working with the Water Element for a little while. The Fire Element of the Soul will unveil itself, as will its counterpart, the emotion of unconditional love. The Sun path represents the sublimation of opposites which occurs on the mental level, which is necessary to rise as high as the Fire Element and the Soul. Essentially, the purpose of the Water Element is to prepare you for the Fire Element and connect you with your Soul.

In the Water Element, you are entirely absorbed in the Waters of Creation and the Sea of Consciousness. As such, the Water Element is also connected to Binah, the Great Feminine Principle of Creation. Therefore, the virtues associated with the Water Element stem from the energy of unconditional love, the highest emotion that connects all Beings in the Universe.

Within Christian theology, the three chief theological virtues are faith, hope, and charity—imparted to us by the Grace of God- the Creator—once we have built up the Water Element into our hearts and minds. Since inner peace comes with unconditional love, patience is another virtue built up by the Water Element. Also, since unconditional love brings out honesty within oneself, you will find yourself always speaking the truth, even if you know it might get you into trouble. Thus, truth is another expression of embodying the energy of unconditional love.

The concept of faith implies a strong belief in God-the Creator, which is intensified when we are exposed to the energy of unconditional love. Faith is also confidence and trust in a person, a concept, or an idea. Thus, you will find yourself examining your inner beliefs often as well as your relationships with other people. In the Water Element, you will rely more on "feeling things out" instead of intellectualizing your emotions (which is more of an Air Element quality).

Hope is an optimistic state of mind based on expectations of positive outcomes. In the Water Element, you will find yourself thinking with optimism, even when a life situation may not be so favourable on the surface. This optimistic state of mind comes from being connected to the Spirit and the energy of unconditional love, which never lets down in the face of adversity. Your problem-solving skills will be enhanced while working with the Water Element if you can embrace the virtues of hope and faith.

Charity is a form of generosity and is considered the greatest of the three theological virtues. Charity involves self-sacrifice, an essential concept for any initiate on the path of Light. You must always be ready to sacrifice yourself for another person if you want to resonate with a higher state of consciousness. In sacrifice, you lose yourself and your identity and reach as high as the Mind of God. Charity is a practice of being benevolent, which involves altruism and selflessness.

The vice associated with hope is despair; when we despair, we feel there are no choices that can yield positive outcomes. Instead of looking for solutions, we give up. Our Ego takes over and brings fear into our hearts and minds. Despair comes after we have lost faith. In losing faith, we start to doubt ourselves and our connection with God-the Creator. We begin to doubt that we are unique and deserve good things in life. Again, it is the Ego that makes us lose faith since once we bring fear in, we immediately lose touch with the unconditional love energy. You cannot simultaneously draw power from unconditional love and fear—the one drowns out the other.

The vice associated with charity is greed, which is also of the Ego. Greed is a form of hoarding, not sharing with others and seeking fulfilment only for oneself. It is the antithesis of charity and love since greed occurs from the fear of being a separate entity from the rest of the world. However, since we are all One, once we allow unconditional love to guide us, we can experience this connection.

Wrath or anger is the antithesis of patience. When you do not feel the love in your heart, anger is apt to come out whenever the Ego does not get what it wants. But when love is present, it is impossible to show anger or wrath since patience is also naturally present.

"Love is patient, love is kind. It does not envy, it does not boast, it is not proud. It does not dishonour others, it is not Self-seeking, it is not easily angered, it keeps no record of wrongs. Love does not delight in evil but rejoices with the truth. It always protects, always trusts, always hopes, always perseveres." — "The Holy Bible" (Corinthians 13:4-7)

When you have love in your heart, the vices are naturally removed from the Self, exalting the virtues. Love truly is the building block of all Spiritual Life and is to be found in the Water Element.

THE FIRE ELEMENT

The Fire Element is the third Chakra, Manipura, located in the solar plexus. In the upright Pentagram symbol, the Fire Element is of the colour red, forming the lower right part of the Pentagram. If we superimpose the human being onto the Pentagram symbol, the Fire Element represents the left leg.

The Fire Element's Qabalistic correspondence is the Geburah Sephira, whose Planetary attribution is Mars. The Fire of Geburah is one of will-power and drive. The Fire Element is the active, masculine part of the Self, as the Water Element is the passive, feminine part of the Self. The Fire Element is the Soul, while the Water Element is consciousness.

The Fire Element is also expressed through Netzach as desire, which is an emotion that is powered by Fire. Desire is often instinctual and involuntary, such as sexual or sensual desire. The Fire Element also stimulates and powers intelligence; hence, it is also expressed through the Hod Sephira—as the strength of mind (fortitude) in the face of fluctuating emotions. Intellect and reason are the driving force of willpower at the lower levels, while the Soul is the driving force at the higher levels. Willpower is most exalted when it is motivated by unconditional love.

The Fire Element is the Father Principle, as the Water Element is the Mother Principle. Fire without Water is tyranny and oppression—it can be uncontrollable and often manifest as anger. Fire needs Water to balance it; otherwise, it can be detrimental to the psyche and other people since it can quickly turn to hostility. Therefore, one must understand the nature of their anger and face the inner pain that is causing it to manifest.

Fire is the motivation; it is the drive, dynamism, the active thought, and the focused willpower underlying every conscious thought and emotion. Thus, Fire is the highest of the Four Elements. Fire is the cause behind the effect, and as such, it is linked more to the Supernals than the other three Elements. Fire without Water would be an effect without a cause. Fire and Water exist in terms of their duality with one another. Willpower always fights in the name of love, whether it is Self-love or unconditional love for all living Beings.

The Element of Fire deals a lot with inner beliefs. With Fire invocations, you can change your beliefs, ideas, and attitude about who you think you are as well as the world around you. Through Fire, you begin to burn away aspects of the Ego that are detrimental to forming the newly elevated consciousness. The same issues with the Ego you encountered with Air invocations are increased tenfold with Fire invocations. With Fire invocations, you are tuning into the Ego and how it expresses itself, including its beliefs about its identity and the world surrounding it.

Pride is the primary vice that shows itself in Fire invocations, as pride is the building block for the Ego's beliefs. Therefore, you must spend a good deal of time invoking Water before embarking on Fire. And there must be a proper mental foundation in Air before starting with Water and the proper stability in Earth before embarking on Air.

It is important to note that you must work through the Elements systematically since you are undergoing a formulated Spiritual Alchemy procedure. The process starts with Earth and moves on to Air, Water, and finally Fire. Working with Fire first without having a solid foundation in the other Elements would be disastrous and would only set you back in your Spiritual Evolution progress.

Fire cannot exist without Air, but it gets put out with too much of it. Therefore, having a good mental foundation is very important before working with Fire since Fire stimulates thoughts. Personal beliefs are most valuable when working with the Fire Element since beliefs determine your reality. Once you change your inner beliefs about yourself, you will also change the world around you.

Gandhi said, "Be the change you wish to see in the world." This means that once you change your concept of who you think you are, the people around you will react accordingly, and your reality will transform positively. Changing your inner beliefs will enable you to tap into your innermost potential, and new opportunities in life will present themselves to you, allowing you to get the most of your life here on Earth.

Mars is attributed to the Fire Element, whose action is symbolically depicted in the Tower card of the Tarot. The Tower card contains an image of a thunderbolt hitting and destroying a Tower, alluding to the Tower of Babel story in the *Book of Genesis*. The Tower represents our beliefs, while the lightning flash is the Yod, the Primal Fire, the Father energy. It signifies the depth of the Fire Element since it is in our Solar Plexus, our core, and has a direct link to the Godhead—the Creator. It is also essential to understand the connection between the Fire Element and Mars and Aries—the Gods of War. The great Spartan King Leonidas is another mythological character that comes to mind as an example of a warrior who fights for love and justice.

Mercury is the God of Wisdom and is the corresponding Planet in Hod. Hod is the Sphere of communication and logic and reason—the workings of the inner Fire acting on the Element of Water and the mind. In the case of Hod, it is Fire (willpower) acted on by Air (thoughts), projecting into Water (consciousness), which forms the intellect. In the case of Netzach, it is Fire acting on Water (in its expression as the emotions), which creates desire. It is no wonder that the Planet Venus is attributed to Netzach, as sensual or sexual stimulation is one of the significant motivating factors for humanity.

In the Golden Dawn tradition, invocations of the Fire Element mean that you are advancing from the Hod Sephira to the Netzach Sephira. Three Tarot paths connect Netzach to the lower three Sephiroth—the Tower, the Star, and the Moon paths. The Tower, as mentioned, represents the beliefs about the world and the application of the destructive Mars energy since the old must be destroyed for something new to take its place.

The Star card is the meditation and stillness of mind necessary to align the individual consciousness to Netzach successfully. The emotions and thoughts must be stilled for the Fire Element energy to infuse Manipura successfully. And finally, the Moon card is the subconscious mind, the back of the head, the deepest of our Water Element and that which needs to transform. As you can see, the idea of transformation is very prevalent while working with the Fire Element.

You will find that you will not need much sleep while working with the Fire Element, and you will be generally disconnected from your dreams, unlike the previous two Elements of Water and Air. Fire is of the Soul, which concerns itself with experiencing life directly through intuition. You will, therefore, experience deep sleep instead of experiencing the images in your mind as you sleep. You will feel disconnected from the inner visual images but more in tune with the Archetypal energy and the feeling behind the images.

Humility is the highest virtue that comes from exalting the Fire Element. Its vice is pride, the foundation of all the other vices and the Ego. You can see how the Fire Element is the core of your Being, your Soul, since it represents the beliefs about the world, deeply rooted in your subconscious mind and difficult to change. With the Fire Element invoked into the Aura, you zero in on the Solar Plexus Chakra, allowing you to reach the deepest, innermost corners of your Soul to make the necessary changes in that area.

Invocations of Fire will make you feel very inspired, creative, active, and engaged. As mentioned, you will not need much sleep to function at your full capacity. There will be a constant heat felt in the Solar Plexus area, and over time you will find your life beliefs are transforming, seemingly without your conscious participation.

The pain that manifests at first will leave the Aura through purging with the Fire Element. Internal pain is something that is lodged within the subconscious mind. It is a part of your memory and belongs to the Water Element. With proper application, the Fire Element will burn away this pain so that the Solar Plexus Chakra is functioning better and radiating more Light energy. This process will align your consciousness with your Soul, in turn distancing you from your Ego.

The Water Element is the emotions, so to purify Water, you need to apply Fire to it in the same way as you would cleanse physical water—you add heat to it until it reaches a boiling point and the impurities evaporate into the air. This process of purifying water can also be applied to the mental and emotional level—As Above, So Below. We apply heat to our thoughts and emotions with the Fire Element to get the desired outcome.

Working with the Fire Element is an excellent time to practice meditation and stillness of mind. By embodying the Fire Element, you will be able to rise above the Ego's mind chatter since the Fire Element is higher on the scale, Spiritually speaking. In silence, the truth is experienced through intuition, and the Fire Element will connect you to your intuition more than any previous Element.

If you have awakened the inner Fire of the Kundalini, you will find that working with the Fire Element is relatively easy as the energy complements the Kundalini energy. The two will often feel like the same thing but do not worry; the Fire Element is still working on different aspects of the Self, while the Kundalini energy is active.

The Fire Element will make you very energized, and you will feel a need to engage in different activities to channel its energy. These can be physical activities as well as mental ones since the Fire Element encompasses the other three Elements of Earth, Air, and Water.

Since Fire enflames the Air Element in you, your creativity and imagination will heighten, as will your level of inspiration about life in general. You will have an unwavering strength of mind (fortitude), which will enable you to apply this energy to activities and see them through to the end. Your level of persistence and determination will be intensified like never before, allowing you to accomplish various tasks with ease.

"The use of the will as the projector of mentative currents is the real base of all mental magic." — William Walker Atkinson; excerpt from "Mind-Power: The Secret of Mental Magic"

Because it is willpower, the Fire Element will enable you to manifest your dreams and goals in an unprecedented way. Manifesting an extraordinary life requires the proper application of the Fire Element, filtered through the Earth Element. There is a back-and-forth, action and reaction, continually occurring between the Fire and Earth Elements when your Soul is your guiding force.

Conversely, if the Ego is your guiding force, the willpower becomes hijacked, and your Earth Element draws its primary energy from the involuntary emotions of the Water Element instead. As mentioned, the Air Element is needed to fuel both Fire and Water, and your thoughts can serve your Soul or your Ego. You do have Free Will, which allows you to choose between the two. However, the average person mostly lets their emotions do their thinking for them, not realizing they have a choice in the matter.

While invoking the Fire Element, people will react well to you, and you will be inspiring to others. Be mindful to remain balanced and not allow the Fire to manifest negatively through anger or impatience. Learning to curb your Ego is a must while working with the Fire Element, which may appear very challenging at times. The lessons learned from working with the previous Elements will need to be applied. For example, if willpower is unchecked by unconditional love, it will result in Self-love, which will bring forth negative Karma that will need to be worked through in the future. So you see, having a good foundation in the Water Element is essential before proceeding to Fire.

Since the Fire Element is the willpower and the expressions of your Soul, you need to spend many months working with Fire before proceeding to the next Element of Spirit. It takes many months to change and purify negative, fear-based emotions through the application of heat and to change unwanted beliefs about the Self and the world. In most cases, it has taken many years to build a belief about something and in turn, it takes a long time to eradicate that negative mindset.

Once infused into the Aura through ritual invocations, the Element of Fire will do what it needs to do to purify the Manipura Chakra. Again, you need to be conscious of your thoughts and actions as this process is taking place so as not to fall prey to the Ego. By remaining balanced in mind, body and Soul, simply bringing the Fire Element into the Aura to purify your thoughts and emotions is all that is required of you to attune your willpower and exalt the Soul over the Ego.

In many cases, you will feel the effect behind the cause, and it will manifest through you, as you will be filtering all of your mental and emotional processes through the Fire Element. With a simple ritual exercise invocation (LIRP), you will find that the energy stays present up to twenty-four hours throughout your day. While in sleep, as you enter the *Alpha State*, the excess energy will dissipate as it filters through all parts of the Self and leaves your Aura entirely.

THE SPIRIT ELEMENT

The English word "Spirit" comes from the Latin word "spiritus," meaning "breath." This correlation between the two words tells us that there is a correspondence between the Spirit energy and the act of breathing the air around us (which is a physical manifestation of the Air Element). To breathe is to receive Spirit. All creatures which have to breathe to sustain their lives are a part of Spirit. Thus, breath is the evidence of life and Spirit. For this reason, breathing techniques are essential in meditation and Ritual Magick.

The Spirit/Aethyr Element is attributed to the Throat Chakra (Vishuddhi), the Mind's Eye Chakra (Ajna), and the Crown Chakra (Sahasrara). In the upright Pentagram symbol, the Spirit Element is white, forming the uppermost part of the Pentagram. If we superimpose the human being onto the Pentagram symbol, the Spirit Element represents the head, our connection with the Divine Source.

"Heaven is the First Element." — Hermes Trismegistus; excerpt from "The Divine Pymander"

In the Qabalah, the Spirit Element represents the Supernals—the Spheres of Kether, Chokmah and Binah. The Spirit Element also encompasses the Sphere of Daath, the invisible eleventh Sphere. Daath is called the Abyss, and it is the point where the duality of the lower seven Sephiroth meets the Non-Duality of the Supernals. The only duality that exists at the level of the Supernals is Chokmah-the Father and Binah-the Mother. However, the three Spheres of Kether, Chokmah, and Binah work as a whole. Chokmah receives its Archetypal energy from Kether, and Binah transforms those Archetypal ideas into Form. The Christian equivalent of the Supernals is the Trinity—the Father, the Son, and the Holy Ghost (or Spirit).

In terms of the Chakras, Daath is found in the throat, represented by Vishuddhi Chakra. As Daath stands for knowledge and the purpose of the throat is to generate the vibration to speak orally, the Word expressed through language links us to the Creator. Therefore, the Word becomes our modus operandi, our connection to God, since we can speak and use words to communicate.

The Throat Chakra is the voice of the body, the mind, and the Soul. It is a pressure valve that allows the energy from the other Chakras to be expressed. If it is out of balance or blocked, it can affect the health of the other Chakras. Consequently, when it is in balance, we can express what we think and feel. Thus, we see the Spiritual quality of this Chakra because Spirit is the unifying factor of the other Four Elements, which serve as the expression of Spirit.

The Throat Chakra, Vishuddhi, is the first point where the lower Four Elements synthesize into Spirit and are expressed through communication. Vishuddhi is directly connected with truth; someone who always speaks the truth should have a well-balanced Throat Chakra. Conversely, someone who lies and manipulates others will have an unbalanced Throat Chakra. Remember always that truth and unconditional love are the two most potent factors when relating to anything Spiritual. Therefore, always telling the truth in life is essential since doing that alone allows you to "walk with God."

Lying is the domain of God's opposite, the Devil, and will yield negative Karma in the Throat Chakra. The Devil is a personification of a concept, an idea, not an entity in and of itself. The idea behind this concept is best portrayed in the Devil Tarot card. Called the "Lord of the Gates of Matter," the title and meaning of this card inform us that, in reality, the Devil is the alluring and energy-binding quality of Matter itself. All things that pertain to attaching our consciousness to Matter instead of Spirit belong to the Devil. This would be the more occult description of the Devil's energy.

> *"And now it stands proven that Satan, or the Red Fiery Dragon...and Lucifer, or "Light-Bearer," is in us; it is our Mind."* — H. P. Blavatsky; excerpt from "The Secret Doctrine: The Synthesis of Science, Religion, and Philosophy"

In *The Torah* and *The Holy Bible*, the name of the Devil is Satan. The name "Satan" was derived from the Planet Saturn, and this is because of Saturn's close association with the World of Matter. As Saturn is the slowest moving Planet in our Solar System, it has been associated with the passage of time and death. As such, Saturn is responsible for the building up of the Ego. Qabalistically, Saturn is associated with Binah, the Great Feminine energy and the Astral blueprint behind all the Matter in the Universe. The Tarot card of Saturn is the Universe card.

The Devil tempts humanity to lie because lies use the energy of fear instead of love. Fear is linked to the World of Matter because of the instinctual defense mechanism used by the Ego to protect the physical body. We usually lie to conceal the truth out of fear that we will get into trouble by revealing it. Or we lie for our Egos to get what they desire, even if that thing is detrimental to our Spirituality. Truth is directly linked to honour and personal integrity, while lies serve to conceal and manipulate others for personal gain. Blockages in the Throat Chakra can manifest as thyroid problems.

The sixth Chakra, Ajna, is our connection to the Divine and Spiritual Worlds. Its gift is "seeing"—not physically though, but Astrally. The energy of this Chakra allows us to experience clear thought and the gifts of Spiritual contemplation and self-reflection.

The Mind's Eye is a doughnut-shaped portal between the eyebrows which can be accessed by focusing your two physical eyes on it once they are closed. As we focus our eyes on this Mind's Eye portal, a magnet-like attraction pulls our attention into it, resulting in the entrance portal naturally opening up. Accessing the Mind's Eye portal this way is considered a meditation and the most popular and effective one. All meditation methods aim to tune you in to your Mind's Eye Chakra.

Ajna is directly linked to Chokmah and Binah; through this Chakra, we access both of these Spheres. Ajna Chakra is the seat of intuition. It allows us to be the observer of events taking place without taking part in them. It also allows us to see and observe ourselves and the world around us in the third-person.

A person who undergoes a full and sustained Kundalini awakening will have "blown open" the Mind's Eye Chakra, where its average doughnut (circular) portal expands to the size of a car tire, figuratively speaking. After this occurs, everything the awakened individual sees with their two physical eyes is now filtered through the expanded Mind's Eye, yielding many transcendental experiences regularly.

Ajna allows us to access inner guidance from Divine Worlds and be in touch with our Holy Guardian Angel—hence Ajna's connection to Chokmah. Ajna enables us to cut through illusion and access more profound truths about life and the Universe, to see beyond the mind and words. It allows us to experience the Archetypal energy behind the images playing in our heads.

Ajna is commonly called the Third Eye, and its full activation occurs when the Pineal Gland and the Pituitary Gland become balanced in the brain. The Pineal Gland is a small cone-shaped gland in the middle of the brain that produces melatonin, a serotonin-derived hormone which modulates sleep patterns. The Pituitary Gland is a small pea-shaped gland closer to the front of the head, along the eye line. Often called the "master gland," its purpose is to secrete many hormones controlling various bodily organs.

The Pineal and Pituitary Glands are inextricably connected with the functions of Ajna—but also the Chakra above it, Sahasrara. Ajna is the vehicle one uses to reach Sahasrara. Also, Sahasrara cannot be achieved without activating Ajna first. When activated, one of the functions of Ajna is to serve as a receiver of information from Sahasrara.

The seventh Chakra, Sahasrara, is the Crown and the culmination of the other six Chakras below it. Its location is at the top of the head. Sahasrara is the last of the Chakras of the Self and the beginning of the *Transpersonal Self*. It is our connection to the Divine Source of all of Creation. At a fundamental level, it is unity and the reconciliation of opposites since it is the Chakra of Oneness. Through Sahasrara, we experience mystical Oneness with everyone and everything in nature. Within this Chakra, we see that All is One and that separation is an illusion.

Sahasrara is a Sanskrit word which means "Thousand-Petaled Lotus." It opens us up like a flower to the vibrations of our Divine Universe. Qabalistically, this Chakra is represented by Kether-the Crown and the beginning of the Three Veils of Negative Existence. Sahasrara is the meeting point between the Finite and the Infinite—it is beyond Time and Space as it is Eternal. Sahasrara is a channel of the Pure Spirit—the Great White Light.

It is important to note that all three of the top Chakras of Vishuddhi, Ajna, and Sahasrara belong to the Spirit/Aethyr Element, but only Sahasrara belongs to Non-Duality. Ajna is the vehicle whereby one reaches the Crown, while Vishuddhi is the connection to Spirit through the spoken Word. Sahasrara, though, is beyond fear and negativity since the Ego cannot reach it. The Ego loses itself entirely in Ajna. It is still present in Vishuddhi, the last place it can access.

The Ego is a by-product of separatedness that ends at Vishuddhi Chakra since it is the Mind's Abyss. On the other hand, Sahasrara is awareness, the "Seed of Truth," and the ultimate reality of the unity of all things. It is the access point of the Divine Realms and Chakras above the Crown. Sahasrara is also the summit of our Spiritual Evolution.

All three Chakras of Vishuddhi, Ajna, and Sahasrara participate in the Spirit Element. They are its conductors and the medium whereby you can access the inner Cosmic Realms. You are to start working with Spirit only after you have spent much time invoking the other Four Elements of Earth, Air, Water, and Fire. The purpose of the Spirit Element invocations is to attune the three top Chakras and synthesize the Four Elements by infusing them with the Spirit energy. Working with the Spirit Element prepares you for Adepthood.

The effects on the physical body through Spirit invocations will be a pervading sense of peace, calm, and Oneness in your thoughts and emotions. The body will feel tender as the Spirit energy is infused in the deepest recesses of your Being. Inspirational dreams, transcendental states of consciousness, and inspired meditation are all by-products of invoking Spirit.

Metaphorically speaking, invoking the Spirit Element daily will make you walk on the Earth while having your head in Heaven, in the clouds. This means that while the Spiritual energy is present in your Aura, the Cosmic Planes become opened up within you as accessible states of consciousness. The Mind's Eye starts to function at a higher level and can sense vibrations beyond the Physical Realm, which registers in your consciousness.

When invoking the Spirit Element, you will notice that people generally respond well to you. However, because Spirit is directly connected to truth, you will have an almost impossible time not speaking your mind at all times, which will often get you into confrontational situations. Managing speaking the truth at all times is the Karma of the Element of Spirit. You are meant to learn to overcome all confrontations with others and develop your character.

The Spirit Element elevates your consciousness to the level of the Fourth Dimension—the Dimension of Vibration. Once your consciousness is elevated, you can read energy through the Mind's Eye and receive vibrations from the outside world, which you will experience through intuition. In addition, invoking the Spirit Element allows you to function through Chokmah and Binah—Wisdom and Understanding.

The Spirit Element invocation is the closest thing to experiencing what a full Kundalini awakening feels like. Full awakening of the Kundalini activates all of the Elements in the body, which is what the Spirit Element does as well. Spirit invocations also fine-tune the three top Chakras. As the Chakras are being tuned through Spirit invocations, blockages will be removed in the head area, enabling the Kundalini energy to better access all the untapped regions of the brain and activate them.

CEREMONIAL MAGICK RITUAL EXERCISES

THE HERMETIC ORDER OF THE GOLDEN DAWN

The ritual exercises I will be presenting to you in this section are from the Hermetic Order of the Golden Dawn. The Golden Dawn was an organization devoted to studying and practising the *Western Esoteric Mysteries*, including the Qabalah and Ceremonial Magick. It was established in 1888 in London, Great Britain, by a group of Freemasons, Qabalists, Rosicrucians, and Theosophists. William Wynn Westcott was the initial driving force behind the establishment of the Golden Dawn—along with two fellow Freemasons, Dr William Robert Woodman and Samuel Liddell MacGregor Mathers. The Hermetic Order of the Golden Dawn's original Temple was called the Isis-Urania Temple.

The Golden Dawn was a Hermetic society of like-minded individuals concerned with their Spiritual development. Its system was based on hierarchy and initiation, like the Masonic lodges. The main difference was that women were admitted into the Golden Dawn Order and were on an equal basis with men. The Golden Dawn was primarily a school of occult knowledge, where the main focus was theurgy (the practice of ritual exercises) and learning about the Mysteries of the Universe. The theurgy portion was supposedly based on the Cipher Manuscripts, which were cryptic notes that included a series of Magickal initiation rituals corresponding to the Spiritual Elements of Earth, Air, Water and Fire.

The Golden Dawn Order had its peak early on and fell apart in 1903 due to internal issues between the members. The Order split into different factions, and other offshoot Orders sprung up from what remained of the original Order. The two main offshoots were the Order of the Stella Matutina and the Order of the Alpha et Omega. The ritual exercises presented in *The Magus* and their knowledge were secret at the time. One had to be initiated into one of these Magickal Orders to partake in the vast amount of knowledge being disseminated to their members.

These ritual exercises were not made public until 1937, when Israel Regardie published *The Golden Dawn*, giving the masses the complete course of study of the Hermetic Order of the Golden Dawn's teachings and practices. The New Age movement was on the rise in Europe and North America at the time, which motivated

Regardie to break his oath of secrecy and make the Golden Dawn knowledge public. By doing so, he provided the foundation for modern Western occultism.

Many other Golden Dawn Orders came after Regardie's *The Golden Dawn* was published, claiming that they held the true lineage of the original Hermetic Order of the Golden Dawn, and many are still in the world today. But the truth is that the genuine lineage was lost in the early 1900s as the principal members of the original Order left. Some even went on to assimilate the Golden Dawn's beliefs and rituals into other existing Magickal Orders, such as Aleister Crowley, who reformed the Ordo Templi Orientis (OTO). In reality, the power and use of these ritual exercises are still relatively unknown to the public, so I am presenting them with the most practical explanation of how and why they work.

HIGH AND LOW MAGICK

Ceremonial Magick is otherwise called High Magick or White Magick. It is Solar Magick and of the Light. It draws energy from the Solar System and infuses Light (at different frequencies) into the Aura through ritual exercises. Ceremonial Magick has a Spiritual purpose rather than a practical one.

Another name for High Magick is Sun Magick since the Sun is the source of the Light and life for us. The energy is drawn directly from the Universe above, and using the air as its medium of transmission invokes this energy into the practitioner's Aura. For this reason, you will often feel a rush of wind on your skin when invoking energy through a Ceremonial Magick exercise.

Low Magick, on the other hand, draws up energy from the Earth—it is often referred to as Earth Magick or Natural Magick. Folk Magick is another common name for it. Low Magick is concerned with achieving a practical, material result—it utilizes natural objects such as plants, animals, stones, fire, water, and anything and everything that can be found in our environment and nature. It often involves charms and spells, consisting of much less elaborate rituals than in High Magick.

Low Magick is the Magick of the Pagan people, Witches, Wizards, sorcerers and wise elders. It can be used to obtain a material item, get money, find love, heal the physical body, and anything else that involves taking care of your bodily, Earthly wants, needs, or desires.

The main difference between High and Low Magick is that they work on different parts of the Self. Low Magick works directly with the physical body and the Sephira Malkuth. On the other hand, High Magick can work on all the Subtle Bodies within the inner Cosmic Planes, as it encompasses the entire Tree of Life.

High Magick can also produce the same results as Low Magick, but only through invoking the Earth Element. Low Magick is a more exact science regarding manifesting in the material world since the symbolic items it incorporates into its rituals work to accomplish specific tasks. High Magick only gives you what your Soul needs to keep advancing Spiritually while Low Magick can be used by the Soul but also the Ego; thus, its results may not always be favourable for you from a Karmic standpoint.

In *The Magus*, we will only be concerning ourselves with High Magick. Therefore, I will not be making the distinction between High and Low Magick from now on but will only refer to the subject as Magick. If you want to learn more about Low Magick, I invite you to do some research on your own. There is no harm from learning about Low Magick or any other type of Magick. However, I advise against invoking energies from other systems while performing one of the Spiritual Alchemy programs from *The Magus*. Doing so may negatively affect the desired results you are trying to achieve through this work.

THE ORIGINS OF MAGICK

The origins of Magick are veiled in mystery and intrigue. According to the *Book of the Watchers* (from the apocryphal *Book of Enoch*), before the event of Noah's Flood, there existed a group of otherworldly Beings called the Watchers. In the Old Testament, the Watchers are said to be Angels who came down from Heaven. The Watchers are organized into an Archangel hierarchy within mystical Hebrew sects, with Michael, Gabriel, Raphael, and Auriel as their leaders. In Ceremonial Magick, these four Archangels are the representatives of the Four Elements.

According to the story, God sent the Watchers to Earth to watch over the humans. After a while, some of them started to lust after human women. Led by the Angels Semyaza and Azazel, two hundred of the Watchers rebelled against God and came down to Earth to live amongst the humans. They took human wives for themselves and taught humans forbidden knowledge against God's will. This group became known as the "Fallen Angels." The story of the Watchers is where this popular term originated from.

The Fallen Angels revealed many occult secrets to humankind, including High and Low Magick. They also taught humans Astrology, astronomy, meteorology, writing, science and technology, various creative arts, agriculture, medicine, and the use of cosmetics. The Fallen Angels also taught humans metallurgy—how to make elaborate weapons of war such as swords, knives, shields, and breastplates.

The Fallen Angels procreated with human women, and their offspring became known as the Nephilim or the "Giants." In the Old Testament (Genesis 6:1-4), the Nephilim are referred to as the offspring of the "sons of God" and "daughters of men." They were called Giants because they were much taller than humans, averaging fourteen feet in height. As a result, humans worshipped them as half-Gods.

With constant wars being waged amongst humans, as well as other forms of lawlessness and sinning, the Earth became very corrupt. To make matters worse, the Nephilim turned on the humans and started eating them once the humans got tired of feeding them their produce. When God saw what was taking place, he sent the Deluge (Great Flood) to destroy the wickedness plaguing the Earth, thus allowing humankind to start again.

According to this story, Magick has its origins in the Watchers. Since the original purpose of the Watchers was to watch over humanity literally, the group that rebelled gave us a Spiritual practice that has the power to attune us energetically and raise our consciousness to Divine heights and levels that are our birthright. Perhaps after falling in love with human women, they felt a personal responsibility to share the knowledge of Magick with us and help us evolve.

In the *Book of Jubilees*, otherwise known as the "Lesser Genesis," the Watchers originally descended to Earth to teach humanity by God's decree—their "Fall" was marked by their procreation with human women and not the dissemination of knowledge. According to this version of the Watchers' story, giving humanity knowledge was not a forbidden act but the primary purpose of their descent onto Earth.

After the Great Flood event, as humanity survived, so did the knowledge they received from the Watchers. Interestingly, the knowledge of Magick became reserved for the select few (upper class and Priesthood) in the thousands of years that followed, and only recently (past one-hundred years) its cloak of secrecy has been removed from the general population. It is as if the powers that have dominated the world stage in the civilizations that followed the Great Flood did not want the average human to have this knowledge. For some nefarious reason, humanity's collective level of consciousness was preferred to be kept in a lower state.

From the story of the Watchers, we see that they are of Divine origin—whether they are Angels, Archangels, or something else entirely. Also, the Watchers were probably the ones who imparted knowledge of the Qabalah to humanity. There is much relation between the Qabalah and Magick as you have seen so far, including the same aim—the Spiritual transformation of the human race. Also, it cannot be a coincidence that both were supposedly handed down to humanity in antiquity by Angelic Beings.

Were the Watchers Aetheric Beings though, or were they something else entirely? We know for a fact that the Watchers had sexual relations with human women and produced physical offspring. It would not be possible for them to do so if they were not flesh and blood since non-physical Beings cannot impregnate human women.

I think that by examining the nature of the Nephilim, we can ascertain more about who the Watchers were. Firstly, the Watchers were the "sons of God" according to the Old Testament. This statement says that they were superior to humans and were Gods themselves. Secondly, they had physical bodies since they could impregnate physical women. And thirdly, their offspring were giants compared to humans, meaning their DNA was different and superior to ours but also compatible.

After many years of research into this matter, I believe that the Watchers were not Angels or Archangels but Extraterrestrials instead. What you are hearing is an unorthodox theory but one that requires further examination since the many pieces of the puzzle fit together perfectly if we can accept this theory as a possibility.

There is ample evidence in Ancient civilizations from all over the world that Extraterrestrials played a part in the creation of modern-day humans hundreds of thousands of years ago and even made us in their image. For example, in the original Hebrew text of the *Book of Genesis*, the word "Elohim" is used in place of God, meaning "the Gods" (plural)—denoting that we were made in the image of our Creators and not our Creator.

Ancient Astronaut theorists believe that humans had contact with Extraterrestrials in the remote past and that our evolution was furthered by them when they mixed our genetics with theirs and gave us intelligence. For this reason, humans are continually advancing on all fronts as a species while other animal species are not. If this theory is correct, then the Watchers were sent to watch over us in the first place because they created us and had a responsibility towards us, as any parents do to their children. However, it is not the purpose of this book to question anthropology but to make the following few points.

When fully awakened to the highest potential of their Spiritual energy, a human being is a Being of Light. The purpose of working with the Five Elements through the Spiritual Alchemy process presented in *The Magus* is to attain Enlightenment—in other words, to realize your highest potential as a Being of Light.

If the Extraterrestrials are the ones who created us and then gave us knowledge of Magick to help us reach our highest potential, then it is highly possible that they also may have been Beings of Light. After all, they made us in their image, and every created thing contains the essence of its Creator. So perhaps they invented Magick to help themselves evolve Spiritually to their fullest potential, and they knew that this practice would help us reach the same goal since we were made in their reflection—from the perspective of energy and consciousness.

Also, our Creators implanted in us a biological mechanism called the Kundalini—whose purpose is to accelerate our Spiritual Evolution process. This mechanism may serve as a "safety switch" since it has the potential to be triggered at any point in time to further our evolution as a species. It is even possible that this switch will get activated on a mass scale in the future, which will usher us collectively into the much-anticipated Golden Age widely talked about in religious scriptures worldwide.

In my experience, I had learned that Ceremonial Magick is the best aid, without exception, in the Spiritual transformation process that began when I had a full and permanent Kundalini awakening. Perhaps this is another reason why we were given Magick by the Watchers —so that when mass Kundalini awakenings occur in the future, we will have a powerful Spiritual practice that we can turn to for help while collectively undergoing this Spiritual transformation.

Once we are fully awakened to our highest Spiritual potential, we will become Interdimensional Beings—with a capacity to experience the inner, Cosmic Planes through our Bodies of Light. We will transcend the World of Matter and remove the shackles of our physical bodies, thereby enabling our consciousness to explore the different dimensions of vibration in the Cosmos.

Whether we were created by God or by Extraterrestrials does not matter to us concerning where we are going collectively as a species. Our destiny is to become Beings of Light, and the purpose of the Qabalah, Magick, and especially the Kundalini mechanism, is to help us get there.

THE POWER OF MAGICK

The main questions people have when hearing about Magick for the first time are how and why Magick works. Firstly, Magick is an invisible, Divine science. The process of Magick rituals involves affecting the Astral World by using your imagination and willpower. As the Astral World is influenced, the corresponding Cosmic Planes are also affected—As Above, So Below. Thus, the Astral World is the "contact point" between the Magus and the Cosmic Planes. We trigger energy to pour in from the Cosmic Planes by consciously affecting the Astral Plane.

Secondly, Magick gets its power through repetition. Once you repeat a particular ritualistic formula, you create an energy field that grows in power with further practice repetitions. Since the mind needs to "see it to believe it," you need to attune the brain to the workings of Magick to be convinced that it works. Once the mind is convinced beyond any doubt, its floodgates are opened up, thus bringing in the desired energy into the Aura more efficiently. In essence, this is how Magick works.

Why it works is a different story entirely. Magick is really what the word implies—Magic. It is a supernatural art form with Divine origins. It is imperative to note the difference between Magick with a 'k' and Magic with a 'c'. Magic is mere card tricks, illusions, and a form of entertainment, while Magick is the art and practice of energy invocation (or evocation) and conforming reality to will. Magick is a Divine practice meant to exalt the consciousness, and it uses the power of the Universal Principles of Creation to accomplish this task. (I will discuss the Principles of Creation in-depth in a later section on Hermetic Philosophy.)

"The occultist does not try to dominate Nature, but to bring himself into harmony with these great Cosmic Forces, and work with them." — Dion Fortune; excerpt from "Applied Magic"

Each of the ritual techniques that I will give you has been tried and tested by many people who came before you. They all work, and they are powerful and effective. At first, you might not feel a thing, but don't let that concern you; it works as long as the correct formula is followed. Sometimes it takes time for your mind to start seeing the manifestations of these ritual exercises and to feel the energy intuitively in your body through the emotions. If you have awakened the Kundalini, you will have a much easier time feeling the energies. In most cases, I have found that people immediately sense the invoked energies.

All Magickal traditions advise the initiate of Light to have determination, perseverance, persistence, and patience. Indeed, it takes time to see Magick working in many cases but let me put your mind to rest—it works. As for why it works, we can sit here and speculate for all Eternity. Our finite minds will never fully comprehend something that belongs to the Infinite Mind of God. If done systematically as the ritual exercises are recommended, you can benefit from them, as they help to tune and heal the Chakras and raise the vibration of your consciousness.

"No one can give you Magickal powers. You have to earn them. There is only one way to do this. Practice, practice, practice!" — Donald Michael Kraig; excerpt from "Modern Magick: Twelve Lessons in the High Magickal Arts."

The purpose of these ritual exercises is to evolve Spiritually. They are presented systematically as part of an Alchemical formula that has existed for thousands of years. Turning lead into gold and obtaining the Philosopher's Stone of the Alchemist is the process of turning base Matter into Spirit and elevating the Magus (You) to Divine levels of consciousness.

These ritual exercises will be of particular interest to the Kundalini awakened individuals. Once the Kundalini has awakened and systematically blown open each of the Chakras on its upwards rise through the hollow tube in the spinal column, it will remain localized in the brain for the rest of the individual's life. This event would result in fully activating their Body of Light and awakening the entire Tree of Life within them.

The fear and anxiety present after a full Kundalini awakening signifies that the Chakras need cleansing and purifying. While living in this condition, these individuals will need a Spiritual practice or tool to help themselves evolve and raise their consciousness past the first Four Elements (or Chakras) and into the Spirit Element of the highest three Chakras.

Magickal ritual exercises provide the necessary practice which effectively combats the emotional and mental negativity that all Kundalini awakened individuals go through following the initial awakening. These exercises work to remove the fear and anxiety that is present in the energy system (Aura) upon awakening the Kundalini.

SPIRITUAL INITIATION

A lot has been written about Spiritual initiation and its importance in Magick. Spiritual initiation does not deal with acquiring further knowledge of a subject—it is not something you get from books. Instead, it is about the death of something old for something new to take its place. As such, Spiritual initiation is closely aligned with the idea of Spiritual Rebirth, as that is its final goal.

Spiritual Rebirth means to be reborn, metaphorically speaking, through the Spirit. It implies the conquering over the Ego by the Higher Self, the True Self, belonging to the Spirit energy. Initiation is the starting point of sacrificing the Ego and its mode of functioning so that the consciousness can rise above the mere material existence that the Ego has imposed on it over time. It, therefore, involves the process of transformation of consciousness.

Spiritual initiation implies that you will not be the same as you were before since there will be a drastic change in your cognitive functions after you are initiated. A fresh outlook on life, new beliefs, and renewed thoughts are all a part of the initiation into the energies of Ceremonial Magick. You will be kinder and more loving towards people and more assertive in your life. Initiation allows you to tap into your highest potential as a Spiritual human being and make the most of your life here on Planet Earth.

The actual initiation process takes place within you, the aspiring Magus, and not as part of some Ceremonial ritual or "rite" imparted to you by other people. By working with the ritual exercises presented in this book, you are Self-initiating into the Cosmic energies to obtain all of the objectives I just mentioned.

"We take Spiritual initiation when we become conscious of the Divine within us, and thereby contact the Divine without us." — Dion Fortune; excerpt from "The Training and Work of an Initiate"

Belonging to a Magickal Order (such as one of the Golden Dawn offshoots or Ordo Templi Orientis) is beneficial for gaining further knowledge and experience in the Western Mysteries. However, it is not necessary to receive the power of Spiritual initiation.

The ritual exercises presented in *The Magus* initiate the individual into the energies of the Five Elements. Let me reiterate that since what I am saying will shatter the belief structures that some of you have about being initiated into a Magickal Order. The rituals presented here, including the Lesser Invoking Ritual of the Pentagram of each of the Four Elements and the Supreme Invoking Ritual of the Pentagram (Spirit), are the very initiatory rituals into those particular energies. You must understand this because most Ceremonial Magick Orders profess that if you would like to receive a Spiritual initiation, you have to become part of an Order that deals with the particular energies that interest you.

Most Ceremonial Magick Orders work on a grading system where each grade corresponds with one of the lower Sephiroth of the Tree of Life. Each of these Sephiroth, in turn, corresponds to one of the Four Elements, including the fifth Element of Spirit. By initiating yourself into the energies of the Elements through the ritual exercises presented in *The Magus*, you are taking full responsibility for your Spiritual Evolution. You bypass having to belong to an Order to receive these all-important Spiritual initiations.

For a complete program of practising the ritual exercises found in this section, see the chapter titled "The Spiritual Alchemy Process." If you adhere to the ritual formulas and their prescribed programs presented in this book, you will walk the path of the Mystic, the Sage, and the Magus.

RITUAL WEAR AND SETTING

Since the dawn of the Western Mystery tradition, much importance has been placed on unique ritual wear and the setting in which Ceremonial Magick rituals were to be performed. As such, a misunderstanding has arisen concerning this subject, which requires clarification before moving forward.

In the Golden Dawn tradition, a black ceremonial robe is worn as part of the regalia, including a Nemyss and a Grade Sash (Figure 29). The Nemyss is a piece of striped headcloth that Pharaohs wore in Ancient Egypt. The Grade Sash represents a student's level in the Order, as each Grade they pass is marked by a symbolic patch on their sash. Once the initiate has reached the Portal Grade, they receive a plain white sash. Other Magickal Orders use different regalia that represents the beliefs of their tradition.

However, to practise Ceremonial Magick with the ritual exercises from *The Magus*, you can wear anything that you consider Holy or sacred. These Magickal exercises work by merely following the ritual formula; thus, what you wear and your setting are only essential to put you in the right mood to be motivated and enjoy the ritual exercise process.

I have found that when individuals are just getting into Ceremonial Magick, a robe or a special outfit helps them get into the right Spiritual mindset before starting an exercise. Then, as time goes by and they work with Ceremonial Magick regularly, they can discard the unique wardrobe since they can reproduce this desired mindset without extra help. Therefore, what you wear when practising ritual exercises is only necessary to get you in the proper mood. Remember that. Whoever tells you otherwise is leading you astray.

Figure 29: Traditional Golden Dawn Regalia (Outer Order)

Most individuals who practice Ceremonial Magick like to create a basic ritual space from simple everyday objects. For example, you could use a small, square table (waist-high) to represent the central altar around which you will be performing your ritual operation. You should then place a pair of candles at the head of the table, one in each corner.

Lighting the candles is a symbolic act of starting the ritual process, as extinguishing them is an act of ending it. Since you will be working with the Five Elements, it is best to use a square or rectangular-shaped space for this venture, where the four surrounding walls represent the Four Elements, while the ceiling and the floor represent the Above and Below, Heaven and Earth.

It helps to have some symbolic representations of each of the Four Elements in the four corners of the altar. In the East, we have Air; in the South, we have Fire; in the West, we have Water; and in the North, we have Earth. The central altar represents Spirit. These are the ritualistic designations of the Elements in space.

In the Golden Dawn tradition, a dagger is used to represent the Air Element, a wand for Fire, a cup for Water, and a pentacle for Earth. If you don't have access to these items, you can get creative and use any items instead that symbolize the Four Elements to you.

If you wanted to go as far as creating an elaborate temple setting, you would need a central altar and four "stations" of smaller altars around it dedicated to the Four Elements. Traditionally, in the Golden Dawn, two pillars (representing Light and Darkness) are placed directly in front of the central altar on opposing sides (North and South), as well as the *Banners of the East and the West*. The Enochian Tablets are placed above the four Elemental stations. The floor is checkered black and white, while the walls are painted black. The entire temple setting has a theme of duality present. The practitioner of Magick, the ritualist, is the source of Light within the darkness of space, symbolically depicted by the black walls.

Figure 30: The Author's Personal Golden Dawn Temple

Within the Golden Dawn tradition, before starting any ritual in the temple, it would be cleansed of any stale, unwanted energy. Traditionally, an aspergillum with Holy water is used to purify the space and a chain censer with incense to consecrate it. Once this is complete, the ritual exercise can commence.

The images in Figure 30 are of the temple I built many years ago in one of the rooms of my house while practising Ceremonial Magick within the Golden Dawn Order. I also created the traditional Golden Dawn temple equipment to add to the authenticity of the experience.

However, I do not want there to be an emphasis on building a personal temple or temple equipment or even having to cleanse the space elaborately. Doing so may deter you from trying the ritual exercises as the entire process can be deemed too laborious, tedious, and challenging overall. The power behind the ritual operations lies in the formulas, not where you perform them or what you wear. The fact is that if you do the ritual formula correctly (irrespective of where you are or how you are dressed), it will work.

Also, if you are in a place where you cannot vibrate the Divine Names of Power out loud, you can intone them silently while performing the ritual formula, and the exercise will still work. The invoked energy will be less in quantity than it would be if you were vibrating the Divine Names out loud, but it would work nonetheless.

I have done these ritual exercises in bathroom stalls of aeroplanes, or restaurants, when I could not find a more appropriate space where I could have some privacy for a few minutes—and it worked. To be the Magus, you must want it and be ready to be unconventional when it is required of you.

To perform these ritual exercises out of the comfort zone of your place of residence, all you need to have with you is a basic compass so that you can always orient yourself towards the East whenever you want to do a banishing or an energy invocation. I don't recommend doing these exercises around strangers in a public setting (since you may feel uncomfortable). Still, a public bathroom stall with enough room to pivot in a circle will suffice. If you believe you can, you are right, and if you think you can't, you are also right. Therefore, have confidence in yourself when working with these ritual exercises, and you will succeed.

THE RITUAL PROCESS

Before starting any ritual exercise, the essential factor to clarify within yourself is its purpose or intention. Why are you doing the exercise, and what are you trying to achieve? Since the ritual exercises in *The Magus* are geared toward Spiritual Evolution, your intention or purpose (in most cases) will be to invoke or evoke particular energy, learn from it, and evolve. Thus, take a moment before starting a ritual exercise to remind yourself of this. After all, our Higher Self is the one who should be guiding our actions in the performance of Magick rituals and not the Ego.

"The first condition of success in Magick is purity of purpose." — Aleister Crowley; excerpt from *"Moonchild"*

As mentioned, it helps to do the ritual exercises in some sacred space you created, but in reality, they work wherever you decide to do them, as long as the right formula is followed. If you can get some privacy, doing the exercises in a park or forest is a great way to ground yourself in nature while working on your energy field (Aura).

It is best to avoid ritual exercises after a big meal. While your stomach is working to synthesize the food into Light energy, your senses will be distracted. Ritual practices are best done a few hours after a meal, once the body has integrated the new energy, and you can concentrate easier. As a beginner, you should follow this rule, and as you get more advanced and can focus on the task at hand more efficiently, you can make your own rules concerning this matter.

Once you have clarified your purpose and decided where to perform the ritual exercise, the next step is to centre yourself. You must be in a well-balanced mental state where you are feeling positive, which will enable any invoked energies to penetrate the Aura better. In terms of ritual invocations, the energy is brought into your Aura from outside of you. After all, these energies are a part of our Solar System and all of Creation. In terms of evocations, you are accessing a type of energy inside of yourself, most often performed for Self-reflection or to remove it from your Aura.

You should perform the Four-Fold Breath to calm your mind and get in the "zone." The technique of performing this breathing exercise is given in this section. Being composed both mentally and emotionally is vital before working with Magick. Just as you would mentally prepare yourself for an all-important game of sports you are participating in, you have to do the same before practising Magick. For this reason, many people like to use incense to make their space sacred and help put them in a meditative state. The most popular scents used to clear any area's energy are Sage, Frankincense, and Sandalwood, but any incense that you find pleasant will work.

All ritual exercises should be performed while standing facing the East. They are to be performed clockwise, following the path of the rising and setting Sun. The Sun rises in the East (attributed to the Air Element), where we start to receive the Light. The Sun is at its highest peak and generates the most Light in the South (attributed to the Fire Element). The Sun then starts to set and finishes its cycle in the West (assigned to the Water Element). The North is attributed to the Earth Element, and as such, it receives no Light—it represents the darkness before the Sun rises and starts its cycle again. For these reasons, when we are invoking or banishing any energies, we follow the path of the Sun symbolically.

Since the Astral World is the contact point for the Magus, it is crucial to apply the use of willpower and imagination for a ritual exercise to work. This process involves visualizing specific images you are given as part of the formula of the exercise and transposing them onto the physical reality around you.

By using the imagination while tracing symbols with your right hand, along with vibrating the Divine Names of Power, energy will be invoked (or evoked) into (or out of) the Aura. It is pretty simple when you know what you are doing and have some practice.

> *"In all forms of Magick, the imagination or image-making faculty is the most important factor."* — Kenneth Grant; excerpt from *"The Magical Revival"*

To clarify, in a ritual "invocation," you are bringing (calling in) a particular type of energy from the outside Universe into your Aura. In a ritual "evocation," you are accessing a specific type of energy from inside yourself for introspection or banishing it from your Aura (as in the banishing Pentagram or Hexagram ritual exercises).

It is imperative to actively use your imagination and willpower during the ritual exercises to give them life. For the Magick to work, a ritualistic formula must be followed that consists of vibrating (chanting) the Divine Names of Power and drawing certain symbols in the air before you.

The drawing of symbols is an imaginary process whereby you are tracing symbols in the air with your right hand by either using a dagger, your fingers, or some other tool you want to use to invoke (or evoke) the energy. What you use in this regard is up to you. A simple placement of the thumb in between the ring finger and middle finger is the technique employed by the Golden Dawn tradition.

The thumb in the middle of the four fingers represents the reconciling factor of the Shin letter in between the Tetragrammaton, whereby it becomes the Pentagrammaton or the name of Jesus Christ. As you draw the symbol of the Pentagram or Hexagram, you are to imagine it present in front of you, thereby giving it power.

Every ritual exercise has its formula that must be followed down to the last detail. Also, it is crucial to vibrate the Divine Names of Power. If you have heard Tibetan monks chant, it is similar to that. Vibrations are to be performed in monotone, natural C, and elongated in pronunciation. Furthermore, the names have to be pronounced as they are written and with a commanding but reverent tone.

The proper vibration of these names will infuse the correct energy into your Aura. Vibrating them in your throat and using the power of the abdomen when chanting them is very important. You should feel your whole body vibrate as you pronounce these Divine Names of Power.

Words are power, and so is our ability to invoke these Divine Names. Our Word is our connecting link to the Worlds beyond the Physical Realm. The vibrations include the many Divine Names of God, Archangels, Angels, and other Holy names, depending on the ritual exercise and its origin. The Divine Names used in these exercises have existed for thousands of years in most cases and are very powerful.

Ceremonial Magick ritual exercises work through repetition, as the mind assimilates the process and creates doorways to allow the invoked energy to enter into the Aura. With these rituals, it is the mind that we are playing tricks on to influence it to tune into energies that are beyond us and bring them into the Aura.

All the ritual exercises presented in *The Magus* employ the Magickal circle. The ritualist creates this circle to construct an area that is protected and sacred. Also, since most of the exercises presented in this work are invocations, the energies you are working with outside you will pour into your Magickal circle and infuse into your Aura.

If other people are present inside your Magickal circle once you have created it, the desired energy will also penetrate their Auras. In a group ritual, one person can do all the work to create the Magickal circle, or others can be actively engaged. The key to absorbing the invoked energies is to be inside the Magickal circle as the ritual exercise is performed.

Your Aura is the Alchemical Alembic where the Spiritual Alchemy process occurs. An Alembic, in Alchemical terms, is an apparatus used in distillation, usually a beaker or a flask. The Aura becomes the Alembic since the energetic changes occur inside it, thereby exalting the Higher Self.

To truly benefit from the ritual exercises over a longer time, though, the Aura must be "Hermetically sealed." This term means that it is essential to keep these rituals a secret, at least for a little while, until you see that the process is working because you do not want the outside world dissuading you from using these exercises. Magick is very foreign to people who have not done it before. Humans are naturally afraid of things they do not understand and will generally shun those things to remove the fear of the Unknown from their life.

Let me state again—these rituals work. They have always worked, and they will still work. You need to be persistent and determined in using them, and I promise you that you will see the results—give it some time. The mind needs some time to adjust to the new realities taking place, but once it does, these ritual exercises have a habit of becoming addictive.

Having the ability to control how you want to feel throughout the day is an incredible power to have over your life. And while they feel fantastic, these exercises also do wonders for your Chakras as they purify the energy of the Elements within them.

How this sacred science is relatively unknown to the outside world is a mystery to me since it is so powerful and valuable. I feel that religious belief has something to do with it, specifically the concept that most religions put forth, stating that they hold the answers to the many questions we have that are Spiritual. Most religions want us to believe that we have to pray to a God outside of ourselves since, according to them, their God is "out there" and not within us.

Conversely, Ceremonial Magick rituals work on the basis that each of us is our own Messiah, Redeemer, and vehicle of transformation from Matter into Spirit. In this way, we are to fully take responsibility for our Spiritual Evolution instead of just doing what we want and hoping that the Universe rewards us. Using Ceremonial Magick rituals allows us to take destiny into our own hands. There is no more effective way to maximize your personal power than by becoming a master of your destiny.

THE MAGICKAL JOURNAL

As you start practising Ceremonial Magick, many fundamental truths about the nature of existence will be revealed to you in your dreams. Also, as you are progressing through the Elements, you may even start Lucid Dreaming regularly. While in a Lucid Dream, you can develop the ability to control your dream content consciously.

As you become the "movie director" of your dreams, you will be developing your Magickal abilities even in dream states. With all of these new experiences taking place, it helps to have a Magickal journal so that you can write down your dreams and keep track of everything happening to you. Over time, you will see patterns in your dreams and be able to interpret symbols that you did not initially understand. Your dreams tell the story of "You," and sometimes, it takes a certain amount of time before you can step back and see the big picture.

By training yourself to write down your dreams, you are aligning yourself more with your subconscious and the ability to see pictures and images inside your mind. As a practising Magi, this is a beneficial skill to have because it helps you gain better control over your thoughts, which will, in turn, influence your ability to better control your life by exercising your willpower.

Instead of writing down the content of your dreams, another method is to use a voice recorder. Doing so is more comfortable in terms of recording information quicker and then going back to sleep to continue dreaming. In the case of waking up in the middle of the night, this method will be optimal. You can always listen to the voice recording in the morning and write down the dreams in your Magickal journal.

By writing down your dreams, you are also stepping into the role of being your own psychologist. The mere act of writing them down is the act of analyzing your psyche. Even with no prior knowledge of basic psychology, you will be able to recognize symbols and see patterns in your dreams. These symbols and patterns of repetition will inevitably tell a story about something that the subconscious mind is trying to communicate to the conscious mind.

The subconscious mind can often act like a wild animal, completely independent in its expression. Because it is usually hidden from us, we might not be able to see its workings unless we shine a magnifying glass on it to zero in on its actions. Writing down your dreams serves as that magnifying glass; by doing it over time, the subconscious will reveal itself to you more and more. It will realize it cannot stay hidden anymore since you have taken an interest in seeing what it is showing you.

By writing down your dreams daily, you will gain better access to your subconscious mind, even in the waking state. You will be able to connect to it at will and see the images it projects and analyze them. In turn, this will help significantly with your Spiritual Evolution. Also, your intuition will increase immensely.

Besides recording your dreams, you should use your Magickal journal to write down the ritual exercises you are performing. Every time you do any type of ritual, you should write it down in your journal. For optimal results, you need to write down the date and the time you did the exercise. The same applies when writing down your dreams.

It is also recommended that you obtain a Planetary Guide (which maps the movement of the Planets and the Moon with respect to the Stars) and write down the Astrological influences on the given day and time you did the ritual exercise. This part is not mandatory, but it helps to do this if you are serious about becoming an advanced Magi.

The Elemental ritual exercises affect the Microcosm, while the Planetary and Moon cycles affect the Macrocosm—As Above, So Below. One affects the other continuously. Therefore, it is essential to be mindful of the movements of the Planets in our Solar System and the Moon cycles so that you have an idea of what Macrocosmic energies are affecting you daily. After you finish the first Spiritual Alchemy program with the Elements, the following program allows you to directly change your Macrocosmic influences through invocations of the Planetary energies.

Once you have written down the ritual exercise you completed, you need to write down how that exercise made you feel and whatever was on your mind before and after its completion. The idea here is to be reflective and write down how the exercise affected you psychologically. At first, you may not feel anything or have any inspiring thoughts about it, but over time this will change. Through repetition of the ritual exercises and exposing your psyche to their energies, your experience of them will heighten as time goes on.

The importance of writing down your thoughts on paper every time you perform a ritual exercise is to see your evolution over time in gaining the ability to connect mentally and emotionally to these exercises. In this way, you can track your progress and development in becoming a Magi.

THE FOUR-FOLD BREATH

The Four-Fold Breath is a stress-reducing, meditative exercise to be performed daily, whether right before or after a ritual practice or at any time during the day when you want to get into a calm, balanced state of mind. Its use will bring very positive results every time since breath control is critical to getting into a meditative state. Furthermore, the performance of the Four-Fold Breath goes side by side with the ritual exercises because being in a calm and balanced mental state helps attune to the energies being invoked and allows them to integrate within the Self more efficiently.

The Four-Fold Breath is a Pranayama Yoga technique known as Sama-Vritti, which in English means "equal breathing." Besides being a preliminary breathing technique for ritual exercises, you can implement it when encountering a stressful situation or dealing with anxiety. Its use will calm you down within a few minutes and enable you to think clearly. Moreover, its performance will shift your consciousness into the Alpha State.

Using the Four-Fold Breath opens up the psychic centre, the Mind's Eye Chakra (Ajna), which, in turn, creates a stronger connection with your Crown Chakra (Sahasrara), thereby aligning you with the Spirit energy. Attuning the Mind's Eye Chakra will bring balance and calmness to mind, body, and Soul over time. The Mind's Eye Chakra is a gate, a "portal" that leads to the inner Cosmic Realms and higher levels of consciousness.

It is important to note that if you have awakened the Kundalini fully and it resides now in the brain, causing a lot of pressure in your head (which is common when in this state), you should skip the following Mind's Eye Meditation and focus on the Four-Fold Breath. Perform the Four-Fold Breath as a simple meditative technique, and send the energy downward instead of upward. You accomplish this by placing your attention and awareness on your abdomen while performing this breathing exercise. As a result, the energy will move downward from your head into the abdomen, releasing the pressure from the head and resulting in a more relaxed and balanced state.

The Four-Fold Breath is to be used to get you into the right state of mind. To perform it, relax your body and exhale to the count of four. Hold your breath out for a count of four. Then, inhale for a count of four. Hold the breath in for a count of four. Simple. Repeat this cycle and continue for at least three to five minutes when first using this exercise. Count at a consistent, comfortable speed as you try to match your natural breathing. It may take a few days of practice until you find a pace that suits your body and obtains the desired result.

The rhythmic breathing of the Four-Fold Breath is necessary as it stimulates the Kundalini energy and Astral Light. It immediately puts you in a meditative state of mind giving you the proper preparation before starting any ritual exercise or other meditation technique. Since you can use the Four-Fold Breath whenever you need to calm yourself down, it should be practised often and made a regular part of your life.

THE MIND'S EYE MEDITATION

The Mind's Eye Meditation is best performed while lying down or in a lotus position, although it can be undertaken at any time when the body is still and in a state of relaxation. The Mind's Eye Chakra is located in-between the eyebrows and just above eye level at about 1/5 of the way towards the hairline. Its location is one centimetre inside the head when looking up at this point with closed eyes. Although there is no physical third eye present in the body, there is a centre of consciousness existing in that area.

The Mind's Eye is a small, circular portal, a window into the Cosmic Realms. When we focus on it, we immediately attain a meditative state. However, when we hold our attention there for a brief time and neglect the chatter of the Ego, we will start to receive visions and images streaming across this area as if on a movie screen.

Perform the Four-Fold Breath while focusing on the Mind's Eye centre. You should start to feel a connection with this centre and a force slowly pulling your eyes towards it. There is a magnetic attraction and a mild strain on your eyes when performing this exercise. You will know that you have made a connection with the Mind's Eye when a pleasant feeling enters your heart. You will then start to see visions streaming across this area. Try to connect with these visions by giving them your utmost attention. Do not hold each image too long as it will be fleeting. Instead, look at it and let it go. If you are performing this meditation after a ritual invocation, the images will pertain in some way to the nature of the energy you invoked.

Your body and mind should now be in an Alpha State while performing the Four-Fold Breath, which is a necessary state for the energy you invoked to start to communicate to you. You will see these thoughts as if in a dream and will realize that the real "watcher" is within you. In other words, you will be able to perceive the Silent Witness inside you. He or she is something different from the body or mind but is a part of you. It is the Higher Self that is part of the pure, undifferentiated Cosmic Consciousness of the Universe.

Be in this state for ten to fifteen minutes. The more time you spend in this state, the better, considering that you will be developing your psychic abilities while at the same time attuning yourself to the Spirit energy. Now, slowly return from this state to a normal one. Release the strain from your eyes and gradually shift them from the Mind's Eye centre to their normal position, allowing your mind to return to normal waking consciousness.

Allow yourself a few minutes to be still so that you can integrate the experience. Think over the images you saw and any messages you received while in this meditative state. Slowly open your eyes. Your meditation is now complete.

This meditation is beneficial in allowing you to channel the energy you are working with through the ritual exercises and attaining Gnosis. It is also instrumental in developing concentration and increasing your intuitive powers. Its use will also stimulate the Kundalini and may result in a spontaneous Kundalini awakening if you have not already had one.

The Mind's Eye meditation is the most basic and effective meditation in existence. It is very powerful because if you perform it daily, you will advance your Spiritual Evolution tenfold in just a few months. This meditation works well with the Four-Fold Breath and the ritual exercises because it enables you to put your mind into a calm and relaxed state whereby the energies can infuse into your Chakras more efficiently.

Other than attaining a very relaxed and balanced state of mind, you are working on opening up your Mind's Eye Chakra and receiving energies from your Supernals, your God-Self. You cannot access Sahasrara on its own but need to use the Mind's Eye as the entry portal. By working with this meditation, you will be accessing the two highest Chakras and opening up to their energies. As such, you will be advancing well on your Spiritual Evolution journey.

LESSER BANISHING RITUAL OF THE PENTAGRAM

This ritual exercise is a type of banishing of both the negative and positive energy influences in your Aura and should be performed at least a few times a day. The Lesser Banishing Ritual of the Pentagram (LBRP) banishes the Microcosm, while the Banishing Ritual of the Hexagram (BRH) banishes the Macrocosm. Although it may seem strange to want to remove positive energy influences, these are still energies that can deter you from achieving your desired goals.

The Microcosm is the human being and is considered a reflection of the Solar System, which is the Macrocosm. In the Hermetic axiom of "As Above, So Below," the Macrocosm is the Above, while the Microcosm is the Below. We implement this Hermetic axiom when performing all Magickal operations.

The Microcosm is the Aura of the human and the Elemental energies it contains within itself, which operate through the Chakras. The Macrocosm is the energies contained within our Solar System, which are the energies of the Seven Ancient Planets, the Twelve Zodiac, and the Elemental energies outside us. The LBRP is the first ritual exercise given to the aspiring Magus, and it focuses on the Microcosm, the human Aura.

It is optimal to perform the LBRP at three specific times during the day—once in the morning (right when you wake up), once during the major daily invocation, and once in the evening (right before you go to sleep). The major invocation in the first Spiritual Alchemy program will include the Middle Pillar ritual, the Banishing Ritual of the Hexagram (BRH) and an Elemental invocation ritual—using the Lesser Invoking Ritual of the Pentagram (LIRP). (You can find these ritual exercises in this section, following the LBRP.)

The LBRP should be done right in the morning because it helps start the morning feeling balanced in mind, body, and Soul since that state usually sets the tone for the entire day. Likewise, the LBRP should be done before sleep because it will banish any negative influences, like adverse thought senders that can keep us up at night. Doing so will aid in falling asleep quicker and having more sound sleep.

The LBRP is very easy to do, and once practised and memorized, you can do this exercise in under a few minutes. This ritual exercise, along with the BRH and the Middle Pillar, is considered the practitioner's "bread and butter"—their foundation. Its purpose is to balance you and put you in touch with your centre, your Soul, which is the primary prerequisite behind any Magickal work. Because, if you are not balanced, bringing in any energies outside of you can affect you negatively as it will activate thought senders that are not of the Light that can quickly overtake the consciousness.

The LBRP is necessary to ground you, as it uses the banishing Pentagram of Earth to remove the dense energies of the three Elements that can weigh you down. In doing so, it brings peace, calm, and balance. It is similar to performing an intense prayer before any Magickal operation to align with the Higher Self with the added component of protecting your Aura. While vibrating the Divine Names of Power in the LBRP, remember to elongate each word in a continuous flow, using one full breath. You must do so to obtain the best results. This ritual exercise has a four-part formula.

As mentioned, the LBRP is the most commonly used exercise along with the BRH, which will be given next as part of the daily banishings. By banishing Earth's dense energies, you raise the vibration of your consciousness while getting in touch with your core and centre, becoming balanced in all parts of Self.

Lesser Banishing Ritual of the Pentagram

Formula 1: The Qabalistic Cross

Stand in the centre of where you will be creating your Magickal circle and face East. If you have Elemental altars and (or) a central altar, stand behind the central altar. The Qabalistic Cross is used to open and close the ritual. Begin by performing the Four-Fold Breath for a minute or two to get you in a calm, balanced state of mind. Close your eyes. Stand with your hands outstretched horizontally, forming a cross with your body. Your two arms form the horizontal part of the cross, while your feet together and your head form the vertical part of the cross.

Imagine a ball of Light the size of a basketball touching your Crown Chakra and hovering above you. It is Kether, the invigorated Sahasrara Chakra. Imagine it swirling and twirling, and feel the heat of the pure White Light which emanates from it. Once you have imagined it well, reach into it with your right hand with the middle and index fingers together. As you reach into it, you still hold your left hand stretched outwards and feet planted together. Now touch your forehead with your right hand while visualizing a Light beam coming out of this Sphere as you carry it into your head. You will carry this Light beam into your body wherever you move your right hand (with your middle and index fingers together).

Vibrate:

Aaaahhh-taaahhh

(Atah: "Thou Art")

Touch the centre of your chest now and then point down to the Earth at your feet while seeing the Light carried from your head to your feet, thereby forming a central column of Light that permeates your physical body. As you make these motions, continue holding your left hand stretched outwards.

Vibrate:

Mahllll-kooot

(Malkuth: "The Kingdom")

Now move your right hand up vertically, and touch the centre of your chest again. Then touch your right shoulder with your right hand and extend it outwards while moving the Light beam to the palm of your hand.

As you make this motion, move your left hand inwards and touch the centre of your chest with the middle and index finger of your left hand. Hold this position and connect with the Light inside of your body. You have formed the central channel of the cross and the right arm.

Vibrate:

vihhh-Geh-booo-raaah

(ve-Geburah: "And the Power")

Move your right hand towards your left and touch the centre of your chest. As you make this motion, extend your left hand outwards yet again. Using your right hand, move the beam of Light to your left shoulder now by touching it, followed by touching the palm of your left hand. (You have now carried the beam of Light through to your entire left arm.) In a sweeping motion, draw the Light across your body horizontally, starting from the left hand and moving across to the right. Your right hand should be stretched outwards yet again. Your physical body should be in the form of a cross as when you began this exercise. The only difference is that a full cross of Light is superimposed over your body now.

Vibrate:

vihhh-Geh-dooo-laaah

(ve-Gedulah: "And the Glory")

Place your hands together in a prayer position in front of your chest while maintaining the visualization of the cross of Light within you.

Vibrate:

Layyy-Ohhh-lahmmm

(Le-Olahm: "Forever")

Now outstretch your hands again in the form of the cross.

Vibrate:

Ah-mennn

(Amen: "So be it.")

If you want to spend a minute and make a prayer to the Lord of the Universe (your conception of The All, or God), you may do so. Any prayer will work as long as it is directed to the Godhead. Performing it would put you more in touch with your Higher Self and solidify your intent behind the performance of the ritual operation.

Formula 2: Formulation of the Pentagrams

Step 1: After you have completed the Qabalistic Cross, stand and face East. Using your Magickal tool for tracing symbols, or simply using your hand with your thumb in between your ring finger and middle finger, draw a Pentagram in a brilliant flaming blue. Draw it right in front of you, of a considerable size, and the distance of one full arm's length. The most important part of drawing a Pentagram is how it is traced since tracing it from one of the five points and directions will produce different Elemental energy and be either an invoking or banishing of one of the Five Elements. In this case, we are using the banishing Pentagram of Earth (Figure 31), so you must trace it accordingly.

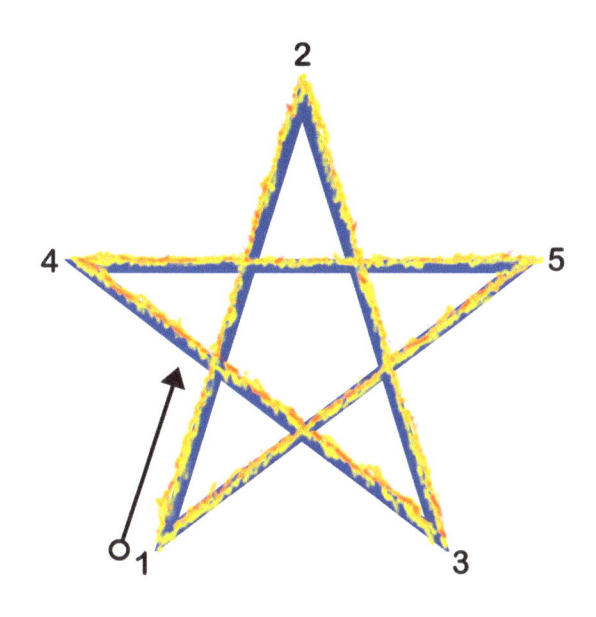

Figure 31: Banishing Pentagram of Earth

Start at the bottom where your left hip is, move up to your head, then to your right hip, across your body to the furthest left side, then across to the right, ending where you began. You have drawn the Pentagram in front of you in flaming blue. If you are making your arm stiff and straight and completing these motions from your right shoulder, it should form the ideal size of the Pentagram.

Step 2: Stand in front of the Pentagram. Inhale through your nose while reaching into the Sphere of Light above your head (Kether). Both of your arms should go up vertically as you do this. Bring this Light down to your chest while moving your hands to the middle of your head, so they are at eye level. Next, project the Light from the tips of your fingers. Your arms should extend before you while pointing directly at the Pentagram. (Your palms should be facing the ground as you do this.)

As you project with your hands, in that same motion, move your left foot forward about a foot in front of your right (Figure 32). The entire motion of Step 2 is a complete symbolic representation of the Projection Sign, otherwise called the Sign of Horus or the "Sign of the Enterer," which you will use to enflame the Pentagrams and Hexagrams in the ritual exercises in this book. See the Light shoot out of your fingers, and as it hits the Pentagram, it makes it go ablaze, almost as if you threw gasoline on an already existing fire.

Vibrate:

Yooohd-Heyyy-Vaaav-Heyyy

(YHVH)

Now the Pentagram is empowered with the Divine Name YHVH and is stronger than ever. As you pronounce the Divine Names, do so with a commanding tone in natural C. Try to connect with this experience as you feel your whole body vibrate with each pronunciation. As you are vibrating, make sure to elongate each word in a continuous flow, using one full breath. With every vibration, you should mentally hear each Divine Name echo throughout the furthest reaches of whichever cardinal direction you are standing in.

Your hands should be outstretched still. Next, start moving them back to your sides and, using your left hand, put your index finger to your mouth in the Sign of Harpocrates. As part of the same motion, move your left foot back to where the right foot is (Figure 32). The Sign of Harpocrates (the God of Silence) is also called the Sign of Protection or the "Sign of Silence." Its purpose is to cut off the energy channel created by charging the Pentagram (or Hexagram) with the Sign of the Enterer.

Step 3: Using your Magickal tool (or your right hand), stab the centre of the Pentagram and transpose a brilliant white line from the centre, moving in a clockwise fashion now to the following cardinal direction. As you move towards your right, you are following the path of the rising and setting Sun. Finish by stabbing the end of the white line in the centre of this next direction in space. You will have formed an arc of ninety degrees with the white line from the last Pentagram you created.

Thus far, you have drawn the flaming blue Pentagram in the East and a white line starting from its centre and connecting with the South. Stand and face the South now.

Step 4: In the South, repeat the same procedure as in Step 1 and Step 2, using the following Divine Name instead:
Aaahhh-dooohhh-nyyyeee
(Adonai)
You have drawn the flaming blue Pentagram in the East and the South and a white line connecting them. Now, repeat Step 3 and move this white line to the West. Stand and face West.

Step 5: In the West, repeat the same procedure as in Step 1 and Step 2, using the following Divine Name instead:
Eeehhh-heyyy-yeyyy
(Eheieh)
Thus far, you have drawn the flaming blue Pentagram in the East, South, and West, and a white line connecting all three in a circular pattern. One-half of your Magickal circle is complete. Now, repeat Step 3 and move this line to the North. Stand and face North.

Step 6: In the North, repeat the same procedure as in Step 1 and Step 2, using this Divine Name instead:
Aaahhh-Glaaahhh
(AGLA)
You have now drawn all four Pentagrams in all four cardinal directions and created three-quarters of your Magickal circle. Now, repeat Step 3, and carry the white line from the centre of the North Pentagram and

connect with the Pentagram in the East. After doing so, you have created the entire Magickal circle with a white line connecting all four flaming blue Pentagrams.

Step 7: While standing facing the East direction, perform the Sign of the Enterer and the Sign of Silence and see all four Pentagrams even more ablaze, including the white line connecting them.

Come back to the centre of the Magickal circle now and face East. If you have a central altar, stand behind it.

Formula 3: The Evocation of the Archangels

Stretch out your arms again horizontally in the form of a cross. Feel the Qabalistic Cross inside of you as you felt when you did it before drawing the Pentagrams. Focus on the East and say:

"Before me,"

Vibrate:

Raaahhh-faaayyy-elll

(Raphael)

Visualize the Great Archangel of Air, Raphael, standing in front of you outside of your Magickal circle with his back to you. He is wearing a yellow robe overlaid with purple highlights. He carries the Caduceus wand in his right hand and stands atop a tall mountain. He is grand in size and has his back towards you, guarding the East. See his giant Archangel wings and allow yourself to connect to the visual image of him and his surroundings as well as you can. Feel a fresh breeze of air now in the East and the essence of the Element of Air. Once you have done so, with your feet still firmly planted in the ground, turn your attention to the West and say:

"Behind me,"

Vibrate:

Gahhh-breee-elll

(Gabriel)

Visualize the Great Archangel of Water, Gabriel, standing behind you outside of your circle with his back to you. He is dressed in a blue robe with orange highlights. He is holding a cup in his right hand while standing with his feet in a lake surrounded by waterfalls. See his giant Archangel wings and feel the moisture in the air while hearing the waterfalls rushing. Connect with the image of Gabriel and feel the essence of the Element of Water. Once you have done so, without moving your feet, turn your attention to the South while giving a little nod with your right hand and say:

"On my right,"

Vibrate:

Meee-khaaaiii-elll

(Michael)

Visualize now the Great Archangel of Fire, Michael, standing to your right and outside of the circle you created, with his back to you. He is dressed in a red robe with green highlights. Michael is holding a flaming sword in his right hand with his giant Archangel wings facing you. Imagine his gigantic presence towering over you as he stands in a fiery pit. Connect to this image and feel the essence of the Fire Element and the heat emanating from the South. Once you have made a proper connection, without moving your feet, turn your attention to the North while giving a little nod with your left hand and say:

"And on my left,"

Vibrate:

Ohhh-reee-elll

(Auriel)

Visualize now the Great Archangel of Earth, Auriel, standing to your left. He is outside your circle and has his back to you. He is dressed in a black robe with citrine, olive, and russet highlights. In his right hand, he holds a wheat sheaf while standing inside a cave. See his giant wings and connect to the image of him and his surroundings. Feel now the Earth Element emanating from the North, the qualities of cold and dryness.

As you have evoked the Archangels to guard the four cardinal directions, say:

"For before me flames the Pentagram,

And behind me shines the six-rayed Star."

Formula 4: The Qabalistic Cross

Repeat the Qabalistic Cross. This completes the Lesser Banishing Ritual of the Pentagram.

***

You will find a sense of peace pervade you after performing the LBRP. You will immediately feel more Spiritual, calm, and serene. This feeling will last until you allow some unbalanced energy to enter your energy field, your Aura. It may last for hours, though, if you practice mindfulness after this exercise. You can perform this ritual exercise many times throughout the day—you can turn to it whenever you feel yourself getting out of balance mentally and emotionally. It will immediately put you back in touch with your centre and remove any negative energy influences in your Aura. Along with the Four-Fold Breath, the LBRP is the perfect exercise to perform if dealing with any stressful situation causing you anxiety.

As mentioned, the LBRP is usually followed by the BRH as part of the standard banishings. When starting to work with ritual exercises, though, you are to use the LBRP only, but the BRH is given soon after as part of your daily practice. Therefore, it is best to learn to do the LBRP first and get comfortable with it before being given a more complicated ritual exercise sequence. I do not want you getting deterred too early on because you are finding the sequences too complex to memorize. Once you have learned the ritual sequences of the LBRP, though, you will have an effortless time with the Lesser Invoking Ritual of the Pentagram since only the direction of tracing the Pentagram, and the orientation of the Archangels are different.

Figure 32: LBRP Magickal Gestures

BANISHING RITUAL OF THE HEXAGRAM

The Hexagram is a powerful symbol representing the operation of the Seven Ancient Planets under the presidency of the Sephiroth and the seven-lettered name ARARITA. While the LBRP serves to banish negative and positive energies on a Microcosmic level of the Chakras, the Banishing Ritual of the Hexagram (BRH) expels unwanted energy on a Macrocosmic level. The Pentagram is the Signet Star, or symbol of the Microcosm, while the Hexagram is the Signet Star of the Macrocosm—As Above, So Below.

The BRH is a banishing of the Planet Saturn, which is the Planet of Karma and time and directly relates to the material world. Since Saturn is the furthest Planet from the Earth in the Qabalistic model, banishing its energies also banishes any unwanted energies from the other Planets in between. The BRH is a banishing of the positive and negative energies of the Seven Ancient Planets, the Twelve Zodiac, and the Four Elemental energies influencing you—from the Macrocosm. Performing it will create a "blank slate," which will give you an excellent foundation to perform Magick.

The BRH puts you in touch with your Solar energy, as the Hexagram represents the Sun. The Lesser Hexagram Ritual is also used to invoke and banish any of the Seven Ancient Planets. (These techniques will be presented in a later chapter called "Advanced Planetary Magick.") By banishing Saturn, you overcome its Karmic influences, which will exalt your consciousness. Doing so will put you in touch with your inner core, your spark of Light—your Soul.

The LBRP and BRH are to be completed one after the other as part of the daily banishings. The banishings can be performed often during the day, as is recommended. The BRH allows the Solar energy and the Light to shine more brightly by removing these unwanted Planetary, Zodiacal, and Elemental energies. Combining the two ritual exercises will put you in the most balanced, centred state. The mere daily use of the LBRP and BRH will do wonders for your Spiritual Alchemy.

You are to vibrate the name ARARITA in all four cardinal directions along with tracing the four forms of the Hexagram that are given. ARARITA is a seven-lettered name of God. It is an acronym, otherwise called a Notarikon. A Notarikon is the reduction of a complete word to one of its component letters, in most cases, the first letter. ARARITA translates in English as "One is his unity, One is his individuality, his permutation is One."

Every time you vibrate the name ARARITA, you are expressing the unity of Divinity. Since this is a Solar ritual operation and there are Seven Ancient Planets, ARARITA being a seven-letter word, also contains one of the Seven Ancient Planets in each letter. Therefore, this word includes unity, which is meant to be evoked. To Saturn is attributed Aleph, Jupiter is Resh, Mars is Aleph, Venus is Resh, Sun is Yod, Mercury is Tav, and Luna is Aleph.

The four forms of the Hexagram are meant to represent the positions of the Elements in the Zodiac. In the East is given the position of Fire in the Zodiac. The South is the position of Earth, with the Sun at its culmination at noon. In the West is the position of Air in the Zodiac. Finally, in the North is the position of Water. (I will further describe the Hexagram symbol in the "Advanced Planetary Magick" chapter.)

Banishing Ritual of the Hexagram

Formula 1: The Qabalistic Cross

Perform the Four-Fold Breath for a minute or two to get you into a calm, balanced state of mind. Stand in the centre of your circle and face East. If you have Elemental altars and (or) a central altar, stand behind the central altar. Perform the Qabalistic Cross as per the formula given in the instructions for the LBRP. At this point, you would have completed the LBRP; therefore, continue holding in your imagination the flaming Pentagrams, the Magickal circle with the white line connecting them, and the forms of the Archangels in all four cardinal directions.

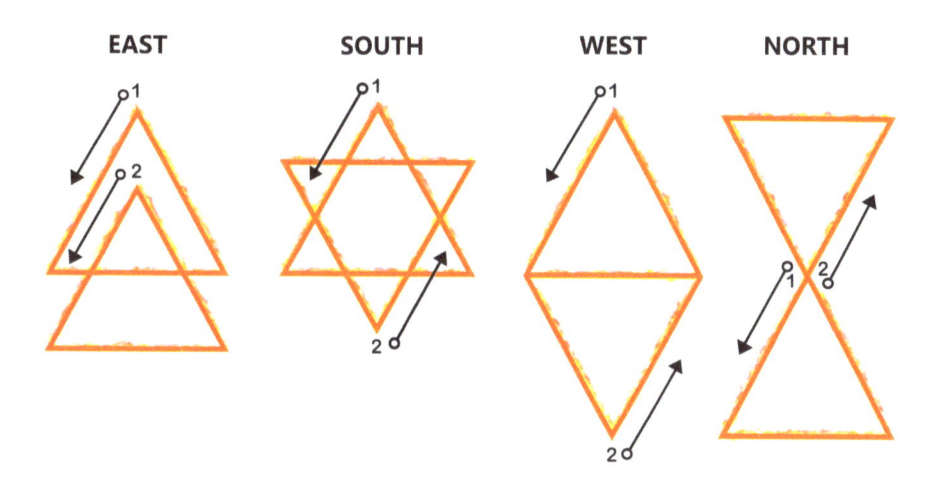

Figure 33: Four Forms of the Hexagram in the BRH

Formula 2: Tracing the Four Forms of the Hexagram in the Four Cardinal Directions (Figure 33)

Move to the East and draw the banishing Fire Hexagram as given. Visualize it in a golden flame (as opposed to a blue flame of the Pentagrams). See it transposed onto the Pentagram that was previously drawn in the LBRP. Inhale while drawing in the energy from the Sphere of Kether above you. Bring down the Light from Kether and thrust your fingers forward in the Sign of the Enterer as given in the LBRP ritual.

To the full extent of your breath, vibrate:

Aaahhh-Raaahhh-Reee-Taaahhh

(ARARITA)

See the Hexagram enflamed. End with the Sign of Silence, as given in the LBRP ritual.

Using your hand or ritual invoking tool, stab the middle of the Hexagram you just drew and carry a white line to the South in the same way as you did in the LBRP. Draw the banishing Hexagram of Earth as is given in the above diagram. See it transposed onto the Pentagram previously drawn there in the LBRP.

Perform the Sign of the Enterer, followed by vibrating the name:

Aaahhh-Raaahhh-Reee-Taaahhh

(ARARITA)

See the Hexagram enflamed. End with the Sign of Silence.

In the same manner, move the white line to the West now. Draw the banishing Hexagram of Air as is given in the diagram above. Again, see it transposed onto the Pentagram previously drawn in the LBRP.

Perform the Sign of the Enterer, followed by vibrating the name:

Aaahhh-Raaahhh-Reee-Taaahhh

(ARARITA)

Again, see the Hexagram enflamed. End with the Sign of Silence. Thus far, you have drawn half the Magickal circle with the white line, connecting the Hexagrams in the East, South, and West. Now move the white line to the North, in the same manner, and draw the banishing Hexagram of Water. Again, see it transposed onto the Pentagram previously drawn in the LBRP.

Perform the Sign of the Enterer, followed by vibrating the name:

Aaahhh-Raaahhh-Reee-Taaahhh

(ARARITA)

See the Hexagram enflamed. End with the Sign of Silence.

Connect the white line from the North to the East, thereby completing your Magickal circle. While standing in the East, perform the Sign of the Enterer and the Sign of Silence, enflaming the Hexagrams and the Pentagrams underneath them, including the white line connecting them.

Come back to the centre of the Magickal circle now and face East. If you have a central altar, then stand behind it.

Formula 3: The Qabalistic Cross

Stand in the centre of your circle now and repeat the Qabalistic Cross. This completes the Banishing Ritual of the Hexagram.

***

Take a minute now to reflect on the LBRP and BRH you just performed and to connect with your core, your Soul centre. As the LBRP serves to calm and quiet the mind, you will find that in combination with the BRH, this feeling of peace and serenity is even more magnified. This meditative state is a prerequisite to continuing with further ritual invocations, such as the Middle Pillar and LIRP. You can also use this time to perform the Mind's Eye meditation if you do not want to invoke any energies at this point. You will find that you will have a much easier time meditating and connecting with the Mind's Eye Chakra than you would if you had not done the LBRP and BRH.

If your purpose was only to ground your thoughts and silence the Ego for the time being, proceed with whatever tasks you have planned for the day. As mentioned, the peace of mind you are experiencing will continue if you do not allow any thought senders to retake hold of your consciousness. Therefore, practice mindfulness.

MIDDLE PILLAR EXERCISE

The Middle Pillar is an effective Light-inducing exercise that develops and heightens your Astral senses. This ritual exercise, along with the LBRP and BRH, is a vital component of the fundamental preparations that must be undertaken before any Elemental or Planetary invocations can take place.

The LBRP and BRH centre and balance you mentally and emotionally while removing all Karmic influences from the Microcosm and Macrocosm. They put you in a meditative state whereby you can work more efficiently in the Astral World, where all Magickal workings occur.

On the other hand, the Middle Pillar infuses or invokes the Light emanating from Kether into the Aura and the Subtle Bodies. This exercise implements the energies of the Middle Pillar of the Tree of Life and invokes their properties. It reconciles all opposites within the thoughts and emotions by bringing in Light energy. After its completion, use the Light energy to power the imagination and willpower to continue whatever major ritual invocation/evocation you intend to perform next.

Alternatively, the Middle Pillar can be done for itself and by itself to infuse Light energy into the Aura and help you move ahead on your journey of Spiritual transformation. The Middle Pillar exercise is best performed after the LBRP and BRH since you must balance the mind before taking on Light energy.

The Middle Pillar of the Tree of Life is the pillar of the Air Element, as all of its Spheres have an Airy quality. As such, you will feel more inspired and creative after completing the Middle Pillar exercise since you will be in touch with your Soul centre and your thoughts. For this reason, the Middle Pillar exercise should be performed after the LBRP and BRH, as all three ritual exercises serve to attune you to the Light of your Soul and remove adverse thought senders.

In the Middle Pillar exercise, the invoked Light enflames your Soul, increasing the overall quantity of Light energy in your Aura. As your Soul becomes enflamed with Light energy, latent energy in your Chakras is activated as well—which then filters into different parts of the Self, related to the Elements of your Being.

Kundalini awakened individuals will find that the Middle Pillar exercise works directly with the Kundalini Fire since both energies are of the Light quality. As the invoked Light energy acts on the Kundalini Fire, further Karmic energy is activated in your life. Whatever Karma awaits you for you to grow and evolve Spiritually will be initiated far quicker with the use of the Middle Pillar exercise than without it.

As you perform the Middle Pillar exercise daily, you will start to have Lucid Dreams—within a few weeks in most cases. Lucid Dreaming, in this case, occurs because the Aura becomes infused with Light energy, whose high vibration vaults your consciousness out into the higher Cosmic Realms. Light energy also awakens your inner imagination during sleep when you are most relaxed and your brain is in the Alpha State. As this happens, you will become conscious and aware while in dream states, enabling you to control the content of your dreams to a great extent.

You will find that vibrating the Divine Names ten times each will suffice to bring in Light energy to use throughout the day. Vibrating the Divine Names more than ten times each will bring in more Light energy since this ritual exercise has a quantifiable effect. If you chant the Divine Names more than twenty times each, you might be infusing too much Light energy into the Aura. In this instance, you may feel lightheaded, dizzy, and so energetically zapped that you may even lose consciousness during the ritual process. I had witnessed this happen in a group ritual setting when the number of vibrations of the Middle Pillar was done in excess.

The Middle Pillar exercise is to be performed at least once a day. You can complete it more times than that, but as a general rule, never before sleep or after 8 PM—since you will not be able to fall asleep with so much Light energy present. If you are doing it more than once a day and feel too spacey (which can happen), it is best to bring it down to only once a day. Too much Light can also make you feel agitated since it is literally" lighting up" all parts of the inner Self, including all positive and negative aspects. Therefore, be mindful of how you are reacting to this ritual exercise and how others are reacting to you, and make adjustments accordingly on how many times per day is best for you to perform it. However, remember that doing it once a day is a prerequisite that never yields negative results.

There are two versions of the Middle Pillar exercise—Basic and Advanced. The Basic Middle Pillar is the same ritual operation but omits the Circulation of the Ball of Light, which is included in the Advanced Middle Pillar. I will give you the technique for the Advanced Middle Pillar, but if you want to use just the Basic Middle Pillar and skip the Circulation of the Ball of Light, it is your choice. The Advanced Middle Pillar will bring more Light into the Aura, but both versions will work. Sometimes, you may not have ample time to do the Advanced Middle Pillar, in which case, do the Basic Middle Pillar.

Middle Pillar Exercise

Formula 1: Prayer or Praise

The LBRP should have already been performed as well as the BRH. While in the centre of your Magickal circle, face West now with your feet together. You should be standing upright with your hands on the sides, palms outwards. Perform the Four-Fold Breath for a minute or two to get yourself in a meditative state.

Start the exercise of the Middle Pillar with a prayer. Below is the praise to God-the Creator by Hermes Trismegistus from *Book I* of the *Corpus Hermeticum*, slightly modified from the original to fit the intended purpose. Any prayer or praise would work here as long as it is sacred and affirms your intention to align with the Godhead and sanctify this Magickal ritual.

> *Holy is God, the Father of All.*
> *Holy is God, whose will is accomplished by His own powers.*
> *Holy is God, who wills to be known and is known by those that are his own.*
> *Holy art thou, who by the Word has united all that is.*
> *Holy art thou, of whom all Nature became an image.*
> *Holy art thou, who is stronger than all power.*
> *Holy art thou, who art higher than all pre-eminence.*
> *Holy art thou, who surpasses praise.*
> *I adore thee and I invoke thee.*
> *Look thou with favour upon me,*
> *As I stand humbly before thee.*
> *And grant thine aid unto the highest aspiration of my Soul,*

So that I may accomplish the Great Work.
And be at One with thee.
Until the end of time.
Amen

This prayer is optional, not mandatory. It is not a part of the formula of the invocation of the Middle Pillar but is there to further put you in that desired state where you are aligned with your Higher Self. If you are short on time for whatever reason and want to skip the prayer, that is fine. The Middle Pillar exercise will still work without it.

Formula 2: Basic Middle Pillar (Figure 34)

Visualize a brilliant white Light above your head, the size of a basketball—as your Kether/Sahasrara Sphere. It is suspended at the top of your head, swirling and twirling. Its placement is just inside the head, as shown in the following drawing. Feel the energy of its presence and vibrate the Divine name of Eheieh ten times. If you do not have much time to perform the exercise, you can vibrate any number of times, but be consistent. For example, if you vibrate the first Divine Name five times, you must vibrate all the other Divine Names five times each. To perform the formula correctly, the Divine Names have to be vibrated the same amount of times because otherwise, the energy that comes in will be unbalanced. The pronunciation of Eheieh is as follows:

Eeehhh-heyyy-yeyyy

(Eheieh)

Now visualize a shaft of White Light extending from Eheieh, the Crown, into your throat area where a smaller ball of Light is located. It is Daath, the Sphere of Knowledge. Its colour is lavender, approximately the size of a tennis ball. Vibrate the following Divine name of YHVH Elohim the same number of times as Eheieh:

Yooohd-Heyyy-Vaaav-Heyyy Elll-oooh-heeemmm

(YHVH Elohim)

Now visualize another shaft of Light extending from Daath, the lavender Sphere, into your Solar Plexus area, and imagine another basketball-sized ball of Light there. It is the Sphere of Tiphareth, your own central Sun, the colour of gold/yellow. Vibrate the Divine name of YHVH Eloah Ve Daath the same number of times as the first two Spheres:

Yooohd-Heyyy-Vaaav-Heyyy Elll-ooo-aaah vihhh-Daaah-aath

(YHVH Eloah ve-Daath)

Bring down another beam of Light from the Tiphareth Sphere into your groin area, where you are to visualize another basketball-sized ball of Light, violet in colour. It is the Sphere of Yesod, your Moon centre. Vibrate the Divine Name Shaddai El Chai the same number of times as the first three Spheres:

Shaaah-dyeee Elll Chaaaiii

(Shaddai El Chai)

Now bring down the Light beam from Yesod into your feet, as you are standing in another Sphere the size of a basketball, the colour black. The top half encompasses your feet, while the bottom half is within the ground on which you stand. It is Malkuth, the Earth. Vibrate Adonai ha-Aretz the same number of times as the other Spheres:

Aaahhh-dooohhh-nyyyeee haaa-Aaah-retz

(Adonai ha-Aretz)

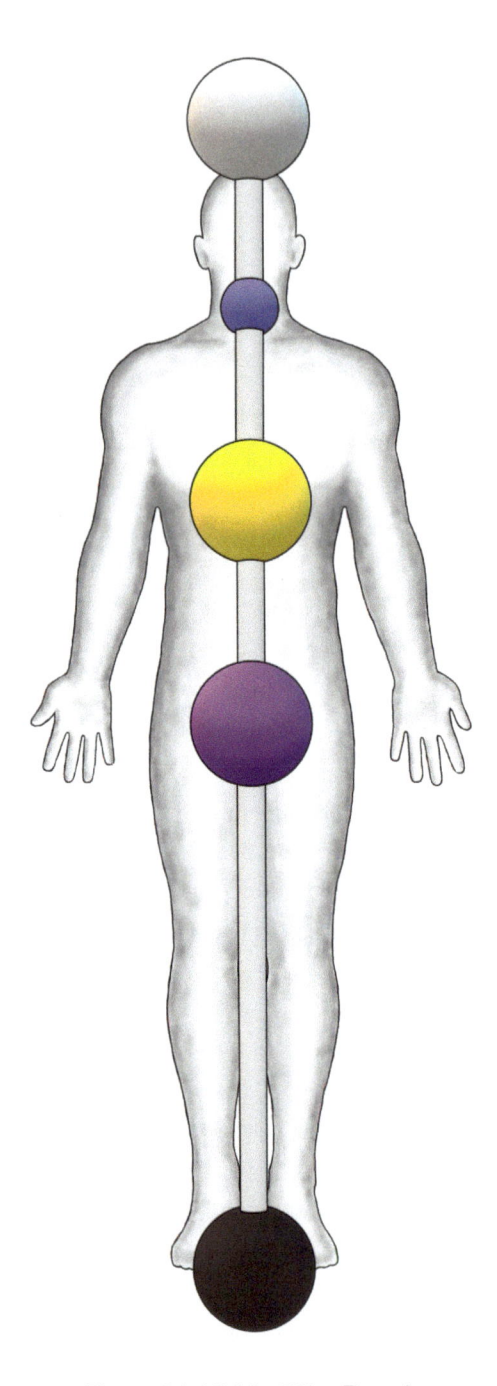

Figure 34: Middle Pillar Exercise

Once you have completed this procedure, you should have five Spheres, each brightly illuminated and connected by one beam of Light. The next part of the Middle Pillar exercise is the Circulation of the Ball of Light, forming part of the Advanced Middle Pillar exercise. Again, you do not have to do this part of the exercise if you are short on time and have a busy schedule that day. I do not want you to feel discouraged if you do not have the time to do this since the central part of the exercise, the invocation of the Light energy of the Middle Pillar, is accomplished at this point. But this next part of the ritual exercise solidifies the process and attunes you more to the Light energy, covering your entire Aura with Light and allowing it to permeate your Chakras further.

Formula 3: Circulation of the Ball of Light

This part of the Middle Pillar exercise involves using the Four-Fold Breath, as you will use it to time the movement of the imaginary Astral ball of Light. Since you have just finished the Basic Middle Pillar, you will begin the Circulation of the Ball of Light in Malkuth at the feet. First, visualise a basketball-sized ball of white Light coming out of the black Sphere of Malkuth and slowly moving up the right side of the body. As it gradually moves, the ball of White Light grazes the physical body on its way upwards to the Crown Chakra. Once it reaches the Crown, it permeates it further with Light energy.

Gradually move the ball of Light out of the Crown, and carry it down the left side of the body. You are to end at the feet again, in Malkuth. The Four-Fold Breath should give you a count of four seconds to move it up, then hold it for four seconds inside the Crown Chakra, then take another four seconds moving it back down, and then keep it in Malkuth for four seconds. Repeat the process in the same way, giving you two times that you circulated the ball of Light along your sides, from your feet to your head and back down again.

Move the ball of Light from Malkuth up the front of your body with the same Four-Fold Breath technique. Then move it back down the backside of the body. Now repeat the process one more time. Move the ball of Light up clockwise along your left side now (instead of counter-clockwise on your right). You are now moving it in reverse order, repeating the entire procedure, the same amount of times, but in reverse. You should have eight complete circulations with the ball of Light as you end off in the same place you began—the Sphere of Malkuth at your feet.

Using the Four-Fold Breath technique, visualize the ball of Light coming out of Malkuth and moving along your body clockwise in a spiral motion, completely covering your whole body and Aura with Light. This part of the exercise is called the "mummy-wrap." Once you have reached the Crown, hold for four seconds, and then reverse the movement of the ball of Light counter-clockwise in a spiral motion until you reach Malkuth. Now do the same procedure, starting counter-clockwise first and then reversing the ball of Light again. Repeat this entire procedure one more time, making it four times that you visualized the ball of Light moving up and down.

As you are again in Malkuth, visualize the ball of Light shooting a stream of Light energy from Malkuth through the column of Light connecting the Spheres of the Middle Pillar and into your Crown Chakra. As it reaches the Crown, the Light energy bursts out of it as if you were a fountain of Light, showering your entire Aura with Light particles. Visualize this for about ten to fifteen seconds as you feel the Light energy surging through your body.

If this part of the exercise is completed correctly, it will stimulate the Kundalini energy into activity, which may even result in an awakening. Since this is the last part of the exercise, it is your choice if you want to spend more time than is recommended on this visualization. By spending a longer time on this visualization, your chances of activating the Kundalini energy will be increased.

The Advanced Middle Pillar exercise is now complete. You can regain full waking consciousness and feel the physical space around you. You do not have to stop feeling the Light in your Aura as it will stay present for most of the day, but you can now continue to the next part of your ritual sequence or end with a Qabalistic Cross if this was the final part of your ritual sequence for the day.

LESSER INVOKING RITUAL OF THE PENTAGRAM

The Lesser Invoking Ritual of the Pentagram (LIRP) is performed in the same way as the LBRP, the only difference being the direction of tracing the Pentagram (Figure 35) and having the Archangels face you instead of having their back to you.

By substituting the Earth banishing Pentagram with the invoking Pentagram of the Element you are calling in, and then having the Archangels face you, you will be pouring the energy of that Element into your Magickal circle as well as your Aura. The LIRP formula might not seem very complicated since you are only tweaking two factors from the LBRP. Still, the energy you will experience after the ritual exercise is complete is like night and day from the LBRP—it is vastly different.

Just the simple change of direction in tracing the Pentagram invokes an entirely different Elemental energy that feels and acts on you completely differently. This process is genuinely Magick—there is no other word to explain it or give it the credit it deserves. Again, you are to use the same formula as the LBRP, the same Divine Names and everything else, except for the direction of tracing the Pentagram and having the Archangels face you.

The final added component in the LIRP is using a Grade Sign particular to the Element you are working with. Grade Signs and the purpose of performing them will be given in a later chapter in the "Great Work" section, titled "Grade Signs of the Five Elements." A Grade Sign is to be used immediately following the completion of the LIRP formula, as you stand in the centre of your circle.

While performing the banishing ritual of the Pentagram, the Archangels have their back to you, causing the direction of the energy flow to go from you to the outside Universe. In a banishing ritual of the Pentagram, the energy of an Element pours out of your Aura. You are banishing (evoking) whatever Elemental energy you choose out of your Aura and out of your Magickal circle and releasing it back into the Universe from whence it came.

Having the Archangels face you, though, along with tracing the Pentagram from a specific direction, gives an entirely different effect. It becomes an invocation, as that energy is brought into your Magickal circle from the outside Universe. In the banishing and invoking Rituals of the Pentagram, the Archangels serve as the conductors of the Elemental energies.

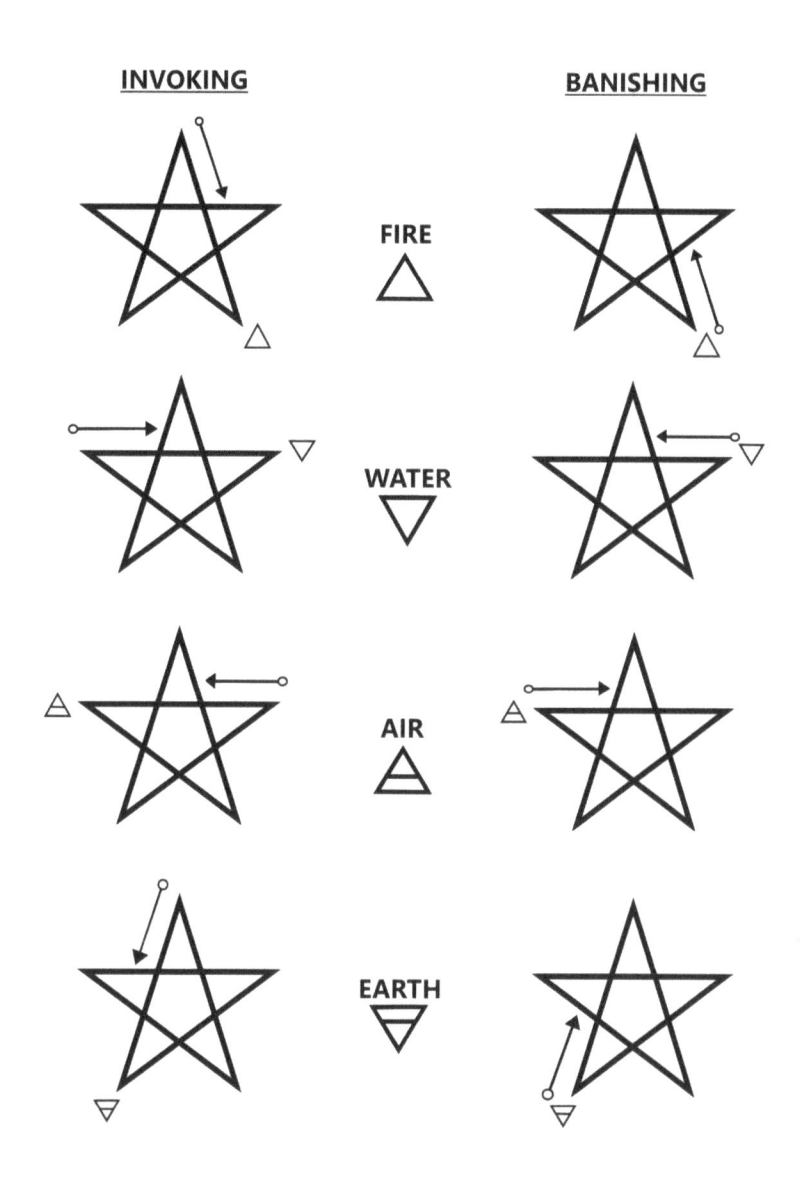

INVOKING		BANISHING
	FIRE △	
	WATER ▽	
	AIR △ (with line)	
	EARTH ▽ (with line)	

Figure 35: Invoking and Banishing Pentagrams of the Elements

The Magickal circle is the boundary between yourself (and other people if they are inside your circle) and the Universe. Within this boundary, the Magickal process occurs. For example, you can evoke a type of energy from within yourself (and other people if they are within your Magickal circle) and release it into the Universe. Or you can invoke a type of energy from the outside Universe and allow it to pour into your Magickal circle and, consequently, your Aura. As new energy is invoked inside your Aura, it will stay there for a while until you use it up throughout the day or release it back into the Universe during sleep.

When you get to working with the Planetary energies in the "Advanced Planetary Magick" section, you will also have the option of banishing the energy of a Planet, which again is considered an evocation. Here you will be employing the Hexagram for the invocations and evocations and creating a Magickal circle. Remember that the methods of evocation and invocation described thus far pertain only to working with the Pentagram and Hexagram ritual exercises. Once you get to Enochian Magick, the entire system presented in *The Magus* is a series of evocations through the Enochian Keys or Calls. These evocations are different from banishings of the Elements or Planets—more on this in a later section on Enochian Magick.

As you are invoking the Elements through the Lesser Invoking Ritual of the Pentagram, keep in mind that every Element you invoke can also be banished—if you are having difficulty managing its energy for some reason. For Spiritual Alchemy purposes, though, the idea is for you to work through the energy of the Element you are invoking instead of merely banishing it once it becomes challenging to work with.

However, in those odd instances when you are having an overwhelming time with an Element you invoke and feel that you cannot deal with its energy at that moment, you can do a banishing of that Element. So it is a beneficial tool to have when working with these energies.

To banish any Element, you must use the LBRP formula but substitute the Earth banishing Pentagram with the banishing Pentagram of the desired Element. After performing the banishing of an Element, you will have expelled the energy you previously invoked and any natural energy you had of that particular Element before the invocation. It will take a few hours at least to rebuild that Elemental energy in your Aura again; therefore, be mindful of this if you choose to banish any Element other than Earth.

Once you have invoked the Element into your circle and the energy has permeated your Aura, you now have a choice whether you want to have communion with the representative of that particular energy, which is one of the four Archangels. Raphael is the Archangel of Air, Gabriel is the Archangel of Water, Michael is the Archangel of Fire, and Auriel is the Archangel of Earth.

The process of communion occurs as a result of your Aura being overtaken by the energy of the Element you invoked, as it acts on your imagination, manifesting as a personified image. The Element is now communicating to your mind and your Soul if you take the time to listen. The technique of visualization is "imagination under willpower." In the case of communion, the willpower becomes suspended as the invoked Elemental energy overtakes the imagination. Therefore, if you listen with your heart and mind, you will receive messages from the representative Archangel of a particular Element.

Communion with an Archangel can be a very enlightening experience. Because the nature of every Element is personal to the psyche (and is different from one person to the next), communion can be very informative. The Archangels will give you messages about yourself and how you can evolve further Spiritually. They will also provide information about the nature of the Element itself—all received through pure Gnosis. As mentioned, Gnosis is the direct communication from Divine energies or any Beings who are not of the Physical Realm, who intend to teach and guide us.

After the communion with the representative Archangel of the invoked Element is complete, you are to salute the Archangel by performing the Grade Sign particular to the Element you invoked. If, for whatever reason, you have decided to skip the communion part of the LIRP, not to worry because the nature of the invoked Elemental energy is to teach and heal us, regardless of if we want to be active participants or not. Therefore, if we decide not to listen during waking hours because our Egos are too involved, we will receive communication when the Ego quiets down, such as during sleep. Remember always that whatever energy you invoke has to filter through the Four Worlds of the Qabalah and find the best way to communicate to you so that you can understand and integrate this communication.

The ability to invoke or banish an Element at will is a powerful tool at your disposal as an aspiring Magus. By learning the ritual exercise sequences, you receive a key to obtaining a level of control over your reality which you probably never thought was possible. However, to become a full-fledged Magus, you must follow the Spiritual Alchemy programs given as part of this work. Once you have carried these programs through to the end, their ritual exercises will be a part of your life forever, and you can use them to control your energy at will whenever you desire to do so.

SUPREME INVOKING RITUAL OF THE PENTAGRAM

The Supreme Invoking Ritual of the Pentagram (SIRP) is to be performed after the other Four Elements have been invoked for the minimum time as prescribed in the Spiritual Alchemy program in the next chapter. The SIRP is the most potent ritual exercise presented so far since it uses the Enochian Divine Names for the Active and Passive Spirit Pentagrams to give them their power. As such, this exercise is an introduction to Enochian Magick—which should only be undertaken once you have practised the SIRP for a sufficient amount of time. Enochian Magick can be very dangerous for those not ready for it; thus, I have put it at the back of the book.

The SIRP recombines the best qualities of each of the Four Elements—now under the presidency of Spirit. After performing this exercise, you will immediately feel a sense of peace and calm, as well as heightened intuitive abilities. This ritual exercise is very mystical—its purpose is to completely awaken your inner sight to the first invisible World, the Astral Plane. Remember that the manifestation process must filter through the Astral World before coming into the Physical World. Since the Astral World is the contact point between the Magus and the Cosmic Planes, by performing the SIRP daily, you will be "walking on Earth, while having your head in Heaven," as the Golden Dawn Adepts would say.

The SIRP transforms the Magus into a "Sky-Walker," a Spiritually enhanced human Being that walks in between the Inner and Outer Worlds—they have one foot in the Astral Plane and the other foot on Earth, metaphorically speaking. The SIRP stimulates and activates the Mind's Eye Chakra, invigorates the Throat Chakra and the act of communication, and creates the doorway to reach the Transpersonal Self in Sahasrara Chakra.

This ritual exercise is a preparation for Adepthood. Embarking on invocations of the Spirit Element will mark a milestone in your career as a Ceremonial Magickian since it is the next level of Spiritual Evolution for you. While you have been "learning to walk" with the ritual exercises presented so far, you are "learning to run" with Spirit invocations.

Spirit is essentially the synthesis of the previous Elemental invocations with an addition of a fifth Element—one that is most mystical and transcendental. Spirit invocations with the SIRP are to be performed for nine months at least, after work with the LIRPs of the Four Elements has been completed. It will balance all parts of your psyche (mental and emotional) and will attune you to the higher workings of the Spiritual energy within you.

Before starting the SIRP, you should have performed at least the LBRP and BRH to banish unwanted energy and prepare yourself for the influx of the Spirit Element. The Middle Pillar is also recommended before starting the SIRP, but it is not mandatory.

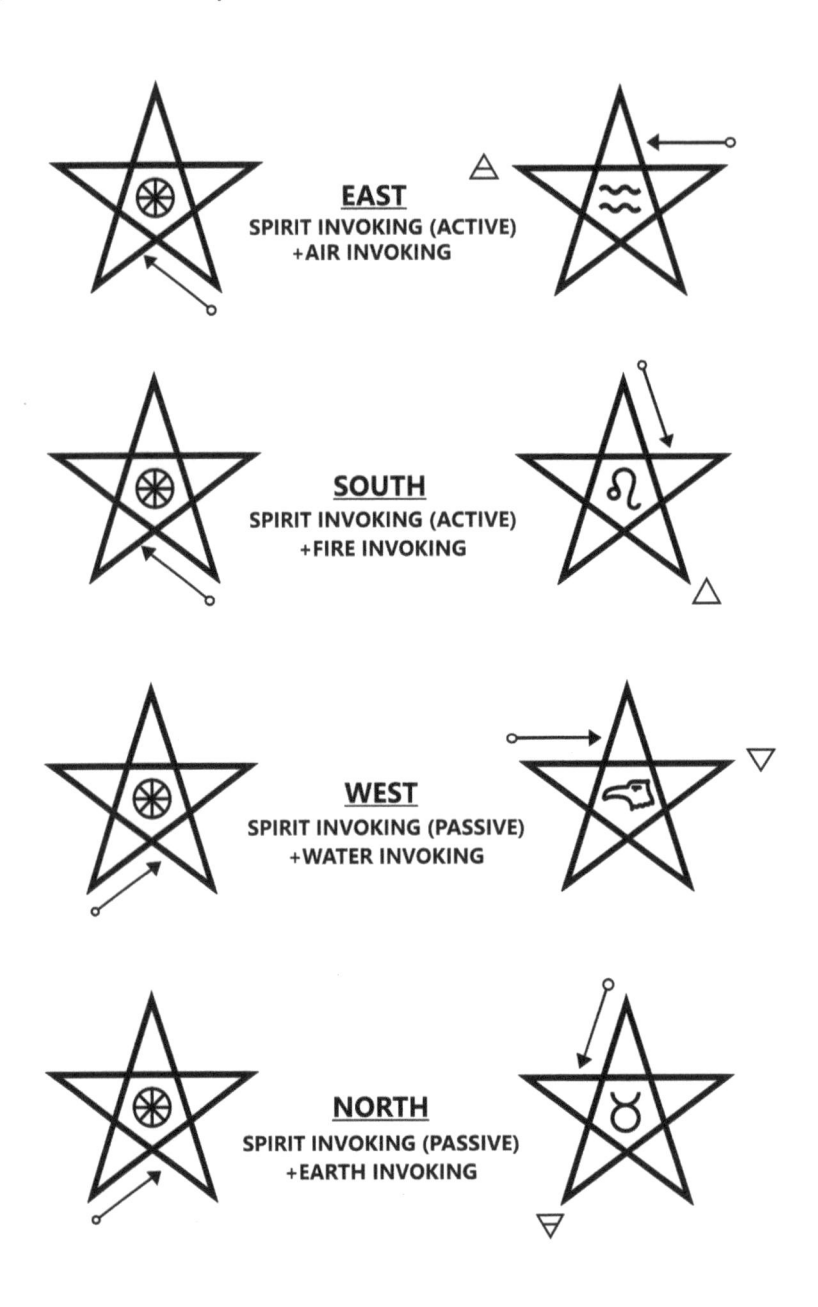

EAST
SPIRIT INVOKING (ACTIVE)
+AIR INVOKING

SOUTH
SPIRIT INVOKING (ACTIVE)
+FIRE INVOKING

WEST
SPIRIT INVOKING (PASSIVE)
+WATER INVOKING

NORTH
SPIRIT INVOKING (PASSIVE)
+EARTH INVOKING

Figure 36: Invoking Pentagrams of the SIRP

Supreme Invoking Ritual of the Pentagram

Formula 1: The Qabalistic Cross

Perform the Four-Fold Breath for a minute or two to get you into a calm, balanced state of mind. Stand in the centre of your circle and face East. If you have Elemental altars and (or) a central altar, stand behind the central altar. Perform the Qabalistic Cross as per the formula in the instructions for the LBRP.

Formula 2: Tracing of the Active and Passive Spirit Pentagrams and Invoking the Elements (Figure 36)

Move now to the East. Draw the Equilibrated Active Pentagram of Spirit in a flaming blue.
While doing so, vibrate:
Exxx-Ahrrr-Peyyy
(EXARP)

See it ablaze as you are infusing it with the Divine Name EXARP. Trace the wheel in the middle of the Pentagram in white Light in a clockwise direction.
While doing so, vibrate:
Eeehhh-heyyy-yeyyy
(Eheieh)

Reach into the Kether Sphere above your head and thrust forward the Light from Kether with the Sign of the Enterer, completely infusing the Pentagram and wheel with Light and seeing it ablaze. Finish with the Sign of Silence. Trace the invoking Pentagram of Air over the Pentagram of Spirit in flaming blue to infuse it with Light.
While doing so, vibrate:
Ohh-Rowww Eee-Bahhh-Hahhh Ahhh-Ohhh-Zooohd-Peee
(ORO IBAH AOZPI)

Trace the Sign of the Aquarius in the middle of the Pentagram in yellow. Trace it in a clockwise direction, from left to right.
While doing so, vibrate:
Yooohd-Heyyy-Vaaav-Heyyy
(YHVH)

Reach into the Kether Sphere and thrust forward the Light from Kether into the Air Pentagram with the Aquarius symbol in the middle, seeing it ablaze as you perform the Sign of the Enterer. Finish with the Sign of Silence. Then, using your Magickal tool, or your right hand, stab in the middle of the Pentagrams and create a white line, which you are to carry forward clockwise towards the South.

Face the South now. Draw the Equilibrated Active Pentagram of Spirit in a flaming blue.
While doing so, vibrate:
Bayyy-Eeee-Tohhh-Ehmmm
(BITOM)

See it ablaze and trace a white wheel in the middle of the Pentagram in a clockwise direction.
While doing so, vibrate:
Eeehhh-heyyy-yeyyy

(Eheieh)

Reach into the Kether Sphere and thrust forward the Light forward with the Sign of the Enterer, infusing the Pentagram and wheel with Light. End with the Sign of Silence. Trace the invoking Pentagram of Fire over the Spirit Pentagram also in a flaming blue.

While doing so, vibrate:

Ohhh-Eee-Payyy Tayyy-Ahhh-Ahhh Payyy-Dohhh-Kayyy

(OIP TEAA PEDOCE)

Draw the Leo sign in red in the middle of the Pentagram. Do this in a clockwise direction.

While doing so, vibrate:

Elll-oooh-heeemmm

(Elohim)

Reach into the Kether Sphere again and thrust forward the Light from Kether into the Fire Pentagram with the Leo sigil, seeing it ablaze while doing the Sign of the Enterer. Finish with the Sign of Silence. Using your Magickal tool, or your right hand, stab the middle of the Pentagrams and carry a white line to the West, thereby making one-half of the Magickal circle so far.

Face the West now. Draw the Equilibrated Passive Pentagram of Spirit in a flaming blue.

While doing so, vibrate:

Hayyy-Cohhh-Maaah

(HCOMA)

See it ablaze and trace a white wheel in the middle of the Pentagram in a clockwise direction.

While doing so, vibrate:

Aaahhh-Glaaahhh

(AGLA)

Reach into the Kether Sphere and thrust forward the Light from Kether into the Pentagram, finishing with the Sign of the Enterer and the Sign of Silence. Then, trace the invoking Pentagram of Water over the Spirit Pentagram in a flaming blue.

While doing so, vibrate:

Ehmmm-Payyy-Hayy Ahrrr-Selll Gahhh-Eee-Ohlll

(EMPEH ARSEL GAIOL)

Draw the Eagle Head sign in the middle of it in blue. Do this in a clockwise direction.

While doing so, vibrate:

Elll

(El)

Reach into the Kether Sphere and thrust forward the Light from Kether into the Water Pentagram, seeing it ablaze while doing the Sign of the Enterer. Finish with the Sign of Silence. Using your Magickal tool, or your right hand, stab the middle of the drawn Pentagrams and continue forming your circle with a white line, now moving to the North.

Face the North now. Draw the Equilibrated Passive Pentagram of Spirit in a flaming blue.

While doing so, vibrate:

Ehnnn-Aaahhh-Ehnnn-Taaahhh

(NANTA)

See it ablaze and trace a white wheel in the middle of the Pentagram in a clockwise direction.

While doing so, vibrate:

Aaaahhhh-Gllaaaaahhh

(AGLA)

Reach into the Kether Sphere and thrust forward the Light from Kether into the Pentagram, finishing with the Sign of the Enterer, followed by the Sign of Silence. Trace the invoking Pentagram of Earth over the Spirit Pentagram also in a flaming blue.

While doing so, vibrate:

Eeee-Mohrrr Deee-Ahhhlll Hekkk-Tayyy-Gaaahhh

(EMOR DIAL HECTEGA)

Draw the Taurus sign in brown colour in the middle of the Pentagram. Do this in a clockwise direction, from left to right.

While doing so, vibrate:

Aaahhh-dooohhh-nyyyeee

(Adonai)

Reach into the Kether Sphere and thrust forward the Light from Kether into the Earth Pentagram, seeing it ablaze while doing the Sign of the Enterer. Finish with the Sign of Silence. Using your Magickal tool, or your right hand, stab now the middle of the Pentagrams and carry your white line to where you started in the East. Your Magickal circle is now complete. Seal the Magickal circle with the Sign of the Enterer and the Sign of Silence. Go to the centre of your circle now. If you have an altar in the middle, then stand behind it.

Formula 3: Invocation of the Archangels

Use the formula of the "Evocation of the Archangels" given in the LBRP (*Formula 3*) but have the Archangels face you instead of having their backs to you, just like in the LIRP (thus making it an invocation). The energy of the Four Elements, under the presidency of the Spirit Element, will be infused into your Magickal circle and, consequently, your Aura.

Formula 4: The Qabalistic Cross

Repeat the Qabalistic Cross as in the beginning.

Formula 5: The Portal Signs

Finish the SIRP by performing the Opening of the Veil Portal Signs. This three-step Sign is given in the "Great Work" section in a chapter titled "Grade Signs of the Five Elements."

***

Note that you can also perform the Supreme Banishing Ritual of the Pentagram (SBRP) if you are having difficulty managing the energies of the SIRP. To do so, you would have to reverse the currents and use the banishing Pentagrams instead of the invoking ones (Figure 37). The only differences from the formula of the SIRP are the direction of the tracings of the Pentagrams, evoking the Archangels with their backs to you, and ending the ritual exercise by using the Closing of the Veil Portal Signs (as given in the "Grade Signs and Their Use" chapter).

Keep in mind that when performing the SBRP, you will be banishing all the Elemental and Spirit energy that you invoked with the SIRP (if you did one previously) and any natural energy you had of the Elements and Spirit before the SIRP. It will then take a good few hours or more until you can naturally rebuild those energies inside of your Aura. The Spirit banishing Pentagrams are given below.

SPIRIT BANISHING (ACTIVE)   **SPIRIT BANISHING (PASSIVE)**

Figure 37: Banishing Pentagrams of Spirit

THE GREAT WORK

> *"Hermeticism is the science of nature hidden in the hieroglyphics and symbols of the Ancient world. It is the search for the principle of life, along with the dream (for those who have not yet achieved it) of accomplishing the Great Work, that is the reproduction by man of the Divine, natural Fire which creates and recreates Beings." — Eliphas Levi; excerpt from "The Kabalistic and Occult Philosophy of Eliphas Levi - Volume 1: Letters to Students"*

The Great Work, or "Magnum Opus," is a term used by Alchemists to describe a conscious effort to achieve the highest state of Spirituality. The goal of the Great Work is Enlightenment and union with the Godhead. The Great Work also refers to the process of Creation. For this reason, the initiate (or practitioner) of Spiritual Alchemy must understand intellectually the nature of the Cosmos and how things work. As the Microcosm is the mirror image of the Macrocosm, the Great Work of the initiate is the process of the Great Work of Creation, but in reverse.

Magnum Opus is a Hermetic term, as is the nature of Alchemy itself. Besides giving you the practice for healing your Chakras (Spiritual Alchemy), this book develops your intellect so that you can comprehend the different aspects of the Universe and the Solar System we live in. Every topic covered so far is an aspect of Creation itself, and learning about it will open doors to your psyche and enable you to understand its workings. Once the intellectual foundation has been laid, the Spiritual Alchemy process can be integrated more easily. In this way, every component of *The Magus* is part of the Great Work.

SPIRITUAL ALCHEMY PROGRAM I—THE FIVE ELEMENTS

0=0: Neophyte Grade (Probationary)

You will begin your Spiritual Alchemy journey by introducing first the Lesser Banishing Ritual of the Pentagram (LBRP) and Middle Pillar as part of your daily routine. You are to do this for two weeks. At least once a day with the LBRP and no more than once a day with the Middle Pillar. These two ritual exercises serve to cleanse your Aura and invoke Light. They are a preparation for working with the Elements.

In the Golden Dawn Order, this is the practice given in the first Grade of Neophyte, as it is the first step of the Alchemical journey. The Grade of Neophyte is considered a preparatory Grade within the Golden Dawn since it does not correspond with any Sephiroth of the Tree of Life, as do the other Grades. For that reason, Neophyte is considered Grade Zero.

The Neophyte Grade and the following four Grades are part of the Outer Order of the Golden Dawn. Since the following four Grades correspond to one of the Elements of Earth, Air, Water, and Fire, the purpose of the Outer Order is Spiritual Alchemy and transformation of the lower four Chakras before embarking on the Element of Spirit, corresponding with the higher three Chakras. The Neophyte Grade's purpose with the LBRP and Middle Pillar is the exaltation of the Soul and Spirit over the Ego.

The LBRP can be performed numerous times during the day, preferably once when you wake up and once when you go to sleep. However, the Middle Pillar is only to be performed once a day during this time period to build up the Light in the Aura safely and efficiently.

The daily ritual exercise sequence for Weeks 0-2 is LBRP, MP.

You must be consistent and do each of these two exercises daily. If you miss a day occasionally, it is quite easy to lose focus of the task at hand and even give up early on. Therefore be determined and persistent in memorizing the ritual sequences of each through repetition daily. The first few weeks are the most difficult because they set the pace for future workings. Also, it is good to employ the use of the Magickal journal right away and keep track of the ritual exercises you are performing as well as your dreams since your dreams will immediately start being impacted by the invoked energy.

1=10: Zelator Grade (Malkuth)—The Earth Element

The Banishing Ritual of the Hexagram (BRH) is to be introduced after the two weeks and is to become a regular part of your ritual practice, always following the LBRP as part of the daily banishings.

The LBRP, BRH, and Middle Pillar can and should be done daily to balance yourself, remove unwanted energy influences from the outside, and infuse Light energy into your Aura. The Lesser Invoking Ritual of the Pentagram (LIRP) is to be performed for Spiritual Alchemy purposes and to do it correctly, there is a formula to be followed.

To start the process of Spiritual Alchemy with the Elements, you need to begin with Earth and perform LIRPs of Earth for a particular amount of time. In the Golden Dawn, this ritual practice is given once the initiate advances to the First Grade, Zelator. Zelator relates to the tenth Sephira, Malkuth, since Earth is where we start our Spiritual journey and go upwards and inwards from there.

The daily ritual exercise sequence for Weeks 2-6 is LBRP, BRH, MP, and LIRP of Earth.

The minimum time you are to spend doing Earth LIRPs is one month. You should do this ritual invocation once daily, preferably in the morning, but any time of the day works fine. It is important to note that the LIRPs of a particular Element should be performed at least three to four times a week. Anything less than that, and you are not infusing the Aura with a specific Element enough. Keep in mind that if you are doing the Middle Pillar exercise right before bed, chances are you will not be able to fall asleep due to the massive influx of Light energy. Therefore, mornings or afternoons are the preferred time for major ritual invocations.

There should be a total of at least 20 LIRPs of Earth completed before you can move on to the next Element of Air. Note again that an LIRP of an Element should never be performed more than once a day. And if you are finding the Earth energy too dense and grounding, you can and should do the LIRP of Earth every two days and not every day. The Aura needs time to be infused with an Element and for it to work on the Chakra corresponding to it. Remember always that this is a process of Spiritual Alchemy, meaning that a strict program and formulas must be followed to succeed.

After the initial two weeks, the Middle Pillar exercise can be performed more times in a day if desired, but doing it too much can make you too spacey and agitated; thus, more than twice a day is not recommended. Once at least twenty Earth LIRPs have been completed, you will be well-grounded, and the Muladhara Chakra will be receiving the right influx of energy from the Earth below you and the minor Chakric points in the soles of your feet. A proper grounding in Earth is necessary before adding the other Elements.

2=9: Theoricus Grade (Yesod)—The Air Element

Now you are ready to start invoking the Air Element through the LIRP of Air. In the Golden Dawn, the Air invocation ritual exercise is given in the Second Grade, Theoricus, corresponding to the ninth Sephira, Yesod. As you scale the Tree of Life upwards, Yesod is synonymous with the Air Element. The ritual sequence to follow is LBRP, BRH, Middle Pillar, and LIRP of Air. You have to spend even more time invoking the Air Element and purifying the Ego than the previous Element of Earth.

The daily ritual exercise sequence for Weeks 6-18 is LBRP, BRH, MP, and LIRP of Air.

The Air Element should be invoked for a minimum of three months with at least 60 LIRPs of Air completed before proceeding to the next Element of Water. The Air Element deals with thoughts, the subconscious mind, and the Ego. Therefore, you need ample time to examine your thoughts and Ego to properly assimilate the lessons of Anahata Chakra and purify your Air Element.

Again, you should not invoke Air more than once in the day through the LIRP, and if you find yourself too Airy and not grounded enough, you should do it every second day instead of every day. Although, in most situations, people enjoy invoking the Air Element since it stimulates creativity, imagination, and inspiration, which is something you can never really get enough of.

3=8: Practicus Grade (Hod)—The Water Element

The next Element in succession is Water, which incorporates the use of the LIRP of Water. In the Golden Dawn, this exercise is given in the Third Grade, Practicus, corresponding with the eighth Sephira, Hod, which is synonymous with the Water Element at this level of the Tree of Life. You need to spend a minimum of two months doing invocations of the Water Element and a minimum of 40 LIRPs of Water during that time. To be purified and exalted, the corresponding Chakra, Swadhisthana, must be correctly infused with the Water Element.

The daily ritual exercise sequence for Weeks 18-26 is LBRP, BRH, MP, and LIRP of Water.

Remember again that you cannot speed up the process of Spiritual Alchemy by performing the LIRP more than once a day. You have to be patient with this practice as it will pay off in the end. If you feel overly emotional and are drowning in the Water Element, you can take down the invocation to once every two days to decrease the influx of Water energy. If, with this practice, you have not reached the minimum of forty-five LIRPs of Water after the allotted two months, then extend the two months. The key is to invoke each Element the prescribed amount of times in total, no matter how often you call-in the Element per week.

The Water Element deals with the emotions and expressions of love. To exalt its Chakra means to overcome personal feelings of love and connect with unconditional love. You must invoke Water in succession with the other two Elements of Earth and Air before embarking on the Element of Fire. It is said in *The Chaldean Oracles*, as part of the Golden Dawn curriculum, "Therefore first the priest who governeth the works of Fire, must sprinkle with the lustral Waters of the loud and resounding sea." What this means is that you must have a strong basis in unconditional love before invoking the very powerful Fire Element; otherwise, you fall prey to the negative expressions of Fire.

4=7: Philosophus Grade (Netzach)—The Fire Element

Once you have completed the necessary time spent invoking Water and have built up a good foundation, you can proceed to work with the LIRP of Fire. In the Golden Dawn, this exercise is given in the Fourth Grade, Philosophus, corresponding with the seventh Sephira, Netzach, which is the Fire Element at this level of the Tree of Life. Remember that through this Spiritual Alchemy process, you are climbing the Tree of Life upwards along the reversed Path of the Flaming Sword so that you can reenter the Garden of Eden again.

You should study and re-examine the different discourses in this book as you work through the Spiritual Alchemy process. You will often get further insight into a subject once you are under the influence of a particular energy that can enlighten that subject. The descriptions of the Elements, in particular, are something you will want to revisit as you invoke them. But since most of the subjects presented here deal with expressions of types of energy, you will learn more and understand different concepts and ideas better as you re-read them many times.

Fire is the most volatile of the Elements and one that burns away at the impurities in the corresponding Manipura Chakra. Manipura deals with expressions of your Soul. The Fire Element also fine-tunes the other three Chakras corresponding with the Earth, Water, and Air Elements since the Soul uses the Elements to express itself. As such, you are to spend a minimum of seven months doing invocations of Fire with the LIRP. At least 140 LIRPs of Fire should be completed before proceeding to work with the Spirit Element.

The daily ritual exercise sequence for Weeks 26-54 is LBRP, BRH, MP, and LIRP of Fire.

The Fire Element is at the core of our Being, in the First World of Atziluth, where the Archetypes lie. It relates to our beliefs about ourselves and the world, which are deeply ingrained within us. Since the Fire Element works through the other three Elements, Fire invocations will bring about the most change in your psychological makeup thus far. For this reason, you are to spend more time invoking the Fire Element than you have the other three Elements since Fire deals with transformation.

Again, if you feel too agitated by the Fire Element (which can happen), and it is causing you to act in a negative, destructive way in your daily life, then do the LIRPs of Fire once every two days instead or even once every three days. You always have to add and subtract an Element within yourself through the ritual exercises given so that you are comfortable with the Spiritual Alchemy process. Always be wary that an Element is not manifesting negatively in your personal life.

It often helps to drop back down to the previous Elements and do more work on those before proceeding with the current one, considering that the last Element you worked with is meant to help with the following one. For this reason, the sequence of the Elements being invoked is critical. A later section on Hermetic Alchemy will shed more light on why the Elements are invoked in this order. Spiritual Alchemy is a proven process that works—as it has been tried-tested-and true for thousands of years by Alchemists and Magi alike.

Veil of Paroketh: Portal Grade—The Spirit Element
Once you have spent the necessary time doing invocations of Fire, you can embark on doing the Supreme Invoking Ritual of the Pentagram (SIRP) and invoking the Spirit Element. This exercise is given in the Golden Dawn in the Portal Grade. The Portal Grade is the precursor to the Adeptus Minor Grade, which corresponds with the Tiphareth Sephira. The purpose of entering Tiphareth is to relive the life, death, and Resurrection of Jesus Christ, Mithras, and Osiris of Egypt and become Resurrected in this Sphere through the Spirit Element. Before entering it, though, sufficient time must be spent working with the SIRP and infusing the Spirit Element into the Aura and the Chakras, and this process begins in the Portal Grade.

The daily ritual exercise sequence for Weeks 54-90 is LBRP, BRH, MP, and SIRP.

Alchemically, this Spirit invocation operation requires nine months, which is the time a fetus gestates in its mother's womb. This process is synonymous with the Christian Resurrection and being born again of the Spirit.

Of those nine months, you need to do at least 180 SIRPs to complete the Alchemical Spiritual process. Completing this many SIRPs will fully assimilate the Spirit Element into your Aura and psyche.

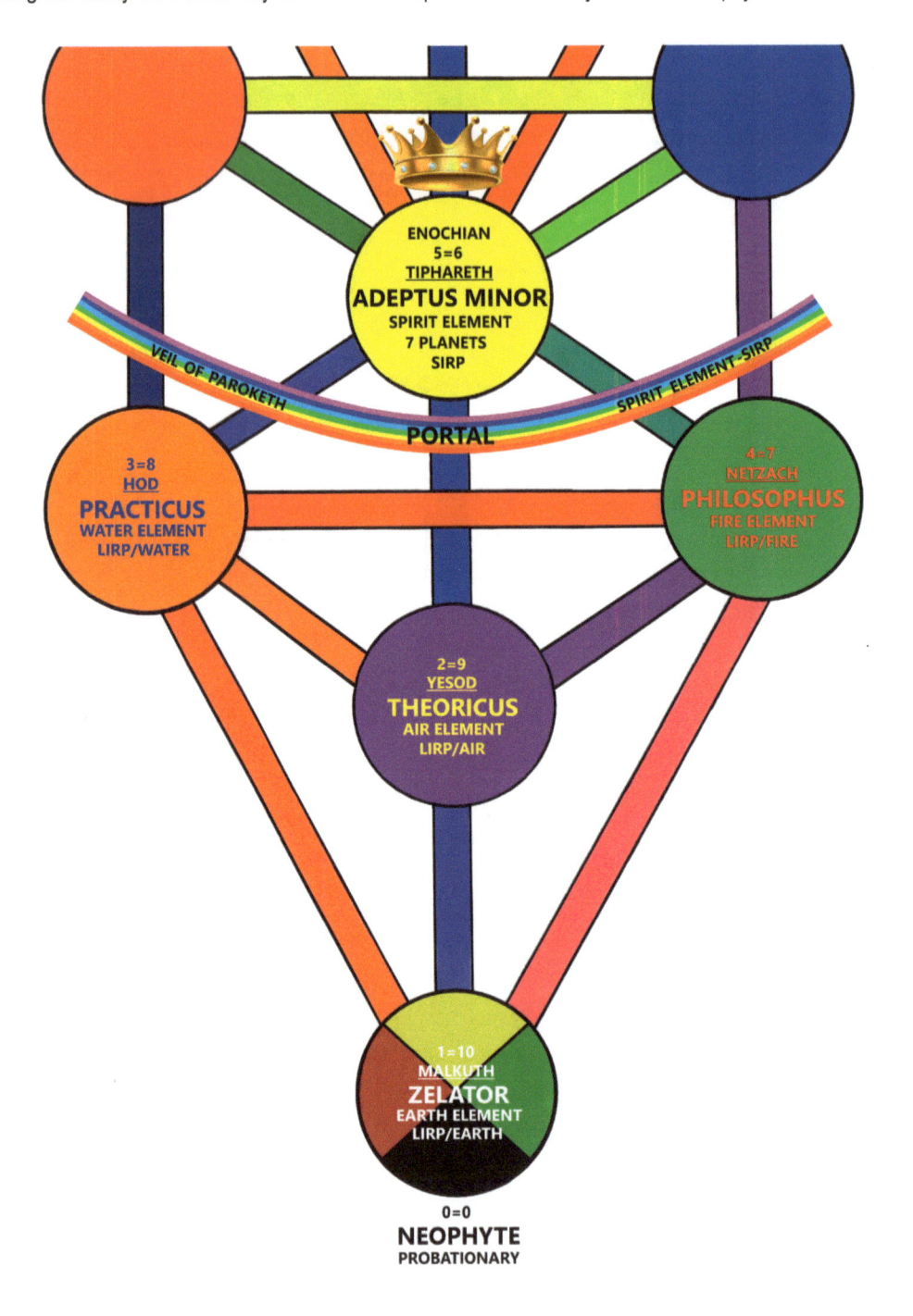

Figure 38: The System of Advancement in "The Magus"

***

At this point in the Golden Dawn, you will have finished the Outer Order (First Order), corresponding to the Four Elements, and will have assimilated the Spirit energy into your Aura. Doing so is a precursor to entering the Second Order, which corresponds with the Grades of the three Sephiroth of Tiphareth, Geburah, and Chesed. The Second Order is frequently referred to as the Inner Order.

The Third Order is also a part of the Inner Order, corresponding with Grades of the three highest Sephiroth of Binah, Chokmah, and Kether. Attaining these three Grades is rare. A discrepancy exists regarding whether a human can achieve the two top Grades while living in the physical body. Some would argue that a full Kundalini awakening, when the energy rises to the Crown and stays in the brain permanently, is the only real initiation into the Third Order.

The Tiphareth Sephira is the separation point between the Inner Order and the Outer Order of the Golden Dawn. All the Sephiroth below Tiphareth belong to the Outer Order, while the Sephiroth above Tiphareth belong to the Inner Order. There is a Veil between the lower Sephiroth of the Tree of Life with Tiphareth and the higher Sephiroth, called the Veil of Paroketh. The Element of Spirit will give you entry through this Veil, which, once penetrated through (by invoking the Spirit Element), will make you an Adept in the Western Mysteries.

An Adept is a person who has mastered the Four Elements of their Being and who solely operates from the Spirit Element. The consciousness of the Adept is elevated as they function from the higher three Chakras of Vishuddhi, Ajna, and Sahasrara. Since these three Chakras are also connected to the Divine Worlds above Sahasrara, this would mean that Divine Beings residing in those Worlds will have direct contact with the Adept and can communicate to them through Gnosis. Being in the Inner Order means to have contact with these Divine Beings, some of whom are considered transcendent Cosmic authorities. The Golden Dawn Order refers to them as the "Secret Chiefs."

Once you have completed your work with the SIRP, this would mark the end of your Spiritual Alchemy process with the Five Elements of Earth, Air, Water, Fire, and Spirit. In reality, though, your journey as a Magus has just begun. There is much more work to be done with the energies of our Solar System for you to complete the Great Work (Figure 38).

The entire process of Spiritual Alchemy with the Five Elements takes just under two years. You have to be patient and determined to do it consistently, which requires a great deal of dedication and effort, but as I said before, it is very much worth it. You will emerge as a much more Spiritually advanced person and someone who has control over their reality. You will be a cause instead of an effect, enabling you to tap into your innermost potential as a Spiritual human being. Your personal power will increase to an unimaginable degree, allowing you to manifest the life you always dreamed of.

What I have presented to you is the prescribed program of the Ritual Magick exercises within the Golden Dawn Order, as it was taught to me many years ago. All Golden Dawn Orders practice Ritual Magick this way simply because the method works. It has worked in the past and will always work in the future. Furthermore, these sequences have been proven to work for many years by many past Golden Dawn students. Therefore, adhering to the timeline I presented is the most optimal way to experience the Spiritual Alchemy process since it will yield the best results.

ACCELERATING THE SPIRITUAL ALCHEMY PROGRAM

Since some of my past students expressed concern regarding the timeline of the Spiritual Alchemy program with the Five Elements, I have decided to offer an alternative, faster-paced version of the same program. If you choose that this second version is for you, follow it instead.

I am presenting an alternative version because many students felt they were ready for the next Element in the Spiritual Alchemy sequence ahead of time. Most often, this happens once they complete 80% of the prescribed LIRPs with an Element. To make the correct judgement, I would ascertain the origin of their feelings and determine whether it is their Ego or their Higher Self that is projecting them. The Ego might feel too challenged by the Elements, and it may give misleading information to avoid these challenges. On the other hand, if it is the Higher Self, perhaps the Spirit is communicating something that should be listened to and even honoured to a certain degree. After all, learning to listen to our Higher Selves is one of the aims of the Great Work.

In most cases, people fall in love with Ceremonial Magick from the very beginning and embrace the Spiritual Alchemy process. Consequently, these people are usually the ones that come to me with this kind of predicament. After all, it is normal for anyone to get excited to advance to the next Element in the sequence once it becomes evident that the Elements are making a positive change in their lives. However, it is crucial to make sure the Higher Self is guiding this process and overseeing the changes that are taking place within you. After all, there is no more exceptional teacher or Spiritual guide than your own Higher Self.

Often, Spiritual stagnation may occur if the lessons with an Element have been learned earlier than predicted—resulting in the Higher Self signalling that you are ready to move on. If this happens, the correct thing to do is to listen. After all, remaining enthusiastic and inspired to do this work is of utmost importance. I would not want you to fall off the path and quit altogether if you are not getting what your Higher Self is asking for.

The method I propose in this case is to allow you to start the next Element in sequence only once 90% of the prescribed LIRPs of an Element are completed. In this case, you do not need to spend the minimum amount of time in an Element but only focus on how many LIRPs you have completed. The prescribed amount of time you are to spend working with an Element is there for you to be able to integrate the lessons of that Element. Still, if you feel you have already done that, then only the number of LIRPs is essential in the Spiritual Alchemy process.

Again, this is solely for students whose Higher Selves communicate this information to them, not their Egos. If you are still dealing with challenges and learning life lessons being imparted to you by the Element you are working with, then you must finish the prescribed work with that Element before moving on. Be honest with yourself since you only will be harming yourself if you are not.

For example, instead of doing twenty LIRPs of Earth, you can do eighteen and move on to Air. And in Air, you can do fifty-four instead of sixty LIRPs. The formula to accelerate the process is to do 90% of the recommended Elemental invocations, but not one invocation less than that. This means that if you are spending every day doing the LIRP of an Element, you can finish your work with it much faster than you normally would if you are invoking every few days, following the first version of the same program.

If you are doing less than 90% of invocations and moving on to the following Element, you jeopardise the entire Spiritual Alchemy process. The Spiritual Alchemy method has to be respected since we are dealing with a precise science of adding and subtracting energy for personal transformation into a Being of Light.

I want you to maintain momentum with this work, but I also want you to gain the benefits of the Spiritual Alchemy process when completed in full. I have seen too many initiates fall off the path because they felt they were stagnating Spiritually, and their mentors were very rigid in their attitudes towards this work. I have also seen initiates move ahead to the following Element far earlier than they should have, which often ends up being catastrophic for their Magickal journey. Their Egos completely take over and drown out their Higher Self, resulting in them turning their back on this work and quitting altogether.

Suppose you are finding yourself stagnant in one Element and you have not completed 90% of the recommended invocations. In that case, you are free to revisit any lower Elements you have done before. Then, when you are ready, you can return and finish the work you left with your current Element. It is recommended that you do this to truly master the Elements within yourself.

You will find that as you gain access to a higher Element, once you drop down to a lower one, new life lessons will emerge for you to learn from. Remember always that the key is tuning and healing the Chakras, removing negative Karma, and becoming a master of the Elements within yourself. Each Element contains many lessons, triggering different parts of the psyche. Thus, be on the lookout to see how this manifests within you.

I implore you again to be determined, persistent, and consistent in performing this Spiritual Alchemy process. Take it very seriously. It does not require more than ten minutes a day to complete the ritual exercises (and as you get good at it, even less time will be needed), but the formula must be followed as given without any deviations. This process can and will be very positive and fun and will pay off in the end for you.

Once you have started the Spiritual Alchemy process, I recommend you devote the time and effort to finishing it. If you quit ahead of time, you will be preventing yourself from evolving further Spiritually and mastering whatever Elements within yourself that you have still not worked with. After all, if you want to become a Master Manifestor of your reality, you need all the necessary ingredients to enable you to become one.

Imagine what would happen if you wanted to learn to play basketball but quit before you learned how to make a layup. Your game would suffer until you learned this skill. In the same way, if you worked with a few Elements but did not reach as high as Water, Fire, or Spirit, you would be missing those critical ingredients within yourself. Therefore, I highly recommend that you finish this Spiritual Alchemy process once you have begun. It is better to take time off and continue the journey at a later time than to quit altogether.

GRADE SIGNS OF THE FIVE ELEMENTS

Each of the Four Elements has a Grade Sign (Figure 39), which is meant to be used at the end of an LIRP. The Spirit Element has a three-step Grade Sign that can be completed in two methods, depending on whether you are performing the SIRP or SBRP. The purpose of the Grade Signs is to assume dominance over the Elemental Kingdom of the invoked Element. By implementing a Grade Sign, you are aligning with the Angels of the invoked Element and repelling the Demons, considering that every Element contains the dichotomy of both.

A Grade Sign can also be used as a key that allows you to commune with an Element's energy in the hopes that you may gain complete control over that energy. These are Magickal gestures that become living symbols and make you, the practitioner, an embodiment of the power of the ritual exercise itself.

Figure 39: Grade Signs of the Four Elements

Sign of Zelator

This is the Sign of the Earth Element, corresponding with the Sephira Malkuth and the LIRP of Earth. To perform the Sign of the Zelator, you must raise your right arm straight up at a forty-five-degree angle from the body, with the hand held flat and thumb facing the Heavens above you. Your left foot should be facing forward as in the Sign of the Enterer. Your gaze should be forwards and upwards towards the sky. The Sign of Zelator alludes to the aspiring Magus, and the left foot forward represents moving towards the Light.

Sign of Theoricus

This is the Sign of the Air Element, corresponding with the Sephira Yesod and the LIRP of Air. To perform this Sign, you must bend both arms at the elbows, with the palms facing upwards, as if supporting the Heavens above. The feet should be square and shoulder-width apart while your gaze is forwards and upwards towards the sky. The Sign of Theoricus alludes to the Light descending from the Heavens Above to the practitioner Below. This Sign is symbolic of receiving the healing power of the Light.

Sign of Practicus

This is the Sign of the Water Element, corresponding with the Sephira Hod and the LIRP of Water. To perform this Sign, you are to form a triangle with your thumbs and forefingers (apex downwards) and place it over your solar plexus. Your feet should be square and shoulder-width apart while your gaze is directly in front of you. The Sign of Practicus alludes to the power of the Waters of Creation.

Sign of Philosophus

This is the Sign of the Fire Element, corresponding with the Sephira Netzach and the LIRP of Fire. To perform this sign, you must form a triangle with your thumbs and forefingers (apex upwards) and place them over your forehead. Your feet should be square and shoulder-width apart while your gaze is directly in front of you. The Sign of Philosophus alludes to the power of the Fires of the Soul.

Opening of the Veil

This is the Sign of the Spirit Element, corresponding with the Portal Grade and the Veil of Paroketh. Another name for this Sign is the Rending of the Veil. This Three-Step Sign (Figure 40) begins with both feet planted together and hands together in a prayer position but with fingers pointing forwards instead of upwards (Step One). In Step Two, you keep your hands in the same place but bring your left foot forward like in the Sign of the Enterer. In Step Three, you separate the hands as if opening a curtain, while bringing your right foot forward and planting it beside the left.

All three steps should be performed in one motion ending with you in the position of the Tav Cross, with your palms facing forward. The Veil you are opening with this Sign is the Veil of Paroketh, which separates the Ethical Triangle from the lower Sephiroth. Performing the Opening of the Veil is symbolic of opening yourself up to the power of your Higher Self.

Closing of the Veil

This is another sign of the Spirit Element, corresponding with the Portal Grade and the Veil of Paroketh. This sign is performed by following the same three steps as the Opening of the Veil but in reverse order. As the Opening of the Veil is used after a Spirit invocation, the Closing of the Veil is used following a Spirit banishing. Performing it is symbolic of closing yourself off from the influx of energy from the Spirit Element, which will sever the connection with your Higher Self for the time being.

Figure 40: Three Steps of the Portal Grade Signs

THE MAGUS EMBLEM

The Red Calvary Cross sitting atop a White Triangle forms the emblem of the Golden Dawn Tradition. Often, but not always, the Cross and Triangle are shown upon a black background. The White Triangle represents the Divine Light, which created the world out of the darkness. It corresponds with the Supernal Triad, a manifestation of the Divine Light and the highest attainable state of consciousness for human beings.

The White Triangle also represents the Alchemical Trinity and the Christian Holy Trinity. The triangle is a powerful Spiritual and occult symbol because it represents two contending forces and one which unites them. It refers to the duality of the World of Matter, reconciled by the Non-Duality of the Spiritual World.

The Red Calvary Cross represents Tiphareth and the Self-sacrifice that is necessary for one to undergo the process of transformation from man into God. Furthermore, since Tiphareth is the Sphere of Resurrection, the Red Cross alludes to the Spiritual rebirth that needs to occur for the individual to unite their consciousness with the Cosmic Consciousness of the Creator. Together, the White Triangle and Red Cross represent Light and Life.

The Magus emblem is modified from the traditional Golden Dawn Cross and Triangle to best represent the many ideas in this work (Figure 41). After all, the purpose of *The Magus* is to bridge the Eastern Spiritual System and the Western Mystery Tradition—the Kundalini and the Golden Dawn.

The Red Cross in *The Magus* emblem is in the shape of the Rose Cross, a symbol of Adepthood and entry into the Second Order of the Golden Dawn. This symbol represents the Tiphareth Grade but also the Rosicrucian influence in the Golden Dawn system.

The Caduceus is superimposed on the Red Cross as a Western symbol for the Kundalini energy. Behind the Cross is a lotus flower symbol with seven layers of petals showing. It represents Sahasrara, the Crown Chakra, containing within itself the totality of the Seven Chakras. On the Tree of Life, Sahasrara corresponds with Kether, the highest Sphere. Each row of petals is in the colour of one of the Chakras, which correspond with the Cosmic Planes. The rows start with red on the outside (Muladhara) and end with Sahasrara (violet) closest to the Cross.

The lotus is open and in full bloom, meaning that the Kundalini energy has risen to the Crown, awakening the Seven Chakras and the entire Tree of Life. In addition, the Body of Light has been fully activated, enabling the Adept to be conscious and present on all levels and dimensions of reality simultaneously.

The Caduceus on the Red Cross also stands for Jesus Christ, sacrificing himself on the Cross of the Four Elements. His sacrifice is symbolic of the fifth Element of Spirit. As mentioned in a previous lesson, Jesus is a prototype for the Kundalini awakening and transformation. This mystery is being further alluded to by the letters of the Pentagrammaton within the White Triangle.

The Hebrew letter Shin, the Threefold Flame of the Soul, is another symbol for the Kundalini Fire. It is exalted atop the rising Sun, the central Star of our Solar System, representing the Soul (Sol) and the Tiphareth Sephira. The Sun also stands for the "Son of Man" and the "Light of the World," which references Jesus Christ in *The Holy Bible*.

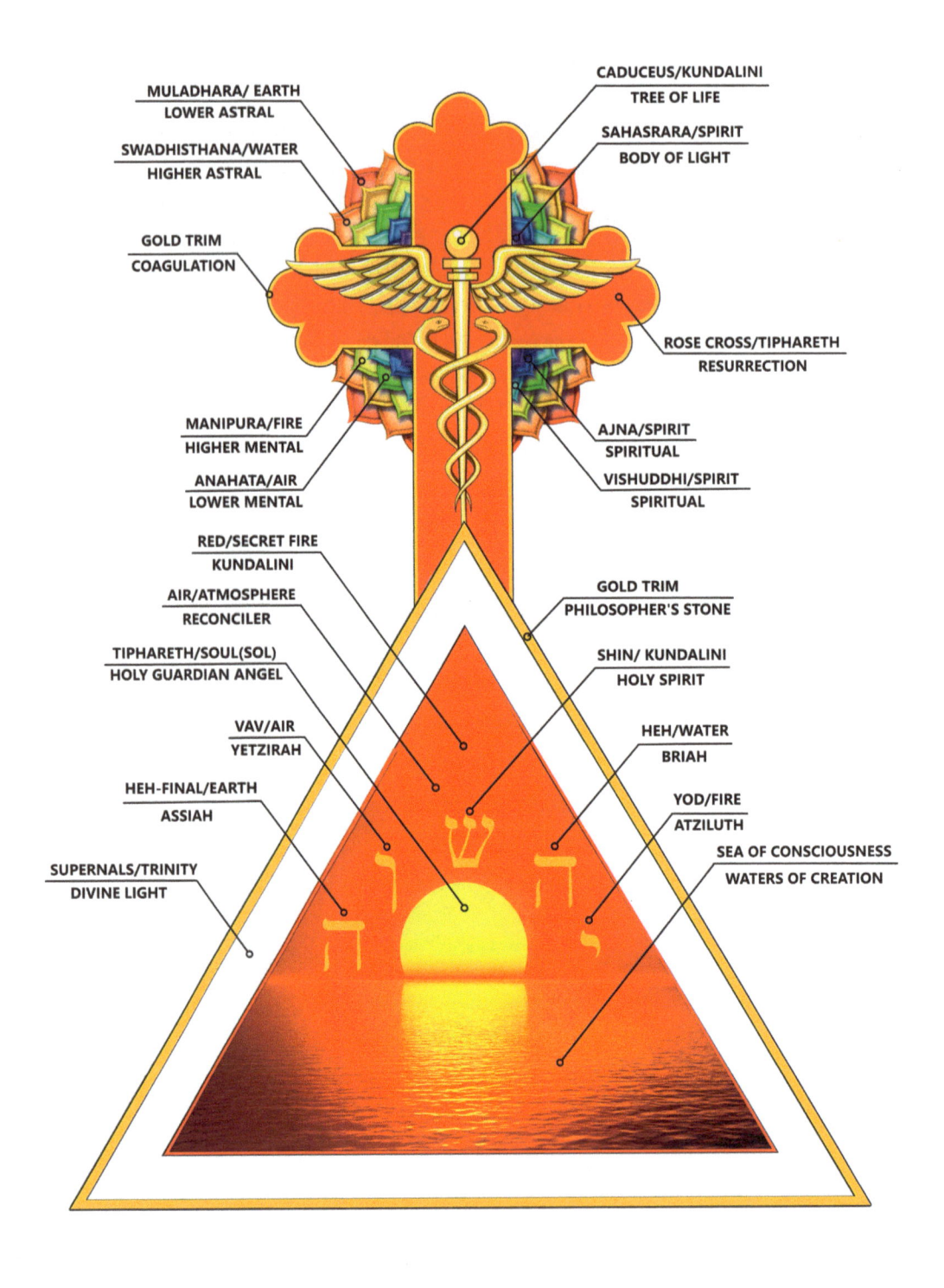

Figure 41: "The Magus" Emblem

The other four letters of the Pentagrammaton are on opposite sides of the Sun, with Yod and Heh (Fire and Water Elements) on one side and Vav and Heh-final (Air and Earth Elements) on the other side. There is a balance between the active and passive, masculine and feminine forces, reconciled by the Shin letter of the Holy Spirit. YHVH also alludes to the Four Worlds of the Qabalah—the Cosmic Planes. It represents the totality of our existence.

Tiphareth is a Sphere of Spiritual healing and illumination. Through Tiphareth, we can make contact with our Holy Guardian Angel from the Supernals, above the Abyss. The rising Sun in the White Triangle represents this connection. The Sun rises on the horizon, above an ocean representing the Sea of Consciousness.

This image portrays a perfect balance between the Fires of the Soul and the Waters of Creation. It represents the Hexagram, a symbol of the Spiritually perfected human. It also alludes to the Hermetic axiom, "As Above, So Below." The Air Element is also present in the image, as the Earth's atmosphere. It serves as the reconciler between the Fire and Water Elements, represented by the Sun and the ocean.

The entire scene portrayed in the White Triangle represents the "Golden Dawn"— the decrease of the darkness and the increase of the Light. It symbolizes the essence of the work in *The Magus*, which is furthering one's Spiritual Evolution. Red colour dominates the scene, indicating that even though the three main Elements (Fire, Water, and Air) are present within the White Triangle, Fire is the dominant Element because of the influence of the Secret Fire of the Kundalini.

The Red Cross and the White Triangle have gold trim around them, representing the perfected Philosopher's Stone. Gold is attributed to the Sun in Alchemy, which signifies the final stage of Coagulation. Symbolically, Malkuth has been raised into Daath, and Spirit and Matter are united and unified as one. The Garden of Eden has been restored. The initiate now functions through perpetual intuition, as their consciousness has been elevated to the Supernals. They have become an Enlightened Adept and have achieved Nirvana in this lifetime.

Englightenment is not an overnight process but requires a constant sacrifice of the Ego and exaltation of the Soul. One needs to purify and consecrate their Chakras to gain mastery over the Five Elements. The Spiritual Alchemy programs contained within *The Magus* are designed for this purpose. Once the body is made into a living temple, the Spirit can descend into the Self, thereby transforming the consciousness. A permanent link with the Holy Guardian Angel will be established, thus completing the Great Work.

As you can see, *The Magus* emblem is loaded with relevant symbolic imagery. There are many Universal mysteries contained within it that work together as a whole. Its essence is at the very core of Creation. The emblem can be used as a meditative symbol, and as such, it should be referred to often to enlighten and solidify the various lessons contained within *The Magus*.

THE NEXT STEP IN THE GREAT WORK

Once you have completed the prescribed Spiritual Alchemy program with the Five Elements and want to continue working further with Ceremonial Magick ritual exercises, you have four options to choose from. The first option is for you to go back to the Earth Element and repeat the same process. This time, you are not limited by the amount of time or LIRPs you need to perform for each Element but can decide on your own based on how much time you feel you need to work on each one.

Again, you are to follow the same sequence as before by starting in Earth, then invoking Air, Water, and Fire. And finally, you are to end with Spirit once you have completed working Fire. In this way, you are working with the Spiritual Alchemy process that has been time-tested and is dependable for optimal results. Performing this sequence again will help you evolve Spiritually further and heal particular Chakras that may require additional work.

The second option is to choose whichever Element you want to work on and stay in it as long as you want. In this case, working through the Elements in succession is unnecessary. Instead, choose whichever Element interests you to work with further to optimize the corresponding Chakra(s) and expressions of Self. You can do this for as long as you want and work on any Elements you desire. Through this process, you are truly becoming a Magus, where you are learning to master the Elements of your Being.

The third option is to keep advancing within the Golden Dawn Order's grade system. As you finish the Spiritual Alchemy of the Portal Grade, your next step is Inner Order work, starting with working with the energies of the Seven Ancient Planets. The purpose of this work, including the description of the ritual exercises and the program to be followed, is given in the "Advanced Planetary Magick" chapter following the discourse on Astrology. Planetary Magick is only offered in the Golden Dawn once the initiate has entered the Adeptus Minor Grade.

The fourth option can technically be undertaken before the third one, although it is recommended that you work with Planetary Magick first. The fourth option is working with Enochian Magick, which is another Inner Order practice in the Golden Dawn system of Magick. This option is the most powerful one and one that you genuinely need to be prepared for.

Within the Golden Dawn, Enochian Magick is given as part of the Adeptus Minor curriculum only after the initiate has worked with Planetary Magick for the prescribed period. Working with Planetary Magick will further prepare you for Enochian Magick. However, in my personal experience and the experience of most of my students, the previous work with the Elements was sufficient. Therefore, you can work with Enochian first and then jump to Planetary Magick afterwards; the choice is yours. As a rule of thumb, if you had a difficult time working with the Elements, it is recommended that you start with Planetary Magick first (since it will give you an even stronger foundation) before beginning to work with the potent Enochian Keys.

It is crucial to gain mastery over the Five Elements of Earth, Air, Water, Fire and Spirit before embarking on Enochian Magick. Jumping into it too early can cause you Spiritual harm since you need to have a proper foundation in the previous ritual exercises to control the powerful forces invoked through the Enochian Keys. Once you are ready, though, Enochian Magick will take your Spiritual Alchemy process to the next level.

The Spiritual Alchemy process with Enochian Magick will be undertaken with a similar formula presented so far. Turn to the "Enochian Magick" section, following Hermetic Philosophy, to learn more about Enochian Magick and find the program to practice the Enochian Keys.

Whether you choose to work with Planetary Magick or Enochian Magick first, you must finish the prescribed program of the option you selected before starting the second one. Working with both simultaneously or moving from one to the other without completing it in full will hinder its intended Spiritual Alchemy. Therefore, I highly discourage you from doing this as it can negatively impact your Spiritual Evolution process and even set you back on your journey.

A WARNING ON ENOCHIAN MAGICK

Enochian Magick is the highest form of Magick in Ceremonial Magick Orders. It offers excellent Spiritual Alchemy, and my experience has been that the Enochian Aethyrs are exceptional for working with the Ida and Pingala Nadis (or currents) in Kundalini awakened individuals. Because of its power, though, and often volatile nature, Enochian Magick is only for the advanced seekers of Magick and practitioners who have advanced well along the Spiritual path. You must have a proper foundation in the other ritual exercises presented so far. I cannot stress this enough.

Just looking over the Enochian Keys or reading them silently to yourself will invoke the energy regardless. Therefore, if you want to read about Enochian Magick and what it is, that is fine. But skip over the Enochian Keys and do not even glance at them until you are ready and confident that you want to proceed in that direction. Heed the warning I am giving you because these Enochian Keys are highly potent. I will keep repeating myself in this regard to ensure that your curiosity does not get the best of you.

I have included the Enochian Keys at the very back of the book, and they are there only for those aspiring Magi who have completed the prescribed program with the ritual exercises presented so far. If you do not have a proper mental and emotional foundation and choose to play around with the Enochian Keys (thereby going against my warning), you will put yourself at risk of opening doors to your mind, which cannot be closed once opened. Just think of what happened in the story of Pandora's Box.

When used haphazardly, the Enochian Keys can create mental and emotional issues, even mania. When I was part of the Golden Dawn Order, I heard of stories where individuals used them recklessly and had to be admitted into a mental institution. Whether this ever happened or was just a way to deter individuals from practising Enochian Magick without being ready will remain a mystery. I can tell you from personal experience, though, that you are dealing with a loaded gun. If used correctly, it can save your life. If misused, it can be Spiritual suicide. You need to be able to control the forces you are unleashing with these Keys.

Having said that, I am not trying to discourage you from using the Enochian Keys. On the contrary, once you have completed the program prescribed with the other ritual exercises, Enochian Magick is the next step in your Spiritual Alchemical journey. The Enochian Magick system stands on its own as something unique and separate from the rest, but also part of it. It is the crowning achievement of becoming a Magus since you will emerge a much higher Spiritual Being out of that work than you were before you entered it.

Working with Enochian Magick will be an exciting venture for you, making you feel like a true Mystic and Sage. Many people I have taught the art of Ceremonial Magick, including Enochian Magick, have enjoyed Enochian Magick the most and made it their home in the end. The Enochian Keys offer incredible states of consciousness that you can tap into to learn more about yourself and the Universe around you. I have spent a great deal of time using Enochian Magick myself, and it has been my preferred work with Ceremonial Magick to date.

PART IV: ASTROLOGY

ASTROLOGY AND THE ZODIAC

"Astrology has no more useful function than this, to discover the inmost nature of a man and to bring it out into his consciousness, that he may fulfil it according to the Law of Light." — Aleister Crowley; excerpt from "The Complete Astrological Writings"

Astrology is one of the oldest sciences of humanity. Its origins can be traced back to Ancient Sumer and even earlier. It is the science that examines the movements and relative positions of the celestial bodies (Planets) and their influence on all human beings on Earth. Astrology gives us a means of divining information about our affairs as well as terrestrial events. It has been recognized and practised throughout history around the world. The Egyptians, Greeks, Romans, Chinese, Hindus, Persians, and the Ancient Mesoamerica civilisations all knew of Astrology's significance.

There are twelve Astrological signs, each of which belongs to a particular Element in one of its states. These states are best described as the Sub-Element of an Element. With this breakdown, we have twelve different yet fundamental vibratory frequencies of energy. These varying energetic qualities provide the overall influence on the Planetary positions at the time of our birth. However, how a Planet's influence will manifest for us depends on which of the Twelve Houses it falls in. The blueprint of these energy influences forms our Horoscope, otherwise called a Natal Chart or Birth Chart.

Astrological signs are the twelve 30-degree sectors of the ecliptic, starting at the Vernal, or Spring Equinox, which is one of the intersections of the ecliptic with the celestial equator. The twelve Astrological signs have been given their names according to the twelve constellations in the night sky. A constellation is a cluster of Stars in the sky grouped in a particular pattern. The Ancients gave them a name according to the visible image they formed in their grouping.

The Tropical Year, called the Solar Year, is determined by the Earth's revolution around the Sun, which takes approximately 365.25 days. The Tropical Year forms the Gregorian Calendar, which is the standard measure of time in our modern-day society. Every month, as the Earth continues its orbit around the Sun, we continually transition from one Zodiac sign to the next.

As the Spring Equinox starts off the Solar Year, the name of the constellation that the Sun is in we call Aries. When we look up at the night sky during this time, though, we cannot see Aries but will have to wait a few months until the Sun has moved a sufficient number of signs away from it. The Zodiac sign that the Sun is in would be the constellation directly behind it if we were to project a straight line from the Earth through the Sun (Figure 42). If we are in Aries, then we would have the best view of its opposite constellation according to the Wheel of the Zodiac.

There are other constellations in the sky beside the twelve Zodiacal ones. However, this work will only focus on the twelve that form the imaginary "belt" or "roadway" in the Heavens surrounding our Solar System.

In Western Astrology, Equinox and Solstice points are measured, relating to equal, longest and shortest days of the Solar year. The Equinoxes occur twice, in spring and autumn, and mark the time of the year when the day length is the same as the night (twelve hours).

The Solstices also occur twice during the year. The Summer Solstice is when the day is longest during the year, while the Winter Solstice marks the time when the night is longest. These two represent the beginning of the summer and winter seasons, as the Equinoxes signify the beginning of the spring and autumn seasons.

The Equinoxes and Solstices are times of the year when the Ancient people performed certain rituals to commemorate the Solar year. Since they represent the time of the year when the Light of the Sun is most and least present on Earth, they are important in all Magickal workings.

THE HOROSCOPE

Every human being is influenced Karmically by the Planets and the Zodiac signs they were in at the time of their birth. According to Astrology, celestial phenomena relate to human activity on the Hermetic Principle of "As Above, So Below." The Zodiac signs represent characteristic modes of expression in humanity. The Ancients teach that the personality's likes and dislikes and the character's aspirations are influenced by the Planetary energies in our Solar System.

These Planetary energies form our overall Self, upon which our life experiences are built. As we are born on a particular day, at a certain hour, in a specific city, we will have a distinct influence from the Zodiac energies influencing our Planets, or storehouses of inner powers, that our Self will have at its disposal throughout our lives. In this way, every human being will be motivated by something different. Couple this with each person's diverse life experiences while growing up, and no person is ever the same as another. We are all unique, which makes us all very special in the eyes of God-the Creator.

The three most vital signs within the Horoscope are the Sun Sign, the Moon Sign, and the Ascendant (Rising) Sign. Along with the Planets, these Signs are "frozen" in their position at that initial moment of birth. The placement of the individual Planets in the Horoscope is given according to the Tree of Life framework.

The Ascendant (Rising) Sign is the Zodiac Sign on the Eastern horizon at the time of our birth. This Sign represents our First House which starts off the Twelve Houses, a separate system that grounds Astrology in Earthly matters. Although the Ascendant is given in all Western Astrology Horoscopes, the rest of the Houses and their Planetary influences are often overlooked; hence they are only included in more advanced readings.

The Sun Sign is our core and general nature and will as individuals. This influence describes our highest aspirations in this lifetime. Our Sun Sign is our "true colours" that we display to the world daily. The Moon Sign is the emotional side of our personality, including the immediate emotional responses to life's events. It is the subconscious Self, as the Sun Sign is the conscious Self. The Moon Sign is expressive of our reactions instilled by past conditioning, memory, and habitual patterns. The Ascendant, or Rising Sign, denotes how we look at life. Often, it is the impression of who we are, perceived by those around us. It is who we consciously present to the world.

I advise you to go online and obtain a free Natal Chart. Doing so will give you a framework of your personality, character, and the energies influencing your psyche since birth. As the Ancient Greek aphorism says, "Know Thyself." Understanding your Horoscope will allow you to understand and accept yourself more clearly. It will enable you to see which challenges you need to overcome in yourself to further your Spiritual Evolution. Remember always that your natural attributes can be seen as the hand you have been dealt in life, but how you play that hand is up to you since you do have Free Will.

THE FOUR ELEMENTS WITHIN THE ZODIAC

Each of the Twelve Zodiac signs belongs to one of the Four Elements. Thus, the Zodiac is grouped into four triplicities of Earth, Air, Water, and Fire signs. These Elements represent the essential type of energy that influences each of us. For Earth signs, we have Taurus, Virgo, and Capricorn. For Air signs, we have Gemini, Libra, and Aquarius. Water signs are Cancer, Scorpio, and Pisces. And Fire signs are Aries, Leo, and Sagittarius.

Earth signs are the most grounded, conservative and practical. On the other hand, Air signs are imaginative, rational, communicative and creative. Water signs are known to be emotional, sensitive, intuitive and loving. And Fire signs are dynamic, passionate, energetic, and inspiring.

The Twelve Zodiac signs are grouped into three quadruplicities to understand better how the energies work. These are the Cardinal, Fixed, and Mutable signs. The Cardinal signs are Aries, Cancer, Libra, and Capricorn. They are called Cardinal signs because they rule the change of seasons. In addition, all Cardinal signs have Fire in their Sub-Element, which makes them behave according to specific guidelines that are being affected by Fire. Therefore, all Cardinal Signs will have many Fire characteristics even though they may not be a Fire sign.

Cardinal signs are associated with being active, Self-motivated, insightful, and ambitious. They are great leaders and know how to initiate change. On the other hand, they can be bossy, inconsiderate, and domineering, as they feel their way is the best for everyone to follow. They also sometimes cannot follow through with the projects they have started.

Fixed signs include Taurus, Leo, Scorpio, and Aquarius. They are called Fixed because they govern the middle month of each season. All Fixed signs have Air as the Sub-Element, which manifests as the desire to have reality stay fixed and as it is. They are stable, determined, persevering, and able to concentrate well. Their goals are reached slowly but steadily. They are highly perceptive and have excellent memories.

Fixed signs are concerned with maintaining something as it is, changing things so they can be the same as before, or stabilizing factors to achieve their initial state. Some negative qualities of Fixed signs include being Egotistical, obstinate, and too firmly ingrained in their ways and opinions.

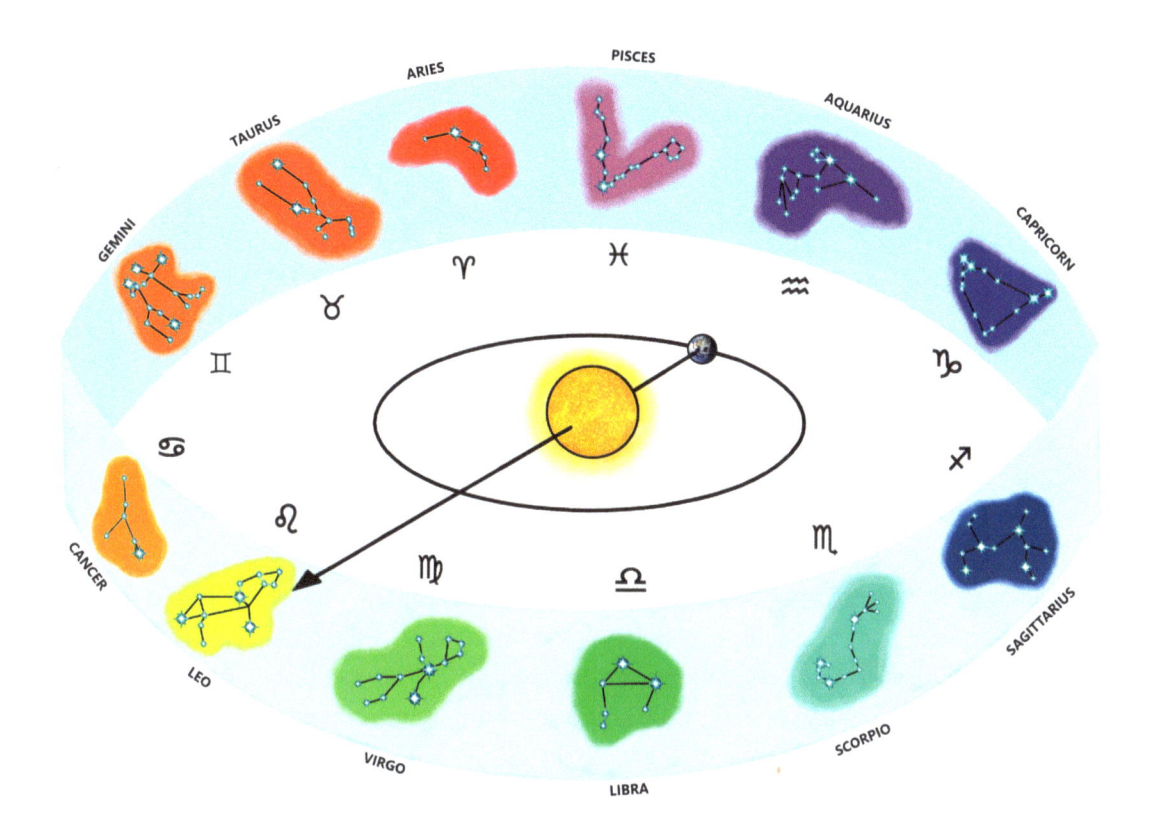

Figure 42: The Twelve Zodiac

Mutable signs include Gemini, Virgo, Sagittarius, and Pisces. These signs rule the closing month of each season. They are also called Common signs, as they govern the completion of the work of one season. They each have Water as the Sub-Element, which is why they are changeable and adaptable to all situations. Mutable signs are overly concerned with changing things into something else, which is not a form of transformation; instead, it is about moving on to the next item in life.

Mutable signs accept change while Fixed signs resist it at all costs. Mutable signs adapt themselves to their environment while the Fixed signs adjust the circumstances to their needs, wants and goals. Mutable signs are very versatile, changeable, flexible, subtle, intuitive, and understanding. Their negative qualities include being unreliable, inconsistent, deceptive, and cunning.

Note that each Zodiac sign has a Divine Name which is derived from a permutation of the Tetragrammaton (YHVH). These Divine Names are to be used in Magickal operations involving the invocation or banishing of the energies of the Zodiac signs. These techniques are presented in the "Advanced Planetary Magick" chapter.

Now, I will share an overview of each of the twelve signs of the Zodiac, outlining their characteristics, inclinations, and unique qualities. Generally, you will find that the descriptions accurately represent you and other people you know who fall under a particular sign.

ARIES—THE RAM

March 21—April 19

The first sign of the Zodiac is Aries, whose constellation spans the 0-30th degree of celestial longitude. As it is the first sign, Aries deals with new beginnings. Because of its powerful fiery nature, Aries exemplifies the need for energetic balance. It is essential to understand that a Zodiac sign's primary energy must always be balanced with its opposite energy. For example, Fire always requires Water for success.

Each Zodiac sign is a by-product of the Element and Sub-Element that govern it. For example, Aries is under the rule of Mars and the Element of Fire, with the Sub-Element of Fire of Fire. For this reason, it is a robust and powerful Fire that, when unbalanced by its opposite (the Water Element), can easily transform into tyranny, oppression, and anger.

Arians are quick to begin new activities, but they must find balance with being consistent and persistent in carrying them out. If not, the novelty of new activities will keep wearing off. Those under this sign are full of creative energy, drive, initiative, and enthusiasm. They are honest, optimistic, competitive, eager, and known for living in the present. They can, however, also be impulsive, which does not always yield a positive outcome. The key phrase describing the Arian is "I am."

Arians have a lot of courage and sharp intuition and are inspirational to others. They are alert, decisive, and direct. Motivated by their excess enthusiasm, they cannot wait to get started on whatever it is they have in their minds to do. They like taking on leadership roles, playing sports, and overcoming physical challenges.

Being a Cardinal Fire sign, Arians are typically impatient when trying to reach their goals due to their excess energy. These attributes are qualities of Fire of Fire and the Planet Mars, as it is the Arian's foundational energy. The Ram represents Aries because of its headstrong and determined nature.

Some of the negative qualities of the Arian can be that they are overly opinionated, Egotistical, hasty, overbearing, foolhardy, quick-tempered, violent, intolerant, and zealot. If the Ego is predominant, the Arian will often use others solely for their self-interest.

In the Tarot, Aries is attributed to the Emperor card. It exemplifies the powerful creative energy and rulership of this sign. Gemstones associated with Aries are Bloodstone, Carnelian, Diamond, Garnet, Red Jasper, and Ruby. Aries governs the face, brain, and eyes in terms of the physical body. Regarding romance, Aries is most compatible with Libra and Leo Zodiac signs.

TAURUS—THE BULL

April 20—May 20

The second Zodiac sign is Taurus, whose constellation spans the 30-60th degree of celestial longitude. Taurus is ruled by Venus in the Earth Element, with the Sub-Element of Air of Earth. Taureans are fantastic practical thinkers and masters of physical matters. They are known for their determination, stability, and power. Because of this, the Bull represents their sign. As Taurus is Air of Earth, their intellect and thoughts are dominant, although aimed towards Earthly matters. As such, the key phrase of the Taurus sign is "I have."

Since they are born under the Planet Venus, Taureans enjoy sensuality and beauty. They are sensitive and loyal to their romantic partners. Other qualities include being generous, affectionate, well-composed, calm, and understanding of their fellow man and woman. They are lovers of pleasure, comfort, and satisfaction on every level. Taureans are known to be down-to-earth, reliable, conventional, and thorough. They are very practical in their thinking, making them productive and ready to tackle any task.

Some negative qualities of those born under the Taurus sign are that they can be stubborn without cause, frugal, overly emotional, reserved, and too fixed in their perspectives (uncompromising). Since Taurus is a Fixed sign, they are very committed to keeping their material wealth—they do not like change in this regard. Taureans are known to use their wealth as a measure of the quality of their life. If the Ego is predominant, a Taurean will seek material rewards for their efforts. They can also be short-tempered, selfish, greedy, overly materialistic, and possessive.

In the Tarot, Taurus is attributed to The Hierophant card—it exemplifies the stability and clear thinking of this sign. Gemstones associated with Taurus are Amber, Rose Quartz, Blood Coral, Golden Topaz, Emerald, Sapphire, and Turquoise. Regarding the physical body, Taurus governs the throat, neck, thyroid gland, and vocal tract. In matters of romance, Taurus is most compatible with the two Water signs of Scorpio and Cancer.

GEMINI—THE TWINS

May 21—June 21

The third Zodiac sign is Gemini, whose constellation spans the 60-90th degree of celestial longitude. Ruled by Mercury, Gemini is of the Air Element with the Sub-Element of Water of Air. Due to the Water Element in Air, the Gemini has an almost dual personality. For this reason, it is represented by the Twins.

Water is a signifier of emotions and the fluidic nature of thought. Therefore, when applied to the Air Element (which represents thought), it gives the Gemini the most powerful intellect of all the signs of the Zodiac. For the Gemini, the intelligence and speed of thought are expressions of their predominant energy. The key phrase to describe the Gemini is "I think."

Geminis are known to thirst for knowledge to expand their intellect continuously. Such desire gives them a high capacity for learning and absorbing information. They are excellent communicators, and using the spoken word is their most exceptional skill. As their mind jumps from one thought to another, the Gemini uses words as anchors to keep them steady. In addition, they possess a great sense of humour and are cheerful and highly intelligent.

As said, Mercury—a Planet of communication, rules Gemini. Mercury relates to the speed of thought, intellect, logic, and reason. Since it is the Planet of the mind, this further affirms the cerebral power of the Gemini. In essence, Geminis are thinkers that use the power of logic and reason to act swiftly. They are skilled in identifying and classifying each of their thoughts.

Gemini is a Mutable sign, meaning they are adaptable to any circumstance, with an absolute versatility that is useful when facing all of life's challenges. Geminis are friendly, resourceful, humorous, expressive, and analytical. They are transparent and objective in their thinking and are often very lighthearted.

Some negative qualities associated with Geminis are that they can be overly silly and immature. They can be chatterboxes (talk too much) as well. Sometimes, they can be insensitive to the emotions of others, seeing that they are primarily concerned with the intellectual instead of the emotional faculty. Their emphasis on the intellect and lack of emotional balance can make them seem cold and aloof, lacking empathy for others.

Geminis can have a short attention span, be scatterbrained (have an unfocused mind), and conniving. Furthermore, Geminis are rather unemotional and sometimes two-faced towards others due to their inability to connect emotionally. Often, they might lie to blend in with the crowd, though they might not mean what they say.

In the Tarot, Gemini is attributed to the Lovers card. This is because it exemplifies the unification of opposites, mainly the emotional and mental nature, which are frequently opposed to one another—hence the dual nature of this sign.

Gemstones associated with Gemini are Aquamarine, Agate, Chrysoprase, Pearl, Moonstone, Citrine, and White Sapphire. Gemini governs the arms, lungs, shoulders, hands, and nervous system in the physical body. In matters of romance, Geminis are most compatible with Sagittarius and Aquarius Zodiac signs.

CANCER—THE CRAB

June 22—July 22

The fourth Zodiac sign is Cancer, whose constellation spans the 90-120th degree of celestial longitude. Ruled by the Moon, Cancer is of the Water Element with the Sub-Element of Fire of Water. The Fire acting on the Water Element shapes the Cancer into who they are. Cancers are of high tenacity and quite sensitive to their feelings. Of all the Water signs, Cancer is the strongest. The key phrase that describes a Cancer is "I feel."

Cancer's continual challenge is distinguishing between emotions that are a projection of their Ego and feelings that are based on reality—the illusory nature of the Moon is always acting on them. Emotional shifts are a challenge that Cancers are often faced with. As they fear criticism and ridicule, they have been assigned the protective shell of the Crab.

Cancers hide in their shell where they can be safe. They are often very psychologically and physically vulnerable and somewhat timid. These qualities will drive them to seek solitude often. Here, the predominant energy is emotional sensitivity and feelings. Cancers possess a well-developed protective and defensive instinct because of the Fire Element within them. They are often very concerned with domestic and household responsibilities.

Cancer is a Cardinal sign; for this reason, they are great initiators with strong wills that help them accomplish their goals. Cancers are very empathetic towards others and are ready to care for them. They can often display psychic abilities and are sensitive and able to tune in to other people's Souls, communicating with them directly. They are often traditional and understanding with excellent memories. Cancers are family-oriented and are willing to protect their family at all costs. In the household, the energy they use for domestic purposes is calming and settling.

Some of the negative qualities of Cancer are that they may become hysterical in the event of overwhelming emotions. They can be self-centred, manipulative, sulky, moody, self-pitying, and overcautious. They can also have illogical, unfounded fears and be very selfish when protecting their Ego. Cancers can be snobby, and when they retreat into solitude, they can become aloof to the desires of others.

In the Tarot, Cancer is attributed to the Chariot card—it signifies power over the illusive nature of thoughts through the conscious use of the will. Gemstones associated with Cancer are Moonstone, Ruby, Emerald, and Pearl. In terms of the physical body, Cancer governs the chest, breasts, stomach, alimentary canal, and lymphatic system. In romantic matters, Cancer is most compatible with the two stable Earth signs, Capricorn and Taurus.

LEO—THE LION

July 23—August 22

The fifth sign of the Zodiac wheel is Leo, the most powerful sign and the only one solely ruled by the Sun. It originates from the constellation of Leo and spans the 120-150th degree of celestial longitude. Leo is a Fixed sign, and as such, Leos need to maintain their personal power at all costs, even if that means making changes in their lives. Leo is of the Element of Fire and the Sub-Element of Air of Fire. This Elemental combination characterizes Leo as very self-expressive since the Air acts on the Fire, making them very much in tune with their thoughts. The key phrase of Leo is "I will."

The challenge for Leo is balancing the Ego with their higher goals and ideals while being mindful not to fall prey to their emotional sensitivity and high expectations of others. Leos are enterprising, dramatic, charismatic, proud, ambitious, confident, and distinguished. In addition, their predominant energy is one of authority, power, and vitality.

Leos are naturally generous and noble. They are strong and ready to give themselves to others when needed. They enjoy talking and being with others but also enjoy solitude to examine their feelings. By nature,

Leos are very emotional, especially if they feel they are being wronged. Nevertheless, they desire to be impressive and creative and maintain relationships with others.

As Leos draw their energy from the Sun, they are vital and energetic, allowing them to be emotionally healing for others. Leos are affectionate, loving, protective, sincere, warm, and inspired by Universal love. They desire always to maintain their dignity. When they are met with disagreement, they are cautious and diplomatic in expressing their opinion. Leos are very protective of their feelings and are noble in stature as the "King of the Jungle." For this reason, Leo is signified by the Lion.

Some negative traits of Leo include vanity and selfishness. They can also be lustful, Egotistical, and overly concerned with their own opinions. Furthermore, they can be arrogant, dictatorial, pompous, domineering, childish, cruel, and excessively conscious of their status. Since they are big romantics, Leos are highly attracted to the opposite sex. They can sometimes get impatient because they detest repetition and constantly need new stimulation.

In the Tarot, Leo is attributed to the Strength card—it signifies unity in the Fire and Water Elements, willpower under the governance of unconditional love. Leos use thoughts and the Air Element to rationalize their emotions and attain balance in mind, body, and Soul. Gemstones associated with Leo are Amber, Tourmaline, Carnelian, Ruby, Sardonyx, Onyx, and Golden Topaz. Leo governs the heart, chest, spinal column, and upper back in terms of the physical body. In matters of romance, Leo is most compatible with the two Air signs of Aquarius and Gemini.

VIRGO—THE VIRGIN

August 23—September 22

Virgo is the sixth sign of the Zodiac wheel and the second-largest constellation in the sky, spanning the 150-180th degree of the Zodiac. Virgo is of the Earth Element, with the Sub-Element of Water of Earth. As the Virgo's mind is aimed at the material world (because they are an Earth sign), they are very focused on their work and being of service to others. Moreover, since Virgo is the Virgin, it represents the natural love and purity of the Spirit.

Virgo's dominant energy is to be analytical and discriminative. They have highly analytical minds and make excellent teachers, as they are both calm and self-reliant. As perfectionists, they are diligent, making them skilled at research and scientific endeavours. To the Virgo, wisdom and knowledge come through hard work and life experience. They are systematic in their thinking and are very oriented toward personal growth. The key phrase that describes the Virgo is "I analyze."

Ruled by the Planet Mercury, Virgos are given the quest for knowledge. They have very sharp attention to detail and are known to be careful and efficient in all of their activities. They are meticulous in work and study and like bringing order out of confusion.

The Virgo is unselfish and very helpful to other people. Generally speaking, their perspective is positive, and they are giving their positivity to others. Virgo is a Mutable sign, and they use their analytical and critical nature to move tactfully from one thing to another, adapting to new environments with ease.

Virgos believe that change will bring personal growth, so they always welcome it. They are lovers of travel and new life experiences. As Virgos appreciate mysterious subjects and inner growth, they are often attracted to the occult. As non-conformists, Virgos follow the beat of their own drum, always.

Some of the negative aspects of the Virgo include being sometimes manipulative to get what they desire. They can be self-centred, meticulous, and snobbish, as well as highly secretive and superficial. Virgos can be overly critical of other people as well as themselves. Also, if they cannot develop their independence, they will eventually become dependent on others, often manipulating them for their gain.

In the Tarot, Virgo is attributed to the Hermit card. The Hermit is wise and receptive to the world around them, as is the Virgo. Gemstones associated with Virgo are Blue Sapphire, Pink Jasper, Carnelian, Jade, Moss Agate, Turquoise, and Zircon. Virgo governs the digestive system, spleen, and intestines in the physical body. Virgo is most compatible with the two Water signs of Pisces and Cancer in romantic endeavours.

LIBRA—THE SCALES

September 23—October 22

The seventh sign of the Zodiac is Libra, whose constellation spans the 180-210th degree of celestial longitude. Libra is of the Air Element, with the Sub-Element of Fire of Air. Libra's predominant energy is that of harmonizing and balancing opposing energies within themselves. Libra's most significant concern is justice and fairness concerning all matters.

As Libras are an Air sign, they are potent thinkers; however, unlike Geminis, who are highly intellectual, Libras are more concerned with the matters of the Soul. Thus, integrity and ethics are essential to them, as they are associated with the higher aspects of a person's Soul. The key phrase to describe Libra is "I balance."

Venus governs the Libra sign. They have very balanced minds, as indicated by their symbol—the Scales. They are charming, graceful, and expressive. Furthermore, they are known to seek the approval of others and enjoy themselves in crowds. Though they enjoy being around people, Libras also enjoy solitude and alone time with their thoughts.

Libra is a Cardinal sign; for this reason, they are good at taking action and beginning new tasks. They are often initiators of activity, and they look for the cooperation of others. Libras are proud and do not enjoy being compromised. Unlike the Arian, the Libra tends to express themselves through words instead of direct action. The Libra is tactful, friendly, persuasive, and diplomatic. Naturally, as they are a very social sign, they require companionship and make great spouses due to their cooperative and peace-loving nature. Libras generally inspire people to be their best.

Some negative qualities of the Libra are that they are often indecisive and can be overly pleasure-seeking due to being ruled by Venus—a Planet of sensuality and beauty. Furthermore, they can be dependent on others and, in some cases, manipulative, causing them to seek relationships for personal gain in an authoritarian way. They can sometimes be sulking, inconsistent, superficial, and deceitful. Libras can also be too inquisitive, ambivalent, and easily deterred from the task at hand.

In the Tarot, Libra is attributed to the Justice card. Here we see a direct reference to the "Scales of Justice" and the conscious weighing of opposites to find balance. Balance is the key to living a healthy life. Gemstones associated with Libra are Lapis Lazuli, Opal, Diamond, Emerald, Rose Quartz, and Peridot. Libra governs the kidneys, skin, adrenals, lumbar region, and buttocks in the physical body. In matters of romance, Libra is most compatible with the two Fire signs, Aries and Sagittarius.

SCORPIO—THE SCORPION

October 23—November 21

Eighth on the Zodiac wheel is Scorpio, one of the most powerful signs. Originating from the constellation of the same name, it spans the 210-240th degree of celestial longitude. Scorpio is a Water sign with the Sub-Element of Air of Water. Scorpio is a Fixed sign; as such, Scorpios are relatively consistent with their emotional reactions. As Mars directly governs this sign, its predominant energy is that of regeneration and transformation on all levels. For this reason, Scorpio is assigned to the Death card in the Tarot (death as a form of transformation). Their key phrase is "I create."

Scorpio's symbol is the Scorpion. Like the scorpion would rather kill itself than be killed, those born under this sign are in ultimate control of their destiny. Scorpios promote their agenda and see to it that things go forward. Scorpios are exceptionally sexual, with high sex drives and desires. They are seekers of justice at all costs, ready to defend it.

In addition, Scorpios are great thinkers and speakers, full of many different ideas about the world. Those born under this sign have great willpower and intense emotional desires. Scorpios are very resourceful also. One of their life challenges is aligning their willpower with their desires, as these two attributes are powerful within them.

To those they love, Scorpios are loyal. They are curious and inspiring, and because they seek alignment with the Spirit, they are attracted to the occult and esoteric arts. Emotion is a dominant attribute of the Scorpio unless it is opposed to their willpower. Scorpios can be pretty intense, passionate, and profound. They enjoy creating in all kinds of ways, though usually through rebuilding. They are known to feel more secure when they are aware of what others are feeling.

Scorpios' negative qualities are that they can be Egotistical and temperamental. They respect their privacy and are known to keep secrets from others. Scorpios can distrust other people until their trust is gained. They sometimes use others for their interests and demand that other people share the same beliefs and thoughts as they do.

Scorpios have the potential to be volatile, turning from positive to negative at any moment. Due to their intense emotions, they can be irritable, intolerant, jealous, resentful, and sometimes destructive to themselves and others. They are prone to violence, as well. Balancing their powerful emotions with logic and reason is one of their challenges in life. For better or worse, Scorpios can also be great seducers.

Gemstones attributed to Scorpio are Aquamarine, Black Obsidian, Garnet, Agate, Topaz, Beryl, Apache Tears, and Coral. In terms of the physical body, Scorpio governs the reproductive system, sexual organs, bowels, and excretory system. Scorpio is most compatible with Taurus and Cancer in matters of romance.

SAGITTARIUS—THE ARCHER

November 22—December 21

The ninth sign of the Zodiac wheel is Sagittarius, whose constellation spans the 240-270th degree of celestial longitude. As the ruling Planet of Sagittarius is Jupiter, these people love to enjoy abundance and are serious about well-being, for both themselves and those around them. Sagittarius is a Fire sign with the Sub-Element of Water of Fire. Their fundamental energy gives them a balance between their emotions and willpower. For this reason, they are usually sincere and direct with others.

Sagittarius is the Archer who flings his arrows, although in this case, it is a Centaur, who is half-man, half-beast. Centaurs were considered the intellectuals of Roman mythology, and the Sagittarius is their modern-day counterpart. They are clear-thinkers who look at the big picture most of the time and seek knowledge always.

Sagittarius' predominant energy is that of aspiration and love of freedom. This sign is mainly concerned with independence since Sagittarius' like to explore all aspects of life. They are philosophical, charitable, ethical, and enthusiastic. They are also concerned with truth and can often be very religious. Sagittarius' are very energetic, with a positive perspective and outlook on life. They love to be inspired, and they love inspiring others as well. The key phrase of the Sagittarius is "I perceive."

As Sagittarius is a Mutable sign, they move around from one thing to the next and cannot stay on one subject for too long, making them highly adaptable to any situation. Because they can see the big picture, they can easily blend in with life and mould themselves to fit any situation.

Some of the negative traits of the Sagittarius are that they are not always able to regulate mind with matter. They can often exaggerate if they are too focused on their personal feelings. They can be loudmouths, sometimes divulging information that they should not. They can also be hotheaded, self-indulgent, disrespectful, impatient, procrastinating, and pushy. They often lack satisfaction no matter what is happening in their life.

In the Tarot, Sagittarius is attributed to the Temperance card—it signifies cutting through the illusion to attain the truth. Gemstones associated with Sagittarius are Turquoise, Topaz, Sapphire, Amethyst, and Ruby. Concerning the physical body, Sagittarius governs the hips, thighs, liver, and sciatic nerve. In romantic matters, Sagittarius is most compatible with Gemini and Aries.

CAPRICORN—THE GOAT

December 22—January 19

The tenth sign of the Zodiac is Capricorn, whose constellation spans the 270-300th degree of celestial longitude. Ruled by the Planet Saturn, Capricorns have excellent intuition. Capricorn is an Earth sign with the Sub-Element of Fire of Earth. As they are an Earth sign, economic stability and security are crucial to them. Capricorn is a Cardinal sign, and for this reason, they enjoy beginning new things but can lack the persistence to finish them.

Capricorn's predominant energy is that of conscientiousness and organization. They are hardworking, prudent, pragmatic, and serious. They must always be motivated, having some mundane task or goal to accomplish. Capricorns are practical thinkers and are always looking to simplify things. They are much happier when they are on the move than when they are still and stagnant. They also long to achieve independence in their lives.

As the symbol for the Capricorn is the Mountain Goat, it symbolizes the ability and drive to climb to the top of the mountain. In the same way, those born under this sign are hard workers and seek to get to the top of whatever field they are in to reap the benefits of success. Capricorns love fame, prestige and money but realize it will take hard work to achieve those things. The key phrase to describe the Capricorn is "I use."

Capricorns are trustworthy and possess a deep Spiritual understanding while being conscious of other people's needs. They are loyal to those they love and are willing to sacrifice themselves when needed. Capricorns are ambitious, always seeking to improve upon how things are.

Some of the negative qualities of Capricorn are that they can be demeaning, arrogant, and dictatorial. If they are in their Ego, they can lack sympathy for others. They can be unforgiving and stubborn, as well. Furthermore, they can also be overly ambitious with unrealistic goals they set for themselves. Just like Leo, the Capricorn can be pretty status-conscious.

In the Tarot, Capricorn is attributed to the Devil card. As the Devil represents the binding of the senses to the World of Matter, this energy is exemplified in Capricorn's ambition and drive, directed at achievement within the material reality. Therefore, Capricorns must step back a bit and re-evaluate the importance of their goals and what they are willing to do to achieve them—the Spiritual reality should never take a backseat to the Material one.

Gemstones associated with Capricorn are Ruby, Black Onyx, Smoky Quartz, Garnet, and Agate. In terms of the physical body, Capricorn governs the knees, joints, and skeletal system. In matters of romance, Capricorn is most compatible with Taurus and Cancer.

AQUARIUS—THE WATER BEARER

January 20—February 18

The eleventh sign of the Zodiac wheel is Aquarius, whose constellation spans the 300-330th degree of celestial longitude. Ruled by Saturn, Aquarius is of the Air Element with the Sub-Element of Air of Air. With this combination comes the highest Spiritual energy and very sharp intuitive skills. Being connected to the Spirit Element at a deep level, Aquarians have excellent knowledge of all that is happening around them. They are very perceptive and wise and directly connect with the truth in all things. The key phrase to describe the Aquarius is "I know."

Aquarians are perfect representatives of the new Age of Aquarius. Those born under this sign have the social conscience necessary to carry us into the new millennium. Aquarians are philanthropists, and making the world a better place is one of their inner motivations. Since the symbol of the Aquarius is the Water Bearer, who pours the pitcher of water onto humanity, in the same way, Aquarians shower the world with innovative thoughts and ideas.

Since they are very Spiritual, Aquarians are drawn to the occult and the esoteric arts. They effortlessly understand complex Spiritual concepts and ideas and value knowledge and wisdom over all things. They are honourable towards all human beings and value speaking the truth. Generally, they are shameless in their expressions and look to the future instead of dwelling on the past.

Aquarius' predominant energy is the quality of being a humanitarian. They maintain high ethical ideals and high hopes for humanity unless they become too immersed in their Egos, which they are prone to doing. Since Aquarius is a Fixed sign, these people are known for always wanting to keep their beliefs, especially regarding humanity, fixed. If they are natural revolutionaries, they will stay that until the end.

Aquarians are independent, and their expressions are unique and original. They value friendship and romance. They are naturally gregarious, social, and have a great sense of humour. Their imaginative and creative abilities strive for goodwill always. Those born under this sign are generally sexually expressive and prone to lust. Aquarians can also be very progressive, understanding, benevolent, and scientific. They are frequently eccentric but highly determined, especially when aligned with their life's purpose.

Some of the negative qualities of the Aquarians are that they can be overly talkative and tend to impose their beliefs and ideas onto others. If they are operating from their Ego, Aquarians can come across as cold and unsympathetic to the feelings of others. They can also be unpredictable, temperamental, and extreme in their thoughts and actions. Some of their ideas can be far-fetched, impractical, and ungrounded, which is the nature of the Air Element that dominates them. Although usually extroverted, some Aquarians can also be very shy.

In the Tarot, Aquarius is attributed to The Star card. As The Star signifies meditation and quiet contemplation to perceive the Spiritual reality, the Aquarius also needs to practice those things if they are to remain balanced in mind, body, and Soul. Meditation comes naturally to the Aquarius if they learn to overcome the constant chatter in their minds.

Gemstones associated with Aquarius are Garnet, Sugilite, Amethyst, Blue Sapphire, Moss Agate, and Opal. In addition, Aquarius governs the ankles and circulatory system in the physical body. Finally, in matters of romance, Aquarius is most compatible with the two Fire signs, Leo and Sagittarius.

PISCES—THE FISH

February 19—March 20

The twelfth and final sign of the Zodiac wheel is Pisces, whose constellation spans the 330-360th degree of celestial longitude. Pisces' Element is Water, with the Sub-Element of Water of Water. Their fundamental energy brings deep emotions, the expansion of consciousness, and with evolution, deep unconditional love and compassion towards all living beings. Ruled by Jupiter, Pisces is symbolized by the Fish. The Water Element makes the Pisces psychic and empathic, receptive to everything happening within their environment.

The Piscean symbol is of two fish, one swimming upstream and one swimming downstream. This symbol implies a stark duality in the emotions. The Pisces can go along with the positive or negative viewpoint and sometimes both simultaneously. Their challenge is to avoid being caught up in their fears, as Water signs are prone to fear and anxiety. The key phrase to describe the Piscean is "I believe."

Those people born under this sign are responsive and sensitive to the thoughts and feelings of those around them. Unconsciously, they absorb the mental outlooks of people they surround themselves with. Piscean's challenge is to develop their willpower. Because of the strong influence of the Water Element in the Piscean, their Fire is prone to be drowned out, causing the willpower to weaken. Thus, they can often look to others for guidance and are easily influenced.

Pisces is a Mutable sign, making these people adaptable to their environments. They are very intuitive and understand the matters of the Soul, which makes them sympathetic to other people's needs and wants. They are also creative and innovative with vast imaginations, making them prone to music and other artistic expressions.

Pisceans tend to work towards high ideals and are often concerned with ethics and morals concerning themselves and others. They will renounce those whom they find unjust. They are playful, joyous, and possess a great sense of humour. Furthermore, they have high Spiritual aspirations and are drawn toward the occult and esoteric disciplines. However, Pisceans seek peace and emotional stability at all costs, seeing that their environment heavily influences them. For this reason, they often seek solitude. In social settings, though, they shine.

Some of the negative qualities of the Pisces are that they seek to control through giving and can often fall victim to their Ego. They are known to talk a lot while being emotionally constrained at times. Pisceans are sensualists in all things, which can be positive or negative, depending on whether their Ego or their Higher Self is guiding them. They have little control over their emotions, which can appear self-centred and selfish. Often, they feel misunderstood by others, causing melancholy.

Pisceans must stay well-grounded, with both feet planted on the ground, lest they fall prey to paranoia, anxiety, and even hallucinations. As a result, they can lack a sense of individuality and be pessimistic, lazy, procrastinating, and unrealistic in their way of thinking. In addition, Pisceans are susceptible to bad moods if they become overwhelmed by negative feelings. They often have a hard time composing themselves without changing their environment.

In the Tarot, Pisces is attributed to the Moon card. As the Moon card signifies the subconscious mind's fears, the Pisces is challenged by the same due to their profound Watery nature. A proper dose of logic and reason, powered by the will, is necessary for the Pisces to overcome these emotional challenges.

Gemstones associated with Pisces are Amethyst, Jade, Aquamarine, Rock Crystal, Bloodstone, Diamond, and Sapphire. Pisces govern the feet, toes, lymphatic system, and adipose tissue in the physical body. In matters of romance, Pisces is most compatible with the two stable Earth signs, Virgo and Taurus.

THE TWELVE HOUSES

The Horoscope is divided into twelve segments, or Houses, where each is ruled by one of the Twelve Zodiac signs in sequence (Figure 43). The Zodiac begins with the First House (Aries) and goes counterclockwise until it reaches the Twelfth House (Pisces). At the moment of our birth, the Ancient Planets (and the two Nodes of the Moon) occupied Zodiac Signs and Houses.

However, the Twelve Houses are not the same as the Twelve Zodiac. The Zodiac Wheel is based on the Earth's yearly revolution around the Sun, while the Houses reflect the Earth's twenty-four-hour rotation around its axis. Thus, the Twelve Signs of the Zodiac are called the "Celestial Houses," while the Twelve Houses are called the "Mundane Houses."

When Astrologers read a person's Horoscope, they look at both the Celestial and Mundane Houses for the most optimal interpretation. Since the Houses shift every two hours, the correct time of birth is essential. The first six Houses are the "Personal Houses," while the last are the "Interpersonal Houses". The energy influences of the Personal Houses are reflected in a broader sense in the Interpersonal Houses—each Personal House has its Interpersonal counterpart directly opposite to them. Thus, the First and Seventh House are related, as are the Second and Eighth, Third and Ninth, Fourth and Tenth, Fifth and Eleventh, and Sixth and Twelfth.

Each of the Twelve Houses is associated with various attributes in one's life, beginning with the Self and expanding outwards into society and beyond. The Houses give us invaluable insight into our personality and character and how we coexist with the world around us. They offer us a roadmap for understanding our past, present, and future and a view into our mental and emotional triggers, facilitated by the movement of the Planets.

When interpreting your Birth Chart, be mindful of which Houses are occupied by Planets. Since each Planet has a different type of influence, it energizes the associated traits of the House it visits. Assessing our Birth Chart allows us to see what part of our lives needs work and how we can counteract the Planetary influence upon us to achieve balance. Since we carry around the Twelve Houses from birth to death, their influences are imprinted in our Aura. Each House mirrors a part of our existence and holds some specific lesson essential for our Spiritual Evolution.

1st House (Aries)

The First House starts the Zodiac, and so it relates to our sense of Self. It is the most important of the Twelve Houses since it represents our Ascendant (AC), or Rising Sign. The Ascendant represents the outer Self that determines other people's first impressions of us. It includes our physical appearance, mannerisms, and general disposition and temperament. Essentially, the First House represents what we put out into the world. It also relates to new beginnings, including projects, ideas, and perspectives.

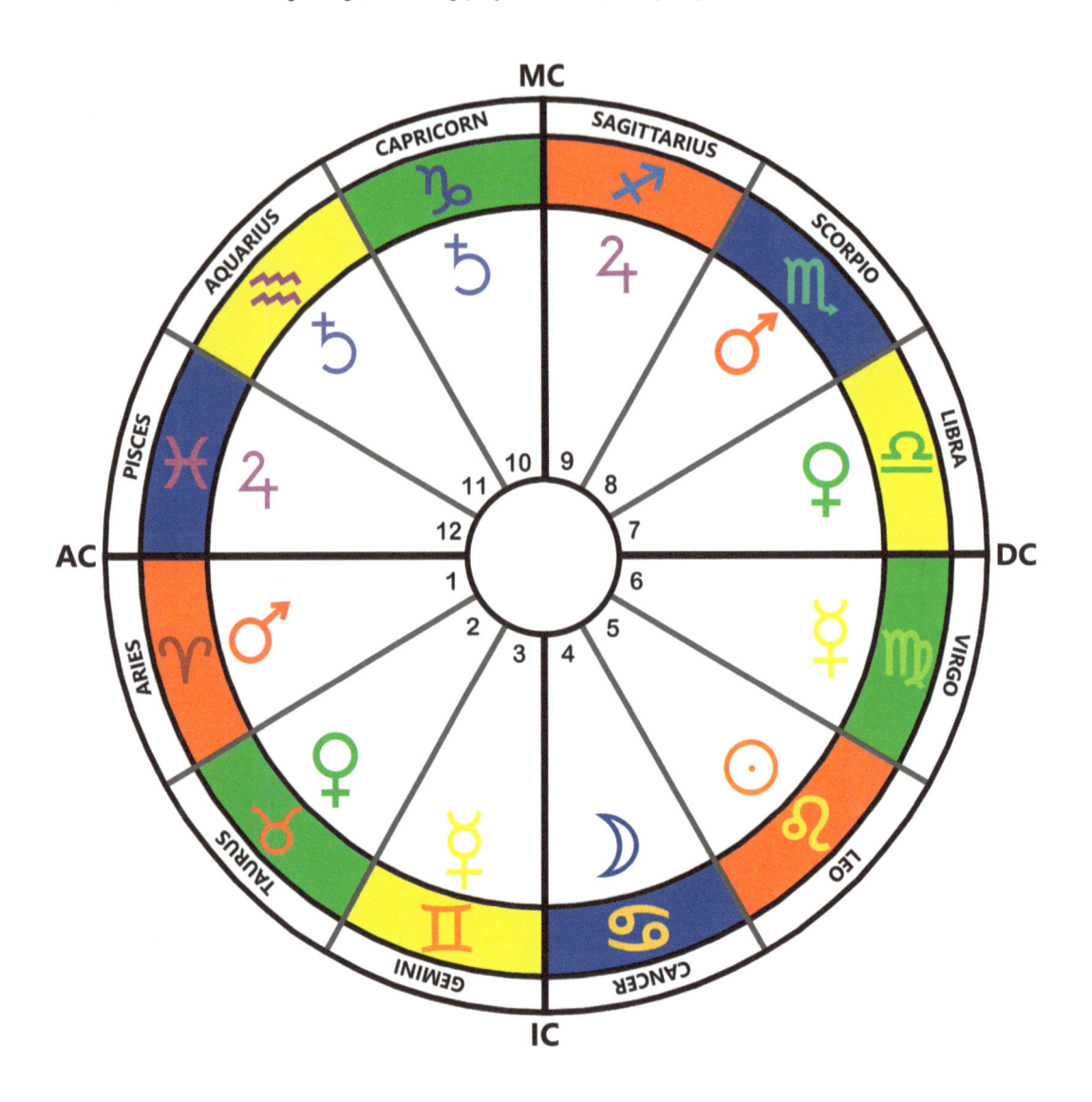

Figure 43: The Twelve Houses and their Correspondences

2nd House (Taurus)

The Second House is related to money, security, and material possessions. It governs our personal belongings, income, and financial prospects, including our capacity to accrue wealth. Our self-worth and self-esteem also come alive in the Second House.

3rd House (Gemini)

The Third House rules communication, logic and reason, transportation, and family ties. It affects our early education and ability to learn and study. Since it governs our thinking processes and cognitive functioning, the Third House affects our style of speech. It also rules the technological devices we use for communication with others and vehicles of transportation for small-distance travel.

4th House (Cancer)

The Fourth House cusp is the Nadir, or Imum Coeli (IC), Latin for "Lowest Point," concerning its position at the base of the Birth Chart. It represents our private persona found in the deepest, darkest, quietest and most personal place in our Birth Chart. As such, the Fourth House is our inner foundation—our emotional foundation and sense of security governing the home and family. In addition, the Fourth House indicates the individual's relationship with their mother and outlook on domesticity.

5th House (Leo)

The Fifth House is related to creativity, joy, and sex. It governs self-expression and everything we do for pleasure and entertainment. The Fifth House is our inner child, so the pleasure we receive from having children is governed by it.

6th House (Virgo)

The Sixth House is related to service and health, including diseases. It indicates our need to help others and be useful in society. It rules the relationships with the people we work with and our state of health, especially of a mental and emotional nature. It also rules our attitude toward routines, organization, and scheduling plans.

7th House (Libra)

The Seventh House is related to marriage and other partnerships, including business. It covers legal unions or contracts we enter into and the attitude we have towards these unions. The Seventh House concerns our ability to work harmoniously with others. Conversely, it also covers our open enemies or adversaries in business and other areas where we have formed a partnership. The Seventh House sits directly across from the First House (Ascendent). It is considered our Descendent (DC), representing the person nearest and dearest to us, mainly our spouse.

8th House (Scorpio)

The Eighth House is related to death, regeneration, and financial assets we receive from other people. Since orgasm is considered a mini-death, the Eighth House also relates to sex. Often referred to as the House of Spiritual transformation, the Eighth House relates to our belief in the afterlife. It also governs psychic powers and occult knowledge.

9th House (Sagittarius)

The Ninth House covers higher learning, life beliefs and philosophy, and international and long-distance travel. This House can be perceived as the extended Third House as mental pursuits, travel, and knowledge are expanded to a higher, more Spiritual level.

10th House (Capricorn)

The Tenth House governs our career, public image, and social standing and achievements in society. It rules our relationship with control structures, authority figures, and our boundaries and discipline to achieve our goals. As the Birth Chart's highest point, the Tenth House cusp is called the Midheaven, or Medium Coeli (MC), Latin for "Highest Point," signifying the height of our societal success. As it is directly opposite the Nadir, the Midheaven represents our Public Persona.

11th House (Aquarius)

The Eleventh House rules our hopes, wishes, friends, and a sense of community. It covers humanitarian pursuits and revolutionary ideas, including technology and innovation. Long-term dreams and goals and pleasures of the intellect are also included in the Eleventh House.

12th House (Pisces)

The Twelfth House rules sorrows, secrets, and self-defeat. It is the most mystical of all the Houses since it covers psychism, dreams, nightmares, and deep emotions. As it relates to the subconscious, the Twelfth House affects the limitations we set upon ourselves through self-destructive behaviour. As such, this House governs our Karma since it contains the rewards and punishments for our actions. On a mundane level, the Twelfth House rules prisons, asylums, hospitals, and secret enemies.

***

Knowledge of the Zodiac would not be complete without mentioning the Astrological Ages. Astrological ages represent a period in Astrology that parallels significant changes in the development of humanity, particularly concerning culture, politics, and society in general. Astrological Ages occur because of a phenomenon known as the Precession of the Equinoxes. One complete precession period is called a "Great Year," or Platonic Year, which is approximately 25,920 years.

Astrologers divide the Great Year into twelve Astrological Ages. These are each of approximately equal lengths of around 2160 years per Age. We currently live in the Age of Pisces, which began around the time Jesus Christ was born. Jesus himself is considered the Archetype of the Piscean, and the birth and rise of Christianity were one of the key events to mark the Age of Pisces. For this reason, you often will see the symbol of Pisces, the Fishes, used by Christians.

As the Age of Pisces slowly ends, we are transitioning into the Age of Aquarius. However, understand that an Astrological Age does not just begin and end on an exact day or year; the transition is a gradual process. This transition period is called a "cusp." So, we are currently on a cusp as we are receiving influences from the energy of the Aquarian Age.

Humanity is being changed at a fundamental level, but for these changes to manifest outwardly, it will take some time. As the Aquarius is the most Spiritual of all the Zodiac signs, the Age of Aquarius will be marked by humanity's Spiritual Evolution. For this reason, the Age of Aquarius is often referred to as the Golden Age.

The purpose of *The Magus* is to aid in accomplishing this goal. Time and again, Hermetic Science has emerged out of obscurity and into the Light. Its purpose is to illuminate the hearts and minds of all of humanity. Those who are ready to receive its lips of wisdom will find this Hermetic doctrine to be the most enlightening in grasping otherwise hard-to-understand concepts concerning the invisible world of the Spirit that we all partake of.

As we usher into the Age of Aquarius, I challenge you to embrace this Hermetic Science and allow it to transform your mind, body, and Soul, as it has for countless Adepts and Sages of the past. By doing so, we may all become Beings of Light and raise the collective consciousness of humanity. After all, the fruits of Heaven are our inherent birthright and our ultimate destiny.

THE PLANETS WITHIN OUR SOLAR SYSTEM

The Planets in Astrology have a different meaning from our modern astronomical understanding of them. In Ancient times, the night sky was thought to consist of two very similar components—fixed Stars called the Zodiac, which remained motionless to each other, and wandering Stars or "Planets," which moved relative to the fixed Stars through the year.

The group of Planets in our Solar System consisted of five, which were visible to the naked eye, and excluded the Earth. During the Middle Ages, the term "Planet" was broadened to include the Sun and the Moon, totalling Seven Ancient Planets (Figure 44). In the Qabalah, they are Saturn, Jupiter, Mars, Sun, Venus, Mercury, and the Moon. The Earth is also a Planet but is considered apart from the Seven Ancient Planets since it never leaves our sphere of experience. Qabalistically, the Planets are direct representatives of the Sephiroth, while the Earth is synonymous with Malkuth.

The Planets are the celestial bodies in our Solar System. Our Solar System has the Sun in the centre, our central Star, while the Planets are the heavenly bodies orbiting around it. The Sun is the visible dispenser of Light in our Solar System and is considered the most important. Therefore, many Ancient traditions have worshipped it as the highest manifestation of God-the Creator in the visible Universe.

The Planets are held in orbit around the Sun by the gravitational effect the Sun has on them. Some Planets move slower, and some faster around the Sun. The speed at which they move and the type of energy each Planet carries influence humanity. The purpose of Astrology is to examine this influence, to understand better who we are.

The Ancients acknowledged the existence of the Deities, or Gods and Goddesses, as they belonged to the order of Creation. The Seven Ancient Planets in the Western Esoteric framework represent several of these Deities, whom the Ancients personified to understand their energy and effect on humanity better.

According to the Ancients, the Planetary Deities constituted the higher powers and aspects of the human psyche. Their knowledge became essential in Astrology, which contains the key to understanding human psychology, including our highest aspirations and other expressions of our inner powers.

Figure 44: The Seven Ancient Planets

It is important to note that the existence of the Deities and their relation to the Planets themselves governs fate, the idea that events in life are beyond a person's control, determined by a supernatural power. According to many Ancient religions and philosophies, this supernatural power is the power of the Deities.

Fate and destiny are often interchangeable, but they are not the same. Fate is based on the notion that there is a natural order in the Universe that cannot be changed. Individual Free Will, in other words, does not affect fate. The common phrase to describe fate is, "It's the Will of the Gods (or God)." Destiny, on the other hand, is your potential waiting to happen. There is an element of choice and Free Will here as we shape our destiny by making active and conscious decisions in our lives. As the Planets represent the "Will of the Gods," you can see how they directly influence human affairs.

In Western Astrology, the Planets represent basic drives, or urges, in the subconscious mind, that can best be described as energy flow regulators. These regulators form the character and personality of the human being as they express themselves with different qualities in the twelve signs of the Zodiac. The patterns of the movements of the Planets make the night sky reflect the ebb and flow of basic human impulses as they represent the fundamental forces of nature.

Because they influence humanity, studying the Planets and the Zodiac is critical. If we can understand the energies of the Zodiac and the Planets, then we can understand our psychological makeup. The energies of both affect our thoughts, emotions, imagination, inspiration, willpower, memory, desire, intelligence, and everything else inside of us that makes us human. Therefore, knowledge of the Planets and the Zodiac goes hand in hand with understanding the Qabalistic Tree of Life better.

The Planets also rule different parts of the body, the knowledge of which is helpful in alternative medicine. A great way to affect and heal different parts of the body is with the use of Planetary ritual invocations. These are presented in the following section called "Advanced Planetary Magick." By invoking a particular Planet, we are also working on healing the corresponding parts of the human body. However, remember that you should not use Planetary Magick until you have finished the Spiritual Alchemy program with the Five Elements.

SATURN

Saturn is attributed to the Sphere of Binah in the Qabalah and has an affinity to the Earth Element. Its energy is comparable to Earth of Air since it stimulates intuitive thinking directed towards the material world. Saturn is the Planet of Karma and the cycles of time. Its affinity to Binah implies the connection between time and the Astral blueprint of the material world (which includes all Forms in existence). Saturn is also known as the teacher and the task maker of the Horoscope.

Saturn has an Airy quality, though it is a grounded type of Air that is very lucid and deep. Saturn's energy is one of constriction as well as crystallization. It is the Planet of faith, and it impacts how an idea from the mind manifests.

Saturn is responsible for the passage of time and the advancement of the ages. In Hebrew, Saturn is known as the Sphere of Shabbathai. To the Greeks, Saturn is known as Chronos (or Cronus), popularly called "Father Time," who wields the scythe that cuts away all things which impede progress. Chronos was the governor of linear, chronological time. He was the ruler of the Titans and the Father of Zeus.

To the Romans, Saturn was the God of agriculture. He was depicted in Greco-Roman mosaics as a man turning the Wheel of the Zodiac. Thus, the passage of time is associated with the Earth progressing through the Zodiac constellations.

Saturn was known as the "Greater Malefic," which means it is a Planet thought to bring bad luck and misfortune to those born within its radius. This is because it is closely associated with the material world, and as we know, any energy that binds us to the World of Matter causes misery and grief in the long run.

Around the world, Deities associated with Saturn include Isis, Ishtar, Brahma, Hera, Nephthys, Ptah, Ninurta, and Harpocrates. Within Astrology, Saturn rules Capricorn and Aquarius. In the Tarot, Saturn is attributed to the Universe card. Gemstones of Saturn are Jet Black Onyx, Diamonds, and Smoky Quartz. The metal corresponding with Saturn is lead, while the day of the week attributed to Saturn is Saturday. The Hebrew Divine Name associated with Saturn is YHVH Elohim.

As Saturn rules time, it also rules both truth and wisdom. It affects one's patience and restrictions in life, keeping one within the bounds of all humanity. Saturn's qualities concerning other Planets indicate how a person can right the wrongs of their past and acquire insight, thereby redeeming the flaws of their nature. Saturn implies a reflection on the past to learn from it and advance Spiritually.

Since Saturn is a Planet of control and structures, it is logical that it rules our physical structure, our bones. Our bones are the only part of us that withstands the passage of time as they are the foundation of our physical bodies. Saturn also rules the teeth, cartilage, glands, hair, joints, and the spleen. An afflicted Saturn can lead to paralysis, weak joints, and other bone issues. It can also create breathing problems, hair loss, rapid weight loss, constipation, and even give you a cold.

The qualities of Saturn and the house it rules (in Astrology) indicate a person's capacity for Self-discipline and how they create structure within their life. Without the well-developed influence of Saturn, a person cannot succeed in life because they will lack discipline. Someone with conflict in Saturn can be selfish and stubborn when it comes to changing their attitudes. This behaviour can be a source of problems in social interactions, leading to many misfortunes and personal setbacks.

Saturn rules over one's goals and career opportunities, as well as their limitations and conservatism. People with a strong influence of Saturn in their Horoscope are ambitious and driven in nature, and Spiritual Evolution is of utmost importance to them. In astronomy, Saturn is the sixth Planet from the Sun and the second-largest in our Solar System, after Jupiter.

JUPITER

Jupiter is attributed to the Sphere of Chesed in the Qabalah. It has an affinity to the Element of Water; however, its energy is best described as feeling like Water of Fire since it stimulates the "Love under Will" Principle. Jupiter is a name the Romans gave for the God of the sky and thunder.

In Hebrew, Jupiter is known as Tzedek. To the Greeks, Jupiter is called Zeus, the King of the Gods of Mount Olympus. In terms of greatness and power, Zeus is second only to Saturn, or Chronos (Cronus). Jupiter was also known as the "Greater Benefic," meaning it is a Planet that brings benevolence and good fortune. This name was given because of its association with the energy of unconditional love and the Spiritual reality— all energies with unconditional love at their core yield positive results.

Around the globe, Deities attributed to Jupiter include Maat, Marduk, Vishnu, Saraswati, Indra, Hapi of the North, Hapi of the South, and Dagda. Within Astrology, Jupiter is the ruler of Pisces and Sagittarius. In the Tarot, Jupiter is attributed to The Wheel of Fortune card. Gemstones of Jupiter are Sapphire, Lapis Lazuli, Turquoise, and Aquamarine. The metal corresponding with Jupiter is tin, while the day of the week attributed to it is Thursday. The Hebrew Divine Name associated with Jupiter is El.

Jupiter is merciful and bountiful, just like the Water Element. It has an affinity to the blue sky and all bodies of water. Jupiter has a responsibility to all of humanity to aid in maintaining their wellbeing. It is known to be a very kind and benevolent energy that affects human interaction and cooperation through unconditional love. Thus, Jupiter rules compassion, the protective impulse, morality, and ethics. It has a powerful influence on a person's character and virtues and is their builder, in a sense. Jupiter also rules one's personal development in life since the best way to grow within society is by giving and receiving.

An aspect of the Fire Element is present in Jupiter because it is known to protect that which it loves and cares for. The underlying energy of Jupiter is the energy of bestowal and expansion, as well as optimism. It is an organizing and majestic power. Jupiter is the lawmaker, the judge, and the benefactor of humankind.

Since Jupiter is an expansive Planet, it governs the physical growth of the body. Jupiter rules the maintenance of cellular development and integration in the human body. The preservation of soft tissues of the body as well as the intestines is under its rule. Jupiter also governs the liver, kidneys, adrenals, sciatic nerves, and digestive processes. It regulates excretion and the clearing out of toxins. Finally, it rules the hips and thighs. An afflicted Jupiter can cause heart and liver problems, weight gain, diabetes, varicose veins, liver problems, and high blood pressure.

Within one's Horoscope, an afflicted Jupiter is indicative of the person having a hard time giving and cooperating with others within society. Jupiter is also the ruler of the higher, abstract mind, one's education, one's philosophy on life, as well as their luck. Jupiter's action is efficient and orderly, fostering growth. Thus, Spiritual growth, as well as religious and Spiritual leadership, is under its governance. One's prosperity and abundance are also under Jupiter's influence, as is one's leisure time, indulgence, wealth, optimism, success, opportunities, and assimilation of thoughts and ideas. In astronomy, Jupiter is the fifth Planet from the Sun and the largest in our Solar System.

MARS

Mars is associated with the Sphere of Geburah in the Qabalah. It has an affinity to the Element of Fire. Its energy is best described as feeling like Earth of Fire since it is dry, scorching fire. This Planet is very powerful, and since it is the Fire Element, the aspects of strength and courage of the body and mind are attributed to it.

Mars is dynamic, vigorous, initiatory, and focused on action. Resolution and enthusiasm are also aspects of Mars, as is passion. Mars is highly masculine, and too much of its energy can bring destruction, which is vital to any renewal since the old must die to give birth to the new. This idea is best portrayed in the Tower Tarot card, to which Mars is attributed.

Mars can also be tyrannous and oppressive if it lacks balance with the unconditional love and mercy of Jupiter. Armies, wars, and physical combat are all associated with Mars. Its Archetypal image is of the warrior.

Mars is the sphere of fraternal fellowship and the voice of the people. It is the sphere of engineering because of its association with iron and steel. Mars bestows the ability to express oneself through powerful and dynamic actions. However, it can also make a person act impulsively without considering the consequences of their actions.

Named after the Roman God of War, Mars was known by the Ancients as the "Lesser Malefic" as it can often be destructive. Mars is called Ares in Greek, where he is also the God of War. In Hebrew, Mars is known as Madim.

Around the world, some other Deities attributed to Mars are Horus, Sekhmet, Ninurta, Agni, Durga, Nergal, and Shiva. Within Astrology, Mars is the ruler of Aries and Scorpio. Gemstones of Mars are Ruby, Garnet, Red Agate, Bloodstone, and Red Coral. The metal corresponding with Mars is iron, while Tuesday is the day of the week attributed to it. The Hebrew Divine Name associated with Mars is Elohim Gibor.

Mars' energy is powerful, so it must be channelled consciously. Those with an afflicted Mars in their Horoscope are susceptible to having ill tempers, outbursts of anger, and resorting to violence. Like Saturn, Mars has a traditional reputation for being a malign Planet in conflict with the others. Furthermore, Mars also rules our animal nature, achievement, competition, strife, strain, adversity, and work. Its action is often disruptive and sudden, as well as forceful. Mars' energy can be used with courage and strength or violence and destruction.

One can earn great respect and honour from others if their use of Mars' energy is balanced. Having a proper balance in the other Planets will enable one to use their Mars energy constructively. For example, Jupiter gives altruistic inspiration, Mercury rationalises, and Saturn gives discipline. Those three Planets especially can be of help to Mars.

Mars is the red Planet, and as such, it rules the red blood cells and natural oxidation in the body. It governs the development and well-being of the limbs in the body. It rules the external organs, such as the nose, ears, eyes, mouth, and the entire face region. It also governs the excretory system. Since Mars is an assertive Planet, it rules the procreative aspects of the body, such as the function of the sexual organs. Also, motor nerves and the gallbladder are governed by it.

An afflicted Mars can lead to blood-related diseases. It can create inflammation in the body, infectious and contagious sicknesses, accidental physical injuries, and haemorrhaging. It can also lead to hyperactive physical or mental diseases. An afflicted Mars can also lead to excessive hormones, leading to erection problems for men.

Mars is related to Venus, as they are both fiery Planets. In essence, Mars rules male sexuality, while Venus rules female sexuality. Mars represents willpower, while Venus represents desire. These two Planets work with each other to fulfil both of their needs. Their Ego desires drive most people, but when they have Spiritually evolved, their willpower falls under the governance of their Soul and Higher Self. They will then operate from a place of ethics and morality, not their desires.

To behave in a balanced and proactive fashion, Mars needs intelligence more than it needs personal desires. When people are aligned with their desires but lack reason and logic, they are more likely to be destructive in their application of Mars' energy. In astronomy, Mars is the fourth Planet from the Sun and the second smallest Planet in the Solar System, after Mercury.

THE SUN (SOL)

The Sun is the Sphere of Tiphareth in the Qabalah, which is the abode of the Saviour Gods, such as Jesus Christ, Mithras, Krishna, Dionysus, Tammuz, and Osiris, the "Risen One." As it is the source of Light in our Solar System, the Sun is very Spiritual. It affects growth and regeneration, both mentally and emotionally. It is the most Spiritual of all the Ancient Planets since it reflects the Sphere of Kether. The Sun's Light manifests the Great White Light of Kether, the source of all life.

The Sun is, in fact, the offspring of the Light of Kether—it is its Son. For us, the Sun is the highest manifestation of the energy of God. It has an affinity to the Air Element. However, its energy can most aptly be described as comparable to Air of Fire since it is the energy of creative and imaginative thinking.

Sol is the Roman name of the invincible Sun Deity. It is the origin of the word "Solar." As the Souls of all living things come from Sol or the Sun, we are simply Beings of Light contained within material bodies that serve as our vehicles within this Third Dimension of Time and Space. The Sun is responsible for the distribution of energy and material for production.

In Greek, the Sun is known as Helios, while in Hebrew, it is known as Shemesh. Other Deities associated with the Sun are Amun Ra, Shamash, Apollo and Surya. In the Tarot, the Sun is attributed to the Sun card. Gemstones attributed to the Sun's energy are Amber, Tiger's Eye, Gold Topaz, Goldstone, and Zircon. The metal corresponding with the Sun is gold, while the day of the week attributed to the Sun is Sunday. The Hebrew Divine Name associated with the Sun is YHVH Eloah ve-Daath.

In Astrology, the Sun rules Leo and gives one vitality, courage, creativity, dynamism, balance, good health, inspiration, leadership, and imagination. The Sun is the fundamental expression of the individual and the inner Self. It is authoritative. The Sun is also known as the ruler of one's fulfilment, identity, command, and capacity for experience. As the Sun is the visible provider of Light to the Earth, it is the most significant influence on our lives throughout the day, just as the Moon is the most considerable influence throughout the night.

When it comes to our Horoscope, the Sun affects our essential selfhood and identity, which drive our willpower. Thus, the Sun requires raw energy and passion from Mars. The Sun is our most basic energy, and a strong Sun in our Horoscope is characteristic of courage and opportunity in life. The Sun is known to be the balancer of the powers of Jupiter and Mars, two opposing energies. It balances them constructively and healthily. The Sun's energy is needed to attain equilibrium and harmony in all things.

The Sun governs the general flow of energy throughout the physical body as well as the various Subtle Bodies within the Aura. It rules the generation and maintenance of Life energy (Prana, chi, mana, Ruach). The heart and the eyes, as well as the upper region of the back, are governed by the Sun. Since it regulates the function of the heart, the Sun also rules the circulation of the blood.

Our vitality, in general, is governed by the Sun, as is the distribution of all vital fluids. An afflicted Sun can create disorders of the heart, angina, palpitations, illnesses of the eyes, spinal and spleen afflictions, as well as high fevers. An afflicted Sun can also impede our ability to heal different aspects of the physical body.

The Sun's warmth and positive energy are vital to our joy and happiness in life. Being in places that are limited to the Light of the Sun is more likely to be a cause of depression compared to being in areas where the Light of the Sun is abundant. Its energy is also healing, as it is of the Air Element and Light. Light is the healing energy of the mind, body, and Soul. The Sun is also symbolic of joy and happiness. It activates endorphins in our brains, giving us vitamin D, which is necessary for happiness and maintaining a positive outlook on life.

In astronomy, the Sun is the Star in the centre of our Solar system. It is a nearly perfect sphere of plasmic energy that radiates heat and Light. As such, it is an essential source of energy for all life on Earth. The Planets within our Solar System all orbit around the Sun, which exerts a gravitational field that holds them together. The Earth's orbit around the Sun is the basis of our Solar calendar, which is how we measure time.

VENUS

Named after the Roman Goddess, Venus is the Planet of love and desire. This Planet is attributed to the Sphere of Netzach in the Qabalah, with an affinity to the Fire Element. Its energy can best be described as comparable to Water of Earth since it is passive, feminine energy with fiery overtones. Venus has an affinity to the Planet Mars as they are both fiery Planets.

The Ancients referred to Venus as the "Lesser Benefic." In Greek, Venus is called Aphrodite, while in Hebrew, it is called Nogah. Deities attributed to Venus are Hathor, Bast, Ishtar, Lakshmi, Chenrezi, Ushas, and Sukra. Astrologically, Venus rules both Libra and Taurus. In the Tarot, Venus is attributed to the Empress card.

Gemstones attributed to Venus' energy are Emerald, Jade, Aventurine, Malachite, Rose Quartz, Green Agate, and Peridot. The metal corresponding with Venus is copper or brass, while the day of the week attributed to Venus is Friday. The Hebrew Divine Name associated with Venus is YHVH Tzabaoth.

Venus is the ruler of friendship as well as how we view beauty and its meaning to us. It is a joyful and benign Planet, bringing luck in terms of one's finances as well as one's love life. Venus governs creativity and artistic expressions such as the visual arts, dance, drama, poetry, and music. The High Renaissance was a period with a high degree of Venetian energy. Artists from various fields were producing beautiful works of art that withstood the test of time.

As Venus is a Planet of love, it is also a Planet of lust. As such, the desires for love and lust can be incredibly powerful if not balanced by Venus' opposite, Mercury—the Planet responsible for logic and reasoning. When the desire is unbalanced, it can be rather destructive to a person's life. It needs a proper dose of logic and reason to manifest successfully. Venus affects our care for the people in our lives. Vegetation and the natural world, in general, are directly influenced by Venus.

Venus is frequently called the "Morning Star" since its positioning to the Sun can be seen just before sunrise or after sunset as a bright morning or evening Star. Jesus Christ often referred to himself as "the bright Morning Star" in *The Holy Bible*. Lucifer, the Light-Bearer, is an often misunderstood figure whose name is based on the Latin name for the Morning Star. Venus is also associated with the Dog Star, Sirius, since they are the two brightest objects in the night sky. Both were used for navigation by the Ancient peoples all over the world.

Venus influences how we attract people into our lives. If Venus is afflicted in our Horoscope, there would be conflicts with our abilities to express ourselves in social and intimate situations. In a male's Horoscope, Venus indicates the type of female he desires, while in a female's Horoscope, it shows how she will relate to her partner.

Venus is a very tactile Planet, so it makes sense that it governs the sensory organs. It regulates our taste, tongue, swallowing function, mouth, throat, and saliva. Since it is the Planet of Desire, Venus also governs the internal sexual organs and the kidneys. Furthermore, it regulates the lymphatic system and the nerves in general. Since Venus rules the sensory perception of touch, it governs our skin, especially its function in breathing, absorption, and exudation. Venus also regulates our muscles regarding tone and relaxation.

An afflicted Venus can lead to tonsillitis and other ailments of the taste organs mentioned above. In addition, it creates maladies affecting nerves and our lymphatic system. Furthermore, certain skin disorders such as dermatitis are associated with having an afflicted Venus, as are sexual diseases and kidney issues.

In a person's Horoscope, Venus indicates a strong desire for companionship. It is indicative of how we express our love to others and the area in our lives where we might have an easy or difficult time relating. Venus influences social, romantic, and sexual urges and how we respond and express them. It is the ruler of sensuality, sociability, interaction, and marriage.

As Venus represents joy and harmony, it also shows our capacity to create material prosperity and beauty in our lives. In astronomy, Venus is the second Planet from the Sun, and the second brightest natural object in the night sky, after the Moon.

MERCURY

Attributed to the Sphere of Hod in the Qabalah, Mercury has an affinity to the Water Element. However, its energy can most aptly be described as being comparable to Water of Air, since Mercury relates to the fluidity of thoughts. Air is thought, and Mercury is directly related to thought processes. Mercury is named after the Roman Messenger God, who is called Hermes in Greek and Kokab in Hebrew. It has an affinity to the Planet Jupiter.

Other Deities attributed to Mercury are Thoth, Anubis, Nabu, Budha, Quetzalcoatl, Viracocha, and Kukulkan. In the Tarot, Mercury is attributed to the Magician card. Astrologically, it rules Gemini and Virgo, both highly communicative signs.

Gemstones attributed to Mercury are Orange Sapphire, Orange Spinel, Tourmaline, Imperial Topaz, Citrine, and Fire Opal. The metal corresponding with Mercury is quicksilver, while the day of the week attributed to it is Wednesday. The Hebrew Divine Name associated with Mercury is Elohim Tzabaoth.

Of all the Planets in our Solar System, Mercury moves the most rapidly around the Sun. This speedy physical movement of the Planet corresponds with the symbolic attributes of Mercury or Hermes. He is the Messenger of the Gods and the medium of communication between the Above (Heaven) and Below (Earth). Since Mercury is related to thought, the speed of thought and the channelling and processing of information are our connecting links between Heaven and Earth. Thus, knowledge and wisdom are channelled from the Divine into humanity through the Planet Mercury. In this way, intelligence in a person is built up.

Mercury is also the Planet of communication. In a person's Horoscope, it influences how they think and the characteristics of their mind. Mercury is expressive of the truth, hence its dualistic qualities, because the truth requires that a person can see "both sides of the coin."

Mercury is neutral in terms of mental communication, reasoning, memory, and perception. The mind and thought processes are the organizing tool or lens through which all other skills and abilities must be focused. As such, one cannot attain success without having a well-developed Mercury in their Horoscope. Mercury, like a trickster, has a certain ambivalent quality. It also sets pitfalls for people to show them their foolishness. Mercury forces a person to engage all of their faculties with total concentration and alertness.

Since Mercury governs mental functions, it influences both hemispheres of the human brain. As such, it regulates the intellect and its clarity, as well as creative thought. It also governs strategic calculations through deduction and reasoning.

Mercury also rules the automatic body functions such as breathing and blinking. In addition, it governs organs of speech, the ears regarding hearing, gestures in terms of communicating, and nervous and muscular coordination. The arms, hands, tongue, and lungs are all governed by it. The bowels are ruled by Mercury as well. An afflicted Mercury can lead to speech disorders, bowel issues, bronchitis, thyroid problems, weak nerves, insomnia, loss of memory, and issues with ears, mouth, arms, and hands.

Mercury is connected directly to the air and the wind within the Earth's atmosphere. Encompassing all opposites within itself, Mercury is androgynous. Therefore, it is independent of a polar opposite. Mercury is also associated with social contacts, family, children, siblings, daily activities, and transportation. Essentially, it is the Planet of intelligence, logic, and reason.

Mercury is the ruler of analysis, teaching, learning, calculations, language, mathematics, and the higher intellectual mind. It rules travel as well, since travel is a way of experiencing, learning about, and absorbing new environments and information. Mercury helps one be adaptable to unique circumstances and situations. In astronomy, it is the smallest Planet in our Solar System and one closest to the Sun.

THE MOON (LUNA)

In the Qabalah, the Moon is attributed to the Sphere of Yesod, with an affinity to the Air Element. However, its energy can be best described as comparable to Earth of Water since it is passive, reflective energy. Also known as Luna (Latin), the Moon is attributed to the Roman Goddess Diana. It is known as Selene in Greek, while in Hebrew, it is Levanah.

Other Deities around the world associated with the Moon are Khonsu, Artemis, Hecate, Sin, Uma, Cybele, Astarte, and Arianrhod. In the Tarot, the Moon is associated with the High Priestess card. Gemstones attributed to the Moon are Moonstone, Pearl, and Beryl. The metal corresponding with the Moon is silver, while the day of the week assigned to it is Monday. The Hebrew Divine Name associated with the Moon is Shaddai El Chai.

The Moon has an affinity to the Sun. While the Sun is masculine, the Moon is feminine. It is changeable, reflective, and nurturing, with a strong influence on growth, fertility, and conception. As the Sun governs the day, the Moon governs the night. It affects our dreams since that which we dream about is representative of the potential realities of our mundane, Earth life.

The Moon is illusory because it reflects the Light of the Sun. Thus, it is filled with what one believes is real rather than what is truly real. For this reason, it is the ruler of the subconscious mind, while the Sun is the ruler of the conscious mind. The subconscious mind contains many fears, suppressed feelings, and primal instincts.

These attributes of the mind all fall under the ruling of the Moon's illusory energy. As such, the Moon is the governor of involuntary emotions.

Astrologically, Cancer is ruled by the Moon. The Moon's energy is highly influential on intuition. When dealing with the Moon, though, we must consciously discern between what is real and what is unreal. Furthermore, the Moon is the ruler of phases, habits, moods, feelings, and personal interests. It can be cold and quick to change while also intense and passionate.

The Air Element is very much present in the Moon's energy, and over time, the Ego is developed through it—as the Ego is merely a reflection of who we think we are. Momentary pleasure, also known as caprice, is under the influence of the Moon.

The Moon influences spontaneity, sudden calls to adventure, and child-like curiosity and wonder. It rules fertility, women's cycles, and the fluctuating tides of the oceans and seas. As over 70% of the Earth is covered in water, the Moon's influence on life on Earth is immense.

The gravitational pull of the Moon on the Earth creates the pendulum-like movement of the waters. In the same way, our emotions are also affected. We swing back and forth between emotional extremes almost automatically, without any conscious effort on our part. The Moon is connected to the Hermetic Principles of Polarity and Rhythm since they describe the nature of the emotions, as will be discussed in detail later in the section on Hermetic Philosophy.

As the Moon orbits around the Earth, influencing the tides of the oceans and seas, the fluids in our physical bodies are similarly affected. Our physical bodies consist of around 60% water. The brain and heart are composed of over 70% water, while the lungs are over 80%. The Moon governs the secretion and utilization of all fluids, including tears, saliva, digestive juices, sexual fluids, etc. It also regulates the liquid substance in our brains, hearts, lungs, stomach, nose, mouth, and eyeballs.

The Moon governs the sympathetic nervous system and the lymphatic system in general. Its energy influences water retention, digestive motion, blood flow, and cellular moisture. An afflicted Moon can lead to disorders relating to accumulations of bodily fluids, abscesses, female diseases, tumours, chest colds, coughs, allergies, pneumonia, stomach problems, asthma, and insomnia.

When looking at a person's Astrological chart (Horoscope), the Astrologer often uses the North and South Nodes of the Moon, Caput Draconis and Cauda Draconis, to glean more specific details about a person's life. For example, aspects of the North Node indicate a person's relationships and common social trends. It is also responsible for influencing one's attitude towards the opportunities for advancement that might present themselves in one's life. For this reason, it is related to the Planet Jupiter.

Conversely, aspects of the South Node are indicators of which habits, picked up from the past, can influence a person's present behaviour. Like this, the South Node reveals the Karmic effect of a person's past actions. As such, we have a Saturn-type influence and connotation arising with the Moon.

The Moon is vital in all Magickal workings and has been studied and followed by occultists from all Ancient traditions. Ritual invocations are performed in the proper Planetary hour and time following the Moon's cycles. Most invocations are done on a waxing Moon, which is when it is getting more prominent in the sky as it transitions from the New Moon to the Full Moon. Banishings are done on a waning Moon when it decreases in size after a Full Moon. A dark Moon or no Moon is usually a time of inner growth, and no rituals are performed at this time.

In astronomy, the Moon is the Earth's only permanent natural satellite, orbiting around the Earth. It is in synchronous rotation with the Earth, and thus it always shows the same side. After the Sun, the Moon is the second brightest visible celestial object in the Earth's sky. Its gravitational pull on the Earth affects the tides of the bodies of water, which slows the rotation of the Earth on its axis, thereby creating the twenty-four-hour time clock.

THE EARTH

Planet Earth is associated with the Sphere of Malkuth on the Tree of Life, and naturally, it has an affinity to the Element of Earth. It is known as Gaia, personified as one of the Greek primordial Deities. Gaia is the Ancestral Mother of all life. She is the Primal Mother Earth Goddess. Earth is also known as "Terra Firma" in Latin, meaning "solid earth" as it is perpetually present, under our feet, here and now. Other Deities around the world associated with Planet Earth are Geb, Demeter, Ceres, Cernunnos, Nerthus, Ganesha, Azaka, and Ochosi.

There are no Astrological or Tarot correspondences with Planet Earth. Gemstones attributed to it are Black Tourmaline, Obsidian, and Hematite. Planet Earth has neither a corresponding metal nor a day of the week. The Hebrew Divine Name associated with it is Adonai ha-Aretz.

Planet Earth is not often portrayed alongside the other Planets because, as mentioned, it never leaves our sphere of experience. It represents the Physical Realm and all mundane matters of the material world. Earth alludes to an individual's purpose and mission in life. "Reality" is the word best fit to describe Planet Earth. Another word that best describes the Earth is "Matter," concerning everything within the Earth's atmosphere.

The Earth's atmosphere is a layer of gases, commonly known as air, which surrounds Planet Earth and is retained by its gravity. All life on Planet Earth depends on air for breathing. Breath sustains and supports all living things. The Earth also feeds us and gives us water for sustenance. Our consciousness is inextricably connected to the consciousness of the Earth—we exist in a symbiotic relationship with it. As the Planet Earth nurtures us, it plays the role of a Mother to us, her children.

In astronomy, the Earth is the third Planet from the Sun and the only astronomical object known to harbour life. The Earth's axis of rotation is tilted to its orbital plane, thereby producing the seasons. As mentioned, the gravitational interaction between Planet Earth and the Moon stabilizes the Earth's orientation on its axis and gradually slows its rotation, creating the twenty-four-hour time clock. The Earth revolves around the Sun for 365 days, a period known as one Earth or Solar year. Earth is the densest Planet in our Solar System.

THE NEW PLANETS—URANUS, NEPTUNE, PLUTO

Since the invention of the telescope in 1608, three new Planets have been discovered. Uranus was discovered in 1781, while Neptune was found in 1846. Lastly, Pluto was discovered in 1930. As these Planets' orbits are slow-moving, they are often regarded as symbols of eras. The effects of these Planets are felt across the whole generations of society.

Additionally, these three new Planets are referred to as the Transcendental Planets. This is because they do not enter into the sevenfold scheme of the different Sephiroth on the Tree of Life. Considered "outer" Planets, they do not have a strong position within the Qabalistic teachings. However, since they are included in modern-day Western Astrology, a brief mention of them is suitable for this discussion.

In Greek mythology, Uranus is the God of the Sky. Otherwise called "Father Sky," Uranus was the son and husband of Gaia, Mother Earth, and one of the Greek primordial Deities. This same God is called Caelus by the Romans. Uranus is said to govern genius and humanitarian and progressive ideals. It rules freedom, ingenuity and originality, including unexpected changes.

Uranus rules all radical and unconventional ideas as well as people, and it is said to have influenced past revolutionary events that disturbed established structures. Considered the higher octave of the Planet Mercury, Uranus' day of the week is Wednesday. In modern-day Western Astrology, Uranus is said to rule Aquarius. The influence of Cauda Draconis, the South Node of the Moon, is likened to that of Uranus.

Neptune is the Roman God of the Sea, called Poseidon by the Greeks. This Planet is deep blue, resembling the ocean, hence how it got its name. Neptune rules dreams, idealism, artistry, and empathy. Because of its association with the Water Element, it has a connection with Jupiter. Since it also rules over illusion and vagueness, it has a relationship with the Moon as well.

Neptune is in the higher octave of the Planet Venus; as such, its day of the week is Friday. In modern-day Astrology, Neptune is said to rule Pisces, the deepest and most emotional of the Water signs. In addition, the influence of Caput Draconis, the North Node of the Moon, is similar to that of Neptune.

In Roman mythology, Pluto is the God of the Underworld, the judge of the dead. As the God of the Underworld, he is associated with the Egyptian God Osiris. Pluto is called Hades by the Greeks. In Greek cosmogony, once the Titan Chronos (Cronus) was overthrown, Hades received the rule of the Underworld in a three-way division of sovereignty over the world. His brother Zeus was given the sky, while his other brother Poseidon was given dominion over the sea.

Pluto deals with transformation on all levels. It represents the part of the individual that destroys to renew. As such, it is linked to the Death card of the Tarot. Pluto is associated with all enterprises that require digging under the surface to bring the truth to light. It is also related to personal power and mastery over the Self. The Great Work is closely linked to Pluto's influence.

Pluto is associated with Mars as it is the higher octave of that Planet in Astrology. As such, its day of the week is Tuesday. In modern-day Astrology, Pluto is said to rule Scorpio, the Zodiac sign associated with transformation.

***

Knowledge of the Elements, the Planets, and the Zodiac is the core of the Hermetic Qabalah. Consequently, these energies form the totality of the Tree of Life. Understanding the information presented in *The Magus* will enable you to see the "big picture" of how the Solar System, the Macrocosm, works. And, as the Hermetic axiom of "As Above, So Below" states, the Macrocosm finds its reflection in the Microcosm. Likewise, the Solar System is reflected in the human energy system (Aura). Therefore, by learning about the energies of the outer Universe, you are learning about the powers comprising your inner Self.

To attain Gnosis, you must commit this knowledge to memory. Gnosis is the direct communication of your Higher Genius with the Soul and Ego. Once you create a link with your Higher Genius, you no longer will need outside teachers or books to learn from. Instead, you will become your own teacher. Therefore, Gnosis is the most optimal method of learning the Qabalah and the correct path to Spiritual growth. The information presented in this book is meant to impart the necessary knowledge to achieve this goal.

You must read and reread this information numerous times to get the most from this knowledge. Every time you read it, you will learn something new. And once it is committed to memory, your Higher Genius will start communicating to you to give you further Qabalistic knowledge through Gnosis.

In this way, true wisdom is built. And once you obtain this Wisdom, you will invariably gain Understanding because one does not exist without the other. Understanding is the highest function of the human Self that establishes a link with the Higher Genius—the Eternal Self. Through Gnosis and the Spiritual Evolution that follows, you can restore the Garden of Eden, thus regaining your inherent birthright given to you by your Creator.

ADVANCED PLANETARY MAGICK

The Ancient Babylonians, Greeks, Romans, and many other cultures and civilizations considered the Planets in our Solar System as the Gods. To them, the Planets were symbolic of the different powers of God-the Creator and represented these qualities or attributes. They recognized the correspondence between the Planets and our higher powers as we are made in the image of God-the Creator.

Since every human being is a Microcosm of the Macrocosm (meaning we carry the energies of the Solar System within ourselves), then the purpose of working with the Planetary energies is to attune those higher powers of the Self and efficiently integrate them within our lives. The Elements you have worked with so far served to exalt the Higher Self over the Lower Self-the Ego and infuse the Spirit energy within your consciousness. The next step in the Great Work is to work with the Planetary powers that express through your consciousness.

You have learned how the Seven Ancient Planets relate to the Tree of life and the Sephiroth. In this section, you will be using the powers of the Planets to help you evolve further Spiritually and tap into your innermost potential. The paths of the Tree of Life open doors inwards, but Sephiroth establish contacts with the limitless Mind of the Creator. Working with the Seven Ancient Planets is crucial in furthering your understanding of the Self and its many intricate components. After all, if every human at the core of their Being is God-the Creator, then by invoking the Planets, we can isolate and examine the different powers that make up the whole.

Regarding their influence on the human psyche, the Planets belong to the World of Atziluth—the World of pure Spirit and the Divine Plane where thoughts of God-the Creator, exist. This association means that the Planets are Archetypal forces emanating from the highest levels of the Divine energy. So now you understand why you needed to work with the lower Elements and the Spirit Element before working with the Planets.

These Planetary powers filter into your Being through the Spirit/Aethyr Element. Thus, working with the SIRP was a preparation for this task. By invoking a Planet, you are going deep within yourself and gaining the ability to alter how its energy impacts the corresponding aspect of your psyche. The Planetary forces are responsible for our intricate behaviours according to the expression of our Souls in the world.

Each Planet has ruling powers (as per Table 4) that constitute the highest of our aspirations but also our limitations. The key to working with the Planets is exalting the Higher Self over the Ego and its expressions.

As mentioned in the previous chapter, we were dealt a hand by God-the Creator the very moment we were born and brought into this world. Macrocosmic energies impacting you at the time of your birth became locked into your consciousness—the type and quality of these energies are dependent on the place you were born in and what signs of the Zodiac your Planets expressed themselves through. Thus, you are predetermined to act in a particular manner right from birth.

These Planetary energies are embedded deep in your subconscious mind and work to regulate the flow of energy in your Chakras and your various Subtle bodies. Although the Seven Ancient Planets and the Zodiac Signs they rule relate to the Seven Chakras, I am reserving the discourse on this subject for my second book, *Serpent Rising: The Kundalini Compendium,* since that work is more in-depth on the Chakric system in general.

The Magus is Qabalistic in nature, so I want to focus only on the correspondences between the Planets and the Sephiroth. You have seen in an earlier discussion how the relationship between the Sephiroth and Chakras is more complex than attributing one Chakra to one Sephira. Thus, I don't want to create confusion regarding the Chakras when working with the Planets through Ceremonial Magick means.

Through Planetary invocations, you are also working with the different energies that form the virtues and vices in your character and personality. Your ethics, morals, and internal beliefs about the world you live in are all impacted by the Planetary energies affecting you. Primarily, your aim with this work is to work on overcoming your vices and other limitations that prevent you from being the best version of "You" possible.

TABLE 4: The Seven Ancient Planets and their Correspondences

Planet	Sephira & Divine Name	Associated Deities	Elemental Affinity	Zodiac & Metal	Expressions/ Powers	Gemstones
Saturn	Binah, YHVH Elohim	Chronos, Isis, Brahma, Hera, Nephthys, Ptah, Harpocrates, Ninurta	Earth; Feels like Earth of Air	Capricorn & Aquarius, Lead	Karma, Truth, Wisdom, Structure, Discipline, Intuition	Jet Black Onyx, Diamonds, Smoky Quartz
Jupiter	Chesed, El	Zeus, Maat, Indra, Vishnu, Saraswati, Hapi, Dagda, Marduk	Water; Feels like Water of Fire	Pisces & Saggitarius, Tin	Mercy, Abundance, Unconditional Love, Morals, Ethics	Sapphire, Lapis Lazuli, Turquoise, Aquamarine
Mars	Geburah, Elohim Gibor	Ares, Horus, Sekhmet, Ninurta, Agni, Durga, Nergal, Shiva	Fire; Feels like Earth of Fire	Aries & Scorpio, Iron	Ambition, Drive, Renewal, Action, Survival, Competition, Passion, Willpower	Ruby, Garnet, Red Agate, Bloodstone, Red Coral
Sun (Sol)	Tiphareth, YHVH Eloah ve-Daath	Helios, Jesus Christ, Osiris, Apollo, Dionysus, Mithras, Surya, Krishna, Tammuz, Shamash, Amun Ra	Air; Feels like Air of Fire	Leo, Gold	Healing, Vitality, Courage, Creativity, Inspiration, Imagination	Amber, Tiger's Eye, Gold Topaz, Goldstone, Zircon
Venus	Netzach, YHVH Tzabaoth	Aphrodite, Hathor, Bast, Ishtar, Lakshmi, Chenrezi, Ushas, Sukra	Fire; Feels like Water of Earth	Libra & Taurus, Copper or Brass	Desire, Creative Expressions, Romantic Love, Friendship, Sensuality	Emerald, Jade, Aventurine, Malachite, Rose Quartz, Green Agate, Peridot
Mercury	Hod, Elohim Tzabaoth	Hermes, Thoth, Anubis, Nabu, Budha, Quetzalcoatl, Viracocha, Kukulkan	Water; Feels like Water of Air	Gemini & Virgo, Quicksilver	Logic, Reason, Communication, Intellect, Learning	Orange Sapphire, Tourmaline, Imperial Topaz, Citrine, Fire Opal
Moon (Luna)	Yesod, Shaddai El Chai	Diana, Selene, Khonsu, Artemis, Hecate, Uma, Sin, Cybele, Astarte, Arianrhod, Chandra	Air; Feels like Earth of Water	Cancer, Silver	Feelings, Emotions, Illusions, Caprice, Fertility, Clairvoyance	Moonstone, Pearl, Beryl
Earth	Malkuth, Adonai ha-Aretz	Gaia, Geb, Demeter, Ceres, Cernunnos, Nerthus, Ganesha, Azaka, Ochosi	Earth	-	Stability, Grounding, Practicality	Black Tourmaline, Obsidian, Hematite

LESSER RITUAL OF THE HEXAGRAM

The Lesser Ritual of the Hexagram (LRH) is an invoking or a banishing of the Planetary powers as they relate to the Four Elements of Fire, Earth, Air and Water. The Banishing Ritual of the Hexagram is just one of fourteen Lesser Rituals of the Hexagram, as each of the Seven Ancient Planets can be either banished or invoked through the four forms of the Hexagram (Figures 45-48).

The Hexagram is a symbol of the Sun, the grand equalizing power in our Solar System and the source of Matter in this Third Dimension we live in. Solar energy condenses in stages to form Matter, and these stages are expressed through the Four Elements of Fire, Air, Water, and Earth. Herein we see the relationship between the Hexagram and the Elements.

As mentioned, the four forms of the Hexagram represent the positions of the Elements in the Zodiac. In the East, we have the Fire Element; in the South, we have Earth; in the West is Air; in the North is Water. The Earth Hexagram is of utmost importance in Magick because it will be used in the Greater Ritual of the Hexagram (GRH). This form of the Hexagram is the Star of David—the symbol of the Macrocosm.

The Hexagram is composed of the two triangles of the Fire and Water Elements in conjunction with one another. Because of this, it is not traced in one continuous line like the Pentagram symbol but by each triangle separately. All the invoking Hexagrams follow the course of the rising and setting Sun, meaning they are drawn from left to right. The banishing Hexagrams are drawn from right to left. They start at the same angle from which they are invoked, contrary to the course of the Sun.

The Lesser Ritual of the Hexagram accesses the Solar Power in all of its various manifestations. These manifestations are the Planetary energies of Saturn, Jupiter, Mars, Venus, Mercury, and the Moon. It is interesting to note that to invoke the power of the Sun, you must invoke all six of the Planets mentioned above in that exact order. This method further affirms how each of the six Planetary forces is, in essence, just one part of the whole, which is the totality of the Solar energy of the Sun. After all, the White Light of the Sun is the highest manifestation of God-the Creator in our Solar System. In it, we find the seven rays, which are the seven colours of the rainbow—corresponding with the Seven Chakras.

Since you are already familiar with the Banishing Ritual of the Hexagram (which banishes Saturn), invoking or banishing any of the other Planets with the four forms of the Hexagram will be relatively easy for you. It is merely a matter of how you trace the triangles (since their form is the same, but the direction of tracings changes from one Planet to the next).

As in the BRH, you are to vibrate the name ARARITA in all four cardinal directions while tracing the four forms of the Hexagram as they are given. Also, the Hexagrams are meant to be visualized in a golden colour, enflamed as you vibrate the Divine Name ARARITA. The formula then for the Lesser Ritual of the Hexagram is the same as the BRH. The minor difference is the change in direction when you are tracing the Hexagrams.

Keep in mind that using the Lesser banishing Hexagrams for any of the Planets (except in the case of the BRH) is unnecessary unless you are having difficulty managing the energy of the Planet you invoked. As you banish a Planet, you will be releasing its invoked energy out of your Aura and any natural energy of that Planet before its invocation. As with the banishings of the Elements, it will take a few hours at least to rebuild that Planetary energy in your Aura again. Although the BRH does remove unwanted energies of all the Planets, it is not as powerful in banishing an individual Planet's energy as when you use that Planet's Lesser banishing Hexagram ritual.

INVOKING

EAST　　SOUTH　　WEST　　NORTH

SATURN ♄

JUPITER ♃

MARS ♂

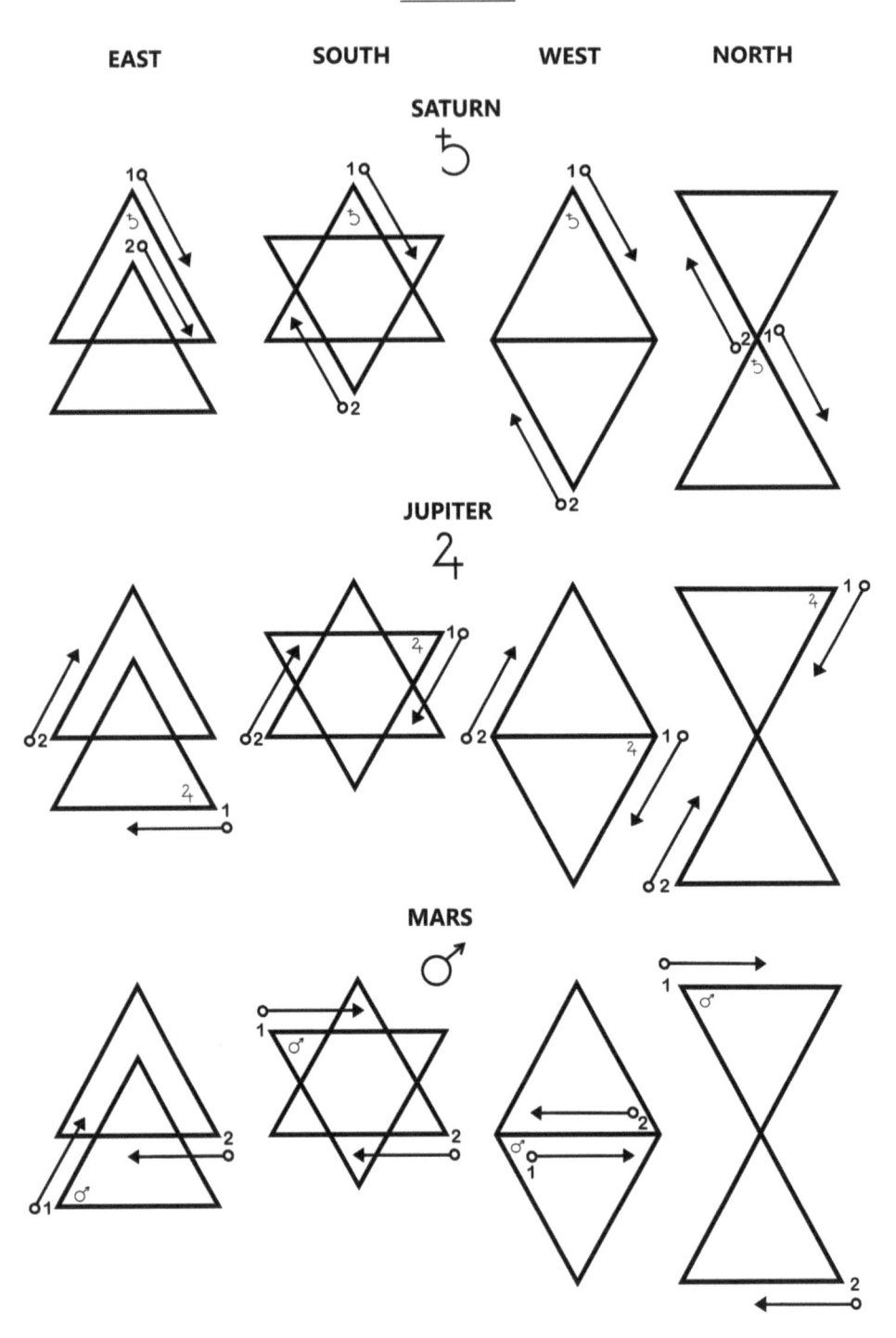

Figure 45: Lesser Invoking Hexagrams for Saturn, Jupiter, and Mars

INVOKING

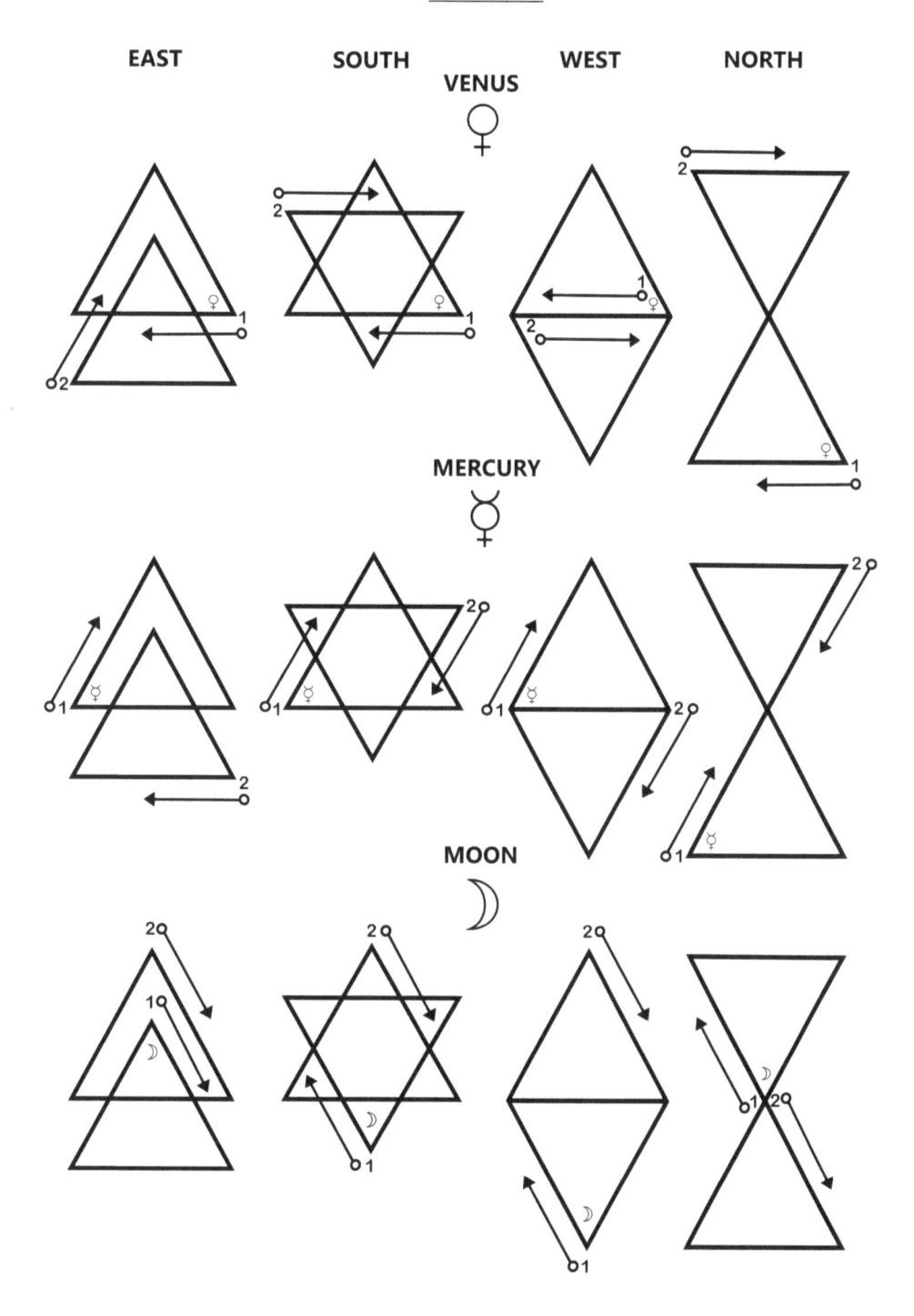

Figure 46: Lesser Invoking Hexagrams for Venus, Mercury, and the Moon

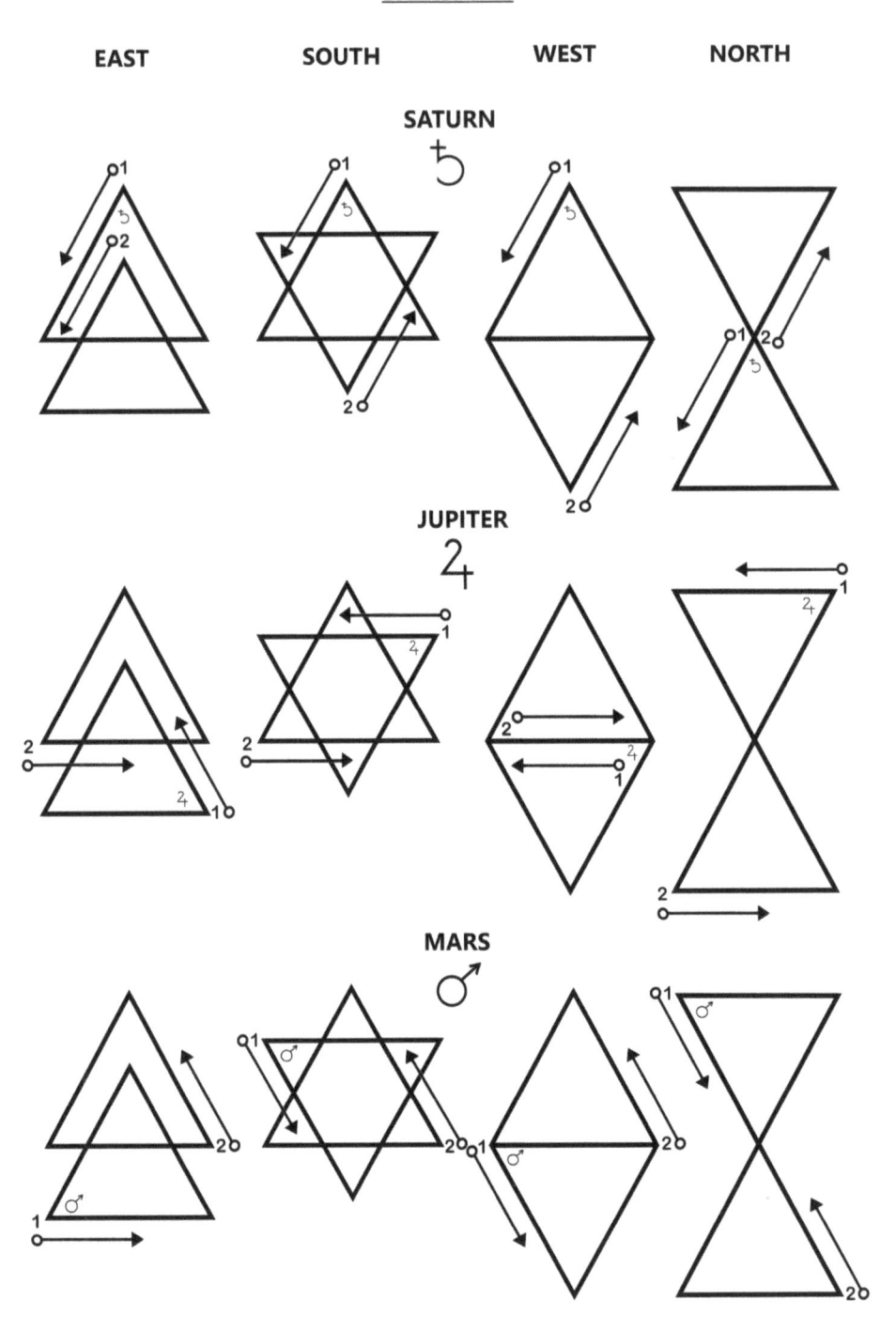

Figure 47: Lesser Banishing Hexagrams for Saturn, Jupiter, and Mars

BANISHING

EAST SOUTH WEST NORTH

VENUS

MERCURY

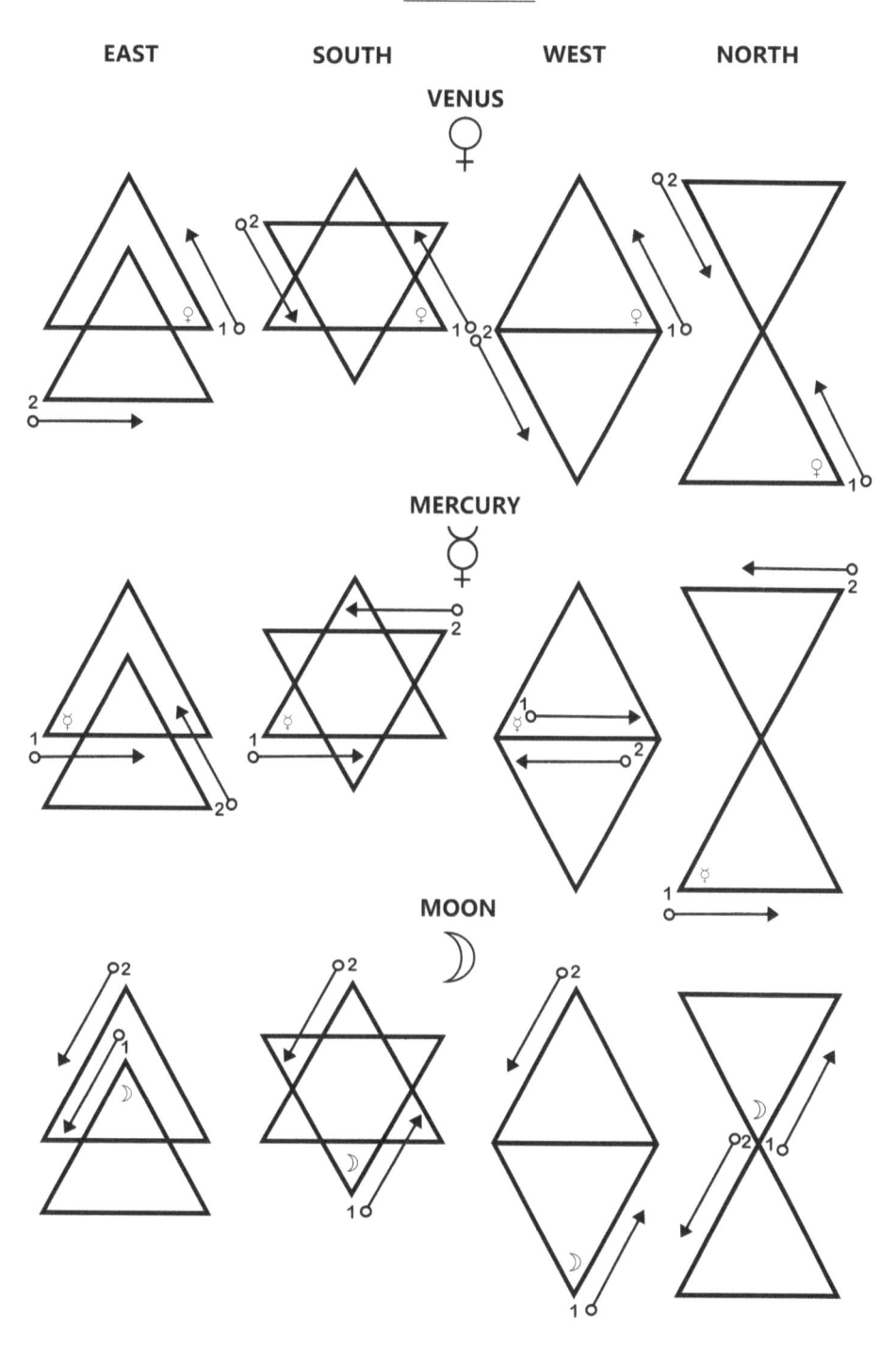

MOON

Figure 48: Lesser Banishing Hexagrams for Venus, Mercury, and Moon

GREATER RITUAL OF THE HEXAGRAM

The Greater Ritual of the Hexagram can be used for working with both the Planets and signs of the Zodiac. Although you will not be working with Zodiacal energies as part of any Spiritual Alchemy program presented in this book, I will give you the ritual exercise formula regardless. You can experiment with its use if you desire, but only once you have finished Spiritual Alchemy Program I and decided to work with the Seven Ancient Planets.

The six Planets of Saturn, Jupiter, Mars, Venus, Mercury, and the Moon are attributed to each angle of the Hexagram (Figure 49). The colour in each corner corresponds with the colour of the Planet's Sephira on the Tree of Life. These colours are in the Briah scale. Saturn is the only exception to this rule. Its colour is indigo, while the Moon is violet, Jupiter is blue, Mars is scarlet (red), Venus is emerald green, and Mercury is orange.

The Sun is in the centre of the Hexagram as the great reconciling force, whose colour is golden yellow. It possesses the power of all the Planets in our Solar System. In the Lesser Ritual of the Hexagram, we use this form of the Hexagram in the cardinal direction of the Earth Element.

Figure 49: Greater Hexagram Planetary Attributions

The order of attribution of each angle on the Earth Hexagram symbol is based on the Sephiroth as you descend the Tree of Life. The uppermost angle corresponds with Saturn but also Daath, while the lowest angle corresponds with Yesod. The other angles correspond with the remaining Sephiroth of the Microprosopus. From this descending order arises the Greater Ritual of the Hexagram (GRH).

In the GRH, the Divine Names of the corresponding Sephiroth are used, including the symbols of the Planets. Thus, its power is more significant than just the use of the Earth Hexagram in the Lesser Ritual of the Hexagram since it invokes the corresponding Sephira in its appropriate colour as well.

The Planets are categorized into superior and inferior Planets. A sympathy exists between each opposing pair as per their placement on the Hexagram symbol. Because of this, the triangles of their invoking and banishing Earth Hexagrams counter-change. The superior Planets are Saturn, Jupiter, and Mars. The inferior Planets are Venus, Mercury, and Luna. The superior Saturn and inferior Moon are sympathetic, as are Jupiter and Mercury, and Mars and Venus. Amid the six Planets is the Fire of the Sun, the source of Light and life in our Solar System.

When performing the Greater Ritual of the Hexagram, you must use the Earth Hexagram of a Planet and trace it in two triangles (Figures 51-52). The first triangle is traced starting from the angle of the Planet, while the second triangle is traced starting from its sympathetic Planet, opposite to it.

While tracing each Earth Hexagram of the Planet with one of the colours given in the above diagram (Figure 49), the Divine Name ARARITA should be vibrated. Afterwards, you are to trace the Planet symbol in the middle of the Hexagram. As you do so, vibrate the Divine Name of the Sephira associated with that Planet.

The Planet's colour should be in the corresponding Tree of Life path colour (Atziluth), as per Table 3. As you trace the Planet symbol in the centre of the Hexagram, make it a proportionate size so it fits its interior. The tracing method is from left to right, again following the course of the rising and setting Sun.

End by enflaming the Hexagram and the Planet symbol with the Sign of the Enterer and the Sign of Silence. Note that the Greater Hexagram of Saturn can also be used to invoke or banish the energies of the Supernal Triad of Kether, Chokmah, and Binah.

The Sun employs the Earth Hexagrams of all six Planets, which should be traced in their descending Planetary order according to their placement on the Tree of Life (Figures 53-54). While tracing each Hexagram, vibrate the Divine Name ARARITA while visualizing it in golden yellow. Then you are to trace the symbol of the Sun in orange in the middle of the Hexagram while vibrating the Divine Name YHVH Eloah ve-Daath.

Repeat this process five more times, as there are six Sun Hexagrams in total. End by enflaming the Hexagrams and Sun symbols with the Sign of the Enterer and the Sign of Silence. This formula is to be used whether invoking or banishing the Sun.

The optimal method of using the GRH is to turn to the quarter of the Heavens where the physical Planet is located. To do this, you would need to create a Horoscope chart of the heavens at the time of the ritual. You can also obtain a Horoscope online. You then would position the Ascendant to the East on the altar, followed by finding the desired Planet's closest quarter on the circle of the chart. By knowing in which quarter the physical Planet is located during your operation, you would incorporate the Greater Hexagram as part of the Lesser Ritual of the Hexagram by tracing it in its quarter after you have traced its four forms.

♈	♉	♊	♋
ARIES	TAURUS	GEMINI	CANCER
♌	♍	♎	♏
LEO	VIRGO	LIBRA	SCORPIO
♐	♑	♒	♓
SAGITTARIUS	CAPRICORN	AQUARIUS	PISCES

Figure 50: Symbols of the Zodiac Signs

To invoke the signs of the Zodiac, use the Earth Hexagram of its ruling Planet while vibrating the Divine Name ARARITA. The colour of the Hexagram is to be in its corresponding Tree of Life Sephira colour (Briah). In this case, you must trace the symbol of the desired Zodiac in the middle of the Hexagram as you vibrate its corresponding Divine Name according to the permutation of the Tetragrammaton.

Again, the Zodiac symbol (Figure 50) should be traced from left to right, in a clockwise fashion, to proportionate size to the interior of the Hexagram. In addition, the colour of the Zodiac symbol should be in the corresponding Tree of Life path colour (Atziluth). A supplementary Table 9 is given in the Appendix with all the information you need to invoke the Zodiac Signs.

INVOKING   **BANISHING**

SATURN

JUPITER

MARS

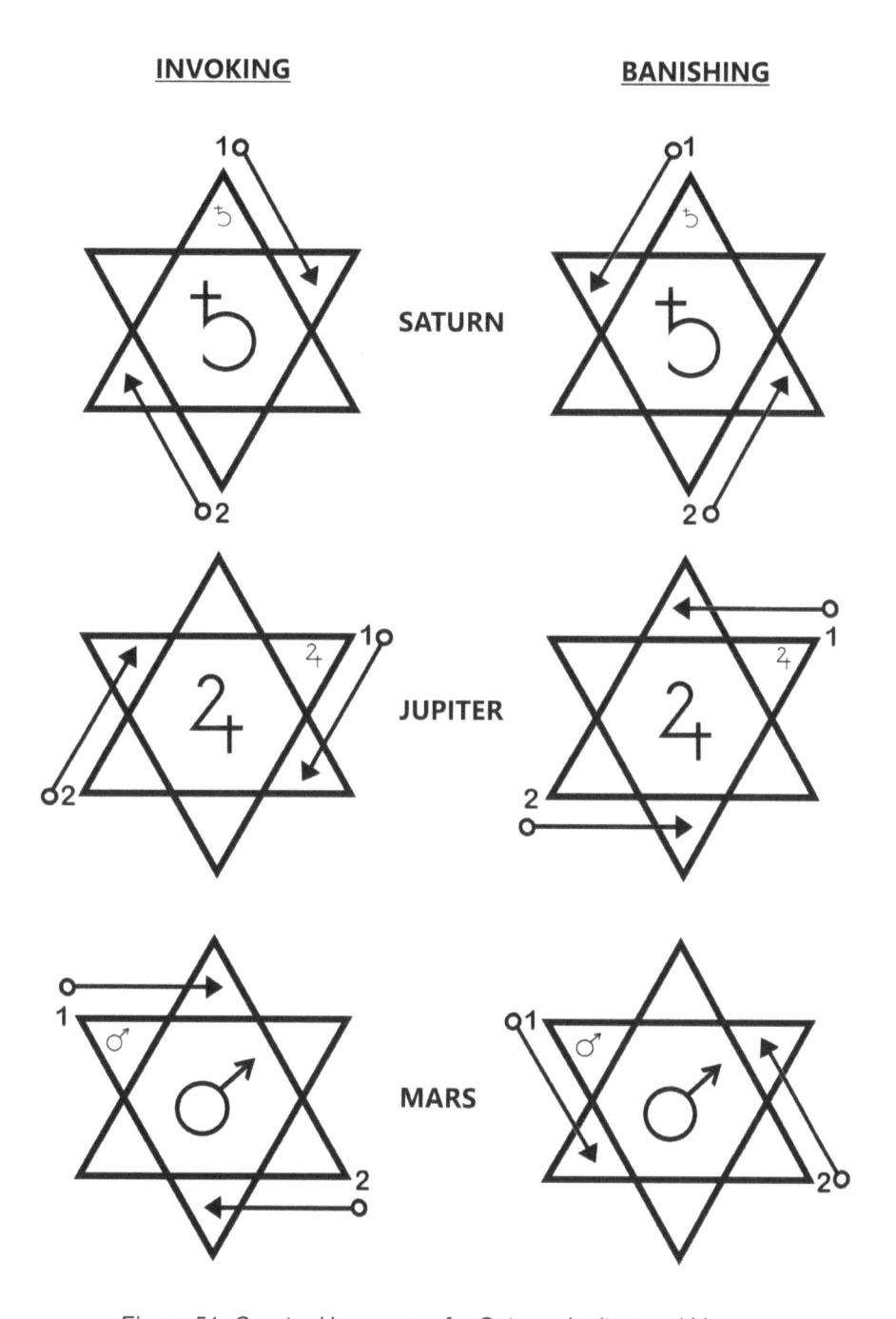

Figure 51: Greater Hexagrams for Saturn, Jupiter, and Mars

INVOKING   **BANISHING**

VENUS

MERCURY

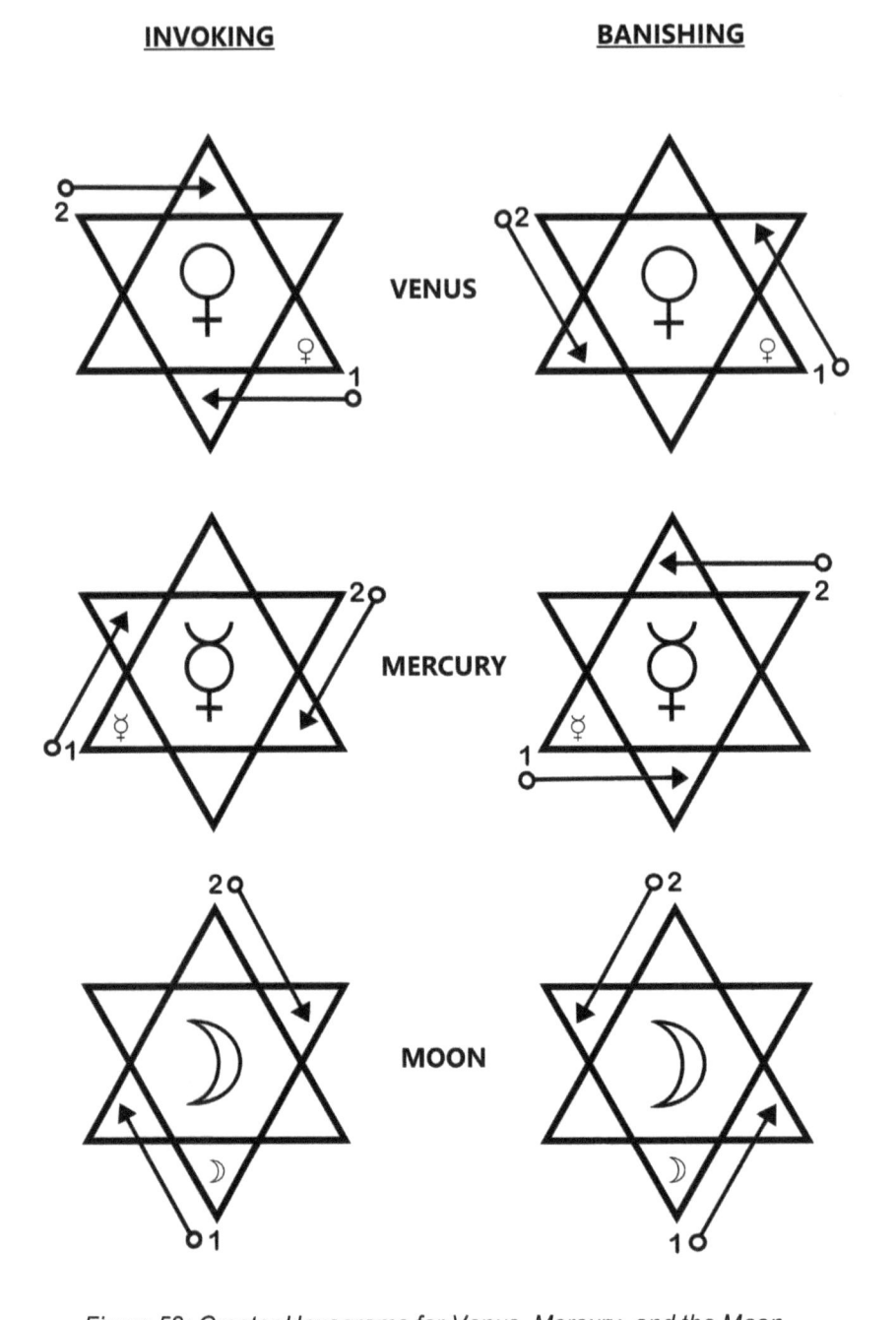

MOON

Figure 52: Greater Hexagrams for Venus, Mercury, and the Moon

SUN INVOKING

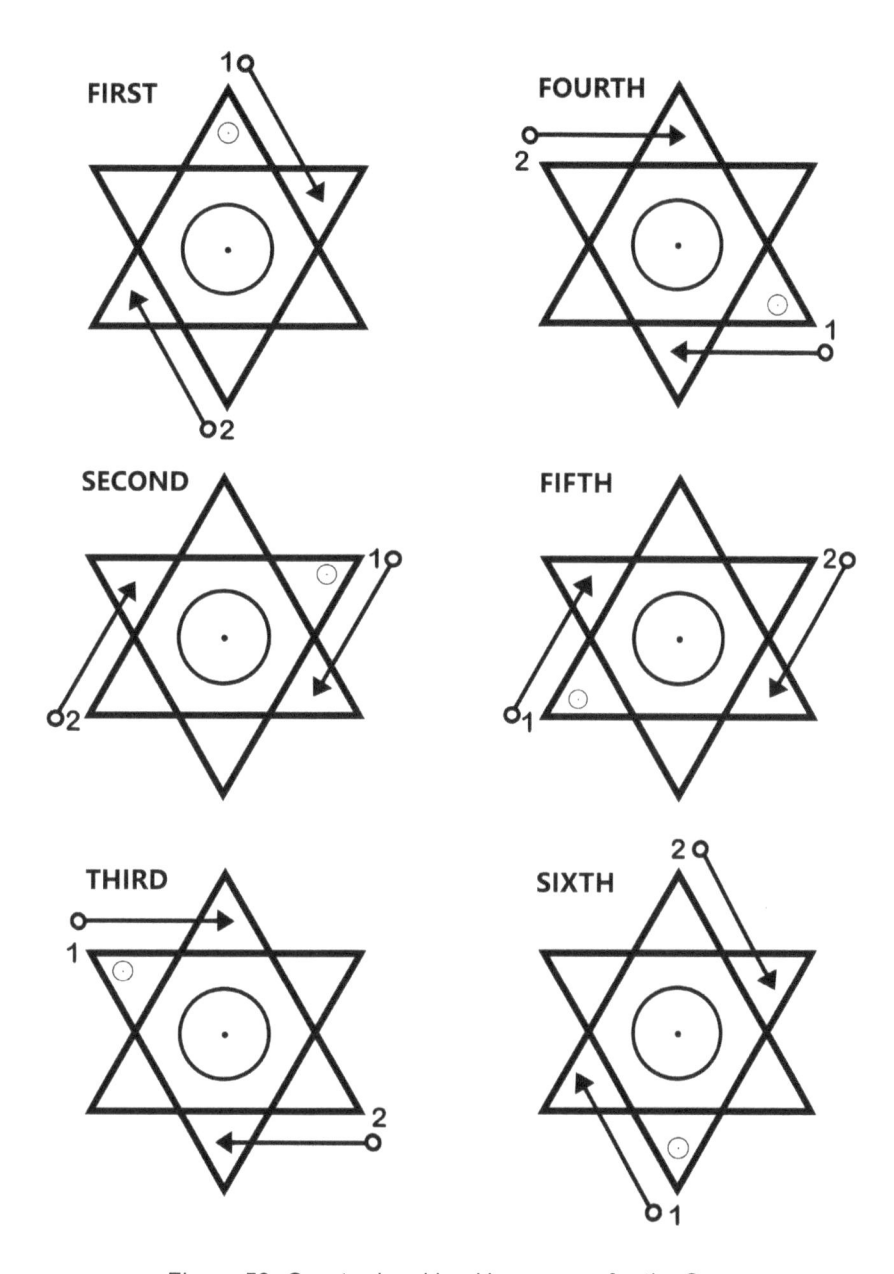

Figure 53: Greater Invoking Hexagrams for the Sun

SUN BANISHING

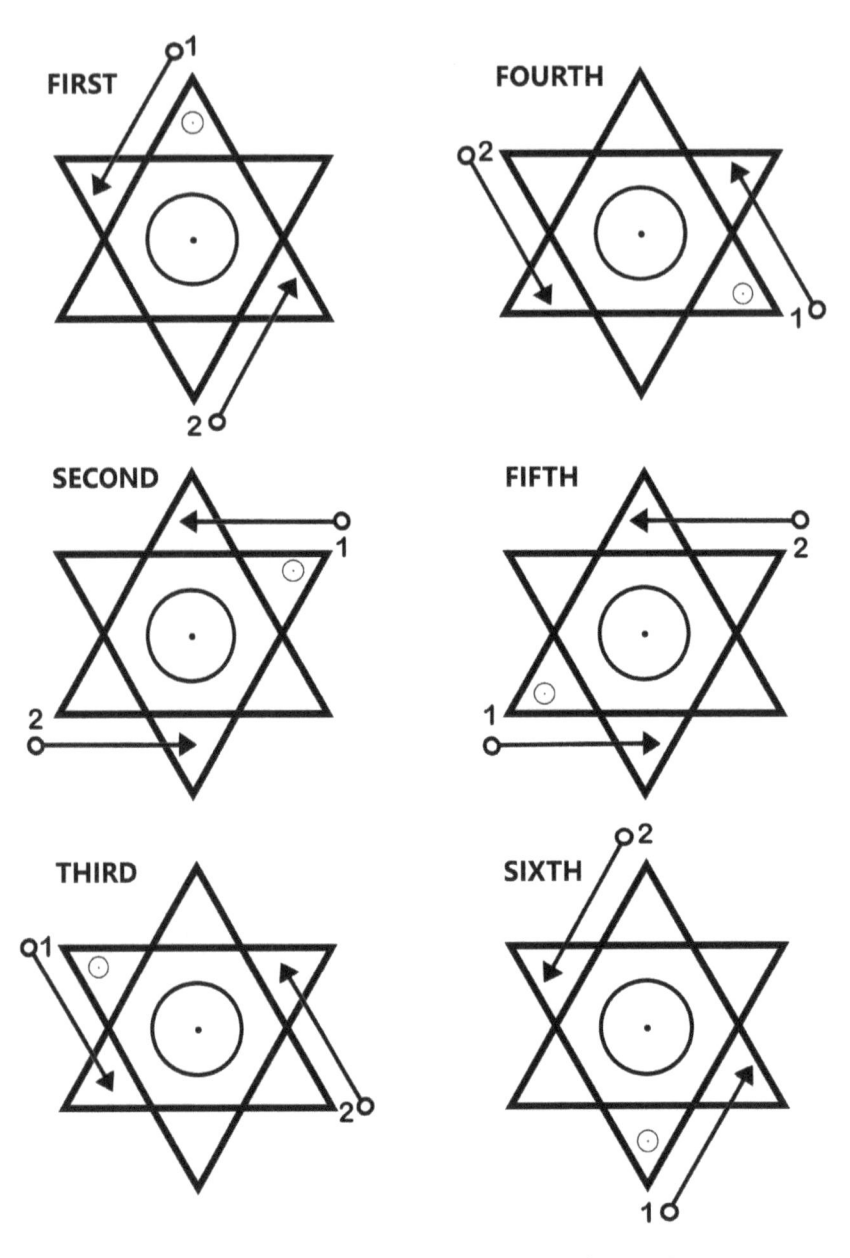

Figure 54: Greater Banishing Hexagrams for the Sun

Ritual of the Hexagram (Lesser + Greater)

Formula 1: The Qabalistic Cross

Perform the Four-Fold Breath for a minute or two to get you into a calm, balanced state of mind. Stand in the centre of your circle and face East. If you have Elemental altars and (or) a central altar, then stand behind the central altar. Perform the Qabalistic Cross as per the formula given in the instructions for the LBRP.

Formula 2: Tracing the Four Forms of the Lesser Hexagrams in the Four Cardinal Directions

Move to the East now and draw the invoking (or banishing) Fire Hexagram (of the Planet you are choosing to work with) as given. Visualize it in a golden flame. Inhale while drawing in the energy from the Sphere of Kether above you. Bring down the Light from Kether and thrust your fingers forward in the Sign of the Enterer as given in the LBRP ritual.

To the full extent of your breath, vibrate:

Aaahhh-Raaahhh-Reee-Taaahhh

(ARARITA)

See the Hexagram enflamed. End with the Sign of Silence (as per the LBRP).

Using your hand or ritual invoking tool, stab the middle of the Hexagram you just drew and carry a white line to the South. Draw the invoking (or banishing) Hexagram of Earth as given.

Perform the Sign of the Enterer, followed by vibrating the name:

Aaahhh-Raaahhh-Reee-Taaahhh

(ARARITA)

See the Hexagram enflamed. End with the Sign of Silence.

In the same manner as before, move the white line to the West and draw the invoking (or banishing) Hexagram of Air as given.

Perform the Sign of the Enterer, followed by vibrating the name:

Aaaahhh-Raaahhh-Reee-Taaahhh

(ARARITA)

Again, see the Hexagram enflamed. End with the Sign of Silence.

Thus far, you have drawn one-half the Magickal circle with the white line, connecting the Hexagrams in the East, South, and West. Now move the white line to the North, in the same manner as before, and draw the invoking or banishing Hexagram of Water.

Perform the Sign of the Enterer, followed by vibrating the name:

Aaahhh-Raaahhh-Reee-Taaahhh

(ARARITA)

See the Hexagram enflamed. End with the Sign of Silence.

Connect the white line from the North to the East, thereby completing your Magickal circle. While standing in the East, perform the Sign of the Enterer and the Sign of Silence, enflaming all four Hexagrams and the white line connecting them.

Come back to the centre of the Magickal circle now and face East. If you have a central altar, then stand behind it.

Formula 3: Tracing the Greater Hexagram in its respective quarter

If you have obtained a chart of the Heavens at the time of the working (either by constructing one yourself or finding one online), determine the position of Planet you have invoked (or banished) thus far. Then, turn to the quarter in which the physical Planet is located and perform the invoking (or banishing) Greater Hexagram of that Planet. You may do so by tracing the Earth Hexagram of the Planet in its corresponding colour while vibrating the Divine Name ARARITA.

Next, trace the Planet symbol in the middle of the Hexagram as you vibrate the Divine Name of its associated Sephira. The colour of the Planet symbol must be in its corresponding Tree of Life path colour (Atziluth) found in Table 3 of "The Qabalah" section. If you don't know what quarter of the Heavens the physical Planet is located, trace the Planet's symbol right in front of you. As you do this, you should be standing in the centre of your circle, facing East. Finally, enflame the Hexagram and the Planet symbol with the Sign of the Enterer. End with the Sign of Silence.

Formula 4: The Qabalistic Cross

Repeat the Qabalistic Cross in the centre of your circle (while facing East).

Formula 5: Perform the Analysis of the Keyword

Perform the Analysis of the Keyword as per the instructions given below. This completes the Ritual of the Hexagram.

ANALYSIS OF THE KEYWORD

The Analysis of the Keyword is given at this point in your Spiritual Alchemy process to be used as part of the Hexagram ritual exercise or an Enochian evocation. Its purpose is briefly taking on the Egyptian Deities associated with death and resurrection, which invokes a transmutation of the inner Self. This involves the transformation of the aspiring but imperfect human's Pentagram into the perfected and balanced Hexagram, metaphorically speaking.

The Keyword itself refers to the letters I.N.R.I., which is an essential acronym in Magick but also in Christianity and Judaism. The letters I.N.R.I. were placed above the head of Jesus Christ on the cross, and they stand for "Jesus Nazarenus Rex Judecorum," which translates as "Jesus of Nazareth, King of the Jews." I.N.R.I thus equates with the "Christ-Force," the redemptive, life/death/resurrection Archetype in the Universe. Within the Golden Dawn context, the Keyword also alludes to the sequence of the seasons of the year. These include the Equinoxes and Solstices.

The Keyword invokes the many names and images associated with this exercise. As part of the invocation, the Latin letters I.N.R.I. are followed by their Hebrew counterparts, Yod, Nun, Resh, and Yod. From the Qabalistic attributions of these letters (Tarot paths correspondences) are derived Virgo (Yod), Scorpio (Nun), Sol (Resh), and Virgo (Yod). These correspond to a trio of Egyptian Deities— Isis, Apophis (Set), and Osiris. These three Deities are the key figures in the Egyptian legend of the dying and resurrected God. The first letters of these Deity names form the name IAO, which is the Gnostic name of God. IAO can be said to represent nature's process of Creation, Destruction, and Resurrection (Rebirth).

The letter "I" (in I.N.R.I.) is the Sign of Virgo as Isis the Mighty Mother—representing the production of the seeds of fruit on Earth, which correspond with Spring and the generative, creative force of nature. The letter "N" is Scorpio as Apophis the Destroyer—the destructive power of nature that represents Winter. The letter "R" is Sol, which relates to Summer—the time of the year when nature is most fruitful and abundant, and the vitality of all living things is at its most optimal level.

The final "I" is Osiris Slain and Risen, which relates to Autumn—the time of the year when life in nature begins the process of slowly dying down, only to be reborn again in Spring of the following year. By pronouncing the Keyword, you are invoking the power of the Sun's Light, the nurturer of all living things, into your Aura.

As part of the Analysis of the Keyword are Magickal gestures which form the Latin word "lux," or LVX, meaning "Light." As you perform these Magickal gestures while making the given pronunciations, you align your consciousness with the cycle of death and rebirth of the Sun, including the Self in its quest for Spiritual Enlightenment. This process is one of continuous renewal and regeneration to obtain Spiritual perfection. These Magickal gestures (called LVX Signs within the Golden Dawn) are also associated with the Egyptian trio of Deities previously mentioned.

The LVX Signs are the Signs given in the Adeptus Minor Grade. At this level, you are attempting to embody the essence of Tiphareth, which includes the sacrifice of all imbalances and destructive impulses necessary to fully become One with the Spirit Element and the Higher Self.

The inner Self must be in perfect harmony before the Spirit can descend and transform the Soul. By using the Grade Signs associated with the Five Elements, you were working with the power of the Light in its different manifestations. With the LVX Signs, you are fully transforming your consciousness and becoming One with your Holy Guardian Angel, as is the nature of the work within the Adeptus Minor Grade.

Analysis of the Keyword

Formula 1: Invocation of I.N.R.I and I.A.O.
Extend your arms in the form of the Tav Cross, with your palms facing forward. Say the following acronym in English by pronouncing each letter with reverence:

"I.N.R.I"

Then vibrate:

Yooohd-Nooon-Rehhhsh-Yooohd

(Yod Nun Resh Yod)

As you vibrate the Hebrew letters, trace them in the air before you (at eye level) from right to left (Figure 55), using your hand or a ritual invoking tool. The letters should be in flaming blue, just like the Pentagrams.

יכני

Figure 55: I.N.R.I. in Hebrew: Yod, Nun, Resh, Yod (right to left)

Return to the Tav Cross position again and say with reverence:
"Virgo, Isis, Mighty Mother!
Scorpio, Apophis, Destroyer!
Sol, Osiris, Slain and Risen!
Isis, Apophis, Osiris!"

As you perform this oration, slowly raise your arms and head towards the sky. Once finished, vibrate:

Eeeeee-Aaahhh-Ooohhh

(IAO)

Formula 2: The L.V.X. Signs (Figure 56)
Return to the position of the Tav Cross and say:
"The Sign of Osiris Slain."

As you perform this Magickal gesture, contemplate the forces of the Equinox when the Light of the Sun and the darkness are equal in power.

Raise your right arm straight up in the air while holding your left arm in the same position as the previous gesture. The two arms should form a ninety-degree angle with open palms facing forward. Their position should resemble the letter "L." Now say with reverence:

"L, the Sign of the Mourning of Isis."

As you perform this gesture, contemplate the Summer Solstice, the time of the year when the Light of the Sun is most potent. This gesture should link you with the Life Force of Osiris.

Raise both arms now overhead to an angle of sixty degrees each. Both arms should be straight, and the palms should be facing forward. The position of the arms should form the letter "V." With this gesture, the head should go slightly back as you are gazing forward and upwards towards the sky. Now say with reverence:

"V, the Sign of Typhon and Apophis."

As you perform this gesture, contemplate the Winter Solstice, the time of the year when the darkness is most powerful.

Cross the arms on the chest with the right arm over the left, thereby forming the letter "X." As you do so, bow your head and say:

"X, the Sign of Osiris Risen."

As you perform this gesture, contemplate the forces of the Equinox and the Solstice, as both energies are present here. The duality of Light and darkness and their relationship create the cycles of life and death and the constant, perpetual regeneration of nature.

Now, repeat the last three Magickal gestures while spelling out each letter from the acronym L.V.X. as you make each gesture. Once you end in the Sign of Osiris Risen say:

Luuuux

(LUX)

Remain in the Sign of Osiris Slain (Tav Cross position) and say the following sentence with reverence:

"The Light…" (Hold arms out in the Tav Cross position while saying this part of the sentence.)

"….of the Cross." (As you say this second part of the sentence, recross your arms on the chest in the Sign of Osiris Risen)

Figure 56: The L.V.X. Signs

***

The Analysis of the Keyword is now complete. After performing this exercise, a powerful Solar energy current from the Astral Realm will be invoked into the Aura. Since this ritual exercise is to be used during a Planetary invocation or an Enochian evocation, continue with the next part of the formula of whatever exercise you are performing.

SPIRITUAL ALCHEMY PROGRAM II—THE SEVEN ANCIENT PLANETS

Since the Planets correspond with the Sephiroth, you will be working with each one systematically, starting from Yesod and moving upwards on the Tree of Life, up to Binah. It is crucial to integrate the powers of each Planet first before moving on to the next Planet. Planetary Magick continues the work done thus far with the Four Elements of Earth, Air, Water, and Fire, and the fifth Element of Spirit. This time, you are zeroing in even closer to the Archetypal forces that make up your psyche.

Invoking a specific Planet (on the hour its influence is maximized) will align you with its energy. As you become in harmony with a Planet's energy, you will be able to learn from it and use its power productively in your own life. Doing so will further make you a master of your destiny, as is the intended purpose of the work presented in *The Magus*.

Planetary hours are not the same as regular daily hours. The way you can determine a Planetary hour is to find the exact time between sunrise and sunset on a particular day (by looking online) and divide that time by twelve. In doing this, you will get the length of the Planetary hours of the day. To find the Planetary hours of the night, divide the time between sunset and sunrise by twelve. The hours of the day and night will be of different lengths, except on the Equinoxes. Use Tables 5 and 6 to find the Planetary hours of the day and night.

Regarding the program to be followed with Planetary invocations, you are only to concern yourself with the hour that a Planet corresponds with. Keep in mind that a Planetary invocation is most potent when a Planet is invoked on the day attributed to it as well as the hour. But since you will be working with one Planet at a time for an extended period, it is only essential that you invoke it during its corresponding hour.

The time that you are to work with each Planet is one month. In other words, you are to do invocations of a Planet as often as you want during the week, for four weeks. Also, the same rule applies as with the LIRPs and SIRP, where you are not to perform a Planetary invocation more than once per day. The banishings (LBRP and BRH) and Middle Pillar can be completed multiple times in a day.

The Spiritual Alchemy program to be followed when working with Planetary forces is not as strict as what you have been presented with so far with the Elements and the SIRP. If you decide you wish to work longer than one month with a Planet, then you may do so. To fully integrate the energy of a Planet, though, you should not work with it for less than one whole month.

You are to start with the Moon, invoking it once a day on its corresponding hour, for four weeks minimum. Employ the Ritual of the Hexagram (Lesser and Greater) to invoke it. Once you have accomplished this, you are to move on to invoking Mercury and do the same formula for one month. Then you are to move onto Venus, followed by the Sun, Mars, Jupiter, and Saturn. The Spiritual Alchemy program with the Planets should take a minimum of seven months to complete. Once you have completed it, you can move on to Enochian Magick unless you have already completed its program.

Keep in mind that you are now working with Adept-level ritual exercises, strictly reserved for the Inner Order of the Golden Dawn, within the Adeptus Minor curriculum. Although the SIRP was, in reality, an Adept-level ritual, it served primarily to bring you up to the level of Adept Spiritually so that you may be ready to work with

Planetary Magick and Enochian Magick. In the Golden Dawn, the SIRP is presented as part of the work of the Portal Grade—the contact point between the Inner and Outer Orders.

After completing the Spiritual Alchemy program with the SIRP, you will have integrated the Five Elements within your Being, thus operating from a higher level of consciousness. Do not be surprised if you channel information from higher realms while working with the Planets and Enochian Magick. If this happens, you have made contact with your Holy Guardian Angel, your Higher Self, the Eternal inner guide and teacher. You will learn a lot from your inner teacher, and your path of discovery concerning the Mysteries of the Universe has only truly begun.

Many Golden Dawn Orders teach their Adepts to use the SIRP daily as part of any major invocation, such as a Planetary one or even an Enochian one. This method is taught once the initiate has reached the Adeptus Minor grade and has officially become an Adept within the Order. The idea behind this method is that the SIRP invokes all five Elements; thus, it will enable the practitioner to be in the most balanced state of mind, body, and Soul before commencing with any major ritual invocations. Also, the SIRP serves as a launch pad into the Astral Realm, where all Magickal operations occur. Therefore, this method will enable you to integrate the energy of any major ritual invocation in the most optimal way possible.

In my personal experience, I have found that using the SIRP before working with a Planet can be an enlightening experience but can also cloud my mind so that I do not feel the Planetary energy as desired. On the other hand, I have found that using the SIRP once or twice a week and focusing on the daily Planetary invocations enabled me to best get in touch with a Planet's energy and learn from it.

However, feel free to experiment with both methods and see what works best for you. If you are having a hard time managing either, keep in mind that you can perform the SBRP or a banishing of a Planet to alleviate the effects of its energy. A large part of being the Magus is knowing when to add or subtract the desired energy to function at your most optimal state and tap into your highest potential throughout the day.

The discourse on the energy work with the Seven Ancient Planets is now complete. Whether you have chosen to work with Enochian Magick or the Planets first, once you have completed their prescribed Spiritual Alchemy program, move on to the second option. Once both options are complete, you can again start any operation presented so far and either follow the prescribed program or experiment with different daily invocations.

I have also included supplementary Magickal work for the Adept in the Appendix, which contains energy work with the potent Olympic Planetary Spirits. It is recommended that you wait until you have finished the Spiritual Alchemy program with the Seven Ancient Planets before starting with the Olympic Spirits. Doing so will give you better control over the Planetary energies as the Olympic Spirits are blind forces that can manifest positively or negatively, depending on what input you give them.

Use the extra material in the Appendix wisely, with care and caution. Remember, you can spend many years working with Ceremonial Magick since many years are needed to become an Enlightened Being and complete the Great Work.

TABLE 5: The Planetary Hours of the Day

Hour	Sunday	Monday	Tuesday	Wednesday	Thursday	Friday	Saturday
1	Sun	Moon	Mars	Mercury	Jupiter	Venus	Saturn
2	Venus	Saturn	Sun	Moon	Mars	Mercury	Jupiter
3	Mercury	Jupiter	Venus	Saturn	Sun	Moon	Mars
4	Moon	Mars	Mercury	Jupiter	Venus	Saturn	Sun
5	Saturn	Sun	Moon	Mars	Mercury	Jupiter	Venus
6	Jupiter	Venus	Saturn	Sun	Moon	Mars	Mercury
7	Mars	Mercury	Jupiter	Venus	Saturn	Sun	Moon
8	Sun	Moon	Mars	Mercury	Jupiter	Venus	Saturn
9	Venus	Saturn	Sun	Moon	Mars	Mercury	Jupiter
10	Mercury	Jupiter	Venus	Saturn	Sun	Moon	Mars
11	Moon	Mars	Mercury	Jupiter	Venus	Saturn	Sun
12	Saturn	Sun	Moon	Mars	Mercury	Jupiter	Venus

TABLE 6: The Planetary Hours of the Night

Hour	Sunday	Monday	Tuesday	Wednesday	Thursday	Friday	Saturday
1	Jupiter	Venus	Saturn	Sun	Moon	Mars	Mercury
2	Mars	Mercury	Jupiter	Venus	Saturn	Sun	Moon
3	Sun	Moon	Mars	Mercury	Jupiter	Venus	Saturn
4	Venus	Saturn	Sun	Moon	Mars	Mercury	Jupiter
5	Mercury	Jupiter	Venus	Saturn	Sun	Moon	Mars
6	Moon	Mars	Mercury	Jupiter	Venus	Saturn	Sun
7	Saturn	Sun	Moon	Mars	Mercury	Jupiter	Venus
8	Jupiter	Venus	Saturn	Sun	Moon	Mars	Mercury
9	Mars	Mercury	Jupiter	Venus	Saturn	Sun	Moon
10	Sun	Moon	Mars	Mercury	Jupiter	Venus	Saturn
11	Venus	Saturn	Sun	Moon	Mars	Mercury	Jupiter
12	Mercury	Jupiter	Venus	Saturn	Sun	Moon	Mars

PART V: THE KYBALION- HERMETIC PHILOSOPHY

INTRODUCTION TO THE KYBALION

The Kybalion: Hermetic Philosophy was initially published in 1908 by Yogi Publication Society by a person or persons under the pseudonym of the Three Initiates. The pages of this book contain the essence of Hermes Trismegistus's teachings on the nature of the Cosmos and the Laws that govern it. The ideas and philosophies contained in *The Kybalion* were so profound at the time that they became one of the founding pillars of the New Age movement in the early 1900s.

Interestingly, *The Kybalion* was published around the same time frame that the original Hermetic Order of the Golden Dawn was practising. Both had a profound influence on society and Spirituality at the time, the effect of which is still felt today.

Many speculations were made in the last century about the identity of the Three Initiates since they chose to remain anonymous. The most credible theory is that *The Kybalion* was authored by one man, William Walker Atkinson, who wrote under many different pseudonyms. Many of his works were published by Yogi Publication Society, of which he was the founder.

Another theory is that Atkinson co-wrote *The Kybalion* with Paul Foster Case and that Case was a Freemason since Yogi Publication Society gave its address as "Masonic Temple, Chicago IL" inside the book. Lastly, there are many theories about the third co-author; some even suggest it may have been a former member of the original Golden Dawn.

Whether William Walker Atkinson was the sole author of *The Kybalion* or co-wrote it with others will always remain a mystery. One thing is for sure, though; *The Kybalion* was and will forever remain one of the most critical and influential occult and esoteric books of all time. Its knowledge is Universal, which is why people have been naturally drawn to it since its inception.

Our society at the present moment is in dire need of the knowledge contained within *The Kybalion's* pages, for it alone can enlighten the mind like no other philosophy in the world. For this reason, I have decided to present its main body of teachings and tie them in with the Qabalah since the two philosophies go hand in hand.

I will be presenting *The Kybalion's* Principles of Creation along with new additions and commentary while relating this timeless Hermetic Philosophy to the Tree of Life and the Chakric system. My presentation of this work is highly comprehensive and modified to fit the needs, general understanding, and language of people in today's world.

As mentioned in the introduction to *The Magus*, these Hermetic Principles are so powerful that their use over a short period graced me with a full Kundalini awakening seventeen years ago. Since then, I have felt a calling from the Divine to bring my knowledge and experience with these Principles to the public so that others may get the same benefit.

Comprehending these Principles is paramount to understanding how we can be in charge of our reality. These are Mental Principles operating along the Mental Plane of existence. Your mind is the connecting link between Spirit and Matter, the Above and the Below. Your mind is also the muscle that needs to be exercised since you can access the inner Cosmic Planes that shape your reality through it. By controlling the internal functions of your mind, you can exert a level of control over your reality that you probably never thought was possible.

The Kybalion presents these Mental Principles that govern how we as human beings manifest in our physical reality. In essence, *The Kybalion* is the manual for mastering the Third Dimension of reality we partake in daily. It is a manual that teaches us how to use our physical bodies to project vibrations into the outside world that would allow us to be a cause instead of an effect. So, for us humans, it is a manual for life itself.

These Principles will give you the framework for how aspects of your inner Self, such as willpower, imagination, memory, inspiration, emotion, desire, logic and reason, work together. With this knowledge, you can take hold of their inner workings to influence reality and the people around you.

Many people, more or less, use these Principles subconsciously. However, comprehending these Principles allows you to use them consciously and with intent and purpose. This knowledge goes hand in hand with everything presented so far about the Qabalah and the Tree of Life since the common aim is to increase your personal power and make you a master of your destiny.

By learning and mastering these Principles of Creation, you invariably obtain governance over your mentality, synonymous with the Sephira Hod, since this Sephira deals with the mind and its power. It is no wonder Mercury, or Hermes is attributed to the Sephira Hod since he is the Roman and Greek God of logic, reason, and primarily the intellect. *The Kybalion* is, after all, a work on the Hermetic Philosophy and mastering the Mental Plane of reality.

The Physical World is a concrete version of the World of Pure Energy, called the Fourth Dimension, the Dimension of Vibration. These Principles operate in this Dimension of Vibration and explain how you can raise your vibration levels to influence the world around you. Knowing these Principles and applying them is the true "Scepter of Power," as stated in *The Kybalion*.

THE WISDOM OF HERMES TRISMEGISTUS

Hermes Trismegistus, otherwise known as the "Scribe of the Gods," is said to be the founder of *The Kybalion* Principles. He lived during the oldest dynasties of Egypt, long before the days of Moses, and was considered by the world to be the "Great Central Sun of Occultism." His wisdom was grand beyond measure, bringing to light the countless teachings that came before his time.

Some scholars regard Hermes as the contemporary of Abraham and claim that Abraham acquired a large portion of his mystical knowledge from him. Yet others claim a connection between Hermes and Enoch and say that one may have been a reincarnation of the other.

All the fundamental teachings found in all esoteric and religious sects are said to be able to be traced back to Hermes Trismegistus. According to legend, many Sages, Yogis, and Adepts travelled from different parts of the world to the land of Egypt. Their mission was to sit at the feet of the Master, Hermes, whom they believed could give them the Master-Key, which reconciled their divergent viewpoints about the Universe and human life. In this way, the Secret Doctrine of the Cosmos was firmly established.

Hermes was called the "Master of Masters" and was the father of occult wisdom. He was the founder of Astrology and the discoverer of Alchemy. His knowledge and wisdom were so far above the rest of the people in the world that the Egyptians deified him and made him one of their Gods—Thoth, the God of Wisdom. Years after, Greeks in the Ptolemaic Kingdom of Egypt also made him one of their twelve Olympian Gods, calling him Hermes by his real name. Soon after the Romans took over Egypt, they syncretized their religion with the Greek religion and referred to Hermes as Mercury (Figure 57).

HERMES/MERCURY **HERMES TRISMEGISTUS** **THOTH**

Figure 57: The Forms of Hermes

The Egyptians revered Hermes' memory for many centuries as he brought all things esoteric and occult to light with his wisdom and shone his lamp in areas which otherwise were unknown. They are the ones that gave him his Ancient title, Trismegistus, which means the "Thrice Great," the "Great-Great," and the "Greatest-

Great." The name of Hermes Trismegistus was revered in all the lands; his name became synonymous with the "Fount of Wisdom."

Hermes was considered the most exceptional World Teacher, and a few Adepts that came after him, including Jesus Christ, are considered by many scholars to be his reincarnation. They believe that the Spirit of Hermes incarnates approximately every 2000 years as the World Teacher to enlighten the world in Spiritual, religious, philosophical, and psychological areas by bringing forth a modern language to teach about the Spirit and God, reconciling all divergent viewpoints.

Students of comparative religions will be able to see the influence of the Hermetic teachings in every religion, whether a dead one or one fully active today. Hermetic teachings serve as the Great Reconciler to all religious thoughts and beliefs. However, his work was to establish a great Seed-Truth instead of creating a new religion. He recognized that religion often leads people astray Spiritually since it can be used for political gain; thus, he sought to keep his philosophy pure.

Wisdom was his driving force to give men and women the keys to being their own teachers and Masters. His great Seed-Truths were handed down by the revered Sages of the time from "lips to ear", and there have always been a few alive initiates in each generation who kept the sacred flame of the Hermetic teachings burning. By this method, has this Hermetic wisdom been passed down. But as tradition holds, they kept these "pearls of wisdom" reserved only for the select few because they believed that wisdom could not be received unless the listener's capacity for understanding is satisfactory.

The Ancient teachers always warned against allowing the Secret Doctrine to become crystallized into a creed or religion because, in this way, it would lose its life, its Spirit. Therefore, whenever the Hermetic wisdom was written down, it was veiled in terms of Alchemy and Astrology so that only those who possessed the keys could read it. To this day, there aren't many books on Hermetic Philosophy, yet it is the only Master Key that will open the doors of all the occult teachings and reconcile all religions.

In the early days, there existed a compilation of certain basic Hermetic doctrines, passed on from teacher to student, known as *The Kybalion.* The word's exact meaning has been lost in antiquity, but many scholars say it correlates with the Qabalah since the two words are similar in sound and the essence of their philosophy. This teaching has descended from "mouth to ear" and was never printed, which was also how the true Qabalah was taught.

The Kybalion was simply a collection of maxims, axioms, and precepts, which were non-understandable to outsiders but readily understood by students of Hermeticism. These Principles constituted the fundamental Principles of the Art of Hermetic Alchemy, which dealt with the mastery of Mental Forces and transmuting/transforming mental vibrations.

This type of Alchemy dealt not with turning physical lead into gold. It was a Spiritual one, and this was the secret. Referring to the transmutation of metals from one form to the next was an allegory veiled to the profane but readily understood by the initiates of the Hermetic mysteries. This legend became known in the old days as the quest for the "Philosopher's Stone."

The Magus aims to bring to light these maxims, axioms, and precepts and give you the Master Key that will enable you to gain the wisdom and understanding necessary to master your mental and emotional states.

By knowing the workings of these Universal Principles, you will become a master of your destiny and will maximize your personal power.

"The lips of Wisdom are closed, except to the ears of Understanding." — "The Kybalion"

On the Tree of Life, the title of Chokmah is "Wisdom," while Binah is "Understanding." These are the two highest aspects of duality that humans partake in. They are our Supernals, the Spirit energy within us that was never born and will never die. They are connected to Sahasrara Chakra, corresponding with the Kether Sephira and uniting us with the realm of Non-Duality, the Great White Light that underlies all existence. One cannot have wisdom without having understanding and vice versa.

"Where fall the footsteps of the Master, the ears of those ready for his teaching open wide." — "The Kybalion"

The Master is your own Holy Guardian Angel. It is that part of you that is God-the Creator. The wisdom of the entire Universe is contained within you. Once you are ready to receive it, the Master will activate and channel his (her) knowledge into your Soul. You need to have the ears of understanding prepared to receive it, meaning you need to bring your Spiritual Evolution to a sufficient level before this can occur. This method of learning about the Mysteries of the Universe falls in line with the following axiom from *The Kybalion*:

"When the ears of the student are ready to hear, then cometh the lips to fill them with Wisdom." — "The Kybalion"

The entire purpose of our existence on Earth is Spiritual Evolution. As such, the impulse to learn about the Mysteries of the Universe is encoded within our DNA. Through our DNA, we can connect to our Higher Self to progress Spiritually. Our undying quest for immortality corresponds with our pursuit of Enlightenment. Through one, we achieve the other.

THE SEVEN PRINCIPLES OF CREATION

"The Principles of Truth are Seven; he who knows these, understandingly, possesses the Magic Key before whose touch all the Doors of the Temple fly open." — "The Kybalion"

I. PRINCIPLE OF MENTALISM

The Principle of Mentalism contains the ultimate truth that The All, which is the substantial reality underlying everything we see and perceive in the material world on Earth (the physical Universe), is, in fact, Spirit. Qabalistically, Kether, the White Light, the Spirit energy, is the substance comprising Malkuth, the manifested Earth.

This Spirit is undefinable by the human capacity but can be considered as the Infinite, Universal, Living Mind. It is a thought projected from God-the Creator. This Thought of God is "God's Dream World" as it is a mental creation contained within its Infinite Living Mind. As such, it is subject to the Principles of Creation, which are mental in nature, since the entire Universe is also a mental creation. In the Infinite, Living Mind of God, we live, move, and have our Being.

"The ALL is MIND; the Universe is Mental." — "The Kybalion"

Once you have grasped the Principle of Mentalism (that everything is mental), you can apply the Mental Laws to your wellbeing and become a master of your destiny and Spiritual advancement. Some individuals will have a full Kundalini awakening once they have grasped the concept of "The All is Mind, the Universe is Mental" because it is the Master Key that opens up the doors of the Inner Temple and inner, Cosmic Planes.

Understanding physical reality as something mental in your head will stimulate a part of you that can remove you from the shackles of the Ego, allowing your Soul to soar into the Light, unfettered.

Once you grasp that the Universe is simply a mental creation and you can create through thought, you will be able to reduce the inner chatter of the Ego to nothingness. We give the Ego power by listening to its opinions, often projected from our involuntary, subconscious mind. With the realization that thought is something that can be controlled and re-created, we can access our subconscious mind to nullify our past thoughts and renew our minds with new ideas, concepts, and beliefs. In doing so, the Ego will drop away and lose power over consciousness. Once the Ego is neutralized, the consciousness will naturally elevate to the highest level, the level of Spirit.

Since we were given the ability to dream and are made in the Creator's image, our waking life is also but a dream, higher in degree than our own dreams, although made of the same mental substance. This concept is best explained with the Principle of Vibration and its various rates or degrees of vibration that comprise everything in the Inner and Outer Universe.

Everything in existence is made up of the same energy—Spirit. However, all things differ in degrees of vibration, giving us many interpenetrating realities, all existing simultaneously and occupying the same space. As such, we have the various inner, Cosmic Planes and levels of Being, which we as humans partake of.

Qabalistically, this is how the Sephiroth were manifested into existence. Kether, the Spiritual Light, is on one end of the extreme, and Malkuth, the physical Universe, is on the other end. In between are the Sephiroth, representing the varying states of consciousness, all vibrating at different frequencies but all interpenetrating and occupying the same Space/Time.

As a "Dream of God," Matter is not real, and we can activate the part of our imagination to perceive its illusion, to remove us from the bonds of past conditioning. In doing so, we step into the "Now"—the present moment. There is a close relationship between the Now and the Spirit energy. Being in the Now will enable you to tap into the field of Pure Potentiality where anything is possible, and you can manifest your dreams by unleashing your highest potential as a Spiritual human being.

Our mind can then become the vehicle that will activate our Spiritual counterpart, our Body of Light, by raising the Kundalini energy to the Crown and awakening us to our ultimate reality. The Holy Guardian Angel, the Higher Self, is the part of you that resonates with the highest Spiritual energy frequency. A Kundalini awakening starts the process of aligning with this frequency over time as your mind becomes raised to its lofty height. Once your consciousness fully attunes to the Spirit, you can perceive the world around you as what it is—Pure Energy.

As we were made in the image of God or "The All," and we create mentally first before putting forth any actions and generating events in the material world, does it not make sense that "The All is Mind, the Universe is Mental?" Stop right here and think and meditate on this concept for five to ten minutes.

Begin the exercise by simply looking around you, imagining that the Physical World is merely a mental creation, a manifestation of thought. Instead of being something separate from you, it is part of you as an extension of your mentality. As you look outwards into this reality, you are, in fact, looking at the back of your head where all visual images from your mind manifest. However, the Outer World exists in a degree of reality that is higher than your mind's contents since the "thought stuff" has solidified into what we call Matter.

Try to blur the lines between your imagination and the Physical World. It helps to unfocus your eyes so you can take in more of your surroundings than usual, primarily through peripheral vision. Though, you are seeing it all as one image, like a postcard, without focusing on one thing or another.

Imagine, if you will, that you are in a video game or "The Matrix," how would this reality look? The Outer World would no longer be something concrete and tangible but have a "thought" component to its makeup, making it appear tenuous, insubstantial, and ethereal.

By piercing the Veil of Maya with this exercise, don't be surprised if you begin to see the Universe's Holographic nature, which appears digital to those who can go in deep with this meditation. Contemplate and hold this vision of the physical reality, which by Hermetic definition is nothing more than a thought projection from an infinite, omnipresent, Divine Being we refer to as God.

Next, ask yourself who you are, and remind yourself that you are not real and that the world around you is simply a mind-trick. Notice how you feel as you do this. There should be a letting-go process within you where the Ego starts getting detached from what it thinks it is looking at. And if you do this exercise correctly, it can be a life-changing experience.

As we were created, we create—mentally. And, as we think, so we are THOUGHT. Conversely, before a person performs any action in the Physical World, they must have first had the thought of doing that thing; otherwise, their bodies remain motionless in Space/Time.

As for people who do not generate their own thoughts due to laziness of the mind, they rely on others to think for them, often unconsciously. As a result, these people will carry out the ideas of others, thinking they are their own. Therefore, people must take responsibility for their reality and use their willpower consciously and with intent if they want to be in control of their life.

As you continue reading this section on *The Kybalion*, I will present you with the keys to living in a state of pure potential, the Now, enabling you to generate any reality you desire, thus becoming a master of your destiny. To tap into your personal power, you must be aware of the Principles and use them consciously instead of being used by them by remaining ignorant of their existence.

At any moment in time, we as human beings can think and believe that we are famous actors, dancers, writers, artists, or whoever and whatever we ever wanted to be. When we realize the mental nature of the Universe, this reality can start to take place.

The Principle of Mentalism is the key to becoming anything you want to be in this lifetime. The other Principles will not work unless you grasp this most important Principle since it is their foundation. An old Hermetic Master wrote long ago that one must understand the mental nature of the Universe if they wish to advance Spiritually. Without this Master Key, mastery is impossible, and the student knocks in vain at the many doors of the Inner Temple.

"He who grasps the truth of the Mental Nature of the Universe is well advanced on The Path to Mastery." — "The Kybalion"

Mental Transmutation

Hermeticists were the original Alchemists, Astrologers, and psychologists, with Hermes having been the founder of these schools of thought. From Astrology has grown modern astronomy; from Alchemy has grown modern chemistry; from the mystic psychology has grown modern psychology. But their greatest possession of knowledge was the art of Mental Transmutation. It is a significant subject matter for us to look into further as it will give you the key to mastering your own life.

"Mind (as well as metals and Elements) may be transmuted, from state to state; degree to degree; condition to condition; pole to pole; vibration to vibration. True Hermetic Transmutation is a Mental Art." — "The Kybalion"

The word "transmute" means to "change from one nature, form or substance, into another; to transform." Therefore, Mental Transmutation implies the art of changing and transforming mental states, forms, and conditions into other ones. It is the most significant key a person can have in becoming the Master of his (her) destiny.

According to the first Principle of Mentalism, "The All is Mind, the Universe is Mental;" meaning that the underlying reality of the Universe is mind, and the Universe itself is a mental creation. Mental Transmutation, then, is the art of changing the conditions of the Universe along the lines of Matter, Force, and mind. It is the Magick that the Ancients have talked about but gave so few instructions on.

If The All is Mental, then by proxy, it means that Mental Transmutation is the tool whereby the Master can transmute mental conditions and thus be a controller of material conditions. In my experience, it is possible to do so, although you would have to generate an immense amount of willpower, which, even to most Masters, is a feat that is nearly impossible to do. Almost impossible, but not impossible.

The stories of Jesus Christ turning water into wine, raising the dead, and walking on water are examples of humans accomplishing supernatural feats. However, as mentioned, one must generate immense, seemingly otherworldly willpower to affect material conditions. As such, there have only been a few Masters in antiquity that could accomplish such feats. According to the scriptures, Moses was another Adept with incredible mental powers that could affect material conditions.

One thing that both Jesus and Moses had in common was that they were directly connected to God and regularly had dialogue with the Creator. Perhaps that is why they could perform miracles—their willpower was aligned with God's. So, in theory, if you desire to affect physical reality, you must raise your consciousness so high that you become the very "Thought of God," enabling you to make a change or alter its manifestation, which is the World of Matter.

For the average person, it is better to focus on how they can master their mental states and themselves instead of seeking to alter the laws of physics. For example, most people want to fly but haven't even begun to learn how to walk. Regardless, this Principle operates on all Planes of Life. Its knowledge gives us the key to understanding the mechanics of how the supernatural feats written about in scriptures were performed.

You must understand that all that we call psychic phenomena, mental influence, and mental science operate along the same general lines since there is but one Principle involved, no matter by what name the phenomena is called. Having said that, tread carefully since Mental Transmutation can be used for good but also evil, as per the Principle of Polarity.

The Karmic effects of using this power for evil are always present and cannot be escaped. For example, if you use Mental Transmutation for evil, you will become evil's accomplice and suffer as a result of that action on the Plane of Being corresponding with where the Karma took place. This power is the true wizardry that is read about in books and seen in movies. However, the quality of one's heart and Soul determines whether they use it to advance Spiritually or merely satisfy the Ego's insatiable desires.

"The possession of Knowledge, unless accompanied by a manifestation and expression in Action, is like the hoarding of precious metals—a vain and foolish thing. Knowledge, like wealth, is intended for Use. The Law of Use is Universal, and he who violates it suffers by reason of his (her) conflict with natural forces." — "The Kybalion"

Once you have learned the Mental Laws, you are beyond the stage of ignorance, and it is the duty that you owe to yourself to use them. If you learn this knowledge, comprehend it, and then neglect it and go back to your old ways, you will suffer as a consequence because these Principles were meant to be used. Everything that is learned on your journey in life that is positive for your Spiritual advancement needs to be respected and applied. This knowledge is real; this knowledge can change your life; and this knowledge can raise you from slavery to materialism into the Adepthood of Light if you spend the time to learn, integrate, and use these Principles.

II. PRINCIPLE OF CORRESPONDENCE

The Principle of Correspondence states that correspondence exists between the Hermetic Principles and manifestation on the various Cosmic Planes of Being. There are Planes beyond our knowing, but when we apply the Principle of Correspondence to them, we can understand much that would otherwise be unknowable to us. Always remember, we use this Principle, and other Principles, through the mind, as it is our vehicle into the Unknown. This Principle operates on all Planes of the material, emotional, mental, and Spiritual Universe. It is a Universal Law.

"As Above, So Below; As Below, So Above." — "The Kybalion"

As mentioned, there are many Planes of Being, all occupying the same Space and Time but different in vibration, overlapping one another. The Planes of Being are synonymous with the Cosmic Planes, which, as mentioned before, are states of consciousness. The Principle of Correspondence enables us to understand the workings of the inner, Cosmic Planes through correspondence with our Plane, the Physical Plane of Matter. Correspondence between the Planes is always in full effect on all levels of vibration.

You can manifest any reality you want in your mind by using the Principle of Correspondence and experience it like it is as real as you and me. The method is to imagine anything you desire to experience, and by raising your power of belief, you will tap into the World of Pure Spirit, which then transposes onto the physical reality through your imagination. Thus, what you imagine, you start to experience as being real.

For example, you can imagine you are a different organic Being, whether a real one or merely imaginary, and by raising your power of belief, you will begin to embody this Being's essence, its energy. Now you cannot imagine you are a snake, let's say, and become one physically, but you could, with the power of belief, tap into the Spirit of the snake and transpose what it feels like to be a snake into your own experience.

By using these Mental Laws, you cannot change the laws of physics and shift your organic form into another. In theory, it is possible once a high enough state of consciousness is reached, but it will not do you any good to focus on that goal at the present moment. To better understand the power of the Hermetic Principles, the idea of imagining something into existence is to feel and embody its Spirit. Since everything in nature is made up of Spirit energy, by envisioning something and inducing your emotions with this image, you change the state of your perception of reality.

The knowledge of the Principles of Mentalism and Correspondence reduces any past conditioning to nothing more than an interpretation of past events through one "lens," or one level of perception. To some extent, past events are a figment of the imagination, considering that you imagined those events as being perceived in one way. In reality, there are many lenses through which we can view reality. We condition our Egos in this way, and over time, the Ego becomes an individual intelligence guiding our consciousness.

Even the Ego is not real but exists due to interpreting reality as a singularity. There are, at any moment, many different lenses available, giving rise to countless potential realities. Here is where we get the idea of parallel realities or Universes. To the experiencer, some lenses perceive reality in a positive way and some in a negative way. The choice is up to us at any given moment. In this way, we condition our Ego and its likes and dislikes. Realizing that the mind has the power to overcome these limitations will provide you with the key to manifesting any reality you desire instead of the one you have been conditioned to experience thus far.

"As Above, So Below" manifests on all Planes of existence. The nature of reality is that we live in the Infinite Living Mind—the Spirit. This Spirit energy pours in through the Sphere of Kether, the Sahasrara Chakra, and it comes into the Aura as Light, emanating all the Inner Planes, or states of consciousness, through the other eight Sephiroth of the Tree of Life, before culminating as Matter in Malkuth.

So, the Four Elements, which can be further broken down into the Seven Planetary energies and Twelve Zodiacal energies, are all contained within the Spirit energy. They manifest physically as our Solar System with our Sun in the centre and the Zodiacal constellations in the night sky as the energies that influence us. These energies comprise the powers of the Four Elements, with the unifying glue—the Spirit. The Five Elements of

Earth, Air, Water, Fire and Spirit comprise all of nature, the Inner and Outer Cosmic Planes. But it is the Spirit which manifests the Elements since it is their very Source. And that Source of all things is God-the Creator.

"As Above, So Below" is the most important of the occult truths and Hermetic axioms because it is the means whereby we can create realities on one Plane of existence, which will, in turn, affect the other Planes below it. Again, these different Planes all exist in the same Space at the same Time, although at varying levels or degrees of vibration. They all exist within the Fourth Dimension of Vibration, otherwise called the "Dimension of Energy."

The permanent awakening of the Kundalini fully activates the Body of Light, through which we can receive vibrations from the Fourth Dimension and access any of the Inner Planes at will. For this reason, Kundalini awakened individuals are the highest level of empaths and telepaths. They relate to the world through vibratory frequencies of energy. As such, they operate entirely on intuition. It is the destiny of all humankind to function in this way, which is why the Kundalini awakening is the next step in human evolution.

Again, I will emphasise that the key to manifesting the Hermetic Principles is the power of belief. If you can get yourself to believe what is being said is real, as real as the person you see in the mirror, you can tap into these Principles and start using them. But, on the other hand, if you do not believe in these Principles, you will not be able to accomplish anything with them.

The Ego holds us back from tapping into the pure potential of the Spirit by confusing us into believing that we are it and only it. Yet, the power of belief is the key to unlocking the mysteries of the mind and manifesting any reality you desire. Through understanding these Principles and accessing the power of the mind, you will be able to re-condition yourself to believe whatever you want about who you are and feel however you choose to about life.

Conversely, if you cannot get yourself to believe these Principles are real, they will remain nothing but mere words for you. Therefore, if you are having a hard time trusting that these Hermetic Principles are authentic and the power of your mind in shaping reality, then spend more time trying to understand the big picture and its various parts. In other words, keep reading and re-reading the intellectual components of *The Magus* until you "get it."

III. PRINCIPLE OF VIBRATION

The Principle of Vibration embodies facts which modern science endorses. Regularly, there are new scientific discoveries that verify this Principle. Quantum physics states that Matter is nothing more than empty space. For example, when it comes to a material object that we see as being "real," once we zoom into its molecules, we find that it is nothing other than electrons, protons, and neutrons held in vibratory motion by "something." This "something" that makes the whole Universe vibrate is The All or God/Spirit energy.

> *"Nothing rests; everything moves; everything vibrates." — "The Kybalion"*

Everything vibrates and can, therefore, be induced or affected by applying the Hermetic Principles. In addition, everything is quantifiable and can be broken down into a number. That number varies according to the subject that is perceiving the number. Quantum physics states that nothing remains as it is for very long, that everything is continuously changing, and that we cannot look at a thing without changing its molecular structure.

Our minds are constantly changing the nature of the Universe around us, as are other environmental factors. An important thing to get from this is that everything is in vibratory motion, and nothing is static. Everything is vibrating, moving, and affecting everything else. Everything in nature is essentially consciousness, and for humanity, our minds are the vehicles for its experience.

The Principle of Vibration states that the only difference between Matter and Spirit is a varying rate of vibration and that the higher the vibration of something is, the higher it is on the scale. The vibration of Spirit is at such a tremendous rate of intensity and rapidity that it is practically at rest; hence, it is invisible to our senses. An analogy to this concept is a rapidly moving wheel that seems to appear motionless, but in fact, it is not. And at the other end of the scale, there are gross forms of Matter whose vibrations are so low that they seem at rest. But, between these poles, there are millions upon millions of varying degrees of vibration.

For humans, these various vibratory states are broken down into the Major Cosmic Planes and their Sub-Planes, which are expressed through the Chakras. As mentioned before, there are six Cosmic Planes of Being: the Physical, Lower and Higher Astral, Lower and Higher Mental, and Spiritual. Then there are Divine Planes beyond the Spiritual Plane. These Planes influence and affect one another according to the Principle of Correspondence. So, for example, what manifests in the Plane above filters and affects the Planes below, and vice versa.

However, the Higher Planes are less affected by the Lower Planes, and this aspect of the Universal Laws is used to perform the "Art of Neutralization" or "Rising on the Planes." I will discuss this concept more in the following Principle of Polarity.

Our mental states, including our willpower and emotions, are at varying degrees of vibration, manifested through the Inner Planes. By understanding how the Principle of Vibration works, you receive the key to controlling your mental vibrations, including those of others. This method is the basis of the art of Mental Transmutation.

> *"To change your mood or mental state, change your vibration." — "The Kybalion"*

You change your vibrations by polarizing yourself in any emotion or thought and holding your attention there through applied willpower and concentration. In doing so, you are neutralizing the effect of the Principle of Rhythm and altering its movement. As a result, the pendulum starts to swing back in the opposite direction towards any emotion or thought you are trying to create and re-create in yourself. It may seem challenging at first, but all that is required of you is to focus your attention and hold in your mind, uninterrupted, the polar opposite emotion or thought of the one you are trying to change.

For example, if you are trying to change the emotion (or thought) of hate into love, you must focus on the idea of love by applying your willpower. Focused willpower starts the backward swing of the pendulum until you notice that the emotion (or thought) of hate has become the emotion (or thought) of love. To accomplish this more successfully, before starting this process, it would help to reason with yourself why you should love someone or something instead of hating them and allow that reason to raise your power of belief so that you can be more effective with this method.

Interestingly, the desired emotion (or thought) will influence all people around you so that they now will feel it or think it as well. However, suppose people already have their own strong emotions or thoughts about something. In that case, you will not be able to entirely change theirs through energy induction, although you will influence them to a high degree.

We are all communicating telepathically since only 7% of communication between humans is verbal. The other 93% is subtle, through body language, which reflects what the mind thinks, and the heart feels. The Principle of Vibration is what produces the phenomena of telepathy, or mental influence, and other forms of the power of mind over mind. I will discuss the workings of this process in more detail as we get further into the other Principles. But, for now, understand that this power is real and that with knowledge, you can use this power as well.

IV. PRINCIPLE OF POLARITY

The Principle of Polarity explains that everything in nature is dual and has two poles or extremes. These extreme poles are different in degree, but their substance, their quality, is the same. All subjective viewpoints can be reconciled since everything is and isn't at the same time.

Everything we perceive visually has an Archetypal structure, giving us the subject on which we apply our past conditioned minds. For instance, you can say that a cup is a cup, but how two people see that cup will be different. One may see a small cup, and the other may see a big cup. Their reference points will differ, but both people will agree that it is a cup.

The Principle of Polarity states that we will be talking about the same thing but that our perception of that thing will be different. In Qabalistic terms, we all agree at the level of the First World of Atziluth, the World of Archetypal Fire. However, once this Archetype filters downwards, our Ego perception takes over, and we naturally choose one side of the extreme.

"Everything is Dual; everything has poles; everything has its pair of opposites; like and unlike are the same; opposites are identical in nature, but different in degree; extremes meet; all truths are but half-truths; all paradoxes may be reconciled." — "The Kybalion"

The famous saying in society is, "There are two sides to everything," or, "Two sides of the coin." These statements are both true since everything in our Physical World is a matter of perspective. And that perspective depends on the past conditioning of the person making the observation. Only unconditioned children see things similar to one another, and this is because their Ego has not developed yet. For them, everything is perceived through innocent eyes and wonder.

The workings of the Principle of Polarity also manifest in our mental and emotional states. For example, when we look at our most basic emotions of love and hate concerning other people, at which point does love end and hate begin? Is there a fine line, or do things blend into one another? Often we find ourselves turning from love to hate and vice versa many times in a day when thinking about someone or something.

Hot and cold is another simple example to explain mental perception. For someone born in Alaska, Canadian weather might be considered very warm, while someone born in Africa would consider Canadian weather freezing and unbearable. It is all just a matter of perspective of the two extreme poles. These poles manifest in everything, and how we experience them is always a matter of perspective. Something that is considered a positive experience for one person is a negative experience for another—perspective.

The Principle of Polarity is essential in understanding the workings of the Universal Laws. Everything we perceive as humans in the Physical World belongs to duality. Hence, we see everything in dual terms, and it is so that we can have different perspectives, giving rise to diversity in humanity. Some views we agree on, some we do not. I am mentioning here the mental and emotional interpretations of these polar extremes, but the same Principle manifests on all Planes.

In terms of the Physical World, is there a fine line that separates black and white, sharp and dull, hard and soft, noise and silence, or high and low? All pairs of opposing viewpoints are manifestations of one idea with varying degrees of vibration between them. And this perspective gives us the mental construct to make interpretations of the world around us.

Concerning mental forces, knowing how this Principle operates gives us the ability to change the vibrations of one emotion or thought in our mind into another, including the minds of others. We accomplish this by using focused willpower and applying the Principle of Polarity, which constitutes the basis of Mental Alchemy. I discussed this method in the previous Principle of Vibration. This Principle works with the Principle of Polarity but also the Principle of Rhythm. Transforming emotions or thoughts into opposites requires using all three Principles. As you polarize yourself on the feeling (or thought) that you are trying to induce in yourself (or another person), and by focusing your willpower and attention on that idea for a short duration of time, you start to feel the old emotion (or thought) transforming into the new one.

Another important application of the Principle of Polarity deals with learning to be in the Now, the present moment. Since all life events can be perceived as positive or negative, the key to staying in the Now is the proper application of the Principle of Polarity. We cannot control what happens to us in life, but we have a choice regarding how we want to interpret that event. By controlling the interpretation, we enable ourselves to stay in the realm of no-thought, which is the realm of pure potential—the Now. To accomplish this, you must align with the Higher Self and interpret everything from the viewpoint of learning lessons in life. If you can see everything that happens in life as a learning experience for the Soul, you can avoid Ego interpretations, which will allow you to stay in the Now and feel the joy and rapture of living your life to its fullest.

In a way, all of the Hermetic Principles of Creation come together to form a Grand Principle which one can say is simply the Law of Duality, but really, it is so much more. Still, thinking of everything in terms of ones and twos will create a mental construct that will unravel the world around you like a flower and open you up to it in ways you have never imagined. Thinking in this way will enable you to apply opposite viewpoints when needed so that you don't get stuck in one extreme long enough for it to become a part of your past conditioning. By doing so, you will be in the "zone," in the Now, riding every wave that life throws before you.

Because our essence is constantly in vibratory motion and affecting each other's mental and emotional states just by being in each other's presence, we can use these Principles on ourselves. In turn, the people around us will also be affected by our newfound thoughts and emotions as we project our vibrations and affect their Auras. All of life is a game, a play. The game's foundation is called Energy, and that Energy is Spirit—the Infinite Living Mind.

V. PRINCIPLE OF RHYTHM

This Hermetic Principle embodies the truth that in everything, there is a measured motion, a swing backwards and forwards (a pendulum-like movement), between the two poles that exist under the Principle of Polarity. Every action is followed by a reaction, every advance by a retreat, and every rising by a sinking.

"Everything flows out and in; everything has its tides; all things rise and fall; the pendulum-swing manifests in everything; the measure of the swing to the right is the measure of the swing to the left; rhythm compensates." — "The Kybalion"

This Principle operates on all Planes of existence—from the Physical to the Astral, Mental, and Spiritual Plane. This Law is manifest in the creation and destruction of civilizations and the birth and death of all living things. Everything that has two poles, or two extremes, will manifest this Principle. Everything that has a beginning will inevitably have an end.

For humans living on the Physical Plane of materialism, everything we can experience with our five senses will manifest this Principle. Someone with a high level of enjoyment also has a high level of suffering. In the same way, he who feels a small amount of pain is capable of experiencing a small amount of joy. This Principle also applies to past lives. Therefore, if you were experiencing a great deal of pain in a previous life, then you may experience a great deal of pleasure in the present one or vice versa.

The Hermeticists concerned themselves most with the application of this Principle in their mental and emotional states. They would apply the Mental Law of Neutralization, otherwise called the "Rising on the Planes," to escape the effects of undesired states. Although the Principle of Rhythm cannot be destroyed, it can be overcome. The key is to learn to live in the Now. By living in the present moment, you are training your mind to continuously rise above the Plane where the Principle of Rhythm is manifesting. That is the key.

Regarding the mental and emotional Planes, the Principle of Rhythm is closely aligned with Ego perceptions. Experiencing a positive emotion, for example, will attract adverse thought senders (Demons) to the Ego to take hold of the consciousness and transform the feeling into a negative one. The Principle of Rhythm will always manifest, but its manifestation is dependent on time. Some things take less time, and some take more time to transform their state. But inevitably, everything changes into its opposite.

To be clear, the Mental Law of Neutralization is the "Rising on the Planes" to neutralize the effects of the Principle of Rhythm. This mental art is different from the willful changing of one type of emotion or thought into its opposite by applying the Principle of Vibration. This second art is called Mental Transmutation. Both mental techniques, though, use willpower to accomplish their goal. Both are also either using or overcoming the Principle of Rhythm. Emotions or thoughts can be willfully changed into their opposite, or time can be the determining factor in achieving this naturally since the Principle of Rhythm will always manifest, no matter what.

Mental Transmutation involves using the Principle of Vibration and transforming one mental or emotional state into another through the application of willpower. All thoughts and emotions have vibrational frequencies; therefore, we use willpower like a Tuning Fork to change vibrations into opposite frequencies. As our consciousness can only be tuned into the vibration of one of the inner Cosmic Planes at one time, the Law of Neutralization, or "Rising on the Planes," is the art of willful attention and concentration on a Higher Plane to raise the consciousness to its level. Focused attention and concentration raise the vibration of willpower, which is then magnetised and capable of performing mental feats.

As mentioned before, your Ego perceptions will determine how you interpret reality and which of the parallel, infinite realities it chooses to accept as a singularity. If you train your mind to live in the Now, you will naturally neutralise the effects of the Pendulum of Rhythm in your mental and emotional states. The Ego perceptions and emotions it triggers are involuntary in most cases since your past conditioning chooses which of the infinite realities it wants to accept as real.

Your Ego conditioning is closely aligned to your Karmic energy. Being in the Now and continually feeling the beauty and joy of living in the present moment (the state of pure, unlimited potential) is a way to rise above the effects of Karma. Karma and Karmic energy can be perceived as the driving force of the Principle of Rhythm within the mental and emotional states. Karma functions through the subconscious mind; therefore, its effects are involuntary. Still, conscious effort and application of willpower do affect the subconscious, and we can successfully raise our consciousness to Higher Planes to escape Karma's effects on the Lower ones.

By learning to live in the present moment, we allow our consciousness to be in a constant state of Becoming, where our consciousness is renewed every waking moment. To be in this state of perpetual Becoming, you must align with the Fire Element on the Higher Mental Plane, the area of the Self where your willpower operates from. By doing so, you avoid the effects of the Planes below it. But even the Higher Mental Plane is below the Spiritual Plane, and therefore those aligned with it fall prey to Spiritual pride.

To be truly liberated from this life, you must align your consciousness with the Spiritual Plane. This can only be done through compassion by applying the energy of unconditional love. In my experience, only truly Spiritual people are happy and lighthearted, where nothing seems to bother them. This is because they are permanently on a Higher Plane of consciousness and do not allow the Lower Planes to affect them since they constantly channel and apply the energy of unconditional love, which liberates them Karmically.

However, understand that rising above Karmic energy does not mean that Karma in a particular Plane does not manifest because it does. I have said this before, and I will repeat it: the Wheel of Karma is always in operation and how you behave determines whether you will get good or bad Karma your way. But by using the Hermetic Principle of Correspondence, you can rise to a Plane above the Plane where that particular Karmic energy manifests, allowing you to escape its mental effects.

Karma manifests on all Planes of Being, which correspond to our Seven Chakras and the Five Elements. Therefore, a significant part of the work presented in *The Magus* is working with Karmic energy and overcoming it. We do so by working with the Elements and mastering them within ourselves through Spiritual Healing practices like Ceremonial Magick.

The Principle of Polarity manifests on all Planes of existence, and it works with the Principle of Rhythm since the two Principles are inseparable from one another. Because of their presence and the reality of the Ego, we have the creation of Karmic energy. Therefore, we must align our willpower with the Spiritual and Divine Planes of existence. By doing so, we avoid creating negative Karma since all our actions will be influenced by the unconditional love that is the base energy of these Higher Planes.

Unconditional love is the only energy that does not yield negative Karma; in fact, it creates positive Karma. This is because the Universe wants us to share love by being aligned with our Higher Selves instead of the Ego, the Lower Self. The Ego can never be destroyed or eradicated since it is closely linked to the physical body's survival. So long as the physical body is alive, so is the Ego. But we can choose not to listen to the Ego's thoughts, ensuring that our actions do not carry Karmic consequences.

One of the biggest challenges in humanity is to overcome the effects of the Principle of Rhythm. I am speaking primarily about how this Principle manifests within human emotions. Unfortunately, most people exhibit very little willpower and let their changeable emotions determine how they should feel and what they should think. In turn, their overall reality is compromised.

Since the influence of the control structures in society is so powerful, most people allow others to do their thinking for them. Their willpower then remains unused for the day, leaving them to rely on their emotions to make life decisions. As such, there is tremendous chaos in their lives as people have no general control over their reality.

People of Earth have not taken responsibility for their own lives as the Creator intended, which in turn keeps the collective consciousness of humanity at a low level. Instead of being guided by Spiritual Principles, humans are generally governed by impulses from material reality, which affect their emotions and control their lives. Things will remain the same until people are awakened to their inner potential and consciously decide to make a change. Never forget, we each have to be our own Messiah, our personal Savior and take complete control over our reality.

VI. PRINCIPLE OF CAUSE AND EFFECT

The Principle of Cause and Effect existed ages before Isaac Newton coined his Third Law of Motion, which states, "For every action, there is an equal and opposite reaction." According to Newton's Third Law, everything that is carried into motion or action will have a corresponding effect on the thing that the action is being performed upon.

> "Every Cause has its Effect; every Effect has its Cause; everything happens according to Law; Chance is but a name for Law not recognized; there are many Planes of causation, but nothing escapes the Law." — "The Kybalion"

The Principle of Cause and Effect, on the other hand, implies that nothing merely ever happens. There is a cause behind every effect. There is no such thing as chance since chance is only a term indicating the existence of a cause that goes unrecognized or unperceived. The Principle of Cause and Effect and Newton's Third Law imply the interconnectedness of all things in existence and their energy transfer process.

Understanding this primary Hermetic Principle is crucial if you are trying to master your life. You have to take responsibility for everything in your life and realize that you are causing things to happen, and they don't merely happen to you by chance. Also, everything you do will affect the world around you, so don't act frivolously with disregard for your actions. Be mindful of what you put out into the Universe because it will affect what you get back.

There are various Planes of cause and effect, and the higher always dominates the lower. Chance is a word that does not have any basis in reality. It is a word that the ignorant use to have an excuse for their ignorance, nothing more. The destiny that occurs as a result of chance is a concept that the layman developed to accept whatever happens to them as part of some grand scheme the Creator intended for them. But in reality, we as human beings can control our existence to a great extent and manifest our desires to a degree unimaginable to the ordinary person.

We cannot have 100% control over our reality because things outside of what we can track as cause and effect in our lives can and do happen. Environmental factors also affect our lives that we cannot predict. Very often, though, things that happen to us are the causes of other people's effects and still definitely not just chance. Everything that moves was moved by something. Therefore everything that is in motion was acted on by a force of some sort. Being a cause instead of an effect means becoming a force that projects and not just a blind receiver of other people's energies.

One can say that it is chance that an effect came to us as a result of someone else's cause, but nothing ever escapes the Law and this Principle. Therefore, it is the Spiritual duty of all of us as human beings to become causes instead of effects, at least in our own lives. We owe it to our Creator to do this. Because if we do not, we fall prey to the willpower of those who are mentally stronger than we are. As human beings, we can become masters of our destinies and dominate our moods and powers and the environment around us.

We must always obey the Universal Laws. Still, we have such a high degree of control that if we can tap into it and be respectful of the Principles ruling cause and effect in our lives, we can truly become anything and everything that we ever dreamed of or desired to be.

Always remember that a cause is something that starts something and an effect is the result of that start. Therefore, be the cause behind an action, not a reaction to someone else's cause. Be a force of change, not a manifestation of someone else's change. Be a Sun of your Solar System and not merely the Moon of someone else's Sun. In other words, rule your life; do not let others rule it. You have this God-given right, but if you are stuck following the thoughts and beliefs of others, then you are merely the effect of their cause, nothing more. You must master yourself and realize your personal power to its maximum.

What does it mean to be a cause and not an effect in your life? How do you achieve this? For starters, you must learn to use your willpower to guide all of your daily actions. You must rise above your lower emotions and not let them guide you.

Willpower uses logic and reason to guide it for the most part, which means that you have risen above the Emotional or Astral Plane into the Mental Plane. Willpower also receives its motivation from the Spiritual Plane, where unconditional love is the impetus. When it only receives motivation from logic and reason, devoid of love, willpower is serving the Ego. When it is motivated by unconditional love, it satisfies the Higher Self—the Spirit.

The lower emotions are involuntary for the most part and changeable. In many cases, they are not even the by-product of your mind and thoughts, but other people's. Remember, we are constantly communicating telepathically. Our lower emotions are triggered by Ego responses to external factors and other people's thoughts and feelings. When these triggers cause disharmony within us, often they compel us to act in a way that is negative to ourselves and others.

The aforementioned lower emotions are usually motivated by thoughts of fear and hate, whether for ourselves or other people. In addition, they often trigger emotional reactions relating to the seven deadly sins: pride, greed, lust, envy, gluttony, wrath, and sloth. If willpower is not in control when we experience these emotions, they will lead our actions, which results in misery and despair in the long run.

Our own negative Karma is what attaches these lower emotions to our Being. The challenge when they occur is to rise above the Astral Plane where these emotions are taking place and let our willpower take over. This is what it means to be a cause instead of an effect. Being a cause and using your willpower means being a Co-Creator with the Creator. You are manifesting your desired reality in this way and are a catalyst for change instead of just a blind automaton.

Regarding adverse Karma, your willpower needs to be motivated by unconditional love not to carry Karmic consequences and receive good Karma instead. As I said before, the application of unconditional love produces good Karma. However, if you are being a cause and using your willpower, but Ego desires motivate you, you may still receive negative Karma.

Understand that being a cause and not an effect means to be the Creator of your reality but does not imply that you are necessarily overcoming negative Karma. We can make the argument that if the Ego is leading the willpower instead of the Higher Self, you are still under the influence of foreign intelligence and are an effect, not a cause. The only True Self is the Spirit, the Higher Self, the cause behind all causes, which operates through unconditional love. Nevertheless, even the Ego leading the willpower and controlling your actions is higher on the scale of reality than lower emotions leading the actions directly.

"Nothing escapes the Principle of Cause and Effect, but there are many Planes of Causation, and one may use the Laws of the higher to overcome the Laws of the lower." — "The Kybalion"

Never forget that at any given moment, you can "Rise in the Planes" and raise your consciousness to a Higher Plane. The key is to be in touch with your willpower since only your willpower can control and manifest your desired reality. If you are to choose Spirit over Matter and the Ego, though, that willpower needs to be motivated by the energy of unconditional love.

VII. PRINCIPLE OF GENDER

The Principle of Gender applies to all Planes of existence, including the Physical, Astral, Mental, and Spiritual Plane. On the Physical Plane, its manifestation is the gender of sexes, while on the Planes above the Physical, the expression takes on different forms. No creation is possible without this Principle.

"Gender is in everything; everything has its Masculine and Feminine Principles; Gender manifests on all Planes." — "The Kybalion"

The Principle of Gender works in the direction of generation, regeneration, and creation. Everything in existence, including every human being, contains the masculine and feminine energies within them. Every male has a female component, and every female has a male part—Yin and Yang, positive and negative.

The Principle of Gender is in all things, and its key is equilibrium—the balance of opposites. Too much feminine energy without enough masculine energy will yield undesirable results and vice versa. If you were born a male, you must balance yourself with your feminine counterpart since by being born as one sex, you are dominant in it and need to work on its opposite for proper balance. This same rule applies if you were born a female.

To generate our own desired destinies, we need a proper dose of willpower and imagination. This Principle of Gender applies to all Planes of existence. However, since our main concern is with its manifestation within the mental forces, we must understand that we need to balance ourselves always. We must readily have willpower at our disposal, as well as imagination, to accomplish our goals and be a Co-Creator of our reality. Being a Co-Creator with the Creator is a natural process of Magick.

Mental Gender

As mentioned, human beings have within themselves masculine and feminine energies. On the Mental Plane, they manifest as the dual minds—the "I" and the "Me" components. The "I" is masculine, objective, conscious, voluntary, and is a Force that projects. The "Me" is feminine, subjective, subconscious, involuntary, and passive as it receives Form. The willpower of the Fire Element of the Soul projects into the imagination, creating a visual image expressed via the Water Element. The Air Element is the thought, which is the medium of expression of willpower and creativity.

Qabalistically, the masculine and feminine energies are the two highest Father/Mother components on the Tree of Life—Chokmah and Binah, Wisdom and Understanding. As a whole, they represent the White and Black Pillars of the Tree of Life—one projects, the other receives. They both exist at the same time and are opposites of each other. They nourish each other and can only be understood with respect to one another. These mental "twins" differ in their characteristics, but each component exists within the other as an opposite.

The "I" aspect can stand outside the frame and watch what the "Me" produces. It recognizes that this perception is nothing more than just a snapshot in time, which is half-true. This perception can be changed with the application of willpower by polarizing itself on any pole of a desired mental state.

The "Me" component is a mental creation in which thoughts, ideas, emotions, feelings and other mental states are produced. It is like a mental "womb" capable of generating mental offspring. But as it is a womb, it must receive some form of energy from its "I" component (or someone else's "I"), as it cannot generate its own thoughts.

In other words, to have a thought or idea, you must first will it into action. The "I" is the aspect of Being, while the "Me" is the aspect of Becoming. The "I" is unchangeable, while the "Me" is continually taking in impressions and reading them. These dual aspects of mind give you a Master Key whereby you can master your own mental states and even induce them into other people's minds.

The tendency of feminine energy is always in the direction of receiving impressions, while the inclination of the masculine energy is in the direction of giving out or expressing. This is because the feminine conducts the work of generating new thoughts and ideas, including the imagination, while the masculine energy contents itself with the work of willpower. However, without an "I" of your own, you are apt to receive mental images that result from impressions from outside of yourself, including other people.

The Ego is a by-product of your "Me" component since your emotions inspire it. The Soul, on the other hand, is your real "I." The Ego seeks to confuse you, though, as it wants to convince you it is your "I" to take over the consciousness. In reality, it is not. The Ego uses the lower emotions to make judgements, and so most of its thoughts and ideas are fear-based. It is highly changeable, while the Soul is not. Hence it is a result of your aspect of "Becoming," while the Soul is your element of "Being." Allowing your Ego to direct you in life will make the willpower of the Soul inactive.

You must continuously be fueling your imagination with your willpower to manifest the most optimal reality for yourself. If you are not creating your reality through your True Self, your Soul, then you are not using your God-given powers, which always leads to unhappy situations in your life. If you are not in touch with your "I," you lose identity in this world. There is no faster way to lose yourself than allowing other people to control your reality or solely relying on your Ego for guidance.

To be truly happy, you must allow your Soul to guide you in life. You must use your willpower to its fullest and always make impressions upon your imagination to manifest your optimal reality. It can be quite a challenge at first, as you will deal with many confrontations with people, as well as your Ego, but it is crucial to overcome these challenges and learn this skill. Your willpower is like a muscle, and as it can be difficult at first to build any muscle, over time, it gets easier until it becomes second nature. Always do your thinking for yourself if you want to lead a happy and fulfilling life and allow that thinking to come from a higher place.

The psychic phenomena of telepathy, thought transference, mental influence, suggestion, and hypnotism all fall under the manifestation of this Principle of Gender. Actors, politicians, orators, preachers, statesmen, and other public figures or performers all employ this Principle by inducing other people's feminine aspect of mind with their own "I." It is the secret to personal magnetism.

Learning to use the Principle of Gender will also make you very attractive to the opposite sex. Using your willpower (as opposed to your emotions) to manifest your reality is the secret to creating attraction. People who use their willpower to its fullest are Alphas, while those who solely rely on their emotions to guide them are Betas.

Alphas are charismatic, charming, and have a great sense of humour. They are calm and collected, meaning they operate from the Alpha State of brain activity, making them more composed. They have a purpose in life and follow the beat of their drum. They are confident in their beliefs, and they pursue their dreams. These are all desirable qualities to the opposite sex. All humans recognize themselves in Alphas and, deep down, want to tap into their own abilities to act the same. These special people permit them to do this. We all naturally gravitate toward people who can help us develop our personal power and Spiritually progress in life.

THE ALL-SPIRIT

If you are to have a better grasp of the Mental Laws, you need to understand the nature of The All-Spirit better. For example, what is it, and how do you relate to it? If you can understand the true nature of The All, then you can comprehend who you are since you are its creation. Furthermore, this knowledge will enable you to raise your power of belief, so you can manifest on the different Planes of existence through the mind since the mind is the connecting link between Spirit and Matter.

"Under, and back of, the Universe of Time, Space, and Change, is ever to be found The Substantial Reality—the Fundamental Truth." — "The Kybalion"

This Substantial Reality is what the Ancients have called the Spirit—the Infinite Living Mind. Substantial means the essential Element, the foundation, that which always exists, in reference to the Primum Mobile—the Source. Reality means the state of being real, genuine, enduring, fixed, permanent, and actual.

The All is unchangeable, Eternal, and unknowable. Hermeticists have postulated that The All, or Spirit, must be all that exists—nothing can exist outside of it. It is Infinite, for there is nothing else to define, confine, bind, limit, or restrict it. It must have always existed and never been created by anything outside of it. It must be Infinite in Space and outside of cause and effect. It must be everywhere at the same time.

For thousands of years, many thinkers from different lands have talked about this Substantial Reality due to the innate feeling of something bigger and more significant existing, along with the rational thinking that as we were created, then it must mean that there is a Creator. They have given this Creator many names over time, including, but not limited to, Deity, Energy, Matter, and most importantly and most widely used—God.

The Hermeticists call God, The All. Therefore, we speak of this Substantial Reality when we use the term The All or God. Most people agree on the intuitional realization of the existence of The All and our relationship to it, understanding that it will forever remain unknowable to us while we are in these physical bodies.

"In its Essence, The All is Unknowable. But the report of Reason must be hospitably received, and treated with respect." — "The Kybalion"

The All must be Infinite in Power, or Absolute, for nothing can limit, constrict, restrain, confine, disturb, or condition it. If we are mainly the creation of something, then it must mean that the Creator is so far above us that it would be impossible to state that it is subject to any other power since it is all-power.

The All must be immutable, not subject to change in its fundamental nature, for there is nothing to modify it, nothing into which it could change nor from which it could have changed. It cannot be added to nor subtracted from, increased or decreased nor diminished, nor become greater or lesser in any respect whatsoever. It must have always been and must forever remain just what it is now, which is The All.

For thousands of years, through all religions, philosophies, and Spiritual sects, all humans have agreed on these primary attributes of The All. *The Kybalion* states that The All, which is Spirit Energy, is the Infinite Living Mind that manifests the Universe mentally. It is through our mind that we can access all of its parallel, interpenetrating Cosmic Planes or Worlds.

The Spirit contains within itself the entire Tree of Life that can be broken down into the Four Elements of Fire, Water, Air, and Earth. And our Chakric system contains these energy vortices that operate in unison to give us the inner workings of the mind and heart, all of which are contained within this Infinite Living Mind called the Spirit.

The Spirit is Light, and this Light pours in through Sahasrara Chakra at the Crown and manifests through the Seven Chakras, which correspond to the seven colours of the visible spectrum: violet, indigo, blue, green, yellow, orange, and red. Each of the Chakras has its corresponding Plane of Being, which is like layers of an onion, interpenetrating one another and comprising the overall energy field of the human being—the Aura.

The Spirit also manifests as Light in the physical reality as it channels through the Star of our Solar System, the Sun. The visible Light from the Sun is the giver of life to all living things on Earth, as it sustains us all. The Light is channelled to us at all times, including when the Earth is facing away from the Sun. In this case, our natural satellite, the Moon, reflects the Light of the Sun to us. The Planets, which are held in orbit by the gravitation field of the Sun, are also a part of Creation, and they emanate energies which power the collective consciousness and the individual Chakras of human beings.

Since Spirit and Matter are made of the same substance but on opposite ends of the spectrum, it must postulate that everything in between is higher than the lowest, which is Matter, the physical reality. On the Chakric system, the Muladhara Chakra that connects us to the Earth is followed by Swadhisthana, Manipura, and Anahata. These three Elements of Water, Fire, and Air are of a higher quality to the mind than the Element of Earth and Matter. Following Anahata, there is the Abyss in the Throat Chakra of Vishuddhi. It serves as the doorway for the Spirit Element and the two Chakras above it, Ajna and Sahasrara.

Qabalistically, it is the Sphere of Yesod, or the Path of Tav, The Universe Card in the Tarot, which opens us up to the entirety of the Infinite Living Mind, the Spirit. *The Kybalion* goes hand in hand with the Qabalistic Tree of Life and the Chakric system. If The All is the Infinite Living Mind, then knowledge of the various states of consciousness and Cosmic Planes between Spirit and Matter is crucial to understanding how you can master your mind and take charge of your reality.

Hermetic Philosophy is more of a science, although physical instruments can not measure it. It is based on logic and reason (attributes of Mercury/Hermes), including examining the workings of the natural world as related to our Solar System. Hermetic Philosophy reconciles the teachings of the East and the West as it contains the essence of both. Although its philosophy is theoretical, it examines the invisible world of energy and presents its workings in a practical way that is useable to human beings. Most importantly, Hermetic Philosophy gives great credence to the power of the mind and the Principle of Mentalism, which is its Master Key that opens up all the other Inner Worlds and Planes we partake of as humans.

THE MENTAL UNIVERSE

The Kybalion states that The All is Spirit—the Infinite Living Mind. The All creates the Universe mentally and pervades its creation, just as we all do when we mentally conceptualize any thought or idea. According to the *Book of Genesis*, Adam, the first human, was created in The All/God's image. Likewise, human beings create the same way as The All/God creates—through the mind and its primary medium of expression—thoughts.

As we think, so we are THOUGHT. Our thoughts are living things insofar as our mental reality is concerned. Our mental reality then transposes onto God's mental reality, which is the physical Universe itself. As such, we become Co-Creators in The All's Creation.

Just as you can create an imaginary Universe in your mentality, The All creates Universes in its mentality. However, our fictional Universe is a mental construct of a finite mind as opposed to the Universes that The All imagines, which are the creation of an Infinite Mind. The two are similar in kind but vastly different in degree.

"The Universe is Mental—held in the Mind of THE ALL." — "The Kybalion"

The Principle of Gender is manifest on all Planes of Life—material, emotional, mental, and Spiritual. Since it is a Universal Law, we find this Principle within everything that is generated or created on all Planes. This rule applies even to the creation and generation of Universes.

However, The All itself is above gender, as well as any other distinction, including those of Time and Space. The All is the Prime Principle from which other Principles proceed and is not subject to them. The All was not created but is the Creator of all things. Therefore, only those things that are created fall under the rules of the Principles of Creation.

Consequently, The All manifests the Principle of Gender in its masculine and feminine aspects as God-the Father and God the Mother. These are the two main aspects of all of its creations. The God-Father component is the "I" of the Universe, and the "Me" component is the Mother. Qabalistically, these two are the Supernal duality of Chokmah and Binah, Force and Form. The Hermetic teaching does not imply a fundamental duality, though, since the All is One—the two components are merely the main aspects of manifestation (Creation).

To better understand this concept, apply the same Principle to your mind. We have an "I," which stands apart and witnesses the mental creations of the "Me" component in our minds. They are quite distinct from one another since the "I" is the witness who can examine the thoughts, ideas, images, and forms of the "Me." The "I" is the masculine, conscious part of the mind, the willpower, while the "Me" is the feminine, subconscious part, the imagination. The "I" projects into the "Me" and is separate but involved in its creation.

Hermeticists say that The All creates the same way and has created countless Universes. According to Hermetic teachings, millions upon millions of Universes exist in the Infinite Mind of The All, our own Solar System just being a part of one. And there are regions and Planes far higher than ours, with Superior Beings that we humans cannot even conceive of in our imagination. Death is not real, even in the relative sense, but it is the birth of a new life, and the Soul goes on and on to even higher Planes of Life for aeons of time until it finally unites back with The All.

"Birth is not the beginning of life—only of an individual awareness. Change into another state is not death—only the ending of this awareness." — Hermes Trismegistus; excerpt from "Hermetica: The Greek Corpus Hermeticum and the Latin Asclepius"

In the Mayan tradition, before death, the individual was wished a safe journey into their next incarnation. Many other cultures followed this example, especially the ones that were most Spiritual at their core. The belief in the afterlife was much different in the past than it is now. They accepted the unreality, or illusion of the World of Matter, accompanied by the joy and excitement of reincarnating into the next life. Death was not feared but was embraced, as the ideals of the Ancient people thousands of years ago were of a much higher quality.

Our muddled beliefs about the afterlife make us fear the Unknown instead of embracing it. The concept of honour has been long forgotten in modern society, while in Ancient times, it was the mode of living. People of those days gladly died for what they believed in and embraced the next life. Those were the days when the heroes of the past lived.

The Christian concept of the good going to Heaven and the bad going to Hell is erroneous in every way. Heaven and Hell are mind concepts and the expressions of life while living, not something that exists in the afterlife. We were born of the Spirit, and we will go back into the Spirit. Only our most Ancient religions and philosophies had the right idea about death. Sadly, their views seem all but lost to antiquity in today's day and age.

Whether we reincarnate on this Planet after death, we do not know, nor can we say. It is possible that once you have learned the lessons needed and evolved Spiritually on Planet Earth, you reincarnate on a different Planet in another Solar System. The Kundalini trigger and mechanism may be the next point of Spiritual Evolution and a necessary step in expanding consciousness so that you can incarnate on a different Planet and begin a new evolutionary process.

However, these ideas are left for theory and speculation. You cannot have an exact answer until you have experienced your next life. But knowing and having faith that the afterlife is not some grim, horrible thing but instead the next step in your Soul's journey through the Universe will remove the unnecessary fear of the Unknown. And doing so will only benefit you to get as much as you can from being alive on Planet Earth.

"Within the Father-Mother Mind, mortal children are at home. There is no one who is Fatherless, nor Motherless in the Universe." — "The Kybalion"

According to *The Kybalion*, we have nothing to fear—we are safe and protected by the Infinite Power of the Father-Mother Mind. People who can fully comprehend this will have everlasting peace in their minds and hearts.

THE DIVINE PARADOX

"The half-wise, recognizing the comparative unreality of the Universe, imagine that they may defy its Laws—such are vain and presumptuous fools, and they are broken against the rocks and torn asunder by the Elements by reason of their folly. The truly wise, knowing the nature of the Universe, use Law against laws, the higher against the lower; and by the Art of Alchemy transmute that which is undesirable into that which is worthy, and thus triumph. Mastery consists not in abnormal dreams, visions, and fantastic imaginings or living, but in using the higher forces against the lower—escaping the pains of the lower planes by vibrating on the higher. Transmutation, not presumptuous denial, is the weapon of the Master." — "The Kybalion"

True wisdom is to be found in this statement. If we accept the unreality and illusion of the Universe, we must also accept its reality. Otherwise, we fall prey to half-truths. After all, we are bound to our physical body for this lifetime. We must respect this fact, even when we accept that the Universe around us is an illusion of the mind.

The Divine Paradox states that while the Universe is "Not," still it "Is." These two poles exist on our Plane because we are, after all, a part of Creation, and this Principle of Polarity manifests in all created things. Only in The All itself, which is the totality of all Laws, it does not manifest. Therefore, everything created out of The All's essence contains the Divine Paradox within itself— the absolute and relative points of view, as One.

We must see everything from opposing points of view at the same time. By doing this, we remain in the Now. Being able to interpret and see everything from dual points of view at once constitutes a form of "Mental Yoga." As soon as we accept one point of view, it becomes a part of our past conditioning and attaches itself to our Wheel of Karma.

The Ego thinks in terms of a singularity. It arose from the consciousness perceiving itself as a separate component from the rest of the world. Before seeing oneself as a separate component, though, All was One— our consciousness immersed itself in the Oneness of Spirit.

By seeing the body as something divided from the outside reality (and our consciousness inhabiting this body), we started associating with the Ego, developing into an individual entity. With this progression, we lost sight of the unity we were once part of as children. We lost our innocence. The innocence was the wonder and beauty of being absorbed in the Spirit. The Ego matured, and only upon its maturation, we lost that grace which once was a part of our lives. This evolutionary process awakened an innate desire of the Soul for the consciousness to evolve back into the Spirit and reunite with the Source.

Our Soul is immortal, as it is a spark of Light from the Sun. It is within us, as well as the Spirit energy, our animating substance. We always had the Soul and Spirit within us; otherwise, we would not know where to look. The Soul is the "I" component, the willpower, the Holy Fire, which is not of this Physical World and contains the memory of being once a part of the Spirit. It is our beacon, our guide in our quest to be reunited with the Spirit again. The Soul and Spirit are distinct components yet work side by side. The Soul is the Light which is manifested and ingrained within the human body.

The Spirit is the animating substance of the Universe, the boundless Sea of Consciousness, the White Light component of all that is—the First Mind. The White Light is everywhere at once and is limitless in size and power. The physical Universe is the Second Mind, the manifestation of the First. In reality, both the First and Second Mind are One, the two extreme poles working together to manifest the physical world and all the Cosmic Planes in between Spirit and Matter. They are the highest manifestation of the Principle of Gender—the Father-Mother Mind.

By recognizing the Universe as half-real, we can accept the other half as the realness of the Spirit from whence we came and into which we must return. Through this comprehension at a deep level, we can remove the chains of the Ego and the physical body. Of course, we must always accept the half-truth—we are bound to our physical body for the duration of our life here on Earth. Still, we do not have to be chained to the Ego and its needs and desires. Instead, we can become liberated in this lifetime.

In essence, human beings are a spark of individual consciousness (spark of Light), localized in a physical body for the duration of its life here on Planet Earth. We experience the world through the five senses of the physical body and the sixth's sense through the Mind's Eye Chakra. Using the mind as a receiver, we can access the Inner, Cosmic Planes of Being and various states of consciousness through the Mind's Eye Chakra. This entire process happens inside the mind, within the human brain.

The Soul is manifested at birth as it enters the physical body, namely the heart chamber. As the Soul localizes in the body, the Ego manifests over time as an intelligence, an individual entity whose primary function is to preserve and maintain the body. As we grow up, the Ego takes over our consciousness and convinces us that we are indeed the Ego. Once this happens, we notice that something is off, something is not right, and we begin to seek our primordial innocence again because this was when we were most happy.

To overcome the Ego and regain our initial pristine state, we turn to the Soul and the Light within to guide us. We seek to raise our consciousness back to its original state when it was part of the Cosmic Consciousness and the Spirit energy. We desire to reenter the Garden of Eden. Here is the essence of the Spiritual Evolution process and the challenge and mission of every single human living on Planet Earth.

The body and the Ego then are only one-half of the truth. Anything that has a beginning and an ending must, in a sense, be unreal and untrue. The Universe and our physical body fall under that category. From the absolute point of view, nothing is real to The All but The All itself. But to humans who live in this cycle of life, death, and rebirth, the Universe must be seen and accepted as real since we live, move, and have our being here.

Absolute Truth is how the mind of God sees things, and we are a part of it through the Spirit. Relative Truth is defined as how the highest reason of humanity can understand things. Therefore, yes, the Universe is a Dream of God, and it is unreal from God's perspective, but as we inhabit our physical bodies, we must respect this fact and respect that the Universe is still real to us while we are here.

The World of Matter is real and needs to be respected, as do the laws of physics that govern this reality. Things in our minds are also authentic to us—our thoughts, emotions, and ideas that we produce with our imagination. The only way we could know the Universe as being more real than it is would be for us to become The All itself, which is an impossibility while living in the physical body. But the higher and higher we rise on the scale of life, moving upwards in our Chakras and on the Tree of Life, we increasingly recognise the Universe's unreality. The closer we rise to the mind of the Creator, the more we see this Universe as a mere illusion of the brain. Only once we are reabsorbed into The All does the vision of the material world vanish.

All things contained within the Infinite Mind of The All are real in a degree second only to the reality concerning the true nature of The All. Knowing this, let all of your fears vanish and understand the Ego for what it is—just your mental creation, one that is built and conditioned by past events over time. Rejoice in being alive, for you are held firmly in the Infinite Mind of The All. As such, there is no power outside of The All that can affect you.

"Calm and peaceful we will sleep, rocked in the Cradle of the Deep." — "The Kybalion"

Calmness and serenity are present once you understand the philosophy of *The Kybalion*. The comprehension of the truths concerning our existence brings forth inner peace. It is the real cause of inner peace—the realization of the Spirit inside of you.

THE ALL IN ALL

"While All is in THE ALL, it is equally true that THE ALL is in all. To him who truly understands this truth hath come great knowledge." — "The Kybalion"

The axiom above yields the highest truth, the cornerstone of all religion, philosophy, and science. It gives the exact relation between The All and its mental creation—the Universe. The Hermetic teaching is that The All (Spirit) is inherent in anything and everything it has created. To us humans, this is everything that the eye can see, the ear can hear, the nose can smell, the tongue can taste, and the body can touch. It includes the countless Galaxies within the Universe and our own Solar System within the Milky Way Galaxy.

To understand how The All creates, let us examine how we as humans create, and through the Principle of Correspondence, we will understand The All better. To begin the exercise, use your imagination to form a mental picture of a person, any person, and mentally give them form, manifesting them into existence within your mind. You see that this person now has a reality in your mind, yet it is also your Spirit, your energy, which permeates your mental creation. The life that you gave the image derives from your mind. Whatever pictures you form, they represent the Spiritual and mental power of you as the Creator of those images.

Although we can postulate that the thought-up image is synonymous with the Creator who gave it life, the image is not identical to the Creator. The Spirit of the Creator is inherent in the mental image, yet the image is not the Spirit as a whole but contains it within its essence. In the same way, we are not The All or God, yet The All is in us as the Spirit energy.

As humans realise the existence of the Spirit inside them, immanent within their Being, they will rise on the Spiritual scale of life. And the best part is that we can come to this realization at any moment, which will change us forever. The consciousness is not just the body. The physical body has within it a body-double, made up of the Spirit energy, which occupies the same Space/Time. It is present within you at this very moment, and it is that which animates you and gives you life, the same way as you can imagine a person in your mind and provide them with life.

This realization can yield a very profound Spiritual experience. The recognition of the Spirit within me seventeen years ago made me the recipient of a full, permanent Kundalini awakening. Granted, other factors were also present to induce this most sought-after experience. Still, realising that the Spirit is present within was the much-needed catalyst to open my mind and heart to the power of all of *The Kybalion's* Principles of Creation.

Through some internal will to create, The All created the Universe. It mentally projected its aspect of Being towards its aspect of Becoming. Its masculine Principle, its willpower, was projected into its feminine Principle, its imagination, to think the Universe into existence. This act started the creative cycle. Keep in mind that the willpower and imagination of God are the same as your willpower and imagination, although vastly different in degree. The Principle of Mental Gender, though, is present in all aspects of Creation.

Once it imagined the Universe into existence, The All stood apart from its Creation and witnessed the lowering of the vibration as Pure Spirit manifested into dense Matter. After Matter was created, The All roused itself from attention, or meditation (the witnessing process), and began the path of Spiritual Evolution, the "coming home" process. The process of Creation of the Universe is called "Involution," sometimes also called the "Outpouring of the Divine Energy," just as the evolutionary stage is called the "Evolution" or "Indrawing of the Divine Energy." Scientifically, the moment the Universe was thought into existence is called the Big Bang. It is when everything in the manifested Universe exploded into being from a singularity, a Oneness.

The Principles of Rhythm and Polarity are manifest within the Creation process. Once Matter was created (one end of the extreme), the pendulum of Rhythm started swinging in the opposite direction towards the other end of the extreme—the Spirit. This process gave rise to the Divine Desire, the impetus to be reunited with the Source (Spirit).

The evolution process, the return back to the Spirit energy, involves the raising of vibrations; therefore, the Principle of Vibration is employed. The use of willpower through the application of the Fire Element raises the vibration. There is a link between the Fire Element and the Source itself—the Holy Fire is a direct manifestation of the Spirit energy. The Principle of Cause and Effect is also present within the Creative process since Spiritual Evolution is the immediate effect of the cause, which is the initial Creation of the Universe itself.

You can see how all the Hermetic Principles are present within the Creative process. If we apply the Principle of Correspondence, we see that these same Principles apply to our creative process in the same fashion. For this reason, Hermetic Philosophy is a science more than anything else. By learning about the Universe, we learn about ourselves, and vice versa.

If you take any object from the World of Matter, raise its vibration, and continue increasing it, it will be reabsorbed back into Spirit from whence it came. Scientific experiments have been performed and documented with this idea in mind. Scientists raised the vibration of objects with technological devices until they witnessed these objects disappearing right before their eyes. Once they disappeared, they were never found again, most likely because they were reunited with the Source—Spirit.

Our purpose as human beings is to raise our vibrations in the same way, only using our minds instead of technological instruments. By using the methods of raising vibrations as detailed in *The Magus*, you can elevate your consciousness above the level of Matter and the physical body and Spiritually evolve. In the future, when humanity catches up Spiritually on a collective level, we will all be reabsorbed into The All—our home.

You are changing and restructuring your DNA at a molecular level by raising your vibration. It has been scientifically proven that DNA is directly affected by consciousness and energy. Spiritual healing modalities like the ritual exercises and other techniques within this book heighten your vibration of consciousness, thus optimizing your DNA and awakening your latent potential.

A Kundalini awakening is a process whereby you raise the vibration of your consciousness and rise upwards in the Chakric system, above the lower Four Elements, and into the Spirit—the three highest Chakras. Spirit vibrates at such a high intensity that it is practically at rest. But this heightened vibration is necessary to raise individual consciousness and have it reabsorb into Cosmic Consciousness.

A Kundalini awakening is the next step in the evolution of humanity as it liberates the Soul from the physical body, thus overcoming the Ego. Herein is the meaning of the Spiritual concept of finally "returning home." There is no Spiritual method which can alter and change your DNA faster than a full Kundalini awakening since it is the greatest of all the Spiritual initiations and experiences.

At the beginning of Creation, the creative forces manifested compactly and as a whole. Yet from the beginning of the evolutionary or Indrawing stage, there existed the Law of Individualization. Everything that was created became separate units of Force whose purpose was to return to their Source as countless highly developed units of life, having risen higher and higher on the scale of life through physical, emotional, mental, and Spiritual Evolution.

The Law of Individualization is the process where each living Being in the Universe was given a spark of individual consciousness and a physical body as a vehicle. Here I am mentioning organic Beings, although there are also Beings which do not have physical bodies but exist within the various Cosmic Planes in the Universe. The purpose of life for every living Being (whether physical or not) is to reunite back with the Source-Spirit and be reabsorbed within it. The Divine Desire for that end-goal is present within all living Beings. In fact, it is the primary impetus behind all of our actions. We are all personally responsible for finishing the Great Work that began when The All manifested the Universe into existence.

This whole process of Spiritual Evolution occupies aeons upon aeons of humanity's time, with each aeon containing countless millions of years. The Illumined, or Enlightened Masters, Adepts, and Sages, inform us that the entire process of Creation, including the Spiritual Evolution of the Universe, is nothing more than the "twinkle of an eye" to The All. The All is, after all, beyond Time and Space. Our own experience of life is just a manifestation of its Divine Principles. We cannot even imagine what it means to be The All, but we must humble ourselves to get even a glimpse of its Divine power.

If we use the Principle of Correspondence, we can understand how our Spiritual Evolution is the only thing that matters for us here on Planet Earth. This fact would explain why for thousands of years, Spiritual and religious people have devoted all of their lives to Spiritual advancement, evolution, and progression. It is almost as if we activate this "returning home" Principle when we realize the indwelling Spirit inside us. It seems natural to want to devote all our energy to furthering this process. We release the shackles of the Ego and begin our upwards journey home, back into the Spirit. This human evolutionary method corresponds with the Hermetic Principles and beliefs about The All, its nature, birth, and the coming home process.

Everything other than Spiritual progression almost seems like a waste of time. Ask yourself how many people you know follow this logic. How many leave society and worldly life and go to Temples and Churches to pray, meditate, and live in seclusion, devoting their lives solely to God/The All/Spirit? And those that do this find a purpose in their lives, often being the only real purpose that ever mattered to them.

The Illumined report that the Spirit of each Soul is not annihilated once this evolutionary process is complete but infinitely expanded—the created and the Creator merge as One. Hermeticists have sought for centuries to try to explain why The All would do this; create Universes only to start the process of withdrawing them back into itself. Still, there has never been a plausible answer to this question. Strictly speaking, there cannot be any reason whatsoever for The All to act, for a reason implies a cause, and The All is above cause and effect.

Let me elaborate further on the idea of multiple Universes, apart from the physical Universe of Matter in which we partake. Many theories are available at the moment about parallel Universes, occupying the same Space/Time and existing at different vibrational frequencies in other dimensions. However, there is no actual proof of this being a fact; it is just a theory. Nevertheless, it is not difficult to believe that this is true, that there are countless Universes in existence, and that we live in what is popularly called a *Multiverse*. After all, The All is limitless in power and can accomplish such a thing. Whatever the case, Hermeticists believe that the Principles of Creation are present within everything that is manifested, which would include multiple, parallel Universes as well.

***

Every human being is a Spiritual warrior in training. Your mission and sole purpose in life are to become an emissary of God/The All. Your mind is the pit, and the Light shines brightly in your heart. However, to rise out of darkness, you must face your fears and reach the other side. You must eventually return home.

However, once you cross the Abyss, you must descend into the Underworld first before becoming a King or Queen in Heaven. Such is the Law. After his crucifixion, Jesus Christ spent three days in the tomb, the pit of darkness, symbolic of his descent into Hell, where he had to obtain dominion over this region before becoming Resurrected into the Light. This mythos is reflected in the story of Osiris of Egypt and other life-death-rebirth Gods such as Tammuz and Dionysus.

Now, it is you who must walk this hero's journey. Your trials and tribulations exist to prepare you for the fruits of Heaven that come next. Therefore, apply the Hermetic Principles in your life and move ahead on your journey of Spiritual Evolution. Embrace your destiny!

PART VI:
HERMETIC ALCHEMY

THE EMERALD TABLET

The Emerald Tablet, also known as "Tabula Smaragdina," is said to be a tablet of emerald or green stone inscribed with the secrets of the Universe, namely the process of Creation. It is a part of the *Hermetica,* which also contains the *Corpus Hermeticum* (known as the *Divine Pymander* in earlier translations of this work). *The Emerald Tablet* is another great pillar of the Hermetic Philosophy, and all three texts are believed to have been authored by none other than Hermes Trismegistus.

The Emerald Tablet is generally regarded as the basis of Western Alchemical philosophy and practice as it is reputed to contain the secret of the Prima Materia and its transmutation. Within Alchemy, the Prima Materia is otherwise known as the "First Matter," the Divine Principle, and the Absolute. It is the Source energy from whence everything came—the Spirit. It is also known as "Anima Mundi"—the World Soul, the only vital Force in the Universe.

Many legends surround *The Emerald Tablet* since there are many myths about Hermes himself. One legend says that the Emerald Tablet was found in a caved tomb under the statue of Hermes in Tyana, tightly held by the corpse of Hermes Trismegistus. Another story says that Sarah, the wife of Abraham, discovered it. A third legend says that Alexander the Great found it, while yet another says it was Apollonius of Tyana.

Whichever narrative is accurate, we might never know. Whatever the case, one thing is clear—the contents of *The Emerald Tablet* contain a pearl of Ancient wisdom that can help liberate the reader from the bonds of material existence and transform them Spiritually. Greats such as Isaac Newton, Madame Blavatsky, Fulcanelli, Jabir ibn Hayyan, and others have tried translating the contents of *The Emerald Tablet* as they have found that it alone can illuminate the mind like no other philosophy.

The contents of *The Emerald Tablet* are presented herein, followed by an analysis of each sentence (or segment). The intention is to bring to Light the wisdom that this cryptic tablet is trying to convey. You will find that the knowledge contained within *The Emerald Tablet* is intimately related to *The Kybalion*, as well as the Hermetic Qabalah, as all three branches form the basis of Hermetic teachings and are the main subjects of study within *The Magus*.

"True, without falsehood, certain and most true, that which is Above is as that which is Below, and that which is Below is as that which is Above, for the performance of the miracles of the One Thing.

And as all things are from One, by the mediation of One, so all things have their birth from this One Thing by adaptation.

The Sun is its Father, the Moon its Mother, the Wind carries it in its belly, its nurse is the Earth.

This is the Father of all perfection, or consummation of the whole world. Its power is integrating, if it be turned into Earth.

Thou shalt separate the Earth from the Fire, the subtle from the gross, suavely, and with great ingenuity.

It ascends from Earth to Heaven and descends again to Earth, and receives the power of the superiors and of the inferiors. So thou hast the glory of the whole world; therefore let all obscurity flee before thee.

This is the strong force of all forces, overcoming every subtle and penetrating every solid thing. So the world was created. Hence were all wonderful adaptations, of which this is the manner.

Therefore I am called Hermes Trismegistus, having the three parts of the philosophy of the whole world. What I have to tell is completed, concerning the Operation of the Sun." — *"The Emerald Tablet"*

ANALYSIS OF THE EMERALD TABLET

The Emerald Tablet holds the keys to understanding the Creation process, but its language is veiled in allegory and metaphor. Every sentence in *The Emerald Tablet* has many hidden meanings that I will now analyze linearly, addressing one sentence (or segment) after the other but with an underlying unity in what is meant in the ideas presented within.

"True, without falsehood, certain and most true, that which is Above is as that which is Below, and that which is Below is as that which is Above, for the performance of the miracles of the One Thing." — *"The Emerald Tablet"*

There is a concept in all religions and Spiritual philosophies about the Inner Reality and Outer Reality. The Outer Reality is simple—it is the Physical World in which we live, move, and have our Being. We see it every time we open our eyes, our material body being a testament to this reality. The Inner Reality, however, is something that we all can agree on once we decide to do some introspection. We think and feel, have imaginative capabilities, remember, get inspired, have desires, rationalize, and will our bodies into action. These are just a few examples of Inner Reality manifestations, though there are many more.

We understand that to do something as simple as walking, we need a combination of inner functions and for them to work in unison. There must be an underlying thought or intent before anything happens in this Outer Reality. In other words, we need to think or will something into existence in the Inner Reality first, which invariably manifests in the Outer Reality as a form of action.

The concept of the "Above" and the "Below" working in unison to accomplish the "miracles of the One Thing" becomes more evident as we examine it in more detail. Two Realities are working together to create the One Reality, and this One Reality is the Outer Universe in which we live. You know you are alive and conscious because you are reading these very words. And you are using your Inner Reality to do so, which will manifest as a change or alteration in the Outer Reality once you realize and comprehend the many concepts and ideas discussed in this book.

Hermes says that the two realities are similar to one another, meaning that there is a correspondence in their quality and type. There is an Inner Reality of thought, which is at the core of imagination, memory, willpower, and other inner faculties. If we experience this Inner Reality through our thoughts, it must mean there is a thought component of the Outer Reality also, since they are "as" each other. There must exist a medium of experience of this One Reality that makes both the Inner and Outer Realities real. And there is—it is the mind.

The mind interprets the Outer and Inner Reality as real. But if the Inner World of thoughts is real and we use the mind to experience it, then it also means that the Outer World must have a thought component as well, since the mind is the faculty with which we interpret and experience thoughts.

And this brings us to an essential concept in Hermetic Philosophy, which is stated in *The Kybalion* as, "The All is Mind, the Universe is Mental." If this is so, then the reality we call "Matter" has a "thought" component that is intangible and etheric, which the Ancients referred to as the Astral World. It is a Pure Energy component, an exact blueprint and double of this reality we call Matter—and we experience it through the mind as being real.

In the Qabalah, the blueprint of the World of Matter is represented by the Sephira Yesod. It contains the Astral duplicate, a replica of all forms in existence made of a tenuous substance that occupies the same Space/Time. This is the foundation upon which all forms are built. It is directly associated with Binah, the Sea of Consciousness and originator of Form, the Great Feminine concept of the Universe.

The Above then comprises all the Sephiroth between Binah and Yesod, which contain the various inner functions that operate through the mind and express through thoughts. They constitute our Inner Reality and crystallize in Yesod as it is the Astral, or "thought" foundation of all of Matter.

To further add to the manifestation process, all the Sephiroth between Binah and Malkuth are projected from Chokmah, the Force—the Great Masculine Principle of the Universe. Beyond Chokmah, we have the first Sephira Kether, the Spirit, the Source from whence everything originated, in varying degrees and states of consciousness.

The physical eyes can not see this Astral double made of thought energy as it is seen only through the mind, the connecting link between Spirit and Matter. The brain experiences the Astral double through intuition, perceived through the Mind's Eye Chakra. Intuition belongs to the Sephira Binah and is the highest level of perception for humanity since it directly reads energy imprints. This energy filters downwards into the other Sephiroth below Binah, activating our other inner functions. In this way, our Inner Reality becomes manifested.

Therefore, the Astral World (Yesod) is the Above, and the World of Matter (Malkuth) is the Below. Together, they accomplish the miracles of the One Thing. What is the One Thing? The following sentence in *The Emerald Tablet* gives us further clues.

"And as all things are from One, by the mediation of One, so all things have their birth from this One Thing by adaptation." — *"The Emerald Tablet"*

One is the first number, the number that precedes all other numbers, and the number that contains all other numbers within itself. In monotheistic religions, there is the essential notion of the One God, and even in polytheistic religions, the many Gods are said only to represent aspects or powers of the One God. One, therefore, is the Source as well as the Creator itself. From the One, come the many.

The One God, the Source of all Creation, is the Spirit. The Spirit is the Quintessence, the substance in which all the other Elements find their existence. It is the highest conception of God for humanity, as it is the Source of everything in the world. The One Thing is, therefore, the Spirit—they represent the same thing. Spirit is the White Light, the Sphere of Kether in the Qabalah. Thus, from the Spirit, proceed all other things.

According to *The Emerald Tablet*, all things have their birth from the One Thing, from Spirit. As already mentioned, Spirit is the animating Principle of all things in existence. Through the mediation of Spirit, everything brought into existence adapts to the Outer Reality. They are the manifested Sephiroth between Spirit and Matter, Kether and Malkuth, that form our Inner Reality and internal cognitive faculties or functions. The Inner World adapts to the Outer World of Matter.

The mind experiences both the Inner and Outer Realities as real and as One. We are all living in this reality of Spirit (the White Light) right now in another dimension of Space/Time, but because we experience reality through our minds, we believe the Outer Universe of Matter is also real. We adapted to this material reality the moment we opened our eyes as babies and saw the world for the first time.

However, since the physical brain processes information, many people have become limited in their understanding of reality as a whole, thinking that the material world is the only thing that is real. Hence why there are more atheists in the world than ever. Scientific progress has advanced us tremendously in many areas but has collectively removed us from our inherent connection to the Spiritual reality.

Because the White Light exists right here and now, people with near-death experiences report seeing it and even being united with it for the time being. They report passing through a tunnel to experience the White Light, which corresponds with the Mind's Eye portal or tunnel, widely mentioned by various Ancient Spiritual traditions. Fittingly, this circular tunnel we experience with our eyes closed links us with Sahasrara Chakra at the Crown, the source of the White Light in our Chakric system. So now you see how interpenetrating, parallel realities exist here and now that work together to accomplish the work ("miracles") of the One Thing—the Spirit.

The Spirit also acts as a mediator between the Above and the Below. The word "mediation" is defined as "acting between two or more parties as to effect an agreement or reconciliation." It implies a process of negotiation in a relationship to resolve differences. So, the Spirit acts as the Creator and the mediator, allowing the Above and the Below to co-exist in harmony.

What is interesting to denote here is that the Spirit is ever-present in all of our daily lives since its very presence is what makes this Universe possible. Our consciousness partakes of both Spirit and Matter and everything in between. Through our minds, we adapt to this complex Universe and its modes of function.

"The Sun is its Father, the Moon its Mother, the Wind carries it in its belly, its nurse is the Earth."
— *"The Emerald Tablet"*

The Sun is the visible dispenser of Light in our Solar System. Hermeticism covers only our own Solar System, not the Universe as a whole since we do not know much about anything outside our Solar System. We know that there are trillions of other Solar Systems in the visible Universe within the billions of Galaxies that exist in space. As the Sun is the dispenser of Light, it is also the source of heat for all living things. Without our Sun, there would be no life. It is as simple as that.

The Sun is the dispenser of Light and a medium of its transmission. The Light is a Fire (the masculine Principle), and the Sun serves as the channel for its dispensation in our Solar System. Because of this, it is called the Father—the Soul component of all living things. It is the animating Principle of all the Planets in our Solar System and all of life found on Earth. As it is the animating Principle, it corresponds with the Spirit, the White Light, although it is not the Spirit in its totality. However, the Light from the Sun is the highest visible manifestation of the Creator in the Physical World. The Sun is the Life Force (Prana, chi, mana, Ruach) that sustains our consciousness and physical bodies.

The Moon is the visible reflector of the Light of the Sun. Without the Moon, we would be in pure darkness at night-time. Therefore, the Moon is crucial to maintaining all of life at night since it allows us to navigate ourselves when the Sun's Light is not available to us directly. Since the Light of the Sun is responsible for our existence (as it is our animating Principle), then by applying the Principle of Correspondence, the Moon acts just like the Sun, but on a lower level. The Moon's Light enlivens our thoughts in the same way that the Sun's Light gives vitality and Life energy to our consciousness and physical bodies.

If we apply *The Kybalion's* Principle of "The All is Mind, the Universe is Mental," then we are living in the Dream of God, and our physical existence is real to us, but to God (our Creator), we are just a thought in its Infinite Mind. This thought, though, manifests via the Light of the Sun. And as the Moon reflects the Light of the Sun, its reflection powers our thoughts in our Inner Reality. In fact, the Moon's Light is responsible for maintaining our entire Inner Reality.

In the Qabalah, the Moon corresponds with the Sephira Yesod, the Astral blueprint of all existence. Conversely, the Sun corresponds with the Sephira Tiphareth, the middle Sephira on the Tree of Life. It acts as the medium of transmission of energies between all the other Sephiroth, as it is connected to every one of them (excluding Malkuth, the Earth).

Tiphareth has a direct connection to Kether, the White Light. It is the only Sephira below the Supernals that has a direct link to Kether. In the Qabalah, Kether is the Father, while Tiphareth is the Son. Hence, the White Light channels through the Sun to give us the visible Light in our Solar System. In *The Emerald Tablet*, the Sun takes on the role of the Father as it carries the seed (Force) that manifests physical reality (Form).

The Moon also regulates all bodies of water on the Earth, including the water in our physical bodies. As mentioned, our body consists of 60% water. This water reflects our thoughts and emotions, as these energies are contained within it. Emotions are passive and involuntary (the nature of the Water Element), while willpower is active and voluntary (the quality of the Fire Element). The Moon is, therefore, the feminine, receptive part of the Self, while the Sun is the masculine, active part. Together, they are the "Me" and the "I" components discussed in *The Kybalion*—consciousness and Soul. For this reason, *The Emerald Tablet* says that the Sun and Moon (the Father and Mother) work together to accomplish the miracle of life.

What role does the wind play, and why does *The Emerald Tablet* say that Creation is carried in the "belly" of the wind? Simply put, the wind is the Air Element, the Sun is the Fire Element, and the Moon is the Water Element. Air is another manifestation of Spirit since it is the breath that sustains all life on Earth. We cannot have life without Air and breath since all living things on Earth need to breathe to survive. We can survive without food and water for a little while, but a few minutes or more without breathing will kill us.

The wind then is the air we breathe, and its containment is within the atmosphere of the Earth. Air is a gas that contains oxygen and nitrogen. We have air everywhere within the Earth's atmosphere, including the Earth's soil and water. Once we step outside the Earth's atmosphere, there is no longer breathable air and, therefore, no life. The belly then, which is mentioned in *The Emerald Tablet*, is the air contained within the Earth's atmosphere. It sustains all of life on Earth.

Air is another manifestation of the Spirit (the Great White Light), although it is an invisible substance unlike the Light from the Sun. Air is an even higher form of Spirit than Fire; for example, the Air Chakra (Anahata) is above the Fire Chakra (Manipura) in the Chakric system. As both the Air and Fire Elements are a manifestation of the Spirit, it would be wrong to say that they are the Spirit in its totality. Spirit is the underlying essence of all that is. It is unknowable, unmovable, and all-pervading, existing on a higher frequency vibration than Air and Fire, which are its derivatives.

The Water Element is also derived from Spirit. The physical manifestation of water is the H_2O molecule, containing within itself oxygen (the primary component of air) and hydrogen, a highly volatile and potent molecule. All three Elements of Water, Air, and Fire connect with the Source (Spirit), yet they are all on a lower manifestation than that of the White Light.

The Earth then is the nurse of Creation, and it is so because of the connection that all living things have to Planet Earth. When we think of the idea of a nurse, we think of healing and caretaking. In the concept of a mother nursing a child, she is sustaining the child's life with the milk from her breasts. The Earth is the sustainer of all physical life similarly. Food from the Earth is the fuel of the physical body. Without it, we would die. Water is from the Earth also, without which we also would die. We need food, water, and air, to sustain all living things on the Earth and the Earth is the nurse since it supplies all three. The trees from the Earth clean the air and release oxygen when acted on by the energy of sunlight.

Energetically also, all living things are bound to the Earth through the force of gravity. A human being contains energy lines that connect us to the Earth, similar to the roots of a tree. These energy lines link us to the Earth through our lowest Chakra, Muladhara, attributed to the Earth Element. Our consciousness is inextricably interwoven with the consciousness of the Earth to produce and sustain life on Earth. The Earth feeds our bodies, nurtures them, and heals them when they are sick.

"This is the Father of all perfection, or consummation of the whole world. Its power is integrating, if it be turned into Earth." — *"The Emerald Tablet"*

The Emerald Tablet concerns itself with the process of Creation, including life on Earth and everything humanity can see and perceive with the senses. Creation is, in a sense, perfect, since it has existed from the beginning of time and will exist until the end. Again, we have a concept of the Father here, but not the Father as the Sun in our Solar System. It is the Father as the Creator himself or itself since the Father, in this case, is beyond duality.

On the physical Matter level, a father begets or multiplies himself by creating offspring from his substance. In the same way, the Creator begets through generating Forms from its essence, which is the Spirit energy. As such, the Father is the Creator of all things as well as their Source. On the Tree of Life, the Kether Sephira is the highest manifestation of the Creator. It is formed once the Limitless Light of Ain Soph Aur has contracted itself into a central point through the process of Tzim Tzum. The essence of this White Light is contained in Kether as purely creative energy.

As far as consummation is concerned, here is a critical concept to impregnate upon the mind—that of a Divine Marriage. The marriage is not complete without an act of sexual intercourse, for only this intercourse creates the consummation. This idea of the Divine having sexual intercourse with itself is present in all religions, philosophies, and creeds. Its manifestation on a lower level is the act of sexual intercourse, which is the means of all of life procreating itself. It is the idea of the two becoming One in the act of experience. This "consummation of the whole world" is the Father and Mother Principle working together to produce all of Matter in the Universe. It is Chokmah and Binah Sephiroth working together to manifest the physical Universe as the Creator aspects of Force and Form.

Once the Father and Mother Principles beget the Solar System, the Earth, and all living things, the power of the total sum of the measured quantity became retained within Creation. This concept was discussed in *The Kybalion* when saying that the Spirit is present within everything since it is the animating Principle of all things. The act of begetting, or sexual intercourse, through a marriage of opposites, yields the total sum of the powers from all aspects and parts of Creation. Thus, Spirit and White Light are contained in all things in existence since everything is an offspring of Spirit and the White Light. The Earth, therefore, has all of these properties within itself on an inner, invisible reality that is taking place right here, right now, as you are reading these very words.

> *"Thou shalt separate the Earth from the Fire, the subtle from the gross, suavely, and with great ingenuity." — "The Emerald Tablet"*

In the sentence above, Hermes is referring to the concept of Alchemy, namely Spiritual Alchemy. Remember always that the Emerald Tablet is the source of Alchemy and its method of practice, separating the subtle from the gross, the Earth Element from the Fire Element. The gross contains the subtle, meaning that the Earth contains the Fire Element. Therefore, through Spiritual Alchemy, we are separating one Element from another, and by doing so, we are discarding old parts of the Self that we do not need anymore. This process of Spiritual Evolution involves raising the vibration of consciousness above the level of Physical Matter.

The Kundalini awakening is a process of separating the Fire from the Earth since it is the inner Fire, which, when released, burns away the dross aspects of Earth and elevates the individual consciousness above the level of the physical body. The Ego is subdued in this process, and the inner Light of the Soul is exalted. By overcoming the Ego and exalting the Soul, the Spirit can descend into the Self. As such, the individual can obtain a link with their Higher Self.

The notion of separating the Fire from the Earth "suavely" means to do it in a sophisticated and gracious manner, as was the case with the Alchemists. Spiritual Alchemy, including working with the energy of the Elements, is a very delicate process. It has to be undertaken with grace and ingenuity. The very word "ingenuity" implies being clever and inventive, as Spiritual Alchemy is reserved for the wise.

> *"It ascends from Earth to Heaven and descends again to Earth, and receives the power of the superiors and of the inferiors. So thou hast the glory of the whole world; therefore let all obscurity flee before thee." — "The Emerald Tablet"*

There is a continuous ascending and descending process between Earth and Heaven (Matter and Spirit) that happens instantaneously to manifest Creation. It is happening consistently and continuously. Through this process, the overall power of the Creator becomes preserved. Everything in-between Earth and Heaven is maintained and integrated within itself.

We understand that everything at the human level requires some time to be manifest since, from our perspective, nothing happens in an instant. The process of Creation, however, since God-the Creator executes it, is instantaneous. It manifests as the visible, Physical World of Matter that we live in. The Creator put in motion a continuous, back and forth, ascending and descending process between the two extreme poles of manifestation (Matter and Spirit) to maintain its Creation.

The *Summum* philosophy is based on *The Kybalion* but interpreted in the language of today's day and age. Within its pages is included the Grand Principle of Creation. A brief mention of this Principle is necessary to better understand the Creation process. This Principle relates to what Hermes is talking about here.

> *"NOTHING and POSSIBILITY come in and out of bond infinite times in a finite moment….therefore creating a series of infinite EVENTS. These infinite EVENTS, held within the finite moment of singularity, manifest as infinite conceptualized energy that is then externalized through phenomenal, inconcievable projections, limitless in number. Among these countless projections, one produced our Universe through an extreme rapid expansion, what has been called the BIG BANG—an EVENT. In essence, there are infinite "Big Bangs" creating infinite Universes whose origin is an Eternal, finite moment of infinite EVENTS, all produced by NOTHING and POSSIBILITY." — "Summum: Sealed Except to the Open Mind"*

The Spirit, which contains within itself all possibilities of reality, projects into the void of Space, the negative pole of existence (No-Thing), to manifest Matter as an event in Time and Space. It is implied that Matter is just an event, and the Physical World would not exist without the objective observer since living things are involved in Creation.

The bonding of Infinity and the finite moment generates all Forms in existence. Infinity is present within the Spirit energy since it is the highest expression of the Creator, who was never born and will never die. The finite moment is part of the mental manifestation of the Creator, and as such, it has a beginning and an inevitable end. As part of its expression, though, the Spirit energy is found, as it is integrated within the Creative process.

There was an initial moment the Universe was created through the manifestation process, scientifically called the Big Bang. The Big Bang is well understood through Hermetic Philosophy if we apply the mental nature of the Laws of the Universe. Keep in mind that this is occurring from the perspective of the Cosmic Consciousness, the Mind of God, as *The Kybalion* calls it. It is our Macrocosm.

Since living things are part of Creation, our experience of being conscious of the world around us plays a role in the manifestation of the Universe. The Universe might not exist at all unless there are living things within it to witness it. This idea ties in with what I will discuss next as part of the discourse on *The Emerald Tablet*.

To explain how the Creative process works on the level of human experience, the Microcosm, we need to apply the Hermetic Principle of Correspondence—As Above, So Below. As we were created in the image of our Creator, then it must mean that our Inner Reality manifests in the same way as the Outer Reality since it is an intricate part of Creation as a whole.

As the human being partakes of both Spirit and Matter, the individual consciousness exists as a localized point within one of the various Cosmic Planes of Being between Spirit and Matter. We are a single point of consciousness oscillating between undifferentiated Spirit and dense Matter. We can access any of the inner Cosmic Planes of Being instantly. It all depends on what we are thinking about and giving our attention to. And by observing the outer Universe, we are changing it in the process.

Individual Free Will gives each of us complete control over our reality and how we experience the world around us. Each moment in time, we have the choice of which one of the inner Cosmic Planes our consciousness aligns with. The bonding between Spirit and Matter produces the Qabalistic Tree of Life as the Cosmic Planes and different states of consciousness for human beings to experience. What manifests outwardly manifests inwardly within human beings. The Cosmic Planes are manifested inside and outside of us. Remember, each human being is a Mini Solar System.

If, over time, our consciousness is too ingrained within Matter and the lower Cosmic Planes, then we are not in tune with the higher ones, and the Light in our Souls grows dim. The concept of Spiritual Evolution involves raising the vibration of our consciousness to come as close as possible to the frequency of Spirit. By doing so, the high vibration of Spirit acts like a Tuning Fork and inducts our consciousness, altering our DNA in the process. The latent potential within our DNA transforms us in mind, body, and Soul.

Through Spiritual Evolution, the Light in our Souls is exalted. Once our consciousness is vibrating at the level of Spirit, the Ego loses its hold over us. This experience brings absolute joy and happiness into our lives. Our lives suddenly have a new purpose, and we can accomplish things we never could before.

Thus, human beings are personally responsible for raising Matter back up to the level of Spirit. The integration process within Spirit ends the mental generation of the Universe by the Creator. It is theoretically possible that once this happens on a grand scale, the Spirit would withdraw all of its Creation. Individual Souls would cease to exist as they are but would be infinitely expanded since the many would become One.

The "Glory of the World" is a concept mentioned first in *The Emerald Tablet* but was often spoken about by Jesus Christ, who came after. When referring to this concept, Jesus was talking about the rapturous feeling you experience in your heart once you have Spiritually evolved. He called the Spirit Realm the Kingdom of Heaven (or God) and said that each human being becomes a King or Queen of their Kingdom once they have been Resurrected Spiritually and were born again. Of course, this second birth is a metaphor for attaining a high level of Spiritual Evolution and becoming Enlightened.

Once we become Enlightened and our consciousness resonates with the vibration of the Spirit energy, we receive the powers of the lower Cosmic Planes and the higher ones. We Spiritualize our Ego and become Co-Creators with the Creator. Our consciousness becomes aligned with the Universal Laws.

Creation is a wonderous process meant to bestow on the individual Spiritual riches, but it is up to us to reach our own Kingdom of Heaven. Once we accomplish this, we will have found the Glory of the World, and the illusion of Matter falls away. We can then see the world for what it is—Pure Spirit.

"This is the strong force of all forces, overcoming every subtle and penetrating every solid thing. So the world was created. Hence were all wonderful adaptations, of which this is the manner."— "The Emerald Tablet"

The Kybalion states, "If All is in THE ALL, then it is equally true that THE ALL is in All." Every tangible thing in existence in the World of Matter and every subtle thing in the Astral World has a Spiritual counterpart, a body-double occupying the same Space/Time. Everything we see before us with our physical eyes is said to be in The All, the Infinite Living Mind of the Creator, which is the World of the Spirit.

According to the Hermetic Teachings, it is equally valid that The All-Spirit is in All, meaning that the World of Matter is imbued with Spirit energy. This strong force of all forces (the Spirit energy) is in every living or non-living thing we see or don't see since it is the animating Principle that brought that very thing into existence. Thus, the Spirit is attached to its Creation.

Everything that has been created in the World of Matter adapted to this world and became bound to it. This concept is especially true of humans, but it applies to everything, living or non-living things. It is through events in the Third Dimension of Space/Time that we became bound to this World of Matter as consciousness within all things awakened and started to observe its Creation.

Consciousness is akin to awareness, being able to see into its Creation. All consciousness needs a vehicle with which it can observe itself. For humanity, this is the physical body with its five senses of sight, sound, smell, taste, and touch. Human consciousness uses the sixth sense of intuition, seeing through the Mind's Eye, to perceive Planes above the physical. Everything in existence has individual consciousness, with differing viewpoints which make up the Cosmic Consciousness in its totality. Consciousness is the process of experiencing these different realities within Creation. It is the "Event" that is talked about in *Summum* when discussing the infinite bond between Nothing and Possibility.

Through Events and the experience of consciousness, all living and non-living things in the World of Matter adapted to this reality and found their life here. It is the very process of Creation that manifested consciousness in the first place.

Why does the Creator choose to create? This all-important question has perplexed the minds and hearts of all philosophers, Spiritualists, and religious people alike. Perhaps it is to be able to experience itself through being conscious. The Creator manifests as an individual point of consciousness within each living thing to consciously experience its Creation. It would explain why all religions and Spiritual philosophies say that at our core, our foundation, we are each God, the Creator. There is no higher truth than this. To those that have ears of understanding— let them hear.

"Therefore I am called Hermes Trismegistus, having the three parts of the philosophy of the whole world. What I have to tell is completed, concerning the Operation of the Sun." — "The Emerald Tablet"

The three parts of the "philosophy of the whole world" that Hermes mentions in this segment are Alchemy, Astrology, and Theurgy. Hermes is considered the father and originator of each of these fields. Some say that he was called Trismegistus, which means "Thrice-Great," because he was the greatest philosopher, the greatest priest, and the greatest King—his Kingship, of course, being one of Heaven. Hermes gave humanity the keys with which they can exalt their Divine nature.

Alchemy without Theurgy is incomplete, just as it is without Astrology. One must study the Stars since they are the very Creation itself, as it pertains to the World of Matter. Alchemy is the actual practice of separating the subtle from the gross, Spirit from Matter and exalting the individual consciousness. But this must be done with the understanding of Astrology since the mind must have a roadmap of how energy works and influences us. Theurgy is the practice of ritual exercises, Magickal in nature, to invoke or evoke energy. All three deal with energy and its understanding, invocation, and transformation to raise the vibration of consciousness.

To sum it all up, Hermes talks about the whole of Creation concerning us as human beings and calls it the "Operation of the Sun." Here, he is referring to our Solar System, consisting of the Sun and the Planets orbiting around it. All the Planets in our Solar System are part of this Operation, and the Sun is the General or the one in charge of distributing Light to everything within our Solar System. This Operation of the Sun is the whole of all of Hermeticism. It is the whole of all life pertaining to human beings living on Earth. The Sun is the Son, the offspring of the First Father—the Mind of the World of Spirit. The whole Solar System is inside the Mind of God as its Creation.

In conclusion, *The Emerald Tablet* is of great importance to Hermetic Philosophy and the Spiritual Evolution of all humanity. The wisdom contained within its contents is unprecedented as it describes the very process of Creation itself. This knowledge goes hand in hand with *The Kybalion*, as both are intricate parts of the Hermetic Philosophy. Since this work aims to give you the keys to becoming a Magus (an Adept in the Western Mysteries), it is essential to see how each subject presented so far is part of the big picture.

Once you have received the knowledge concerning the mysteries of Creation, you can use this knowledge to help further your Spiritual Evolution. This Western Mysteries path is about getting the most out of this life and maximizing your personal power. It is about attuning your consciousness to the highest in you, the Spirit, and realizing your true nature. Never forget, you are God, the Creator, living the life of a human, to consciously experience your Creation. Here is the great mystery of the world and the very cause behind our immortality. We are all God-the Creator.

THE ART OF ALCHEMY

"For the Alchemist, the one primarily in need of redemption is not man, but the Deity who is lost and sleeping in Matter." — Carl Jung; excerpt from "The Collected Works of C.G.Jung: Psychology and Alchemy"

Alchemy is one of the branches of Hermetic teachings. Along with Astrology, it is one of the most Ancient and most significant sciences of humanity and the precursor to modern-day chemistry. With its basis in both multiplication and nature's natural growth phenomenon, Alchemy's purpose is to enhance and improve upon Creation itself. Although it can be applied to all of Creation, its primary focus was always on human beings. For thousands of years, Alchemy has been used to raise human vibrations and Spiritually evolve.

The exact origin of the word "Alchemy" is a mystery to this day, but most scholars agree that it comes from the root word, "khemi," which stems from the Coptic name for the great nation of Egypt—Khem. Scholars believe that Khem means "black" regarding Egypt as the "Black Land," but it also may mean "wise."

The first two letters, "Al," is an Arabic article that means "the" in English. But "Al" may also relate to Allah (God of Islam) or correspond to the Hebrew "El," for God. In the most literal sense, Alchemy means "that which pertains to Egypt." The Egyptian religion was considered the source of many religions that followed, and Alchemy was one of its most sacred practices.

Another possible origin of the word "Alchemy" is from the Greek word "chemeia," which means the "art of casting metal." The third possible origin is also Greek, from the word "chumeia," meaning the "art of extracting juice or medicinal properties of plants." Although the Egyptians are considered the founders of Alchemy, it was the invading Greek and Arabic societies that conserved this most sacred Art.

Many specialized sciences such as medicine, chemistry, natural sciences, and herbalism evolved out of Alchemy. These fields serve as present-day testaments to the scientific contribution and legacy of the Egyptians.

According to folklore, the origins of Alchemy are attributed to Hermes Trismegistus. His most significant work, *The Emerald Tablet*, contains the original Alchemical teachings upon which all others are based. Alchemists often refer to themselves as "sons of Hermes" since his wisdom is the source of all Hermetic teachings.

Scholars are unsure who the first Alchemist was, although it is believed that the first group to work with the Art of Alchemy were metalsmiths. The most notable Alchemist of the past is Paracelsus. He thought that the primary goal of Alchemy was to cure illnesses. His work revolutionized both medicine and Alchemy and planted the seeds for modern-day homoeopathy.

Today, the notion of Alchemy is often naively understood to be merely about the effort to transmute base metals into gold. This misunderstanding arose over time since the Art of Alchemy was veiled to the profane at its very inception, as was the true meaning of the Tarot Cards. This teaching method was applied to protect the practitioners of these sacred arts from persecution. Also, to single out those worthy of their true teachings. To this day, most people still believe that Alchemy only has material implications, but this is far from the truth. The true potential of Alchemical processes is magical, mystical, and Spiritual.

The reality is that the idea of transmuting base metals into gold serves as a metaphor for the Spiritual process involving transforming a human being's level of Spiritual Evolution. Alchemy is a Spiritual process whereby it is the Alchemist who is turning him or herself into gold. They are seeking to transform their consciousness and become Enlightened. The legend surrounding this process was called the "search or pursuit for the Philosopher's Stone."

The idea of Alchemy as a means of producing gold serves as a metaphor to represent manifesting within oneself the qualities of gold. As base metals are known to be impure, while gold is understood to be pure and unable to be tarnished, this idea of transmutation serves as the perfect metaphor to represent the transformation of an impure Self into the Spiritual Self.

Pure gold represents the aim of the Alchemist—purity, illumination, liberation, and perfection. Hermetic Alchemy then encompasses the Great Work, which is the basis of this book. It also covers the mastery of mental forces and transmutation of one kind of mental vibrations into others, as discussed in *The Kybalion*.

Alchemical imagery is extraordinarily rich and filled with symbolism. Apart from the Tarot (which is drawn from the same tradition), there is no other esoteric system filled with as many images and symbols. Moreover, since the purpose of symbols is to activate Archetypes within our subconscious, they are useful in conveying certain truths about the Universe and ourselves.

Often the impact of a symbol or image may produce subtle inner effects that raise the consciousness into Higher Planes of Being. Alchemy's symbols make us realize that we are not separate from the Universe, but that the outer processes of the Universe correspond with our inner processes—As Above, So Below.

Many of the symbolic themes within Alchemy involve the struggles of love and separation, death, and eventually Resurrection. These themes are found in many of the old and new religions of the world. These include the Egyptian and Hindu religions, as well as Christianity. The process of Alchemy is Universal and applies to all human beings, no matter what religion or culture they originate from. In that sense, Alchemy transcends all religions and can be viewed as the ultimate purpose of all of them.

Most Spiritual and religious philosophies offer certain types of practices to complete the Great Work. Some of them rely on prayer and others on meditation practices. Some even provide ritual exercises with the same goal. Hermetic Alchemy gives you an actual scientific method whereby you can achieve the highest state of Spirituality in this lifetime and accomplish the Great Work. The ritual exercises presented in *The Magus* are all aimed at achieving this goal. Their systematic practice is the Art of Alchemy, geared toward Spiritual Evolution.

THE OUROBOROS

The beginning and end of the Great Work are to find the Prima Materia. This Divine Principle is the primary energy that the world is built upon. It is the Creative Principle operating from the Cosmic Consciousness of the Universe. It stems from the Absolute—The All. The most common name in society for this primary energy is the Spirit, and becoming reunited with Spirit is the overall goal of the Alchemist.

In Alchemical symbolism, the representation of the Divine Principle is the Ouroboros—the snake eating its tail. It is the number "I" and the "O," signifying the beginning and the end of the Great Work. It is potentially both male and female, but also neither since it is beyond duality.

The Ouroboros represents the Source. As the "I" had no way to comprehend itself, it needed to multiply. But to multiply itself, it became necessary to sacrifice its undivided unity. Through meditation, the "I" became the "O," which is not a "No-Thing," but instead a figure that does not define quantity.

As all numbers proceed from the "O," all things proceed from the Womb of Creation, which it represents. The "O" is thus the feminine, passive, receptive Principle—the Great Mother. The "I" is the Great Father and the masculine, projective Principle of Creation.

Figure 58: The Ouroboros—Orphic Egg

The All, or God-the Creator, is pictured in Alchemical symbolism as an egg with a serpent tightly coiled around it. It is a second form of the Ouroboros, otherwise called the Orphic Egg (Figure 58). In its visual depiction, the "I" (the serpent) is coiled around the "O" (the egg), as God the Mother ready to receive the inseminating Light of God the Father. This form of the Ouroboros is the potential of Creation before realization. The sexual intercourse of the Great Mother and the Great Father represents the Divine Marriage, which needs to take place to manifest the Universe.

Qabalistically, Kether splits itself into two to form Chokmah and Binah; Chokmah is the Force behind all of Creation, and Binah is the Mother of Form. The projection of Chokmah into Binah is what creates the Universe. The Universe materializes through a gradual process of manifesting the Cosmic Planes. Qabalistically, this process is described as the manifestation of the Sephiroth following the Path of the Flaming Sword. Materialization becomes complete in Malkuth as the World of Matter, the tangible world in which we live and move and have our physical existence.

The initial Divine sacrifice of the Creator's undifferentiated unity created the first duality in the manifested Universe. Through this sacrifice, the "I" became the "i," thereby assuming one pole of the extreme in duality, the masculine Principle. It is the Logos, the Word of God, and the seed that fertilizes the egg. The Divine Marriage has taken place between God the Father and God the Mother, Chokmah and Binah. The egg has been fertilized.

The Sun, the Star of our Solar System and the Light of God, originated from the Womb of Creation. The Alchemical symbol for the Sun is the O with a point in the middle, the symbol of gold and the highest achievable Spiritual state for humanity. For this reason, the Alchemist is looking for gold in him (herself), since gold (the Light of God) is the highest essence found in our Solar System. It is our connection to the Prima Materia, the Spirit—the initial Source of all of Creation.

THE PHILOSOPHER'S STONE

The Philosopher's Stone is a legendary Alchemical substance capable of turning base metals (such as mercury) into gold or silver. It is a symbolic representation of achieving perfection through Spiritual Alchemy and achieving Enlightenment. The attainment of Enlightenment is equated with Sainthood, the highest calling of all religions. The concept of Enlightenment corresponds to the various Alchemical and Qabalistic terms relating to the ultimate purpose and goal of all Spiritual practices. This goal is to reunite the Self with the Spirit and accomplish the Great Work.

The Philosopher's Stone is another term used to denote the most sought-after goal of Alchemy, the Spiritual transformation. When you hear that an Alchemist has found the Philosopher's Stone, it means that they have completed the Great Work. They have rejuvenated themselves energetically and have achieved immortality. Of course, their physical body will die since that cannot be avoided, but the Spirit with which their consciousness has now aligned will live forever. For this reason, the Philosopher's Stone is frequently called the "Elixir of Life."

Alchemists believe that there is an inner essence within every human. We lost touch with this essence once Adam and Eve were expelled from the Garden of Eden. This essence, of course, is the Prima Materia, the Spirit. Another name for it is Azoth, whose symbol is the Caduceus. It is no wonder that the Caduceus (the symbol of the Kundalini energy in the West) is considered the highest Spiritual initiation and the next step in the evolution of humanity. Humanity's destiny is to expand our consciousness by attaining the Philosopher's Stone.

You have already seen how the Qabalistic perspective of the Garden of Eden story is significant regarding Spiritual Evolution. As we seek to reenter the Garden of Eden, we are mainly seeking the Azoth, to free it from the bonds of Matter and purify it. It is the Great Work of the Alchemist. If you have experienced a Kundalini awakening, then you have already begun the Spiritual Alchemy process and your quest for the Azoth, the Spirit.

There is much correlation between the various Alchemical terms presented so far, and they relate to the same thing in many cases. Many words denoting the Spirit energy are often used interchangeably, and this is to confuse the profane since only those people seeking this knowledge would know the truth. For a long time in history, it was dangerous to be out in the open with this esoteric knowledge since Alchemists were considered heretics by the dominant power of the last two millennia, the Catholic Church.

For your understanding, it is good to see how these different terms relate, which will reconcile your divergent viewpoints about the Spiritual reality. All humans are built the same, and race, culture, and religion do not make us any different regarding the Spiritual Alchemy process. The quest for the Philosopher's Stone is a journey each of us undertakes at some point in our lives, as it is the duty we owe to our Creator to complete the Great Work.

DUALITY AND THE TRINITY IN ALCHEMY

The Alchemists were aware of the Divine origin of the Universe. They knew that all aspects of Creation emanate from one Divine Source; thus, All is One and interconnected. Furthermore, they understood that all of Creation exists in harmony with the Principle of Polarity. The Principle of Polarity expounds that every aspect of Creation exists in relationship with its opposite. As mentioned in *The Kybalion*, the Principle of Polarity is the most crucial Principle that stands behind everything in the manifested Universe.

In *Book I* of the *Corpus Hermeticum*, Hermes recounts the vision of Creation given to him by Poimandres, the *Nous*, or Mind of God. Here we see the first manifestation of the Hermetic Principle of Polarity.

> *"I beheld a boundless view; All had become Light, a gentle and joyous Light; and I was filled with longing when I saw it. After a little while, there had come to be in one part a downward moving darkness, fearful and loathsome, which I experienced as a twisting and enfolding motion. Thus it appeared to me. I saw the nature of the darkness change into a watery substance, which was indescribably shaken about, and gave out smoke as from fire, culminating in an unutterable and mournful echo. There was sent forth from the watery substance a loud, inarticulate cry; the sound, as I thought, was of the Light."* — *"Corpus Hermeticum"*

This excerpt describes the process of separation of the One Thing spoken about in *The Emerald Tablet*. The Divine Principle, The All, separates into two to form the Matrix, the Womb of Creation, which generates all Forms in existence. The Divine Principle, the White Light (the Spirit), thus gave birth to the darkness of Space. Light and darkness are, therefore, the first duality of Creation. Time is the unifying factor between the two as it is linear, meaning it has a beginning and an inevitable end. In this way, duality came about, and opposites manifested within everything in existence in Space/Time.

Duality is represented by the number two, as it exemplifies the Law of Opposites and the dynamic tension of the created Universe. Two represents desire because all things born in duality naturally seek their mate, their other half. These couples are represented alchemically by Sulfur and Mercury—the Red King and the White Queen, symbolized by the Sun and the Moon. For this reason, Alchemy contains a plethora of Sun and Moon symbolism. As mentioned, the Sun is the Light of God and the Great Father (Sulfur), while the Moon represents the Great Mother (Mercury) in Alchemy. These masculine and feminine components, or Principles, naturally seek union with each other as all opposites within nature seek unity.

Sulfur is also called the Red King, while Mercury is called the White Queen. Once the Divine Marriage between the Red King and White Queen has taken place, a third substance is created—Salt. Sulfur, Mercury, and Salt form the Trinity in Alchemy which corresponds with the Holy Trinity of Christianity—God-the Father, God-the Mother, and God-the Son as found in all of Creation.

Sulfur is the Soul present in all living things in the Universe. It comes from the Sun as the Light of God and is the masculine Principle, the Great Father. Mercury is the Spirit, the Prima Materia; although concerning the Trinity, it is in a sub-mode of it. Found within the polarity with Sulfur, Mercury is bound to it and is defined and specified. It takes on the role of the feminine as the Great Mother, the Principle of consciousness. Salt is the Body, the manifested Form of everything in existence. Salt is Matter itself.

Keep in mind that Sulfur, Mercury, and Salt are Philosophic Principles in Alchemy, not to be confused with the physical substances with the same name. These three Principles are present within everything in the manifested Universe. Salt is the vehicle of material manifestation and the Third Dimension of Time and Space. The other two Principles are subtle, operate on an inner level, and are contained within Salt. Thus, we can find Sulfur and Mercury within our physical bodies.

Mercury unites the Sulfur and Salt Principles, which are controlled through a natural heat created by our Pranic energy. Prana is the Life Force we get mainly through the intake of food. Food is essential to our survival. The consumption of water moderates the Mercury Principle as the water supports consciousness. The dynamic between the three Principles of Sulfur, Mercury and Salt allows the manifested Universe to exist. These three Principles are also behind Hermes' designation as "Thrice-Greatest," for he is the master behind the triple mystery of Creation. He is the messenger of this Divine knowledge as the one who brought it to humanity.

Alchemy shares a lot with the Hindu practice of Yoga. The Yogic concept of the Kundalini and the various channels, or Nadis, that the Kundalini energy flows through corresponds with Alchemical Principles. Pingala, the masculine red channel in the Hindu system, is frequently called the Sun channel—relating to Sulfur. Ida, the feminine blue channel, is called the Moon channel—corresponding with Mercury. Sushumna, the central channel running through the spinal cord and connecting to the brain, is the Brahma channel. It equates to the "Secret Fire" in Alchemy—that which the Alchemists seek to locate within themselves and work with.

The Secret Fire is equivalent to the Hebrew letter Shin, the reconciler between the Four Elements, as the Holy Spirit. Therefore, awakening the Kundalini energy is essentially the goal of Alchemy since it represents the release of the Secret Fire, the Holy Spirit, whose purpose is to expand the consciousness and unite the individual with The All-God.

ALCHEMICAL STAGES AND PROCESSES

There are various stages and processes involved in the Art of Alchemy. By observing the Alchemical processes of nature, such as the phenomenon of seeds being transmuted into fully grown plants, the earliest Alchemists looked up to nature as the original master of Alchemy. By studying nature, the Alchemists saw that everything within it continually moves towards a predetermined state of perfection. Inspired, they aimed to replicate these natural phenomena within the scientific laboratory. However, they intended to achieve similar results in much less time. To accomplish this, within their experiments, they sped up the processes they copied from nature.

Each Alchemical undertaking, be it Spiritual or practical, must involve three fundamental processes—separation, purification, and cohobation (recombination). These three essential processes are also always present within the Alchemical phenomena of nature itself. Within the science of Alchemy, all physical manifestations of Creation can be categorized into either mineral, animal, or vegetable. These three categories are known as the Three Kingdoms. Moreover, each physical manifestation within the Three Kingdoms is comprised of Spirit, Body, and Soul. Together, these three components form the Alchemical Principles.

One of the intentions of Alchemy is to remove impurities and energetic blockages from the Aura of the practitioner. Doing so will reveal the truth of oneself and our connection with the Divine Source. This book is concerned only with Spiritual Alchemy instead of a purely chemical art. The Alchemical processes can theoretically be applied to transform metal into gold, but this was never truly accomplished by anyone. Throughout history, many have tried, but there is no actual proof of anyone succeeding.

Within *The Magus*, the initiation into Spiritual Alchemy begins with the Lesser Banishing Ritual of the Pentagram (LBRP), whose purpose is the removal of all negative and positive energies of the Earth Element. Thus, the separation and purification process begins with the LBRP and BRH. The invocation of the Elements follows it in the successive order they are given in. The Middle Pillar is presented as a Light inducing exercise whose Alchemical purpose is to stabilize the Sulfur—the Soul.

The Element of Earth serves as the stabilizer of the Alchemical Trinity. As part of the Alchemical processes, it is the Salt of the undertaking. However, within the Air Element, the process of separation occurs, allowing you to discern between the impurities of the body, mind, and Soul that influence your thoughts and emotions, which in turn affect your behaviour. Conversely, the Element of Water contains the process of purification. During this process, you must sublimate the aspects of the Self that are in touch with the unconditional love of the Soul. The Water Element is fluidic, as is the Mercury Principle.

The Element of Fire serves to purify the system of its negativities further while elevating your willpower above the emotions. Along with Air, Fire is the Sulfur stage of the Alchemical process, although this stage began with the introduction of the Middle Pillar. Air and Fire are both White Light at different degrees of manifestation; hence, they both have a connection to the Sun, the representative of the Alchemical Principle of Sulfur.

The invocation of the fifth Element of Spirit is the process of cohobation or recombination during which the different Elemental components of the Alchemist's energetic system are united into a refined state of wholeness. Along with Water, Spirit is the Mercury phase of the Alchemical process. In Alchemical symbolism, the Moon represents the Water Element and the Spirit Element since they are both related to consciousness.

The three-part process of Alchemy is not a one-time endeavour, however. Once the process has been understood, the Alchemist must then practice incorporating it into their daily life to transmute their impurities into Spiritual Gold on an ongoing basis.

Each of the four stages of the Alchemical process is assigned a colour. Black represents the Soul in its initial, original condition before any Alchemical work. Upon the beginning of the Alchemical practice, after the first transmutation has taken place, white, or quicksilver, is attributed to this next stage. Following this stage comes a period of passion, represented by Sulfur. The colour red symbolizes this passionate stage. Finally, the last stage of Spiritual purity is represented by gold.

THE THREE PRINCIPLES IN NATURE

The three Alchemical Principles of Sulfur, Mercury, and Salt are the three fundamental substances that exist within all physical manifestations of Creation (Figure 59). They are analogous to Soul, Spirit, and Body, and together, they are understood to be an undivided whole.

The state of union between these three substances is present only before the beginning of the process of Alchemy. Therefore, your duty as the Alchemist is to practice discerning between the three substances within your energy system while undergoing the transformational process of Spiritual Alchemy. Through this process, Sulfur, Mercury, and Salt are recombined into a more highly exalted and valued form—the Secret Fire or Philosophic Mercury. This substance is needed to make the Philosopher's Stone.

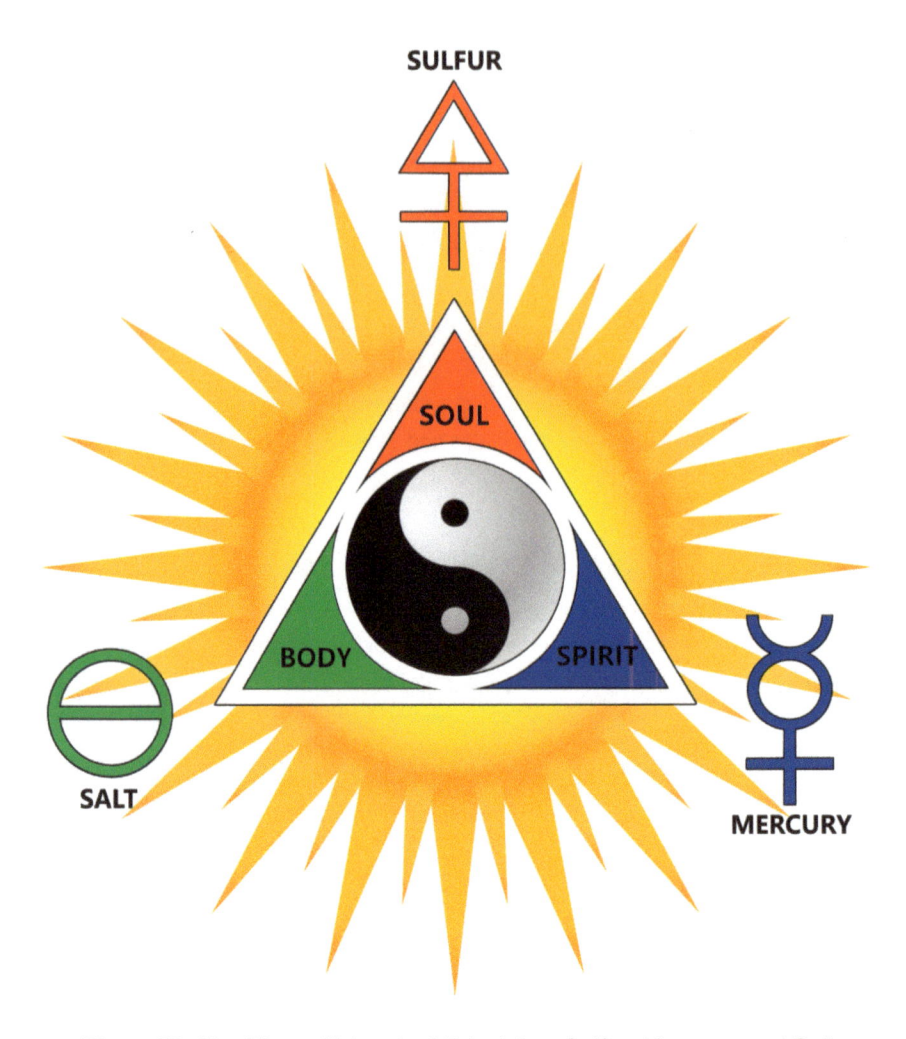

Figure 59: The Three Alchemical Principles: Sulfur, Mercury, and Salt

Principle of Salt

Being part of the essence of all metals and due to its heaviness and torpor, Salt is the Principle that signifies substance and Form. It is the physical body. Sulfur and Mercury are grounded and fixed within Salt, which serves as their vehicle or body. Salt represents the crystallization and hardening of all three Principles together. The Salt stage of the Spiritual Alchemy process is the first Elemental invocation of Earth through the LIRP of Earth.

You are to spend the allotted time invoking this energy because there needs to be a grounding of the other three Elements present in you. This grounding is, therefore, the first step in the Alchemy process. The Elements will solidify into a crystallized whole. Once this is complete, you can start adding and subtracting Sulfur and Mercury.

Principle of Sulfur

The complete process of Alchemical transmutation is dependent on the Principle of Sulfur and its proper application. Found within the Fire Element, Sulfur is the masculine, vibrant, acidic, active, dynamic Principle—the Soul aspect of all living things. As it represents our desire to achieve Spiritual Evolution and growth, it serves as the emotional drive and passion that moves and animates all of life. Sulfur serves to stabilize Mercury, out of which it is extracted and into which it returns. Sulfur is also the physical manifestation of the inspiration invoked by Mercury.

Sulfur represents the Soul and the Fire of the Sun. Within Ceremonial Magick, Sulfur is represented by the invocation of the Fire Element through the Lesser Invoking Ritual of the Pentagram (LIRP) of Fire. However, the Sulfur stage begins with the LIRP of Air since the Air Element is Light at a different frequency than the Fire Element. Both the Fire and Air Elements then represent the Sulfur stage of the Spiritual Alchemy process.

Principle of Mercury

Within the Alchemical process, Mercury itself is the transforming substance. Therefore, it is the most essential of the three Principles. Its role is to bring balance and harmony between the other two, Sulfur and Salt. The Principle of Mercury is the creative Principle that symbolizes the entire process of the Alchemical act of transmutation. Permeating all living forms, Mercury is the Life Force, the Spirit, although in a lower form than the Spirit as Prima Materia. In this form, Mercury takes on the fluidic, feminine Principle that is symbolic of the notion of consciousness. We are working with Mercury at this first stage by performing the LIRP of Water.

Within practical Alchemy relating to chemistry, Mercury exists in two states, both liquid. The first state is volatile before Sulfur has been removed. It is referred to as quicksilver. The second state is fixed, which is after the Sulfur has been returned once again. This latter state is known as Philosophic or "Prepared" Mercury, otherwise known as the Secret Fire—the goal of the Alchemist. We are working with the Mercury Principle at the second stage when performing the Supreme Invoking Ritual of the Pentagram (SIRP).

***

"*Solve Et Coagula*" is an Alchemical axiom which means "dissolve the body and coagulate the Spirit." It relates to the entire process of Alchemy, which is separation, purification, and cohobation (or recombination). The volatile needs to become fixed, and the fixed needs to become volatile. The Spirit or Philosophic Mercury will not dwell in the body until the body is made as subtle and "thin" as the Spirit. Alchemically, things need to break down and be reconstructed, which is not a one-time endeavour but a cyclic process and one that needs to be repeated time and time again.

Throughout life, we have built up our Inner World through our inner faculties and have created blockages in our Aura so that the Spirit, which was a part of us, is not flowing through us anymore. Instead, it is present within, but we need to break down our Elements first and then recombine them into a greater whole. Only then can the Philosophic Mercury dwell in us again, and our consciousness can operate at its highest potential.

THE FOUR ELEMENTS AND THE QUINTESSENCE

The four philosophical Elements are what comprise all physical aspects of Creation. They are Fire, Water, Air, and Earth. These Four Elements arise from the Trinity of the three philosophical Principles of Sulfur, Mercury, and Salt (Soul, Spirit, and Body). The Trinity is responsible for animating all aspects of the material world, beginning with the Four Elements. This Trinity, on the other hand, arises out of the duality of Light and darkness. And finally, the duality arises out of the unity of The All-God.

In this context, the Four Elements do not correspond with the Elements described in the scientific field of chemistry. For example, the Fire Element is not just flame, and the Water Element is not just H2O. Instead, these Four Elements, in varying combinations, are found within all aspects of manifested Creation.

The Four Elements possess the potential to be transformed within all material forms. This dynamism is dependent on the fact that each Element shares its qualities with another. For instance, Fire and Air are the two masculine Elements, while Earth and Water are the feminine Elements. Fire (being hot and dry) is the most volatile Element, while Earth (being cold and dry) is the most stable. Similarly, Water is cold and moist while Air is hot and moist.

Each of the Elements can be transformed in its material manifestation. For example, an Earth-type solid can be melted into a Water-type liquid. Next, it has the potential to be transformed into a flammable gas that can once again be condensed back into a liquid form or burned as a flame.

Found within the three Principles of Alchemy is the notion of the fifth Element—the Element of Spirit. The Spirit Element is also referred to as Philosophic Mercury, the Secret Fire, or the Quintessence. The Quintessence can be found within the Four philosophic Elements themselves. The Quintessence is not a product of the Four Elements, as it is not an aspect of material Creation. Instead, the Quintessence precedes the Four Elements. It is the Trinity of the three philosophical Principles as the Divine Principle and the Prima Materia. The Spirit is the substance used to create the Philosopher's Stone. The symbol of the Spirit, or the Quintessence, is the Pentagram itself, hence its use in Ceremonial Magick. Within *The Magus*, one can experience the Quintessence through the SIRP exercise.

AS ABOVE, SO BELOW

The Hermetic Principle of Correspondence points to a relationship between the Stars and Planets in our Galaxy and all physical manifestations on Planet Earth. By understanding the map of the Heavens, we know how those components reflect themselves on Earth, especially within the makeup of human beings. With this notion comes the connection between Astrology and Alchemy. All Alchemical practices share their aspects in some way with Astrological understandings.

We obtain vast knowledge by understanding the powers of the different Planets in our Solar System. According to Alchemists, the movements and qualities of the celestial bodies in our Solar System represent the unfolding of life on Earth. This knowledge is coupled with understanding the energies of the Stars that form the different constellations. These energies form parts of the human psyche that influence and shape our character and personality. They must be purified and their challenges overcome as we move forward on our Spiritual journeys.

Our Solar System can be likened to a single body. Qabalistically, it is Adam Kadmon. Just like the human body, the Solar System contains vital components. These components correlate with the organs within the human body and the Archetypal aspects of the psyche. In the same way, both the Solar System and the human body contain masculine and feminine energies. Within our Solar System, the Sun represents the masculine Principle (Sulfur) while the Moon represents the feminine Principle (Mercury).

In the same way that each person has a unique balance of the Four Elements within themselves, each person also contains a special balance of the different Planetary qualities. The great Alchemist, Paracelsus, brought insight into how these Planetary qualities correspond to various diseases in the human body, as well as their remedies. For instance, if a person experiences joint pain, this reflects an imbalance in the energy of Saturn within their body. All health issues related to the bones are due to a weakness of Saturn's energy. For further Planetary correspondences with diseases in the body, refer to "The Planets Within Our Solar System" chapter.

Paracelsus emphasized the significance of working with Astrological understandings. He stressed that those practising Alchemy should understand the nature of the different celestial bodies and their qualities, just as a doctor must understand the various organs and components comprising the physical body.

Through knowledge presented thus far in *The Magus*, including the Planetary correspondences, you can use Planetary Magick to help with physical ailments but also emotional and mental ones. To gain true mastery over the Self and tap into your highest potential, you must work with the Planets to integrate your higher powers and aspirations. If you have finished the prescribed Spiritual Alchemy program with the Five Elements, the next step includes working with Planetary Magick for Spiritual Evolution purposes or for healing physical ailments.

THE ALCHEMICAL METALS

Those practising Alchemy understand that metals belong to one of the Three Kingdoms, namely minerals. With this perspective, they consider metals as living substances comparable to animals and vegetables. It is a unique view compared to the modern-day geologist or metallurgist. Like plants and animals, metals also hold within themselves their equivalent of a seed intended to promote further growth.

The Alchemist understands that metals, just like all other aspects of Nature, must be subject to birth, growth, and increase. When the natural conditions are right, metals can be transmuted. However, this is only under the right natural conditions and not under the influence of the Alchemist's efforts. For this reason, one is encouraged to allow the process to unfold at its own pace, without interference.

Each celestial body is recognized to be associated with a particular metal due to each Planet's form and qualities. The Moon is associated with silver. Jupiter is associated with tin. Copper, or brass, is attributed to

Venus. Iron is attributed to Mars. Lead is the metal of Saturn and quicksilver is the metal of Mercury. Lastly, gold is the metal associated with the Sun. The metals are the physical manifestation of the Planets on Earth.

THE STAGES OF ALCHEMY

In the Great Work, the Ladder of the Wise, also known as "Jacob's Ladder," is used to represent the different Alchemical stages on the path to Spiritual perfection. Through imagery, Jacob's Ladder is often depicted as a stepladder or staircase leading from an Earthly temple (representing the Below) to a place in the clouds (representing the Above). Thus, the Ladder is the connecting link between Heaven and Earth, the Above and the Below.

The Ladder of the Wise leads to the Inner Temple, spoken of often by Jesus Christ in his teachings. To reach it, you must purify and consecrate the Alchemical Principles within yourself. The Phoenix resurrecting out of the ashes is symbolic of the new Self emerging from the old Self. Renewal, regeneration, and transformation are at the core of all the Alchemical processes.

The Great Work involves seven stages, which correlate with the Seven Chakras, although one phase may encompass more than one Chakra. The stages also correspond with the Seven Ancient Planets; however, some steps can also be attributed to more than one Planet. Since *The Emerald Tablet* of Hermes Trismegistus deals with the process of Alchemy, the seven stages also correspond with different parts, or phrases, of *The Emerald Tablet*, as will be discussed.

In Alchemical literature, these seven stages are presented as laboratory processes, mainly through imagery. The purpose of this method is to veil the real meaning from the profane. It is also to help understand the processes better by giving a symbolic representation of each stage. After all, most people believed that the legend of the Philosopher's Stone dealt with turning physical lead into gold.

According to the Alchemists, the sequence of the stages on the Ladder of the Wise varies for each person. After all, we are all at different levels in our Spiritual Evolution process and require specific inner work on our path to Enlightenment. Furthermore, for some people, certain Alchemical steps may not even be necessary for the Great Work to be complete and Spiritual perfection attained.

It is important to recognize here that the order of the stages and processes of the Great Work have never been expounded upon explicitly by the great Alchemists. The exact details of the sequence have never been shared in writing. This method was to bring confusion to those that are just curious about this work and not sincere.

Keep in mind that Alchemy was mainly practised before the advent of the Golden Dawn. The method of Spiritual Alchemy presented by the originators of the Golden Dawn has proven to stand the test of time. I have included their procedure as part of the discourse on the Alchemical stages for the most optimal understanding of this subject. Also, the following descriptions of the Alchemical stages are presented in the sequence that best resembles the Golden Dawn method of Spiritual Alchemy. With that said, the following are the seven stages of the Ladder of the Wise.

CALCINATION

"All our purifications are done in Fire, by Fire, and with Fire," said the twentieth-century Alchemist, Fulcanelli, in *The Mystery of the Cathedrals*. The process of Calcination represents the purification of the Ego and destroying all parts of the false personality. Symbolically, this process involves burning up that which we intend to transform with Sulfur through the Fire Element. The Alchemists held Fire in high esteem, believing it was the most potent agent of transformation and necessary for their work. For this reason, they were often called the "Philosophers of Fire."

Symbolically, the process of Calcination was depicted visually as a lion consuming a snake. Here, the lion represents the powerful Fire of the Soul (the Sulfur) and the courage and desire necessary to overcome the darkness. The snake represents the unprocessed Mercury of the false personality—the Ego.

Calcination involves the application of heat and the Fire Element, which corresponds with Manipura Chakra. This process begins in the Root Chakra, Muladhara, since it is a mild, steady Fire that is obtained once the energies in the Aura are grounded through the LIRP of Earth. The Calcination stage is associated with the power of Saturn as there is a firm mystical connection between Saturn and Earth. Saturn represents Time and Space, through which the Ego was formed.

Calcination commences the breaking down process of the old Self. *The Emerald Tablet's* phrase corresponding to the Calcination stage is, "The Sun is its Father." It references the masculine Principle, Sulfur, the Fire Element of transformation.

As the process of burning up is carried out, the Ego's systematic destruction is underway, consuming one's attachments to the material realm. After being challenged by life's difficulties, the process of Calcination is humbling for the seeker undergoing this purification.

Calcination continues through the LIRP of Fire and the Fire Element since, through purification, the old Self burns away, leaving only ashes behind. The "Salt of the Stone," the Eternal Soul, can be found within the ashes. Keep in mind also that when working with the LIRP of Fire, the lower four Chakras are involved in the process since Fire also purifies the Elements of Earth, Air, and Water.

Upon awakening the Kundalini, once the Inner Fire has been released, Calcination is the first stage in the process of transformation. Once this stage has begun, it may take years for the gradual burning up of the negative aspects of the Ego to take place before the Higher Self can be exalted. This first step with the application of Fire aims to release the Ego from bondage to the material world. The process unfolds in this fashion since the Ego is the lowest form of the Self. Therefore, as we rise from Below to Above, the transformation process must begin with the lowest aspect of manifestation—the physical foundation.

DISSOLUTION

In the context of "Solve Et Coagula," Dissolution is the "Solve" part of this Alchemical axiom. Dissolution of the body is necessary so that the Spirit can permeate it after. Following Calcination, Dissolution is the second stage of the process of Alchemical transformation.

Symbolically, a green lion, signifying the component of Mercury within ourselves yet to be perfected, represents Dissolution. This green lion is also a symbol of the initiate, who has been through the first stage, tried by the Fire of the Earth, and is now ready to be illuminated by the bright Light of Solar consciousness.

After going through the intense heat of the Calcination stage, the initiate must be cooled down. This cooling down brings a time of reflection and femininity. Before the Soul can be transformed, it must first become a recipient of grace. It is at this time that the initiate experiences the Water Element through the LIRP of Water. The green lion is depicted as going towards a water spring, ready to drink it. After working with the Fire in the previous stage, he wants to cool down and regenerate.

As the Water moves through the system, it continues the purification process. This stage, attributed to Jupiter, the bearer of Water, becomes a process of sobbing and tears for the initiate. Within *The Emerald Tablet*, the phrase, "The Moon is its Mother," relates to the Dissolution stage. It is a reference to the feminine Principle of Creation—Mercury, the Water Element.

As far as the Chakric energy system is concerned, this stage corresponds with the second Chakra, Swadhisthana—the Sacral Chakra. Swadhisthana is the Water Chakra, closely connected to the subconscious, the buried and often rejected part of the psyche. During this Dissolution process, the conscious mind is opened to allow the previously suppressed material and energy of the subconscious to surface and be dissolved.

SEPARATION

During the previous stage of Dissolution, there comes a profound surrender of the Soul. This process can create an imbalance, causing the Spirit to feel threatened and in conflict with the willpower. During the Calcination period, unwanted aspects of the psyche were burned up, but their remnants may still linger. During the Separation stage, they must be removed for good to bring harmony between the Spirit and the Soul.

Following the Fire of the Calcination stage and the Water of the Dissolution stage comes the Element of Air in the Separation stage. We are undergoing the process of Separation by working with the LIRP of Air. Within *The Emerald Tablet*, the phrase, "The Wind carries it in its belly," relates to the Separation stage.

The imagery used to represent this stage is rather interesting. It includes a man and woman in a quarrel, with a youthful Hermes coming between them to bring reconciliation. One the side of the man is the Sun, and on the side of the woman is the Moon—representing the opposing masculine and feminine energies. Hermes holds a Caduceus in each hand to indicate to the man and the woman that they must be their reconciler of opposites. This image represents the purpose of this Alchemical stage—the reconciliation of all dualities within the initiate.

As we move forward here, we can begin to reap the rewards of the Alchemical process. As there is an increase in the amount of the Air Element moving through the system, the intellect (which the mind uses to understand the world) becomes sharpened. Though all of these processes can be challenging, this stage, in particular, can be rather painful. However, it is vital to remain patient, calm, and imaginative to find new perspectives that will allow us to move forward.

Separation is a conscious process through which we review all hidden aspects of the Self and decide what to discard and what to reintegrate into our refined personality. It is the letting go of the self-inflicted restraints to our true nature, so the Light of the Soul can shine through. It involves breaking down thoughts and emotions, including beliefs, prejudices, neuroses and phobias.

Although the Air Element is associated with the Heart Chakra, Anahata, the Separation process is Alchemically attributed to the Planet Mars and the Fire Chakra, Manipura. In the context of the Chakric system, this is the third Chakra upwards, starting from Muladhara. Mars is the ultimate destroyer and transformer of the Ego and old modes of functioning. It is through Separation that we are removing the clutches of the Ego once and for all.

The Air Element fuels the Water and Fire Chakras, attributed to the Mercury and Sulfur Principles. The final traces of the Ego must be extracted from Spirit and Soul, the two opposites. The Air Element is also the reconciler between these two Alchemical Principles, represented by the Water and Fire Elements. As such, the Separation process encompasses the three Chakras of Swadsthihaha, Manipura, and Anahata.

CONJUNCTION

The Conjunction stage completes the process of reconciliation that began in the previous step of Separation. Here, the Soul and Spirit can finally merge into a harmonious union. Similarly, the masculine and feminine components of the initiate, the Sun and Moon energies, become harmonized and balanced.

Symbolically, the man and woman who were in a quarrel in the previous stage are now conjoined in Holy Matrimony by a more mature Hermes. He is portrayed with a smirk since he knows their union will mark their inevitable death, represented by the following Alchemical stage. Earth and Heaven with a rainbow stretching over them are also depicted in the imagery of this stage. The seven rainbow colours represent the Seven Ancient Planets and the Seven Chakras in equilibrium.

The process of Conjunction uses the body's sexual energy to fuel this stage of the Alchemical transformation. True equilibrium between the masculine (Sun) and feminine (Moon) energies is discovered in the Heart Chakra. Remember that the Water and Fire Elements are below the Heart Chakra (attributed to the Air Element). As the initiate's consciousness gradually aligns with Anahata Chakra, the Water and Fire Elements become balanced through the Air Element. A balance between the inhale and exhale is obtained, bringing coherence to the body.

The Emerald Tablet's phrase, "Its nurse is the Earth," relates to the Conjunction stage. The Planet attributed to the Conjunction stage is Venus, the Planet of Love. This attribution is fitting since love is the true reconciler of all opposites and their unifying energy—love is the ultimate transformer. Unconditional love is attributed to the Heart Chakra, Anahata, although Conjunction is achieved when all four lower Chakras have been balanced and are in harmony. After all, the Sun and Moon energies express through all of the Chakras.

The Conjunction stage begins when the initiate has sufficiently purified all parts of the Self through the LIRP of Fire. However, this stage is embraced when the initiate embarks on working with the Spirit Element through the SIRP. The Conjunction stage is the beginning part of the integration process that occurs once the initiate starts to bring in the unifying glue of the Elements—the Spirit. This stage does not last long, though, and Conjunction is the precursor to something magical that occurs in the following Alchemical stage.

The process of Conjunction brings empowerment of one's True Self as the masculine and feminine Principles (Sulfur and Mercury) find harmony. As a result, a new mode of operating begins, focusing on the intuitive capability instead of the intellect. Now, a significant degree of the initiate's consciousness has been expanded, yielding a more considerable amount of power than ever before. However, Spiritual perfection has not been attained just yet. For this reason, the Alchemists described those that reached this stage as having achieved the "Lesser Philosopher's Stone."

FERMENTATION

The stage of Fermentation, also known as Putrefaction, marks the beginning of the initiate's descent into darkness, eventually undergoing an Alchemical death. This stage is known as the Dark Night of the Soul. The Sun and the Moon, after finding harmony in the Conjunction stage, are now eclipsed as their passion initiates the next process—one of fermentation, death, and decay. This fermentation process will produce Philosophic Mercury, the Spiritual essence that will transform the body, which contains the Sun and Moon energies. As individual qualities, they will each be changed before merging completely, resulting in an essence that is higher in vibration and more transcendent than ever before.

The Fermentation process, the Dark Night of the Soul, is synonymous with the three days Jesus Christ spent in Hell before his Resurrection. It is also equivalent to Osiris's period in the Underworld before his Resurrection. All life-death-Resurrection mythologies of the past involve this same process. In nature, the process of fermentation involves breaking down sugars into ethyl alcohol, producing what we call "Spirits." All Spiritual operations find their reflection in nature's processes—As Above, So Below.

Symbolically, the stage of Fermentation is visually depicted with the image of a skeleton standing over the eclipsed Sun and Moon while a Resurrection, or transformation, occurs. It is not physical death but a metaphysical one that brings forth a new life as the Philosophic Mercury transforms the initiate.

The Dark Night of the Soul can be an incredibly painful, horrifying experience for the initiate, and only those that are balanced will overcome this stage. If the initiate lacks equilibrium at this point, they are likely to fall victim to an array of mental issues since the mind becomes restless and uncontrollable as it undergoes this death process. However, strong-willed individuals who persevere through this stage will be rewarded with the immortality of their Souls and a Resurrection into the Spirit. As such, the Dark Night of the Soul will be overcome.

For those experiencing a Kundalini awakening, the Dark Night of the Soul typically begins with the release of the Inner Fire as it starts burning away the negative aspects of the personality and Ego that keep the Soul from attaining liberation. The Inner Fire, also called the Secret Fire by the Alchemists, corresponds with the Sushumna Nadi. After many years, the Secret Fire is transformed into a cooling, liquid Spirit energy that powers the entire Kundalini system of the awakened initiate. The integration of this transcendental God-like energy signals the attainment of the Elixir of Life. Once it is obtained, the final Alchemical stage of Coagulation has been reached.

The Throat Chakra, Vishuddhi, is attributed to the Fermentation stage. Vishuddhi is the first of the Spiritual Chakras, the Chasm representing the division between Spirit and Matter. Since Fermentation requires the right quality of heat or Fire, it is not the volatile Fire of Mars that is needed here, but instead, the calm Fire of Mercury. For this reason, Mercury is the Planet attributed to this process. In *The Emerald Tablet*, the line "Thou shalt separate the Earth from the Fire, the subtle from the gross, suavely, and with great ingenuity" relates to the Fermentation stage.

Fermentation is achieved through various activities that bring inspiration from higher realms and connect us to the Spirit within. These include but are not limited to ritual exercises invoking the Spirit Element, devotional prayer, transpersonal therapy, transcendental meditation, and psychedelic drugs. If done correctly, there will be a brilliant display of colours and meaningful visions experienced through the Mind's Eye. This phase of the Alchemical process is called "Peacock's Tail."

With the ritual exercises presented in this book, the SIRP (invocation of the Spirit Element) is the process that begins the Fermentation stage. As mentioned, the first step of working with the SIRP will be Conjunction, which will be followed by Fermentation soon after. The initiate needs to spend at least nine months working with the SIRP as part of the Spiritual Alchemy program since this period is equal to the time it takes to give birth to a newborn baby. This time period and practice symbolise the Soul's Resurrection and rebirth into the Spirit. This time, however, for the initiate, the resurgence is more significant than ever, having learned the lessons of life from the previous Alchemical stages.

DISTILLATION

The process of Distillation, also known as Sublimation, is the stage in which the stable becomes unstable, and the unstable becomes stable. It is the process of purification that involves freeing the volatile essences from their material ties and then recondensing them. By adding Fire, these liquid volatile essences are transformed into Air. Next, via condensation, they have liquefied into Water once again, only now they are purified. Chemically, this process involves the boiling and condensation of the fermented solution to increase its purity.

The imagery used to depict this stage includes a distillation train, usually shaped like the Caduceus of Hermes, meant to distil the Aqua Vitae, the "Water of Life." Through Distillation, the initiate purifies the Soul as well as the Spirit. Distillation requires constant circulation and a necessity for the process to be repeated time and again. Through Distillation, the power of the Above and the Below are integrated into a cohesive whole within the initiate. The line in *The Emerald Tablet* referring to Distillation is, "It ascends from Earth to Heaven and descends again to Earth, and receives the power of the superiors and of the inferiors."

Before the following and final stage in Alchemy, the initiate's psyche must be distilled to remove the impurities of the Ego and false personality even further. Keep in mind that Karmic residue from the Ego will require that the initiate repeat the Spiritual Alchemy process many times more by revisiting the lower Elements and working with them.

Distillation is a time of introspection to raise the psyche to the highest possible level, completely cut off from the emotions and everything related to one's sense of personal identity. Because of the inner reflection necessary to complete this process, the Moon Planet is attributed to the Distillation stage. Since it is meant to bring about the Transpersonal Self, Distillation is said to culminate in the Mind's Eye Chakra, at the level of the Pituitary and Pineal Glands. Through the Mind's Eye Chakra, the Light from Sahasrara is brought into the initiate.

COAGULATION

Coagulation is the final stage of the Great Work, accomplished when the full Alchemical transformation has occurred within the initiate. It is now that the Philosopher's Stone is perfected, being immutable and incorruptible, which the initiate has now attained. Upon completing the Great Work, Spirit and Matter are united and unified as one. Earth and Heaven are the same now to the initiate. The truth of the Alchemical dictum, "As Above, So Below," is known directly. The serpent and the lion are one.

With this experience, the initiate is now the Adept, immortal, Enlightened, and beyond duality. Visually, this stage is signified by the Tree of Life, whose fruits produce the Elixir of Life. The glory of the Macrocosm of Heaven is reflected in the Earthly Paradise of the Microcosm. Malkuth has been raised into Daath, and Matter has become Spirit. The initiate now functions through the Supernals where wisdom and understanding are obtained through perpetual intuition, the highest of the inner faculties.

In the Kundalini awakening process, the Coagulation stage begins when the Inner Fire reaches the Crown Chakra, Sahasrara, fully activating the Body of Light. After that, it takes many years for the consciousness to align with the Spiritual Body and for the Higher Self, the Holy Guardian Angel, to manifest as a living presence. Over time, the Kundalini awakened initiate reaches their goal and becomes Enlightened. Achieving this goal is the ultimate destiny of every individual who experiences a full and permanent Kundalini awakening.

Coagulation is attributed to Sahasrara Chakra, the highest of the personal Chakras. With Coagulation comes unshakeable confidence and a permanently elevated state of consciousness that expresses itself through the highest of aspirations and states of mind.

The Light Body, synonymous with the Philosopher's Stone, is now attained and fully activated, enabling the Adept to be present and conscious on all levels and dimensions of reality simultaneously. Through a full Kundalini awakening, Ambrosia in the brain secretes over time, serving as Heavenly food for the body, nourishing and rejuvenating the cells. This Ambrosia is the Elixir of Life. It is attained when the Secret Fire of the Prima Materia has been liberated from its material bonds and purified within the physical body, the Alembic. Coagulation ultimately brings Nirvana, an entirely rapturous and ecstatic emotion felt in the Heart Chakra, Anahata. The initiate becomes able to practice *Samadhi* at will.

In *The Emerald Tablet*, the line relating to Coagulation is, "So thou hast the glory of the whole world; therefore let all obscurity flee before thee. This is the strong force of all forces, overcoming every subtle and penetrating every solid thing."

The Coagulation stage is attributed to the Sun, which is fitting given that at this stage, the Alchemist has found their gold and has achieved the "Greater Philosopher's Stone." Coagulation signifies the return to the Garden of Eden; only now, the Adept is in tune with Cosmic Consciousness and forms part of the Universal Laws.

THE MAGUS SPIRITUAL ALCHEMY FORMULA

The three-part formula of separation, purification, and recombination is what we must follow when embarking on our inner journey of Spiritual Alchemy with the Five Elements. The Alchemical process starts with the Earth Element, where we must stabilize and ground our energy. We achieve this by working with the LIRP of Earth for a certain amount of time. Invoking the Earth Element first marks the beginning of the Calcination stage, where a mild, steady heat is obtained that starts breaking down the old Self. The Calcination stage continues in the Fire Element as Fire is the Element of purification and transformation.

Considering that Air is Light and that Light is the ultimate healer of mind, body and Soul, the Element of Air is the next step after Earth, where we are to infuse new ways of thinking and imagination. Again, we must work with Air for a certain amount of time, this time longer than working with the Earth Element. Here, we work on the Ego and transform any adverse thought senders present in the subconscious mind since the Air Element allows us to go deep and examine the content of our innermost thoughts. This process begins the Separation stage that will unveil our Soul to us. The Dissolution stage starts at the end of working with the Air Element and continues into the next phase of working with the Water Element.

As the Water Element is brought in next, it marks the continuation of the Dissolution stage, where the Soul is exalted, and the Ego is subdued. This part of the process involves the application of the energy of unconditional love through the "Waters of Creation." Here, the Spirit and Soul are separated, to be reunited in the next stage of Conjunction.

Before Conjunction, though, purification through the Fire Element is necessary. The blazing Fire of Manipura Chakra burns away unproductive thoughts, emotions and beliefs about the Self and the external world, thereby renewing and transforming the Self on many levels.

Conjunction occurs after sufficient work is completed with the Fire Element and the Self has been renewed. Since the Fire Element operates through the Earth, Water, and Air Elements, a unification of those parts of Self occurs once the energies become grounded and no more purification is necessary at this stage of the Great Work. Conjunction continues once the initiate recombines the masculine and feminine components through invocations of the Spirit Element, as the Soul and Spirit are reunited again. It is short-lived, though, because the following stage of Fermentation is brought on by continuing to invoke the Spirit Element.

All of these stages of Spiritual Alchemy take specific amounts of time. Therefore, the allotted time for each stage must be followed to have success. To do this correctly, you must work with Fire for much longer than the other three Elements before it, since by invoking Fire, you are also purifying the previous three Elements.

Fermentation follows Conjunction and results from the Soul and the Spirit being reunited through the energy of unconditional love. Fermentation begins the Dark Night of the Soul, where we are to be reborn, metaphorically speaking. It is the recombination stage where the purified Four Elements are rejoined into an even greater whole, now under the presidency of Spirit and the Higher Self. As this process is one of recombination, which takes some time to accomplish, the Spirit is meant to be invoked for an even longer time than the Fire Element.

The next step of Distillation is the process of working with the Alchemical formula repeatedly to "perfect the Stone," as the Alchemists would advise. Working with the Elements in successive order just once is not enough, as this cycle must be repeated time and again. You can spend a lifetime working with this Alchemical formula, and each time, you will move further ahead on your journey of Spiritual Evolution.

The last step of Coagulation is the attainment of the Philosopher's Stone when no more work can be done, and the individual consciousness has been united with Cosmic Consciousness. They have found the Elixir of Life. This stage marks the completion of the Great Work and the attainment of Enlightenment. It is the Kingdom of God made manifest in this lifetime. Coagulation is hard to attain, and many will spend a lifetime working with the Spiritual Alchemy formula trying to achieve it.

Keep in mind that Alchemical authors have deliberately mixed up the exact processes of Spiritual Alchemy because the order of steps to be undertaken is not always sequential. Nonetheless, the Spiritual Alchemy formula we follow in *The Magus* (with the five Elemental invocations of Earth, Air, Water, Fire, and Spirit) has been proven to work for over a century by Ceremonial Magick Orders such as the Golden Dawn and Ordo Templi Orientis. I have seen these rituals working in my life and the lives of countless others I have met on my Spiritual journey. For this reason, I have presented the Spiritual Alchemy program with the Five Elements that must be followed in the exact sequence given for optimal results.

Figure 60: Ceremonial Magick of the Golden Dawn

PART VII: ENOCHIAN MAGICK

THE ENOCHIAN MAGICK SYSTEM

Enochian Magick is the highest form of Ceremonial Magick that exists today, whose power and efficiency in furthering an individual's Spiritual Evolution is immense. Since a big part of any Magickal system is the removal of Karmic blockages in the Chakras, consider the following analogy about the power of Enochian Magick. Imagine that Karmic blockages are a giant rock at the seashore. The ritual exercises presented in the "Ceremonial Magick" section can be likened to water in a tide continually working upon this rock and eroding it over time. Enochian Magick would be compared to a wrecking ball smashing into the rock.

Now, you may be thinking that it must be a good thing to remove Karmic blockages in the fastest way possible, but this is not always the case. The mind must be ready to receive these new influxes of energy that Enochian Magick opens the doors for because once they are open, there is no closing them. The mind must work through these new states of consciousness and safely and efficiently integrate them into the psyche.

In the Jewish tradition, it is customary for the Qabalah not to be presented to rabbis before the age of forty because of its power to open the doors of the mind. What do you think can be said of Magick then, especially Enochian Magick? These Enochian Keys are very potent, and one must tread carefully upon this path.

Due to its power, Enochian Magick should only be practised after the Spiritual Alchemy program with the Five Elements is complete. Enochian Magick offers the aspiring Magi a new level of Spiritual Alchemy. It allows you to go even deeper into the mind, body, and Soul, as well as the Chakras. Enochian Magick is considered "Shadow Work" because through its use; you are working with the darker aspects of the Self and transforming them. For this reason, you need to have a strong foundation in the Five Elements of your Being.

Enochian Magick is a vast system with many intricate parts. The area of Enochian Magick we will concern ourselves in this work are the Nineteen Enochian Keys, or Calls, often called the Angelic Keys. Each Key serves as a *Mantra* that must be spoken aloud and vibrated to attain the desired effect. These Nineteen Keys are broken down into the two Spirit Keys (Active and Passive), four Elemental Keys, and three Sub-Elemental Keys per each of the Four Elements. The final Nineteenth Key, called the Aethyr Key, is an operation in and of itself. This Key contains the Thirty Aethyrs. It relates to the layers of the Aura that are much like the layers of an onion.

Before proceeding with the work of invoking the Keys, it is vital to give you some background about Enochian Magick, including its history, its different components, its goals, and everything else you may need to know to aid in your understanding of this subject.

JOHN DEE AND EDWARD KELLEY

John Dee served Queen Elizabeth I as her court Astrologer. He was not only a praised Astrologer but a Magi as well who devoted much of his life to studying Alchemy, Divination, and Hermetic Philosophy. Edward Kelley was Dee's psychic associate and partner at the time. Together, Dee and Kelley are the originators of Enochian Magick.

The Enochian Magick system was channelled to Dee and Kelley by a group of Angels that they contacted via the method of scrying. These Angelic communications lasted from 1582-1589. The Angels that Dee and Kelley contacted revealed themselves as inhabitants of the Subtle Realms, called the Watchtowers and the Aethyrs. Dee and Kelley believed that their visions gave them access to secrets contained within the apocryphal and Biblical text called the *Book of Enoch*.

To channel means to receive information from otherworldly entities, such as Archangels, Angels, Demons, or other non-physical Beings that exist in the Divine Planes of reality. To scry means to look into a particular medium (such as a Crystal or Black Mirror) to obtain meaningful messages, insights, or visions from the Cosmic Planes.

Kelley was responsible for conducting the scrying and receiving the channelled messages, while Dee was responsible for recording the information. Kelley's method of scrying and channelling was by using a shewstone. This shewstone was a black Crystal, roughly the size of an egg, otherwise known as a Crystal Ball.

ENOCHIAN (ANGELIC) LANGUAGE

John Dee and Edward Kelley were able to channel a series of Tablets from the Angels that they were in communication with. These enigmatic Tablets are referred to as the Four Watchtowers and the Tablet of Union. They form the basis of the Enochian system. Each Tablet is divided into squares, with each square containing a unique rune (symbol). The runes comprise the Enochian Alphabet. Dee and Kelley also brought forth a set of Magickal seals and talismans depicting Enochian letters. Magickal work with these is reserved for the advanced students of Enochian Magick.

The Enochian language is one of a kind. Each letter corresponds with a specific Magickal meaning and a Gematria number. Using the power of Divine Names, one can evoke specific Deities from the Watchtowers. Divine Names, in this case, are different sets of Enochian letters that are put together based on each letter's meaning.

There is a whole wealth of knowledge contained in the Enochian Alphabet. It is not necessary to learn it as part of this work, though, since we will be working only with the phonetic pronunciation of the Enochian Keys. Using the phonetic pronunciation will evoke the energy of each Key. It is essential to pronounce each word in the correct way it is written to obtain the desired effect of evoking the Key's energy.

According to Dee's journals, the Enochian language was described as "Angelic", often being called the "Language of the Angels" or the "First Language of God-Christ." He even called the Enochian language "Adamical" since, according to the Angels who channelled it, this language was used by Adam in the Garden of Eden. The name "Enochian" was finally given to this language since, according to Dee's assertion, Enoch (the Biblical patriarch) was the last human before Dee and Kelley to know and speak it.

THE FOUR WATCHTOWERS AND THE TABLET OF UNION

The Four Watchtowers each represent one of the Four Elements of Earth, Air, Water, and Fire, while the Tablet of Union represents the fifth Element, the Quintessence—Spirit (Figure 61). Each of the Four Watchtowers is attributed to one of the four cardinal directions, and together with the Tablet of Union, they encompass our Planet Earth.

"Regardless of their origin, these Tablets and the whole Enochian system do represent realities of the Inner Planes. Their value is undoubted, as only a little study and application prove."— Israel Regardie; excerpt from "The Golden Dawn"

Each square of the Watchtower Tablets signifies a particular area of the inner, Cosmic Worlds. Each Watchtower is under the control of a hierarchy of Divine Beings. These Divine Beings vary in nature, as some are Angels; some are Demons, while others are associated with the Deities of the Egyptian pantheon. Together, these various Divine Beings belong to the Inner Planes and are a representation of the Hermetic Principle of Correspondence.

For simplicity, we will not be working with the Enochian Tablets directly. Instead, we will be working only with the Enochian Keys. Nonetheless, you may experience an encounter with some of these Deities through the use of the Keys.

Through the Four Watchtower Tablets and the Tablet of Union (along with assistance from the Angels themselves), Dee and Kelley were able to present the Forty-Nine Enochian Keys. These Keys were written in the Enochian language to be pronounced aloud, phonetically. As stated, this means they must be read as they are written.

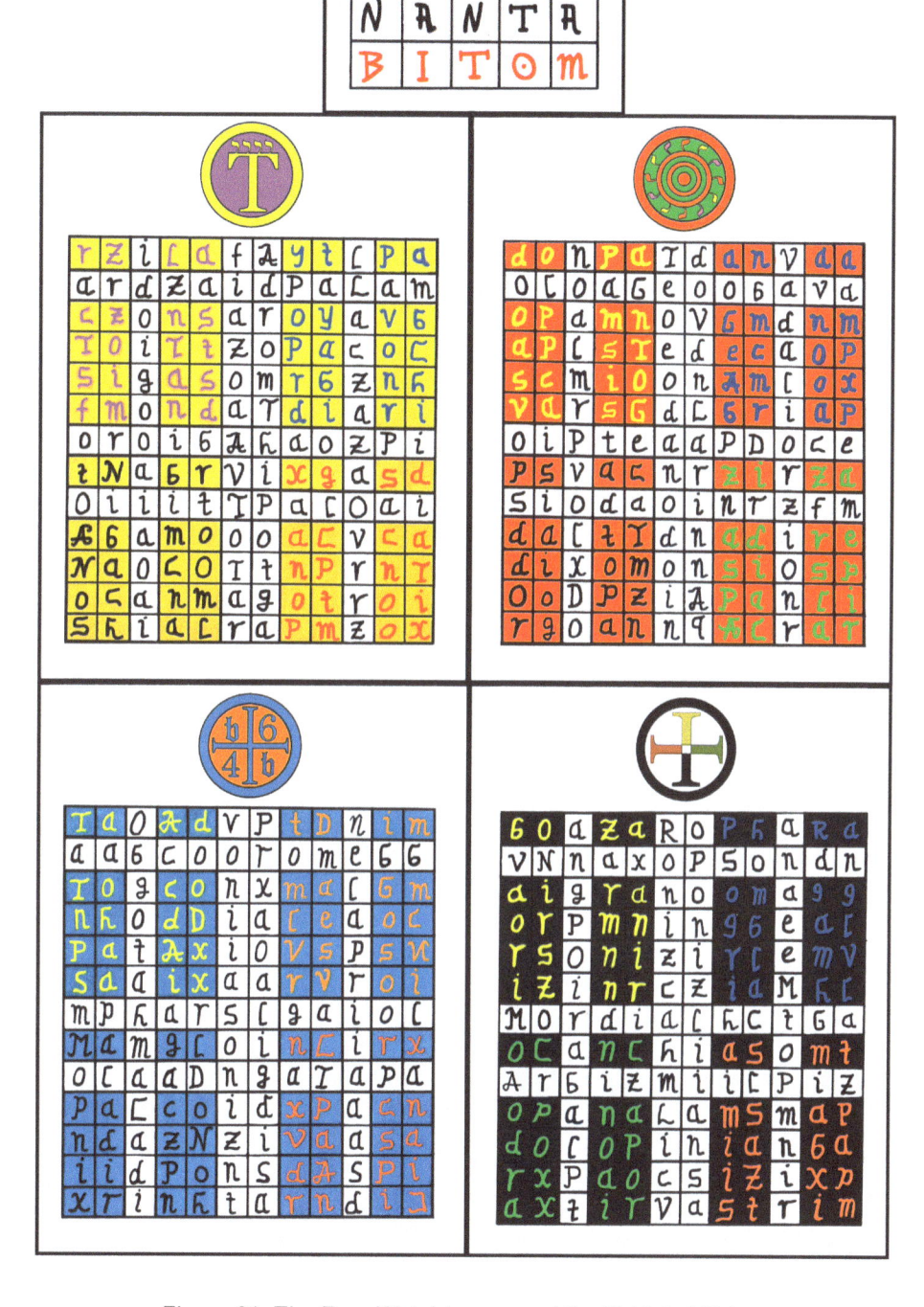

Figure 61: The Four Watchtowers and the Tablet of Union

To tap into the energy of an Enochian Key, all that you must do is phonetically recite it. To clarify, the Enochian Keys are evocations (not invocations), meaning that the energetic states of consciousness they allow us to enter are a part of us. In an evocation, the energy does not pour into the Aura from the outside Universe. Instead, we are accessing a doorway into a particular state of consciousness within us. Once we enter this state, we tap into the Angelic and (or) Demonic energy present. For this reason, Enochian Magick is considered "Shadow Work" since you are accessing a part of yourself (good and bad) and learning and evolving from it.

In the same way as with the Pentagram and Hexagram invocation rituals, the energy we evoke through the Enochian Keys stays in the Aura for the entire day until we go to sleep and allow our consciousness to project out from the state it inhabited after the recitation of the Enochian Key. Before this happens, though, a series of visions or dreams will flood the consciousness.

THE GOLDEN DAWN AND ENOCHIAN MAGICK

After Dee and Kelley passed away, Enochian Magick fell to obscurity. Then, their work was rediscovered in the late nineteenth century by an esoteric brotherhood of Adepts, known as the Hermetic Order of the Golden Dawn. It was the first time Enochian Magick was given attention in hundreds of years.

S.L. MacGregor Mathers, W. Wynn Westcott, and Dr. W. Robert Woodman of the Golden Dawn were responsible for this revival of Enochian Magick. Seeing its power to help one Spiritually evolve, they included it within their Ceremonial Magick system. These men continued the development of Enochian Magick by correlating it with the Qabalah and the Tarot. Through this relationship, they could map the Enochian Magick system onto the Tree of Life.

Within the system of Spiritual advancement in the various Golden Dawn Orders of today, Enochian Magick is included as part of the work once the initiate has reached the level of Adeptus Minor and has completed the Outer Order. The initiate is first introduced to Enochian Magick energies through the SIRP (Portal Grade), which uses the Enochian Tablet of Union to invoke the Spirit Element. From the inception of the Hermetic Order of the Golden Dawn until now, Enochian Magick is considered the crown jewel of the Inner Order in the many Golden Dawn Mystery schools that exist today.

Israel Regardie first introduced Enochian Magick to the general public through his most influential work, *The Golden Dawn*. Years later, another member of the original Hermetic Order of the Golden Dawn, Aleister Crowley, scryed each of the Thirty Aethyrs and published his experiences in his book, *The Vision and the Voice*, further exposing the general public to Enochian Magick. After leaving the Golden Dawn, Crowley joined Ordo Templi Orientis, reorganizing it and making Enochian Magick a part of their system as well.

THE AIM OF ENOCHIAN MAGICK

Enochian Magick's essential teaching is that Divinity's expression is systematic. All manifestations of Creation begin in the Spiritual World and express through the Cosmic Planes until they reach the dimension of Space and Time, thereby affecting the Physical World. The Planes and Sub-Planes between the Spiritual World and the Physical World cannot be experienced with the five physical senses. Instead, they can only be accessed through the Mind's Eye Chakra.

The five major Planes in the Enochian Magick system correspond with the Five Elements. Each is represented by one of the Four Watchtower Tablets and the Tablet of Union. Interpenetrating these Planes are the Thirty Aethyrs. They are considered the Spiritual experiences and Soul lessons of the Five Elements and the Cosmic Planes they pertain to. Through practising the evocations of the Enochian Keys, one can access each of these Planes via the Light Body within the Aura. Through these practices, the initiate has access to invaluable lessons and knowledge about the Universe and oneself. As a result, they can continue their journey of consciousness expansion and Spiritual Evolution.

The intention of Enochian Magick and these practices is for the initiate to merge their Microcosm with the Macrocosm—in other words, to unite one's subjective Self with the objective Universe as a whole. It is the grand, final goal of Enochian Magick. However, a more immediate and accessible goal is gaining control over one's life.

Through the progressive practice and experience of the Thirty Aethyrs, the goals of Enochian Magick can be realized. Along the way, the initiate will gain access to their Holy Guardian Angel, their Higher Self, to further their Spiritual Evolution. Through this work, we are purifying ourselves, shedding that which no longer serves us while strengthening our valuable qualities. Thus, the purpose of Enochian Magick is Spiritual development with Enlightenment as the final goal, as is the goal of all beneficial Spiritual practices.

The Thirty Aethyrs are sequenced progressively, and those who move through them, one by one, can progress further on their Spiritual journey, eventually coming to the truth and essence of reality. The road itself is a journey through the Five Elements and beyond. It is a journey towards the Source of all of Creation—God.

Note that your work with the Elemental ritual exercises invoked through the LIRP and the SIRP will prepare you mentally and emotionally for this Enochian Magick journey. As mentioned, the SIRP was an introduction to the Enochian Magick energies since the God names from the Tablet of Union are used in each cardinal direction.

With practice, as you make the progressive journey through the Aethyrs, you will cultivate discernment and be able to see through illusion. By this process, you will be aligning with your True Will and leaving behind parts of the Self that no longer serve you. Since you are working with your Shadow Self, you will have to face the dark aspects of your Being directly and learn to overcome them.

It is essential to understand that Enochian Magick has its basis in the Law of Karma. Therefore, those seeking to practice this Magick for reasons other than Spiritual development must reconsider their motives or else they will be subject to suffering. Enochian Magick expands on the goals of the previous ritual exercises presented in this work. These goals include consciously controlling your thoughts, emotions, and actions. Your external circumstances (in both waking and dreaming states) reflect your inner state. As such, your conditions can be consciously controlled by your inner will. Life lessons such as these are continually being taught on the path of Magick.

THE COSMIC PLANES

The Cosmic Planes model is present within the Enochian Magick system, which attests to its validity as a comprehensive system containing all of Creation. The Physical Plane is the lowest in a progressive series of Cosmic Planes that make up all existence. It is the densest of all the Planes. There exist multiple invisible Worlds surrounding the Planet Earth, parallel realities that exist simultaneously with our physical reality. As Hermes states in *The Emerald Tablet*, these Worlds function in unison to "accomplish the miracles of the One Thing."

After the Physical Plane, next is the Lower Astral Plane. As it is very close to the Physical Plane, it corresponds with the Earth Element, though it is, in fact, a more ethereal realm. As such, is it often called the Etheric Plane. The Earth Element corresponds with the Root Chakra, Muladhara, and contains four Sub-Elements within itself. These Sub-Elements are Earth of Earth, Water of Earth, Air of Earth, and Fire of Earth. Within the Enochian system, the Keys which correspond to the Element of Earth are the Fifth, Thirteenth, Fourteenth, and Fifteenth. Keep in mind that the Earth Element expresses the Lower Astral Plane but also the Physical Plane as the two Planes blend into one another.

Following the Lower Astral Plane is the Higher Astral Plane, which is associated with the Water Element. It is often called the Emotional Plane. The Water Element corresponds with the Sacral Chakra, Swadhisthana, and contains the Sub-Elements of Water of Water, Earth of Water, Air of Water, and Fire of Water. The Enochian Keys which correspond to the Water Element are the Fourth, Tenth, Eleventh, and Twelfth.

After the Higher Astral Plane comes the Lower Mental Plane, which is associated with the Air Element. It corresponds with the Heart Chakra, Anahata, and contains the Sub-Elements of Air of Air, Earth of Air, Water of Air, and Fire of Air within itself. The Enochian Keys which correspond to the Air Element are the Third, Seventh, Eighth, and Ninth.

Next in sequence is the Higher Mental Plane. The Elemental correspondence here is Fire, associated with the Solar Plexus Chakra, Manipura. Within the Fire Element are found the Sub-Elements of Fire of Fire, Earth of Fire, Water of Fire, and Air of Fire. The Enochian Keys connected with the Fire Element are the Sixth, Sixteenth, Seventeenth, and Eighteenth Keys.

As we progress further, we come to the Spiritual Plane that naturally corresponds to the Spirit Element. There are three Chakras associated with the Spirit Element. They are the Throat (Vishuddhi), the Mind's Eye (Ajna), and the Crown (Sahasrara). The Enochian Keys which correspond to the Spirit Element are the First and Second Keys.

Beyond the Spiritual Plane are Planes that are unfathomable to the human mind, exceeding all descriptions. These are the Divine Planes. These Planes are associated with the Transpersonal Chakras that exist beyond

Sahasrara. Within the Enochian system, the Aethyr of LIL has the potential to offer a small glimpse of these Planes, but not more than that. It is essential to mention the existence of the Divine Planes since they are genuine indeed, but because we cannot define them, we will group them all into one Divine Plane for clarity and understanding.

There are seven Planes of existence in total, including the Physical Plane and Divine Plane. The first five have been described, while the Divine Plane is beyond description. And don't forget that the Divine Plane is plural, as there are many. The five Inner Planes beneath the Divine Plane are accessible to human beings. However, most people only recognize the densest and lowest Physical Plane, the Plane of Matter.

The six Cosmic Planes encompass our Physical World. Like the layers of an onion, these Planes are concentric, with each Plane containing the lower ones beneath it. Each Plane's boundary is impassable by an Element that is tied to the Plane that precedes it.

THE BODY OF LIGHT AND THE SUBTLE BODIES

Just as each human has a physical body, we each have a Body of Light or Light Body. We were born with one, and it is a part of us as long as our physical body is alive. Stemming from the top of the head on the physical body is a non-physical silver cord connected to the Body of Light. Throughout our lives, this connection remains, until the moment of death when it is severed. After death, our physical body returns to the Earth from whence it came, while the Light Body continues on its journey to the next incarnation.

In our early years as children, our Souls were free, and through this freedom, our consciousness could experience the Body of Light. As our physical bodies started to grow, the Ego began to develop as the protector of the physical body. The vehicle of the Soul is the Body of Light, while the vehicle of the Ego is the physical body. Through the development of the Ego, our individual consciousness naturally started to align with the physical body and its needs. This process severed our connection with the Soul and the Body of Light.

For this reason, many people report having had Out of Body Experiences as children but then lost this ability as they entered their early teens and adulthood. One of the purposes of the full and permanent Kundalini awakening is to fully activate the Body of Light, thereby awakening all of its latent potentials. By awakening the Kundalini and raising it to the Crown, the individual consciousness is freed from the hold of the Ego and the physical body, enabling it to re-align with the Soul and the newly activated Body of Light.

As mentioned in a previous chapter, the Body of Light is synonymous with the Rainbow Body. Different frequencies of Light comprise the different colours of the rainbow. These colours express themselves through the Chakric system, which is integral to the Body of Light. When the Kundalini Fire invigorates the Body of Light during the awakening process, the Chakras begin to function at their optimal level. The consciousness can then experience the totality of all the Chakras instead of being stuck in one Chakra or another.

The Body of Light serves as a vessel, a vehicle through which the Soul can traverse and explore the various Planes of existence beyond the Physical. Through the Enochian Keys, along with focused willpower and imagination, the Soul can travel through these different Cosmic Planes and Sub-Planes with the Body of Light.

This type of travelling is called Astral Travel or "Travelling in the Spirit Vision." It is a consciously induced Out of Body Experience, as opposed to Lucid Dreams, which are involuntary Out of Body Experiences.

It is essential to understand that you do not have to awaken the Kundalini energy to use your Body of Light. Remember, you were given one at birth, and it is with you your whole life. The Kundalini energy activates all of the latent potentials in the Body of Light and aligns your consciousness to it. However, even without this full activation, you can still use the Body of Light to a high degree.

Since Light is a tenuous substance, its form is not fixed, which means that the Body of Light can be transformed with your willpower and imagination. Any visualization exercise where you imagine what it is like to embody the Spirit of an animate or inanimate object is an exercise of using the Body of Light.

Another frequent exercise in Magickal Orders is the ability to assume the form of the different Gods or Goddesses from various Spiritual pantheons. To do so, you must imagine the God or Goddess of your desire and apply your willpower to shift to that form. By maintaining focus and holding the vision in your imagination over just a short period, you will assume the God-form. You will feel the God-form and experience a glimpse of what it is like to be that God or Goddess.

While the human Aura is the Microcosm, the external world (notably our Solar System) is the Macrocosm. Inside the Aura, the Body of Light can transform itself into one of the Subtle Bodies, which serve as vehicles that the Soul uses to experience the corresponding inner Cosmic Planes (each Subtle Body corresponds with one inner Cosmic Plane). The Aura is thus a mirror, reflecting and containing the different energies of the entire Solar System within the human system.

In essence, human beings are a point of consciousness localized within a physical body, with a centre that is nowhere and a circumference that is everywhere. Our centre is our Microcosm, while the totality of our consciousness is the Macrocosm—one reflects and contains the power of the other. The known Universe is a manifestation of the Cosmic Planes that comprise it, and we can explore the Universe by having our consciousness inhabit one of the Subtle Bodies of one of the Cosmic Planes (or Sub-Planes).

It is crucial to understand that these Cosmic Planes all occupy the same Time and Space as the physical body. They are on varying rates or frequencies of vibration that the consciousness aligns with to experience them. They do not exist somewhere outside of you but inside. The Enochian Magick Keys serve as Tuning Forks that tune us into these different frequencies of vibration, which are the Cosmic Planes and their Sub-Planes.

Since the Body of Light takes on a different form respective to each of the Cosmic Planes of existence, through the evocation of an Enochian Key, we can zero in on the chosen inner Cosmic Plane we want to visit and experience this Plane with the Subtle Body corresponding to it. The Enochian Magick system is a complete system that encompasses the totality of all the Cosmic Planes, and each Enochian Key opens the doorway to a Cosmic Plane (or a Sub-Plane) that you can explore with its Subtle Body.

To explore a Cosmic Plane (or Sub-Plane), you do not need to have a Kundalini awakening to activate your Body of Light fully but do the evocation of a corresponding Enochian Key. Doing so will shift your consciousness to the Subtle Body of that Cosmic Plane. This shift occurs as your Aura is permeated by the evoked energy of the chosen Enochian Key. Once the evocation is complete, this process occurs naturally, with or without your conscious participation. Note that one Subtle Body corresponds with a Cosmic Plane and its multiple Sub-Planes.

The Lower Astral Body is the initial Subtle Body, which lies just above the physical reality and the physical body. It is often called the Etheric Body (and even Astral Body within some Spiritual circles). Everything within manifest Creation has a subtle, Etheric Body. The Etheric or Astral form is part of the vibrating, interconnected web of energy that makes up a person's or an object's energetic blueprint. Because the Lower Astral Plane's vibration is higher than that of the dense Physical Plane, this Plane is beyond the five senses. The Lower Astral Body is connected to Muladhara Chakra and the Earth Element.

The next Subtle Body is the Higher Astral Body, which is used to travel within the Astral Plane. It is within the Higher Astral Body that our feelings and emotions are stored, including unsettled issues from our past and even previous incarnations. These emotions, in the form of memories and thought patterns, are collected in our Higher Astral Body, where they can be involuntarily triggered to the surface in response to events we may experience in our daily lives. Swadhisthana is the Chakra associated with the Higher Astral Body (Emotional Body), whose Element is Water.

Next, the Lower Mental Body is used to traverse the Lower Mental Plane. Here is where all thought patterns and psychological processes are held and transmitted. It is also the area of imagination and creativity. This Subtle Body is of the Element of Air, corresponding with Anahata Chakra.

The Higher Mental Body follows the Lower Mental Body, used to travel in the Higher Mental Plane. This Subtle Body is associated with our willpower. Thus, it is one level higher than the preceding Emotional and Lower Mental Body, as willpower can overcome emotions and thoughts and is higher on the vibration scale. The Higher Mental Body is associated with the Fire Element and Manipura Chakra.

The final Subtle Body is the Spiritual Body of the Spirit Element and the higher three Spiritual Chakras, Vishuddhi, Ajna, and Sahasrara. To travel in the Spiritual Plane, the Body of Light takes on the form of the Spiritual Body. Each of the different expressions of the Body of Light (Subtle Bodies), from the Etheric to the Spiritual, is unique and necessary for our consciousness to experience the various Cosmic Planes of existence.

THE COSMIC ELEMENTS

Within the Enochian Magick system, the Five Elements indicate the density of the different aspects of reality, namely the Planes and the Subtle Bodies. As physical Matter is the densest, with its vibration being close to being at rest, we can perceive it with our senses. The higher Cosmic Elements, however, are invisible to our senses though they can be perceived through Ajna, the Mind's Eye Chakra. This is because the energies of the Elements correspond with the inner Cosmic Planes of existence.

Emotions are experienced and felt with our Astral Bodies (Lower and Higher) within the Astral Plane. Feelings, being composed of the Water Element, are tangible. Similarly, thoughts are also tangible, being made up of the Air Element. We can experience our thoughts through the Mental Bodies (Lower and Higher) in the Mental Planes of existence. It is through our Spiritual Body and the Spirit Element that we can experience the

Spiritual Plane. The experiences of the Spiritual Plane are Archetypal, presented as tangible images that can be felt or seen, often only intuitively.

Irrespective of what Cosmic Plane an experience occurs, emotions and thoughts are always impacted. If, for example, an experience occurs on the Mental Plane, it will influence the Astral Plane and vice versa. When something happens on one Plane, it affects the other Planes to a certain degree since the Principle of Correspondence is in full effect at all times.

Keep in mind, though, as *The Kybalion* states, the tendency of the creative impulse is for the Higher Planes to dominate the Lower Planes. As such, the Higher Planes are less impacted by the Lower ones. For this reason, the real, lasting change in consciousness happens when you are working mainly with the Higher Planes.

As you practice Enochian Magick, you will have your own unique experience with the Keys. Each Enochian Key and its evocation will tap into a single Plane of existence pertaining to a Watchtower, the Tablet of Union, or an individual Aethyr. You cannot experience multiple Planes simultaneously. Furthermore, no two Magi will experience any of the Subtle Planes in the same way. Certain signposts within each Plane are consistent, as the symbols themselves are consistent, which everyone can experience. However, beyond that, everyone will experience the energy of each evocation uniquely. How your experience unfolds will vary according to your past conditioning and Karma.

Regardless of which Enochian Key, Plane, or Subtle Body you are encountering in your practice, you will begin to grasp, through direct experience, that the Universe around you is a mirror reflecting the thoughts and emotions that lie within you. Moreover, you will learn that your thoughts and feelings result from your conditioning, affected by the people around you. You will see precisely how you are influenced and motivated by your external environment and how you can attain personal power by actively controlling the interpretation of your circumstances. With these methods, you will be able to tap into the power that lies within you that often goes overlooked. This understanding will come as you work directly with the Enochian Keys.

Enochian Magick is one of the most excellent practices or tools for inner exploration I have ever encountered, if not the greatest. Also, the level of control you can achieve over your own life is extraordinary. By working with the Enochian Keys, you are walking the true path of the Magus. You must master the Elements within yourself and gain complete control over your life by exercising your willpower to its fullest. Until you do this, you will not be tapping into your highest potential as a Spiritual human being.

ENOCHIAN MAGICK AND DREAMS

Through the evocations of the Enochian Keys, your experiences of the Watchtowers and the Aethyrs will be similar to the experience of watching a movie, complete with symbols, metaphors, unique characters, and events. However, more than just watching a movie, you will also experience yourself as the director and star in the film. The experiences will all be a manifestation of whatever Cosmic Plane you are visiting. These experiences, like any good movie, can be both intense and revealing. Expect in-depth Gnosis about yourself and your reality to be bestowed upon you.

Usually, after a recitation of a Key, you will feel a wave of its energy permeate your Aura. This wave of energy will remain present until it finds some way to filter through the Four Worlds and manifest as a thought or emotion so that you can experience it, learn from it, and evolve past it. As a result, you will notice that throughout the day, you will be overtaken by thoughts and emotions that sometimes feel foreign to you, although they are projections from your inner consciousness.

These emotions or thoughts will build and influence how you think, feel and relate to the world around you. They will affect your actions and reactions to people as well as events that you are experiencing throughout the day. By the end of the day, you will frequently feel tired and welcome a good night's sleep. Here is where you can get most in touch with your thoughts and emotions and travel in these different Planes by using one of your various Subtle Bodies. Remember always, the energy you invoke (or evoke) needs to find some way to filter through the Four Worlds inside your Aura, and until it does, it will be present within it.

By understanding the qualities of your dreams, you can understand more about your consciousness and where it goes during sleep. While we sleep, our consciousness leaves the physical body and enters one of the Subtle Bodies.

If a dream has a very emotional quality, your consciousness has likely entered your Light Body, which has taken the form of the Higher Astral Body, in the Higher Astral Plane, where the Water Element is dominant. Similarly, if a dream lacks emotion yet has a very intellectual kind of experience, you are likely experiencing the Lower Mental Body in the Lower Mental Plane, within the Air Element.

If you are in a deep, dreamless sleep, your Light Body has likely taken the form of the Higher Mental Body in the Higher Mental Plane, where the Fire Element is dominant. If you are experiencing a Lucid Dream, during which you are consciously able to control and influence its content, you are likely in the Spiritual Plane and have assumed the form of the Spiritual Body. If the quality of your dreams feels Divine, perhaps with the presence of Divine Beings in beautiful, unseen before places (whether in a Lucid Dream or not), you have likely had the fortune of experiencing the Divine Planes. Regardless of the quality of your sleep and dreams, including dreamless sleep, your consciousness will return to your physical body when you awaken.

With the same method as with the other ritual exercises presented in *The Magus*, it is recommended that you have a Magickal journal where you can write down your dreams and experiences while working with these Enochian evocations. In the case of working with Enochian Magick, you will have more vivid dreams than ever with themes that seem out of a Hollywood movie. Enochian Magick is very theatrical. In that way, it is also enjoyable and entertaining and will leave a lasting impression on your consciousness.

ASTRAL TRAVEL

Once you have recited one of the Enochian Keys in phonetic, you can also perform the Astral Travel technique. As mentioned, the evoked energy must filter through the Four Worlds before leaving your Aura for good. You can allow it to stay with you throughout the day and filter through you during sleep while you are in a dream state. Or you can deliberately try to access one of these Cosmic Planes by consciously entering into the respective Plane (or Sub-Plane) to which the evoked Key pertains. The mechanics are the same as entering into this Plane during sleep; only, in this case, you are doing it deliberately.

It requires you to shift your consciousness in some way to the desired Cosmic Plane. You need to be in a state of meditation to accomplish this. The mind has to shift from normal waking consciousness with mental activity (in the *Beta State* of brain activity) to a deeper state called the Alpha State. When this occurs, your consciousness will leave your body and enter into the Cosmic Plane to which the evoked energy pertains.

To induce a meditative state, perform the Four-Fold Breath while either lying down or sitting in a lotus position. Your physical body has to be in its most relaxed state if you are planning to transfer your consciousness into one of the Cosmic Planes. By accomplishing a state of comfort in your physical body and using the Four-Fold Breath to enter into a meditative Alpha State, you should be able to project your consciousness inwards by merely allowing this experience to happen.

There is a Veil between the waking consciousness and the inner Cosmic Planes. Shifting your consciousness from one to the other and slipping through this Veil happens almost instantaneously. As mentioned, this is the same mechanism as going into a dream state during sleep, only, in this case, you are doing it consciously and with intention.

Once you have accomplished this, you will be able to consciously experience one of the Cosmic Planes while using its corresponding Subtle Body and learn the lessons from that particular Plane. Because you are tapping into this energy directly, you will release some of it from your Aura. However, some of the energy will still stay present within you for the day until you get a full night's sleep, and it leaves your Aura entirely.

ENOCH AND HERMES

Enoch is one of the Biblical patriarchs and the subject of many Jewish and Christian writings. He is the great-grandfather of Noah and is considered the author of the *Book of Enoch*. The first part of this book describes the Watchers, whereas the second part describes Enoch's visits to Heaven in the form of travels, visions, dreams, and revelations.

The Holy Bible says that Enoch lived for 365 years before being "taken" by God. Genesis 5:24 says, "And Enoch walked with God: and he was not, for God took him." Many Christians interpret this as Enoch entering Heaven alive and ceasing to exist in physical form, which is impossible since one can only do this after the physical body perishes.

The Ancient Astronaut theorists who believe that the Watchers were Extraterrestrials believe that Enoch was taken off-Planet by them. Whichever interpretation is closer to the truth is open to debate. Still, if Enoch actually lived for 365 years as the scriptures say (and we take this meaning literally), then there is a strong possibility that he was of Extraterrestrial origin himself. These theories are unorthodox, but they are worth examining since Enoch is clothed in more mystery and interpretation than any other prominent figure in *The Holy Bible*. Moreover, there are a lot of credible scholars who make Extraterrestrial associations with his story.

Perhaps the most plausible theory, though (if you are against the existence of Extraterrestrials), is that Enoch and Hermes/Thoth may have been the same Being (or the reincarnation of one). All three were revered figures associated with the invention of writing and the promulgation of sacred books and inscriptions. All three also had Astrological connections, as Hermes is said to have written 36,525 books. Considering that Enoch predates Hermes/Thoth and is Antideluvian (before the Great Flood), it means that the Spirit of Enoch reincarnates time and time again as the World Teacher to teach humankind about who they are and their origins.

According to John Dee, Enoch was the last person who spoke the Enochian language before this language was long forgotten. The Enochian Keys presented here are then of the Spirit of the World Teacher since their purpose is to further the Spiritual Evolution of humanity (as was the purpose of Enoch's work and that of Hermes/Thoth). The Enochian language may very well be of the highest authenticity and authority. After all, Enoch was considered the highest source of Spiritual wisdom and knowledge rivalled only by his successor, Hermes Trismegistus.

It is even possible that the Enochian language is the language of the Extraterrestrials Beings, the Watchers, from the *Book of Enoch*. It cannot be a coincidence that the Elements in Enochian Magick are represented by the Watchtowers, presided over by Angelic and Demonic Spirits. Some Ceremonial Magi believe that the Spirits of Enochian Magick are the Watchers (Angels) and the Nephilim, the Fallen Angels (Demons) from *The Book of Enoch*. As you practice the Enochian Keys, you will learn of their power and realize that you are dealing with something exceptional indeed.

ENOCHIAN ARMIES OF ANGELS

When I began working with Enochian Magick many years ago, I received a vision of an army of Angels on horseback the very first night. It was not a modern-day army with guns and tanks but one reminiscent of medieval times. Perhaps this is because of the time in which Dee and Kelley channelled Enochian Magick. This army carried swords, bows, and other medieval weapons, stamping across a barren land with force. Before having this vision, I did the evocation of the First and Second Key (Spirit Active and Passive) earlier in the day. Although I felt a cooling Spirit energy inside my Heart Chakra immediately after the evocation, it was during the night when I was drifting off into sleep that this energy became personified in visual form.

The most impactful part of this vision was the army general, a man with a white rabbit head, exacting and fierce. He had a metal plate on his face like Kano from Mortal Kombat and carried the Scythe of Saturn in a futuristic form and design. Led by the general, the army came upon a God-form of Horus, which personified my Ego personality at the time. Upon seeing Horus, the general dismounted his horse and slew him with his Scythe. After slashing him with the Scythe, he said, "I always hated that guy."

Interestingly, I very much disliked who I was and had become prior to having this vision. I believe that the general was a manifestation of my Higher Self since the white rabbit was a pet I owned that I related to at the time. Another prominent connection to the rabbit was the first street I lived on in Canada called Lappin Avenue, "lapin," meaning "rabbit" in French, Canada's second language.

The Scythe of Saturn that the general carried is a tool used by the Grim Reaper to bring death and transformation to everything it cuts. Weeks passed after this experience, and the armies of Angles manifested almost nightly in my dreams. Finally, I realized their purpose was to destroy everything old inside me, which was not serving my Higher Self. In this way, the armies of Angels sought to remake me entirely.

These armies are mighty, and I continued to see them in my dreams in visions during the time that I practised the Elemental and Sub-Elemental Keys. In addition, I found that the Elemental and Sub-Elemental Keys (numbered One to Eighteen) carry combatant, warrior energy. For this reason, I saw armies of Angels often.

How the energy of the Enochian Keys of Elements and Sub-Elements will manifest to you depends on the personification of your *Ancestral Energy*. For example, you may not see armies of Angels at all but something else entirely. But many people I have taught Enochian Magick in the past have reported compelling visions with themes of conquest and war. Thus, be on the lookout for their manifestation in your dreams as you begin working with the Keys.

Interestingly, I have found that how the Keys manifested usually remained uniform while working with the Elemental and Sub-Elemental Enochian Keys. The energies of the Thirty Aethyrs, on the other hand, manifested differently. Remember, the Enochian Keys energy seeks to transform you and discard old parts of Self that no longer serve you. So do not be afraid of your experiences while working with Enochian Magick.

ANGELS AND DEMONS IN ENOCHIAN MAGICK

Many practitioners of Enochian Magick have said that the Spiritual entities they encountered in their dreams and visions are Demonic. To clarify, Enochian Magick contains both Angelic and Demonic Spirits since it is up to us to learn to command both parts of the Self. As such, these Angelic or Demonic Spirits are personifications of forces within us. So now you understand why it was crucial to finish the Spiritual Alchemy program with the Five Elements before embarking on Enochian Magick. If you jump into this before having a proper foundation, the Demonic energies could easily tear you apart mentally and emotionally.

The Demonic parts of the Self are the Fallen Angels. It is up to us to give them back their wings, metaphorically speaking. We must learn to command and use our Demons for good instead of being used and abused by them. Through Enochian Magick, you are learning to control your Geburah aspect, the Inner Fire of the Self, which also contains the part of you that is often termed Demonic. Demonic does not necessarily mean evil, though, since we have Free Will. It is up to us to discern between positive, loving actions in life and negative, evil ones.

Because of this dichotomy of Angels and Demons, Enochian Magick reaches the deepest parts of the Self, where it taps into both. Having the experience of the previous ritual exercises presented in *The Magus*, namely the LIRPs of the Elements and the SIRP, will give you the necessary mastery over your Elements so that when your personal Demons confront you, you will know how to approach them.

Let this not confuse you nor deter you from working with Enochian Magick, though. After completing the Spiritual Alchemy program with the Five Elements, this is the next step in your Ritual Magick evolution. This method has been practised for over 120 years within different Golden Dawn Orders. Learning to master your dichotomy of Angelic and Demonic energy is part of being human since we live in a world of duality. Strength of mind and heart can only be achieved when you learn to command both aspects, as it is the path towards true mastery of Self.

DEFEATING DEMONS IN YOUR DREAMS

As you encounter Angelic and Demonic Spirits in your dreams and visions, you may also have to overcome a Demon occasionally, to progress further on your Spiritual journey. Often, Demonic Spirits bar the way to a succeeding Elemental or Sub-Elemental Plane or Aethyr. Once you defeat one, your consciousness can rise to a Higher Plane naturally. Do not be alarmed because, in your dreams, you will be given guidance on how to accomplish this. Very often, you will obtain knowledge of how to defeat a Demon instantaneously the moment you are confronted with one.

From personal experience, defeating Demons usually involves using Light and love and projecting this energy into the Demon until they are destroyed (or, to be more accurate, transformed). Sometimes the technique involves "slaying" it with a sword or another symbolic weapon. Other methods include tools and implements such as a cross, a Bible, the name of Jesus Christ, a Pentagram, a Hexagram, or some other symbolic item or symbol representing the power of Light and love. The methods of performing an exorcism prevalent in Hollywood movies work in real life. The Banner of the West is also often used by Ceremonial Magi to command Demons since its image represents dominion over darkness.

Your dreams may even personify the Demon into a Vampire; therefore, to trap it, you may need to use garlic, while to defeat it, you may need to drive a stake in its heart. This representation of a Demon is not uncommon. Your imagination will personify how the Demon appears to you and the method of defeating it. The personified image will be based on your past conditioning and what your Soul is comfortable with. Remember that your Soul will never be tested beyond what it can handle.

Be on the lookout in your dreams and visions, and the first thing you must do when you encounter a Demon is not fear it. This part is crucial. By fearing them, you are feeding them energy since it is your fear that they try to use against you, as that is what gives them power over you. Don't forget that personal Demons are just a projection of your mind and your inner fears. Thus, overcoming them is a symbolic event of mastering that part of yourself.

Often, all that is required of you is to confront the Demon instead of running from it. Showing courage by engaging it will allow you to integrate its energy into your Heart Chakra and dissolve it into love and Light. As such, their state will change permanently. Now, whatever power they had over you in the past, you will have over them.

Welcome these experiences as positive ones in your life, since by overcoming a Demon, you will be enhancing your personal power. Defeating a Demon means overcoming something in yourself that causes you to fear in life. Remember always that Light is love and every Being within the inner Cosmic Planes bows down to love. Thus, when you embark on this Enochian Magick journey, your faith in the Divine and the power of love is an essential tool at your disposal.

THE ENOCHIAN ELEMENTAL AND SUB-ELEMENTAL KEYS

In the following chapter, the First to Eighteen Enochian Keys are presented. These Keys will feel something like the LIRP energy you have worked with thus far, but with a more theatrical element in your visions that is typical of Enochian Magick. The energy will feel like it has permeated your Being more than the LIRP. Enochian Magick reaches the deepest levels of the subconscious, activating the Demonic parts of the Self. These Demonic parts of Self rest in your subconscious as parts of the Self that you cast away because you could not command them. The fear you have of them is a fear of lacking the ability to control them.

The use of these Keys will give you very unusual and challenging dreams. The energy that is evoked through them will test your Soul by bringing out your innermost desires—the good, the bad, and the ugly. You will see every facet of yourself and have to confront it. Enochian energies will communicate to you through symbols. They will try to use your weaknesses against you. Fear not, for all they are doing is bringing to the surface that which lies buried in your subconscious. All of your fears and secrets will be revealed to you through this work.

These parts of Self are activated by the Enochian energy, which will feel hot and fiery at times, even if it is an energy that is its opposite. Evocations of the Enochian Keys will tap into one of the Worlds of the Four Watchtowers of the Elements or the Tablet of Union. As such, you will be using the Subtle Body that relates to whatever Element or Sub-Element you are invoking to "surf" its corresponding inner Plane.

The Sub-Elements will have the underlying energy of the primary Element they pertain to, with the addition of another Element in a smaller degree of energy. These Sub-Elements and Elements correspond with the Planetary and Zodiacal energies to a certain degree.

The setting of each Element and Sub-Element will be a personification of its overall energy. The Air of Air Key may be a high mountain top, or somewhere elevated off the ground where you can feel the cool breeze of the air around you. The Water of Water Key might be on or near a lake, or ocean, or a body of water where you can feel the water present. The Fire of Earth Key might be an erupting volcano, where you can feel the

Fire acting on the Earth. The Water of Air Key might manifest as a mist, where you can feel the Water Element within the Air Element.

These are just a few examples, but it is important to note that these manifestations in your visions may be entirely different for everyone. Depending on what your Ancestral Energy is, it will be powered by the Enochian Angels and Demons. Enochian Magick is meant to make you tough, both mentally and emotionally. Therefore, look at everything you see and experience as a test. If you persevere and face this test without fear in your heart, you will succeed.

THE EIGHTEEN ENOCHIAN KEYS

IF YOU HAVE NOT FINISHED THE PRESCRIBED SPIRITUAL ALCHEMY PROGRAM WITH THE FIVE ELEMENTS, DO NOT USE THE ENOCHIAN KEYS! DOING SO WITHOUT THE RIGHT FOUNDATION MAY BRING HARM TO YOUR SPIRITUAL, MENTAL, AND EMOTIONAL WELL-BEING.

Even though you may not understand why I caution you at the moment, you must heed my warning. There is a reason why I have placed Enochian Magick as the very last section of this book. Therefore, do not glance nor read over the Enochian Keys presented below but instead skip over this section entirely if you wish to keep reading about Enochian Magick. It is my final word of warning on this subject. You must be prepared for this work in mind, body, and Soul before undertaking it.

For those ready to begin this work, you will be working with the Enochian phonetic translations, which you are to recite individually with utmost care and solemnity. Anyone who mocks these Keys with an impure mind and heart shall be liable to bring serious physical and Spiritual harm unto themselves. Remember, the phonetic translation is meant to be pronounced as it is written and vibrated with your vocal cords in a projective, energising tone.

These Eighteen Keys are attributed to the Tablet of Union and the Four Watchtower Tablets. The First and Second Keys are assigned to the Tablet of Union and pertain to the Spiritual Plane.

The Third, Seventh, Eighth, and Ninth Keys are attributed to the four quadrants of the Watchtower of Air in the Lower Mental Plane. The Third Key can be used for the Watchtower of the Air Tablet as a whole and is representative of the Air Element.

The Fourth, Tenth, Eleventh, and Twelfth Keys are attributed to the four quadrants of the Watchtower of Water in the Higher Astral Plane. The Fourth Key also can be used for the Watchtower of Water Tablet as a whole and is representative of the Water Element.

The Fifth, Thirteenth, Fourteenth, and Fifteenth Keys are attributed to the four quadrants of the Watchtower of Earth in the Lower Astral Plane. The Fifth Key is for the Watchtower of Earth Tablet as a whole and is representative of the Earth Element.

The Sixth, Sixteenth, Seventeenth, and Eighteenth Keys are attributed to the four quadrants of the Watchtower of Fire in the Higher Mental Plane. The Sixth Key can be used for the Watchtower of Fire Tablet as a whole and it represents the Fire Element.

It is believed by many practitioners of Enochian Magick that there is also a Zero Key, which is of the Godhead and therefore cannot be expressed. Once you have completed the entire Eighteen Enochian Keys operation, though, along with the Thirty Aethyrs operation, the Zero Key may reveal itself to you as a tangible energy source. Many seasoned Enochian Magick practitioners believe this to be true, and some report to have even experienced it. Therefore, if you have the privilege of experiencing the Zero Key while working with the Enochian system, consider it the highest of blessings from the Divine.

S.L. MacGregor Mathers and Aleister Crowley studied the documents left by John Dee and Edward Kelley on Enochian Magick. Each of them developed translations of the Enochian Keys, including the phonetic pronunciation of each Key. Both versions are slightly different from each other. Crowley's interpretations are more attuned to the Thelemic energy current, while Mathers' are along the Golden Dawn lines. I have found that Crowley's version of the Keys evokes the same energy but in a more grounded, less Aetheric way, making it more challenging to surf the energy of each Key.

After working with both translations numerous times, and since *The Magus* holds to the Golden Dawn teachings, I have decided to use Mathers' Enochian Keys as part of this work. It is the complete version from his manuscript titled *The 48 Angelical Keys of Calls* by G.H. Frater D.D.C.F. (S.L. MacGregor Mathers).

I include the Enochian, English and Enochian (Phonetic) versions of each Key, edited by me so that all three parts correspond. The Enochian version is the actual Key as was channelled to Dee and Kelley by the Angels. The English version presents the meaning behind each Key, while the Enochian (Phonetic) is the ritual exercise evocation, the Mantras, that evokes the energy of each Key.

In the diagram following the Enochian Keys (Figure 62), I have also given you the general associations of the Zodiacal and Planetary energies to the energies of the Elements and Sub-Elements of the Keys. You will find that it is a very accurate representation of the energy of each Zodiac, and it is presented here to further your understanding of this subject. In addition, these associations will cross-reference with any other experiences you may have had with the Zodiacal and Planetary energies through other Magickal ritual invocation and evocation techniques.

1st Key—Spirit (Active)

Enochian:

Ol Sonf Vorsag Goho Iad Bait, Lonsh Calz Vonpho Sobra Z-OL.

Ror I Ta Nazps, Od Graa Ta Maiprg:

Ds Hol-Q Qaa Nothoa Zimz Od Commah Ta Nobioh Zien;

Soba Thu Gnonp Prge Aldi Ds Vrbs Oboleh G Rsam;

Casarm Ohorela Taba Pir; Ds Zonrensg Cab Erm Iadnah.

Pilah Farzm Znrza Adna Gono Iadpil Ds Hom Od To h;

Soba Ipam Lu Ipamis;

Ds Loholo Vep Zomd Poamal, Od Bogpa Aai Ta Piap Piamol Od Vaoan.

Zacare Eca Od Zamran. Odo Cicle Qaa! Zorge Lap Zirdo Noco Mad, Hoath Iaida.

English:

I reign over you Saith the God of Justice. In power exalted above the firmament of Wrath.

In Whose hands the Sun is as a sword and the Moon as through-thrusting fire:

Who measureth your garments in the midst of my vestures and trussed you together as the palms of my hands:

Whose seats I garnished with the fire of gathering:

Who beautified your garments with admiration:

To Whom I made a law to govern the Holy Ones: Who delivered you a rod with the Ark of Knowledge.

Moreover Ye lifted up Your voices and sware obedience and faith to Him that liveth and triumpheth:

Whose beginning is not nor end cannot be: which shineth as a flame in the midst of your Palaces and reigneth amongst you as the balance of righteousness and truth.

Move therefore and show yourselves. Open the mysteries of your creation! Be friendly unto me. For I am the servant of the same your God, the true worshipper of the Highest.

Enochian (Phonetic):

Oh-el Soh-noof Vay-oh-air-sahjee Goh-hoh Ee-ah-dah Bahl-tah, Elon-shee Kahi-zoad Von-pay-hoh: Soh-bay-rah Zoad-oh-lah.

Roh-ray Ee Tah Nan-zoad-pay-ess, Oh-dah Jee-rah-ah Tah Mahi- peer-jee:

Dah-ess Hoh-el-koh Kah-ah No-thoh-ah Zoad-ee-mah-zoad Oh-dah Koh-mah-mahhay Tah Noh-bloh-hay Zoad-ee-aynoo;

So-bah Tah-heelah Jee-noh-noo-pay Peer-jee Ahi-dee; Dah-ess Ur-bass Oh-boh-lay Jee Rah-sah-may;

Cahs-armay Oh-hor-raylah Tah-bah Peer; Dah-es Zoad-oh-noo-ray-noo-sah-jee Kahbah Air-may Ee-ad-nah.

Peelah-hay Far-zoad-mee Zoad-noo-ray-zoad-ah Ahd-nah Goh-noh Ee-ah-dah-pee-ayl Dah-ess Hoh-may Oh-dah Toh hay;

Soh-bay Ee-pah-may Loo Ee-pah-mees; Dah-ess Loh-hoh-loh Vay-pay Zoad-oh-Maydah Po-ah-may-ell, Oh-dah Boh-jee-pay Ah-ah-ee Tay-ah Pee-ah-pay Pee-ah-moh-ayl Oh-dah Vay-oh-ah-noo.

Zoad-a-kah-ray Ay-kah Oh-dah Zoad-a-mer-ahnoo. Oh-dah Kee-klay kah-ah! Zoadorjee Lah-pay Zoad-eer-raydoh Noh-koh Mahdah, Hoh-ah-tah-hay Ee-ah-ee-dah.

2nd Key—Spirit (Passive)

Enochian:
Adgt Vpaah Zong Om Faaip Sald, Vi-I-V L, Sobam Ial-Prg I-Za-Zaz Pi-Adph;
Casarma Abrang Ta Talho Paracleda, Q Ta Lorslq Turbs Ooge Baltoh.
Givi Chis Lusd Orri Od Micaip Chis Bia Ozongon.
Lap Noan Trof Cors Ta Ge O Q Manin Ia-Idon.
Torzu Gohe L. Zacar Eca C Noqod. Zamran Micaizo Od Ozazm Vrelp, Lap Zir Io-Iad.

English:
Can the Wings of the Winds Understand your voices of wonder. O You the Second of the First, Whom the burning flames have framed within the depth of my jaws:

Whom I have prepared as cups for a wedding or as the flowers in their beauty for the Chamber of the Righteous.

Stronger are your feet than the barren stone and mightier are your voices than the manifold winds.

For ye are become a building such as is not save in the mind of the All-Powerful.

Arise, saith the First. Move, therefore, unto thy servants. Show yourselves in power and make me a strong seer of things, for I am of Him that liveth forever.

Enochian (Phonetic):
Ahd-gee-tay Oo-pah-hay Zoad-oh-noo-jee Oh-mah Fah-ah-ee-pay Saldah, Vee-ee-vee Ayl, S oh-bah-may Ee-ahl-peer-jee Ee-zoad-ah-zoad-ah-zoad Pee-ahd-pay-hay;

Cah-sarmah Ah-brahn-jee Tah-hoh Paraclaydah, Koh Tah Lor-es-sel-koh Toor-bay-ess Oh-oh-jee Bahi-toha.

Jee-vee Kah-hee-sah Loos-dah Ohr-ree Oh-dah Mee-cal-pah Kah-hees-ah Bee-ah Oh-zoad-oh-noo-goh-noo.

Lah-pay Noh-ah-noo Troh-eff Corsay Tah Jee Oh Koh Mah-nee-no Ee-ah-ee-doh-noo.

Tohr-zoad-oo Goh-hay Ayl. Zoad-a-kar-ray Ay-Kah Kah Noh-Kwoh-dah. Zoad-amerah-noo. Me-kah-el-zoad-oh Oh-dah Oh-zoad-ah-zoad-may Oo-rel-pay, Lah-pay Zoadee-ray Ee-oh Ee-ah-dah.

3rd Key—Air of Air

Enochian:
Micma! Goho Mad. Zir Comselha Zien Biah Os Londoh. Norz Chis Othil Gigipah, Vnd-L Chis ta Pu-Im Q Mospleh Teloch, Qui-I—N Toltorg Chis I Chis-Ge In Ozien, Ds T Brgdo Od Torzul.

I Li E Ol Balzarg Od Aala, Thiln Os Netaab, Dluga Vonsarg Lonsa Cap-Mi Ali Vors CLA, Homil Cocasb; Fafen Izizop Od Miinoag De Gnetaab Vaun Na-Na-E-El; Panpir Malpirg Pild Caosg.

Noan Vnaiah Bait Od Vaoan.

Do-O-I-A p Mad; Goholor Gohus Amiran. Micma Iehusoz Ca-Cacom Od Do-O-A-In Noar Mica-Olz A-Ai-Om, Casarmg Gohia; Zacar Vnigiag Od Im-Va-Mar Pugo, Piapii Ananael Qa-A-An.

English:
Behold saith your God. I am a Circle on whose hands stand Twelve Kingdoms. Six are the seats of Living Breath, the rest are as sharp sickles or the horns of Death, wherein the creatures of Earth are and are not, except Mine own hands which also sleep and shall rise.

In the first I made you stewards and placed you in the seats Twelve of Government, giving unto every one of you power successively over Four, Five and Six, the true Ages of Time: to the intent that from the highest Vessels and the corners of your governments ye might work My power: Pouring down the Fires of Life and increase continually upon the Earth.

Thus ye are become the Skirts of Justice and Truth.

In the Name of the same your God lift up, I say yourselves. Behold, His mercies flourish and His Name is become mighty amongst us, in Whom we say: Move, Descend and apply your selves unto us, as unto the Partakers of the Secret Wisdom of your creation.

Enochian (Phonetic):
Meek-mah! Goh-hoh Mah-dah. Zoad-eeray Kohm-sayl-hah Zoad-ee-ay-noo Be-ahhay Oh-ess Lon-doh-hah. Nohr -zoad Kah-heesah Otheeiah Jee-jee-pay-hay, Oon-dah-iah Kah-heesah Tah Poo-eem Kwo-Mohs-piay Tayiohk-hay, kwee-eenoo Tohl-torjee, Kahees Ee Kah-hees-jee Ee-noo Oh-zoad-ee-ay-noo, Day-ess Tay Bray-jee-dah Oh-dah Tor-zoad-oo-lah.

Ee-Lee Ay Oh-Lah Bahl-zoad-ahr-jee Oh-dah Ah-ah-iah, Tay-heeinoo Oh-ess Nay-tahah-bay, Dah-loo-gahr Vohn-sahrjee Lohn-sah Cahpeemee-ahiee Vor-sah Cah Ayl Ah, Hoh-meei Koh-kahs-bay; Fah-faynoo Ee-zoad-ee-zoad-oh-pay Oh Dah Mee-ee-noh-ahjee Day Jee-nay-tah-ah-bah Vah-oo-noo Nah-nah-ay-ayl; Pahn-peer Mahi-peerjee Pee-el-dah Kah-ohs-gah.

Noh-ah-noo Oo-nah-iah Baitah Oh-dah Vay-oh-ah-noo.

Doo-oh-ee-ah-pay Mah-dah, Goh-hoh-ior Goh-hoos Ah-mee-rah-noo. Meek-mah Yehhoo-soh-zoad Kah-Kah-komah Oh-dah Doh-oh-ah-ee-noo Noh-ahr Mee-kah-ohl-zoad Ah-ah-ee-oh-mah, Kah-sarmjee Goh-hee-ah;

Zoadah-kah-ray Oo-nee-giah-jee Oh-dah Eem-vah-mar Poojoh, Plahplee Ah-nah-nahayl Kah-ah-noo.

4th Key—Water of Water

Enochian:
Othil Lusdi Babage Od Dorpha Gohol:
G-Chis-Gee Avavago Cormp P D Ds Sonf Vi-vi-Iv Casarmi Oali MAPM Soham Ag Cormpo Crp L:
Casarmg Cro-Od-Zi Chis Od Vgeg, Ds T Capmiali Chis Capimaon, Od Lonshin Chis Ta L-O CLA.
Torzu Nor-Quasahi, Od F Caosga; Bagle Zire Mad Ds I Od Apila.
Do—O-A—Ip Qaal, Zacar Od Zamran Obelisong, Rest-El-Aaf Nor-Molap.

English:
I have set my feet in the South and have looked about me saying:
Are not the Thunders of Increase numbered thirty-three which reign in the Second Angle?
Under Whom I have placed Nine Six Three Nine, Whom None hath yet numbered but One:
In Whom the Second Beginning of things are and wax strong, which also successively are the numbers of Time, and their powers are as the first.
Arise ye Sons of Pleasure and visit the Earth: For I am the Lord your God which is and liveth for ever.
In the Name of the Creator, move and show yourselves as pleasant deliverers that you may praise Him amongst the Sons of Men.

Enochian (Phonetic):
Oh-thee-iah Loos-dee Bah-bah-jee Oh-dah Dor-pay-hah Goh-hoh-lah:
Jee-kah-hees-jee Ah-vah-vah-goh Kohr-em-pay Pay-Dah Dah-ess Sohnoof Vee-vee-eevah Kas-ahrm-ee Oh-ah-lee Em-Ah-Pay-Em Soh-bah-mah Ah-gee Kohr-em-poh Kah-arpay Ayl:
Kah-sahrmjee Kroh-oh-dah-zoadee Kah-heesah Ohdah Vah-jeejee, Dah-ess Tay Kahpee-mah-lee Kah-heesah Kapee-mah-ohnoo, Oh-dah Lon-sheenoo Kah-heesah Tay-ah Aylo-oh Kay-El-Ah.
Tor-zoad-oo Nohr-kwah-sahee, Oh-dah Eff Kah-ohs-gah; Bah-glay Zoad-eeray Mahdah Dah-ess Ee Ohdah Ahpeelah.
Doo-ah-ee-pay Kah-ah-lah, Zoad-a karah Oh-dah Zoadamerahnoo Oh-bayleesonjee, Raystellah Ah-ah-eff Nohr-moh-lahpay.

5th Key—Earth of Earth

Enochian:
Sapah Zimii DUIY od noas ta quanis Adroch, Dorphal Caosg od faonts Piripsol Ta blior.
Casarm am-ipzi nazarth AF od dlugar zizop zlida Caosgi toltorgi:
Od z chis e siasch L ta Vi-u od laod thild ds Hubar PEOAL,
Sobo-Cormfa chis Ta LA, Vls od Q Cocasb. Eca niis, od darbs.
Qaas F etharzi od bliora. Ia-lal ednas cicles. Bagle? Ge-lad I L.

English:
The mighty sounds have entered in the Third Angle And are become as Olives in the Olive Mount, Looking with Gladness upon the Earth, and dwelling in the Brightness of the Heavens as continual comforters.
Unto Whom I fastened 19 Pillars of Gladness and gave them Vessels to water the Earth with all her creatures:
And they are the brothers of the First and the Second, and the beginning of their own Seats which are garnished with 69636 Continual Burning Lamps, whose numbers are as the First, the Ends, and the Contents of Time.
Therefore come ye and obey your creation. Visit us in peace and comfort.
Conclude us Receivers of your Mysteries, For why? Our Lord and Master is the All One.

Enochian (Phonetic):

Sah-pah-hay Zoad-ee-mee-ee Doo-ee-vay, Oh-dah Noh-ahs Tay-ah Kah-nees Ah-drohkay, Dohr-pay-hal Kah-ohs-gah Oh-dah Fah-ohn-tay-ess Pee-reep-sohl Tay-ah Blee-ohr.

Kah-sarmay Ah-mee-eep-zoad-ee Nah-zoad-arth Ah-eff Oh-dah Dahloo-gahr Zoad-eezoad-oh-pay Zoad-leedah Kah-ohs-jee Tohi -torjee;

Oh-dah Zoad Kah-heesah Ay-See-ahs-kay Ayl Tah vee-oo-Oh-dah Ee-ah-ohdah Tayheeldah Dah-ess Hoobar Pay Ay Oh Ah Ayl.

Soh-bah Kohr-em-fah Kah-heesah Tay-ah El-ah Vah-less Oh-dah Koh-Koh-Kahs-bay. Ag-kah Nee-ee-sah Oh-dah Dahr-bay-ess.

Kah-ah-sah Eff Aythar-zoadee Oh-dah Blee-ohr-ah. Ee-ah-ee -ah-ayl. Ayd-nahss Keeklay-sah. Bah-glay? Jee-Ee-Ahdah Ee-el!

6th Key—Fire of Fire

Enochian:

Gah S diu chis Em, micalzo pilzin; Sobam El harg mir Babalon od obloc Samvelg:

Dlugar malprg Ar Caosgi, Od ACAM Canal sobol zar fbliard Caosgi, od chisa Netaab od Miam ta VIV od D.

Darsar Solpeth bi-en. Brita od zacam g-micalza sobol ath trian lu-la he od ecrin Mad Qaaon.

English:

The Spirits of the Fourth Angle are Nine, mighty in the firmament of waters: Whom the First hath planted a torment to the wicked and a garland to the Righteous:

Giving unto them fiery darts to Vanne the Earth, and 7699 Continual workmen whose courses visit with comfort the Earth, and are in government and continuance as the Second and the Third.

Wherefore, hearken unto my voice. I have talked of you and I move you in power and presence; Whose works shall be a Song of Honour and the Praise of your God in your Creation.

Enochian (Phonetic):

Gah-hay Ess Dee-oo Kah-heesah AY-Em, Mee-kahl-zoadoh Peel-zoadeenoo; Soh-bah may Ayl Harjee Meer Bah-bah-lohnoo Oh-dah Oh-bloh-kah Sahm-vay-lanjee:

Dah-loogar Mah-lah-peerjee Ahray Kah-ohsjee, Oh-dah Ah Kah Ah Em Kah-nahl So-bolah Zoad-ah-ray Eff Blee-ahr-dah Kah-ohs-jee, Oh-dah Kah-heesay Naytah-ah-bay Oh-dah Mee-ah may Tay-ah Vee-ee-vah Oh-dah Dah.

Dahr-sahr Sohi-pet-hay Bee-aynoo. Bay-reetah Oh-dah Zoad-ah-kahmay Jee-meekahel-zoadah So-boh-lah Aht-hay Tre-ah-noo Loo -EE-ah Hay Oh-dah Aykreenoo Mahdah Kah-ah-ohnoo.

7th Key—Water of Air

Enochian:

Raas i salman paradiz, oecrimi aao Ialpirgah, quiin Enay Butmon od I Noas NI Paradial casarmg vgear chirlan od zonac Luciftian cors ta vaul zirn tolhami.

Sobol londoh od miam chis ta I od ES vmadea od pibliar, Othil Rit od miam.

C noqol rit, Zacar zamran oecrimi Qaada! od O micaolz aaiom! Bagle papnor i dlugam lonshi od vmplif vgegi Bigl IAD!

English:

The East is a House of Virgins singing praises amongst the Flames of First Glory, wherein the Lord hath opened His mouth and they are become 28 Living Dwellings in whom the strength of man rejoiceth, and they are apparelled with Ornaments of brightness such as work wonders on all Creatures.

Whose kingdoms and continuance are as the Third and Fourth, strong towers and places of comfort, the Seat of Mercy and continuance.

O ye servants of Mercy, Move, Appear, Sing praises unto the Creator! And be mighty amongst us! For to this remembrance is given power, and our strength waxeth strong in our Comforter!

Enochian (Phonetic):

Rah-ahs Ee Salmahnoo Pahr-ahdeezoad, Oh-ay Kah-reemee Ah-ah-oh Ee-ahl-peergah, Kwee-ee-ee-noo Ayn-ah-yee Boot-mohnah Oh-dah Ee Noh-ah-sah Nee Pahr-ah-deeahlah Kah-sahr-emjee Vay-jee-ahr Kah-heer-lahnoo Oh-dah Zoad-oh-nah-kah Loo-keeftee-ahnoo Kohr-say Tay-ah Vah-oo-lah Zoad-ee-raynoo Tohl-hahmee.

Soh-boh-lah Lohn-d-do-hah Oh-dah Mee-ahmay Kah-heesah Tay-ah Dah-Oh-dah Ay-ess, Oomah-day-ah Oh-dah Pee-blee-ahray Otheelah, Reetah Oh-dah Mee-ahmay.

Kah-noh-kolah Reetah, Zoadakahray Mee-kah-ohl-zoad Ah -ah-ee-ohm! Bahglay Pahp-nohr ee Day-loo-gahm Lon-shee On-dah Oomplee-fah Oo-gay-jee Beeglah Eeah-dah.

8th Key—Earth of Air

Enochian:
Bazm ELO, i ta Piripson oln Nazavabh OX, casarmg vran chis vgeg, ds abramg baltoha goho lad,
Soba mian trian ta lolcis Abaivovin od Aziagiar nor.
Irgil chis da ds paaox busd caosgo, ds chis, od ipuran teloch cacrg oi salman loncho od voviva carbaf.
Niiso! Bagle avavago gohon!
Niiso! Bagle momao siaion od mabza IAD OI as Momar Poilp.
Niis! Zamran ciaofi caosgo od bliors, od corsi ta abramig.

English:

The mid-day, the First, is as the Third Heaven made of hyacinthine Pillars 26, in whom the Elders are become strong, which I have prepared for my own Righteousness, Saith the Lord.

Whose long continuance shall be as buckles to the Stooping Dragon and like unto the Harvest of a Widow.

How many are there which remain in the glory of the Earth, which Are, and Shall not see Death until this house fall, and the Dragon sink?

Come away! For the Thunders have spoken!

Come away! For the Crown of the Temple and the robe of Him that Is, Was, and Shall be Crowned are divided.

Come! Appear unto the terror of the earth and unto our comfort and of such as are prepared.

Enochian (Phonetic):

Bah-zoad-em Ayloh, Eetah Peeripsohnoo Ohlnoo Noh-zoad-ah-vah-bay-hay Oh-Ex, Cah-sarm-jee Oo-rahnoo Kah-heesah Vah-jeejee, Dah-ess Ah-brahmjee Bahi-toha Goho Ee-ah-dah, Soh-bah Mee-ahnoo Tree-ahnoo Tay-ah Lohl-kees Ah-bah-ee-voh-veenoo Oh-dah Ah-zoadee-ahjee-ahr Ree-ohray.

Eer-jeelah Kah-heesah Day-ah Dah-ess Pa-ah-Oh-Ex Boos-dah Kah-ohs-goh, Dah-ess Kah-heesah, Oh-dah Ee-poor-ahnoo Tay-lohk-ah Kah-karjee Oh-ee Sahl-mahnoo Lohnkah-hoh Oh-dah Voh-vee-nah Kar-bahfay.

Nee-eesoh! Bahglay Ah-vah-vah-goh Goh-hoh-noo.

Nee-ee-soh! Bahglay Moh-mah-oh See-ah-see-ohnoo Oh-dah Mahb zoad-ah Ee-ah-dah Oh Ee Ahsah Moh-maray Poh eelahpay.

Nee-ee-sah, zoadamerahnoo Kee-ah-oh-fee Kah-ohs-goh Oh-dah Blee-ohr-sah, Oh-dab Kor-see Tay-ah Ah-brah-meejee.

9th Key—Fire of Air

Enochian:

Micaolz bransg prgel napea lalpor, ds brin P Efafage Vonpho olani od obza, sobol vpeah chis tatan od tranan balie, alar lusda soboin od chis holq c Noquodi CIAL.

Unal alson Mom Caosgo ta las ollor gnay limlal.

Amma chis sobca madrid z chis. Ooanoan chis aviny drilpi caosgin, od butmoni parm zumvi cnila.

Dazis ethamza childao, od mire ozol.

Chis pidiai collal.

Vicinina sobam vcim. Bagle? IAD Baltoh chirlan.

Par. Niiso! Od ip efafafe bagle a cocasb i cors ta vnig blior.

English:

A mighty guard of fire with two-edged swords flaming, which have eight Vials of Wrath for two times and a half, whose wings are of wormwood and of the marrow of Salt, have settled their feet in the West and are measured with their 9996 Ministers.

These gather up the moss of the earth as the rich man doth his treasures.

Cursed are they whose iniquities they are. In their eyes are millstones greater than the Earth, and from their mouths run seas of blood.

Their heads are covered with diamonds and upon their hands are marble sleeves.

Happy is he on whom they frown not! For Why? The God of Righteousness rejoiceth in them. Come away! And not your vials, for the time is such as requireth comfort.

Enochian (Phonetic):

Mee-kah-ohl-zoad Brahn-sahjee Peer-jee-lah Nah-pay-tah Ee-ahl-poh-ray, Dah-ess Bree-noo Pay Ay-fah-fah-fay Vohn-pay-ho Oh-lah-nee Oh-dab Ohb-zoad-ah, Soh-bohlah Oopah-ah Kah-heesah Tah-tahnoo Oh-dah Trah-nah-noo Bah-lee-ay, Ah-laray Loosdah Soh -bohlnoo Od-dah Kah-heesah Hohi-kew Kah Noh-koh-dee Kah-ee -ah-lah.

Oo-nahl Ahl-dohnoo Moh-mah Kah-ohs-goh Tay-ah Lah-sah Ohi-loray Jee-nayoh Lee-may-lah-lah.

Ahm-mah Kah-heesah Soh-bay-kah Mah-dreedah Zoad Kah-heesah. Oo-ah-nohahnoo Kah-heesah Ah-veenee Dree-lahpee Kah-ohs-jeenoo, Oh-dab Boot-mohnee Parmay Zoad-oomvee Kah-neelah.

Dah-zoad-eesah Ayt-hahm-zoadah Kah-hil-dah-oh Oh-dah Meer-kah Oh-zoad-ohlah

Kah-hees-ah Pee-dee-ah-ee Kohl-lah-lah.

Vahl-kee-neenah Soh-bahmay Ookeemay. Bahglay? Ee-ah-dah Bahi-toha Kar-heerlahnoo.

Pahray. Nee-ee-soh! Oh-dah Ee-pay Ay-fah-fah-fay Bahglay Ah Koh-Kahs-bay Ee Korsay Tay-ah Oo-neegay Blee-ohrah.

10th Key—Air of Water

Enochian:

Coraxo chis cormp od blans lucal aziazor paeb sobol ilonon chis OP virq eophan od raclir, maasi bagle caosgi, di ialpon dosig od basgim;

Od oxex dazis siatris od saibrox, cinxir faboan.

Unal chis const ds DAOX cocasg ol oanio yorb voh m gizyax, od math cocasg plosi molvi ds page ip, larag om dron matorb cocasb emna.

L Patralx yolci matb, nomig monons olora gnay angelard.

Ohio! Ohio! Ohio! Ohio! Ohio! Ohio! Noib Ohio! Casgon, bagle madrid i zir, od chiso drilpa.

Niiso! Crip ip Nidali.

English:

The thunders of Judgement and Wrath are numbered, and are harboured in the North in the likeness of an oak whose branches are 22 nests of Lamentation and Weeping laid up for the Earth, which burn night and day.

And vomit out the heads of scorpions and live sulphur, mingled with Poison. These be the thunders that 5678 times (in ye 24th part of a moment) roar with an hundred mighty earthquakes and a thousand times as many surges, which rest not, neither know any echoing time herein.

One rock bringeth forth a thousand, even as the heart of man doth his thoughts.

Woe! Woe! Woe! Woe! Woe! Woe! Yea Woe! Be to the earth, for her iniquity is, was, and shall be great.

Come away! But not your mighty sounds.

Enochian (Phonetic):

Koh-rahx-oh Kah-heesah Kohr-em-pay Oh-dah Blah-noos Loo-kahlah Ah-zoad-ee-ahzoad-ohra Pah-ay-bah Soh-bohlah Eeloh-nohnoo Kah-heesah Oh-pay Veer-kwoh Ay-ohfahnoo Oh-dah Rah-cleerah, Mah-ahsee Bahglay Kah-ohs-jee, Dah-ess Ee-ah-la-pohnoo Doh-seejee Oh-dah Bahs-jeemee.

Oh-dah Oh Ex-Ex Dah-zoadeesah See-ah-treesah Oh-dah Sahlbrox, Keenoo-tseerah Fah-boh-ahnoo.

Oo-nah-lah Kah-heesah Koh-noo-stah Dah-ess Dah-Ox Koh-kasjee Oh-eli Oh-ah-nee oh Yohr-bay Voh-heemah Jee-zoad-ee-ax, Oh-day Ay-orsah Koh-kasjee Pay-loh-see Mohi-vee Dah-ess Pah-jay Ee-pay, Lah-rah-gee Oh-em Dah-rohl-noo Mah-tor-bay Kohkasjee Em-nah.

Eli Pah-trah-laxa Yohi-kee Maht-bay, Noh-meegee Moh-noh-noos Oh-loh-rah Jeenah-yee Ahn-jee-lar-dah.

Oh-hee-oh! Oh-hee-oh! Oh-hee-oh! Oh-hee-oh! Oh-hee-oh! Oh-hee-oh! Noh-eebay Ohhee-oh! Kah-ohs-gohnoo, Bah-glay Mah-dree-dah Ee, Zoadeerah, Oh-dah Kah-heesoh Dah-reel-pah.

Nee-eesoh! Kah-ahr-pay Ee-pay Nee-dah-lee.

11th Key—Earth of Water

Enochian:

Oxyiayal holdo, od zirom O coraxo dis zildar Raasy, od Vabzir camliax, od bahal.

Niiso! Salman teloch, casarman hoiq, od t i ta Z soba cormf I GA.

Niiso! Bagle abrang noncp.

Zacar ece od zamran. Odo cicle qaa! Zorge lap zirdo noco Mad, hoath laida.

English:

The mighty seat groaned aloud, and there were five thunders which flew into the East, and the Eagle spake and cried with a loud voice.

Come away! And they gathered themselves together and became the House of Death, of whom it is measured, and it is 31.

Come away! For I have prepared for you a place.

Move therefore and show yourselves. Open the mysteries of your creation! Be friendly unto me, for I am the servant of the same your God, the true worshiper of the Highest.

Enochian (Phonetic):

Ohx-ee-ah-yah-iah Hol-doh, Oh-dah Zoad-eer-oh-mah Oy Kohr-ahxo Dah-ess Zoad-eeldar Rah-ahs-ee, Oh-dah Vahb-zoad-eer Kahm-lee-ahx Oh-Dah Bah-hahi.

Nee-ee-soh! Sahi-mah-noo Tay-ioh-kah, Kah-sahr-mahnoo Hohei-koh, Oh-dah Tay Ee Tay-ah Zoad Soh-bah Kohr-em-fah Ee Gee-ah.

Nee-ee-soh! Bah-glay Ah-brahn-jee noh-noo-kah-pay.

Zoad-akarah Ay-kah Oh-dah Zoadamerahnoo. Oh-doh Kee-klay Kah-ah! Zoad-orjee Lah-pay Zoadeereedoh Noh-koh Mahdah, Hoh-ah-tah-hay Ee-ah-ee dah.

12th Key—Fire of Water

Enochian:

Nonci ds sonf babage, od chis OB Hubardo tibibp, allar atraah od ef!

Drix fafen MIAN, ar Enay ovof, sobol ooain vonph.

Zacar gohus od zamran. Odo cicle qaa!

Zorge lap zirdo noco Mad, hoath Iaida.

English:

O You that reign in the South, and are the 28 Lanterns of Sorrow, bind up your girdles and visit us.

Bring down your train 3663, that the Lord may be magnified, Whose Name amongst you is Wrath.

Move, I say, and show yourselves. Open the mysteries of your creation!

Be friendly unto me! For I am the servant of the same your God, the true Worshipper of the Highest.

Enochian (Phonetic):

Noh-noo-kee Dah-ess Soh-noof Bah-bah-jee, Oh-dah Kah-heesah Oh-bay Hoo-bardoh fee-bee-bee-pay, Ah-lah-lahr Ah-trah-ah-hay Oh-day Ay-eff!

Dah-reex Fah-fah-aynoo Meeah-noo, Ah-ray Ay-nah-ee Oh-voh-fah, Soh-oh-lah Doo-ah-ee-noo Ah-ah Von-payhoh.

Zoad-ah-kahray Goh-hoo-sah Oh-dah Zoad-ah-mer-ahnoo. Oh-doh Kee-klay Kahah!

Zoadorjee Lahpay Zoadeereedoh Noh-koh Mah-dah, Hoh-ah-tah-hay Ee-ah-ee-dah.

13th Key—Air of Earth

Enochian:

Napeai babage ds brin VX ooaona iring vonph doalim: eolis ollog orsba, ds chis affa.

Micma Isro Mad od Lonshi Tox, ds i vmd aai Grosb!

Zacar od zamran. Odo cicle qaa!

Zorge lap zirdo noco Mad, hoath Iaida.

English:

O you Swords of the South, which have 42 eyes to stir up the Wrath of sin: making men drunken, which are empty.

Behold the promise of God and his power, which is called amongst you a Bitter Sting!

Move and show yourselves. Open the mysteries of your creation!

Be friendly unto me! For I am the servant of the same your God, the true worshipper of the highest.

Enochian (Phonetic):

Nah-pay-ah-ee Bah-bah-jee Dah-ess Bay-ree-noo Vee Ex Oo-ah-oh-nah Lah-reen-gee Vohn-pay-hay Doh-ah-leem: Ay-oh-leesah Oh-loh-jee Ohrs-bah, Dah-ess Kah-heesah Ahf-fah.

Meek-mah Ees-roh Mahdah Oh-dah Lohn-shee Toh-tza, Dah-ess Ee-Vah-mee-dah Ah-ah-ee Grohs-bay!

Zoad-a-kah-rah Oh-dah Zoad-a-mer-ahnoo. Oh-doh Kee-klay Kah-ah!

Zoad-orjee Lah-pay Zoad-eer-eedoh Noh-koh Mah-dah, Hoh-ah-tah-hay Ee-aa-ee-dah.

14th Key—Water of Earth

Enochian:

Noromi baghie, pashs O lad, ds trint mirc OL thil, dods tol hami caosgi homin, ds brin oroch QUAR.

Micma bialo Iad! Isro tox ds I vmd aai Baltim.

Zacar od zamran. Odo cicle qaa!

Zorge lap zirdo noco Mad, hoath laida.

English:

O you Sons of Fury, the Child of the Just, which sit upon 24 seats, vexing all creatures of the earth with age, which have under you 1636.

Behold the Voice of God! The promise of Him who is called amongst you Fury or extreme Justice.

Move therefore and show yourselves. Open the mysteries of your creation! Be friendly unto me, for I am the servant of the same your God, the true worshipper of the Highest.

Enochian (Phonetic):

Noh-roh-mee Bahg-hee-ay, Pahs-hay-sah Oh-ee-ah-dah, Dah-ess Tree-ndo-tay Meerkay Oh-el Tah-heelah, Doh-dah-sah Tol-hah-mee Kah-ohs-jee Hoh-mee-noo, Dah-ess Bay-ree-noo Oh-roh-chah Kwah-ah-ray.

Meek-mah Bee-ah-loh Ee-ah-dah! Ees-roh Tohx Dah-ess Ee Va-mee-dah Ah-ah-ee Bahl-tee-mah.

Zoad-a-kah-rah Oh-dah Zoad-a-mer-ahnoo. Oh-doh Kee-klay Kah-ah!

Zoad-orjee Lah-pay Zoad-eer-eedoh Noh-koh Mah-dah, Hoh-ah-tah-hay Ee-aa-ee-dah.

15th Key—Fire of Earth

Enochian:

Ils tabaan L Ialpirt, casarman vpaachi chis DARG ds oado caosgi orscor:

Ds oman baeouib od emetgis Iaiadix!

Zacar od zamran. Odo cicle qaa!

Zorge lap zirdo noco Mad, hoath laida.

English:

O Thou, the Governor of the First Flame under whose wings are 6739 which weave the earth with dryness;

Which knowest the great name Righteousness and the Seal of Honour!

Move and show yourselves. Open the mysteries of your Creation!

Be friendly unto me, for I am the servant of the same your God, the true worshipper of the Highest.

Enochian (Phonetic):

Ee-lah- sah Tah-bah-ah-noo Ayl Ee-ahl-peer-tah, Kas-ahr-mah-noo Oo-pah-ah-chee Kah-heesah Dahr-jee Dah-ess Oh-ah-doh Kah-ohs-jee Ohrs-koh-ray:

Dah-ess Oh-Mahnu Bah-ay-oh-oo-ee-bay Oh-dah Ay-mayt-gees Ee-ah-ee-ah-dix!

Zoad-a-kah-rah Oh-dah Zoad-a-mer-ahnoo. Oh-doh Kee-klay Kah-ah!

Zoad-orjee Lah-pay Zoad-eer-eedoh Noh-koh Mah-dah, H oh-ah-tah-hay Ee-aa-ee-dah.

16th Key—Air of Fire

Enochian:

Ils viv Iaiprt, Salman Bait, ds a croodzi busd, od bliorax Balit, ds insi caosgi iusdan EMOD, ds om od tiiob.

Drilpa geh us Mad Zilodarp.

Zacar od zamran. Odo cicle qaa!

Zorge lap zirdo noco Mad, hoath Iaida.

English:

O Thou of the Second Flame, the house of Justice, Who hast Thy Beginning in glory, and shall comfort the Just, Who walkest on the Earth with 8763 feet, which understand and separate creatures.

Great art Thou in the God of Conquest.

Move therefore and show yourselves. Open the mysteries of your creation! Be friendly unto me, for I am the servant of the same your God, the true worshipper of the Highest.

Enochian (Phonetic):

Ee-lah-sah Vee-ee-vee Ee-ahl-peert, Sahi-mahn-oo Bal-toh, Dah-ess Ah Cro-oh-dahzoad-ee Boosdah, Oh-Dah Blee-ohr-ahx Bah-lee-tah, Dah-ess Ee-noo-see Kah-ohs-jee Loos-dah-noo Ah-Em-Oh-Day, Dah-ess Oh-Em Oh-dah Tah-lee-oh-bah.

Dah-reei-pah Gay-hah Ee-lah-sah Mah-dah Zoad-ee-loh dahr-pay.

Zoad-a-kah-rah Oh-dah Zoad-a-mer-ahnoo. Oh-doh Kee-klay Kah-ah!

Zoad-orjee Lah-pay Zoad-eer-eedoh Noh-koh Mah-dah, Hoh-ah-tah-hay Ee-aa-ee-dah.

17th Key—Water of Fire

Enochian:

Ils D Ialpirt, soba vpaah chis nanba zixiay dodseh, od ds brint TAXS Hubardo tastax ilsi.

Soba Iad i vonpho vonph.

Aldon dax il od toatar.

Zacar od zamran. Odo cicle qaa!

Zorge lap zirdo noco Mad, hoath Iaida.

English:

O Thou third Flame whose wings are Thorns to stir up vexation.

And who hast 7336 living lamps going before Thee.

Whose God is Wrath in Anger.

Gird up thy Loins and hearken.

Move therefore and show yourselves. Open the mysteries of your creation! Be friendly unto me, for I am the servant of the same your God, the true worshipper of the Highest.

Enochian (Phonetic):

Ee-loh-sah Dah Ee-ahl-peer-tah, Soh-boh Oo-pah-ah-hay Kah- Heesah Nah-noo-bah Zoad-eex-lah-yoh Dohd-say-hah, Oh-dah Dah-ess Bay-reen-tah Tah-ah-ex-sah Hoo-bahr-doh Tahs-tax Ee-lah-see.

Soh-bah Es-ah-dah Ee Von-pay-hoh Oon-pay-hoh.

Ahl-doh-noo Dahx Eelah Oh-dah Toh-ah-tahray.

Zoad-a-kah-rah Oh-dah Zoad-a-mer-ahnoo. Oh-doh Kee-klay Kah-ah!

Zoad-orjee Lah-pay Zoad-eer-eedoh Noh-koh Mah-dah, Hoh-ah-tah-hay Ee-aa-ee-dah.

18th Key—Earth of Fire

Enochian:

Ils micaolz Olprt od lalprt, bliors ds odo Busdir O Iad ovoars caosgo, casarmg ERAN la Iad brints cafafam, ds I vmd Aglo Adohi Moz od Maoffas.

Bolp como bliort pambt.

Zacar od zamran. Odo cicle qaa!

Zorge lap zirdo noco Mad, hoath Iaida.

English:

O Thou mighty Light and burning Flame of Comfort which openest the Glory of God unto the centre of the Earth.

In Whom the 6332 secrets of truth have their abiding, that is called in Thy Kingdom Joy, and not to be measured.

Be Thou a window of comfort unto me.

Move therefore and show yourselves. Open the mysteries of your creation! Be friendly unto me, for I am the servant of the same your God, the true worshipper of the highest.

Enochian (Phonetic):

Ee-loh-sah Mee-kah-ohl-zoad Ohl-peertah Oh-dah Ee-ahl-peertah, Blee-ohr-sah Dah-ess Oh-doh Boos-dee-rah Oh-ee-ah-day Oh-voh-ahrsah Kah-ohs-goh, Kass-armjee Ay-rahnoo Lah ee-andah Breen-tas Kah-fah-fay-may, Dah-ess EE Ooo-may-day Ahk-loh Ah-doh-hee Moh-zoad Oh-dah Mah-oh-fah-fah-sah.

Boh-lah-pay Koh-moh Blee-ohrta Pahm-bay-tay.

Zoad-a-kah-rah Oh-dah Zoad-a-mer-ahnoo. Oh-doh Kee-klay Kah-ah!

Zoad-orjee Lah-pay Zoad-eer-eedoh Noh-koh Mah-dah, Hoh-ah-tah-hay Ee-aa-ee-dah.

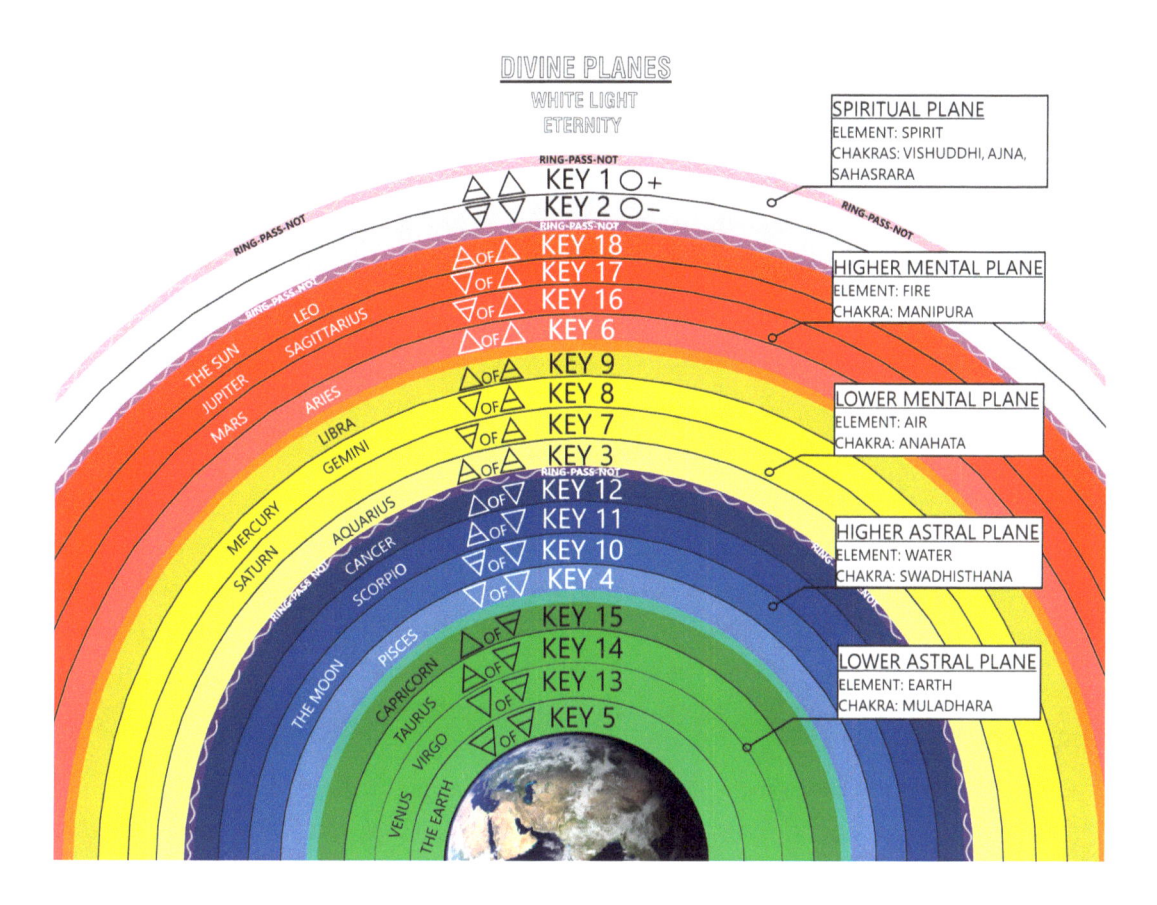

Figure 62: The Eighteen Enochian Keys

THE THIRTY AETHYRS (19TH ENOCHIAN KEY)

Otherwise known as the "Aires," the Thirty Aethyrs comprise the layers of the Aura. The Aethyrs are different from the Elements in the Elemental Planes, yet they are simultaneously a part of them. The best way of describing the Aethyrs is as the Spiritual experiences and Soul lessons of the Elements and Sub-Elements in the Enochian Watchtowers. The lowest of the Aetheric layers is of Earth. The other Aethyrs exist in an outward progression, beginning with Earth, with each being lower in density and higher in Spiritual experience than the one below it.

Again like the layers of an onion, the Aethyrs form concentric circles, overlapping one another. As such, the Aethyrs must be evoked and experienced systematically and progressively. You must begin with the lowest Aethyr, the one closest to Earth, and move upwards one at a time until you reach the highest. This sequence must be honoured to accomplish the Thirty Aethyrs operation correctly.

Keep in mind that these Aethyrs exist at different vibration frequencies, occupying the same Space and Time as your physical body. By raising your consciousness to the desired rate of vibration, you become attuned to that Plane or Sub-Plane of reality.

The Enochian Aethyrs and the Qabalistic Tree of Life represent the systematic structure of the Cosmic Planes and Sub-Planes of existence that are beyond our physical senses. They are subtle but very real indeed. Each Aethyr represents one of these different Planes, with unique qualities and energy. Some Aethyrs are intelligent, existing as separate and outside of ourselves. Yet others only exist as a projection of the Self. All Aethyrs, though, can be tapped into and experienced by our consciousness.

The Aethyrs are comparable to the Sephiroth of the Tree of Life and the Tarot paths, though not completely identical. You could say that the Aethyrs are the subjective experiences of the Sephiroth of the Tree of Life, though not the Sephiroth in and of themselves. The only complete correlation between the Aethyrs and the Tree of Life is the Tenth Aethyr, ZAX, representing the Abyss of the eleventh Sephira, Daath.

The Aethyrs do fully correspond with the Chakras and the Cosmic Planes. The Sephiroth, on the other hand, are more complex in their function since, in most cases, one Sephira operates through multiple Chakras. Regardless, there is a great deal of similarity between the Aethyrs and the Tree of Life, as each Aethyr embodies a state of consciousness akin to the Spiritual experience of a particular Sephira or Tarot path.

Performing the Thirty Aethyr operation is similar in experience to rising up the Tree of Life following the Path of the Flaming Sword in reverse. The middle and higher Sephiroth represent states of consciousness that are more advanced than the lower Sephiroth. Thus, they require us to experience multiple Aethyrs to learn their intended lessons and experience their initiations.

As mentioned in an earlier chapter, the Aethyrs surround our physical Planet, Earth. The densest and material-based is the Aethyr of TEX, while the highest and most Spiritual one is LIL. The sequential order of the Aethyrs must be respected since each of the Aethyrs serves as an initiation into the next one. Similar to how the ritual exercises you encountered so far served to initiate you into those particular energies, the Aethyrs also serve as initiations into these different aspects and levels of Self.

While working with particular Aethyrs, you are likely to encounter Spiritual entities. These entities are manifestations of the different parts of the Self. They may be Angelic, but they also may be Demonic. In the latter's case, they may challenge you, blocking the way to the next Aethyr until they are overcome. By overcoming these challenges, you become initiated into the next Aethyr. At the same time, you can also face the aspects of yourself that are often overlooked. After discovering these aspects and overcoming them, you can tap into more of your personal power.

As you make your way progressively and systematically through the Aethyrs, your experience will become less and less dense while also becoming increasingly joyful. Naturally, true happiness and joy are a consequence of Spiritual Evolution. In the final and highest Aethyr, LIL, one merges with Non-Duality of God-the Creator. This experience is one of pure bliss. It is the ultimate goal of Nirvana, of the liberation of the Soul. At this point, the Great Work has been completed.

As you are under the influence of an Aethyr's energy, you may frequently be downloading information about the Universe and life while in a dream state or during a vision. Most often, this will happen in the background while you are experiencing a dream or a vision. You may even notice your inner voice speaking to you and other, unknown voices. As this work is meant to tune you into your Holy Guardian Angel, it also allows other higher Spiritual entities to channel information to you. This work results in pure Gnosis, and it expands your ability to understand and perceive the higher wisdom about our Cosmos. It is a true gift from the Divine.

The Thirty Aethyrs operation is a very Shamanic aspect of Enochian Magick, as each Aethyr will offer unique visions and mystical experiences. You will also experience hidden parts of the Self revealing themselves to you while the corresponding Chakras become fully invigorated. You might feel movements of different energies inside of you, and some of you may even have a full Kundalini awakening due to working with the Aethyrs.

SEXUAL ENERGY CURRENTS IN THE AETHYRS

Each of the Thirty Aethyrs carries a particular sexual energy current. Some Aethyrs contain a combination of masculine (+) and feminine (-) sexual currents, while others consist of just one, in varying intensities and degrees. The dominant quality of the masculine sexual current is awareness or consciousness, without emotion or feeling, with an emphasis on willpower. The masculine component of one's Being is focused on taking action and powering the intellect.

The ruling quality of the feminine sexual current, on the other hand, is blind emotion along with bliss, devoid of intelligence. The feminine portion of one's Being is focused primarily on feeling and emotion. While the masculine can be viewed as uncaring, purely logical, and intellectual at times, the feminine can sometimes appear irrational and overly emotional.

The qualities of the masculine and feminine sexual energy currents will shift and change as you progress through the Aethyrs, experiencing each one directly and evolving in the process. When it comes to experiencing the Aethyrs that are solely either masculine or feminine, the goal is to use the opposite sexual energy, to evoke it within yourself and balance the experience. In turn, this method will bring harmony to your inner Self.

The different combinations of the masculine and feminine energies encountered in the Aethyrs are a consequence of the division of the *Monad*. The Monad is the aspect of ourselves that is Non-Dual. This realm of Non-Duality is synonymous with the energy you can experience through the first Aethyr, LIL. The direct experience of LIL is likened to experiencing the Transpersonal Chakras that exist beyond Sahasrara. Both LIL and these Chakras are Non-Dual.

The masculine and feminine sexual energy currents within Enochian Magick also relate to the Ida and Pingala Nadis of the Kundalini system. If you have an awakened Kundalini, you will experience progressions in the Ida and Pingala Nadis as you work with the Aethyrs. Some Aethyrs release tremendous sexual energy once evoked. Since there is a direct correlation between sexual energy and the Kundalini, awakened individuals will have many Kundalini-related experiences while working with the Aethyrs.

As you are progressing through the Aethyrs, you will notice that you are more and more inspired. This inspiration correlates with the level of sexual energy and current each Aethyr carries. The highest Aethyrs are so inspiring that you might unlock hidden abilities within yourself, skills such as creative expressions, or increased wisdom that you may not have known existed inside of you.

After the descriptions of each Aethyr, I will give you the pronunciation of the individual Aethyrs and the Nineteenth Enochian Key—the Call of the Thirty Aethyrs. You are to pronounce and vibrate the Call phonetically as it is written while inserting the individual Aethyr you wish to visit into it.

BABALON IN ENOCHIAN MAGICK

Babalon is a Goddess from the mystical philosophy of *Thelema*. Aleister Crowley founded Thelema, whose fundamental beliefs and principles are based on *The Book of the Law*. Babalon is the Great Mother of Thelema, also known as the Scarlet Woman. She represents the liberated woman and the female sexual impulse. She is identified with Mother Earth and the Sephira Binah, as she represents Matter and the Sea of Consciousness.

Babalon is the chief Goddess of Enochian Magick. Dee and Kelley channelled her in their communications with Enochian Angels. Many of her forms are found within the Enochian Aethyrs. As mentioned, the Enochian

Aethyrs contain strong sexual currents. Babalon will be encountered in certain Aethyrs, as her power will gradually be revealed to you.

Babalon's primary symbol is the Chalice or Grail, otherwise known as "Sangraal" or the *Holy Grail*. As initiates of Light, we are to pour our blood (metaphorically speaking) into her cup, as a form of sacrifice and sacrament, to evolve Spiritually and gain everlasting life. By doing so, we will obtain compassion and unconditional love.

Babalon's consort is Chaos, the Father of Life and the male aspect of the Creative Principle. Babalon herself is the Cosmos. While Chaos represents Force, Cosmos represents Form. Babalon is often described as riding the Beast, with whom Aleister Crowley personally identified his whole life.

While working with the Thirty Aethyrs, Babalon is symbolic of the liberation of your sexual energy. This sexual energy moves through different parts of your Being. On the other hand, the Beast is your Lower Self and your untamed consciousness, devoid of Spirit. The idea is to infuse Spirit into your Lower Self and exalt it, thereby raising the vibration of your consciousness. As such, you are making yourself a conduit for the energy of the Higher Self or Holy Guardian Angel. In this way, a transfiguration occurs, and your consciousness transforms permanently.

Sexual energy is transformative energy of consciousness, as all Kundalini awakened individuals know. Visions of Babalon in the descriptions of the Aethyrs are meant to help you understand how your sexual energy is revealing itself to you and how it is influencing parts of you and your consciousness.

If your consciousness is aligned with one religion or Spiritual pantheon, it is possible to encounter visions of Babalon personified by a Goddess from your faith. Babalon is, after all, a representation of the Goddess, and the Goddess has many forms. No matter how she presents herself to you, it is crucial to understand the idea behind the vision you are encountering and the quality of the sexual current particular to the Aethyr you are working with. Having the correct understanding of the experience of Babalon will aid in the purpose of the operation itself, which is the transformation of individual consciousness and Spiritual Evolution.

DESCRIPTIONS OF THE ENOCHIAN AETHYRS

Since Magick uses numbers and symbols to communicate to you (Archetypal ideas), they will manifest through your subconscious thoughts and emotions. Be aware of images in your visions that are personifications of these ideas to try to understand what the energy is attempting to communicate to you. Archetypal ideas are the result of the energy of the Aethyr, which will be the same for everyone who visits that Aethyr. Your past conditioning and knowledge gained in life will personify these forces through images particular to you and only you. In this way, we may see different visions of the same Aethyr, but the message will be the same for everyone.

I am incorporating my personal experiences with the Thirty Aethyrs from the third time I did the thirty-day operation. I include the third operation because it was this time that I officially crossed the Abyss. Due to my Kundalini awakening before getting into Magick, my consciousness was already at a high level. Still, I needed to align and purify my Subtle Bodies of the lower Elements first before successfully crossing the Abyss. My experiences with the Aethyrs then offered energetic transformations where the Kundalini energy would align in my Light Body, eventually resulting in my consciousness crossing the Abyss and aligning with Cosmic Consciousness. These energy transformations were happening through the Seven Chakras and the three primary Nadis of Ida, Pingala, and Sushumna.

As mentioned, each Aethyr carries Archetypal energy, but the visions each person gets will be different. Regardless, it helps to know the symbolic ideas and energy behind each Aethyr as you visit it. This information will give you a roadmap for assimilating whatever knowledge and lesson an Aethyr is meant to impart to you.

My experiences with the Aethyr energies came with a direct intuitive feeling which enabled me to feel the energy as a quantifiable essence in my Heart Chakra and, through intuition and logic, put it into words. Depending on the sexual current and its power within each Aethyr, it may or may not have offered me transformational experiences with the Kundalini energy, as these transformations depended on which Plane the Aethyr pertained to and whether I needed energy alignments in that area.

In my descriptions of each Aethyr below, I did not focus on elaborate depictions of visions since those, as mentioned, will be different for everyone. Instead, I focused on describing the feeling generated by the energy of each Aethyr and how it impacted my mind, body, and Soul.

I would be remiss if I did not mention the two great Adepts in Enochian Magick, Gerald and Betty Schueler, whose work has greatly influenced my work in the same area. Unfortunately, since Enochian Magick is not widely practised outside of Magickal Orders, there aren't many books or information on it, especially when it comes to working with the Enochian Keys.

The work of the Shuelers, especially on the Thirty Aethyrs operation, had served to illuminate my path many years ago when I was exploring these Enochian Keys. As such, my visions and experiences of the Aethyrs are influenced by their descriptions of the same. Since my primary objective while working with the Thirty Aethyrs was to further my Kundalini awakening process, I have added the component of feeling the energy intuitively and allowing it to work with my Kundalini system.

30th Aethyr—TEX

The English translation of TEX is "the Aethyr that is in four parts." As the lowest of the Aethyrs, it is on the bottom part of the Lower Astral Plane within the Element of Earth, corresponding with the Root Chakra, Muladhara. TEX is the closest Aethyr to our own physical Earth. This Aethyr naturally oscillates between the Physical World of Matter and the Lower Astral Plane. The two are inextricably connected and intertwined.

I felt a potent Karmic feel in this Aethyr relating to the limitations of how I perceived myself. I experienced these limitations in my actions the entire day, and my desire to be a Co-Creator in my reality decreased. I also felt a sense of silence in my mind and a restriction of my cognitive abilities. As the evoked energy was relatively dense, I felt a lack of ability to express myself fully in this Aethyr and a sense of purgatory or limbo of the Self. TEX carries both sexual energy currents and is likened to the experience of Malkuth on the Tree of Life. Because of the overall dense energy and mild sexual current, I did not have any significant transformative experience in this Aethyr.

29th Aethyr—RII

The English translation of RII is "the Aethyr of the mercy of Heaven." It is in the highest part of the Lower Astral Plane within the Element of Earth. As in TEX, we use our Lower Astral Body to travel in RII. Also, RII is related to Muladhara Chakra, the same as TEX, since they are both of the Earth Element. RII and TEX are closely related but separate. RII is the region that contains the Heavens and Hells of the world's religions, and as such, it is the area of the Inner Planes that is fabricated and based on erroneous thinking.

There was a sense of Karmic judgement in this Aethyr. Similar to TEX, I felt that my cognitive abilities were decreased. This Aethyr has an intense daydream feel to it. It felt Airy at times, although my thoughts seemed more in passive mode. I realized that I sometimes enter RII subconsciously throughout the day when I need a mental break from what I am doing. Both masculine and feminine sexual energy currents are present in RII. This Aethyr is likened to experiencing the highest part of Malkuth on the Tree of Life, bordering on entering Yesod. Again, as in TEX, I did not experience any significant transformation with the Kundalini energy. I believe this is due to the density of the energy of the Aethyr and the relatively mild sexual current.

28th Aethyr—BAG

The English translation of BAG is "the Aethyr of doubt." This Aethyr is located in the lowest Sub-Plane of the Higher Astral Plane within the Water Element, related to the Sacral Chakra, Swadhisthana. The Higher Astral Body is often called the Emotional Body. We use our Higher Astral Body to travel in this Plane. As physical water comprises 60% of our bodies, it carries memories and emotions within it.

The Ego exists because of how we processed these past events in our lives. As such, it has fear, doubt, and guilt attached to who it thinks it is because its existence is based on erroneous thinking. Here, you must confront that part of the Ego that projects fear into the world.

The sexual current present in BAG was strictly a masculine one. In a Kundalini awakened person, this Aethyr works with the Pingala Nadi. It is similar to entering the Sphere of Yesod on the Tree of Life.

I felt a sense of purgative suffering here. The emotionality of this Aethyr was powerful. I had to face the complexes in my subconscious as they were being presented to me throughout the day. The part of the Ego present here is the mirror of the Soul (Figure 63). It is its reflection, but not the Soul in and of itself. In this way was this emotional part of the Ego created, since it is I who have given it life and manifested it in this realm. In BAG, I had to face that part of myself and overcome it.

I felt that my self-doubt and negative memories were preventing me from maximizing my personal power. This limitation came with sorrow since identifying any part of myself with the Ego meant that I was not identifying myself with the Soul. This action restricted my Soul and took away its joy, preventing its Light from radiating at its total capacity.

As I encountered this part of the Ego, I could see it for what it is—an illusion of the mind. It did not show itself to me in a vision but more as an intuitive feeling inside my Heart Chakra. I immediately noticed how I viewed myself and knew what I was dealing with. My Ego used fear tactics to try and scare me, but I remained firm in the inner silence I generated within myself. There were no transformations with the Kundalini energy that evening. However, I learned to quiet my mind while experiencing the emotion of fear as a method of neutralizing the fear and overcoming it.

Figure 63: The Ego as a Reflection of the Soul in BAG

27th Aethyr—ZAA

The English translation of ZAA is "the Aethyr of solitude." There was a pervading sense of loneliness in this Aethyr. ZAA is in the lower part of the Higher Astral Plane within the Water Element, corresponding with the Sacral Chakra, Swadhisthana. Here, I got the feeling of being alone with myself, devoid of emotions and feelings. This feeling is natural, accompanied by the development of the Ego.

Because we are each an individual entity existing in the Universe, we are forever alone with our mental reality and ourselves. The idea of being a separate entity from the Universe brings this feeling of loneliness. It is an illusion, but in this Aethyr, all other parts of the Self will be stripped away to deal with this reality. I had to mentally cultivate compassion and rationalize what was happening to me with whatever cognitive abilities were available.

This Aethyr has a Lunar nature, and I felt my mental components opening up slightly while my emotional capacity became entirely subdued. ZAA has a very Lunar feel, similar to invoking the Air Element or the Moon Planet, but without any tangible cognitive abilities available for me to use. The consciousness of ZAA can be likened to Yesod on the Tree of Life as it is the continuation of overcoming the Ego that originated in BAG. In this case, the Ego's sense of identity created this feeling of aloneness with itself.

ZAA isolates the feeling of being alone with yourself and apart from the Universe so that you can deal with this idea and overcome it. We have all felt this emotion of aloneness at some point in our lives. By experiencing it continuously throughout our lives, this emotion grew and became more powerful. In ZAA, this emotion has to be directly confronted.

The sense of loneliness in ZAA results from distorted thinking because we are individuals; however, we are not alone but a part of the Universe. The emptiness of emotion and loneliness in ZAA also brings forth the feeling of the abundance of Space. I could feel the Space around me as a form of darkness with no limits. In this sense, I could feel Yesod's connection to Binah, the originator of Space and Form.

The sexual energy current in ZAA is feminine. In a Kundalini awakened person, this Aethyr works with the Ida Nadi. Due to the mild sexual current, there was no Kundalini transformation. From the previous two times doing the Thirty Aethyrs operation, I noticed that the strength of the sexual energy current affects my level of inspiration, which in turn affects the power of the Kundalini energy. These lower Aethyrs carry little joy, and Kundalini needs inner happiness to be fully active for it to operate at its full capacity.

26th Aethyr—DES

The English translation of DES is "the Aethyr that accepts that which is." After the solitude of ZAA, I was prepared to understand the limitations of the mind and its cognitive abilities. This Aethyr is focused on logic and reason but is devoid of intuition. It is located in the upper region of the Higher Astral Plane within the Water Element, corresponding with the Sacral Chakra, Swadhisthana. The Ego is present here, as it is present in all Astral Plane workings.

Duality is present in this Aethyr because of its logical nature. The Ego exists because of the interpretation of life events through the lens of duality. All experiences in life are categorized into good or bad components and filed away in a filing cabinet that is the human mind. The intelligence, the Ego, has complete control of the lower Aethyrs below it but does not reach into the higher Aethyrs.

Truth cannot be perceived by logic and reason alone, and here I could recognize and feel these limitations. There is a lot of discrimination in this Aethyr, and because of the intellectual component, life is taken very seriously. On the Tree of Life, this Aethyr is similar to entering the Sphere of Hod. Thus, it is very Mercurial. I had to learn to overcome logic and reason and rise above it so that I could try to perceive through intuition. It was the main challenge of this Aethyr.

Intuition is what the Higher Self uses to communicate. It is our link with the Higher Self. The innate desire generated within the Self to perceive through intuition allows you to overcome this Aethyr. Human life is merely a Divine play and the mind can rise above logic and reason to function through intuition alone.

The sexual energy current in this Aethyr is masculine. In a Kundalini awakened person, this Aethyr works with the Pingala Nadi. In DES, I did not experience any energetic Kundalini transformations.

These lower Aethyrs are the necessary preparation for the higher ones because they put the mind in a state where cognitive limitations are experienced. Once these limitations are removed, it can result in a powerful Spiritual experience in the higher Aethyrs. As you progress through the Aethyrs, joy and inspiration are increased along with a stronger sexual energy current, all of which move and power the Kundalini energy.

25th Aethyr—VTI

The English translation of VTI is "the Aethyr of change." It is in the upper region of the Higher Astral Plane within the Water Element, corresponding with the Sacral Chakra, Swadhisthana. VTI is characterized by the feeling of change in cognitive abilities. A newfound sense of intuition replaced the logic and reason of the intellect. It was the first time since I started the Thirty Aethyrs operation that I had access to my intuition, which I used to deduce the reality around me. We can perceive truth directly, but the intuition that is present in VTI is quite unruly and undisciplined because it represents a state of consciousness just above the Ego.

This region is the first stage of what Crowley called the "Beast". Spiritual pride is present in this Aethyr because consciousness at this level is still joined to the lower personality and the physical body. The work of the higher Aethyrs is to purify this state of consciousness and exalt the Higher Self. In this sense, the Beast within us will grow and mature. In the lower Aethyrs, we must refine our lower nature and gain experience to achieve this task.

VTI can also be seen as a reflection of my Holy Guardian Angel, although I was not to meet him until the higher Aethyrs. The sexual energy current in this Aethyr is feminine. A Kundalini awakened person is working with the Ida Nadi in this Aethyr. The state of consciousness of VTI is likened to entering Netzach on the Tree of Life as Hod's intellect is left behind and replaced by intuition.

The atmosphere of this Aethyr is still in the Astral Plane but is now starting to reach higher than the Water Element alone. Here, the intuition had a persistent Airy quality to it. I did not experience any Kundalini transformations in VTI, as the energy here is still too dense. All the sexual energy currents thus far have been very mild.

24th Aethyr—NIA

The English translation of NIA is "the Aethyr of travelling." Its location is at the apex of the Higher Astral Plane, bordering the Lower Mental Plane. It is a region of initiation into travelling in the Body of Light. NIA contains the influence of the Mental Plane above it, and because emotions and thoughts of the Ego do not weigh down the Body of Light, it is in flight mode. This Aethyr is the preparation for the Aethyrs above it that are higher in vibrational frequency than those below.

I experienced a complete emotional release in this Aethyr. I felt my consciousness was freed to experience the boundlessness of Space. As this feeling came on, I felt entirely disconnected from the Ego. There is a sense of joy in the NIA Aethyr, which is a prime component of Spiritual Evolution.

In NIA, I encountered the first Ring-Pass-Not, which establishes a clear division between the Aethyrs below it and those above. The Ring-Pass-Not is a term coined by Madame Blavatsky in *The Secret Doctrine* and pertains to phases or states of consciousness. It is synonymous with the Qabalistic term "Veil," as related to the different Veils found on the Tree of Life. It is a division line between one state of consciousness and another. It means that which is in a lower state of consciousness cannot pass into a higher state. The Ring-Pass-Not is the boundary that keeps particular states of consciousness separate. The Ring-Pass-Not in NIA corresponds with the Veil of Paroketh on the Tree of Life.

Within Enochian Magick, the Ring-Pass-Not separates the various Planes of Being from one another. In terms of the Lower and Higher Astral Planes, they are indivisible and considered as one Plane. The same applies to the Lower and Higher Mental Planes.

In a sense, NIA is a summary of the Aethyrs below it, combining the best characteristics of each. It carries with it both masculine and feminine sexual energy currents. Qabalistically, it is similar to the higher region of Netzach on the Tree of Life, bordering on the Veil of Paroketh.

The Aethyrs past NIA feel like a gift from the Divine, with a substantially higher level of Spiritual joy present in each of them. The weight of the Ego's emotions does not permeate the Aethyrs above NIA, as they are limited to the Water Element.

The night of working with NIA, I had Lucid Dreams in which I was flying. I did not experience anything transformative here, though. Having completed the Thirty Aethyr operations twice before, I knew that the transformational experiences began in the middle Aethyrs, which I was now heading into.

23rd Aethyr—TOR

The English translation of TOR is "the Aethyr that sustains the Universe." It is the first Aethyr of the Lower Mental Plane in the Air Element, corresponding with the Heart Chakra, Anahata. The Ring-Pass-Not in the region separating TOR and NIA is there to prevent the Astral Body from crossing into the Mental Plane. In TOR, I took on my Mental Body for the first time. An active Earth energy is present in TOR, and the overall Aethyr has a theme of work or physical labour. I felt that work (on various levels) is the very thing that sustains the Universe.

The atmosphere in TOR was heavy and dark. It is work which creates stability, which in turn influences change. Man and the Universe are the effects of the labour of an infinite number of components, all working together to create change and evolve. As Matter evolves from Spirit, it does not rest there but continues the process of involution. The process of motion and change is present here and unending.

The sexual energy current is masculine as the concept of Force is ever-present in this Aethyr. The consciousness of TOR is similar to an Earthy aspect of Tiphareth. I experienced an influx of different forces that converge in Tiphareth on the Tree of Life.

The energy of the Aethyr reminded me of the Zodiac energy of Taurus, which is the Sub-Element of Air of Earth. While embodying TOR's grounded energy, I was steadfast in completing all the goals I set out for myself that day. As I was now in the Lower Mental Plane, I was able to use my intellect, as well as intuition, to a great extent. I did not experience a significant pull in the sexual energy current I encountered, and the buildup of sexual energy was relatively mild. However, I felt more of my Spiritual and mental faculties slowly opening up and becoming available for me to use, which was refreshing.

22nd Aethyr—LIN

The English translation of LIN is "the Aethyr of the Void." It is the second Aethyr in the Lower Mental Plane within the Air Element, corresponding with the Heart Chakra, Anahata. This Aethyr is the first direct experience of Spirituality as my consciousness has risen upwards while visiting the Aethyrs. I experienced a glimpse of Samadhi here, the mystical and meditative awareness.

In LIN, Form meets the Form-less. The idea of the Form-less becomes more apparent in the Aethyrs above LIN. The Form-less is the beginning of Non-Duality. It is an endless Void, which is where the Aethyr gets its name. On the other hand, form can be viewed as an extension in Space in the endless Void. As such, the Mental Plane is boundless.

LIN put my consciousness in a naturally meditative state. Listening to music felt more transcendent than ever before while in this Aethyr. At moments, I would completely lose myself in Time and Space and become absorbed in any activity I was doing. The immense expanse of the Void felt like it went on endlessly in all directions.

The sexual energy current permeating this Aethyr is feminine. For the Kundalini awakened individuals, LIN allows you to experience the Ida Nadi in its natural passive, receptive state. This Aethyr carries a cooling sensation with it and a connection to the Spiritual component within the Air Element.

LIN's energy reminded me of the Aquarius Zodiac sign or the Star path of the Tarot. The consciousness of LIN was similar to an Airy aspect of Tiphareth. Since I am an Aquarius, this Aethyr felt like home. I could feel the cold air on my skin throughout the whole day. I felt an energy alignment in the Kundalini system occur that evening as I went into a dream state. The sexual energy current was becoming noticeably more potent compared to the lower Aethyrs.

21st Aethyr—ASP

The English translation of ASP is "the Aethyr of causation." It is the third Aethyr in the Lower Mental Plane within the Air Element, which corresponds with the Heart Chakra, Anahata.

ASP is the Aethyr of the Reincarnating Ego. It is the part of us that takes on manifestation into the lower realms of existence to express itself through Time, Space, and Form. It reincarnates from one life into the next and learns lessons from a long series of life experiences. As the personal Ego is an expression of the Self, linked to the physical body in this lifetime, the Reincarnating Ego is the Higher Ego, the impersonal sense of I-ness at the Soul level.

I saw glimpses of what could have been my past lives in my visions of this Aethyr. I was in places in the world I had never been to and doing activities I don't remember ever doing in this lifetime.

The Reincarnating Ego cannot see into the Aethyrs above ASP but only manifests through the Aethyrs below it. It is the reflection of the Higher Self and the Universal Consciousness present within us. The Reincarnating Ego is the distorted version of our true Spiritual nature projected through the Mental Plane. It is that which animates the physical body which gives rise to the personal Ego over time.

There is very little joy present in this Aethyr as there is a permeating sense of desolation, which felt like the continuation of the loneliness in ZAA. It is a result of identifying ourselves with our personal Egos. The challenge here is to shift your identity from the personal Ego to the Reincarnating Ego, which has many lifetimes. By doing so, you will feel a sense of liberation and freedom, knowing that once you die, your Soul will continue its journey into the next life.

ASP is a dense Aethyr compared to the higher Aethyrs in the Mental Plane. The sexual energy current is masculine. To the Kundalini awakened individuals, this Aethyr corresponds with the Pingala current. The consciousness of ASP is similar to a Fiery aspect of Tiphareth, as the Reincarnating Ego is related to the Soul's identity through incarnations. The Reincarnating Ego descends from Kether into Tiphareth, expressing as the masculine principle of this Sphere. I felt an energy alignment that evening in my Heart Chakra as I lay in my bed, trying to fall asleep. It felt dense and of the Solar quality, just like the overall feel of the Aethyr.

20th Aethyr—KHR

The English translation of KHR is "the Aethyr of the wheel." It is the fourth Aethyr in the Lower Mental Plane within the Air Element, corresponding with the Heart Chakra, Anahata. This Aethyr is an expression of the cycles that are a part of life. As such, it is closely associated with the Wheel of Fortune path of the Tarot.

In my visions, I always saw a symbol of a wheel present. This wheel relates to the cycles of time, as well as Karma. KHR relates to the Chesed Sephira, as the masculine energy of Jupiter is tempered by the feminine energy of Juno (wife of Jupiter).

All religious and Spiritual traditions have the idea of the wheel and cycles as part of their overall philosophy. This turning wheel is our Universe. It teaches life lessons as we go through the many periods, especially the Solar and Lunar cycles. A surplus of the Water Element is present in this Aethyr, which I noticed immediately upon entering it. However, the energy was balanced since all Four Elements are within KHR and form part of the wheel. With an influx of energy from Chesed, KHR's consciousness is akin to a Watery aspect of Tiphareth.

The idea of fate, as well as destiny, is present in KHR. The atmosphere is both joyous and melancholy—there is a duality present. The sexual energy current is both masculine and feminine. I felt a powerful connection to the boundlessness of consciousness. The energy felt quite heavy emotionally and mentally; thus, I did not experience any energy transformations that evening.

19th Aethyr—POP

The English translation of POP is "the Aethyr of division." It is in the middle of the Lower Mental Plane within the Air Element, corresponding with the Heart Chakra, Anahata. This Aethyr's energy is similar in quality and type to the High Priestess path of the Tarot. POP channels the White Light of Kether from the Crown Chakra into the Heart Chakra. Qabalistically, your consciousness is akin to being in Tiphareth still, working through the many lessons and initiations surrounding this Sphere.

POP embodies the expression of the "Priestess of the Silver Star." She is called Isis by the Egyptians and Mary by the Christians. She is also Shekinah of the Hebrew tradition. She personifies the Spiritual impulse in its feminine aspect. As such, POP is an Aethyr of initiation into the feminine Spiritual current coming directly from the Godhead. If you are a male practising Magick, the initiation in POP will be a major one, as it was for me. The three Elements of Water, Air, and Spirit are present in this Aethyr.

POP imparts to the mind that the duality of good and evil is a part of human existence. There is a struggle between life and death in POP. Spirituality is a way to rise above that duality and experience the Oneness of Spirit. This Aethyr is of the feminine sexual current and for the Kundalini awakened, it serves to purify the Ida Nadi and remove any blockages that impede its flow. There is a stillness in thoughts and emotions in this Aethyr as the mind becomes wholly passive and ready to receive the initiation of the Spiritual feminine current.

As I lay in my bed the evening of the evocation, I felt stirrings of energy in my head and heart. It led to the most profound transformational Kundalini experience I have had thus far with the Aethyrs. The same occurrence happened in POP the first two times I completed the entire Thirty Aethyr operation.

This Aethyr has proven to be profoundly transformational for me. In all three instances, I felt the Ida channel saturate with Pranic energy and ultimately align with its exit point at the top of the head. Therefore, the connection between my heart and my head was aligned, and a cooling Spirit energy permeated the left side of my body and entered my physical heart. It was rapturous and put me in a tranquil state of mind like never before.

The initiation of this Aethyr represents the act of accepting and receiving the feminine Spiritual current. Every time I have encountered POP in the future, this alignment further expanded my consciousness.

18th Aethyr—ZEN

The English translation of ZEN is "the Aethyr of sacrifice." This Aethyr is in the second half of the Lower Mental Plane within the Air Element, corresponding with the Heart Chakra, Anahata. As POP was the initiation into the feminine Spiritual current, ZEN is the initiation into the masculine one. It holds the esoteric meaning of the "Initiation of the Crucifixion."

As I entered this Aethyr, I noticed that my thinking and emotional faculties were subdued entirely. There was a stillness inside of me that felt sacrificial of my Soul. For most of the day, I spent time alone in a meditative state and quieted down my interior. The thoughts I chose to contemplate were compassionate ones, indicative of the personal sacrifice necessary to initiate myself into the masculine Spiritual current of ZEN. I let go of the past, including any regrets or attachments and was ready to receive this all-important initiation.

The initiations of ZEN and POP are necessary to comprehend and assimilate the Aethyrs above them since they become more and more Spiritual as you go upwards. The vision in this Aethyr is a crucifixion, which is a two-step process. The first step is the sacrifice of Jesus on the cross of the Four Elements, symbolized by the Hanged Man card of the Tarot. It incorporates the inner compassion and unconditional love you need to contemplate to let go of all parts of the Self that no longer serve you.

The second step is the sacrificial tomb of the King's Chamber (referring to the Great Pyramid in Egypt) and the silence of the mind that needs to be induced through this experience (Figure 64). These two steps are meant to free the consciousness from the body and unite it with Cosmic Consciousness.

The idea is to sacrifice the old Self to be reborn into the new Spiritual Self. The cross is the willful action to sacrifice the Self in the name of the Spirit. The tomb is the time in darkness and silence that serves to withdraw the bodily senses and free the consciousness. These two methods induce a transmutation and transformation of the lower parts of the Self into the higher Spiritual parts.

The new Spiritual Self, which comes out of this experience, embraces the suffering of humankind and works to help them at all costs. The unconditional love within the Self ultimately awakens once this process is complete.

ZEN impresses on the Soul and the mind that life is a series of sacrifices. The old must always be ready to die for there to be an evolution in the thoughts and emotions. Through self-sacrifice and applying the energy of unconditional love, change is ever-present, as well as a transformation into something better and higher on the scale of life.

Within the Golden Dawn Order, ZEN is representative of the *Vault of the Adepti,* in which the initiate must lie for three days and three nights, symbolic of the death of Jesus Christ, who lay in a tomb for the same amount of time before being Resurrected. You must spend time in the cocoon before transforming into a beautiful butterfly, metaphorically speaking.

You should embrace the energy of this Aethyr instead of running away from it. Naturally, your old cognitive faculties will drop away, which may initially seem scary. Still, if you remain patient, you will integrate the masculine Spiritual current and transcend past this Aethyr.

Qabalistically, the Aethyr of ZEN is directly related to the Hanged Man card of the Tarot that leads from Hod to Geburah. As such, once you have successfully integrated the initiations of POP and ZEN, you will have finally advanced beyond the state of consciousness of Tiphareth and are ready to explore the following Sphere, Geburah.

POP initiated me further into the Ida Nadi (Water) energy current, while ZEN was the initiation into the Pingala Nadi (Fire) energy current. As POP was feminine sexual energy, ZEN was masculine. I felt Ida active and aligning along the left side of my body, near my physical heart, while Pingala was aligning on the right side. The result was a further activation of the *Spiritual Heart*, on the opposite side of the physical one, beside the right breast. After the initiations of these two Aethyrs, POP and ZEN, I felt renewed in every way, and my Kundalini was functioning at a much higher level.

Figure 64: The King's Chamber Initiation of ZEN

17th Aethyr—TAN

The English translation of TAN is "the Aethyr of one's equilibrium." It is located on the highest Sub-Plane of the Lower Mental Plane within the Air Element, corresponding to the Heart Chakra, Anahata. TAN represents the harmonizing forces of Karma that always work toward preserving justice in the world. The vision of this Aethyr will be some symbol representing balance and duality. As such, this Aethyr is related to the Justice path of the Tarot, connecting Tiphareth and Geburah.

The main symbol of the Justice card is the scales, alluding to the Zodiac Libra, the representative energy of this path. Before you can experience the Geburah Sphere, your Karmic burden must be weighed and made fully known to you. You may even see the Egyptian scales of balance in the Hall of Maat, otherwise known as the "Hall of Two Truths." This symbolic item weighed the heart of the initiate against the feather of Maat. Anubis operated the scales while Thoth recorded the results, after which Horus took the initiate to Osiris for judgement.

Concepts of morality and ethics are prominent in TAN since by embodying the higher virtues, good Karma is gained, and bad Karma is avoided. Karma is a natural Law or Principle that acts on all the Cosmic Planes. All opposing forces of duality below the Aethyr LIL contain Karma within them since Karma is, in essence, the by-product of duality. All thinking in terms of opposites creates Karma. Accepting any dual idea without considering its opposite produces Karma, according to the perception of that event. Only unity in all things creates non-Karmic events.

While in TAN, I thought about the concepts of good and evil, right and wrong. I understood that I must always be checked by a moral and ethical outlook, where all of my actions are for the good of the whole and not just me. Otherwise, I will be judged, and negative Karma will be attached to my Wheel of Karma that is continuously operational since I live in a world of duality. It is through the mind that we interpret these events in a relative sense. Things are actual only concerning the consciousness that experiences them. Therefore, all imbalances in this Aethyr are considered evil, and the scales of justice seek to equalize them.

Newton's Third Law states: "For every action (Force) in nature, there is an equal and opposite reaction." Karma is the by-product of this Law when it is applied to the context of human actions. We must right every wrong when we see it; otherwise, we become evil's accomplices. As humans, we must learn to use our Mercy and our Severity—the two opposing pillars on the Tree of Life. If not applied correctly, harmful or bad Karma is created. If used successfully, positive or good Karma is created, which brings forth more positivity in our lives since the Universe rewards ethical and moral actions.

Bad Karma attaches itself to our Wheel of Karma, to be repeated in the future until the action is corrected and balance or equilibrium is struck. Because there is an equal amount of dual-energy in this Aethyr, both masculine and feminine sexual energy currents are present. TAN is meant to create equilibrium in the Lower Mental Plane before proceeding further since it is the last Aethyr of the Air Element. I did not experience any Kundalini energetic transformations in this Aethyr.

16th Aethyr—LEA

The English translation of LEA is "the first Aethyr of the Higher Self." LEA is the first Aethyr of the Higher Mental Plane corresponding with the Fire Element. As such, I took on my Higher Mental Body to experience this Aethyr. The corresponding Chakra is the Solar Plexus Chakra, Manipura.

In LEA, I began to identify as a Spiritual human being. The Fire Element is the highest I have experienced in the Thirty Aethyrs operation so far since it is closest to Spirit. I could feel the Fire energy in my heart as a tangible substance. LEA results from the initiations in POP and ZEN of the masculine and feminine Spiritual currents. In this Aethyr, you connect with the Fire of your Soul, which is the next step once the two opposing energy currents have been integrated.

There is seductive energy permeating this Aethyr, and I could feel my consciousness being pulled in all directions, like an unruly animal needing discipline. Thus, the theme of this Aethyr is "Babalon and the Beast." The consciousness of LEA is akin to the Sphere of Geburah, although due to the high influx of sexual energy, it reminded me of the Strength card of the Tarot. Crowley's interpretation of this path is called "Lust" because of the intense sexual current. He describes the Aethyr's energy as that of the Great Goddess Babalon, riding a Beast (animal), who is frequently portrayed as a lion or a bull.

The duality here is the objective and subjective nature of the Universe and the force of attraction between them. Babalon represents objectivity, which is the real Universe around us. The Beast is the consciousness that is subjective to the one perceiving the Universe. Because the Universe is seductive and beautiful, the consciousness is moved in all directions, trying to grasp and embrace everything the Universe has to offer, like a child looking at the world with wonder for the first time. The Soul is that which needs to take control of the consciousness, subdue it, and make it fall in line with its True Will—this is the challenge of this Aethyr.

LEA also offers an initiation, which is the initiation of the Fire of the Soul. Since you are now in the Higher Mental Plane of the Fire Element, you must embrace the energy of Geburah and integrate it within yourself.

The theme of life and death is apparent in LEA, and its energy often reminded me of the path of the Tower in the Tarot. After all, Mars is assigned to the Tower card, corresponding with Geburah. There is an influx of Fire in LEA accompanied by the destruction of old beliefs and modes of thinking. Change is the only constant in the Universe, and it requires the death of the old Self so that the new Self can be reborn every waking moment. Life is a series of little deaths and changes that manifests on all Planes of life.

The environment in LEA is very alluring. The lust that is felt is a result of the strength of the sexual current present, which is feminine. Furthermore, because we are now dealing with willpower, an aspect of Geburah and the Fire Element, it is a step higher than the other Planes of emotions and thoughts.

LEA is the first Aethyr of the Higher Self; entering it offered a powerful transformational experience. A stream of Kundalini energy rose from Muladhara into my Solar Plexus Chakra, Manipura. Afterwards, my connection with the Fire Element strengthened, which I could feel through my Heart Chakra, Anahata.

LEA made me see that the sexual energy serves to unite the Inner and Outer Worlds into one cohesive whole. It is the sexual energy that makes us excited about living in the world and causes us to see it as enticing and beautiful. In LEA, non-Kundalini awakened individuals may experience a Kundalini awakening of the Inner Fire through Sushumna into Manipura Chakra because of the power of the sexual current present.

15th Aethyr—OXO

The English translation of OXO is "the Aethyr of dancing." It is in the lower region of the Higher Mental Plane within the Fire Element, corresponding with the Solar Plexus Chakra, Manipura. The shared vision in this Aethyr is that of dancing as an expression of the ecstatic joy of obtaining Spiritual consciousness. The purpose of life is to live, and that in and of itself is a joyous activity.

The proportion of the movements of the Planets has been called the "Music of the Spheres" by the Ancients. There is beauty in the mechanism of the Solar System, and the very joy and bliss present in OXO are the creative expression of this idea.

In this Aethyr, I felt the integration of the lower initiations of POP, ZEN, and LEA. As I achieved a higher state of consciousness due to those initiations, my Soul was overjoyed. Now in OXO, I could partake in the harmony of the Universe in its creative expression. By obtaining a higher sense of Spiritual consciousness in LEA, I felt bliss in OXO. Becoming Spiritual and rising in the vibration of consciousness is a route to achieving real and lasting happiness in your life.

In this Aethyr, life is seen as a Divine dance, the "Lila" of Hinduism. Living on Planet Earth is a joyous game as Matter flows from Spirit and back again due to its creative Divine nature. Life is an endless cyclic expression in Time and Space, where the ultimate purpose is to be alive and be part of it. This Aethyr's energy put me in touch with the beauty of music, and I spent the better portion of the day listening to all the songs that moved me emotionally. They sounded even more epic while I was surfing the energy of this Aethyr.

Successful experience of OXO can result in another initiation, which is the unity of the masculine and feminine Spiritual currents as One. Within the Golden Dawn, this experience is symbolized by the Rose Cross. It relates to the Heart Chakra, where the opposing Spiritual currents merge and fuse. This symbol represents the union of opposites and the dualism in nature.

Since LEA was an initiation of the Fire of the Soul, the masculine current is still present in OXO. The bliss of OXO, though, is a result of the feminine sexual current that characterizes the base energy of this Aethyr. If the Ego is subdued and does not rebel against the bliss experienced due to obtaining Spiritual consciousness in LEA, you may achieve this initiation of OXO. Spiritual consciousness transcends time and is above logic and reason, the Ego's modes of expression.

The consciousness of OXO is akin to Geburah, with a powerful influx of the feminine sexual current. The next few Aethyrs are preparing you for entry into Chesed by infusing the necessary energies into your Soul. The Ego has been stripped away at this point, although you must still abolish all desire and instil the essential ethical and moral outlooks to exalt your Higher Self thoroughly. As Geburah deals with your willpower, Chesed deals with unconditional love and compassion.

That evening, in the blissful state I was in, I embraced the feminine sexual current of OXO. I had another transformative experience with the Kundalini energy, where joy and bliss permeated my physical heart. I was cleansing my Heart Chakra and also removing any remnants of Ego desires that would ultimately prepare me for an integration of the energy of compassion and unconditional love.

14th Aethyr—VTA

The English translation of VTA is "the Aethyr of semblances." This Aethyr is in the lower region of the Higher Mental Plane within the Fire Element, corresponding with the Solar Plexus Chakra, Manipura. There is a feeling of darkness in this Aethyr, including stern thoughtfulness and solemnity. The Fire Element is abundant in VTA and can be felt strongly as soon as you enter it. The pervading darkness, which feels like an ocean, is due to VTA being in close proximity to Binah.

In this Aethyr, no desires are present, and the sexual energy current is entirely masculine. Kundalini awakened individuals are working with higher aspects of the Pingala Nadi in VTA. Willpower becomes enhanced, as does the ability to follow logic and reason, devoid of emotions and feelings.

The vision you might have here is of the "City of the Pyramids," which contains Adepts who have abolished desire and lust for life to attain solemnity. The Pyramids were considered initiation chambers which the initiate enters to extinguish all personal inclinations and evolve Spiritually.

There is a strong feeling of death in the darkness that pervades VTA. The consciousness of VTA is akin to the Fire of Geburah, although one can feel the darkness of Binah and Daath as well. This Aethyr is best visited at night due to its dark nature. It has a connection to the ZEN Aethyr and its energy, only with more of the Fire Element present, which burns away all desires and feelings/emotions. Thus, the initiation in VTA is one of the abolishment of desire. Still, since this Aethyr is devoid of feeling, it also is devoid of compassion, which is the necessary aspect you need to acquire to rise in consciousness above VTA. And since this Aethyr lacks empathy, the Ego is still present. Only through compassion and empathy can the Ego be overcome entirely.

Due to the incredibly mystical feeling present in VTA, I enjoyed being in this Aethyr, although it did not offer any Kundalini energy transformations. There is no joy of life; instead, the solemnity of death and darkness are ever-present. Still, the mystical element was so strong that I revisited this Aethyr often in the future.

13th Aethyr—ZIM

The English translation of ZIM is "the Aethyr of application or practice." This Aethyr is in the middle region of the Higher Mental Plane within the Fire Element, corresponding with the Solar Plexus Chakra, Manipura. The vision here may be of an Ascended Master, a Silent Watcher of humankind. The purpose of the Ascended Master is to help other people realize their Spiritual potential. They are Adepts who have undergone a series of initiations and who serve God by keeping the Spirit of love, goodwill, and compassion towards all living things alive.

ZIM naturally follows VTA because the Adepts in VTA have renounced all desires but lack compassion, the main ingredient in accessing all the Aethyrs above it. Here in ZIM, compassion is present, as are all the other attributes acquired and learned in the lower Aethyrs. This compassion feels quite heavy on the heart as the unconditional love energy is increased in this Aethyr to impart some higher Spiritual truths to us. As such, the consciousness of ZIM is akin to entering the Chesed Sphere. The energy allowed me to see that helping others is a sacred duty since we all need to evolve Spiritually and expand our consciousness. Until we all do so, the collective consciousness of humanity will stay as it is.

The lesson in this Aethyr is service to others as a sacred duty to our Creator. We are all personally responsible for our Spiritual Evolution but also the collective evolution of all humankind. Therefore, once you have climbed to the top of the mountain, it becomes your duty to alight the path for all those people climbing the mountain themselves—the student must become the teacher, such is the Law.

The sexual energy current in this Aethyr is both masculine and feminine. I did not have a transformative experience with the Kundalini. Regardless, now that I was starting to embody the higher expressions of unconditional love, I knew I was being prepared for a major initiation in a higher Aethyr. Once you access the consciousness of Chesed, the next step is getting past the Abyss to enter the Supernals. Before getting there, though, the lessons of Chesed have to be integrated fully.

12th Aethyr—LOE

The English translation of LOE is "the first Aethyr of Glory." This Aethyr is located in the upper region of the Higher Mental Plane within the Fire Element, corresponding with the Solar Plexus Chakra, Manipura. The vision of "Babalon and the Beast" seen in LEA is also present here, although intensified. The connection with the Fire of the Soul is present also.

LOE is the Aethyr of the "Cup of Babalon," Sangraal, the Holy Grail. This Cup is filled with wine, which is symbolic of the blood of Jesus Christ, as it represents unconditional love and sacrifice. In LOE, the attachment to desire has been renounced (as per the lesson in VTA). As such, the element of compassion and empathy is increased.

The consciousness of LOE is akin to the Sephira Chesed, with an influence of Binah past the Abyss. After all, Binah is the Sea of Love and compassion, the Great Feminine aspect of Divinity. In LOE, I had to shed the last bit of my Ego before proceeding to the following two Aethyrs in the Fire Watchtower. The initiation present here is that of shedding your blood, symbolically speaking, into the Cup of Babalon and obtaining the understanding of Divinity.

Those who cling to their Ego will assemble here and be unable to rise higher. To be fully initiated into this current, you must sacrifice all personal desires to attain sincere compassion. Consequently, as it is the Aethyr of Glory, here is felt the Glory of God spoken of by Jesus Christ, when referring to a state of Being attained once you have renounced all desire and surrendered your Ego to unconditional love and compassion. However, you must achieve a healthy balance between Mercy and Severity, Chesed and Geburah, to reach this state.

The Beast is the individual consciousness now being able to perceive the mystery of Babalon for what she truly is, Universal Love. In this Aethyr, the compassion and love for others are seen as a sacred duty, a Holy trust. The feeling present in the previous Aethyr, ZIM, has the added sense of glory that becomes the emotional reward for accepting the sacred duty of helping others on their Spiritual paths. The Spiritual consciousness attained in LEA has now been given its primary mode of expression, compassion. The sacrifice of the Self and the Ego is necessary to activate compassion and to feel the Glory of God.

This Aethyr promotes the idea of being a Spiritual warrior, fighting in the name of God-the Creator. We are all brothers and sisters since we all come from the same Creator. This Aethyr emphasizes the value of good deeds, being kind to others, and sacrificing yourself for the greater good. If you see an injustice being done to your brothers and sisters, you must stand up for them and protect and defend them. We are all equal in the eyes of our Creator, irrespective of our race, religion, or creed.

The sexual energy current in LOE is feminine, and those who are Kundalini awakened will be working with the Ida Nadi in its highest aspect of unconditional love. Because of my connection to this Aethyr and the strong sexual current, I had a transformative experience that evening in which the energy of compassion became further ingrained in me. I cried a large portion of the night while I felt empathy and love for all humanity, realizing that we are all One.

LOE is a powerful Aethyr to make you understand the value of compassion. Because of my experience with this Aethyr, I became a more Spiritual person overall, being able to love everyone equally.

11th Aethyr—IKH

The English translation of IKH is "the Aethyr of tension." It lies in the upper region of the Higher Mental Plane within the Fire Element, corresponding with the Solar Plexus Chakra, Manipura. The tension in IKH is a result of being at the precipice of the Abyss, which is the next Aethyr above it. IKH is the highest Aethyr attainable by the human mind since crossing the Abyss means rising above the Mental Plane of duality into the Spiritual Plane of unity. The consciousness of IKH is akin to the highest part of Chesed, bordering on Daath.

Cognitive faculties must be surrendered, starting in this Aethyr and the one above it, to learn to function entirely on intuition. Logic and reason are faculties of the mind, and they find their last mode of operating here in IKH, although due to the tense feeling in this Aethyr, they will be relatively subdued. IKH is the final frontier of human consciousness, and the tension felt is created by the Ego, which knows it is about to die and disperse fully in the next Aethyr, ZAX.

The Great Abyss of the Mind is immediately above this Aethyr, as is the *Archdemon* Khoronzon, the personification of the Devil himself. The Devil is your Ego and the source of the duality of the human mind through which it functions. Khoronzon is the Master of Demons, which are the personifications of your negative aspects of personality and character. They are your negative thoughts fuelled by fear, the antithesis of love.

As there is tension present here, fear is present as well. It is the fear of the Unknown and the fear of the death/transformation of the Ego. I was spending a lot of time in contemplation and away from other people in this Aethyr (and the next Aethyr above it, ZAX). I was learning to quiet the mind in IKH so that I could cross the Abyss successfully. The previous two Thirty Aethyr operations helped me because I knew what to expect, but I believe that I had not passed the Abyss successfully in those operations. I had worked on silencing my mind up to this point and preparing myself further for ZAX.

What awaits on the other side of the Abyss is Non-Duality and the ability to induce silence of mind at will. Consciousness will be localized fully in the Spiritual Plane if the Abyss is crossed successfully. This experience marks the end of being emotionally affected by fear and anxiety.

The sexual energy current present in this Aethyr is masculine. Kundalini awakened individuals are working with the Pingala Nadi in its aspect of mentality and Ego duality. I did not experience any transformations in this Aethyr with the Kundalini energy.

10th Aethyr—ZAX

The English translation of ZAX is "the Aethyr of the One with a Great Name." It lies at the Sub-Plane of the Great Outer Abyss. Qabalistically, ZAX is the eleventh Sephira, Daath, the Veil of the Abyss. It separates the

Supernals from the lower parts of the Tree of Life. It is the Abyss of the Mind, the part of you that is the Eternal Spirit separated from the part of you that is the Ego and the physical body. The sexual energy current in ZAX is both masculine and feminine.

The Abyss separates the World of Spirit from the World of Matter. It acts as a bridge between the Above and the Below. The Ego is formed via the human mind through a singular perception of duality. To rise above the Ego means to eradicate it in the Abyss. What remains afterwards is an elevated state of higher consciousness that is inherently Spiritual, functioning solely through intuition.

The Great Archdemon Khoronzon is a personification of the Ego, and he will be encountered in ZAX, as that is the abode and source of the Ego. He contains within himself the forces of dispersion and annihilation of the thoughts and ideas of the Ego. Therefore, you must not listen to his chatter. Instead, you must quiet your mind to raise your consciousness into the Spiritual Plane.

There is a Ring-Pass-Not between ZAX and the higher Aethyrs in the Great Spiritual Plane. The Higher Mental Body is to be left behind as you take on the Spiritual Body as the vehicle in the following ten Aethyrs. ZAX is the last Aethyr of the Higher Mental Plane, corresponding with the Solar Plexus Chakra, Manipura. The sexual current found here is both masculine and feminine. The Aethyrs above ZAX all pertain to the three highest Chakras of Vishuddhi, Ajna, and Sahasrara.

If you have successfully entered the Aethyrs preceding ZAX, you should be ready for this critical initiation. All of your Karma from the previous Aethyrs must be overcome while quieting the mind in a meditative state of Samadhi. You cannot use logic and reason, nor compassion, against Khoronzon. The silence of mind is the only way to pass through this Aethyr successfully.

The forces in this Aethyr will appear chaotic. The attuning of the part of the Self that comprehends the truth in silence will help you align with the Higher Self to pass through this Aethyr. It helps to invoke the Egyptian Child-God, Hoor-Paar-Kraat, otherwise known as Harpocrates, who is the God of Silence. Contemplate his energy and meaning and use him to help quiet your mind.

Vestiges of personality from the lower Subtle bodies will tend to speak up, but if you hold silence of mind firmly against all forces present in this Aethyr, you should pass safely through the Abyss. Furthermore, it is best to eradicate all fear in the Aethyrs before ZAX because Khoronzon will use your fear against you and amplify it to an unimaginable degree.

The safe passage of this Aethyr will allow you to have complete contact with your Holy Guardian Angel and converse with him (her). The HGA is the part of the Self that speaks to you through the silence of the mind. It channels information from the Spiritual Plane through your intuition. He or she (depending on the polarity of your Soul) gives you the wisdom and understanding to comprehend Spiritual truths about yourself and the Universe. Your sense of identity must be extinguished to accomplish this task since the Higher Self exists as a Monad found in the unity of all things.

Once the Ego has dispersed in the Abyss and Khoronzon has been defeated, you will obtain a permanent connection with your Holy Guardian Angel. In doing so, you will abandon all teachers other than him (her), for you will fully become both the student and the teacher as One. At that point, true Gnosis concerning the Mysteries of the Universe will begin to be imparted to you.

Upon entering this Aethyr, I heard many thoughts come to me at once, with no apparent connection between them. My mind was in complete disarray, which caused incredible chaos in my interior. I focused on quieting my mind and not allowing these random thoughts to take hold of my consciousness. This required a great deal of concentration and application of my willpower. I had to reconcile and quiet every thought or idea that came in. If I tried to rationalize these thoughts, I failed. Thus, I could not spend any time examining my thoughts but had to induce silence from one moment to the next.

It was evident that Khoronzon was trying to use the energy of fear to bind my consciousness to whatever he chose to project at me. Everything that related to my Ego, its likes and dislikes, its experiences in life, was being used against me. The only way to not allow fear to take over was to induce silence of the mind.

I found that the best method of producing unwavering stillness of mind is using my faith in God-the Creator. Khoronzon would try to fool me by projecting fearful thoughts that required rationalizing, but I was steadfast in overcoming them through faith in what I was trying to accomplish. At all costs, Khoronzon attempted to convince me that I am it and not the Higher Self that exists in silence, but I chose not to listen and stayed firm in my task.

That evening, having induced unyielding silence in my mind, I lay still in my bed with perfect concentration and my attention placed on my Heart Chakra, where the source of my inner silence came from. After a few minutes, I felt a pull in my consciousness as a stream of energy rose upwards into my head. After it filled my brain area with a cooling Spirit energy, it projected out of my Crown Chakra and the Bindu Chakra at the top back of my head. It seemed an energy alignment had occurred, and I had successfully crossed the Abyss.

After this process was complete, I noticed right away that the chatter of the Ego was minimized, and a blissful feeling permeated my Heart Chakra. Negative thoughts did not affect me emotionally anymore as I felt my consciousness was in a higher place now. I had attained peace of mind that I had never experienced before.

After this experience, I began to function on intuition alone, and logic and reason would not have an emotional impact on me anymore. I would not get caught up in the Ego's chatter since I could induce silence at will. Remember, you cannot annihilate the Ego while living in the physical body, but you can learn to produce silence at will and overcome it—you can become its master instead of being its slave.

Every time I visited and revisited the Aethyrs and went through ZAX, I induced silence and more of my consciousness would be pulled upwards through the Crown Chakra, thus aligning with the Bindu Chakra, which resulted in an even more blissful state. Since I now function through intuition in my day-to-day activities, including in my interactions with others, I developed greater empathic and telepathic skills over time. Merely listening to energy and allowing it to speak to my heart enabled me to focus more on what matters in life. It helped me to further my virtues and discard my vices.

Crossing the Abyss linked me to my own Holy Guardian Angel, who became my Spiritual teacher for the rest of my life. To this day, he teaches me through pure Gnosis, which is now a regular part of my life. He communicates to me when I need or consciously ask for his help. He speaks through wisdom and understanding and imparts knowledge about the Universe to help me advance Spiritually. My Holy Guardian Angel is the part of me that is God, the Divine. The main body of work in *The Magus*, as well as my other writing works, was channelled to me by my Holy Guardian Angel. Having this connection with him has been the greatest blessing in my life.

9th Aethyr—ZIP

The English translation of ZIP is "the Aethyr for those who are void of Ego." This Aethyr is directly above the Abyss, in the lowest Sub-Plane of the Spiritual Plane within the Spirit Element. The Spirit Element corresponds with the three highest Chakras of Vishuddhi, Ajna, and Sahasrara. In ZIP, as well as all the Aethyrs above it, you will use your Spiritual Body for travel. This Aethyr will appear very beautiful upon entering it since the tension of the previous two Aethyrs will be overcome and left behind. As the energy of ZIP took over me, a blissful feeling permeated my Heart Chakra, and it intensified as the day went on.

There is a powerful feminine sexual energy current in this Aethyr. It made me perceive the world around me as an illusion while my interior and Spiritual reality was the only thing substantial and real. When I closed my eyes, I saw glimpses of a beautiful woman I had never seen before. This beautiful woman is none other than the Shakti or the Kundalini energy itself in its feminine aspect. As such, the energy of this Aethyr carries the different elements of the Great Goddess and feminine energy in general.

ZIP is a region of great harmony, peace, and beauty. Qabalistically, this Aethyr is similar to entering Binah on the Tree of Life. No initiations or energy transformations were present here, but I felt a great sense of accomplishment to have reached such lofty heights of Divinity. ZIP felt like the reward for overcoming all the previous Aethyrs. Kundalini awakened individuals will behold the glory and beauty of the Ida Nadi in its most elegant essence.

8th Aethyr—ZID

The English translation of ZID is "the Aethyr of one's inner God." This Aethyr lies in the lower region of the Spiritual Plane within the Spirit Element, attributed to the Chakras of Vishuddhi, Ajna, and Sahasrara. The consciousness of ZID is akin to entering Chokmah on the Tree of Life. It is the region of the Holy Guardian Angel, the expression of the Higher Self. The truth of your Spiritual nature will directly be confronted here.

The Aethyrs of the Spiritual Plane operate differently than what we've seen so far since they seem to swing back and forth between Binah and Chokmah, for the most part, to impart on you the lessons of the Supernals. Force cannot exist without Form to register its ideas, and Form needs Force to impregnate thoughts upon it. The paths connecting these two of the Supernal Sephiroth are also significant when visiting the Aethyrs of the Spiritual Plane.

Chokmah and Binah are the highest expressions of the masculine and feminine (Father and Mother) Principles within the Self. Aethyrs akin to Binah channel the energy of love, while those who relate to Chokmah impart wisdom and knowledge. Aethyrs that connect any two of the Supernals carry a combination of energies relating to love, truth, and wisdom, the highest expressions of Spirituality.

As you faced the Goddess Shakti in the previous Aethyr, ZIP, this next Aethyr reveals your highest masculine component, your Holy Guardian Angel. By aligning with your Higher Self, your True Will will be revealed to you. As such, you may discover your real purpose in this lifetime. Interestingly, your life's purpose is not something that you have created but something you must discover about yourself. Once you find it, you will embrace your True Will as the essential guiding force in your life.

This Aethyr is the direct opposite of the preceding Aethyr; thus, the sexual energy is masculine. Confronting your Higher Self, or Higher Genius, will bestow upon you authority over all parts of your Being. By aligning yourself to your True Will, you will have control over the Four Elements of your Being and become their Master. Your consciousness will experience continuous awareness where you see both your conscious and subconscious thoughts simultaneously and can manipulate both to carry out your True Will.

When I entered ZID, I immediately felt the bliss from the day before vanish, and a sober yet very Spiritually uplifted outlook replaced it. I decided to meditate and tune into the silence that I had gained (since I could now induce it at will after crossing ZAX successfully). When I shut down my senses and quieted my mind, I heard the voice of my Holy Guardian Angel, which was my own voice but not spoken by my Ego, but by a different, Higher part of me.

The connection to my Higher Self made me wish to explore this Aethyr further in the future, and I did. I felt I had reached a new high in my Spiritual Evolution. There were no Kundalini energy transformations for me in ZID. Instead, I was receiving information about my True Will and purpose in life, which is to guide and teach other people, especially those on the Kundalini path seeking answers, as I did when I had a Kundalini awakening many years ago. I also felt strong compassion for all of humanity, which was strange since the current is entirely masculine. Nonetheless, the compassion made me tune into the Spiritual needs of others, which aided my mission and purpose in life.

7th Aethyr—DEO

The English translation of DEO is "the Aethyr of Spiritual selfishness." This Aethyr lies in the lower region of the Spiritual Plane within the Spirit Element, corresponding with the highest three Chakras of Vishuddhi, Ajna, and Sahasrara. As I entered DEO, I felt love being the predominant feeling—the love of myself and other people.

The love of Self is not a selfish kind of love but one based on a misunderstanding of perception of the world around you. If you regard the world as Maya, a mere illusion, you will lack compassion and will see others as an illusion also. If you have compassion, though, you will see the Souls of others as something real, to be honoured and respected. The world of Matter may be an illusion of the mind, but the Soul and Spirit are real and Eternal. They are above the Abyss and do not belong to duality. As such, they were never born and will never die.

It is Venus, or Aphrodite, the Goddess of love, who is present in this Aethyr, and she may take many forms in your visions. She is also Shakti, the feminine energy of the Kundalini. The power of love in this Aethyr is extreme, as is the creative component that comes with it. I found myself inspired to paint the entire day.

DEO was the most creative Aethyr I had encountered so far. The Spiritual Fire I felt in this Aethyr was extraordinary. It seemed to intensify my natural Kundalini energy to a high degree. Because the love current was so strong, I found myself inspired to show affection to the people in my life, especially those closest to me. Qabalistically, the consciousness of DEO is akin to the Empress path of the Tarot.

The lesson to be learned in this Aethyr is to integrate compassion as your mode of communication with other human beings, which will enable you to rise to the Aethyrs above this one. Otherwise, you will fall prey to Spiritual selfishness where you may have integrated the lessons of Spirit and Soul but have not taken the next step in cultivating compassion towards others.

Compassion, which is a reaction to unconditional love, unites us all. It is the critical component of a true Adept or Sage. All the Prophets and Saints of the past were compassionate towards their fellow humans and sought to help them expand their consciousness and evolve Spiritually. Altruism and charity are the virtues to be learned in this Aethyr before proceeding further.

The sexual energy current here is feminine, and Kundalini awakened individuals are working with the Ida Nadi. This Aethyr did not offer anything regarding energy transformations, but it was an absolute creative joy to partake of its energy the entire day while it was present.

6th Aethyr—MAZ

The English translation of MAZ is "the Aethyr of appearances." This Aethyr is located close to the middle of the Spiritual Plane within the Spirit Element. As ZIP and ZID are opposites, MAZ can be seen as the opposite of the Aethyr before it, DEO. As DEO contains the creative feminine energy, MAZ provides creative masculine energy. The consciousness of MAZ can be likened to an aspect of the Chokmah Sphere on the Tree of Life.

I felt an expansion in consciousness as I entered the energy of this Aethyr. It had the right combination of Spiritual faculties present and available at the same time. The bliss was nonexistent unless I focused on a blissful idea or thought. If I focused on something negative, this feeling was heightened instead.

MAZ had a Karmic component, similar to the two previous Aethyrs, KHR and TAN. MAZ can be seen as the extension of those Aethyrs, with a profoundly higher sense of Spiritual consciousness. It is the last Aethyr dealing with one's personal Karma. Because of this, this Aethyr felt heavy at times. The Water and Fire energies were balanced in this Aethyr, filtered through the Spirit Element.

All the Aethyrs in the great Spiritual Plane have a much higher Spiritual consciousness than anything below them. This means that they each have a sense of mysticism and transcendence. Things move slower in them, music sounds more enhanced, and moral and ethical character components are increased. There was no Kundalini energy transformation in this Aethyr for me.

5th Aethyr—LIT

The English translation of LIT is "the Aethyr that is without a Supreme Being." It is located in the middle of the Spiritual Plane within the Spirit Element, corresponding to the Vishuddhi, Ajna, and Sahasrara Chakras. There is a strong sense of Eternity and Infinity permeating this Aethyr, as well as the concept of freedom and, most importantly, truth. The energy of this Aethyr is feminine, although it is not the Fire of love that is present, but the sobriety of truth. The consciousness of LIT is akin to an aspect of the Binah Sphere, the source of intuition—the direct experience of the truth in reality.

LIT felt like a release and relief after entering MAZ since it felt lighter and more Aetheric. The Air Element was predominant. There was a heightened feeling of honour and glory in the idea of truth. As such, the Sun energy was also present, but it was transcendental. I saw a vision of the feather of Maat, which symbolizes truth. This vision summed up the energy of the entire Aethyr for me—the power and beauty of truth.

> *"The truth is like a lion. You don't have to defend it. Let it loose and it will defend itself."* — Anonymous

In this sense, truth is likened to the king of the jungle—the lion. As all animals bow down to their king, all things in life bow down to the truth. Truth is objective, and when we speak it, all those who hear it naturally align with it. They do not have to accept it, but everyone must respect it. In this way, truth is a guiding Light in our lives. Those that align with it become its agents.

> *"God is a Spirit; and they that worship him must worship him in Spirit and in truth."* — *"The Holy Bible"* (John 4:24)

The Holy Bible is filled with quotes about truth and its importance in our lives. The Supreme Deity is Unknowable to humanity, but we align ourselves to it through the truth. By always being truthful to ourselves and others, we walk in the Light and embody the Spirit. That's all it takes. Truth, the Light, and the Spirit are all corresponding ideas that give rise to one another. By aligning to one of them, we align with all three. And even though Light and the Spirit are relatively elusive, the truth is easily accessed throughout the day.

> *"I am the way, the truth, and the life; no man cometh unto the Father, but by me."* — *"The Holy Bible"* (John 14:6)

I felt very inspired in this Aethyr, but not in a creative way. I was motivated to develop my character further to be a beacon of Light for others. As I have been a truthful person my entire life, this Aethyr very much resonated with my personal beliefs and felt like home. The beauty of truth is that it allows you to sleep with a clear conscience every night and always be yourself. It enables you to continually live in the Now since you cannot be in the present moment unless you are aligned with the truth.

As I felt very much in the moment while surfing this Aethyr, the sounds around me were heightened, as was my inner stillness. Also, my interactions with other people were inspiring and enlightening. My state of mind seemed to induce other people around me, who also felt more inspired to be themselves and be honest.

There is a high power to be gained by living and walking in truth, and I integrated the lessons of this Aethyr further into my personality and character. That evening, I felt a pull in consciousness and alignment along the Ida channel. This Aethyr allows you to integrate the Light energy into yourself if you let it. The sexual energy current in this Aethyr is feminine, and Kundalini awakened individuals will be working with the Ida Nadi.

4th Aethyr—PAZ

The English translation of PAZ is "the Aethyr of impending expression." It is located in the upper regions of the Spiritual Plane within the Spirit Element, corresponding with the Vishuddhi, Ajna, and Sahasrara Chakras. This Aethyr combines the feminine and masculine sexual forces and can be viewed as their source.

PAZ contains the two aspects of life that keep everything in balance—the feminine aspect of love and the masculine element of will. In this sense, Aleister Crowley's Magickal axiom of "Love is the Law, Love under Will" is exemplified in this Aethyr. These two opposites are found in the lower Aethyrs in different modes of expression.

Love is an expression of Babalon in the form of the Cosmos. Love also represents Space and is the builder of Form in the Universe. Will is the Force, its opposite component, expressed through Time. Will also represents Chaos, the formless Matter supposed to have existed before the creation of the Universe. Together, they are Chokmah and Binah, Time and Space, Force and Form—Chaos and Cosmos. The attraction between these two opposites ultimately leads to their union, which is the base energy permeating this Aethyr.

PAZ depicts the original separation of the polar forces of duality and their ultimate reunion. As I entered this Aethyr, I felt a powerful energy present, including a balance of the Fire and Water Elements. I could express myself thoroughly to others and felt a connection to all things.

This Aethyr seemed like a compilation of the best qualities of the Spiritual Aethyrs. There was a heightened consciousness present here. I found that due to the abundance of the Fire and Water energies, I sometimes was moved in both directions simultaneously and often, my views would seem opposed. I also felt the energy of PAZ was making me aggressive at times. Thus, I tried not to overthink while in this Aethyr and focused on the high level of consciousness present.

Qabalistically, this Aethyr is akin to being somewhere between Chokmah and Binah but far higher than the Empress card of the Tarot. The sexual energy current, as mentioned, is both masculine and feminine. Kundalini awakened individuals are working with both the Ida and Pingala Nadis. Due to the heaviness of the energy present, I did not have any Kundalini energy transformations that evening.

3rd Aethyr—ZOM

The English translation of ZOM is "the Aethyr of Self-knowledge." This Aethyr is located in the upper regions of the Spiritual Plane within the Spirit Element, corresponding with Vishuddhi, Ajna, and Sahasrara Chakras. Qabalistically, the consciousness of ZOM is akin to being somewhere along the path of the Magician in the Tarot. Thus, if you have accessed this Aethyr correctly, you will become the "Master of the Elements," otherwise known as "The Magus."

The lesson in this Aethyr is that all objective reality is related to how you perceive the world through the subjective Self. Our consciousness, our essence, is like a circle whose centre is nowhere and whose circumference is everywhere. As you have learned your True Will in ZID, in ZOM, you are given the ability to carry it out. It is the purpose of the Magus to carry out their True Will, which is why they are called the "Master of the Elements." You carry out your True Will with the help of your own Four Elements of Being since now you know how to use your Elements efficiently.

You also learn to plant seeds in the minds of others by the use of your Elements and *The Kybalion* Principles, namely the Principle of Mental Gender. When you are tuned into your True Will, its rate of vibration will be very high since it is of the Spirit Element. As such, when you project your thoughts into the minds of others, they will conform to your True Will seemingly effortlessly. By being tuned into your True Will, you are consciously creative and can create whatever mental realities you desire.

All the people of the past who were leaders of humanity, through politics or other means, were also Magi, whether they were working their Magick consciously or unconsciously. These men and women were Adepts, whether Adepts of Light, such as Mahatma Gandhi and Mother Theresa, or Adepts of Darkness, such as Adolf Hitler and Napoleon. All these people used their Light energy creatively by controlling their own Four Elements of Being, whether their intention was for good or evil. They were using their True Will through the conscious expression of their inherent qualities and characteristics, manifested through the Subtle Planes and the Aethyrs.

In ZOM, the world is seen as a projection of the Self and is therefore under its direct control. Here, you have the power to cut through any illusion to get to the truth and mentally create realities and have other people adopt your mental realities as theirs.

The sexual energy current of this Aethyr is masculine, and the Kundalini awakened individuals are working with the Pingala Nadi. I had no Kundalini energy transformations in this Aethyr. Nevertheless, I often revisited ZOM due to its potent nature in manifesting my True Will.

2nd Aethyr—ARN

The English translation of ARN is "the Aethyr of fulfilment." This Aethyr is located in the higher region of the Spiritual Plane within the Spirit Element, corresponding with Vishuddhi, Ajna, and Sahasrara Chakras. ARN is the home of Babalon, and in this Aethyr, the totality of her energy is revealed to you. She was first seen in LEA, then again in LOE, and finally, her daughter was seen in ZIP. All of these were manifestations of the overall energy of Babalon, which is found in this Aethyr.

ARN is the highest level of feminine sexual energy out of all the Aethyrs. Babalon is the personification of the powerful force of attraction between the subjective Self and the objective non-Self. It will manifest to you as an attraction to sound, as the true beauty of sound will be unveiled to you in this Aethyr. Therefore, I highly recommend you spend some time listening to music that you enjoy, as you will find your whole Being dancing to it while in this Aethyr.

There is an intense bliss present in this Aethyr. If you have performed the Spiritual Alchemy programs up to this level, ARN will be the most prominent high you have ever experienced while performing Ceremonial Magick. The beauty of Non-Duality will make itself known to you, although the actual experience is not revealed until you enter the next Aethyr, LIL.

ARN represents ultimate duality, as all the other Aethyrs below it are expressions of this one. The struggle you felt between the subjective Self and objective non-Self in PAZ is now a gentle and loving sharing between Cosmos and Chaos. ARN is the highest expression of Binah and Chokmah as the source of all duality on the Tree of Life. It is somewhere between these two Spheres, well above the Empress card and PAZ Aethyr.

There are tremendous desires and ecstasy present in this Aethyr, which may make you incredibly sexually excited. The mere sexual excitement in this Aethyr can trigger a Kundalini rising if you haven't already had one. For the Kundalini awakened individuals, you will be tapping into the highest essence of energy present within the Ida Nadi. The creative powers of this Aethyr are potent indeed.

ARN represents the bliss that accompanies Spiritual consciousness. There was no Kundalini energy transformation awaiting me that evening, possibly because I had already been exposed to this high level of sexual energy upon my initial awakening many years ago. However, I did come back to this Aethyr often because of the intense, blissful energy present in it. I found that it greatly magnified my Kundalini energy.

1st Aethyr—LIL

The English translation of LIL is "the First Aethyr." It is located in the highest region of the Spiritual Plane in the Spirit Element. Right above it is a Ring-Pass-Not, which means that the Spiritual Body cannot pass beyond this Aethyr. This Ring-Pass-Not separates the Spiritual Plane from the Divine Plane above.

LIL is the first Aethyr of Non-Duality. Every thought and emotion immediately becomes reconciled with its opposite through the energy present in the Aethyr. The influence of Kether's energy induces this incredible transcendental state of mind. The Ego is not present in this region at all. With this reconciliation process occurring from moment to moment, you will feel at One with the Universe in an unprecedented way. Because there is no discrimination of thoughts and feelings, there is an inner silence in this Aethyr. And through this silence, all truth is conveyed.

The vision of this Aethyr, as well as its representative symbol, is Horus the child, Hoor-Paar-Kraat, the embodiment of innocence and purity. He is the transformed Beast. Seen as unruly and wild in the lower Aethyrs, he has become the child again.

Becoming Hoor-Paar-Kraat is the culmination and completion of the Great Work. As we are born and our Ego develops over time in our teenage years, taking hold of our consciousness, it becomes our duty to reverse the cycle and become the innocent child yet again. Only this time, we have the wisdom and knowledge we gained along the way. The Fool has become the Magician, Qabalistically speaking.

Beyond LIL is the Divine Plane of existence, of which not much can be said since it is incomprehensible to the human mind. LIL is the highest stage of the human Spirit and the perfect state conceivable to the consciousness. As it is the only Aethyr of Non-Duality, you will genuinely feel at One with the world. The sexual energy current in LIL is masculine. Kundalini awakened individuals are working with the Pingala Nadi. Although this Aethyr is Non-Dual, the energy of the Ida Nadi is present as well, in a state of unity with Pingala.

Qabalistically, this Aethyr is akin to the path of the Fool card of the Tarot, although one has complete access to Kether once the mind becomes still. And if you stay in this Aethyr long enough and learn to silence the mind completely, you will even get glimpses and visions of the Divine Plane. As such, this Aethyr is the most mystical and transcendental of all the Aethyrs. Samadhi is easily obtainable while surfing this Aethyr.

The Thirty Aethyrs' Names and their Phonetic Pronunciations

30. TEX (Teh-etz)—The Aethyr that is in four parts.
29. RII (Ree-ee)—The Aethyr of the mercy of Heaven.
28. BAG (Bah-geh)—The Aethyr of doubt.
27. ZAA (Zodah-ah)—The Aethyr of solitude.
26. DES (Dess)—The Aethyr that accepts that which is.
25. VTI (Veh-tee)—The Aethyr of change.
24. NIA (En-ee-ah)—The Aethyr of travelling.
23. TOR (Tor-rah)—The Aethyr that sustains the Universe.
22. LIN (El-ee-en)—The Aethyr of the Void.
21. ASP (Ahs-peh)—The Aethyr of causation.
20. KHR (Keh-har)—The Aethyr of the Wheel.
19. POP (Poh-peh)—The Aethyr of division.
18. ZEN (Zod-en)—The Aethyr of sacrifice.
17. TAN (Tah-en)—The Aethyr of one's equilibrium.
16. LEA (Eleh-ah)—The first Aethyr of the Higher Self.
15. OXO (Oh-tzoh)—The Aethyr of dancing.
14. VTA (Veh-tah)—The Aethyr of semblances.
13. ZIM (Zodee-meh)—The Aethyr of application or practice.
12. LOE (El-oh-eh)—The first Aethyr of Glory.
11. IKH (Ee-keh)—The Aethyr of tension.
10. ZAX (Zod-ahtz)—The Aethyr of the One with a Great Name.
9. ZIP (Zodee-peh)—The Aethyr of those who are void of Ego.
8. ZID (Zodee-deh)—The Aethyr of one's inner God.
7. DEO (Deh-oh)—The Aethyr of Spiritual selfishness.
6. MAZ (Em-ah-zod or Mah-zod)—The Aethyr of appearances.
5. LIT (Lee-teh or El-ee-teh)—The Aethyr that is without a Supreme Being.
4. PAZ (Pah-zod)—The Aethyr of impending expression.
3. ZOM (Zod-oh-em)—The Aethyr of Self-Knowledge.
2. ARN (Ar-en)—The Aethyr of fulfillment.
1. LIL (El-ee-el or Lee-el)—The First Aethyr.

THE CALL OF THE AETHYRS (19TH KEY)

Enochian:

Madriaax ds praf (NAME OF AETHYR) chis micaolz saanir caosgo od fisis balzizras laida!

Nonca gohulim: Micma adoian Mad, Iaod bliorb, soba ooaona chis Lucifitias Piripsol, ds abraassa noncf netaaib caosgi od tilb adphaht damploz, tooatnoncfg Micalz Oma Irasd tol glo marb Yarry Idoigo od torzulp laodaf gohol:

Caosga tabaord saanir od christeos yrpoil tiobi busdir tilb noaln paid orsba od dodrmni zylna.

Elzap tub parm gi Piripsax, od ta qurist booapis.

L nibm ovcho symp od christeos ag toltorn mirc q tiobi I el. Tol paomd dilzmo as pian od christeos ag L toltorn parach asymp.

Cordziz, dodpal od fifalz L smnad; od fargt bams omaoas.

Conisbra od avavox, tonug. Orsca tbl noasmi tabges levithmong. Unchi omp tibi ors.

Bagle? Modoah ol cordziz. L capimao izomaxip, od cacocasb gosaa. Baglem pii tianta a babalond, od faorgt teloc vovim.

Madriiax, torzu! Oadriax orocho aboapri! Tabaori priaz ar tabas. Adrpan cors ta dobix. Iolcam priazi ar coazior, od Quasb Qting.

Ripir paoxt sa la cor. Vml od prdzar cacrg aoiveae cormpt.

Torzu! Zacar! Od zamran aspt sibsi butmona, ds surzas tia balta.

Odo cicle qaa, Od ozozma plapli ladnamad.

English:

The heavens which dwell in the (NAME OF AETHYR), are mighty in the Parts of the Earth, and execute the judgement of the Highest!

Unto you it is said: Behold the Face of your God, the beginning of Comfort, whose eyes are the Brightness of the Heavens, which provided you for the Government of Earth and her Unspeakable Variety, furnishing you with a Power of Understanding to dispose all things according to the Providence of Him that sitteth on the Holy Throne, and rose up in the beginning saying:

The Earth, let her be governed by her parts and let there be division in her that the glory of her may be always drunken and vexed in itself.

Her course, let it round (or run) with the heavens, and as an handmaiden let her serve them.

One season, let it confound another, and let there be no creature upon or within her one and the same. All her members let them differ in their qualities, and let there be no one creature equal with another.

The reasonable creatures of Earth, or Man, let them vex and weed out one another; and their dwelling places, let them forget their names.

The work of Man and his pomp, let them be defaced. His buildings, let them become caves for the beasts of the field! Confound her understanding with Darkness.

For why? It repenteth Me that I have made Man.

One while let her be known, and another while a stranger. Because she is the bed of an harlot, and the dwelling place of Him that is Fallen.

O ye Heavens, Arise! The lower Heavens beneath you, let them serve you! Govern those that govern. Cast down such as Fall. Bring forth with those that increase, and destroy the rotten.

No place, let it remain in one number. Add and diminish until the Stars be numbered.

Arise! Move! And appear before the Covenant of His Mouth which He hath sworn unto us in His justice. Open the Mysteries of your creation, and make us partakers of the Undefiled Knowledge.

Enochian (Phonetic):

Mah-dree-ahx dah-ess pay-rah-fay (NAME AETHYR) Kah-hees mee-kah-ohl-zoad sah-ah-neer kah-ohs-goh oh-dah fee-see-sah bahl-zoad-ee-zoad-rah-sah Ee-ah-ee-dah!

Noh-nooh-kah goh-hoo-leem: mee-kah-mah ah-doh-ee-ah-noo Mah-dah, Ee-ah-oh-dah blee-ohr-bay, soh-bah oo-ah-oh-nah kah-hees Loo-kif-tee-ahs Pee-rip-sohlah, dah-ess ah-brah-ahs-sah noh-noo-kah-fay nay-tah-ah-ee-bay kah-ohs-jee oh-dah teelah-bay ahd-phah-hay-tah dah-mah-ploh-zoad, too-ah-tah noh-noo-kah-fay jee meekahl-zoad oh-mah ayl-rah-sahd toh-lah jee-loh-hah em-ah-bay yah-ree Ee-doh-ee-goh oh-dah tor-zoad-ool-pay Ee-ah-oh-dah-eff goh-hol:

Kah-ohs-gah tah-bah-ohr-dah sah-ah-neer oh-dah krees-tee-ohs eer-poh-eelah tee-ohbe boos-deer teel-bay noh-ahl-noo pah-ee-dah ohrs-bah oh-dah doh-dahr-mee-nee zoad-ee-lah-nah.

Ayl-zoad-ah-pay teel-bay pahr-mayjee Pee-reep-sax, oh-dah tah kew-rel-saht boo-ah-pees.

Ayl nee-bah-may oh-vah-choh see-mah-pay oh-dah krees-tee-ohs ah-jee tohl-tor-noo mee-rah-kah goh tee-oh-bel Ayl ay-lah. Toh-ah pah-ohm-dah deel-zoad-moh Ah-ess peeah-noo oh-dah krees-tee-ohs ab-jee Ayl tol-tornoo pah-rah-chah ah-seem-pah.

Kohr-dah-zoad-ee-zoad, doh-dah-pah-lay oh-dah fee-fahl-zoad Ayl ess-mah-noo-ahd; oh-dah fahr-gee-tah bah-em-sah ohm-ah -oh-ah-sah.

Koh-nees-brah oh-dah ah-vah-vah-ohtza, toh-noo-gee. Ohrs-kah tee-bay-ayl noh-ahsmee tah-bay-jee-sah lev-ee-thah-moh-noo-jee. Oo-noo-chee oh-may-pay tee-bay-ayl ohr-sah.

Bah-glay? Moh-doh-ah oh-el kohr-dah-zoad. Ayl kah-pee-mah-oh ee-zoad-ee mahx-eepay, oh-dah kah-koh-kahs-bay goh-sah-ah. Bah-glay-noo pee-ee tee-ahnoo-tah ah bahbah-loh-noo-dah, oh-dah fah-ohr-jee-tay tay-lohk-voh-veem.

Mah-dree-ahx, tor-zoad-oo! Oh-ah-dree-ahx ohr-ochoh ah-boh-ah-pree! Tah-bahohree pree-ah-zoad ah-ray tah-bah-sah. Ahd-ray-pahnoo Kohr-sah tay-ah doh-beex. Eeohl-kah-mah pree-ah-zoad-ee-ah-ray koh-ah-zoad-ee-ohr-ray, oh-dah kew-ahs-bah kewtee -noo-gah.

Ree-pee-rah pah-ohx-tay essah ayl-ahkohr. Oo-may-lah pray-dah-zoad-ah-ray kahkahr-jee ah-oh-ee-vay-ah-ay koh-em-pay-toh.

Tohr-zoad-oo! Zoad-ah-kah-ray! Oh-dah zoad-ah-mer-ah-noo ahs-pay-tah see-bay-see boot-moh-nah, dah-ess soo-ray-zoad-ahs tee-ah bahl-toh-noo.

Oh-doh kee-klay kah-ah, Oh-dah Oh-zoad-oh-zoad-mah plah-plee Ee-ahd-nah-mah-dah.

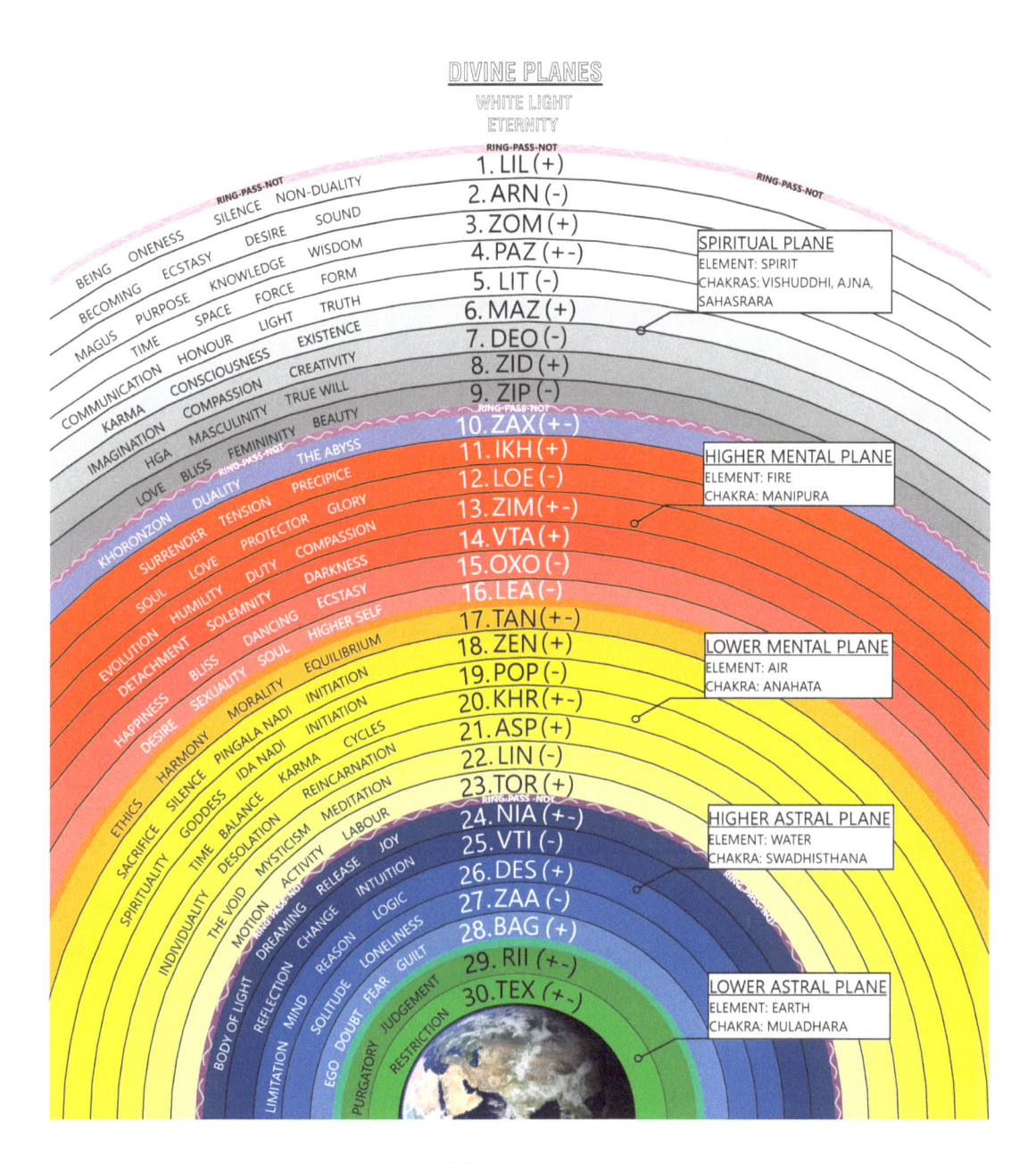

Figure 65: The Thirty Enochian Aethyrs

WORKING WITH THE ENOCHIAN KEYS

The Spiritual Alchemy formula for working with the Enochian Keys follows the same systematic progression through the Elements as what you have worked with previously with the LIRPs and SIRP. You are to start with the Earth Element and work with its Sub-Elements, followed by Water, Air, Fire, and Spirit. Once the two Spirit Keys are completed, you are to start the Enochian Aethyrs in reverse, beginning with the thirtieth, TEX, and working your way up to the first Aethyr, LIL.

You will notice that you are not working with the Air Element after Earth, but Water instead. The Higher Astral Plane of Water follows the Lower Astral Plane of Earth in sequence. The Lower Mental Plane and Higher Mental Plane of the Air and Fire Elements are next. So the course of progression in Enochian Magick is a little different from when we are working with the Qabalistic Tree of Life through the LIRPs and SIRP.

In Enochian Magick, we are working progressively with the Chakras, corresponding with the layers of the Aura. When working with the LIRP's and SIRP, though, we are rising up the Tree of Life following the Path of the Flaming Sword sequence in reverse.

As mentioned, the states of consciousness of the Sephiroth do relate to the Chakras. However, they are more sophisticated in how they function, as one Sephira, in many cases, expresses through multiple Chakras. The Eastern and Western systems fully correspond with the Elements, which is the unifying factor between the two. If you are still confused about how this works, I highly recommend you revisit some previous lectures in *The Magus*.

The entire Enochian operation will take forty-eight days to complete. It encompasses the two Spirit Keys, the sixteen Keys of the Elements and their Sub-Elements, and the Thirty Aethyrs. While working with the Keys, it is recommended to spend more time in meditation. Working on some scrying techniques to receive visions would also be beneficial. Enochian Magick is very mystical, and each Key will have its vision of the World or Plane of Being you enter. Therefore, being in the Alpha State is vital where you are lucid enough to receive and see images in your Mind's Eye Chakra.

SCRYING THE KEYS AND THE AETHYRS

The best way to enter the Alpha State is through meditative breathing techniques (Pranayamas) while relaxing your physical body. To achieve this, you should be sitting in a lotus position or lying down on your back. The Four-Fold Breath is designed to get you into the right state of mind for ritual exercises; thus, you are also to use it here.

A scrying Crystal works best to help you receive visions of the Enochian Planes, Sub-Planes, and Aethyrs. A Black Mirror works as well for this purpose. These two items are designed to draw in your consciousness so that you can see visions on their surface. Without their use, these visions would occur somewhere in the back of your head. Therefore, they are difficult to see unless you are adequately trained.

With a Natural Stone (Crystal), it needs to be big enough to draw in your energy. Quartz Crystals are most often used for this purpose, but many other Crystals also work. Something the size of 1.5-2" diameter at the minimum would work well. Some people opt-out for larger Crystals, otherwise known as Crystal Balls. I am sure you have seen an example of these in movies or if you have ever received a reading from a Spiritual medium.

You must hold the Crystal in your hand, or you can have it in front of you on a table surface. If you hold it in your hand, you will directly draw energy from it, which will amplify your natural energy. To receive visions, it helps if you are looking down slightly at the Crystal. Not in such a way that you have to tilt your head down too much, though.

Gaze at the Crystal while performing the Four-Fold Breath to keep yourself in a meditative state. While gazing, unfocus your eyes so that you are not looking directly at the Crystal but somewhere right behind it. In this way, the Crystal is drawn into your consciousness. After a minute or two, you should start to see visions or images on the surface of the Crystal. This method of scrying Crystals is optimal and will yield the best results.

A Black Mirror has a reflective black surface upon which you can vaguely see yourself. Once you unfocus your eyes and see right behind it with the same method as with a Crystal, your consciousness will be drawn into it, and you will start to receive visions and see images in the Mirror.

A Black Mirror works best if you are naturally prone to visions. However, because the Crystal Ball emits a large amount of energy, it may be a more desired medium since this energy will serve to change your vibration and put you into an altered state of consciousness. Some people need this extra burst of energy to shift out from normal waking consciousness and go within themselves.

A Black Mirror works well if you already have a lot of energy built up, making your consciousness oscillate naturally between the conscious and subconscious minds. As I did, Kundalini awakened individuals may even get a better outcome with a Black Mirror than a Crystal. Since there is already so much energy built up through the Kundalini, more energy may not be needed to go within and see visions.

SPIRITUAL ALCHEMY PROGRAM III—THE ENOCHIAN KEYS

Once you have completed the necessary work with the SIRP or finished working with Planetary Magick and deem yourself ready for Enochian Magick, you are to follow the prescribed program outlined here. However, remember that you do not need to start with Enochian Magick immediately after finishing the program with the LIRPs and SIRP. Instead, you can choose one of the other three options presented in "The Next Step in the Great Work" chapter in the "Ceremonial Magick" section.

Working with the other two options of revisiting the LIRPs and SIRP can be repeated as often as you want in your life, and you will always learn something new and further evolve Spiritually. Or suppose you have chosen to work with Planetary Magick first. In that case, you will strengthen your mental and emotional foundation even more, which will help control the potent Enochian energy forces.

As with all Magickal workings, you must start the ritual sequence by performing the Four-Fold Breath for a few minutes to get yourself into a meditative state. The next step is to clear your space, your Magickal circle, with the LBRP followed by the BRH. Afterwards, you have an option to do the Middle Pillar exercise or not. If you do, you are invoking Light into your Aura, which may be beneficial since it will make the following process of scrying better and easier. Remember, though, that you do not have to perform the scrying method, but it is an option since it will help you get in touch with your visions more clearly.

Once you have done the Middle Pillar exercise (or if you have decided to skip it), you are ready for the evocation, the oration of one of the Enochian Keys in phonetic. Each Key is to be read once only, not more. Sufficient energy is evoked with just one reading. Reading it more than once can result in too much energy being evoked and is highly discouraged. Considering Enochian Magick is Adept-level, you are to end the ritual sequence by performing the Analysis of the Keyword. While working with the Enochian Keys, the sequence of the evocations must be strictly followed. This part is essential.

Enochian Keys: 1 to 18

Lower Astral Plane—Earth/Muladhara:
Day 1—Key 5 (Earth of Earth)
Day 2—Key 14 (Water of Earth)
Day 3—Key 13 (Air of Earth)
Day 4—Key 15 (Fire of Earth)

Higher Astral Plane—Water/Swadhisthana:
Day 5—Key 4 (Water of Water)
Day 6—Key 11 (Earth of Water)
Day 7—Key 10 (Air of Water)
Day 8—Key 12 (Fire of Water)

Lower Mental Plane—Air/Anahata:
Day 9—Key 3 (Air of Air)
Day 10—Key 8 (Earth of Air)
Day 11—Key 7 (Water of Air)
Day 12—Key 9 (Fire of Air)

Higher Mental Plane—Fire/Manipura:
Day 13—Key 6 (Fire of Fire)
Day 14—Key 18 (Earth of Fire)
Day 15—Key 17 (Water of Fire)
Day 16—Key 16 (Air of Fire)

Spiritual Plane—Spirit/Vishuddhi, Ajna, Sahasrara:
Day 17—Key 2 (Spirit—Passive)
Day 18—Key 1 (Spirit—Active)

Once you have completed the program with the Enochian Keys of the Elements and Sub-Elements, you are to start the Enochian Aethyrs (the Nineteenth Key). To evoke an Aethyr, insert its phonetic pronunciation into the Nineteenth Key, which also is to be recited in phonetic. The Aethyrs are again to be visited with the formula of entering the layers of the Aura from the Lower Astral to Higher Astral, then Lower Mental, onto Higher Mental, and finally to the Spiritual Plane. You will notice that the Aethyrs offer much more to work with regarding the Spiritual Plane. Because of the powerful sexual energy currents and transformative power, the Thirty Aethyrs are one of the best forms of Magick for Spiritual Evolution. Kundalini awakened individuals will particularly like the Thirty Aethyrs and find their use very beneficial in their transformation process.

Enochian Key 19 (Thirty Aethyrs)

Lower Astral Plane—Earth/Muladhara:
Day 19—TEX (30th Aethyr)
Day 20—RII (29th Aethyr)

Higher Astral Plane—Water/Swadhisthana:
Day 21—BAG (28th Aethyr)
Day 22—ZAA (27th Aethyr)
Day 23—DES (26th Aethyr)
Day 24—VTI (25th Aethyr)
Day 25—NIA (24th Aethyr)

Lower Mental Plane—Air/Anahata:
Day 26—TOR (23rd Aethyr)
Day 27—LIN (22nd Aethyr)
Day 28—ASP (21st Aethyr)
Day 29—KHR (20th Aethyr)
Day 30—POP (19th Aethyr)
Day 31—ZEN (18th Aethyr)
Day 32—TAN (17th Aethyr)

Higher Mental Plane—Fire/(Manipura:
Day 33—LEA (16th Aethyr)
Day 34—OXO (15th Aethyr)
Day 35—VTA (14th Aethyr)
Day 36—ZIM (13th Aethyr)
Day 37—LOE (12th Aethyr)
Day 38—IKH (11th Aethyr)
Day 39—ZAX (10th Aethyr)

Spiritual Plane—Spirit/Vishuddhi, Ajna, Sahasrara:
Day 40—ZIP (9th Aethyr)
Day 41—ZID (8th Aethyr)
Day 42—DEO (7th Aethyr)
Day 43—MAZ (6th Aethyr)
Day 44—LIT (5th Aethyr)
Day 45—PAZ (4th Aethyr)
Day 46—ZOM (3rd Aethyr)
Day 47—ARN (2nd Aethyr)
Day 48—LIL (1st Aethyr)

Once you have completed day forty-eight, you will have created a direct line of communication with Realms beyond the Spiritual Plane, namely the Divine Realms. It is possible and has been reported by numerous practitioners of Enochian Magick that you will receive entry into the Divine Planes and have visions and experiences of them.

The first Aethyr, LIL, is the only true Aethyr of Non-Duality and the states of consciousness reminiscent of the Divine Planes of existence. By creating a link with the Godhead through a systematic evocation of the Aethyrs, you may experience a stream of energy from a Divine Plane entering your Being. If this happens, welcome this event because it may be your life's most exceptional Spiritual experience.

For the Kundalini awakened individuals, systematically traversing the Enochian Keys from the ground up will optimise the channels (Nadis) and pathways of the Light of the Kundalini by removing any blockages that may be causing the Light to stagnate. Once Day 48 is completed, you may decide to visit and revisit the Enochian Keys, including the Elements and Sub-Elements, as well as the Aethyrs. I recommend that you do so.

In my experience, I have found the Thirty Aethyrs to be very mystical and transcendental, and their use helped me to evolve immensely Spiritually. Also, they were inspiring and fun to work with. I have spent many months visiting and revisiting the Aethyrs, sometimes systematically from the lowest to the highest, and periodically visiting only the ones I felt I wanted to experience more. To this day, I have never come across Magick rituals (in any form) that are more powerful, fun, and exciting than the Thirty Aethyrs.

EPILOGUE

The purpose of this work has been to give you the keys to maximizing your true potential as a Spiritual human being. As we each have a Divine spark of Light inside us, many of us lose touch with this inner Light as the Ego develops. And we cannot avoid having an Ego since it evolves as we grow up and our consciousness acclimates to our newly formed physical bodies.

The Ego's purpose is to protect the physical body and help us avoid danger. It is an intelligence, though, apart from the Soul, and it becomes its adversary over the years. After all, by tending to your physical body too much, your consciousness aligns with it and loses touch with the Soul.

As the Ego assumes dominance over the individual consciousness, it also allows fear to enter your energy system. The childlike innocence and wonder that we were born with becomes lost. Sadness soon sets in, as does confusion about who we have become over the years.

But even when the Ego has taken a complete foothold over a person's consciousness, the inner Light can never be fully extinguished. Instead, it starts to communicate to us in silence to let us know that it is our home and who we are. Thus, it is inevitable for every single human being to desire to reunite their consciousness with their inner Light. The challenge for all of us is overcoming our Egos and the darkness we accrue while growing up. The Ego and the Soul are a part of us for as long as we live on Earth, but we can only truly align our consciousness with one of them.

We were born as Beings of Light, and it is our destiny, our sacred duty, to regain our innocence. If we are to draw energy from the Spirit, we must get in touch with the Soul first. Once we regain a connection with the Soul, we can allow the Spirit energy to descend into us and transform us permanently. Through this process, we can find the everlasting happiness we all seek.

In essence, this is the process of the Great Work and the means of becoming Enlightened. To accomplish this, though, we must bathe ourselves in the Elemental energies, starting at the lowest, Earth, and progressing higher and higher through the inner Cosmic Planes. The process of Spiritual Alchemy is systematic. The purpose of the work presented in *The Magus* is geared toward bringing you closer to this goal. Every lesson and ritual exercise is a piece of the puzzle you need to complete the Great Work.

I hope that you have taken the keys I have given you in *The Magus* and applied them to your own life. This work is meant to be a manual for the Western Mysteries with the added component of cross-referencing the Eastern Chakric System. It is a manual for Ceremonial Magick and purifying and cleansing the Chakras while enflaming your Aura with Light. Because if you are to maximize your personal power, you must remove the

Karmic energy blocking you from operating at your optimal level. In doing so, you will overcome your Ego's impulses and align your consciousness with your Soul and Spirit.

This work is not meant only to be read once and put away forever after that. Instead, it is a "working" manual intended to be used as a reference for the various subjects discussed. I have aimed to turn you into a seeker of the Light and the Mysteries of the Universe so that you can continue to explore these subjects on your own by seeking further knowledge about them. And by aligning with your Holy Guardian Angel through this work, you will get direct access to guidance and wisdom you need to always remain on the path of Light.

If you have started the Spiritual Alchemy program with the Five Elements, you are well on your way to completing the Great Work. However, once you complete this program, don't stop there but keep going further. There is much to be gained from working with the Ancient Planets and especially the Enochian Keys. And as an Adept in the Western Mysteries, don't forget to utilize the additional material in the Appendix, including pertinent work with the Olympic Planetary Spirits.

If you have read this far but have not tried any of the ritual exercises yet, I implore you to try them. You will not be disappointed with the results. The intellectual knowledge contained in this work is enlightening, but the real essence is the ritual exercises. The intellect is, after all, only the third Sephira (Hod) on the Tree of Life, and there are still seven higher Spheres that you need to access within yourself.

Thank you for giving me your time to share the wisdom, knowledge, and experience I have acquired on my Spiritual journey through the Western Mystery tradition. If you are a Kundalini awakened individual, I hope that Ceremonial Magick serves you well on your journey, as it did for me on mine.

In closing, we are each a Magus in the making. Our life's purpose is to evolve Spiritually and tap into our innermost potential. It is our destiny to gain control over the Elements of our Being and become masters over our realities. In doing so, we serve God-the Creator since we are meant to be Co-Creators of our realities. We are intended to return to the Garden of Eden; it is our inherent birthright. Thus, keep your feet on the ground at all times, but have your head in the clouds. Work hard on improving yourself every single day. Seek growth and wisdom at all times. Most importantly, always stay inspired. And in time, you too will become—The Magus.

APPENDIX

ADDITIONAL ADEPT MATERIAL

SUPPLEMENTARY TABLES

Note: The following Tables are included as general information or to be used in Magickal work. Each of the Divine Names represents particular Deities or powers that can be invoked or evoked by vibrating their names. Magickal work with these Tables is Adept-level; it should not be undertaken until you have completed the Spiritual Alchemy program with the Five Elements.

TABLE 7: Divine Names Attributed to the Seven Ancient Planets

Name of Planet	Name of Planet (Hebrew)	Angel	Intelligence	Spirits	Olympic Planetary Spirits *
Saturn	Shabbathai	Cassiel	Agiel	Zazel	Arathor
Jupiter	Tzedek	Sachiel	Iophiel	Hismael	Bethor
Mars	Madim	Zamael	Graphiel	Bartzabel	Phalegh
Sun (Sol)	Shemesh	Michael	Nakhiel	Sorath	Och
Venus	Nogah	Hanael	Hagiel	Kedemel	Hagith
Mercury	Kokab	Raphael	Tiriel	Taphthartharath	Ophiel
Moon (Luna)	Levanah	Gabriel	Malkah be Tarshisim ve-ad Ruachoth Schechalim	Schad Barshemoth ha-Shartathan	Phul

* Olympic Planetary Spirits require the use of their sigils.

TABLE 8: Divine Names Attributed to the Sephiroth

Sephira	Divine Name (Atziluth)	Divine Name Meaning	Archangelic Name (Briah)	Archangelic Name Meaning	Choir of Angels (Yetzirah)	Choir of Angels Meaning
Kether	Eheieh	I am	Metatron	Angel of the Presence	Chayoth ha-Qadesh	Holy Living Creatures
Chokmah	Yah	Lord	Raziel	Secret of God	Auphanim	The Wheels
Binah	YHVH Elohim	The Lord God	Tzaphqiel	Contemplation of God	Aralim	The Thrones, or Mighty Ones
Chesed	El	God	Tzadqiel	Righteousness or Justice of God	Chashmalim	Shining Ones
Geburah	Elohim Gibor	God of Power	Kamael	Severity of God	Seraphim	Flaming Ones
Tiphareth	YHVH Eloah ve-Daath	Lord God of Knowledge	Raphael	Healer of God	Melekim	The Kings
Netzach	YHVH Tzabaoth	Lord of Hosts	Haniel	Grace or Love of God	Elohim	The Gods
Hod	Elohim Tzabaoth	God of Hosts	Michael	He who is like God	Beni Elohim	Sons of the Gods
Yesod	Shaddai El Chai	Almighty Living God	Gabriel	Strength of God	Kerubim	The Angels, or Strong Ones
Malkuth	Adonai ha-Aretz	Lord of Earth	Sandalphon	Co-brother (referring to his twin brother Metatron)	Ashim	The Flames, or Souls of Fire

TABLE 9: Invocation of the Forces of the Zodiac Signs

Zodiac Sign	Permutation of YHVH	Tribe of Israel	Angel	Colour (Atziluth)
Aries	YHVH	Gad	Melchidael	Scarlet (Red)
Taurus	YHHV	Ephraim	Asmodel	Red-Orange
Gemini	YVHH	Manasseh	Ambriel	Orange
Cancer	HVHY	Issachar	Muriel	Amber
Leo	HVYH	Judah	Verchiel	Greenish Yellow
Virgo	HHVY	Naphtali	Hamaliel	Yellowish Green
Libra	VHYH	Asshur	Zuriel	Emerald
Scorpio	VHHY	Dan	Barchiel	Green-Blue
Sagittarius	VYHH	Benjamin	Advachiel	Blue
Capricorn	HYHV	Zebulun	Hanael	Indigo
Aquarius	HYVH	Reuben	Cambriel	Violet
Pisces	HHYV	Simeon	Amnitziel	Crimson

OLYMPIC PLANETARY SPIRITS

The Olympic Planetary Spirits were first mentioned in the *Arbatel of Magic*—a Latin grimoire of Renaissance Ceremonial Magic that was published in 1575 in Switzerland by an anonymous author. The *Arbatel of Magic* is Christian in nature and focuses on the relationship between humanity and the celestial hierarchies. This work was highly influential on the occult community then, and many inspiring figures, including John Dee, mentioned it in their works.

The Olympic Planetary Spirits found their way into the Hermetic Order of the Golden Dawn's system of Magick. Although the Golden Dawn's students were introduced to them early on, actual work with the Olympic Spirits was reserved for the Adept, as was all work with Planetary energies or Spiritual Intelligences.

There are seven Olympic Planetary Spirits, one for each of the Seven Ancient Planets. At first glance, you will notice a correlation in their name to the Olympian Gods from the Greek pantheon. Although no clear correspondence between the two exists, some Magi believe that the seven Olympic Spirits are the seven main Greek Gods that rule over the Seven Ancient Planets. These are Chronos, Zeus, Ares, Apollo, Aphrodite, Hermes, and Selene. It is just a theory, of course, since no actual proof exists of this being the case.

The Olympic Planetary Spirits are traditionally considered to be blind forces which are volatile and can manifest negatively if the practitioner is not prepared for their power. Thus, you must have control over the Elements of your Being so that you can stay firm in your intent and use your willpower to guide these powerful forces. Experimenting haphazardly with the Olympic Spirits can cause havoc in your consciousness; therefore, I strongly advise against it. Instead, adhere to the evocation formula presented here.

Since the Olympic Spirits are blind forces, their energies are respective to the positive or negative nature of the particular Planet involved. For this reason, you should complete the Spiritual Alchemy program with the Seven Ancient Planets before undertaking work with the Olympic Spirits. Doing so will make you more familiar with the individual Planetary energies, which is helpful if you encounter any pitfalls with this work.

Traditionally, the practitioner is advised to evoke the Divine Name hierarchy of the Olympic Spirit's associated Sephira, including the Intelligence of the Planet. Doing so gives one more significant control over the Olympic Spirit's energy. Tables 7 and 8 contain all the necessary information for this task. The Planetary Intelligences are considered good (according to tradition), while the Olympic Spirits are deemed evil. This viewpoint, in my opinion, is subjective, but I want you to err on the side of caution regardless.

In my experience, I have not found anything negative about using the Olympic Spirits and have enjoyed the mystical states of consciousness they provided. I found the Planetary energy far more transcendental than when invoked with Planetary Hexagrams. Many enlightening visions ensued from this work, akin to the Enochian Keys, although more lucid. As with all ritual exercises presented in *The Magus*, the evoked energy stayed with me for the entire day. It dissipated out of my Aura during sleep, usually accompanied by exciting and revelatory dreams.

Olympic Spirits are straightforward to work with and offer something new for the aspiring Magus since it is the first time you will be working directly with Spiritual entities. Their use will heighten your knowledge of Planetary energies but also of Alchemy. Since there is no official Spiritual Alchemy program to be followed when working with the Olympic Planetary Spirits, this is an excellent opportunity to allow your Higher Self to take over and guide you with this work. After all, a big part of becoming the Magus is tuning into your Higher Self, your Holy Guardian Angel, and allowing him/her to "run the show."

Evoking the Olympic Planetary Spirits is simple and easy. Everything that you need for this task is in the Appendix. Each Olympic Spirit has its sigil (Figure 66), which serves as a doorway, or portal into its energy. When working with an Olympic Spirit, you will need to have its sigil on hand as you will be scrying them to access their energies.

At this point, you should already be familiar with the Planetary Hour system. In the same fashion as with Planetary Hexagram invocations, you should evoke a particular Olympic Spirit during its associated Planetary Hour, preferably the first one of the day, although he can be called up at night also. Refer to Tables 5 and 6 for this information. For best results, it also helps to evoke an Olympic Spirit on the day that corresponds with its Planet.

As with all major invocations or evocations, only work with one Olympic Spirit per day so you can focus on it and learn from its energy. To start the evocation, perform the LBRP and BRH to balance yourself and clear your Aura of unbalanced energies. If you wish to do a Middle Pillar, you may do so. Afterwards, sit comfortably or stand behind your central altar (facing East) and perform the Four-Fold Breath to shift your mind into the Alpha state.

When ready, vibrate the Divine Names of the Sephira and Planet associated with the Olympic Spirit you chose to evoke. For example, if you are working with Och, you must vibrate the Divine names corresponding with Tiphareth and the Sun Planet. The order to be followed is Divine (God) Name, Archangel, Choir of Angels, and Planetary Intelligence. You are the vibrate each of these names only once. The Planetary Angel and Spirit are not necessary since the Olympic Spirit is substituting their functions.

Take a moment now and read aloud the following prayer from the *Arbatel of Magic*. The prayer is slightly modified to fit the context of *The Magus* best. Vibrate the name of the Spirit once as you insert it into the prayer.

"O Eternal and Omnipotent God, who hast ordained the whole Creation for Thy praise and glory, and for the salvation of man, I beseech Thee to send Thy Spirit (NAME OF SPIRIT) of the Solar Order, who shall inform and teach me those things which I shall ask of him. Nevertheless, not my will be done, but Thine, through Jesus Christ. Amen."

Pick up and hold the sigil of the Olympic Spirit in front of you at around the same distance that you would scry a Crystal. Gaze at the sigil while getting immersed in the image. As you do this, begin to vibrate the Spirit's name repeatedly. Remember to perform the vibrations solemnly and keep your mind clear as you are doing so. The effect of doing this is quantitative, meaning that the longer you gaze at the sigil while vibrating the name of the Spirit, the more energy will be evoked into your Aura. Usually, no more than a minute or two is needed to generate the right amount of energy. Proceed at your discretion.

Once the energy has permeated your Aura, you are to perform the Mind's Eye Meditation from the "Ceremonial Magick Ritual Exercises" section. It helps to be sitting or lying down while doing this. Silence your mind and allow the evoked energy to communicate to you either through visions or by speaking with you directly. Do not be surprised if you hear the sound of your own voice in your head, disclosing new knowledge to you in an inspired tone. After all, the Olympic Spirit is blind energy your mind personifies when you call it up.

Most often, the Olympic Spirit will inform you of what your Soul needs to know to advance further Spiritually. Thus, it is not pertinent to directly ask questions but only to tune into the Spirit's energy with an open mind and heart. Although you may ask questions if you desire, the mere act of silencing the mind will allow the Olympic Spirit to speak to your Soul.

The Olympic Spirits speak to us through the World of Atziluth, thus, whatever comes from your Soul and your True Will, the Olympic Spirit will address, while what comes through your Ego will usually be ignored. Remember also that the nature of the Olympic Spirits is particular to the essence of their associated Planets, as is the knowledge and wisdom gained from working with them.

If you feel you are not getting any communication from the Olympic Spirit, you should try working on scrying techniques using either a Scrying Crystal or a Black Mirror. These techniques will aid in bringing out the communication from your subconscious to your conscious mind. You can find the scrying techniques in the Enochian Magick section. After you have finished the conversation with the Olympic Spirit and feel satisfied with the results, you must perform the following prayer: the licence to depart.

"For as much as thou camest in peace and quietly, having also answered unto my petitions, I give thanks unto God, in whose name thou comest. And now thou mayst depart in peace unto thy orders; and return to me again when I shall call thee by thy name, or by thy order, or by thy office, which is granted from the Creator. Amen"

End your session with an LBRP and BRH. Even though you have officially ended your communication with the Spirit, you will still have some of its energy lingering in your Aura. If you are having difficulty managing this energy at any point during the day, you can perform the LBRP and BRH. You cannot banish the energy of an Olympic Spirit once you evoke it, so you should use the Divine Names from Tables 7 and 8 to help guide it.

The *Arbatel of Magic* lists the Olympic Planetary Spirits, including their powers. According to this work, the Heavens were at one time divided into a total of 196 provinces or districts that the seven Planetary Angels ruled. The seven Planetary Angels are, in fact, the Olympic Planetary Spirits. Each Olympic Spirit had a seal or sigil that the Ancient Magi inscribed on talismans or amulets that they used in their Magickal operations.

The *Arbatel of Magic* also informs us that the Olympic Planetary Spirits are responsible for whole epochs of history since each Spirit rules for 490 years at a time. Bethor ruled from 60BC to 430AD, Phaleg ruled until 920, followed by Och until 1410, and then Hagith until 1900. The current ruler then is Ophiel, which makes sense when we consider the massive technological leap we had in the last century.

Also, each Olympic Spirit has command over legions of lesser Spirits in a hierarchal system of the nature of the Planet they rule. The sigils and associated powers of the Olympic Planetary Spirits are given below. Keep in mind that some of the obscure powers of the Olympic Spirits are obvious Alchemical blinds.

Arathor

The Olympic Spirit of Saturn, who rules over 49 provinces. Arathor's powers include changing any living organism into stone, imparting the secret of invisibility, bestowing long life, and making the barren fruitful. Arathor is the teacher of Alchemy, Magick, and medicine. He can also change coal into treasure and treasure into coal, confer familiars and reconcile underground Spirits to men.

Bethor

The Olympic Spirit of Jupiter who rules over 42 provinces. Bethor's powers include reconciling the Spirits of Air to man so that they are truthful, transporting precious stones from place to place, and composing medicines with miraculous effects. Bethor can prolong life to 700 years (subject to the Will of God) and give familiars of the firmament. He can also grant wealth and friendships to kings and influential people.

Phalegh

Governs all things that are attributed to Mars and rules 35 provinces. Otherwise known as the "Prince of Peace," Phalegh can give one great honour in military affairs. He can also give dominion over others and victory in war.

Och

The Olympic Spirit of the Sun who rules 28 provinces. Och's powers include imparting great wisdom and converting everything into gold and precious stones. He also confers excellent familiar Spirits, teaches perfect medicines, and offers 600 years of perfect health. Whoever possesses his character will be worshipped as a God by the world's kings.

Hagith

Governs all affairs attributed to Venus and rules 21 provinces. His powers include converting copper into gold and gold into copper in an instant. Hagith gives faithful Spirits. Whoever possesses his character will be adorned by beauty. They will be abundant in love and friendships.

Ophiel

The Olympic Spirit of Mercury who rules 14 provinces. Ophiel's powers include teaching all the arts and conferring familiar Spirits. He enables the possessor of his character to change quicksilver immediately into the Philosopher's Stone.

Phul

Rules 7 provinces and all things governed by the Moon. Phul's powers include transmuting all metals into silver and healing dropsy. He confers Spirits of the Water, who serve men in corporal and visible form. He destroys evil Spirits of Water and prolongs life to 300 years.

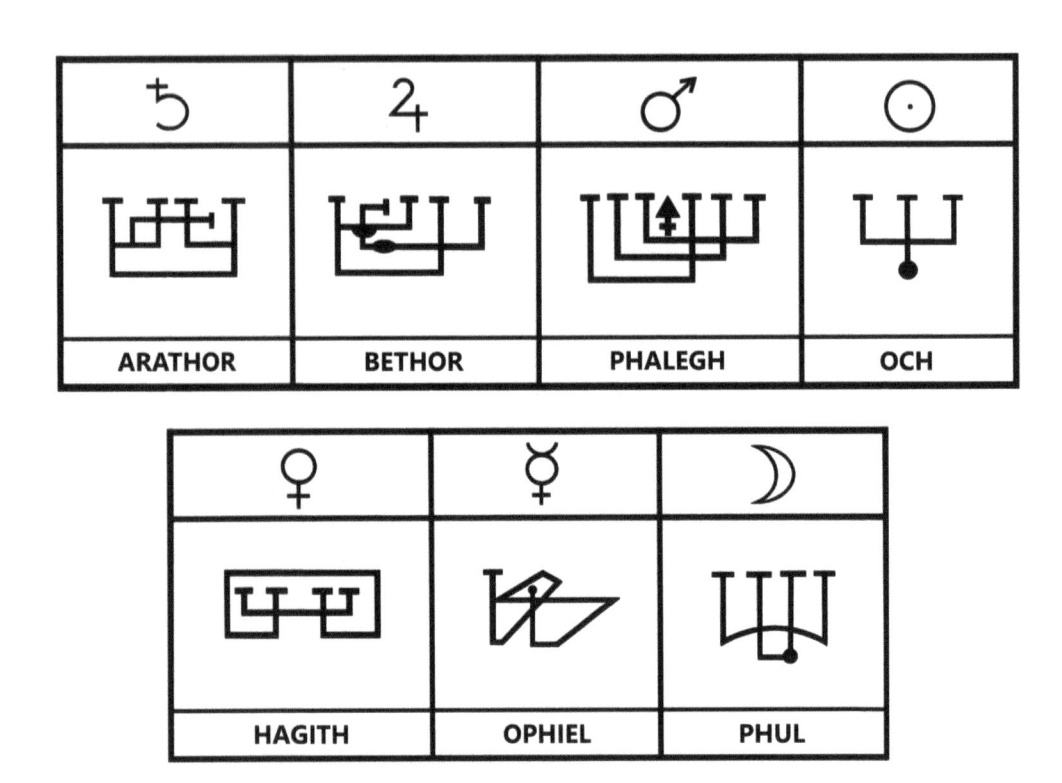

Figure 66: The Olympic Planetary Spirits

KUNDALINI AWAKENING ARTICLES BY THE AUTHOR

Note: The following articles will give you insight into the significant inner changes I underwent after awakening Kundalini and the Spiritual gifts that unfolded during my lengthy transformation. If you are interested in reading more, obtain a copy of my second book, "Serpent Rising: The Kundalini Compendium."

THE NATURE OF THE KUNDALINI

<u>Originally Published by The Kundalini Consortium—October 26, 2016.</u>

We live in a Holographic Universe that occupies the same Time and Space as other, infinite, parallel Universes. The human Soul decides in which direction to take our reality from one moment to the next. However, to align with the Soul, one must learn to live in the Now, the present moment, bypassing their Ego. This state of Being will be natural for us all once we Spiritually evolve.

As the energy rose up my spinal column during my initial Kundalini awakening, I saw the Holographic world around me with my physical eyes once the Kundalini energy entered my brain. Once there, it kept rising until it blew open Sahasrara Chakra, awakening the Thousand-Petalled Lotus. However, the experience wasn't finished.

Next, the Kundalini cracked the Cosmic Egg at the very top of the head, releasing a liquid Ambrosia, which poured over my body from the top-down, activating the 72 000 Nadis of my Body of Light (Figure 67). Due to the intensity of this experience, I shot up in my bed and opened my eyes. To my amazement, I beheld the room around me as a Holographic blueprint of the very room I was in a few minutes before.

To clarify, this was not some inner vision of my Mind's Eye, but I saw it with my two physical eyes. After seeing the painting above my bed suspended in mid-air, I looked down and saw my hands and arms as pure, golden Light. At that moment, I knew that the nature of the Universe around us is simply empty space, nothing more. And I realized our pure form as Beings of Light.

The average, everyday human cannot perceive the Holographic Universe with their physical eyes. After all, the material world vibrates at a much lower frequency than our Spirit energy and our biological brains are made up of Matter. Nevertheless, our consciousness crystallizes our experience of reality, and as such, we accept it as being real.

As infants, up until our Ego and memory started to form (thereby impacting our consciousness and localizing us in Time and Space), we saw the world for what it is—a Hologram. This theory would explain the nature of a child as they look out into the world with innocent, unbiased eyes and pure wonder and imagination streaming into their consciousness perpetually. But unfortunately, we cannot ask a child what it sees and experiences, and as they get older, they naturally forget the first few years of their lives.

The Ego evolved as the body's defence mechanism whose purpose is to protect us from the Elements in nature. The reptilian brain gave rise to the Ego. Once the Ego was formed as an intelligence of the body, we lost our innocence and consciousness fully localized within the physical body. Spiritual Rebirth aims to reverse the process and return us to that innocent state we were in as children. Only this time, we will have all of our cognitive faculties available for us to use.

The shedding of the Ego triggers a rising in consciousness towards the Spirit and away from the physical body. The Ego and Spirit are both points of awareness in the spectrum of consciousness, but they function at two opposite levels of vibration.

Consciousness is awareness in the Now of the internal process. Once liberated from the body through a Kundalini awakening, consciousness travels as awareness into the Spirit. This rise in consciousness is brought on by the Astral Light built up inside the Body of Light in the Kundalini awakened individual. Pranic energy from food and water and our sexual energy sublimate/transform into Astral Light that nourishes the Body of Light. As the Light "grows" inside the Body of Light, and consciousness attunes to the Spiritual Body over time, we begin to "lose ourselves within ourselves," transcending Time and Space to experience the realm of Eternity—the Spiritual Realm.

This mystical state is the goal and the inspiration of every Yogi, Sage, Magi, Adept, Shaman, and Spiritualist. The synthesis of Light in the Body of Light occurs continuously as the Kundalini awakened individual eats nutritious food while saving their seed by withholding ejaculation so that the sexual energy builds. For this reason, even after the initial awakening, it takes about two to three months for the person to start having metaphysical, transcendental experiences. These occur as the Astral Light builds up inside the energy system, fueling the Chakras and expanding the consciousness.

In this Kundalini transformation process, the Ego starts losing itself, which gives rise to fears in the subconscious mind since that is the Ego's domain. The Ego knows it is dying, so it fears this metamorphosis, looking for any way to get the consciousness to side with it and turn away from the Soul and Spirit. Remember, the Ego is tied to the physical body. Thus, any kind of Spiritual practice that purifies the Ego also draws the consciousness away from the physical body.

The veil between the conscious and subconscious minds starts to dissipate over time, and a person becomes attuned to the Oneness of all existence and the Universal Laws. One of these Laws is the Law of manifestation since human beings have the innate ability to manifest whatever reality they want or desire, provided it is in line with their True Will. True Will is different from the Ego (the lower Will) as it seeks to satisfy the Spirit in the realm of Eternity instead of tending only to the physical body's needs.

As the Astral Light grows and expands, awakened individuals become more attuned to the air around them since it creates a vacuum in which the Ego can no longer operate. The 72,000 Nadis, which are likened to tree branches as they carry the liquid Ambrosia inside the Body of Light, become optimized, turning them into antennas for outside vibrations. These vibrations use the air around us as a transmission medium, which the consciousness picks up through psychism. They are received the same way as radio signals; only we pick up thoughts, emotions, and willpower impulses from living beings around us.

However, before one can reach this state, they must first cleanse their Chakras of any dark, Karmic energy clouding their inner Light. When the Light can shine brightly, the individual consciousness can fully integrate and align with the Body of Light. In most cases, it takes many years to achieve this after awakening the Kundalini.

In a full and permanent Kundalini awakening, the energy rises up the Sushumna channel, awakening all the Chakras along the way, including Sahasrara, the Crown. Depending on the intensity of its rise, though, the Kundalini does not end there. Instead, it continues surging upwards towards the Heavens. This event makes the individual lose full consciousness of the physical body, resulting in the experience of being united with the White Light temporarily. Experiencing the White Light in an Out-of-Body-Experience is akin to being One with the Mind of God. However, since this Spiritual experience cannot be sustained while living, the individual consciousness re-enters the physical body soon afterwards.

The full and permanent Kundalini awakening has two distinct symptoms that become everlasting once the energy has localized in the brain: the constant buzzing in the ears and the constant presence of Astral Light in the head (Figure 67). The latter transposes itself onto the physical reality, so the person sees Light in all things with their physical eyes. On the other hand, the vibration or inner hum inside the head results from the Kundalini energy residing in the brain permanently.

In a partial awakening, the Kundalini rises up the spine but doesn't reach the top of the head. In most cases, it tries to blow open Ajna Chakra but, due to blockages or improper meditation methods employed, is unable to do so. As it cannot reach the brain entirely, it goes back down to coil itself three and a half times like a snake around Muladhara Chakra. Often, it drops back down to the Heart centre, Anahata Chakra, allowing the person to experience heart expansions and feel the nature of genuine empathy towards all living beings in the world.

As the Kundalini works its way into the Heart Chakra, it expands one's capacity for experiencing unconditional love, which gradually disengages the individual consciousness from the Ego. However, the Kundalini always aims to finish the awakening process by rising to Sahasrara Chakra, represented in the Tantric system as the feminine Shakti Principle rising to meet the masculine Shiva Principle at the Crown, thereby awakening one to Cosmic Consciousness. Once achieved, the Kundalini enters the brain's Third Ventricle area, called the "Cave of Brahma," facilitating the optimization of the Pineal and Pituitary Glands and the Thalamus and Hypothalamus.

A partial Kundalini rising can occur if the Ego holds on too firmly, inducing fear, which pulls the energy back down, preventing it from blowing open Ajna Chakra. Instead, the Kundalini energy enters the Heart Chakra to expand one's knowledge of the True Self and diffuse the Ego over time.

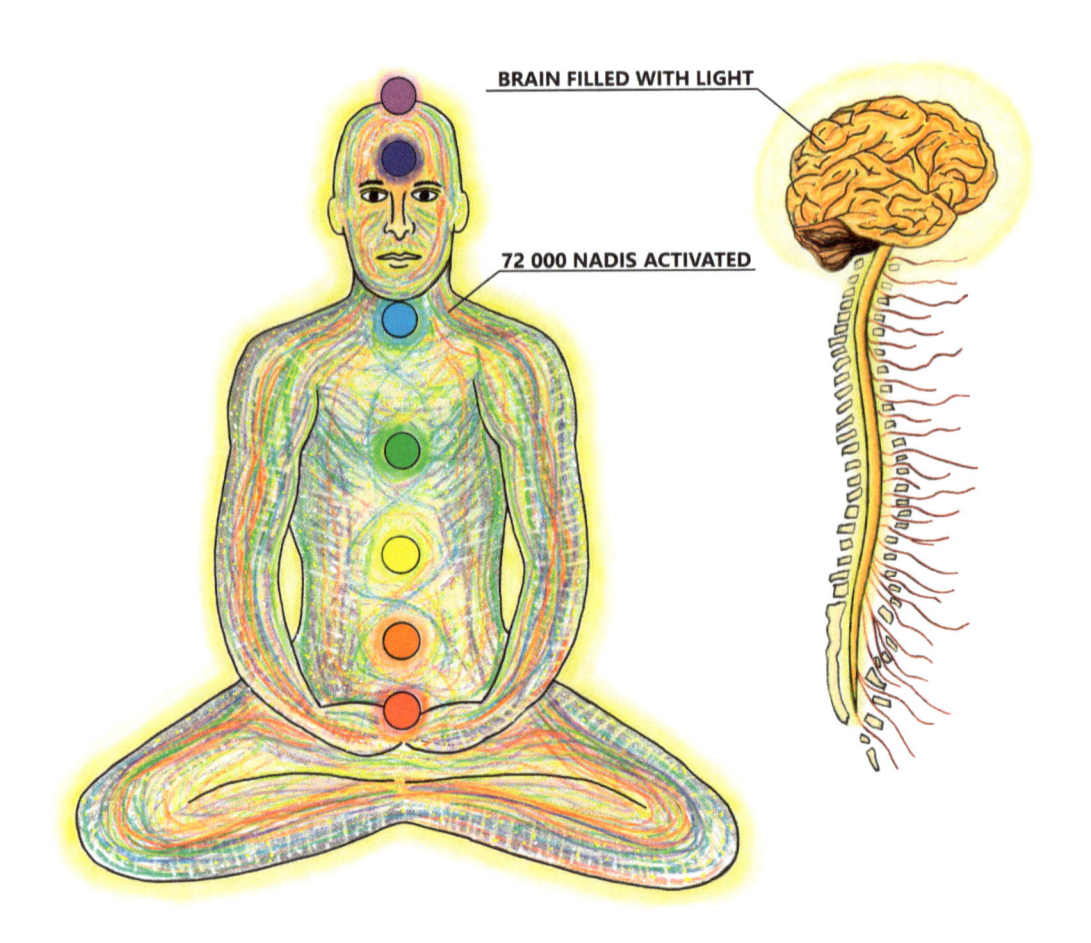

Figure 67: A Permanent Kundalini Awakening

All Kundalini risings carry sublimated Pranic and sexual energy up the spine, representing its initial, unrefined form. However, the Kundalini transforms over time into a fine Spirit energy which is the cause behind the transcendence achieved via the Spiritual Plane, corresponding with Sahasrara Chakra. Once the Kundalini drops back down into the Heart Chakra, it leaves a lingering effect that often plunges the individual into an inspired or Out-of-Body-Experience until the sublimated Prana dissipates completely.

Some Kundalini initiates perform Kriyas, speak in tongues, or do inspirational writing or painting. However, these states usually last ten to fifteen minutes until the person's heightened creative energy becomes depleted. In a fully awakened individual, though, the Kundalini energy is operational 24/7 and is at their disposal. This person channels creativity non-stop, continually expressing the inspired state. They literally become lost in space and time as activities like listening to music or beholding a beautiful landscape transport them into a wholly transcendental or metaphysical reality. This higher reality is incomprehensible to someone who has no experience of it, just as one cannot truly explain Light to someone born blind.

Once the Kundalini is permanently active in the energy system, it also changes how we dream. Since the brainwaves continually oscillate at the Alpha frequency, consciousness is always relatively lucid, meaning it is awake, even during sleep. This heightened awareness gives rise to Lucid Dreams, characterized by the dream feeling real and one controlling the experience.

Lucid Dreams feel similar to the experience of physical reality, although to a degree less. Perhaps this is because consciousness is more used to the physical body than the Light Body, although the individual is fully awake and aware in both experiences. Regardless, through our Light Body, we can see, touch, and feel as we do with the physical body but are not bound by the laws of physics since there is no density to objects in the inner Cosmic Planes—everything is made of Light, which is a tenuous substance. Therefore, we can fly, walk through walls, levitate objects with our minds, and generally teleport ourselves to any place simply by willing it.

The Body of Light is the Soul's vehicle for travel when surfing the inner Cosmic Planes. The Divine Planes of consciousness are often depicted as strange and beautiful lands beyond description and unmatched in their wonder and awe. Experiencing them affirmed that I left our Planet through consciousness. Simply being able to reach and share in the energy of these other worlds has been one of the greatest gifts of the Kundalini awakening.

KUNDALINI TRANSFORMATION—PART I

Originally published by The Kundalini Consortium - March 28, 2017.

Since my Kundalini awakening in 2004, many mind, body, and Soul changes have occurred. However, the most notable change happened when I optimised my Kundalini circuit in the seventh year. As a result, my consciousness began "funnelling" through the Bindu Chakra at the top-back of my head.

The key is not merely to awaken the Kundalini; it is to evolve past the Karma of the Chakras, mentally and emotionally, to the point where consciousness is unobstructed and untainted by fear. Only then can the Kundalini circuit become complete, allowing the energy to funnel out of the Bindu point at the top-back of the head and circulate throughout the body without cessation. I use the word "funnel" because it represents the process of a substance being moved through a small opening. In this case, this movement is continuous, facilitating the circulation of sublimated Kundalini energy in the body.

The key to this process is the Bindu Chakra since it is the point of Non-Duality, where the mind's thoughts and emotions are siphoned into, which cuts off one's connection with fear energy. And by being shut off from fear, the Ego loses its hold on the consciousness since fear energy is what sustains it.

At this point, the Kundalini circuit becomes complete (Figure 68) and exists in a self-sustaining mode. The mind becomes bypassed because it is through the mind that we experience duality, resulting in the raising of vibration of consciousness. Now, nutritious food is transformed into Pranic fuel, powering the entire system in a new way that allows one to experience the Spiritual Plane every second of every day.

The Spiritual Plane represents the highest state of rapture and the ultimate feeling of being happy and alive. The concept of Jesus Christ's Kingdom of Heaven becomes manifest, a far happier state than having millions of dollars. Money cannot buy the emotional rapture that this Spiritual experience triggers.

My experience of Eternal love and joy is unimaginable to most people who are not in this state. The mere act of listening to music is a transcendental event like being on cocaine, ecstasy, or other "feel-good" enhancement drugs, which often brings such rapture in my heart that it makes me clench my teeth because of how euphoric I feel.

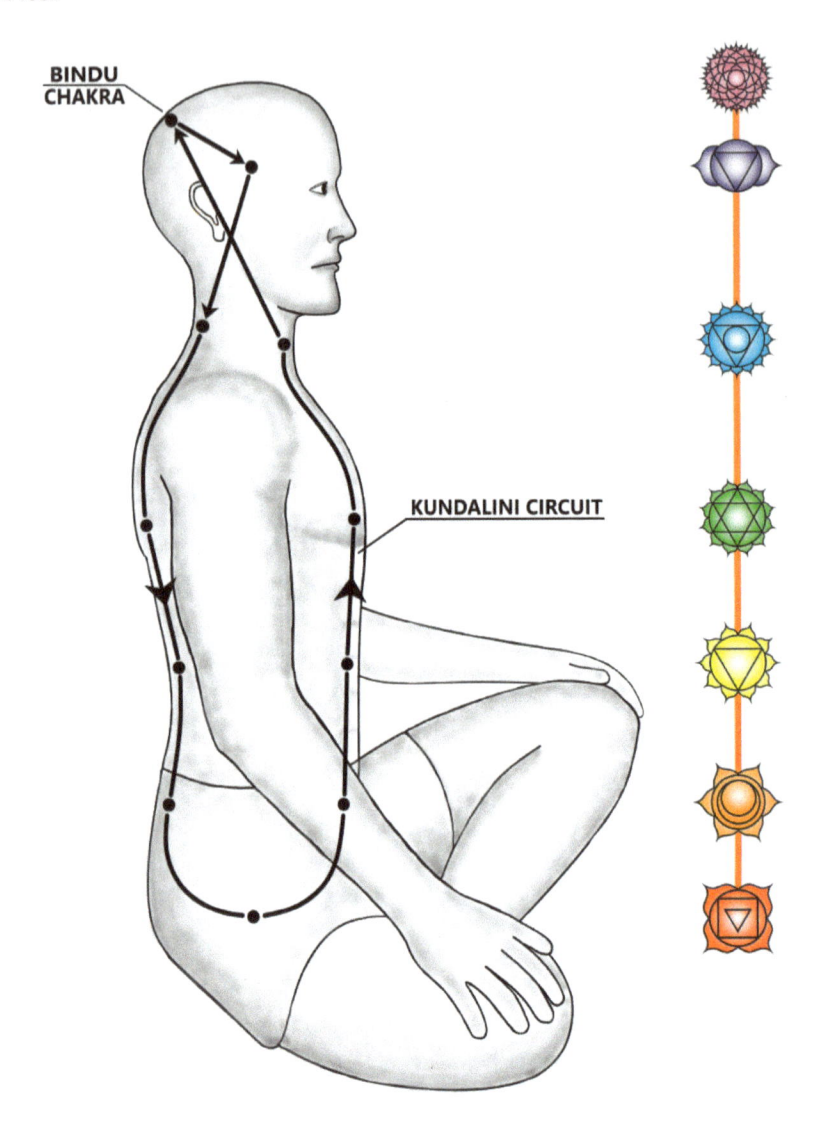

Figure 68: The Bindu and the Kundalini Circuit

Once the whole Kundalini circuit was optimised, I began losing consciousness of my physical body. It felt like my entire body received a shot of novocaine, a numbing agent. I essentially rose above the physical body while still being in it, akin to an Out-of-Body experience, only permanent. If I cut or bruise myself, I do not consciously feel the pain. Instead, I've transcended it. Since my consciousness is somewhere outside of me while being present simultaneously, I no longer feel the pain of being a human being like before the awakening. This is how I live now, and this lifelong adventure began during the seventh year of my Kundalini awakening.

On a mental level, I function solely on intuition. I can still use all of my inner functions, like logic and reason, but I do so in a detached way where I go inwards when I need to, but then I come right out to continue experiencing the perpetual present moment, the Now. I relate to the world through intuition since I am directly connected to the Fourth Dimension of Vibration/Energy. However, getting to this point in my Kundalini transformation has taken me many years of purging and preparing my consciousness. It was mentally and emotionally excruciating as I had to lose myself entirely to find my True Self. Now I am in a state where past events have no more hold on me, and I can dismiss negative memories like it wasn't me they happened to. The new me understands the world's unreality and doesn't take things too seriously.

I learned that if I cling to an expectation of what might happen in the future, the past prevents me from being in the Now. But that only occurs when I think in terms of the past and future, which was my old way of functioning before the Kundalini transformation took me to this high level of consciousness. Through the Bindu Chakra, the concept of past and future dissolve into Nothingness. In Nothingness, its opposite is found—Pure Possibility, represented by the Now, the present moment.

Over the years, I have also experienced massive changes in my character. For one, I am compelled to speak the truth always. Lying has become a foreign concept, which keeps my consciousness clear and unfettered, although the people around me often consider me naïve like I am revealing too much. People who don't walk in my shoes are under the impression that lying is a part of life and that there is no other way to live but to tweak the truth to get what you want. However, this is wrong on so many levels. Living in truth allows me to address every life situation to the best of my ability as it happens. I don't need long-term memory in the same way that I used to. My mind gives me what I need at the moment that I need it.

These are the natural expressions of the level of Kundalini progression that I am at now. It has been seventeen years in the making, bringing more changes every year. After a while, I noticed that my memory started to eradicate and shed itself. When I close my eyes, I still see past events as fleeting memories that have no hold over me anymore. Their emotional and mental pain has been dissolved, as I am operating from a permanent state of inspiration.

This process has weakened the hold that the Ego has over me since the Ego has survived due to the memories that bind it to the physical body. If memories have no hold on the consciousness, the Ego has nothing to cling to, and the person can be in the Now 24/7 to experience life to its fullest. Therefore, I have no regrets about things that pass and take life as a transient experience, which exists for the moment and nothing more. A Spiritual human being is meant to be in the Now.

However, I am not saying that I don't fall prey to the Ego; I do. I am not a Saint, and the Ego cannot be annihilated while living since one must physically die to destroy it. I enjoy mostly the same things in life as everyone else, but my concept of unconditional love, ethics and morals is heightened. And most importantly, I am permanently in the "zone," in the Now.

It takes many years for the Ego to become subdued, the Higher Self exalted, and the mind, body, and Soul to adjust to living in a world of Pure Energy. This is not a short-term process by any stretch of the imagination. For most Kundalini awakened individuals, it takes up to two dozen years to adjust to their new Selves. Even then, the transformation process is not finished because consciousness continues to expand exponentially, meaning new lessons must be integrated constantly.

Through this transformation, my visual sight has also been altered as I now see Light in all things. It appears as a silvery glow in all objects I perceive with my physical eyes. My visual experience of the world now can be likened to advancing from a PlayStation 2 game console, my old Self, to PlayStation 5, which is my new Self. There has been a considerable jump and advancement in graphics and the overall engine that powers the game system, an analogy for my newly expanded consciousness. If my bio-energy field, or Aura, was like a battery that functioned at 100 volts before the awakening, figuratively speaking, its capacity has been increased to 100 000 volts.

Kundalini as a field of scientific study is relatively new. Nevertheless, it is safe to conclude that the increase in Kundalini awakenings could signify a dramatic turn in human evolution. Of course, I speak primarily from personal experience and observation based on my Kundalini journey. Nevertheless, the current interest in Kundalini appears to be driven by what Gopi Krishna called the "evolutionary impulse."

Many Kundalini awakened individuals will not understand what I'm talking about since they haven't experienced the same changes yet. However, others will know exactly what I am describing. Kundalini awakenings vary in intensity level, the overall transformation process, and how the evolution of consciousness is affected. It takes many years to complete, as I said. Awakening the Kundalini is but the starting point of the transfiguration journey.

Planet Earth is meant to be experienced with an awakened Kundalini because it is a fact that the material world is alive and is Pure Energy. Even science corroborates this, but our Ancient Ancestors knew this all along. And in my case, I can see this every waking moment of my life with my physical eyes, which still amazes me to this day.

In the same way that someone might see the world on LSD or magic mushrooms, I see it without any drugs in my system. It's a permanent part of my life now. As I have described many times, there is a Holographic, Pure Energy blueprint, a double of the material world, existing simultaneously and occupying the same space. However, because our brains are composed of Matter, human beings cannot perceive beyond the physical reality without the vibration of their consciousness being raised somehow.

My transformation in how I perceive the physical reality is partly due to the infusion of Light in my head that is always present. This Light transposes onto all things that I look at, hence the appearance of the silvery glow in everything. It de-materialises objects before my very eyes when I focus my attention on them for a little while.

Another reason why I see things the way I do is because of the expansion of my Mind's Eye that allows me to view the outer reality from a much higher source. For example, if I am downtown looking at the buildings around me, my vision will enable me to see that same downtown as an architectural model as if I was standing in the clouds above it. It is a tricky phenomenon to describe accurately since you have to experience this to truly understand what I mean.

Every time I turn my attention to an external object, I become so absorbed in it that I leave my body the moment it happens. The Oneness of all existence that the Ancient Sages have discussed is far more than just a concept for me now. I get to live it every day, and it takes no effort on my part for it to manifest.

I can encompass everything that I see with my physical eyes as if I am looking at it from a bird's eye third-person perspective. I believe this is possible because my Mind's Eye expanded exponentially as the Kundalini energy pierced it with intense force during my initial Kundalini awakening. As a result, the typical doughnut-shaped and sized Mind's Eye portal has been expanded to the size of a car tire, figuratively speaking.

This transformation allows me to step out of myself the moment I view something external to my physical body. And as I step out of myself, I can see myself in the third person—I see my face and my body via my Mind's Eye, and I can control the vibrations I send out to others through my body language. I liken this to being a director and an actor at the same time and crafting the play of life itself.

You can imagine how much fun I have visiting new cities. Seeing New York Times Square at night for the first time was like Alice stepping into Wonderland. Travelling to Ancient and modern cities has become one of my favourite activities since it brings many metaphysical experiences. I feel so blessed to live with these inner changes that I am often brought to tears and would give anything to share this personal life experience with others.

It's most wondrous at night because all the lights are enhanced, especially LED signage, traffic and car lights, and the lighting in houses and buildings. The nighttime also transforms the surface of many objects, which begin to shine like velvet, and their edges appear sharper and more defined. This entire vision comes with a sense of wonder, the same as you would feel if you were transported to another Planet in a different galaxy and viewed that world for the first time. The best way to describe how I see the external world now is with the word "Intergalactic," since it is entirely out of this world yet also existing here and now at the same time as you, the reader, are reading these words.

KUNDALINI TRANSFORMATION—PART II

Originally published by The Kundalini Consortium - April 26, 2017.

During my seventeen-year Kundalini transformation, my connection to sound has been expanded. When I still my mind's activity, different sounds I take in from my environment are accompanied by images in my Mind's Eye that stream across the consciousness in an undulating fashion, like waves in the ocean.

Every sound has a thought behind it, and once you slow down your inner chatter and induce absolute silence, you can connect with that thought and see it as a visual image. Sound moves in waves that the psychic senses can perceive when one is sufficiently Spiritually evolved.

After this transformation in how I process sound vibrations, I feel like I am simultaneously in Heaven and on Earth. The stillness inside me enables me to pick up vibrations around me like a radio receiver. It feels ethereal, almost like I am walking on clouds. Hollywood movies depict Heaven as a place up in the clouds for a reason. This state of Being is accompanied by complete inner silence because only when the mind is still can the consciousness reach high enough to experience Eternity.

I remember how I used to experience the world before the Kundalini transformation, and I can safely say this is Planet Earth 2.0. When combining these phenomena with my new sense of sight, it is almost as if I was given a permanent virtual reality headset to wear 24/7. I live in the same world as everyone else but see and experience it vastly differently.

The expansion of my physical sight occurred five months after my awakening in 2004. It was one of the first gifts of the Kundalini awakening. By now, I am entirely used to it, but I am often reminded of how awesome it is when I look at new landscapes or visit new cities. The first thing I always do is walk downtown to experience the city's bright lights and architecture.

There are moments when I am so immersed in my visual experience and out of my body that I start to see the outer world as a two-dimensional beam of Light coming from the Sun. I can scry inside this vision and see parallel Universes that exist here and now but are invisible to regular human sight. This entire experience is a form of rapture, as my consciousness gets swooped up to have this vision. It comes over me like a wave, and I become pure consciousness embracing it. These visions often transport me to medieval times for some reason, only a much smaller-scale version than the modern world. I believe that parallel worlds exist here and now inside the Light, and once you're able to alter your vibration, you can perceive them.

Due to the expansion of my Mind's Eye, if I focus on a human being for ten seconds or so, I begin to slip out of myself and see the colours of that person's energy. If I carry this vision further, I start changing states of consciousness and see the person from the perspective of a smaller creature, like an ant, or a taller one, like a giraffe. The longer I keep them in focus, the more my visual sight continues to change. I can even see animals and different Beings superimposed on people's faces. Often these Beings look humanoid, but not entirely human.

Every living Being in the Cosmos is composed of Light and pure consciousness. Since a Kundalini awakening is the evolution of consciousness and Light, it enables me to see more of the Universe than what I am limited to by my physical senses.

Soon after the initial awakening, I once experienced an altering of my vibrational frequency, which changed the condition of the physical Universe right before my eyes. Usually, I hear the Kundalini in my ears as a continuous buzzing of a swarm of bees or the sound of radiation (electromagnetic noise), which changes pitch as I take in food. One time I was able to tap into the source of the vibration and change its pitch to a low growling sound, like the engine of a Mustang. When this occurred, I saw the world in front of me as a Hologram, with transparent walls and objects suspended in space. This vision lasted for about ten seconds until my Ego took over, and the vibration changed back to its familiar sound, bringing my consciousness down to the level of Matter.

Again, these visions and experiences I am describing are not seen inside my head when I close my eyes. That would not be unique since I would only be using my imagination. Instead, these visions occur through physical sight. And they often happen when some external object grabs my attention, and I become absorbed in it. Immediately, an internal rapture process unfolds, allowing some visual phenomenon to occur.

Another essential life transformation that I described in a previous article has been Lucid Dreaming, a nighttime version of Astral travel. Once the Light Energy had built up inside me over time, I started to Lucid Dream regularly. Since gravity is not a factor in the Astral World, pure consciousness is the Law that governs it. As mentioned, you can fly, walk through walls, transport yourself to any place on the Earth instantly, perform telekinesis, and fulfil any desires you usually couldn't satisfy in real life.

The best part is that in a Lucid Dream, consciousness is completely awake and aware in the same way as in waking physical life. The difference is only a matter of degree, but the concept and experience are the same. It is pure imagination and desire feeding itself through its experiences. The source of our Souls is imagination and Light.

As for Astral Travel, which occurs during Lucid Dreams, I visited breathtaking and intricate Worlds, beautiful to behold. I travelled to different galaxies, talked to Extraterrestrial Beings, and received information about myself, the world, and our future as a human race. Often, my Lucid Dream would be so powerful that I could not wake up from it. I would have to sleep for up to twelve or sixteen hours at a time in a state of "sleep paralysis" until my consciousness had enough. If I tried to wake up during this time, the potency of the dream would sometimes be so intense that it just threw me back down onto the pillow.

I have spent hours on end downloading information from otherworldly Beings and Ascended Masters and Deities, similarly to how Neo was downloading computer programs in The Matrix. In one hour, I had the privilege of downloading twenty books worth of information. Through these downloads, I have received certain truths about humanity and the world we live in that I would not be able to attain otherwise.

Over time, I also developed the ability to use my Mind's Eye portal like a camera lens in a Lucid Dream. I can change the aperture to shift into a reality that I term hyper-consciousness, a heightened state beyond the realm of human consciousness, including dream states. This state is similar to a DMT or Peyote trip but different because there's a futuristic, steampunk feel.

These are some of the gifts that unravel after awakening the Kundalini. We truly live in the Matrix, where your potential for life experience is so incredible that you cannot even imagine it until it happens to you. Everything around us is consciousness and Light. Once you awaken the Kundalini, which is Light and love, you begin to behold the Universe around you as it truly is.

The inner Light contains many different states of consciousness with varying degrees of experience. This rapture is meant for everyone once we can lose ourselves and go beyond the Ego. It can sometimes happen to unawakened people during meditation, which in my case, has become a permanent state since every act of focusing my attention on something has become a form of meditation.

Many people have had Kundalini awakenings, but few have reported experiences like those I have had in their overall transformation. What separates the type of Kundalini awakening I have had from a spontaneous one or Shaktipat (a transmission of Spiritual energy upon one person by another) is that you must raise enough Prana during the initial awakening to blow open and expand the Mind's Eye as I did. The sexual energy a visualization meditation can generate is the key to successfully doing this. That is why most awakened people do not experience the world the same as I or Gopi Krishna did.

Gopi Krishna is one of the few people I have read about who lived in the same new world as I do after his awakening. Reading his work really helped me at peak points of my transformation process. I have been researching Kundalini extensively for seventeen years, spoken to hundreds of people on social media or in person, and found only a handful who report the same accounts as myself. I do not say this to brag because I never asked for any of this, but I mention it to explain the varied Kundalini experiences. I believe that through my account, you can get a good idea of the Kundalini's overall purpose, which can dispel any improper information you previously received on this subject.

The breaking of the Cosmic Egg at the top of the Crown Chakra by the Kundalini results in the "electrocution" effect, as the 72 000 Nadis become infused with Light energy, fully activating the Body of Light. Furthermore, the infusion of the Light into the Chakras expands and optimises one's toroidal energy field (torus), whose geometric depiction is the Merkaba (Figure 69). It features two counterrotating Tetrahedrons whose rapid rate of spin forms a sphere of Light around the physical body, enabling the Soul (also of spherical shape) to leave the body at will. The Merkaba is a supplement to the Body of Light as each plays a critical function in providing the Soul with a vehicle for travel across the Universe and other dimensions of Space/Time through consciousness. (For a complete discourse on the torus and the Merkaba, consult *Serpent Rising: The Kundalini Compendium*.)

Figure 69: The Merkaba—Optimised Torus

The breaking of the Cosmic Egg can happen if you intentionally try to awaken the Kundalini, during a spontaneous awakening, or through Shaktipat. However, to awaken the Mind's Eye and expand it during the initial Kundalini rising, you must perform a proven energy cultivation technique to generate enough Prana coupled with a visualization meditation to blow open Ajna Chakra.

Although we get Pranic energy from the Sun, we also receive it through oxygen intake. For this reason, all living Beings breathe air to survive. Air is a manifestation of Spirit, although at a lower Plane than the White Light underlying all existence. Prana can be stimulated in many ways, including the Yogic practice of Pranayama (breath control) and thereby increased to a more significant quantum.

Visualization meditations with a sexual component can consciously generate Prana, and if it results in a Kundalini awakening, it can be powerful. In my case, I was doing a form of Tantric sex practice by imagining a sexual experience that was so potent that it triggered continuous internal orgasms whose ecstasy of emotion awakened my Kundalini. The intensity at which the Kundalini blew open all of my Chakras was incredible, culminating in momentarily uniting with the White Light.

Kundalini Science is a reality. Unfortunately, the physical sciences have no means of measuring or studying it other than listening to and possibly compiling the many anecdotal accounts worldwide. The tipping point for science is always a critical mass. There must be enough accounts that share the same triggers and effects. Unfortunately, there are too many variations and variables at the moment.

Some variables are the same; some are different. For example, our biological composition and the pathways of the Kundalini, the Nadis (channels), are the same for all humans. However, although our energy system is the same, the triggers, effects, experiences of risings, and manifestations are not. But since the core of all Kundalini experiences is the evolution of consciousness and complete liberation from the physical body, as more people become Enlightened through this process, there will be a more unified understanding of the Kundalini science.

Once more people become aware of the full potential of the Kundalini, it can get the respect it deserves and become a part of the mainstream, allowing us to study it through scientific means of measuring the intensity and level of the experience. But unfortunately, even though the Kundalini is the most important thing on our Planet, most people are still unaware of it or think it is just a type of Yoga.

Instead, Kundalini is the source of individual consciousness and the key to awakening us to Cosmic Consciousness. As predicted by the Ancients, we may be at the precipice in human history when people will become awakened on a mass scale, ushering the Planet into the much-anticipated Golden Age. If this happens, we will have the answers to who we are and the purpose of living on this Planet with this embedded, yet currently dormant, Kundalini mechanism. We are still at the dawn of our destiny as Spiritual human beings in the Cosmos. And that is very exciting indeed.

CEREMONIAL MAGICK TESTIMONIALS

Note: The following testimonials are from five individuals whom I have mentored in the past. All of them have significantly benefited from Ceremonial Magick, especially from working with the Five Elements; thus, I have asked them to describe their experiences.

"Upon first being initiated into a Golden Dawn Order, I was primarily interested in learning about all the mystical secrets and in developing more of my extra-sensory abilities. What I found, however, was that it was the Elemental Magickal work we did that profoundly changed my perception, and I would go so far as to credit it with having shifted the direction of my life. I would recommend this work to anyone who has a sincere interest in working towards living more authentically. The ritual exercises are empowering, and when used in conjunction with meditation work, there are no limits to what one might achieve with it."

VH Soror LIA (HOGD Adept)

"The Golden Dawn system is a safe, tried and true path of exploration designed to expand upon your theoretical and practical knowledge of Magick. It is organized in a way that allows the practitioner to progress through the various Elemental grades, thereby improving associated aspects of the personality through the integration of Spiritual practices and experiences. The banishing, invoking, and meditation exercises systematically presented at the various levels of attainment are transformational and provide a firm foundation for more advanced Magickal practices, such as Enochian Magick. I would recommend the Golden Dawn system to any serious student or practitioner of Western Esotericism."

Angela Seraphim /VH Soror VLM (HOGD Adept)

"Life gives you many opportunities for growth, but it is up to you to recognize when these opportunities present themselves and fully take advantage of them. After the preliminary work in preparing myself mentally and emotionally (with the use of LIRP's and SIRP) was complete, I began working with the Enochian Keys in earnest. I isolated myself for two months in the countryside of the island of Granada in the Carribean for this task.

My experience with Enochian Magick began with dreams and visions, which were tests to my mind, body, and Soul. I was revealed many insights about my inner nature as well as the Universal Mysteries, which humbled me daily. My Spiritual Evolution was immediate and pronounced. It did not come without a price, though, as with anything of real value. My Ego was torn apart as I was shedding my skin daily, getting more renewed with every Enochian Key. This process was often terrifying but also enlightening at the same time.

Enochian Magick tests your Soul and Spirit to the extreme. I found myself battling with internal and external Demons to master all parts of the Self. After devoting myself wholeheartedly to finishing the Spiritual Alchemy program with the Enochian Keys, I can safely say that I came out on the other side a much more Spiritually evolved person. I highly recommend Enochian Magick to all those individuals who are willing to sacrifice everything in the name of their Spiritual development and evolution."

Prometheus

"Since I started using the LBRP and BRH, my life improved dramatically. Have you ever felt like you had a negative force preventing you from living a full and satisfying life? Well, that is how I felt before practising these ritual exercises. Once I started doing them, things started changing for me in a very positive direction.

The negative force and inertia started to dissipate. This also included confusing and obsessive thoughts. Often, I could feel the negative energy diffuse and scatter. This would allow me the peace of mind and opportunities to progress in all areas of my life.

I have been doing these exercises for over a decade, and let me tell you; this is an indispensable tool that I have incorporated into a routine that fights against these negative forces. I also use these ritual exercises to clear the space around me, including my Aura, of all negative Spiritual entities as well as energy. This creates a sacred space where I could do my Spiritual work. I cannot imagine my life without doing these exercises.

As for the Middle Pillar, this exercise infuses my Aura with a lot of beneficial energy. It gives me the right foundation for me to work on the other ritual exercises so that I can get the most from my day.

We are all severely affected by other people's energies, interpenetrating our Auras constantly. These Magickal rituals banish all these adverse and unwanted energies. This prevents burn out and helps us live a happy and constructive life.

As for the LIRP ritual exercises of the Elements, they infused my Aura with the Element that I was working with, safely and efficiently. I experienced some changes and fluctuations in my mental and emotional life, probably because I was balancing and integrating that Element in me. It takes some adjustment but do not worry, you will emerge victorious, as I did."

Sam Benchimol/Frater AC (EOGD Initiate)

"After only reading about Ceremonial Magick and the Golden Dawn, I decided to start practising the ritual exercises myself. With Neven's help and guidance, accompanied by the Spiritual Alchemy program that he gave me, I started doing the daily banishings (LBRP and BRH), along with the Middle Pillar exercise. I noticed that the banishings and the Middle Pillar immediately put me in a balanced state of mind, which helped me focus on my school work better.

I saw right away that there is something to all this Magick stuff, and I became excited to start working with the Elements. I started working with the LIRP of Earth, and like clockwork, the manifestations began to occur. The first week of working with the Earth energy, I got a new girlfriend and a new job.

After I finished the prescribed program with Earth, I started working with the LIRPs of Air. After day two of invoking Air, I felt very creative and inspired, and so I started writing. I locked myself up in my room and wrote day and night for two weeks, obsessively. I was amazed at how much creativity was pouring out of me, and I wanted to harness it all. The connection I had to my thoughts was unreal. During those two weeks, I also had my first ever Lucid Dream. It was one of the most amazing experiences and one I will never forget. This Lucid Dream experience repeated itself 3-4 more times in the next few months.

I finished the prescribed program with the Air Element and then started invoking Water. The first time I invoked it with the LIRP, I felt an intense rush of water energy fill my heart. It felt like a wave that took over me. I was overtaken with such a strong feeling of love and bliss that I fell to my knees. I could not believe that I felt so good as a result of a Magickal exercise. That night, including many other nights while invoking the Water Element, I lay in my bed with tears in my eyes thinking about how much love I felt for the people in my life. I realized that the tears were a process of purging my emotions and purifying them.

As the Air Element allowed me to express myself better to the people in my life, the Water Element strengthened my relationships with them since it allowed me to connect with my emotions, especially the feeling of compassion. I kept invoking the Water Element until I finished the prescribed program with it, after which I moved on to the Fire Element.

Once I started working with the LIRP of Fire, I felt an immediate shift in my energy. The rush of Water was gone, replaced with a strong Fire energy current felt in my heart. This Fire energy immediately gave me more vitality and raw power for me to complete all of my daily tasks. My ambition and drive were increased tenfold. As I was working on developing my willpower, I was also challenged by my anger. I realized that my anger is the result of not using my willpower to its fullest, so I tried to focus on being more assertive, which curbed my anger for the most part.

I spent many months invoking Fire, and I learned many lessons on how to express myself to the best of my ability. The manifestations of the Fire Element reminded me a lot of Air, only a lot more intense. After I finished the prescribed program with Fire, I was ready to start invoking the Spirit Element.

The first night of using the SIRP, I felt peaceful, yet transcendental energy of the Spirit take me over. It was mystical and very potent. It prompted me to meditate on my Mind's Eye Chakra for a few hours, which is something I repeated every day after that.

After about a week of invoking the Spirit Element and meditating daily, I had a breakthrough. The Kundalini energy rose from the bottom of my spine and into my Heart Chakra, where I felt an expansion take place. I was overtaken with such a powerful feeling of bliss that I lost consciousness for about five minutes. During those five minutes, as I was immersed in the Ocean of Consciousness, I felt unity with all things in existence. After this experience was finished, I was never the same again, and the bliss became a permanent part of my existence. I worked with the SIRP for the prescribed period and learned how to integrate the different lessons from the previous Elements into my life.

I am very thankful to Neven for urging me to start and finish the Spiritual Alchemy program with the Five Elements. It was a transformational experience on all levels and one that I will cherish for the rest of my life. I had only read about the Kundalini until I started working with the Elements, and I feel very blessed to have had a Kundalini rising and awakening of my Heart Chakra. I very much recommend this Spiritual Alchemy program to anyone who wants to evolve and find everlasting happiness in their lives as I did."

Lucias

GLOSSARY OF SELECTED TERMS

Note: The following is a selection of terms that are either undefined in the original body of text or require further definition. Use this section to help further your knowledge of the given subjects.

Aethyr, the: In physics, the Aethyr is a formless and invisible medium, or substance, that permeates the Cosmos. It is a transmission medium for information. In the context of *The Magus*, the Aethyr is synonymous with the Spirit Element. In the Enochian System, the Thirty Aethyrs are interpenetrating circles or layers of the Aura that pertain to the Spiritual experiences of the Cosmic Planes.

Adept, an: A Spiritually evolved individual who is a master of the Elements of their Being. An Adept is proficient in their knowledge concerning the Sacred Mysteries of Creation. Their consciousness operates from the three higher Chakras of Vishuddhi, Ajna, and Sahasrara, of the Spirit Element. An Adept receives Gnosis from the Divine Realms, and they serve God-the Creator. They are in direct communication with their Holy Guardian Angel. Adepts from history include, but are not limited to, Jesus Christ and the Buddha.

Alpha State: A relaxed state of mind that allows you to be more open, receptive, and creative. This state is reached when your brain waves slow to between 8 and 12 Hz, which most often happens when daydreaming and during sleep. The Alpha State can be consciously induced through mediation. Being in this state will heighten your memory recall and intuition while lessening anxiety. The Alpha State of brain activity occurs between being awake with mental activity (Beta State) and sleep (Theta State). It is during later stages of sleep, when the body and brain are rested, that the Alpha State is reached. This experience brings on the involuntary phenomenon of Lucid Dreaming. The Alpha State is the contact point between the practitioner of Magick and the inner Cosmic Planes. Being in an Alpha State during normal waking consciousness allows you to have control over your reality since your connection to your Higher Self is greater. Thus, you can use the Universal Laws consciously and with intent.

Ancestral Energy: An Ancestor is any person from whom an individual has descended. Every person is linked to their Ancestors through their DNA. Depending on the race and ethnicity of your Ancestors, you would be predisposed to certain traits that affect your personality and character development. However, Free Will supersedes all DNA predispositions of one's Ancestral Energy.

Ankh, the: An Ancient Egyptian hieroglyphic symbol that resembles a cross but has a loop instead of the top arm. The Egyptians used it in writing and art to represent the word for "life" or "breath of life." Since the Egyptians believed that one's Earthly existence was only part of the Eternal life of the Soul and Spirit, the Ankh symbolizes both mortal life and the Afterlife. After the Egyptian polytheistic religion fell, the Christian Coptic Church adopted the Ankh symbol as a form of the cross, calling it the "crux ansata," which translates to "cross with a handle."

Archangel, an: This word is derived from the Greek "Arkhangelos," which means "chief Angel." An Archangel is a Spiritual entity of high rank in the celestial hierarchy. The most common Archangels in Judaism and Christianity are Raphael, Gabriel, and Michael. Along with Auriel, these four are the Archangels guarding the four cardinal directions as part of Ceremonial Magick ritual exercises. Each represents the energy of one of the Four Elements of Earth, Air, Fire, and Water. To these four is added the Archangel Metatron, who is often called the "highest of the Angels" because he is the Archangel of the Kether Sephira and the Spirit Element.

Archdemon, an: A Spiritual entity of high rank in the infernal hierarchy. An Archdemon is considered a leader figure by the other Demonic entities. In essence, Archdemons are the evil counterparts of the Archangels. The same as Demons, they are considered the Fallen Angels, or Angels that fell from the Grace of God. The most popular Archdemons in Judaism and Christianity are Lucifer, Beelzebub, and Satan. This work mentions the Archdemon Khoronzon, who is the personification of the Devil as the individual's Ego.

Banners of the East and the West: Two banners that hang on opposite sides (East and West) of a traditional Golden Dawn Temple. The Banner of the East represents Light and the rising of the Sun, and is placed in the South-East corner of the Temple. The Banner of the West represents darkness and the setting of the Sun and is placed in the North-West corner. These two banners represent duality, the same as the Pillars of Light and Darkness (Jachin and Boaz), also used in a traditional Golden Dawn Temple.

Becoming: The concept of "Becoming" originated in Ancient Greece with the philosopher Heraclitus of Ephesus, who said that nothing in this world is constant except change and the process of "Becoming." Becoming relates to evolution, individual and collective. It implies that in every moment, the individual, or the collective state of humanity, is more evolved than the moment before. Evolution does not only include living things but also Planets, Solar Systems, and Galaxies as well. The antithesis of Becoming is "Being." The act of Being is an expression of the Fire Element since it is Eternal and fixed in its ways. On the other hand, the process of Becoming is an expression of the Water Element, as it is changeable and continuously transforming. One is Soul, and the other is consciousness.

Beta State: A state of mind associated with normal waking consciousness and a heightened state of alertness, critical reasoning, and logical thinking. When your brain waves are between 12.5 and 30 Hz, this state is reached. The Ego uses the Beta State to rationalize its existence. While experiencing the Beta State of brain activity, the individual consciousness is susceptible to emotional and mental turmoil. Therefore, to alleviate anxiety, it is imperative that the individual slows down the brain activity and reaches the Alpha State.

Body of Light, the: Synonymous with the Light Body and Rainbow Body. It is a vehicle through which we can experience the inner Cosmic Planes. Raising the Kundalini energy to the Crown will break the Cosmic Egg and fully activate the Body of Light, awakening all of its latent potential. Every human's goal is to raise their

Kundalini in their lifetime. Doing so will liberate the Soul from the physical body and unite the individual consciousness with Cosmic Consciousness.

Cosmic Consciousness: Synonymous with God-Consciousness as pertains to our Solar System. It is the highest achievable state of consciousness for human beings since it is the collective consciousness of the human race. It makes us at One with the Universe. Cosmic Consciousness is described as a higher level of consciousness that can perceive all things at once through unity. Clairvoyance and other psychic abilities become possible through it. Regarding the Qabalah, Cosmic Consciousness belongs to the Kether Sephira and Sahasrara Chakra. Whether Cosmic Consciousness extends beyond our Solar System or is limited to it is a matter of debate. All initiates of Light aim to unify their individual consciousness with Cosmic Consciousness. Through this unification, Enlightenment is achieved.

Cosmic Egg, the: A container of energy that resides at the top of the head, in the centre. When pierced by the Kundalini energy on its upwards rise through the spinal column and the brain, it releases liquid Ambrosia which fully activates the Body of Light, thereby infusing the Seventy-Two Thousand Nadis with Light energy. As this process occurs, it first feels like someone cracked a giant egg over your head, followed by the feeling of being mildly electrocuted as the Ambrosia pours downwards from the top, centre of the head.

Cherubim, a: A Hebrew word from the Old Testament that stands for an Angelic Being who directly attends to God. The Cherubim have many roles, although their primary duty was to protect the Garden of Eden. In *The Magus*, the Cherubim represent the Four Elements as the man (Air), eagle (Water), bull (Earth), and lion (Fire). They are the watchful protectors and representatives of those Elements in The Universe Tarot card.

Christ Consciousness: The word "Christ" is based on the Greek translation of the word "Messiah." Messianic figures in history are considered as living Deities and embodiments of the God-Spirit energy. As such, Jesus of Nazareth was given the title of "Christ" to denote his Godhood. Christ Consciousness represents a state of awareness of our true nature as the Sons or Daughters of God-the Creator. This state implies the integration of Spirit within Matter and equilibrium between the two. In the Qabalah, Christ Consciousness represents the state of consciousness of the Tiphareth Sephira. The Spirit energy is brought in through the path of the High Priestess in the Tarot since it is our link to the Kether Sephira. Christ Consciousness is the individual's state of consciousness once a relationship with Cosmic Consciousness has been achieved. It implies the influx of unconditional love in Anahata, the Heart Chakra since that is where the individual operates from when in this state.

Creation: The process or action of bringing something into existence. In the context of *The Magus*, it refers to the process of God-the Source manifesting the physical Universe into being. Since this work is Hermetic, this term often refers to the Tree of Life as the blueprint of all Creation.

Dark Night of the Soul, the: A period of desolation that an individual undergoes when they are rapidly evolving Spiritually. During the Dark Night of the Soul, all sense of consolation is removed, creating a type of existential crisis for the time being. The individual is meant to face the dark side full-on and embrace the mental and emotional turmoil before transforming Spiritually. It is not uncommon for the individual to isolate themselves from other people during this time and shed many tears while purging old emotions. After this period is complete, the clutches of the Lower Self will have lessened, and the individual becomes more aligned with their Higher Self. The Dark Night of the Soul is a necessary phase of suffering on the path towards Enlightenment.

It is not a one-time process, however, but may be encountered numerous times on one's path of Spiritual Evolution.

Dimension of Vibration, the: The Fourth Dimension, or Dimension of Energy. Since all things in existence are held in vibratory motion, this Dimension is the realm where each object, thought, or emotion has a quantifiable essence (energy). It can be perceived by the Mind's Eye and the intuitive faculty of a human being.

Divine Names of Power, the: In this work, this term applies to the many Divine names of God, Archangels, Angels, and other Holy names used to invoke or evoke Divine energy. By vibrating a Divine Name, the practitioner connects to its power through the frequency of sound, thereby giving them complete control over that energy current through synergy. As such, the energy of a Divine Name permeates the Aura of the practitioner, and the more times a Divine Name is vibrated, the more energy is brought in. Vibrations have a cumulative effect on the quantity of energy brought in. In *The Magus*, we are mainly concerned with the Hebrew and Enochian Divine Names. The Hebrew Divine Names are derived from the Qabalistic system, while John Dee and Edward Kelley directly channelled the Enochian Divine Names. The power of Divine Names extends to Demonic entities, such as the Goetia. By vibrating the names of one of these entities, the practitioner is given authority over them and can command them to do their bidding.

Esoteric Order of the Golden Dawn, the: A Western Mystery school based upon the teachings of the original Hermetic Order of the Golden Dawn. Recently renamed the *Golden Dawn Ancient Mystery School*. Imperator General is G.H. Frater P.D.R. (Robert Zink).

Fallen Angels, the: Synonymous with Demons. Religion scholars believe these are Angelic Beings who were cast out from Heaven for sinning against God. Satan is considered their leader, who is the antithesis of God. The idea behind the term "Fallen Angels" was derived from the apocryphal *Book of Enoch*. It mentions how the offspring of the Fallen Angels, the Nephilim, or "Giants," were drowned in the Great Flood for endangering the survival of the human race. Some scholars on religion believe that the disembodied Spirits of the Nephilim still roam the Earth. These "evil" Spirits look for humans whose Free Will they can overtake and get them to do their bidding. To these scholars, this is the cause of the current dichotomy between Angels and Demons in the modern world. Their war is waged within the inner Cosmic Planes, through which they have the power to affect human thinking and actions. The Spiritual progress of all of humanity is a direct result of their war. Its outcome will determine whether we fall deeper into materialism or are raised collectively Spiritually, thereby ushering us into the much-anticipated Golden Age.

Gaia: Corresponds with the Sephira Malkuth as the personification of Planet Earth. Gaia is the primal Mother Earth Goddess, the Ancestral Mother of all living things. In Greek mythology, Gaia is one of the Greek primordial Deities from whose sexual union with Uranus (the sky), she gave birth to the Titans and the Giants (not to be confused with the Nephilim). The primordial sea Gods were born from Gaia's sexual union with the Pontus (the sea).

Geomancy: A practice of Divination by reading the signs of the Earth, or more appropriately, by a method of relating sixteen figures made up of a number of points or dots. These sixteen figures are given various meanings and are associated with Zodiac signs, Planets, Elements and more. Through these meanings, a Divination can be extracted by the Diviner.

Glory of God, the: The word "glory" comes from the Latin "Gloria," which means "fame, renown." According to the Hebrews and Christians, this word is used to describe the manifestation of God's presence within humanity. Since humans are made in God's image, according to the *Book of Genesis*, we can experience the Glory of God as a reachable state of consciousness while living in the physical body. The Glory of God is an ecstatic feeling in one's heart that transcends the pain and suffering of living in this world of duality. To experience it means that we have aligned with our Higher Self and have transcended the Ego. The Glory of God is the fruit of God's Kingdom (Kingdom of Heaven), and all who embody the life principles taught by Jesus Christ can experience it. These principles include living in truth, being righteous, upholding a moral and ethical attitude, and showing compassion for all living Beings.

Godhead, the: Synonymous with God, as the Source of all Creation. All religions and philosophies consider God to be omnipresent and omniscient. The Spirit energy is God's medium of expression. The Godhead is the undivided unity of God that is the Ain Soph Aur—the Limitless Light. It is the substantial impersonal being of God that is the totality of the Christian Trinity (Supernals) of the Father (Kether), Son (Chokhmah) and Holy Spirit (Binah). Cosmic Consciousness is of the Godhead.

Grim Reaper, the: A skeleton figure, cloaked in a hooded black robe, carrying a scythe. This figure is the personification of death. The Grim Reaper first appeared in Europe during the fourteenth century when one-third of its entire population perished due to the Black Death plague. The skeleton is symbolic of death, and the black robe is reminiscent of the clothing that religious figures of the time wore during funerary services. The scythe alludes to the Scythe of Saturn, which is used in this case to harvest human Souls.

Heaven: The Spiritual Realm where Archangels and Angels are said to reside. Traditionally, this place is depicted as being in the sky, up in the clouds. Heaven is reachable not only as a state of Being after death but also while living. It represents the transcendental state of expanded consciousness and union of Spirit and Matter. Once this occurs, the human being has reached Enlightenment, and their head is up in the clouds while their feet are on solid Earth. The Ancient peoples used the term "Heaven" or "Heavens" to refer to the vault in the sky. It includes the Stars above and the Sun, Moon, and Planets. This is the original and oldest use of the term.

Hell: The Demonic Realm where Archdemons and Demons are said to reside. In religious traditions and folklore, Hell is an afterlife location, often representing a place of punishment and torment. Some religions depict Hell as an Eternal destination, while others only as an intermediary period between incarnations. In Christian theology, Hell is synonymous with the Underworld. Thus, the ideas and meanings associated with both words are the same. In the context of *The Magus*, Hell is a state of mind. Outside of the brain, Hell does not exist.

Hermeticism: A philosophical, religious, and esoteric tradition based primarily upon the works of Hermes Trismegistus. Hermeticism is an invisible science that encompasses the energies of our Solar System and their relation to human beings. Hermetic writings have greatly influenced the Western Esoteric tradition, namely the Golden Dawn Order.

Higher Self, the: Your God-Self that is of the Spirit Element. The Higher Self is often confused with the Holy Guardian Angel, although the latter is the expression of the former. The Higher Self is found in the Kether

Sephira, which corresponds with Sahasrara Chakra. In Qabalistic terms, the Higher Self is the Yechidah. Its opposite is the Lower Self—the Nephesh and the Ego.

Holy Grail, the: Otherwise called Sangraal. The word "graal" comes from Old French, which means "a cup or bowl of earth, wood, or metal." The Holy Grail is a treasure that serves as an essential motif in Arthurian legends and Christianity. Arthurian legends describe the Holy Grail as a cup, dish, or stone with miraculous powers that provide Eternal life, happiness, and infinite abundance. Christians believe that the Holy Grail was the vessel Jesus Christ used at the Last Supper to serve wine. Thus, drinking from it means becoming one with Jesus Christ since he referred to the wine as his blood during the Last Supper. The Holy Grail has gained symbolic meaning over time as an elusive goal sought after because it can give one Eternal life. The fact that it is "Holy" means it has a Divine source. Therefore, to drink from the Holy Grail means to partake of the bounty and magnificence of God's Eternal, Divine energy. We are all, in essence, seeking the Holy Grail, meaning we are all trying to Spiritually evolve and align with our Higher Self (which was never born and will never die, since it is of the Spirit). By doing so, we will have drank from the Holy Grail and gained everlasting life, symbolically speaking.

Holy Guardian Angel, the: It is the expression of the Higher Self or God-Self. Masculine in nature, the Holy Guardian Angel is related to the Chokmah Sephira since it is the Force aspect of the White Light Principle, which is the Godhead-Kether. The Holy Guardian Angel communicates to us through Gnosis, which is the direct imparting of knowledge that is otherwise unknown to us; hence it is our inner teacher. For this reason, it is often referred to as the Higher Genius. Every human has a Holy Guardian Angel, and it is the goal of every human to establish a link with it, to learn their True Will and purpose in life.

Holy Spirit, the: In Judaism, the Holy Spirit is synonymous with the "Spirit of God," implying the oneness of God. In Christianity, however, the Holy Spirit is one personality of God in the Trinity. It is referred to as the "Spirit of Christ" and is portrayed as a dove. In Stoicism, the Holy Spirit is the Anima Mundi (World Soul) that unites all people. While in the Qabalah, the Holy Spirit manifests as the Great Feminine Principle through the Sephira Binah. And finally, in Alchemy, the Holy Spirit is the Secret Fire—the Kundalini energy awakened and risen to the Crown Chakra.

Kingdom of God, the: Synonymous with the Kingdom of Heaven. The Kingdom of God is one of the critical elements in the teachings of Jesus Christ. It is a state of mind akin to Christ Consciousness, where there has been a descent of Spirit into Matter, and they are now One. In Christian teachings, one has to be Resurrected, metaphorically speaking, to enter into the Kingdom of God. The Kingdom of God implies that one is a King or Queen of their own reality, and they have full sovereignty over the Elements of their Being. The "fruits" of the Kingdom of God is the ecstatic transcendence and joy felt in the Heart Chakra once this state has been achieved. Within this book, the term "Kingdom of God" is used to describe the lofty state of higher consciousness attained once the Kundalini energy has risen to the Crown and the Body of Light has been fully activated within the Self. The individual, in this case, has their head in Heaven and their feet upon the Earth. They have aligned their consciousness with their Higher Self.

Light-Bearer, the: Any Deity or human being who helps humanity by bringing them sacred knowledge, wisdom, and technology to help them evolve. Light-Bearer figures across different traditions include Lucifer,

Prometheus, Enki, Enoch, Hermes, Jesus Christ, and the Buddha. In the Tarot, the Hermit is the Light-Bearer, as he represents the "Word of God," the message from the Higher Self.

Logos, the: A Greek word meaning "word," "reason," "plan." The English word "logic" is derived from "logos." Logos is the Divine reason implicit in the Cosmos, expressed through the truth of its nature. It is the expression of the Universal Laws which govern the Cosmos. Logos is also found in humanity in their intellect, expressed through logic and reason. In *The Holy Bible*, Logos is the "Word of God." Jesus Christ came to preach the "Word of God" to humans and was, in essence, the embodiment of the Word.

Lower Self, the: In Qabalistic terms, the Lower Self is the animal Self, called the Nephesh. It is the subconscious mind, the "Shadow Self," and the dark side of the personality. The Ego is often referred to as the Lower Self in *The Magus* since tending to the Nephesh is one of its primary functions. The adversary of the Ego is the Soul since the Soul's prime objective is to unify the individual consciousness with the Higher Self.

Lucid Dreams: Heightened dream state where the individual uses their Body of Light to travel in the higher, inner Cosmic Planes. A Lucid Dream is an Out of Body Experience (OBE). Comparable to Astral Travelling, although not consciously induced, since the individual will most often enter a Lucid Dream seemingly by chance. They will be conscious they are dreaming and have a high degree of control over their dream world reality. Since the body appears weightless in a Lucid Dream, one can fly effortlessly.

Macroprosopus, the: Otherwise known as the "Vast Countenance," or "Arik Anpin." It is God in Heaven, as opposed to the Microprosopus, who is God on Earth. The Macroprosopus is the Kether Sephira, the Grand Architect of the Universe. Often it contains the following two Sephira with it, Chokmah and Binah, although the Macroprosopus is beyond duality.

Mantra, a: A Sanskrit word that means "a tool of the mind" or "an instrument of thought." This word is used to describe any thoughts, songs, utterances, or other sequences of words or sounds that have a Spiritual effect on an individual's emotional or mental state of Being. A Mantra is a ritual exercise "tool" that can evoke (and invoke) energy into the Aura, much like the Pentagram and Hexagram ritual exercises. Mantras are not specific to any one religion or Spiritual tradition.

Matter: A physical substance which occupies space and possesses mass, distinct from mind, Spirit, and energy. In the context of *The Magus*, Matter relates to the Physical World, including everything that we perceive with our physical senses. Quantum physics states that the nature of Matter at a molecular level is empty space. In the Qabalah, the World of Matter relates to the Sephira Malkuth.

Maya: a word in the Hindu culture that literally means "illusion." It is a Spiritual concept denoting that which exists but is continually changing and is thus unreal in a Spiritual sense. Maya implies the Principle or power that conceals the true character of the Spiritual reality that is the foundation on which the World of Matter is built.

Microprosopus, the: Otherwise known as the "Lesser Countenance," "Zeir Anpin," or "Small Face." It is God on Earth, in contrast to the Macroprosopus, who is God in Heaven. The Microprosopus is comprised of the Chesed, Geburah, Tiphareth, Netzach, and Hod Sephiroth. It relates to the inner functions that make up a human being.

Monad, the: From the Greek "monas," which means "singularity" or "alone." In cosmogony, this term refers to the Supreme Being of God-the Creator. The Pythagoreans coined this term, which refers to a single Source, the first cause behind all causes and effects. The Monad also relates to the Non-Dual Self. It is the part of every human that is of the Godhead.

Multiverse: Also known as the Omniverse, Maniverse, Megaverse, Metaverse, and Meta-Universe. It is a theoretical concept implying that within the known Universe of Matter, there are multiple, parallel Universes on different vibration frequencies in other dimensions but occupying the same Space/Time. The Multiverse is a philosophical notion rather than a scientific hypothesis since it cannot be empirically verified nor falsified.

Nadi, a: Singular for Nadis. Sanskrit root word is "and," meaning "channel," "stream," or "flow." Nadis are pathways for the distribution of Pranic energy. When applied to the Kundalini system model, Nadis most often relate to three primary Nadis of Ida, Pingala, and Sushumna.

Nirvana: An Eastern term that is commonly associated with Jainism and Buddhism. Nirvana is a transcendent state of Being in which there is no suffering, desire, or sense of Self as being apart from the rest of the world. It is the release from the effects of Karma and the cycle of death and rebirth. As the final goal of Buddhism, Nirvana signifies the alignment of individual consciousness with Cosmic Consciousness. If someone has achieved the state of Nirvana, they have ascended and attained full Light Body activation. They have united with their Higher Self and have re-integrated the Spirit energy. Nirvana implies that one has reached Enlightenment. As such, it is comparable with two other Eastern terms—Satori and Samadhi.

Non-Duality: A state of Being characteristic of God-the Creator and the Spirit energy. Since God-the Creator is defined as being omnipresent and omniscient, Non-Duality implies that everything within this state of Being lives in undifferentiated unity. In *The Magus*, this term is often used regarding mental and emotional states that accept both opposing dual viewpoints as being real simultaneously. In the Non-Dual state of mind, every thought or emotion is reconciled by its opposite at any given moment. Thus, the state of Non-Duality is a state of mind transcendence. Once the mind is transcended, the Spiritual Realm of Unity can be accessed.

Nous: Nous is synonymous with the Mind of God, which gives forth the Logos, or the Word of God. The Word of God is Reason. Nous and Reason are One, and their union is Life. Nous is the Father of the Word who gives rise to the Thought of God, synonymous with Thoth, the Egyptian God of Wisdom and Knowledge. In Book I of the *Corpus Hermeticum*, Nous is another name for Poimander, the Great Dragon, or Eternal Teacher, who taught Hermes Trismegistus the mysteries and secrets of God's Creation. Nous is the cause of all of existence and is synonymous with the Supreme Good. According to Hermeticism, all men and women are born with Nous, but not all die with it since Nous only comes to pious and religious men. Creatures of the Earth who are lower than humanity do not possess Nous, according to Hermetic teachings.

Now, the: The present moment. The field of pure potential within Cosmic Consciousness. This state of mind is achievable once you have quieted the mind-chatter of the Ego and have transcended beyond perceiving through duality. By entering into the Now, you are entering the frequency of the Spirit energy. Therefore, being in the Now yields the most joy and raw excitement of being alive.

Osiris Onnofris: God of the Underworld in the Egyptian tradition, as well as one of its Pharaohs. Also known as the God of life, death and rebirth. Thus, his myth is similar to the story of Jesus Christ. In the case of Osiris, it was his wife and sister Isis who Resurrected him after his evil brother Set killed him to take his place as the Pharaoh of Egypt. His title of "Onnofris" is derived from "Onnofri," meaning "the perfect or complete Being." This title shares a similar meaning to the title of "Christ."

Rainbow Body, the: In Tibetan Buddhism, the Rainbow Body is a level of realization. It is synonymous with the full activation of the Light Body, or Body of Light. The Rainbow Body phenomenon is reported as being the actual transfiguration of the physical body into a Rainbow Body.

Reiki: A popular Japanese energy healing technique. The word "rei" means Soul, Spirit, while the word "ki" means "vital energy." Reiki incorporates "hands-on-healing" whereby Universal energy (Life Force) is transferred through the palms of the practitioner to the patient. With this healing method, the practitioner can target the patient's physical body or their Chakras to encourage mental, emotional, and Spiritual healing. The Qabalistic version of hands-on-healing comparable to Reiki is called Ruach Healing. The main difference between the two is that in Ruach Healing, the practitioner never makes physical contact with the patient.

Samadhi: An Eastern term that is commonly associated with Buddhism, Hinduism, Jainism, and Sikhism. Samadhi refers to a state of meditative consciousness where the subject and object become One. It is signified by merging the individual consciousness with the Non-Dual Cosmic Consciousness. The Ego's chatter is transcended as the individual enters the field of pure potentiality of the Spirit energy. Samadhi creates an ecstatic feeling in one's Heart Chakra through the blissful energy it draws into the Self. Samadhi is the precursor to attaining Nirvana. It accompanies the expansion of consciousness after one has awakened the Kundalini and risen it to the Crown. In this high state, the individual has to give an external object attention only for a brief time before becoming absorbed within it and entering into Samadhi.

Satori: A Japanese Buddhist term for "awakening," "comprehension," and "understanding." In Zen Buddhism, Satori refers to the experience of "Kensho," which is seeing into one's true nature. Both "Kensho" and Satori are commonly translated to mean Enlightenment, which is the realization of the Spiritual Self. Satori may be short-lived, though, since realization implies something that happens in an instant. Nirvana is the same concept, but it represents a permanent state of consciousness or Being.

Seventy-Two Thousand Nadis, the: Energy channels or meridians in the Light Body that carry Prana, or Life Force energy. The Light Body contains a network of energy channels similar to a tree in appearance. The Seventy-Two Thousand Nadis are like branches emanating from the central trunk of the tree (the Chakric column), especially the heart and navel regions. The Seven Chakras, in turn, are powered by the Ida, Pingala, and Sushumna Nadis, which serve as the primary distributors of Prana in the Light Body.

Scythe of Saturn, the: A symbolic tool used by the Roman God Saturn (Greek Chronos), which represents the nature of the cycles of time. It also symbolizes the impermanence of all living things and their life-death-rebirth cycle. Death is a necessity for the renewal of life and is a natural part of the passage of time. The Scythe of Saturn also represents harvest, as this tool is used to cut down plants, which feed animals and humans. The glyph that represents the Planet Saturn in Astrology resembles a scythe. It has a cross on the top and a half-circle on the bottom.

Shakti: The consort of Lord Shiva. Shakti is considered Shiva's feminine, Divine energy. In Hinduism, Shiva's Shakti is the Goddess Parvati. In the context of the Kundalini, Shakti is called Kundalini Shakti, and it rises up the Sushumna Nadi to meet Shiva at the top of the head. Their union is a Divine Marriage that represents the union of the individual consciousness with the Cosmic Consciousness. Their union also signals the liberation of the Soul from the physical body. It is followed by the full activation of the Body of Light.

Shemhamphorash, the: The seventy-two fold name of God related to the Tetragrammaton (YHVH). Each of the seventy-two names is an Angel with certain powers. According to Qabalah legends, the Shemhamphorash Angels can cast out Demons, heal the sick, prevent natural disasters, and even kill enemies. Moses allegedly used the Shemhamphorash to cross the Red Sea. They are the balancing and counteractive forces to the seventy-two Demons of the Goetia. The Shemhamphorash were also used by S. L. MacGregor Mathers in his works for the Hermetic Order of the Golden Dawn and became a part of the overall system.

Shiva: Otherwise known as Lord Shiva, he is a God in the Hindu pantheon. Shiva is the consort of Parvati—Shiva's feminine energy, or Shakti. In the context of the Kundalini, Shiva represents the ultimate God-Consciousness, called Cosmic Consciousness. He also represents Oneness and the Spirit energy.

Spiritual Heart, the: As the Ida Nadi crosses through the physical heart on the left side of the body, the Pingala Nadi crosses through the Spiritual Heart on the right side of the body. The Spiritual Heart feels like a pocket of energy, directly opposite to the physical heart, beside the right breast. It contains a soothing flame since the Pingala Nadi is related to the Fire Element of the Soul. As the physical heart regulates the circulation of blood in the physical body, the Spiritual Heart governs the flow of Pranic energy in the Body of Light. The Spiritual Heart is transcendental, and it regulates thoughts and emotions that are of a Non-Dual quality. It is fully awakened only when the individual has integrated the Spirit energy within themselves. The Spiritual Heart is connected to the Bindu Chakra at the back of the head.

Thelema: A new religious philosophy/movement developed in the early 1900s by Aleister Crowley. It forms part of the Western Esoteric Mysteries. Thelema is the result of Crowley allegedly contacting a non-corporeal Being in Cairo, Egypt, in 1904, that dictated to him *The Book of the Law*, which outlines the Principles of Thelema. The fundamental tenet of Thelema is called the "Law of Thelema," which says, "Do what thou wilt shall be the whole of the Law." The word "Thelema" is an English transliteration of the Koine Greek noun for "will." The primary belief of Thelemites is that they must follow their True Will in life and find their purpose. Ritual Magick is emphasized as a means of obtaining this goal. Since Crowley's Magickal career started with the Hermetic Order of the Golden Dawn, he reformed their Magickal practices and integrated them into Thelema. He also included different Eastern methods as part of the curriculum as well. Like the Golden Dawn, Thelema's principal Gods and Goddesses are drawn from the Ancient Egyptian religion. Thelema was integrated as part of the Ordo Templi Orientis by Crowley, where it is currently practised today.

Tower of Babel, the: One of the stories, or myths, in the *Book of Genesis* that is meant to explain why the people in the world speak different languages. According to the story, after the Great Flood, human beings lived in a centralized area, and all spoke the same language. They built a city and a tall tower in the midst of it to reach Heaven. The Lord God observed what humans were doing and considered the tower's construction as a hubristic act of defiance. He destroyed the tower so that the people would leave this centralized area and scatter worldwide, thereby allowing the one language to mutate over time and become many. Because of this, according to the story, the people of the world speak many different languages.

Transpersonal Self, the: Synonymous with the Higher Self of the Spirit energy. This part of the Self extends beyond the Ego and any personal sense of identity or individuality and encompasses broader aspects of humanity, life, and the Cosmos. The Transpersonal Self is our connection to the Divine Source of all Creation.

It is experienced through Sahasrara Chakra but extends beyond it to the Transpersonal Chakras above the head. It is our God-Self.

Underworld, the: The world of the dead in various religious traditions. The Underworld is depicted as a place below the world of the living. Hence why it is often portrayed as being under the Earth. In Christian theology, it is called Hell, which is also the Demonic Realm or Kingdom. After his death at the crucifixion, Jesus Christ descended into Hell to bring salvation to all righteous people who have perished since the world came into existence. In Christian theology, this event is called the "Harrowing of Hell," or the "Descent of Christ into Hell." By spending three days in Hell (symbolized by being in the tomb for three days), Jesus had to establish his dominance over the Demonic Kingdom and become a King there before being Resurrected and becoming a King in Heaven. In the Egyptian tradition, Osiris underwent a similar process after his death. He had to descend into the Underworld before being Resurrected by his wife Isis.

Universal Laws, the: The Spiritual Laws that govern and maintain the Cosmos (Universe). In the context of it being a singular term (the Law), it refers to the Spiritual Law that holds all things together in harmony. This Law can be said to be the Law of Divine Oneness, implying that all things come from the same Source-God, and are governed by the Spirit energy. The Principles of Creation in *The Kybalion* are Universal Laws, as is the Law of Divine Oneness, Law of Karma, Law of Light and Love, and Law of Attraction, to name a few. It would be impossible to understand all the Spiritual Laws that govern the Universe since to do so you would have to become God-the Creator itself, which is not possible while existing in physical form.

Vault of the Adepti, the: A seven-sided room used for initiation into the Inner Order within the Golden Dawn system. It forms part of the Adeptus Minor ritual, where the candidate is being initiated into the Tiphareth Sephira of the Second Order. All the furniture in the room is symbolic, containing symbolic images and glyphs on the surfaces of the furniture, floor, ceiling, and walls.

Veil, a: A boundary that separates different states of consciousness from each other. Synonymous with the Ring-Pass-Not from the Enochian Magick model. Since the Tree of Life represents different states of consciousness, particular states are separated from each other by a Veil. Firstly, there are the Three Veils of Negative Existence: the Ain, the Ain Soph, and Ain Soph Aur. These three Veils exist outside the Tree of Life, right above the Kether Sephira. Next is the Veil of the Abyss, separating the Supernals from the lower parts of the Tree of Life. Following it is the Veil of Paroketh, which separates the Ethical Triangle and everything above it from the lower parts of the Tree of Life.

Western Esoteric Mysteries, the: A term that encompasses a wide range of related ideas within movements that developed in Western society, particularly in Europe. The term "esoteric" refers to knowledge concerning the mysteries of the Cosmos that has been rejected by science and religion. The earliest esoteric traditions came about during late antiquity, including Hermeticism, Gnosticism, and Neoplatonism. Jewish Mysticism and Christian theosophy were on the rise during the Renaissance in Europe. Rosicrucianism and Freemasonry in the seventeenth century followed this, and new forms of esoteric thought emerged in the eighteenth century. The nineteenth century saw an emergence of new trends that came to be known as "occultism." Prominent groups such as the Theosophical Society and the Hermetic Order of the Golden Dawn fall under the label of occultism. Religious movements within occultism were developed, which included Wicca and Thelema. Lastly, the New Age phenomenon emerged in the 1970s.

White Light, the: Pure Spirit energy permeating all of the manifested Universe. White Light is the first manifested Principle originating from God-the Creator. It is the foundation of all things in existence and their animating Principle. Qabalistically, the White Light refers to the Sephira Kether and the Light brought in from the Ain Soph Aur through the process of Tzim Tzum. In the Chakric system, it relates to Light brought in through Sahasrara Chakra.

Yang: In Chinese philosophy, Yang is the masculine, active Principle of the Universe. It is the light swirl in the Yin-Yang symbol. In addition, it contains a dot of the opposite colour, symbolizing that within every masculine is the feminine Principle and vice versa.

Yin: In Chinese philosophy, Yin is the female, passive Principle of the Universe. It is the dark swirl in the Yin-Yang symbol. In addition, it contains a dot of the opposite colour, symbolizing that within every feminine is the masculine Principle and vice versa.

BIBLIOGRAPHY

Note: The following is a list of books from my personal library that served as resources and inspiration behind the present work. Every effort has been made to trace all copyright holders of any material included in this edition, whether companies or individuals. Any omission is unintentional, and I will be pleased to correct any errors in future editions of this book.

THE GOLDEN DAWN

Cicero, Chic and Sandra Tabatha (2019). *Golden Dawn Magic: A Complete Guide to the High Magical Arts*. Woodbury, Minnesota: Llewellyn Publications

Cicero, Chic and Sandra Tabatha (2012). *Self-Initiation into the Golden Dawn Tradition*. Woodbury, Minnesota: Llewellyn Publications

Cicero, Chic and Sandra Tabatha (2004). *The Essential Golden Dawn: An Introduction to High Magic*. St. Paul, Minnesota: Llewellyn Publications

Cicero, Chic and Sandra Tabatha (1998). *The Magical Pantheons: The Golden Dawn Journal- Book IV*. St. Paul, Minnesota: Llewellyn Publications

Cicero, Chic and Sandra Tabatha (1999). *The Magician's Craft: Creating Magical Tools*. St. Paul, Minnesota: Llewellyn Publications

Cicero, Chic and Sandra Tabatha (2000). *The Magician's Art: Ritual Use of Magical Tools*. St. Paul, Minnesota: Llewellyn Publications

King, Francis (1997). *Ritual Magic of the Golden Dawn*. Works by S.L. MacGregor Mathers and Others. Rochester, Vermont: Destiny Books

Mead, George Robert (2011). *The Chaldean Oracles*. London, Great Britain: Aziloth Books

Regardie, Israel (1971). *The Golden Dawn*. St. Paul, Minnesota: Llewellyn Publications

Unknown (2003). *Esoteric Order of the Golden Dawn: 0=0 Neophyte to 4=7 Philosophus*. Grade Manuals. Added to by G.H. Frater P.D.R. Los Angeles, California: H.O.M.S.I.

Unknown (Unknown). *Roseae Rubeae Et Aureae Crucis: 5=6 Zelator Adeptus Minor*. Free Online PDF. Posted by G.H. Frater P.C.A.

Zalewski, Pat (2006). *Inner Order Teachings of the Golden Dawn*. Loughborough, Leicestershire: Thoth Publications

Zalewski, Pat (2002). *Talismans and Evocations of the Golden Dawn*. Loughborough, Leicestershire: Thoth Publications

Zink, Robert (2006). *Unleashing the Adept Within*. Audio. Robert A. Zink (G.H. Frater P.D.R.)

THE QABALAH

Ashcroft-Nowicki, Dolores (1997). *The Shining Paths: An Experiential Journey through the Tree of Life*. Loughborough, Leicestershire: Thoth Publications

Bardon, Franz (2002). *The Key to the True Kabbalah*. Salt Lake City, Utah: Merkur Publishing, Inc.

Bonner, John (2002). *Qabalah: A Magical Primer*. Boston, Massachusetts: Red Wheel/Weiser, LLC

Fortune, Dion (2000). *The Mystical Qabalah*. Boston, Massachusetts: Red Wheel/ Weiser, LLC

Grant, Kenneth (1995). *Nightside of Eden*. London, England. Skoob Books Pub Ltd.

Hall, Manly P. (2018). *The Qabalah, the Secret Doctrine of Israel*. CreateSpace Independent Publishing Platform

Levi, Eliphas (2000). The *Mysteries of the Qabalah: Or Occult Agreements of the Two Testaments*. York Beach, Maine: Samuel Weiser, Inc.

Mathers, S.L. MacGregor (2002). *The Kabbalah Unveiled*. Boston, Massachusetts: Red Wheel/ Weiser, LLC

Matt, Daniel C. (1983). *The Essential Kabbalah: The Heart of Jewish Mysticism*. New York, New York: Harper-Collins Publishers

Regardie, Israel (1980). *The Tree of Life: A Study in Magic*. New York, New York: Samuel Weiser, Inc.

Regardie, Israel (2004). *A Garden of Pomegranates: Skrying on the Tree of Life*. Edited and Annotated with New Material by Chic Cicero and Sandra Tabatha Cicero. St. Paul, Minnesota: Llewellyn Publications

Seidman, Richard (2001). *The Oracle of Kabbalah: Mystical Teachings of the Hebrew Letters*. New York, New York: Thomas Dunne Books

Zink, Robert (2006). *Power of Q*. Audio Series. Robert A. Zink

MAGICK AND THE OCCULT

Agrippa, Henry Cornelius (1992). *Three Books of Occult Philosophy*. St. Paul, Minnesota: Llewellyn Publications

Alvarado, Luis (1991). *Psychology, Astrology & Western Magic*. St. Paul, Minnesota: Llewellyn Publications

Barret, Francis (2013). *The Magus, or Celestial Intelligences: Books 1&2 Combined*. CreateSpace Independent Publishing Platform

Craig, Donald Michael (2010). *Modern Magick: Twelve Lessons in the High Magickal Arts*. Woodbury, Minnesota: Llewellyn Publications

Crowley, Aleister (1986). *777 and Other Qabalistic Writings of Aleister Crowley*. Edited with an Introduction by Israel Regardie. Boston, Massachusetts: Red Wheel/ Weiser, LLC

Crowley, Aleister (2004). *Aleister Crowley's Illustrated Goetia*. Tempe, Arizona: New Falcon Publications

Crowley, Aleister (1995). *Magick in Theory and Practice*. New York, New York: Castle Books

Crowley, Aleister (2000). *Moonchild*. York Beach, Maine: Samuel Weister, Inc.

Crowley, Aleister (1981). *The Book of Lies*. San Francisco, California: Red Wheel/ Weiser, LLC

Crowley, Aleister (1976). *The Book of the Law*. Boston, Massachusets: Red Wheel/ Weiser, LLC

Crowley, Aleister (2003). *The Book of Wisdom and Folly*. Boston, Massachusets: Red Wheel/ Weiser, LLC

DuQuette, Lon Milo (2003). *The Magick of Aleister Crowley: A Handbook of Rituals of Thelema*. San Francisco, California: Red Wheel/ Weiser, LLC

Fortune, Dion (2000). *Applied Magic*. York Beach, Maine: Samuel Weister Inc.

Fortune, Dion (1955). *The Training and Work of an Initiate*. London, England: The Aquarian Press

Grant, Kenneth (2010). *The Magical Revival*. London, England: Starfire Publishing

Hulse, David Allen (2004). *The Eastern Mysteries: The Key of it All, Book I*. St. Paul, Minnesota: Llewellyn Publications

Hulse, David Allen (2000). *The Western Mysteries: The Key of it All, Book II*. St. Paul, Minnesota: Llewellyn Publications

Klein, Victor C. (1997). *Hermes and Christ: The Occult Unveiled*. Metairie, Louisiana: Lycanthrope Press

Kynes, Sandra (2013). *Llewellyn's Complete Book of Correspondences*. Woodbury, Minnesota: Llewellyn Publications

Levi, Eliphas (2018). *The Kabalistic and Occult Philosophy of Eliphas Levi-Volume 1: Letters to Students*. Printed in United States: Daath Gnostic Publishing

Levi, Eliphas (1990). *Transcendental Magic: Its Doctrine and Ritual*. York Beach, Maine: Samuel Weiser, Inc.

Mathers, S. L. MacGregor (1975). *The Book of the Sacred Magic of Abramelin the Mage*. Mineola, New York: Dover Publications

Mathers, S.L. MacGregor (1997). *The Goetia: The Lesser Key of Solomon the King*. San Francisco, California: Red Wheel/ Weiser, LLC

Mathers, S.L. MacGregor (2000*). The Key of Solomon the King (Clavicula Solomonis)*. Boston, Massachusets: Red Wheel/ Weiser, LLC

Peterson, Joseph (2001). *Arbatel: Concerning the Magic of Ancients*. A reprint of the original Arbatel of Magic. Lake Worth, Florida: Ibid Press

Regardie, Israel (2013). *The Middle Pillar: The Balance between Mind and Magic*. Edited and Annotated with New Material by Chic Cicero and Sandra Tabatha Cicero. St. Paul, Minnesota: Llewellyn Publications

Regardie, Israel (2013). *The Philosopher's Stone: Spiritual Alchemy, Psychology, and Ritual Magic*. Edited and Annotated with New Material by Chic Cicero and Sandra Tabatha Cicero. Woodbury, Minnesota: Llewellyn Publications

Waite, A.E. (2011). *The Book of Ceremonial Magic*. Eastford, Connecticut: Martino Fine Books

Zink, Robert (2005). *Personal Magic*. Audio Series. Robert A. Zink (G.H. Frater P.D.R.)

HERMETIC PHILOSOPHY

Amen Ra, Summum Bonum (1975). *Summum: Sealed Except to the Open Mind*. Salt Lake City, Utah: Summum

Anonymous (1997). *Hermetic Triumph and the Ancient War of the Knights*. Whitefish, Montana: Kessinger Publishing

Anonymous (2005) *The Emerald Tablet of Hermes*. With Multiple Translations. Whitefish, Montana: Kessinger Publishing

Bardon, Franz (1971). *Initiation into Hermetics*. Wuppertal, West Germany: Dieter Ruggeberg

Benoist, Luc (2003). *The Esoteric Path*. Hillsdale, New York: Sophia Perennis

Chandler, Wayne B. (1999). *Ancient Future: The Teachings and Prophetic Wisdom of the Seven Hermetic Laws of Ancient Egypt*. Atlanta, Georgia: Black Classic Press

Copenhaver, Brian P. (2000) *Hermetica: The Greek Corpus Hermeticum and the Latin Asclepius in a New English Translation, with Notes and Introduction*. New York, New York: Cambridge University Press

Deslippe, Philip (2011). *The Kybalion: The Definitive Edition*. Attributed to William Walker Atkinson writing as Three Initiates. New York, New York: Jeremy P. Tarcher/Penguin

Doreal, M. (Unknown). *The Emerald Tablets of Thoth the Antlantean*. Nashville, Tennessee: Source Books

Everard, John (2019). *The Divine Pymander*. Whithorn, Scotland: Anodos Books

Faivre, Antoine (1995). *The Eternal Hermes: From Greek God to Alchemical Magus*. Grand Rapids, Michigan: Phanes Press

Hall, Manly P. (2007). *The Secret Teachings of All Ages*. Source text for "Poimandres, the Vision of Hermes." Radford, Virginia: Wilder Publications

Kingsford, Anna B., and Edward Maitland (2005). *Virgin of the World of Hermes Mercurius Trismegistus*. Whitefish, Montana: Kessinger Publishing

Jung, Carl Gustav (1968). *The Collected Works of C. G. Jung: Psychology and Alchemy*. Princeton, New Jersey: Princeton University Press

Levi, Eliphas (2013). *The Key of the Mysteries*. Eastford, Connecticut: Martino Fine Books

Melville, Francis (2002). *The Book of Alchemy*. Hauppauge, New York: Barron's Educational Series, Inc.

Newcomb, Jason Augustus (2004). *The New Hermetics*. Boston, Massachusetts: Red Wheel/ Weiser, LLC

Paracelsus (1983). *Hermetic Astronomy*. Printed in United States: Holmes Pub Group Llc

Raleigh, A. S. (2005). *Hermetic Fundamentals Revealed*. Whitefish, Montana: Kessinger Publishing

Roob, Alexander (2015). *The Hermetic Museum: Alchemy & Mysticism*. Hohenzollernring, Koln, Germany: Taschen

Salaman, Clement (2004). *The Way of Hermes: New Translations of the Corpus Hermeticum and the Definitions of Hermes Trismegistus to Asclepius*. Other translators are Dorine Van Oyen, William D. Wharton, and Jean-Pierre Mahe. Rochester, Vermont: Inner Traditions International

Three Initiates (1940). *The Kybalion: Hermetic Philosophy*. Chicago, Illinois: Yogi Publication Society

Walter, William W. (2005). *Hermetic Philosophy Vol. II*. Whitefish, Montana: Kessinger Publishing

THE TAROT

Anonymous (2002). *Meditations on the Tarot*. Translated by Robert Powell. New York, New York: Jeremy P. Tarcher/ Putnam

Cicero, Sandra Tabatha and Chic (2001). *Golden Dawn Magical Tarot*. Tarot Cards. St. Paul, Minnesota: Llewellyn Publications

Cicero, Chic and Sandra Tabatha (1996). *The New Golden Dawn Ritual Tarot: Keys to the Rituals, Symbolism, Magic & Divination*. St. Paul, Minnesota: Llewellyn Publications

Cicero, Chic and Sandra Tabatha (1994). *The Golden Dawn Journal: Book I- Divination*. St. Paul, Minnesota: Llewellyn Publications

Crowley, Aleister, and Lady Frieda Harris (2006). *Aleister Crowley's Thoth Tarot Deck*. Tarot Cards. Stamford, Connecticut: U.S. Games Systems, Inc.

Crowley, Aleister (1986). *The Book of Thoth: A Short Essay on the Tarot of the Egyptians*. York Beach, Maine: Samuel Weiser, Inc.

Duquette, Lon Milo (1995). *Tarot of Ceremonial Magick*. York Beach, Maine: Samuel Weiser, Inc.

Louis, Anthony (2016). *The Complete Book of Tarot: A Comprehensive Guide*. Woodbury, Minnesota: Llewellyn Publications

Martinie, Louis, and Sallie Ann Glassman (1992). The *New Orleans Voodoo Tarot*. Tarot Cards and Book. Rochester, Vermont: Destiny Books

Schueler, Gerald and Betty, and Sallie Ann Glassman (2000). *The Enochian Tarot*. Tarot Cards. St. Paul, Minnesota: Llewellyn Publications

Schueler, Gerald and Betty (1992). *The Enochian Tarot*. St. Paul, Minnesota: Llewellyn Publications

Wang, Robert (1989). *An Introduction to the Golden Dawn Tarot*. York Beach, Maine: Samuel Weiser, Inc.

Wang, Robert (1978). *The Golden Dawn Tarot*. Tarot Cards. Illustrated under direction of Israel Regardie. Stamford, Connecticut: U.S. Games Systems, Inc.

Waite, Arthur Edward (1911). *The Pictorial Key to the Tarot*. Illustrations by Pamela Colman Smith. London, England: W. Rider

ENOCHIAN MAGICK

Crowley, Aleister (1972). *The Vision and the Voice*. Boston, Massachusetts: Red Wheel/Weiser, LLC

Laycock, Donald C. (1994*). The Complete Enochian Dictionary*. York Beach, Maine: Samuel Weiser, Inc.

Schueler, Gerald J. (1988). *An Advanced Guide to Enochian Magick*. St. Paul, Minnesota: Llewellyn Publications

Schueler, Gerald J. (1987). *Enochian Magic: A Practical Manual*. St. Paul, Minnesota: Llewellyn Publications

Schueler, Gerald J. (1988). *Enochian Physics: The Structure of the Magical Universe*. St. Paul, Minnesota: Llewellyn Publications

Schueler, Gerald and Betty (1990). *Enochian Yoga: Uniting Humanity with Divinity*. St. Paul, Minnesota: Llewellyn Publications

Schueler, Gerald and Betty (1996) *The Angels' Message to Humanity: Ascension to Divine Union*. St. Paul, Minnesota: Llewellyn Publications

Tyson, Donald (1997). *Enochian Magic for Beginners: The Original System of Angel Magic*. St. Paul, Minnesota: Llewellyn Publications

Zalewski, Pat (1990). *Golden Dawn Enochian Magic*. St. Paul, Minnesota: Llewellyn Publications

KUNDALINI AND ENERGY

Butler, W.E. (1987). *How to Read the Aura, Practice Psychometry, Telepathy and Clairvoyance*. Rochester, Vermont: Destiny Books

Jung, Carl Gustav (1996). *The Psychology of Kundalini Yoga: Notes of the Seminar Given in 1932 by C. G. Jung*. Princeton, New Jersey: Princeton University Press

Leadbeater, Charles W. (1987). *The Chakras*. Wheaton, Illinois: The Theosophical Publishing House

Lembo, Margaret Ann (2017). *The Essential Guide to Crystals, Minerals and Stones*. Woodbury, Minnesota: Llewellyn Publications

Ostrom, Joseph (2000). *Auras: What they are and How to Read Them*. Hammersmith, London: Thorsons

Paulson, Genevieve Lewis (2003). *Kundalini and the Chakras.* St. Paul, Minnesota: Llewellyn Publications

Saraswati, Swami Satyananda (2007). *Kundalini Tantra*. Munger, Bihar, India: Yoga Publications Trust

McKusick, Eileen Day (2014). *Tuning the Human Biofield: Healing with Vibrational Sound Therapy*. Rochester, Vermont: Healing Arts Press

Permutt, Philip (2016). *The Crystal Healer: Crystal Prescriptions That Will Change Your Life Forever*. London, England: Cico Books

Powell, Arthur E. (1987). *The Etheric Double: And Allied Phenomena*. London, England: Theosophical Publishing House

NEW AGE SCIENCE AND PHILOSOPHY

Atkinson, William Walker (2016). *Mind and Body*. San Bernardino, California: Amazon's Timeless Wisdom Collection

Atkinson, William Walker (2010). *Mind-Power: The Secret of Mental Magic*. Hollister, Missouri: Yogebooks by Roger L. Cole

Atkinson, William Walker (2016). *Mystic Christianity*. San Bernardino, California: Amazon's Timeless Wisdom Collection

Atkinson, William Walker (2016). *Reincarnation and the Law of Karma*. San Bernardino, California: Amazon's Timeless Wisdom Collection

Atkinson, William Walker (2016). *The Arcane Formulas: Or Mental Alchemy*. San Bernardino, California: Amazon's Timeless Wisdom Collection

Atkinson, William Walker (2016). *The Astral World*. San Bernardino, California: Amazon's Timeless Wisdom Collection

Atkinson, William Walker (2010). *The Secret of Success*. Hollister, Missouri: Yogebooks by Roger L. Cole

Atkinson, William Walker (1996). *Thought Vibration or the Law of Attraction in the Thought World.* Whitefish, Montana: Kessinger Publishing

Bucke, Richard Maurice (1991). *Cosmic Consciousness: A Study in the Evolution of the Human Mind.* New York, New York: Penguin Books

Da Vinci, Leondardo (2008). *Leonardo Da Vinci Notebooks.* Edited by Thereza Wells. New York, New York: Oxford University Press

Levi (2001). *The Aquarian Gospel of Jesus the Christ.* Marina del Rey, California: DeVorss & Company

Narby, Jeremy (1999). *The Cosmic Serpent: DNA and the Origins of Knowledge.* New York, New York: Jeremy P. Tarcher/Putnam

Ramacharaka, Yogi (1907). *A Series of Lessons in Gnani Yoga (The Yoga of Wisdom).* London, Great Britain: Yogi Publication Society

Tolle, Eckhart (2016). *A New Earth: Awakening to Your Life's Purpose.* New York, New York: Penguin Books

Zukav, Gary (1980). *The Dancing Wu Li Masters.* New York, New York: Bantam Books, Inc.

WESTERN ESOTERICISM

Achad, Frater (1971). *Ancient Mystical White Brotherhood.* Lakemont, Georgia: CSA Press

Aivanhov, Omraam Mikhael (1982). *Man, Master of his Destiny.* Izvor Collection Number 202. Laval, Quebec: Prosveta Inc.

Aivanhov, Omraam Mikhael (1982). *Sexual Force or the Winged Dragon.* Izvor Collection Number 205. Laval, Quebec: Prosveta Inc.

Aivanhov, Omraam Mikhael (1992). *The Seeds of Happiness.* Izvor Collection Number 231. Laval, Quebec: Prosveta Inc.

Aivanhov, Omraam Mikhael (1985). *The True Meaning of Christ's Teachings.* Izvor Collection Number 215. Laval, Quebec: Prosveta Inc.

Aivanhov, Omraam Mikhael (1986). *Toward a Solar Civilization.* Izvor Collection Number 201. Laval, Quebec: Prosveta Inc.

Blavatsky, H. P. (1972). *The Key to Theosophy.* Wheaton, Illinois: Theosophical Publishing House

Blavatsky, H. P. (1999). *The Secret Doctrine: The Synthesis of Science, Religion, and Philosophy*, California: Theosophical University Press

RELIGIOUS TEXTS

Ashlag, Rav Yehuda (2007). *The Zohar.* Commentary by Rav Michael Laitman PhD. Toronto, Ontario: Laitman Kabbalah Publishers

Berg, Philip S. (1974). *An Entrance to the Zohar.* Attributed to Rabbi Yehuda Ashlag. The Old City, Jerusalem: Research Centre of the Kabbalah

Charles, R.H. (2018). *The Book of Jubilees.* South Carolina, United States: The Best Books Publishing

Faulkner, R. O. (1985). *The Ancient Egyptian Book of the Dead.* Austin, Texas: University of Texas Press

Lawrence, Richard (1995). *The Book of Enoch the Prophet.* San Diego, California: Wizards Bookshelf

Moses (1967). *The Torah: The Five Books of Moses* (Otherwise known as the Old Testament). Philadelphia, Pennsylvania: The Jewish Publication Society of America

Rosenroth, Knorr Von (2005). *The Aesch Mezareph: Or Purifying Fire*. Edited by W. Wynn Westcott. Whitefish, Montana: Kessinger Pub Co.

Westcott, W. Wynn (1893). *Sepher Yetzirah: the Book of Formation, and the Thirty-Two Paths of Wisdom*. London, England: The Theosophical Publishing Society

St. John of the Cross (2003). *Dark Night of the Soul*. General Editor Paul Negri. Mineola, New York: Dover Publications, Inc.

Various (2002). *The Holy Bible: King James Version* (Includes the Old and the New Testament). Grand Rapids, Michigan: Zondervan

ASTROLOGY

Anrias, David (1980). *Man and the Zodiac*. New York, New York: Samuel Weiser, Inc.

Burgoyne, Thomas H. (2013). *The Light of Egypt: The Science of the Soul and Stars*. Mansfield Centre, Connecticut: Martino Publishing

Butler, Hiram E (1943). *Solar Biology*. Applegate, California: Esoteric Fraternity Publishers

Crowley, Aleister (1974). *The Complete Astrological Writings*. London, England: Gerald Duckworth & Co. Ltd.

Howell, Alice O. (1991). *Jungian Symbology in Astrology*. Wheaton, Illinois: The Theosophical Publishing House

Kent, April Elliot (2011). The *Essential Guide to Practical Astrology*. San Diego, California: Two Moons Publishing

Lewis, James R. (1994). *The Astrology Encyclopedia*. Detroit, Michigan: Visible Ink Press

Phillips, Osborne and Denning, Melita (1989). *Planetary Magick: The Heart of Western Magick*. St. Paul, Minnesota: Llewellyn Publications

Riske, Kris Brandt (2007). *Llewellyn's Complete Book of Astrology: The Easy Way to Learn Astrology*. Woodbury, Minnesota: Llewellyn Publications

Riske, Kris Brandt (2011). *Llewellyn's Complete Book of Predictive Astrology: The Easy Way to Predict Your Future*. Woodbury, Minnesota: Llewellyn Publications

Spiller, Jan (1997). *Astrology for the Soul*. New York, New York: Bantam Books

Woolfolk, Joanna Martine (2008). *The Only Astrology Book You'll Ever Need*. Plymouth, United Kingdom: Taylor Trade Publishing

ONLINE RESOURCES

Astrolabe - Free Horoscope and Astrology report (www.alabe.com)

Biddy Tarot - Reference page for Tarot cards (www.biddytarot.com)

Chakra Anatomy – Reference page for the Chakras, Auras, and Reiki

(www.chakra-anatomy.com)

Encyclopedia Britannica - Reference page and compendium for all branches of knowledge (www.britannica.com)

Esoteric Order of the Golden Dawn - The official website of the Esoteric Order of the Golden Dawn (www.goldendawnancientmysteryschool.com)

Hermetic Order of the Golden Dawn - The official website of the Hermetic Order of the Golden Dawn (home of authors Chic and Sandra Tabatha Cicero) (www.hermeticgoldendawn.org)

Hermetics Resource Site - A library of online books on Western Esotericism (www.hermetics.org/library.html)

Internet Sacred Texts Archive - A collection of books on religion, mythology, folklore, and the esoteric arts (www.sacred-texts.com)

Raven's Tarot Site - Reference page for the Tarot and other Hermetic teachings (www.corax.com/tarot)

The Kundalini Consortium - Articles on the Kundalini and human energy potential (www.kundaliniconsortium.org)

Wikipedia-The Free Encyclopedia - Reference page and compendium for all branches of knowledge (www.wikipedia.org)

Vibrational Energy Medicine - Reference page for Chakras, Aura, and energy therapies (www.energyandvibration.com)